Lecture Notes in Computer Science 2675

Edited by G. Goos, J. Hartmanis, and J. van Leeuwen

T0223549

Springer
Berlin
Heidelberg
New York
Barcelona
Hong Kong
London
Milan
Paris
Tokyo

Michele Marchesi   Giancarlo Succi (Eds.)

Extreme Programming and Agile Processes in Software Engineering

4th International Conference, XP 2003
Genova, Italy, May 25-29, 2003
Proceedings

 Springer

Series Editors

Gerhard Goos, Karlsruhe University, Germany
Juris Hartmanis, Cornell University, NY, USA
Jan van Leeuwen, Utrecht University, The Netherlands

Volume Editors

Michele Marchesi
University of Cagliari
Dept. of Electrical and Electronic Engineering
Piazza D'Ami, 09123 Cagliari, Italy
E-mail: michele@diee.unica.it

Giancarlo Succi
Free University of Bozen/Bolzano
Center for Applied Software Engineering
Piazza Domenicani 3, 39100 Bozen/Bolzano, Italy
E-mail: Giancarlo.Succi@unibz.it

Cataloging-in-Publication Data applied for

A catalog record for this book is available from the Library of Congress

Bibliographic information published by Die Deutsche Bibliothek
Die Deutsche Bibliothek lists this publication in the Deutsche Nationalbibliographie;
detailed bibliographic data is available in the Internet at <http://dnb.ddb.de>.

CR Subject Classification (1998): D.2, D.1, D.3, K.6.3, K.6, K.43, F.3

ISSN 0302-9743
ISBN 3-540-40215-2 Springer-Verlag Berlin Heidelberg New York

Springer-Verlag Berlin Heidelberg New York
a member of BertelsmannSpringer Science+Business Media GmbH

http://www.springer.de

© Springer-Verlag Berlin Heidelberg 2003
Printed in Germany

Typesetting: Camera-ready by author, data conversion by Olgun Computergrafik
Printed on acid-free paper   SPIN: 10927526   06/3142   5 4 3 2 1 0

Foreword

This book contains most of the papers presented at the 4th International Conference on Extreme Programming and Agile Processes in Software Engineering (XP 2003), held in Genoa, Italy, May 2003.

The XP 200n series of conferences were started in 2000 to promote the exchange of new ideas, research and applications in the emerging field of agile methodologies for software development. Over the years, the conference has become the main world forum for all major advances in this important field.

Also this year the contributions to Agile Methodologies and Extreme Programming were substantial. They demonstrate that the topic is continuing to gain more and more momentum. In spite of some criticism of agile methodologies, everyone agrees that they address some unresolved needs of software practitioners. People still do not know how to develop software on time, with the desired features, and within the given budget!

This volume is divided into several thematic sections, easing reader's navigation through the content. Full papers are presented first, followed by research reports, papers from the Educational Symposium, and papers from the Ph.D. Symposium. The presentations given during three panel sessions held at the conference conclude the book.

The section on *Managing Agile Processes* includes contributions highlighting the sometimes difficult relationship between agile methodologies and management, and includes approaches and suggestions that should facilitate the acceptance of agile methodologies at the different levels of management.

The section on *Methodology Issues* presents papers on general-interest methodological issues, covering topics such as design in agile methodologies, RUP and XP, and dynamic models of the agile software development process.

The section on *Extending Agile Methodologies and XP* deals with applying XP to real-time and embedded systems, and, at a more abstract level, with extending XP toward important software engineering topics such as the CMM and formal methods.

The section on *Methods and Tools* includes papers on agile development and naked objects, and on continuous integration, refactoring, and process support tools.

The section on *Teaching and Introducing Agile Methodologies* reports experiences, studies and guidelines that will be surely useful to those practitioners wishing to adopt agile methodologies.

Three sections on more specific XP and agile development practices follow: *Testing*, *Pair Programming*, and *Other XP Practices*. These papers discuss the state-of-the-art of agile design, programming, and project management techniques. We are confident that they will be of utmost interest to researchers and practitioners.

The section on *Experience Reports* completes the first part of the book, presenting successful experiences on the introduction of agile methodologies in industry.

The next two sections present short papers discussing trials, novel and hot ideas, and research plans. They are divided into *Methods and Tools* and *Experience Reports*. We believe that these short, sharp, easy-to-read papers give a taste of what is really going on in the field of agile methodologies.

The section on the *Extreme Educational Symposium* includes papers and short communications on teaching and learning agile methods presented at this symposium held at XP 2003.

The section on the *Ph.D. Symposium* includes short communications presented by Ph.D. students at this symposium held at XP 2003. They document the work done now by the people who will become the leaders of the discipline in the near future.

The last section documents the three panels that were presented at XP 2003, on the hottest topics related to agile methodologies. It includes position papers by some of the most prominent leaders in the field.

We are grateful to all contributors for their excellent papers and to those members of the Program Committee who participated in the review process.

We thank Jutta Eckstein for organizing the Educational Symposium and reviewing the related papers, Paul Grünbacher for organizing the Ph.D. Symposium, and Steven Fraser for setting up the panels.

We also thank Marco Melis and Katiuscia Mannaro for their contribution to the preparation of these proceedings.

We express our appreciation to the Free University of Bolzano-Bozen, the University of Cagliari, and the University of Genoa. They made the XP 2003 conference possible!

We thank Microsoft (10,000 Euro), ThoughtWorks (5000 Euro), the Agile Alliance (1000 Euro) and eXoftware (1000 Euro) for sponsoring XP 2003.

Special thanks also go to the members of the Organizing Committee, Alberto Sillitti (Chair), Matteo Canessa, Paolo Vernazza, Marco Scotto and Sara Picardi for their essential contributions to the XP 2003 Website management and local organization.

March 2003   Michele Marchesi
                                                          Giancarlo Succi

Organization

 Center for Applied Software Engineering, Faculty of Computer Science, Free University of Bolzano-Bozen

 Dept. of Electrical and Electronic Engineering, University of Cagliari

 LIPS, Dept. of Communication, Computer and System Sciences (DIST), University of Genoa

Executive and Program Committee

General Chair: Jim Highsmith (Cutter Consortium, USA)

Program Chair: Giancarlo Succi (University of Bolzano-Bozen, Italy)

Tutorial Chair: Michele Marchesi, Italy
Organizing Chair: Alberto Sillitti, Italy
Workshop Chair: Jose Canós Cerda, Spain
Ph.D. Symposium Chair: Paul Grünbacher, Austria
Activity Session Chair: Leon Moonen, The Netherlands
Panel Chair: Steven Fraser, USA
Educational Symposium Chair: Jutta Eckstein, Germany
Publicity Committee Chair: Erik Lundh, Sweden
Co-chair (Northern Europe): Mike Holcombe, UK
Co-chair (Southern Europe): Ernesto Damiani, Italy
Co-chair (Australia): Steve Hayes, Australia
Co-chair (New Zealand): Robert Biddle, New Zealand
Co-chair (Asia): Yoshihide Nagase, Japan
Co-chair (US and Mexico): Laurie Williams, USA
Co-chair (Canada): Luigi Benedicenti, Canada
Co-chair (Central and South America): Moacir Pedroso, Brazil

Scientific Committee

Scott W. Ambler (USA)
Ann Anderson (USA)
Dave Astels (Canada)
H. Glenn Ballard (USA)
Kent Beck (USA)

Luigi Benedicenti (Canada)
Robert Biddle (New Zealand)
Jose H. Canós Cerda (Spain)
Jens Coldewey (Germany)
Ernesto Damiani (Italy)

Jutta Eckstein (Germany)
Khaled El-Emam (Canada)
John Favaro (Italy)
Steven Fraser (USA)
Steve Freeman (UK)
Gerhard Friedrich (Austria)
Arrigo Frisiani (Italy)
Andrew Fuqua (USA)
Paul Grünbacher (Austria)
Jim Highsmith (USA)
Andrea Janes (Italy)
Ron Jeffries (USA)
Martin Lippert (Germany)
Eric Lundh (Sweden)
Tim Mackinnon (UK)
Leon Moonen (The Netherlands)
Yoshihide Nagase (Japan)
Jim Newkirk (USA)

Moacir Pedroso (Brazil)
Witold Pedrycz (Canada)
Joseph Pelrine (Switzerland)
Mary Poppendieck (USA)
David Putnam (UK)
Václav Rajlich (USA)
Rachel Reinitz (USA)
Linda Rising (USA)
Bernhard Rumpe (Germany)
Barbara Russo (Italy)
Ken Schwaber (USA)
Alberto Sillitti (Italy)
Arie van Deursen (The Netherlands)
Christian Wege (Germany)
Don Wells (USA)
Frank Westphal (Germany)
Laurie Williams (USA)

Organizing Committee

LIPS, Dept. of Communication, Computer and System Sciences (DIST),
University of Genoa

Alberto Sillitti
Marco Scotto
Matteo Canessa
Sara Picardi
Paolo Vernazza

Sponsored by (as of March 28, 2003)

 Microsoft Corp. (www.microsoft.com)

 ThoughtWorks, Inc. (www.thoughtworks.com)

 Agile Alliance (www.agilealliance.com)

 eXoftware (www.exoftware.com)

Table of Contents

Managing Agile Processes

Methodology Issues

Extending Agile Methodologies and XP

Methods and Tools

Teaching and Introducing Agile Methodologies

Testing

Pair Programming

Other XP Practices

Experience Reports

Research Reports: Methods and Tools

Research Reports: Experience Reports

Extreme Educational Symposium

Ph.D. Symposium

Panels

XP after Enron – Can It Survive?

Mike Holcombe

Joint Chair - Genesys Solutions, University of Sheffield, Department of Computer Science
Sheffield, S1 4DP United Kingdom
m.holcombe@dcs.shef.ac.uk

Abstract. The recent financial scandals involving Enron, WorldCom etc. have resulted in major changes in the way companies manage their financial activities, not just in the USA but in Europe, also. Chief Executives and Finance Directors are now being made much more accountable for the way that budgets are set and expenditure approved. This raises awkward questions for XP. Can it evolve to provide business customers a more rigorous and auditable process that will stand up to the scrutiny of accountants and lawyers when justifying the allocation of budgets and the validation of expenditure? Can XP relate to this and evolve in a way that will ensure its survival? Some experiences of adapting XP to meet these issues in a software house are described.

1 Introduction

The recent corporate and financial scandals in the USA have led to a significant change in the way in which businesses are expected to operate. The approval of expenditure has always been subject to audit by supposedly independent financial experts but in recent years the tangled web of corporate accounting, consultancy and audit has resulted in serious and spectacular fraud. This now manifests itself in a much greater demand, from potential customers and their lawyers, for greater clarity and detail concerning what the project will deliver and at what price. The idea that there can be an informal relationship between the customers and the developers which allows both sides to explore the issues together without committing to a detailed inventory of what will be delivered for the price negotiated is looking more and more unsustainable. This has now led to significant changes to both the procedures and culture of large business behaviour.

It is no longer possible for Chief Executives or Directors of Finance to approve significant expenditure without documentary evidence that appropriate procedures have been followed. Audit and accountability are important for the purpose of satisfying statutory requirements but are also vital in terms of civil litigation also. Voas, [1], highlights that unreliable and unsuitable software is the subject of numerous and increasing lawsuits in the USA.

There is also survey evidence to indicate that many customer companies are demanding a clearer statement about the software process used and for some projects suitable industry level certification is required. The CMM model is now making im-

M. Marchesi and G. Succi (Eds.): XP 2003, LNCS 2675, pp. 1–8, 2003.

pact in industries where, previously, little attention was paid to standards and certification. I have personal experience whereby a group of large US banks forced a software house to drop XP because of these concerns. Some XP software companies are trying to get into the software development business for industries where safety and reliability are important and coming up against national and international regulatory requirements. The issue of ISO9000 and its derivatives are also an impact on the software business and it is not clear where XP fits into all of this. [2] raise important issues about the potential scope of agile methods in general and some of the problems that may lie ahead. It is obvious that software developers have to recognize these realities and adapt in order to survive. Will the informal approach be sustainable in a climate where contracts and transparency will be major drivers? Some Agile Methodologies already try to address these issues, for example DSDM has a much clearer planning and documentation policy. Is there anything to learn from this? Where does certification fit in. Increasingly customers are asking questions about CMM, ISO9000 accreditation, in many critical application domains there are regulatory processes that are mandatory. These all demand documentation, rigorous audit processes etc.

2   Extreme Programming

XP prides itself with its lack of bureaucracy and agility. Documentation is kept to a minimum and in its traditional form there is often no document that serves as a requirements document, no design documents and so on. This keeps overheads down and removes obstacles to the changes which will affect most projects. However, the lack of some types of documentation and defined quality process is making things difficult for those wishing to use XP.

The requirements document, according to the IEEE standard, provides much more than a list of prioritized functional requirements. It also includes the non-functional requirements - a vital component of any system and often critical to its success, as well as context and dependencies statements and a glossary. Since XP is all about communication and feedback it is strange that both the glossary and the review of a requirements document are not part of the XP process. A requirements document does not have to be a rigid document, it can be an evolving and flexible one which is maintained as the project develops and provides a snapshot of the target system. The functional requirements will change as the stories develop and the priorities will be reflected in the way in which stories are chosen for implementation. Such a document also acts a part of the system metaphor. Certainly, our experience is that a lightweight document that provides the most basic information is not a hindrance to change.

I have managed a number of XP projects and one consistent issue is the requirements document. Nearly all my customers have demanded such a document after the initial investigative phase. This has then been used by the customer to obtain support and approval for the project from senior managers and budgetary approval from finance directors for the expenditure on the project. This is going to be increasingly the case since audit will require a justification of the expenditure and evidence that the approval was given through due diligence.

XP does have some advantages when it comes to the project itself. The regular delivery of increments provides evidence of progress in the project which can be used by customers for their own project control process. Here XP is definitely in a strong position. However, the reliance on collective responsibility is a potential weakness since this is as strong as the weakest link and in teams of mixed abilities, experience and motivation a project could be threatened by the, possibly unintended, incompetence of an individual. Debra Caldow [2] points out *"..DSDM is partly in line with XP on this topic in that it says that quality is the day-to-day responsibility of teams. However, the DSDM roles of Technical Co-ordinator and Visionary have the ultimate responsibility for the technical and business quality of what is produced. Because of the deliberate lack of clear responsibilities, XP works best for small projects. Indeed DSDM is equally successful in small projects, but the roles and responsibilities defined in DSDM mean that it is more easily scaled up to larger developments"*.

The issue of certification, however, requires much more research. There are a number of issues here. Firstly we have to consider how XP relates to standards such as CMM, ISO9000, TickIt and so on. Many of these may be compatible with XP but the case has to be made. It is likely that XP will have adapt slightly in order to be acceptable. As mentioned above, the documentation issue will be key. Many of these certification and standards processes evolved at a time when design was the major activity in engineering projects and a design phase is often an expectation, if sometimes an unwritten one. There is a need for some careful presentation of XP to overcome this problem. There has been a trend in ISO and also in financial audit to replace a bureaucratic box ticking process by one based on principles and which allows flexibility in terms of how the standard is implemented. This is a good thing since a rigid approach to a quality process does not guarantee a quality product. A lot more research is needed in this area but this philosophy should suit XP.

Another issue that may become important is that of whether a company is actually carrying out an XP approach. There is a lot of circumstantial evidence that some companies are claiming to be using XP when in fact they are not, perhaps they are just using a few practices, perhaps they are doing XP in an unsympathetic or unsuccessful way. If this becomes a problem then perhaps there needs to be some sort of XP certification process, so that XP companies would have a badge of approval by some independent assessment organization that their XP process has been audited and approved. There is a lot of experience in this sort of quality process audit, particularly in the UK, and it may be a way forward as long as it is a sympathetic and lightweight approach.

3   Some Possible Ways Forward

During the course of a number of projects carried out in Genesys Solutions and its related companies we have tried to evolve a number of solutions to these problems. These are extensions or adaptations of the traditional XP approach and may be regarded as too bureaucratic or lacking in sympathy with the more *free and easy* attitudes that can be found in the XP community. However, the bottom line is the need to develop a way of working that will be acceptable to our paying customers or else take the risk that business will slowly dry up as other, more auditable, methods are chosen.

Some useful innovations include the development of *dynamic requirements summaries*, a *partially independent quality assurance process* and a simple *process modelling language* to provide metaphor and data for test set generation and resource estimation, see [3, 4. 6] for details of the modelling and testing approach.

3.1   Dynamic Requirements Summaries

These are based on a subset of the IEEE standard but cut down to essentials. Each story card provides a simple statement of the basic requirement together with a suitable tracking number and version. These are listed in related subsections. These may well change but information on the cards will provide details of the story's relationship to other stories so that this should be included in the requirements summary - what other stories interact with the given story. The initial analysis of a story is to identify the business process that it refers to. To do this consider two basic things, what is being done and to what. In other words, there is some operation described in the story that is prompted by some intervention - normally a user action but it could be a signal from an external component or system, such as a sensor or something similar. This operation will affect some aspect of the system or its data and will usually produce some observable effect.

Now we create a card for each story, this will provide some basic information about the story and allow us to plan out our work. Recall that we gave a simple tabular description of each story. The columns define the following aspects of the story.

1. Its name.
2. what is the event that begins the story process.
3. what is the internal knowledge that is needed for the story.
4. what is the observable result,
5. how is the internal knowledge updated as a result of the story
6. what is the current priority of the story,
7. what is the estimated cost of the story.
8. what is the likelihood of the story being changed or dropped?

A story card should be created for each of these with the information described. A template for story cards used in Genesys Solutions is given in Figure 1.

The story card template illustrated has been carefully designed and trialled in the company. It contains more than traditional XP cards but everything is there for a purpose. In particular, areas that have been a cause of difficulty in inexperienced teams such as estimation and test set generation are supported by the inclusion of information on the card that will assist greatly in these tasks.

Customer story card	Project title

| Date _____ | Project phase/iteration ____ |
| Requirements number ____ | Story name ____ |

Task description

Initiating eent

Memory context

Observable result

Risk	Change factor

Related stories

Notes

Story name

Resourestimates

Function/object point total ____   Man-hours total __

Functional tests

Quality attrib

Fig. 1. A story card template

Notice that the story card includes no information about non-functional requirements and so another section of the requirement summary has to be devoted to this. Finally it is useful to have brief sections on the dependencies and assumptions for the system and a glossary. All of these are critical to both an understanding of the system and its context. Since they are available for both customers and developers they can help to provide a wider and clearer understanding of the project. After all, the on site customer may not fully understand what others in the customer's organization, such as CEO, Director of Finance, may think and it provides a document that they can have access to, giving them a bundle of cards is clearly inappropriate.

The format for a dynamic requirements document is constructed from the background material about the project together with a structured list of stories, together with a note of their priorities. This part is usually the dynamic part and a new requirements document is generated whenever there has been a significant change in the nature of the stories or some other fundamental alteration in the project has occurred. This is naturally an aspect where some judgement and experience is needed but a useful principle is to build a new document if there is any doubt about whether the client and the client's backers are concerned about where the project is going.

Introduction - a statement of the required system's purpose and objectives
Dependencies and assumptions - things that will be required for your system to meet its specification, but which are outside your control and not your responsibility
Constraints - things which will limit the type of solution you can deliver, e.g. particular data formats, hardware platforms, legal standards
Functional requirements - with the priorities for the requirements into:
  − mandatory
  − desirable
  − optional

Non-functional requirements - with accurate definitions and an indication of how they are to be measured and the level required.

User characteristics - who will the users be?

User interface characteristics - some indication of how the interface needs to be structured and its properties.

Plan of action - defining milestones - key points in the project deliverables - an indication of when increments will be ready times when these events will occur.

Glossary of terms - any other information such as important references or data sources etc.

3.2   Partially Independent Quality Assurance Process

We have noticed that many pressures encourage developers to be rather less than rigorous or critical when evaluating their deliverables, whether it is code or other material. The introduction of a support team - Research and Development team - into the organization's structure has improved things greatly. The role of R & D is to be present at group meetings to act as technical consultants, to prepare software tools and other resources that might help the development team and to review their work. we have in- house quality check lists that provide a simple and quick method for recording the status of a deliverable - passed, pending revision and the fail points etc. For example, the R&D member will check code against the company coding standards and report non- compliance back to the team. All this activity s recorded on the project database, it is not overly bureaucratic but it is essential in order to have any chance of complying with standards and quality processes such as CMM, etc. The cards provide information that allow estimation to be carried out in a consistent and repeatable manner. A real problem is that unless you are an experienced developer you have no information on which to base any estimates and so it becomes guesswork. That may be unavoidable but failing to record these guesses and reviewing how reliable they were will not ensure that the process of estimation gets better.

To overcome the problems faced by XP teams in the testing of their code and in the variable quality in the other deliverables a separate section called Research and Development (R&D) was created from amongst the most motivated and technically able members of the company. This team (6 strong) was tasked with support and review of he individual XP projects in the company (there are 7 such projects). So, R&D attend key meetings of the XP teams - but not any meetings involving customers, to see how the project can be supported. This might involve the development or selection of tools to support some aspect of the project - specialist test tools, research into some technology aspect and presentations to the team on this, but also the R&D member reviews all of the teams work independently - the story cards - are they properly filled in? the test sets - are they sufficiently testing? the code - is it compliant with the company's coding standards? are the GUIs representing best design practice etc. This the R&D is not just a QA section but is a *support* group, coach, technology consultant as well. This has proved very positive and seen a considerable increase in quality without some of the problems of resentment and alienation often found with developers and independent QA teams.

3.3   Simple Process Modelling for Test Generation and Metaphor Description

We use a simple generalization of a finite state machine to describe what each story does in terms of suggests and processes. The card provides places for the identification of the system inputs and outputs involved in the operation of the story and of the system context (internal memory) that is concerned. The benefits of this is that when a group of stories are defined that form part of a coherent and deliverable increment it is straightforward to create powerful functional tests from this information. See [3], [4], [6].

For each requirement, which should be properly numbered in the requirements document, we will generate a set of tests. The details should be kept in a suitably designed spreadsheet or test management tool. We can do this by identifying, from the stories, what is prompting change (inputs), what internal knowledge is needed (memory), what is the observable result (output) and how the memory changes after the event. We also try to identify the risk that the story will be changed during the course of the project as a means of trying to manage its evolution.

Table 1. Requirements table (part)

story	function	input	current memory	output	updated memory	change risk
1	click(customer)	customer button click	-	new customer screen	-	low
1	enter(customer)	customer details entered	current customer database	confirmation details screen	-	medium (nature of details liable to change)
..	.....					

We build up a simple model like a state machine. Each state has associated with it an appropriate screen with buttons, text fields etc. Of course, the model is simple and crude, there is no distinction between entering a new customer's details and editing an existing one but it is enough to explain the method. We will can create test sets which will exercise the system, further details in [4, 6]. An obvious starting point is to try to check out the paths through this system (machine), this means looking for the conditions and activities that will force the system through paths made up of sequences or arrows.

4   Conclusions

If XP does not engage with these issues then there will be many problems ahead. The objection by some in the XP community to recording anything will damage its credibility and practical application in the ever changing software industry. It could be that the XP community does not have the foresight and the initiative to address issues such as certification and audit and is too inflexible in its approach. If that turns out to be the case then XP will soon be relegated to a footnote of history. However, other, more professional approaches, will benefit from adopting and adapting some of the XP practices and building a more *consistent* development process. We have explored a number of ways that improve the quality of our products and management, that enables clients other than on-site customers, to feel that they were more informed of the project prospects and progress, without loosing the most valuable aspects of XP. In fact, none of our activities increase bureaucracy in any significant or unnecessary way. We exploit all of these activities whether it is exceptionally powerful testing or more accurate estimation. They are part of our attempt to forge an *engineering quality* XP process and to make it more *business friendly*.

References

1. Voas, J.M, "Software quality tradeoffs, return on investment and software safety, 20th International System Safety Conference, Denver, Aug. 2002.
2. Mikael Lindvall, Vic Basili, Barry Bohem, Patricia Costa, Kathleen Dangle, Forrest Shull, Roseanne Tesoriero, Laurie Williams, Marvin Zelkowitz, Empirical Findings in Agile Methods XP/Agile Universe 2002, LNCS 2418, pp. 197-207, 2002
3. Debra Caldow, "DSDM and Extreme Programming (XP)", DSDM web site: <www.dsdm.org>
4. Mike Holcombe, "Extreme Programming for Real : a disciplined, agile approach to software development", To be published by Prentice Hall, 2003.
5. Mike Holcombe, M. Gheorghe, K. Bogdanov, Functional testing for Extreme Programming. Proceedings of XP2001.
6. Mike Holcombe & Florentin Ipate, Correct Systems - building a business process solution, Springer, 1998.

Trailing-Edge Management

David Putman

EXoftware - Ireland House - 150/151 New Bond Street
London W1S 2TX
www.exoftware.com
davidputman@davidputman.com

Abstract. The last thirty years has seen incredible growth in the computer industry, both commercial and technological. However, during that same period, there have been various studies asserting that somewhere between sixty and eighty percent of all software projects fail and the blame for these failures is most often laid at the door of the project manager or the project workers. This paper asks if the project manager and his team really are to blame and points out some similarities to historical events in other industries.

1   Introduction

Not many people in the traditional software world seem to be that worried about the high percentage of project failure quoted, probably because they assume that everybody else is in the same boat. If everybody's projects are failing, we're no different to anybody else. Our customers can't go elsewhere because they will get the same results there as they do here.

There are many excuses given for failure:

- Poor user input
- Stakeholder conflicts
- Vague requirements
- Poor estimation
- Mismatched skill sets
- Hidden costs
- Failure to plan
- Communications breakdown
- Poor architecture
- Missed warning signals

But if we think about it, wouldn't it make sense to just employ someone to make sure that all of these things are taken care of or done properly? What do you mean, we already do? We employ a *manager* to take care of all these things. He follows our processes to the letter, he makes sure all the boxes are ticked and he produces all the documentation we ask for – but still the projects fail/come in late/go over budget. This is why the development manager's position is known as the *poisoned chalice*. The

M. Marchesi and G. Succi (Eds.): XP 2003, LNCS 2675, pp. 9–15, 2003.

rewards for doing the job are excellent but failure is far too common and the price of failure is high.

Some of the most respected writers in software development have been telling us for a long, long time, there is usually only one reason a project fails and that reason is poor management. Poor management is seen as *the* major cause of project failure.

"The single most important factor in the success of a software project is the talent of its project manager" [1]

But isn't this a bit unreasonable, to blame the failings of a *team,* that can consist of anywhere between 8 to 800+ members, on one person? We work in a technologically leading-edge industry and we have well-defined processes that we follow faithfully. We make sure that all the necessary checks and balances are in place and provide reams of documentation to prove that they are not bypassed.

The problem is not that we have bad managers. The managers are doing things exactly the way we think they should but our projects are still failing. Maybe it's not how we implement management that is the problem, maybe it is how we define management that is the problem?

2   Why Management?

A lot of software companies start small. Sometimes just one or two people solving a problem for just one customer. They find that their solution works for other companies in the same industry and before you know it, they have 5,000 customers and a hundred employees.

This is about the time when the owners of the company start to realise that dealing with things in an ad-hoc manner just doesn't work anymore. They find that they need to be able to quantify what they are doing and to be able to predict outcomes and delivery dates.

If they have had the luxury of a programming or software engineering education, they may remember something about this from their course. If not, there are many consultants out there that will be only too happy to advise them on the *best* way to run software development projects and there are plenty of books on the subject too.

Probably 90% or more of all software development companies end up adopting some variation of the waterfall method, first proposed in 1970 and commonly known in the UK as Structured Systems Analysis and Design Methodology (SSADM).

In 1970 the IT industry was characterised by a few large companies selling mainframe computers and software development being performed by large programming teams. The useful life of a system then was estimated at around five years. That means you had five years to develop the next version of your application. That is certainly not the case for most applications today, and has not been the case for many years. Why do we expect techniques that were designed for such an environment to work today?

3   Acceptable Failure

Over thirty years later, we find that most of the industry is still using those same techniques and believes that they are still applicable. Of course, they have been modernised slightly, automated where possible and have been nicely packaged by some of the big consultancies and vendors but they remain essentially the same. Imagine that, an industry that prides itself on the speed of its technological progress is the same industry that clings to thirty-year-old beliefs and techniques.

As for the people involved in the process - the attitude of the consultants and vendors seems to be that the employees are plug-and-play. It doesn't matter who they are or what level of skills they have - as long as they produce the documentation required by the process, they have succeeded in their task. Being *efficient* is more important to these people than being *effective*. [2] Performing the process correctly is much more important than the success of the project. Thus, the tail wags the dog – does that sound very rational to you?

One of the reasons that this state of affairs has gone on for so long is risk. Psychologists have demonstrated that people would rather have an *acceptable way of failing* than a risky way of succeeding. Every other software company is using the same methods and suffering from exactly the same problems that we are. To change means adopting a different method to the rest of the industry. The perception is that different means risky and so easy solutions are sought, especially those that give benefit in the short-term.

4   Organisational Dysmorphic Disorder

There is a range of common diseases in Western society today that fall under the general label of Body Dysmorphic Disorders (BDD). Sufferers with these complaints have great difficulty seeing their body shape as it really is and imagine themselves to be either overweight or underweight. Anorexia Nervosa is one of the most well known forms of BDD and causes the sufferers to imagine that they are overweight, whereby they continue dieting and/or exercising until they become extremely ill or, in some cases, they die.

In business there seem to be a great many managers who also have difficulty seeing their organisational shape as it really is and so could be said to be suffering from Organisational Dysmorphic Disorder (ODD). This applies especially to the process mavens, who seem to believe that doing something badly more efficiently is an improvement.

5   The Sickness

Looking at the software industry as it stands today, I believe we can draw some parallels with manufacturing industry in the 1970s. At that time W Edwards Deming identified the seven diseases of management [3] that he believed were crippling Western business:

1. Lack of constancy of purpose.
2. Emphasis on short-term profits.
3. Evaluation of performance, merit ratings and annual reviews.
4. Mobility of management; job-hopping.
5. Management by use only of visible figures.
6. Excessive sickness costs caused by stress.
7. Excessive legal costs caused by liabilities.

5.1   Lack of Constancy of Purpose

According to Deming's fourteen points for managers, the purpose of the organisation is to stay in business and provide jobs for its employees. How does this fit with to-day's marketplace? Today's objective seems to be to get big enough to go public and then sell out.

5.2   Emphasis on Short-Term Profits

In the stock market, there are two general strategies for profit-making; trading and investing. Traders operate in the short-term and, although they tend to make a greater percentage in profit, their strategy is much riskier as they need to buy and sell frequently. Investors on the other hand, may make a lower level of profit overall but win in the long term because their strategy is robust enough to weather fluctuations in stock prices. Management should look at this and decide whether they should be traders (acting in the short-term) or investors.

5.3   Performance Ratings and Annual Reviews

Performance ratings are a demotivator, especially if averages are used. By definition, some of the participants have to be below the calculated average. It doesn't matter how much improvement the department makes each year, it is a mathematical fact that a proportion of the staff will be below the performance average. How can anyone have pride in their work when told they are below average?

5.4   Mobility of Management

The knowledge that short-term profits are the main objective encourages managers to job-hop. The largest gains always occur at the beginning of the exercise, whether it is an increase in productivity or a decrease in costs. Once this has occurred it is difficult, if not impossible, to continually improve the system at the same rate. The only answer is to move on.

5.5   Management by Visible Figures Only

We're back to performance ratings. Take the defect rate for example. Why don't we list our developers in order of how many defects they produce per week? This will allow us to pay special attention to those that produce the most defects, Either give them extra training or maybe even sack them. What the list doesn't tell us is why the individuals are creating more defects. Is it because they are lazy and incompetent or is it because they are the ones brave enough to tackle the most difficult problems?

5.6   Excessive Sickness Costs Caused by Stress

It's a myth that stress and burnout are executive diseases, these ailments are even more prevalent among the workers. Research has shown that those who have little or no control over how they work and the environment they work in are most susceptible to stress related diseases [4]. The fact that stress and burnout are still prevalent in our industry is borne out by the Cutter IT Journal [5] devoting a whole issue to it in 2002.

5.7   Excessive Legal Costs Caused by Liabilities

Virtually every week we read in the newspapers of another company being sued by an employee that was reduced to ill health by overwork.

6   The Recovery

It wasn't until the beginning of the 1980s that Western manufacturing learned to abandon their old management methods and embraced Deming's concepts that have now become known as quality management. Some never managed the transition and exist no more but there is hardly a manufacturing or logistics manager today that doesn't understand and use the concepts and practices of quality management.

Somehow, most of the software industry seems to have missed the management revolution of the 1980s and is still managing in a very 1960s style. Taylorism and management by objectives are still commonplace although they are often re-badged as 'new' management techniques such as business process re-engineering.

7   Disruptive Technology

There is a story from the early days of computing about an executive from one of the first computer manufacturers claiming that one day computers would be so powerful that there will only be a need for five of them world-wide. It was imagined that because these machines would be so powerful, five would be sufficient to satisfy everybody's needs. Progress in computing in those days meant every new computer was bigger, better, faster and could accommodate more users.

However, what this oft-quoted individual failed to realise was that there might be other ways of delivering computing power to individual desktops other than hooking them up to a giant mainframe. Mainframe manufacturers were caught out when the personal computer took off in the 1980s; some of them weren't able recover and went bankrupt or were taken over.

In this case, the personal computer was a *disruptive technology*.[6] Although related, the technologies behind mainframes and PCs are different. At first inspection there would seem to be no area in which they would compete. Connect a few PCs together in the right way, however, and you have a network. They form a network that is capable of satisfying the computing needs of many individuals and even some organisations. Very few people in the computer world were able to foresee this in the 1980s and so their organisations don't exist anymore.

Similar things happened in the US motor and the UK motorcycle industries in the late 1960s and early 1970s. Companies from the Far East were able to flood Western markets with better quality and cheaper competitive goods, forcing many well-known and established manufactures out of business.

The disruptive technology in this case was known as lean manufacturing. Ironically, lean manufacturing was a set of management and engineering practices developed and taught to Eastern manufacturers by US management gurus, such as W. Edwards Deming, his colleague Walter Shewart and others.

8   Agile Development

Although generally perceived as being led by developers, agile development techniques would be recognised by any experienced manager as the embodiment of lean production and quality management.

Concepts such as:

- Building in quality at every stage
- Customer collaboration
- Streamlined processes
- Continuous improvement

Are at the foundation of the agile movement.

Companies that have adopted agile methods have found them to be of great benefit and more and more companies are looking to them as the economic climate worsens. Agile methods may be prove to be the next disruptive technology.

9   Conclusion

More and more development companies are choosing the agile route and there are many agile methodologies to choose from. As the success of the movement snowballs it is becoming more and more likely that agile methodologies will be the next major disruptive technology in software development. Those companies that refuse to acknowledge this, the companies that believe that *efficiency* will solve their problems, will be in the same position that the motor car and motor cycle industries were in the 1970s . Some will make it, some won't. Companies that already recognize *effectiveness* as much more important than efficiency have a head start.

According to a Computer Weekly survey in 2002 [7], nearly two-thirds of organisations admit that they have suffered from failed projects within the past year, at an average cost of eight million pounds. Some failed projects have cost organisations up to a hundred and thirty three million pounds, raising serious questions about the strength of their project management and nearly 70% of companies quoted believe that their project management functions need to be improved.

Even in the face of these facts, many companies refuse to accept that change is necessary and believe that the problems are due to an inefficient workforce. It does seem anachronistic that we invest thousands, if not millions, of pounds making sure that our developers have the latest tools and the latest training in the latest technology, while at the same time we try to manage them with the tools and techniques of yesteryear?

The problem is not poor individual managers; the problem is the inability of management to recognise true nature of the problem. The future will see the gap between *effectively managed* and *efficiently managed* companies widening.

Acknowledgements

I would like to acknowledge my colleagues at eXoftware [8] and the members of the London eXtreme Tuesday Club (XTC) [9] for their many useful contributions and suggestions.

References

1. Brooks, F, The Mythical Man-Month (Addison-Wesley 1995).
2. DeMarco, T, Slack (Broadway Books 2001)
3. Deming, W.E, Out Of The Crisis, (MIT 1982).
4. Ridley, M, Genome (Fourth Estate 1999)
6. Christensen, C, The Innovator's Dilemma (Harvard 1997)
7. Computer Weekly (http://www.computerweekly.com 2002)
8. http://www.exoftware.com.
9. http://www.xpdeveloper.com

Value Based Management and Agile Methods

John Favaro

Consulenza Informatica, Via Gamerra 21, 56123 Pisa, Italy
jfavaro@tin.it

Abstract. Agile methods strive for clarity at the level of operations. Value Based Management is an integrated strategic and financial approach to the general management of businesses that strives for clarity at the level of the business. This paper discusses how they complement each other, presenting and discussing five principles. Particular attention is focused on metrics for measuring value creation and efficient resource usage.

1   Introduction

Agile methods such as Extreme Programming [1] are essentially focused on the operations of a business: in practice they are executed within the overall context of strategic and financial principles embodied either explicitly or implicitly in a particular management approach. However, they do contain elements of strategy and finance (such as a defined interaction with a Business actor) that give rise to biases that can make them more compatible with one management approach than another.

Value Based Management (VBM) is an integrated strategic and financial approach to the general management of businesses [2]. Value Based IT Management (VBIM) was introduced in 1998 as an approach to managing investment in reusable software, and has since been applied to other types of IT investment. The principal extension with respect to general VBM is the inclusion of options-oriented valuation techniques. We recapitulate here the five principles of VBIM that were introduced in [3]:

A. Economic value maximization drives IT investment strategies.
B. Strategy drives selection of IT investments.
C. IT Investments are structured to maximize embedded strategic options.
D. Both traditional discounted cash flow (DCF) and options-based techniques are used to capture the full value of IT investments.
E. Metrics are used to measure and guide performance.

2   The Tomato Garden Metaphor

We begin with Principle C, which expresses the concept of *active management for strategic options*. The view of XP as an options-driven process was introduced as early as the white book [1]. In another perspective, Luehrmann [4] compares the management of a portfolio of strategic options to growing a garden of tomatoes in an

M. Marchesi and G. Succi (Eds.): XP 2003, LNCS 2675, pp. 16–25, 2003.

unpredictable climate: "Walk into the garden on a given day in August, and you will find that some tomatoes are ripe and perfect. Any gardener would know to pick and eat those immediately. Other tomatoes are rotten; no gardener would ever bother to pick them. These cases at the extremes (now and never) are easy decisions for the gardener to make. In between are tomatoes with varying prospects." Walk into an XP project on a given day and you will find a set of stories with varying prospects (Figure 1). Some can be scheduled for immediate implementation. A few might be clearly impossible to implement and are discarded.

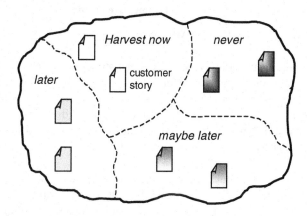

Fig. 1. The tomato garden metaphor

"Some are edible and could be picked now but would benefit from more time on the vine." That is, some stories would benefit from deferral to later iterations (e.g. until requirements become clearer).

"A purely passive gardener ... picks the ripe tomatoes and goes home. Active gardeners [not only] watch the garden but, based on what they see, they also cultivate it: watering, fertilizing, weeding." Active management of an XP project involves continuous cultivation through techniques such as refactoring, automated tests, and daily builds in an effort to maximize the strategic options available at any time.

"Of course, the weather is always a question, and not all the tomatoes will make it. Still, we'd expect the active gardener to enjoy a higher yield in most years than the passive gardener." Although external uncertainties can always undermine a project, we expect the active management of strategic options through agile practices to produce better results than a traditional "fire and forget" methodology.

3   The Role of Strategy

Principle B concerns the role of strategy in driving the business. It is nearly always futile to try to predict with confidence the economic benefits of a single action on an individual project (or tomato garden) due to the multitude of unknowns (and even "unknown unknowns," the so-called *unk-unks*) facing it at any time.

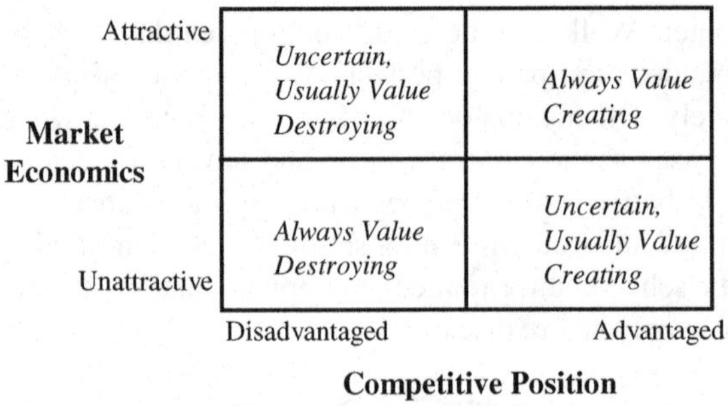

	Attractive	Uncertain, Usually Value Destroying	Always Value Creating
Market Economics			
	Unattractive	Always Value Destroying	Uncertain, Usually Value Creating
		Disadvantaged	Advantaged

Competitive Position

Fig. 2. ME/CP framework

In such a climate of uncertainty, a higher-level strategic framework that links entire strategies to value creation at the level of the business is needed.

The ME/CP framework (Marakon Associates) was described in detail in 1999 in the context of a strategic analysis of application framework development [8]. As seen in Figure 2, there are two (and only two) primary determinants of business value creation: market economics and competitive position.

Market Economics. Over time, the average tomato gardener working in the fertile soil of southern Italy will be more profitable than the average gardener working in the arid soil of the Sahara desert. Likewise, a software enterprise working in a market where the average participant is profitable (such as the mutual fund industry) is more likely to experience business value creation than a participant in a market with less attractive economics. At the operational level, agile methods support the creation of strategic options both for entry into profitable market situations, and exit from unprofitable ones, as discussed in detail in [6].

Competitive Position. Notwithstanding the vast literature on competitive practice, the ME/CP framework tells us that there are ultimately only two ways to improve competitive position: through a lower economic cost position or through successful differentiation. The financial contribution of lower costs (and the operational contribution of agile methods in this respect) is well understood. But the value-based interpretation of differentiation is often misunderstood: the gardener who succeeds in producing the most delicious tomatoes in the world has not achieved differentiation if he cannot exploit this achievement either to (a) sell his tomatoes at a higher price or (b) hold prices while gaining market share.

Differentiation provides a good illustration of the difference between the operational and the strategic/financial levels. Operational skills offer *support*, but differentiation occurs at the level of the business. In the case of tomatoes, it might be the bright red color rather than the flavor that enables differentiation (try a tomato from Holland sometime); in the case of software it may be a particular feature that customers are willing to pay for. The search for differentiating features occurs at the level of the business, through the chosen framework that guides the business toward value-adding strategies; agile methods are particularly good in *supporting* that search for differentiation through feature-oriented practices (especially the organization of projects along user stories at the granularity of individual features).

4   Valuation

Although operational methodologies offer support in the pursuit of business value, it is the job of the strategic/financial framework to provide the definition of "value" that becomes the basis for evaluating a project. This is the subject of principle D.

Value based management provides such a definition, in terms of Present Value: the expected future period i cash flows C_i of a project, discounted back to the present at the opportunity cost of money k. The familiar basic formula is:

$$PV = \frac{C_1}{(1+k)} + \frac{C_2}{(1+k)^2} + ...$$

A comparative analysis in 1996 illustrated how the Present Value approach is superior to other techniques for project valuation such as "time to payback" or "cost-benefit ratio" [14]. Option theoretic techniques that augment Present Value techniques to capture the value of strategic options have been introduced in VBIM and were discussed at length in [6].

5   Economic Value Maximization

The subject of Principle A is the governing objective of an enterprise. Every company has a governing objective, often only implicitly expressed in the way it conducts its business. At first glance, it may seem like some kind of abstract "mission statement" for a company, but its role is actually a very practical one—to provide a decision-making and conflict-resolution principle to the hundreds, usually thousands of business decisions that are carried out every day at all levels in the enterprise, from company headquarters all the way down to the business units and individual projects.

There is a strong tendency for a company to set a strategic, or product-market oriented governing objective:

- achieving the highest possible quality
- maximizing growth of the business
- maximizing customer satisfaction

There are several management styles that support these kinds of governing objectives. An alternative governing objective is financial: maximizing the economic value of the company (or business unit) over time. This is the governing objective supported by VBM. What is meant by "economic value"? Principle C gives us a precise definition: the discounted present value of future cash flows.

Some argue that a strategic and a financial governing objective are effectively equivalent—that each automatically leads to better financial performance. To see why not, let's take a concrete example. Phrases such as "Customer Value" often arise in discussions of agile methodologies. Suppose that our declared governing objective is "maximizing customer value." Such a governing objective generally contains the assumption, often only implicit, that maximizing customer satisfaction will automatically lead to superior financial performance. Paul Allaire, CEO of Xerox, once put it this way: "If we do what's right for the customer, our market share and our return on assets will take care of themselves." [9]

This assumption is more tenuous than it appears, though. In fact, conflicts between customer satisfaction and economic return arise continuously in practice, as was illustrated in 1996 in a graph (Figure 3) that shows four possible scenarios [12]. Scenarios 1 and 4 are the extreme cases and also the simplest: more satisfied customers lead to better economic returns and vice versa. But the other two scenarios are much more common. Scenario 2 illustrates the case where the effort and expense invested have paid off in terms of customer satisfaction, but the economic returns have been insufficient to cover the investment. When a product has overshot the peak, it is effectively subsidizing the customer. The only recourse is to try to move back up the curve, as in Scenario 3, by providing a better balance between value and price. Often this involves removing features that are not essential to customer satisfaction—for example, providing a "lite" version of the product that retains an adequate level of customer satisfaction but lowers production costs.

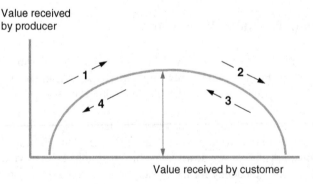

Fig. 3. Producer and customer value conflicts

Customer Value (or any other purely strategic objective) is not suitable as a top-down, corporate-level objective. A business unit, or even a project, should receive only the instructions from upper management to maximize its economic value. It is up to the business unit or project to determine—in its own context—whether customer value should become a strategic weapon in pursuit of that objective. The operational elements of agile methodologies are well suited to supporting this economic objective, with their approach of continuous feedback and re-estimation of both customer and producer value, yielding the information needed by decision-makers in the conflict resolution process. For example, agile methodologists stress the importance of identifying explicit costs with requirements at the individual level [5]. In another example, on program optimization, Fowler writes that "one value of an explicit optimization phase is that the cost of getting fast performance is more explicit, so businesses can trade it against time to market or more features." [11]

6   Value Based Metrics

"The basic XP management tool is the metric [1]." Principle E concerns metrics. We will dwell a bit longer on this topic because it is currently a subject of much interest in the agile community, and because metrics based on value are not yet described elsewhere in the literature on VBIM.

A number of metrics are cited in the agile method literature, such as the ratio between estimated development time and calendar time, unit test scores, and functional test scores. These metrics play a highly visible role in agile methods for measuring and providing feedback on *operational* performance, helping to provide a signal of how well the project is proceeding. Similarly, in VBM, metrics play a highly visible role in measuring and providing feedback on *financial* performance, helping to provide a signal of whether business value is being created or destroyed. As discussed in earlier sections, these metrics are at the level of the business, whereas operational metrics like those mentioned above only give indirect support. Nevertheless, as mentioned in the beginning of this paper, the agile approach to software development has given rise to some biases that makes it particularly well aligned with value-based thinking about business value creation. We are beginning to see this bias in a new set of measures being proposed within the agile community.

One type of new measure that has been gaining credence from several different sides in the agile community is related to the idea of "software inventory." An example is the metric Beck calls "software in process," suggesting an analogy to the "work in process" term used for classifying inventory [13]. The Lean Software Development paradigm [10] is also closely associated with the analogy to inventory management. The preoccupation with inventory in both cases is indicative of a general preoccupation in agile methods with efficient use of resources, manifested in principles of small teams, small documentation, and minimized upfront design.

Let us see now how this emerging way of thinking about agile performance is compatible with the financial performance metrics used in VBM. What is "performance" in a value-based sense? Principles A and D together give us the answer: creating economic value. This leads to the next question: how can economic value creation be measured? We need a financial metric that is aligned with the principle of maximization of economic value (that is, discounted cash flows) and at the same time measures (and encourages) efficient and effective use of capital resources.

Measuring Profitability. In essence, all financial metrics concern the measurement of profitability. In its most basic expression, profit is simply earnings (E) after costs are subtracted. Similarly, in its most basic expression, Return On Investment (ROI) consists simply of the ratio of earnings to the amount invested (I):

$$\text{ROI} = \frac{E}{I}$$

For example, a project with $1000 invested and earnings of $100 each month has an ROI of 10% per month.

Economic Profit. Businesses often measure profitability using this definition of ROI. But in doing so, they are measuring *operating* profits, which are missing one key element of value creation: they don't take into account the cost of the capital (labor, equipment, etc.) that was employed in generating those profits. This is the key characteristic of the metric used in VBM, known as Economic Profit (EP) [2].

EP has its origins in the idea of *residual income*, a concept that is well over a century old. Writing in 1890, Marshall noted that "what remains of [a manager's] profits after deducting interest on his capital at the current rate may be called his earnings of undertaking or management." [7] The use of residual income as a financial metric has been popularized most in recent years in a variation that was promoted (and copyrighted) by the firm Stern Stewart as Economic Value Added or simply EVA©. It is conceptually equivalent to EP.

Economic Profit deducts a charge for the capital employed in generating operating profits. Why? Because capital *does* have a cost. That cost is k, the opportunity cost of capital that appears in the present value formula. Economic Profit is defined as

$$EP = C - I \times k$$

Where C is the cash flow (earnings) of the project; I is the amount of the investment; and k is the cost of capital. The $I \times k$ term is the "capital charge" on earnings.

In order to understand this idea, let us go back to the basic concept of opportunity cost: it is the return that investors demand from the project. If a project is earning an ROI of 10%, as in our example, it is fine if the investors only demanded an 8% return. But if they demanded a 15% return, then business value is not being created for them: it is being destroyed. An equivalent formulation of EP makes this idea clear:

$$EP = I \times (\text{ROI} - k)$$

This formulation demonstrates that value is being created only if the project has an ROI above its cost of capital. In our example, if investors demanded an 8% return, then

$$EP = \$1000 \times (10\% - 8\%) = \$20$$

But if investors demanded a 15% return, then

$$EP = \$1000 \times (10\% - 15\%) = -\$50$$

In each case, the *operating* profit is $100; but the *economic* profit after the capital charge reveals that only in the first case is business value being created for the investors—that is, profit over and above the minimum rate of return expected by them.

Making the Cost of Capital Explicit. The Economic Profit metric is completely aligned with the definition of value in VBM: in fact, it can be shown that representing project value as a stream of economic profits is equivalent to representing it with the standard discounted cash flow formula (see the Appendix for details).

Why, then, not directly use the discounted cash flow formula as a metric? The reason is that DCF, as a forward-looking calculation, cannot give an ongoing signal about what is happening in the project¾in particular, about whether value is being created or destroyed; and *neither* do traditional metrics like ROI or earnings. Reporting that a project is earning -\$50 in Economic Profit sends a much stronger signal about what is really happening than reporting that a project is earning \$100 or has an ROI of 10%, even though all of these metrics are communicating the same information. Analogous to Fowler's example of optimization in the previous section, the Economic Profit metric *makes the cost of capital explicit.*

Monitoring Efficient Resource Usage. Making the cost of capital explicit forces a manager to think twice before lavishing a project with more resources than are needed to accomplish its goals. On the contrary, it encourages him to eliminate waste in any form, from needless man-hours spent in upfront design to bloated programming teams to unneeded office space.

The results in management behavior obtained from switching over to this type of financial metric can be dramatic, whether in software or any other industry. Consider this observation about the effect on management practices within the Quaker Oats Company: "… its businesses had one overriding goal—increasing quarterly earnings. To do it, they guzzled capital. They offered sharp price discounts at the end of each quarter, so plants ran overtime turning out huge shipments … the pernicious practice known as trade loading (because it loads up the trade, or retailers, with product) and many consumer product companies are finally admitting it damages long-run returns. An important reason is that it demands so much capital. Pumping up sales requires many warehouses (capital) to hold vast temporary inventories (more capital). But who cared? Quaker's operating businesses paid no charge for capital in internal accounting, so they barely noticed." [15] (The problem went away when the capital charge metric was introduced.)

The alignment of many of the operating principles promoted by agile methods with this financial principle is remarkable: use all the resources you need, but *only* the resources you need. Agile metrics monitor the effects on operations; Economic Profit monitors the effects on business value.

Profitability and Growth. Software development managers, like those in any business, are often obsessed with growth: bigger teams; more powerful equipment; more investment in support software; elaborate, labor-intensive processes—effectively, a governing objective of "maximizing growth." One financial motivation for this phenomenon of "empire building" is that a larger capital base makes it possible to boost earnings. As a simple illustration, at the same level of ROI in our example, a manager could invest another \$1000 and double his earnings to \$200 per month.

But the agile movement has instinctively understood that not all growth is necessarily good. From an operating perspective, agile principles tell us that undisciplined growth can cause a project to reel out of control, and admonishes us to "start small." From a financial perspective, VBM tells us that unprofitable growth will destroy value and admonishes us to measure Economic Profit before making a decision to grow. In our example, doubling the invested capital when the project is earning below its cost of capital will double the economic loss.

Conversely, not all growth must be bad: measuring Economic Profit makes it possible not only to avoid value-destroying growth, but also to identify value-creating growth opportunities. If a project has a high level of Economic Profit on low invested capital, then an opportunity to increase capital expenditure and generate higher profits has been identified.

7   Conclusions

The operating principles embodied in agile methods make operating parameters explicit; the financial and strategic principles embodied in Value Based Management make profitability parameters explicit. They make a good pair.

References

1. Beck. K., Extreme Programming Explained: Embrace Change, Addison-Wesley, 1999.
2. McTaggart, J. M., P.W. Kontes, and M.C. Mankins, The Value Imperative, The Free Press, 1994.
3. Favaro, J.M., K.R. Favaro and P.F. Favaro, "Value-based software reuse investment," Annals of Software Engineering 5, pp. 5-52, 1998.
4. Luehrman, T. A., "Strategy as a portfolio of real options," Harvard Business Review, September 1998.
5. Favaro, J.M., "Managing Requirements for Business Value," IEEE Software, March 2002.
6. Erdogmus, H. and J.M. Favaro, "Keep your options open: Extreme Programming and the economics of flexibility," in Extreme Programming Perspectives, M. Marchesi, G. Succi, D. Wells and L. Williams, Editors: Addison-Wesley, 2003.
7. Marshall, A., Principles of Economics, Vol. 1, MacMillan & Co., New York, 1890.
8. Favaro, J. M. and K. R. Favaro, "Strategic Analysis of Application Framework Investments," in Building Application Frameworks: Object Oriented Foundations of Framework Design, M. Fayad and R. Johnson, Editors: John Wiley and Sons, 1999.
9. Harari, O., "You're Not in Business to Make a Profit," Management Review, July 1992, pp. 53-55.
10. Poppendieck, M., Lean Development: A Toolkit for Software Development Managers, Addison-Wesley, 2003.
11. Fowler, M., "Yet Another Optimization Article," IEEE Software, May 2002.
12. Favaro, J.M., "When the Pursuit of Quality Destroys Value," IEEE Software, May 1996.
13. Beck, K., "Software-in-Process: A New/Old Project Metric," September 2002, working paper, http://groups.yahoo.com/group/softwareinprocess
14. Favaro, J. M.,"A comparison of approaches to reuse investment analysis," Proc. Fourth International Conference on Software Reuse, IEEE Computer Society Press, Los Alamitos, CA, pp. 136-145.
15. Tully, S., "The Real Key to Creating Shareholder Wealth," Fortune, 20 September 1993.

Appendix

In this appendix we demonstrate more formally that the Economic Profit metric is fully aligned with the definition of value creation in Value Based Management. We will take the simple case of a project where there is a single initial investment I followed by cash flows C_t over an indefinite number of time periods. The cash flows are *discounted* at a rate k, corresponding to the *cost of capital* for the project. According to the DCF formula, the value of the project (its *present value*) is

$$\text{PV} = \frac{C_1}{(1+k)} + \frac{C_2}{(1+k)^2} + \frac{C_3}{(1+k)^3} + \dots$$

In order to arrive at an expression of cash flows in terms of Economic Profit, recall the definition of Economic Profit:

$$\text{EP} = C - I \times k$$

Therefore, in any time period t,

$$C_t = \text{EP}_t + I \times k$$

Now we substitute into the present value formula:

$$\text{PV} = \sum_{t=1}^{\infty} \frac{C_t}{(1+k)^t} = \sum_{t=1}^{\infty} \frac{\text{EP}_t + I \times k}{(1+k)^t}$$

$$= \sum_{t=1}^{\infty} \frac{\text{EP}_t}{(1+k)^t} + \sum_{t=1}^{\infty} \frac{I \times k}{(1+k)^t}$$

$$= \sum_{t=1}^{\infty} \frac{\text{EP}_t}{(1+k)^t} + I \times \sum_{t=1}^{\infty} \frac{k}{(1+k)^t}$$

Noting that the last summation involves an infinite geometric series and converges to 1, we have

$$\text{PV} = I + \sum_{t=1}^{\infty} \frac{\text{EP}_t}{(1+k)^t}$$

Therefore, the value of a project can be expressed *either* as the present value of all future cash flows (more appropriate for use in forward-looking valuations) *or* as the initial investment plus the present value of all future economic profits (more appropriate for use in period-by-period measurement of value creation).

Lean Management – A Metaphor
for Extreme Programming?

Michela Dall'Agnol[1], Andrea Janes[1],
Giancarlo Succi[1], and Enrico Zaninotto[2]

[1] Center for Applied Software Engineering, Free University of Bolzano-Bozen, Italy
{michela.dallagnol,andrea.janes,giancarlo.succi}@unibz.it

[2] University of Trento, Italy
enrico.zaninotto@economia.unitn.it

Abstract. This work focuses on the analogies and the differences between Lean Management and Extreme Programming. Lean Management (LM) is a management strategy that continuously tries to improve business processes focusing only on activities that provide value to the customer. The word lean means that only activities that increase the provided value for the customer are performed. Any additional activities that can be avoided are cancelled, that influences not only production-related processes but also to management structures. XP is a discipline of software development based on the principles of Agile Methodologies. The term agile describes "the ability to both create and respond to change in order to profit in a turbulent business environment [1]."

1 Introduction

A metaphor is "an expression which describes a person or object in a literary way by referring to something that is considered to possess similar characteristics to the person or object you are trying to describe" [2].

That means that a metaphor points out similar characteristics between two things. It establishes a system boundary that helps to decide what attribute the described object does or does not include.

XP and Lean Management have been often compared (e.g. [3]), in this paper we try to establish a metaphorical relationship between LM and XP and to deepen our understanding of analogies and differences.

Metaphors have been used by XP as a vehicle to convey information between people who do not share the same working language, e.g. developers and customers.

In this way XP experts and LM experts will be able to properly define their respective scopes of actions and identify additional areas for improvement.

We use this view of *is* or *is not* suggested by Kent Beck on OOPSLA 2002 to focus on where similarities and differences between Lean Management (LM) and Extreme Programming (XP) exist.

M. Marchesi and G. Succi (Eds.): XP 2003, LNCS 2675, pp. 26–32, 2003.

2   Background

2.1   Lean Management

LM has become a well-known and a successful management strategy. Its principles are those explained by Taiichi Ohno in his book The Toyota Production System [4].

LM and the underlying thinking model are based on an integrated set of industrial principles and methods. Its beliefs are these: value, value stream, flow, pull, and perfection.

The first step in Lean Thinking is to understand what value is and which resources are absolutely necessary to create value. Once this is understood, everything else is muda – the Japanese word for waste.

To eliminate muda it is necessary to focus on the value stream. You must divide the several steps in three kinds of actions: those that add value, those that do not directly add value but are also necessary, and those actions that do not add value: they must be eliminated [9].

Moreover, emphasis is put on a constant flow of production: set up times of machines are kept short, buffers are downsized and employees in form of teams are entitled to be active in problem-solving: if a problem occurs, worker are allowed to stop the line and to search for the real roots of the problems.

Pull means that production is not based on forecasts; the production is delayed until demand is present to indicate what the customer really wants. It may seem that lean system is fragile, because there is not a definitive plan. Instead, the Lean Production is forceful because it acts when the flow of information is maximized and does not anticipate the future.

The last principle is perfection: it is impossible to eliminate every kind of waste. You must come near it through incremental steps. The result is a better quality, a decrease of costs, deliveries on time and satisfied customers.

2.2   Extreme Programming

XP was first described by Kent Beck [5], where he describes XP as a "lightweight methodology for small- to medium-sized teams developing software in the face of vague or rapidly changing requirements."

XP let the customer pull the development of the product. XP assumes that the customer has detailed knowledge about the problems to solve, but not about the solution to develop. Only when the development of the solution has started and the outcome becomes visible and understandable the customer starts understanding how his/her problems could be matched to proposed solutions. Then he/she can advise what is missing and what is misleading in the solution.

3   Analogies between LM and XP

In this section we discuss analogies between LM and XP, in section 4 we discuss the differences.

3.1   Methodologies

"XP manages teams that produce software; LM manages companies that produce goods." – this was our first thought when we started to think about the relation of the two subjects. XP is a methodology – "a system of ways of doing, teaching or studying something", LM talks about management – about the "control and organization of something" [2].

So in this view they are very similar: they both teach you how to improve the quality of the desired output – whatever it is – software, cars or other goods. Both developed from the need and for this reason they are very practical. The recommendations they make consider primarily their specific problem domain – XP was introduced for software development, LM as a management strategy to lead producing industries.

3.2   Wicked and Tame Problems

To point out that the two subjects deal with the same class of problems we consider the categorization of problems into "wicked" and "tame" [6].

Some problems are obvious to solve. An example for this type of problems could be the writing of the New Year's greeting letters. Even a child understands that you are faster if you separate the task into different phases (buying sheets and envelopes, writing the letters, putting the letters into the envelopes, putting a stamp on every envelope).

The separation of the task into different phases is an intuitive way to master apparently difficult tasks. In the mentioned example it was possible because it was a so called "tame problem", i.e. problems that can be analyzed and solved with already well-known techniques in a straightforward way.

This "divide and conquer" approach can only be used if the problem can be planned in every detail. If it is not clear what consequences a certain activity has, the mentioned method does not work well. So called "wicked problems" have this characteristic. They can not be described entirely in every step. And therefore it is not possible to solve them perfectly but only to measure the grade of solution. Every proposed solution to a wicked problem is unique. For that reason there is no immediate and no ultimate test of a solution to a wicked problem.

Both, XP and LM deal with wicked problems. The one right solution is not possible to find so both have to improve their solutions continuously.

3.3   Muda

Lean Management addresses wicked problems in enabling the company to adapt rapidly to changing demands of the market. The basis is the absolute elimination of activities that are not needed to accomplish required tasks and that hinder the company to adapt to changing demand. Those unnecessary activities are profoundly exposed by Just-in-time Manufacturing.

JIT can be described as a Pull from Demand strategy: Only activities that are required from demand are performed. And they are performed exactly the moment they are needed.

XP addresses the same idea in different ways: the Planning Game helps to identify requirements continuously and allows easily changing, adding, or removing requirements. The customer is directly involved: with Customer-on-site it is guaranteed that even during development the customer can be asked if important decisions have to be made. The use of metaphors helps to establish a common vocabulary between customer and developer so that an efficient communication between the two is possible.

Testing in XP is performed before coding so that the test is used to define the required functionality. After writing the test (that in this case works as the specification for one feature) the minimum necessary code to satisfy the test is written. In this way developers concentrate only on creating the needed functionality and the phenomena of Featuritis can be avoided. "Software is growing far too complex ... Each new release of an application is festooned with gratuitous options and an army of tiny icons, the meanings of which I no longer remember [7]." This outline of Featuritis describes exactly the kind of waste Lean Management tells us to avoid.

Collective ownership and Refactoring in XP can be seen as the counterpart to "continuous pursuit of perfection [8]," a characteristic of the lean movement. Lean Management implies that the company should continuously try to improve the ability to avoid waste and to improve changeover times. Refactoring in XP has this objective: to constantly improve the code in the sense that waste (wrong, superfluous or difficult-to-read code) is eliminated.

Collective ownership guarantees that failures and bugs are quickly corrected. This practice can be found in Lean Management too: everyone has the right to stop the production when a problem arises without having to ask a superior.

3.4   Teamwork

Working together can help to avoid mistakes, to solve emerging problems and to focus on essential activities. The practice of Pair programming in XP and the empowered teams in LM address this matter.

By programming in pairs the knowledge about the code is better distributed and the problem field better understood. Teams in LM have similar purposes: The team is directly involved in the process. Tacit knowledge has to be leveraged and for this reason the team is used for problem solving.

Human resources play a very important role in both areas, for this reason too much overtime has to be avoided: the "40 hour practice" in XP helps to avoid mistakes done because of tired developers and keeps the team fresh and energetic.

In Lean Production also it is stressed that human resources are a vital part of the whole system. For this reason the working place should be clean and everything should be in place. LM states that in that case you should be more motivated workers, and that so accidents at the working place can be avoided.

The reaction to employees not willing to integrate in the team – not willing to adopt the new culture is the same in both systems: this employee has to leave the company – even if he or she was a very skilled worker.

3.5   Iterations

Lean Management is very determined to ensure a constant flow of production. This is to avoid extensive buffers between the different stations. The measure to establish is the "Takt time" – a German word meaning "beat" or "cycle" – it describes the speed at which products are ordered by customers and it helps to level production and to avoid excessive capacity costs.

In XP the planning game has the task to set the amount of features to develop during the next iteration. Before each iteration completed and planned tasks are compared so that the "velocity" (it could be described as a "tasks per iteration ratio") is determined. To find out the "velocity" – the speed of the development team helps to "level the production" – that means to constantly develop with a certain stable speed. This (together with the "40 hour principle") leads to higher quality and to higher job satisfaction.

3.6   Quality

In Lean Management quality is verified after every production step. If a problem arises it is cheaper to stop the production in order to reveal the root cause of the problem instead of fixing the problem afterwards on thousands of defect parts. Lean Management advises always to ask five times "Why" to really identify the root cause of an error. XP deals with quality issues using tests. Unit tests are made by programmers to ensure the correct working of a piece of software, acceptance tests are made by customers to confirm that the implemented functionality corresponds to the required features. The practice "Costumer on site" has the same purpose.

4   Differences Between XP and LM

4.1   Knowledge Transfer

If we consider the environments in which XP or LM should be adopted, and the way in which the ideas are implemented, the two are indeed very different: XP describes a set of practices primarily thought for developers. It wants to ease the tenseness often experienced between developer and customer because of conflicting aims. LM is addressed to the upper-management of a company and sees his task in the optimization of the whole company.

In XP the knowledge transfer usually is initiated by convinced developers. They use XP to improve the quality of their software. Often management is not easy to convince to adopt XP because of certain practices that seem to be against common sense like pair programming or refactoring. LM on the other side is a top-down approach. It is a decision of the management to implement lean thinking in their company, to change current processes – it is not only a slight optimization but a radical reorganization of the whole company.

In the software word the manager is also a software expert: the idea is that a developer can become a manager. In XP there is a flat system: the manager is seldom been a high-quality developer. Infect, the XP manager must know the software discipline and he can not be only acquainted with the management subjects.

In the other side, in LM a worker can not often become a manager. The LM manager has high skills of problem solving and he does not work in the manufacture process. There is a clear division between the chief and the other employees, even if a worker can stop the process if there is a problem.

4.2 Measuring

The productivity of a software team is difficult to measure. You can not use the lines of code written by developers in an hour without controlling the quality of these. You can not estimate the ability of a team considering only the time spent in a day to program. Often, the XP teams work less hours, but they produce software with high quality. Some manager has not understood this aspect and they has dismissed the XP developers even if the final result was optimal.

In LM it is simpler to valuate the quality of a product: you can check the physical defects. The productivity of a team can be determined by the numbers of items produced in an hour without defects. The manager has a clear vision about the capacity of a manufacture team.

4.3 Cost Structures

In XP the percentage of labor cost respects of overhead costs are higher than in LM. In LM many costs are linked with machineries, instead in XP many costs derived from the number of developers needed in a project. It is more difficult guess the labor costs in a XP project: every software product is different and every product requires different effort. In LM the costs of human resources are considered fixed costs and so they are simpler to calculate.

5 Summary

We think that many ideas that led to the development of Lean Thinking are directly related to fundamental principles of XP. To deal with wicked problems both approaches try reduce complexity by delaying decisions about produced goods with significant consequences to a point where the answer is easy to find: exactly to the moment when the good is really needed – just in time.

The underlying principles of both approaches are analogous: both underline the "Pull principle", in both cases it is important to banish waste in form of unnecessary work and to empower those who are holding the knowledge about the produced good.

References

1. Jim Highsmith: Agile Software Development – Why It Is Hot! In: Michele Marchesi, Giancarlo Succi, Don Wells, Laurie Williams: Extreme Programming Perspectives. The XP Series, Pearson Education, Indianapolis (2002) 9-16
2. Cambridge Dictionaries Online. Cambridge University Press (2002). Available at http://dictionary.cambridge.org, visited on January 10, 2003
3. Mary Poppendieck: Lean Toolkit (2003). Available at http://www.poppendieck.com/ld.htm, visited on March 10, 2003.
4. Taiichi Ohno: Toyota Production System. Diamond Inc, Tokyo (1978), English translation published by Productivity Inc (1988)
5. Kent Beck: Extreme Programming Explained: embrace change. Addison-Wesley (2000)

6. Mary Poppendieck: Wicked Problems (2002). Available at
   http://www.poppendieck.com/wicked.htm, visited on January 10, 2003
7. Nicholas Negroponte: Information Overbundling by a Monopolist (1998) available at
   http://www.mit.edu/~mcadams/papers/featuritis_talk_spring_1998-9.ppt, visited on January
   13, 2003
8. Bruce A. Henderson, Jorge L. Larco, "Lean Transformation: How to Change Your Business into a Lean Enterprise," Oaklea Press, 1999
9. James P. Womack, Daniel T. Jones: Lean thinking: banish waste and create wealth in your
   corporation. Simon and Schuster, New York (1996)

Metaphor Design Spaces

Martin Lippert, Axel Schmolitzky, and Heinz Züllighoven

Software Engineering Group, Faculty of Computer Science, University of Hamburg &
it Workplace Solutions, Ltd., Vogt-Kölln-Straße 30, 22527 Hamburg, Germany
{lippert,schmolitzky,zuellighoven}@acm.org

Abstract. The importance of using a good metaphor within projects was demonstrated by Kent Beck in his keynote talk at OOPSLA 2002. While the role of metaphors seems to be accepted, the process of finding the right metaphor is a demanding task. Letting the metaphor guide you to a suitable system architecture is even harder. Wouldn't it be nice to have a good starting point for finding and using a metaphor? We introduce the concept of a metaphor design space. This provides a set of proven design metaphors and combines them with architecture patterns similar to Martin Fowler's Enterprise Application Architecture (see [3]). The basic concept has evolved over the past ten years while working on metaphor-based object-oriented systems. We illustrate the concept using examples from the Tools & Materials approach (see [9]).

1   Introduction

Metaphors can be useful when implementing a software system. Kent Beck illustrated this in his keynote talk at OOPSLA 2002. In XP (see [1]), metaphors are mainly used to *facilitate communication* and to *identify the key elements and their interactions* in the system – the architecture. While it is accepted that metaphors can serve these purposes, finding the right metaphor for a specific project is a demanding task[1]. Letting the metaphor drive the development team towards an architecture is even harder. How can a metaphor lead to a conceptually matching and technically appropriate architecture?

The paper presents the concept of metaphor design spaces, using an example from the Tools & Materials approach. The approach was conceived in the early 1990s and has since been used in a number of professional projects (detailed information on the approach can be found in [9]). While the complete Tools & Materials approach goes well beyond metaphor design spaces, here our attention is confined to this topic.

2   Metaphor Design Spaces

Metaphor design spaces are like toolkits or frameworks for metaphors. They contain elements that help us to find metaphors for a system and use them to drive its architecture.

---

[1] Examples for metaphors used within XP projects can be found in [8].

M. Marchesi and G. Succi (Eds.): XP 2003, LNCS 2675, pp. 33–40, 2003.

Toolkits come in different varieties. They are differently equipped to support different tasks. A specific toolkit is typically chosen for a certain task. The same applies to metaphor design spaces. Different design spaces help us to develop different kinds of applications. We have to choose the right one.

To offer support in finding and using the right metaphors, metaphor design spaces consist of:

1. a set of interrelated metaphors and
2. a set of patterns and guidelines indicating how to concretize the metaphors into an architecture.

3   Metaphors in a Design Space

A metaphor design space contains a number of metaphors. An important aspect here is that the metaphors are related to each other – they are coherent. This means that the metaphors fit an overall context and have well-defined relationships. They enhance each other and do not confuse their user. They can be arranged into a picture that intuitively makes sense to everyone using them. The relationships between the metaphors are important because a mere collection of metaphors is not automatically a metaphor design space.

If the metaphors in a design space are to help us develop good software, they must relate relevant characteristics of a well-known object or concept (the "source" of the metaphor) to aspects of the software system. The desktop metaphor, for example, transfers the well-known characteristics of a real office desktop to the software domain. This means that the software's GUI has the look and feel of directly handling and arranging documents on the top of a desk.

Establishing the metaphor for software works best when several important characteristics can be transferred to the software. It makes little sense to use a metaphor if the software does not exhibit these characteristics. A software wastepaper basket that immediately "shreds" electronic documents or that ejects a floppy disk does not demonstrate intuitive behaviour. A software lever arch file in which the lever has to be operated before a document can be inserted is a metaphor overdone.

Metaphor design spaces are even more ambitious in terms of this transfer aspect. A design space should always be created on the basis of common everyday experience. This usually means that it addresses a group of people who handle their tasks in a similar way. The metaphors of a design space are thus task-oriented and not merely related to a common domain, like banking, insurance, payroll, etc.

3.1   Example: A Design Space for the Expert Workplace

The metaphor design space of the Tools & Materials approach focuses on the *expert workplace* where people perform their daily work using a computer in a highly interactive manner. The workplace is equipped with the proper tools for doing the job and is designed for people who know how to handle the different work tasks that make up their job. The expert is the actor; the workplace merely offers the means to an end. The Tools & Materials approach calls this general viewpoint the *Guiding Metaphor* or *Leitmotif.*

The different metaphors of the approach fit into this overall picture of an expert workplace: Tool, Material, Automaton, and Work Environment (see Figure 1). Obviously, these metaphors originate from the context of self-determined human work. When working, people intuitively distinguish between the things that represent their work objects and the things they use to get their jobs done. The metaphors are therefore concrete enough to let the users and developers associate useful ideas. On the other hand, the metaphors are easily transferable to different application domains.

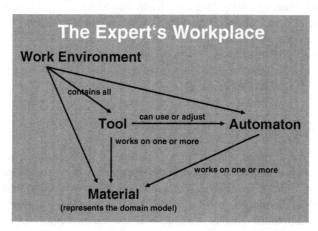

Fig. 1. The Key Metaphors of the Tools & Materials Metaphor Design Space

3.2   Example: The Metaphors in More Detail

A *tool* supports recurring work processes and actions. It is normally useful for a distinct set of tasks and objectives. A tool is handled by its users according to the requirements of the situation and is put aside when not needed. It does not prescribe fixed work steps or processes. If it is a software tool, it allows users to manipulate work objects interactively.

A *material* is a work object that is manipulated such that it will eventually become the work result. Materials are manipulated by the use of tools. Software materials embody »pure« domain-specific functionality. They are never used directly and are never active on their own. A software material is normally characterized by its behaviour rather than its structure.

An *automaton* performs a task that has been fully specified in advance and produces a defined result in defined variants. Once parameterized, an automaton can run without intervention over a lengthy period of time. Automatons often perform bulk operations.

A *work environment* is the place where work is carried out and the required work objects and tools are provided. Work environments embody a spatial concept and order principles. We distinguish between personal workplaces, allowing privacy and an individual arrangement of tools and work objects, and generally accessible rooms in a work environment.

The approach includes further design metaphors which address more specific tasks (such as office work) or work contexts (e.g. cooperative work in a small group) that are beyond the scope of this paper.

All metaphors fit the context of the expert's workplace. In this context, the relationship between the metaphors is explicit and easy to understand. Everyone (within this context) can imagine work as dealing with tools, materials, and automatons within an individual or shared work environment. Software systems designed using this metaphor design space are typically flexible to use and support the tasks of the user without a strict workflow.

While these design metaphors are concrete enough to evoke ideas about handling the elements of a software system, they have to be concretized for each project. Section 5 look at this topic in more detail.

4   From Metaphors to Architectures

The power of the metaphor design space is unleashed if the design space guides us to a matching software architecture based on these metaphors. A metaphor design space is not, then, an isolated set of related metaphors that can be used to build a system. It always helps its developers to find a matching architecture by means of concrete construction guidelines. This is possible because the metaphors of a design space relate to a model architecture and a set of well-defined design patterns.

In our experience, it is useful to have model architecture sketches within a metaphor design space of two different granularities:

- *An Architectural Big Picture:* This includes a common layering scheme, an idea of the basic elements of a proven architecture and/or a basic component model.
- *Design Patterns:* A number of design patterns that spell out the metaphors and their relationships to the level of concrete construction units (similar to the GOF design patterns, see [4]).

4.1   Example: An Architectural Big Picture

The general layering architecture of the Tools & Materials approach (see Figure 2) is based on [2]. The layering provides a basic structure for modularizing a complete application or product line. This architecture is built for large-scale software engineering (e.g. for the entire software architecture of a bank) but is also applicable to small-scale applications. It thus allows small applications to be scaled up without the need to redefine the architecture[2].

---

[2] The issue of architectures and frameworks vs. no upfront design is discussed in more detail in
    [6].

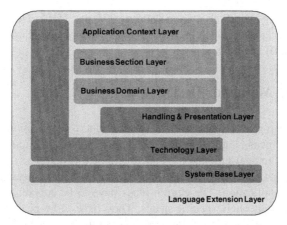

Fig. 2. General Layering Architecture Related to the Tools and Materials Approach

In addition to this general layering scheme, the architectural picture of the metaphor design space contains an outline for client/server in combination with multi-channeling front-ends. For this purpose, the architecture contains the idea of domain-specific services (similar to Service Layer in [3], pp. 133; see also [7]) in addition to the provided metaphors.

4.2 Example: Matching Design Patterns

The design patterns of this metaphor design space show how to move from metaphors to concrete implementations. For example, if you have chosen a tool as a design metaphor, you have several constructive design options. One is to construct a tool using a specific version of the Model-View-Controller pattern (see [3], pp. 330). To realize a complex material, there are container and role patterns to choose from.

Giving a detailed description of the architecture with these patterns would be beyond the scope of this paper. Section 5 uses an example to illustrate a possible application of the architecture.

4.3 Patterns of Enterprise Application Architecture

The architecture and the design patterns we use within the Tools & Materials approach are neither new nor revolutionary. They are based on our experience of building large-scale object-oriented systems. It is not surprising, then, that the architecture nicely matches the patterns of Enterprise Application Architecture, as described by Martin Fowler in [3].

The materials of our design space come very close to the Domain Model (see [3], pp. 116), utilizing Domain Value Objects (see [3], pp. 486). The architecture is completed by a Service Layer (see [3], pp. 133) via the domain services. The domain services are used by front-end applications. In this article, we have focused on tools (using a specialized MVC pattern, see [3], pp. 330). A different front-end channel can be realized by using Web Presentation Patterns ([3], pp. 329ff). The services typically connect to the database, which is why common mapping patterns ([3], pp. 143ff, 183ff, 215ff, 305ff) are used.

5   Applying Metaphor Design Spaces

A metaphor design space is tailored to a specific kind of application without limiting the domain. This means that the design space must maintain a middle course between being too abstract to be useful and too concrete to be transferable.

The result is that a metaphor design space contains generic metaphors for the core elements of the application. The central ideas have to be concretized and the metaphors adapted to suit one's specific needs. They have to be geared to the goal and domain of the concrete project. This is similar to the task of building an ontology. The general concepts are defined. They are then redefined and interpreted to match the specific situation. The result of this process is a set of concrete metaphors for the project in hand. These concepts are oriented to both the application domain and goal of the project, and to the core concepts of the design space.

5.1   Example: A Design Space for the Banking Domain

Based on our substantial experience in the banking sector, we use an example from this domain to illustrate how to apply the metaphor design space of the Tools & Materials approach.

In an ongoing project, we are developing an application to integrate third-party financial products into the general banking software. The software allows a customer consultant to sell bank products together with third-party products using a single desktop application. This product integration yields the greatest benefits if a consultant can compile and sell a mixed financing using a single application.

In the course of the project, we talked to domain experts about their work, about typical tasks and the relevant work objects they handle. The result was an initial sketch of materials: Product File, Product Description and Product Application Form. We asked them about the typical tasks they have to perform in their daily work: selecting the right products, combining them into a portfolio, calculating the financing, looking for the customer's other contracts, and so on. This led us to develop specialized tools for these tasks: a Product Selector (to browse the product file and select a product), a Customer Finder (to search for the customer and display the related contracts), a Calculator (working on the portfolio of product application forms to calculate the complete financing), and a Product Requester (to actually apply for a product or product combination).

The next step is to concretize the architecture. Services are introduced (e.g. to connect the Customer Finder with the back-end system). A number of domain value objects have to be implemented to serve as a base for the materials (e.g. amount of money and customer id). In addition, a simple desktop tool is created representing the work environment.

5.2   Example: Wrap-up

The example shows how the general idea of a material or tool can be adapted to a specific project. This seems quite natural. Experienced programmers might arrive at the same result without using the metaphor design space provided by the Tools & Materials approach, but the general guidelines of the approach can be applied nicely to the metaphors, providing a coherent overall picture: users work with tools to create, modify and combine materials; they choose the right tools at the right moment and decide which materials to work on; the relations between these components of the software system are clear and understandable within the domain, and they are predefined in terms of the metaphor design space.

6   Conclusion and Outlook

We have used the described metaphor design space for more than ten years with considerable success. It provides us with a vocabulary for communicating our ideas about architectures and systems under construction, beyond each individual project. We have experienced all the benefits of metaphors as described by Kent Beck in his talk on metaphors, without the trouble of having to find the right ones.

We believe that the general idea of a metaphor design space can be applied to more areas outside the Tools & Materials approach. We are currently engaged in more comprehensive research on the idea of using ontologies to help developers structure and find the key elements of their software systems.

In addition to the described example design space we reified parts of it as a framework using Java and the Eclipse Runtime Platform (see [5]).

Acknowledgements

The authors would like to thank the members of the Software Engineering Group at the University of Hamburg as well as the team of it-wps Ltd. for their ongoing work on the approach. Special thanks go to Stefan Roock for his comments on draft versions of this paper.

References

1. Kent Beck, Extreme Programming Explained – Embrace Change, Addison-Wesley, 1999.
2. Dirk Bäumer, Guido Gryczan, Rolf Knoll, Carola Lilienthal, Dirk Riehle, Heinz Zülligho-ven, Framework Development for Large Systems. Communications of the ACM, October 1997, Vol. 40, No. 10, pp. 52–59.
3. Martin Fowler, Patterns of Enterprise Application Architecture, Addison Wesley Signature Series, 2003.

4. Erich Gamma, Richard Helm, Ralph Johnson, John Vlissides: Design Patterns – Elements of Reusable Object-Oriented Software, Addison-Wesley, 1994.
5. JWAM Framework Web Site On-line at: http://www.jwam.org/.
6. Martin Lippert, Stefan Roock, Henning Wolf, Extreme Programming in Action – Practical Experiences from Real-World Projects, Wiley & Sons, 2002.
7. Martin Lippert, Henning Wolf, Heinz Züllighoven, Domain Services for Multichannel Application Software, in Proceedings of Hawaii International Conference on System Sciences 2001, HICSS 34, IEEE Computer Society, 2001
8. Wiki Web Site for example metaphors: http://c2.com/cgi/wiki?EightSystemMetaphors
9. Heinz Züllighoven, The Object-Oriented Construction Handbook, Morgan Kaufmann, to be published 2003.

An Experiment Working with RUP and XP[*]

Patricio Letelier, José H. Canós, and Emilio A. Sánchez

Department of Information Systems and Computation
Valencia University of Technology
Camino de Vera s/n, 46020 Valencia, Spain
{letelier,jhcanos,emsanchez}@dsic.upv.es

Abstract. We describe an experiment carried out to compare the use of
the Rational Unified Process and eXtreme Programming in the development of an information system, from a learning and training perspective.
The experience was carried out with upper-level undergraduate students
of the School of Computer Science at the Valencia University of Technology. We summarize the results obtained, from which some interesting
conclusions can be obtained.

1 Introduction

The raising of agile methodologies (AMs) in the last years has led the academic
community to seriously consider including AMs into the software engineering
curricula. However, changing common practice is difficult, especially if there is
no clear evidence that the new one will represent a real improvement in the
learning process. To help in the assessment of AMs in an academic environment,
we performed an experiment with fifth-year students of the School of Computer
Science at the Valencia University of Technology (UPV). We used the "Information Systems Laboratory" (LSI) course [3], in which students have to work
in teams to carry out a software project during one term. We worked with six
teams of 6-8 students each. All the teams were requested to develop the same
case study, consisting of the information system of a virtual store. Like in former
editions of the course, only a brief description of the problem was given by the
instructors. After a short preliminary study of the problem (a couple of hours) a
consensus was reached to develop only two subsystems, namely sales and stock
management.

The main difference with former editions of the course was that, instead of
having all teams using the Rational Unified Process (RUP) [7] as development
methodology, we decided that two teams would use RUP and the other four
would use XP [2]. We chose XP because it is the AM for which one can find the
most comprehensive documentation, even in Spanish.

The aim of this work is to compare RUP and XP regarding how easily they
are learned and applied for students (beginners in software process). In this

[*] This work has been supported by CICYT (Project DOLMEN-SIGLO) TIC2000-
1673-C06-01.

M. Marchesi and G. Succi (Eds.): XP 2003, LNCS 2675, pp. 41–46, 2003.
© Springer-Verlag Berlin Heidelberg 2003

paper we outline the main conclusions we obtained from a technical viewpoint. Though some comparisons between RUP and XP exist [8], [4], [5], and some adaptations to RUP to be used as an AM have been done (see e.g. [1]), but we have not found results based on actual experiences. That is why we think that some of the lessons learned during our experience can be the basis for more detailed experimental frameworks.

The rest of the paper is organized as follows: in section 2 we comment the project settings in the LSI context, in section 3 we describe some results of the experiment, and eventually, in section 4 we present the conclusions and future works.

2   Project Settings

The LSI course has been taught since 1997, with an average audience of 40 students divided in two groups. Classes are conducted in a laboratory with 20 computers. For each group, there are two 2-hour sessions a week. Students have a good knowledge about object-oriented modeling (with UML) and implementation, according to the contents of the previous courses. Furthermore they have some practice with unit testing techniques and tools. However, they are beginners regarding software development processes. Thus, the rough goal of LSI is to make students capable of facing a software development project, using a software engineering approach based in the notation-tool-process trilogy. Basically, the work consists of the development of several case studies along the course; some of them are small, solved in a couple of sessions using CASE tools (specifically, System Architect and Rational Rose) and the Unified Modelling Language (UML). The main part of the course corresponds to the development of a larger software project following a methodology.

Our LSI course has evolved from a schema very focused on teacher-guided problems towards the recreation of a software development project, emphasizing teamwork. Currently, the project is about 70% of the course duration. This, in the one hand, provides students with experiences closer to reality; in the other hand, there is an enforcement of several skills that are not covered by other courses in the Computer Science curriculum, like teamwork, playing roles with real responsibilities, scheduling tasks, goal negotiation, presentation of results, etc. All these skills have already been enforced in previous years using RUP, but we felt that using an agile methodology we could even improve them. However, as we found valuable our former experiences, we decided to keep two teams working with RUP, and create four teams that would use XP. Additionally, using two software development processes should help students to critically evaluate their process during the project development and, especially, to compare their achievements and failures with the ones of students working with different software process. Students were asked to present to their colleagues the state of the artefacts they generated, as well as a demo of the product they developed at the end of each iteration. Regarding XP, as the artefacts produced during the life cycle were very few, and mostly code, the students were requested to explain in details the activities carried out in the iteration.

At the beginning of the course, the basics of software processes, RUP and XP were taught by the instructors in four 2-hour sessions. During the development of the projects, the XP teams performed three iterations, whereas the RUP teams performed four: inception, elaboration and construction (x2). To synchronize RUP and XP software developments, we made the inception and elaboration phases in RUP(1 and 2 weeks long, respectively, to correspond in time with the first XP iteration. Each iteration was three weeks long. Two instructors worked as customers for each development team, working with them at least 6 hours a week. One instructor acted as coach, giving advice about methodological aspects to the team members. The average workload for each team member was about 12 hours a week.

Inside each team a number of different roles were assigned: Manager (x1), Tester/Tracker (x1) plus 4 or 6 programmers. The artefacts used in XP were User Stories, Tasks, User Interface Prototypes (throw-away) , Class Diagram (throw-away), Test Cases (functional tests) and the Code. In RUP, the artefacts were: Software Development Plan, Glossary, Business Use Case Model, Use Case Model, Vision, Use Case Specifications, Analysis and Design Model, User Interface Prototype, Data Model, Implementation Model, Test Cases (functional tests) and the Product.

The student assessment consisted of two marks assigned to the team at the end of each iteration. One mark was equal for everybody. Another mark was obtained by means of a number that the manager had to hand out among the team members.

3   Some Results

The experience was very well evaluated by the students, who initially were very eager to learn about RUP and XP, and at the end of the project they worked with and understood most of its core practices. Particularly, students that worked with XP provided their opinion about XP practices. Table 1 summarizes their answers to a questionnaire (the value between 0 and 10 represents a scale from low to high degree of application, difficulty or impact). Next we present some results or lessons learned from the experiment.

- In words of students, a remarkable fact associated to XP was its simplicity (from teaching and learning perspectives), reduced volume of documentation and intuitiveness and sound sense of many of the practices. However, positive aspects were said about RUP, specifically the detailed enumeration of artefacts to develop and the apparently more controlled development.
- The first iteration in XP presented many problems. In general, the productivity of the teams was under the estimated because the teams did not consider aspects like getting acquaintance with the development environment. However, from the second iteration on, productivity of the teams was rather predictable and planning was fairly accurate.

Table 1. Summary of students' opinion about XP practices

XP practice	Degree of application during the project	Difficulty to learn	Influence on the product quality
Planning game	9	4	9
Small releases	9	3	9
Metaphor	5	5	6
Design simple	8	5	8
Testing	7	8	9
Refactoring	6	8	8
Pair programming	7	4	8
Collective code ownership	8	6	8
Continuous integration	8	5	9
40 hours week	8	6	8
On-site customer	7	5	9
Coding standards	5	6	8

- The RUP projects ran smoothly during the first two phases, so the teams could reach the corresponding milestones (i.e. vision and architecture of the system). However, it was at the first implementation iteration when the problems appeared, so that the teams had to re-negotiate the terms agreed initially.
- Apparently, at the beginning XP teams had a higher productivity, implementing more functionality than RUP teams during the first two iterations. But eventually, after the last iteration all teams reached an equivalent result.
- The expected benefits of using one iteration in RUP to define the architecture of the system were not perceived, as the project was not completely finished. However, two of the XP groups requested the instructors to grant extra time to perform refactoring. This can be seen as an indication of problems in the system design.
- The precise definition of the different artefacts in RUP, as well as the templates provided, guided the teams in the information gathering process. However, in some cases the information was too detailed, even redundant (i.e. the Vision document), and produced a negative effect. In the XP projects, the students used the few examples that appear in the XP literature to prepare templates for describing user stories and tasks, though they contained information that was not used. The instructors provided a format to specify functional test cases (essentially composed of the following sections: execution conditions, input data, expected result and evaluation of the test).
- In the second construction iteration of the RUP processes, the artefact updating effort was greater than in XP, as one could expect from the higher number of artefacts to handle and the details required in RUP.
- Requirements management in the RUP processes was supported by Rational's RequisitePro [6], which allowed establishing traceability relationships between the different artefacts. The use of RequisitePro was optional in the XP processes, and only one team used it (and apparently with positive

results). All the other XP groups used a word processor to create all the artefacts other than code and UML models. Thus, obviously, the more artefacts
created, the more difficult was the traceability.
- The wide scope of RUP made us to adapt it to our small case study (this is
  not an easy task), thus, only partial aspects of RUP were studied. We used
  almost every core practice of XP.

4   Conclusions and Future Work

From the point of view of the teaching and learning experience, students and
instructors agreed that the experiment was very interesting and enjoyable. From
a technical point of view we can point out the following conclusions:

- No matter the assigned software process, there were good and bad teams
  (or not as good as others). This is a natural phenomenon and it does not
  depends only on the individual students' capacity but also it is caused by
  the group dynamic achieved by the team. The two best teams (and projects)
  were a RUP and a XP team.
- As expected, RUP teams needed more mentoring but they began the work
  without big troubles (while they were not programming!). XP teams immediately dealt with some problems (technical and also between team members),
  but most of those problems could be solved.
- Evidently, it is easier to have a software process ready to use according to
  the characteristics of our project (XP), instead of having a more universal
  software process (RUP) that must be adapted to the project.
- There are many open issues not covered in our experiment and comparisons.
  For instance, the impact on "software maintenance". This is an important
  aspect to take into account in a comparison because most of the advantages
  of the so-called heavy methodologies (like RUP) are perceived during this
  activity. RUP provides better conditions for maintenance due to a good
  and updated software documentation. This does not occur in XP where we
  essentially have code. Another interesting issue could be to consider using
  XP practices in RUP or vice versa.
- Although in XP it is emphasized that the better results are obtained applying
  all the practices, it is not clear what the impact on productivity or quality
  would be if some practices were used in a lower degree or if some practices
  were directly discarded. A similar reflection would be done about RUP.
- Associated to the previous point, maybe "customer on-site" is one of the
  practices with more inconveniences. RUP offers a more practical (or affordable) relationship between developers and the customer by means of traditional interviews and meetings.

It is obvious that our experiment, the results and the conclusions we have
extracted are limitated by context of LSI. Our concern in this first application of
XP was not focused on obtaining formal metric or conducting rigorous empirical
research. However, the informal observations we have derived can help to carry

out a more precise comparison between RUP and XP. This is our next step, and now we are preparing a more controlled experiment to assess the difficulty of learning and applying RUP and XP. Furthermore, next year we will begin working with XP in a similar subject in a lower-level undergraduate course.

References

1. A draft version of a book chapter illustrating the adaptation of RUP using agile principles can be found at objectmentor.com/resources/articles/RUPvsXP.pdf
2. Beck K., Extreme Programming Explained: Embrace Change, Addison-Wesley, 1999.
3. Information Systems Laboratory course homepage (in Spanish): www.dsic.upv.es/asignaturas/facultad/lsi/
4. Pollice G., RUP and XP Part I: Finding Common Ground. therationaledge.com/content/mar_01/f_xp_gp.html
5. Pollice G., RUP and XP Part II: Valuing Differences. therationaledge.com/content/apr_01/f_xp2_gp.html
6. Rational RequisitePro homepage: www.rational.com/products/reqpro/index.jsp
7. Rational Unified Process homepage: www.rational.com/products/rup/index.jsp
8. Smith J., A Comparison of RUP and XP. Rational Software White Paper. www.rational.com/media/whitepapers/TP167.pdf

Bridging Cognitive and Social Chasms
in Software Development
Using Extreme Programming

Orit Hazzan[1] and Yael Dubinsky[2]

[1] Department of Education in Technology & Science, Technion, Israel
[2] Department of Computer Science, Technion, Israel

Abstract. Extreme programming (XP) is one of the agile software development methodologies. It achieves its goals by the implementation of twelve practices, all aimed at reducing risks in software development and improving software quality. This paper presents two chasms inherent in software development processes - a cognitive chasm and a social chasm - and describes, based on our experience, how the twelve XP practices can help bridge these chasms.

1 Introduction

Software development is a very sophisticated activity from both a cognitive and a social perspective. Indeed, when examining common problems faced by software developers, both cognitive challenges (such as program comprehension) and social difficulties (such as the need to meet customer requirements or communication problem between teammates) can be found.

By reviewing each of the twelve eXtreme Programming (XP) practices, this paper examines XP from both a cognitive and a social perspective. Specifically, we explain how each of the twelve XP practices helps reduce cognitive and/or social complexities involved in software development.

2 The Abstraction Chasm and the Satisfaction Chasm

In this section, we present two terms that will be used throughout the article: the *abstraction chasm* and the *satisfaction chasm*. The ways by which XP helps bridge these two chasms are examples of how XP practices help reduce cognitive and social complexities of software development. In future work we intend to examine other means by which XP may reduce cognitive and social complexities.

The Abstraction Chasm: In the process of software development, software developers are required to think on various levels of abstraction and move between abstraction levels. In other words, programmer must move from a global view of the system (high level of abstraction) to a local, detailed view of the system (low level of abstraction), and vise versa. For example, when trying to understand customers' requirements during the first stage of development, developers must have a global view of the application (high level of abstraction).

M. Marchesi and G. Succi (Eds.): XP 2003, LNCS 2675, pp. 47–53, 2003.

On the other hand, when coding a specific class, a local perspective (on a lower abstraction level) should be adopted. Obviously, there are many intermediate abstraction levels in between these two edges that programmers should consider during the process of software development. However, the knowledge of how and when to move between different levels of abstraction does not always come naturally, and requires some degree of awareness. For example, a programmer may remain in too low a level of abstraction for too long a time, while the problem he or she faces could be solved immediately should the problem be viewed on a higher level of abstraction. The shift to that higher abstraction level might not be made naturally, unless one is aware that this may be a step towards a solution. The chasm in this case is observed between the inherent need in software development to move between local and global views of the application and the tendency to remain on one level of abstraction for too long a time.

In Section 3, we illustrate how XP helps reduce part of the cognitive complexity of software development by guiding programmers in the transition between levels of abstraction. This is referred to, in what follows, as bridging the **abstraction chasm**, the extremes of which are **local** and **global** views of the application.

The Satisfaction Chasm: In the process of software development, software developers must alternate between satisfying their current needs and supporting their teammates. For example, when trying to understand a specific piece of code, the programmer must first concentrate on his or her needs and consider what he or she does not understand; After completing the development of a specific class, developers must then consider their teammates' perspective and check whether the code can be improved in order to make it more accessible to the minds of others who did not participate in its development. However, how and when to alternate between satisfying ones individual needs and those of the others, with respect to software development, is no trivial matter. For example, one may continue coding as long as the code passes all tests, without realizing that the code is incomprehensible to others who did not participate it the development of that piece of code. The chasm in this case is observed between the inherent need to move between considering the individual needs and those of the collective and the tendency to deal only with the individual's needs with respect to software development.

In Section 3 we illustrate how XP helps reduce part of the social complexity of software development by guiding programmers in the transition between satisfying their own needs and considering the needs, perspectives and mental processes of others who are involved in the process of software development. As will be illustrated, some of the XP practices encourage the programmer to postpone satisfaction of immediate personal needs and first to dedicate additional efforts to the satisfaction of collective needs. By doing so, the software becomes more mentally accessible to the entire team, and time, money and work hours are eventually saved. This will be referred to, in what follows, as bridging of the ***satisfaction chasm***, the extremes of which are ***individual*** and ***collective*** needs.

Table 1. Mapping the XP practices according to technical and human aspects & levels of awareness

Awareness	Technical Perspective	Human Perspective
High	Refactoring Simple design	Metaphor Collective ownership
Intermediate	Coding standards Testing	Pair programming Planning game
Low	Small releases Continuous integration	40-hour week On-site customer

3   How Does XP Bridge the Chasms?

This section shows how each of the XP practices helps bridge the abstraction chasm and the satisfaction chasm. Specifically, we will illustrate how XP guides the transition between different levels of abstraction and between the consideration given both to individual and collective needs during the process of software development. Our claim is that while these two transitions should be inherent in any software development process, in many cases the natural tendency of human being is to behave in an opposite manner, i.e. to fail to think on different levels of abstraction and to fail to consider both individual and collective needs. We believe that these two human tendencies are the source of some of the major problems that are common in the world of software development. Furthermore, we believe that the strength of XP is in the fact that its twelve practices provide very specific guidance on how to bridge the abstraction and satisfaction chasms. We suggest that such analysis helps in understanding the strength of XP.

The twelve practices are presented below according to the XP practices mapping suggested by [2]. The mapping highlights both the social and cognitive aspects of XP, and, for each specific XP practice, reflects the level of awareness required for its implementation (see Table 1). Specifically, the twelve XP practices are mapped along two dimensions: 'Aspect' and 'Awareness'. On the 'Aspect' dimension, the XP practices are classified as addressing either a technical aspect or a human aspect of software development. The second dimension, 'Awareness', maps XP practices according to the level of awareness required to implement each of the practices throughout the software development process.

In the following explanation, we start with the more easily implemented practices (requiring a low level of awareness, e.g., 40-hour week) and move up in Table 1. We believe that such mapping assists the organization of what follows in the process, since it introduces the complexity in stages: First, the simple-to-implement practices are introduced, and later on the more complicated practices are addressed. In this paper we have restricted our analysis to the two chasms described above, and do not discuss other benefits of XP discussed in the literature (for instance, in [1]).

40-Hour Week. As described in XP books, the purpose of this practice is to maintain freshness. Interestingly, even this simple-to-implement practice contributes to the reduction in the cognitive complexity involved in software development. The work framework that this practice establishes, in which programmers develop software for only 8 hours per day, enables programmers to detach themselves from the details involved in software development and to take a more distanced look at the software after they finish the actual 8-hour development process. In contrast, when software developers spend 12 (and more) hours each day engaged in software development activities, they have no opportunity to reflect on the software from the "outside". This practice, therefore, helps one examine the developed software without being overwhelmed by details. In other words, the 40-hour week practice may enable the programmer, in many cases unconsciously, to consider the software development in terms of higher levels of abstraction, i.e. to bridge the abstraction chasm. We believe that the ability to view the system on a higher level of abstraction improves the code that is to be developed the following day.

In addition, this practice helps bridge the satisfaction chasm as well. The 40-hour week practice allows the programmer to dedicate more time to his or her personal life without having to fulfill other people's expectations by working long hours. In other words, this practice helps one decide whose satisfaction and expectations to fulfill. Since the entire team works according to this practice, it is assured that no conflict will exist that must be overcome.

On-site Customer. The fact that a real customer is part of the team and is available full-time to answer questions, enables developers to avoid making decisions regarding the customer's needs without checking first with the customer what is really needed and whether the decisions made are correct. That is, in addition to the importance of this practice from the customer's perspective, the immediate feedback that the on-site customer gives the developers helps them overcome a tendency to make decisions on their own (without the customer) in order to fulfill their need to proceed with the development process. In this way, this practice helps bridge the satisfaction chasm.

Small Releases. This practice promotes transitions between levels of abstraction. In a release planning, a global view is obtained. Details are added only with respect to the customer stories that are intended to be implemented in the forthcoming release. The recommended time period that leads to small releases (every 4-6 months) enables the programmer to move between levels of abstraction without spending too much time in abstraction levels that are too high (requirement analysis) or too low (coding).

Continuous Integration. This practice as well promotes transitions between levels of abstraction. In this case, the movement between abstraction levels depends on the results of the tests. If all the tests are passed together with the integrated code, the developer can remain on the same level of abstraction throughout the coding phase, since it is appropriate to stay on that level of abstraction. If the tests fail, the developer must gain a more global view of the system. He or she has to examine the application on a higher level of abstraction in order to find the source of the problem and the way in which the integrated code affects the rest of the code, as well as to consider possible solutions.

Pair Programming. This practice specifies that any code segment must be written by two developers, each of which has a different role. The developer with the keyboard and mouse must consider what the best way to implement a specific task is, while the other partner must think in a more strategic manner. It is easy to see how this practice can help bridge the abstraction chasm. Since the two individuals work on different levels of abstraction - the driver thinks locally; the navigator thinks globally - the same task is considered on two different levels of abstraction *at the same time.*

However, pair programming contributes also to the bridging of the satisfaction chasm. In this case, the chasm is represented by the gap between the individual tendency to move on as soon as the code is running (sometimes without testing it or rendering it more readable), and the benefits that the collective can gain from this practice, i.e. a code that is comprehensible by a greater number of people. In addition, pair programming also helps to stay focused on the task, while the individual tendency may be to engage in other activities (email, for instance), to skip testing, and so on.

Planning Game. In addition to its significant role in meeting the customer needs, the planning game, like the small releases practice, leads software developers to move between different levels of abstraction several times within the course of the development process. The release planning game is carried out on high levels of abstraction, while the iteration planning game takes place on lower levels of abstraction. Further details (such as development tasks and time estimations for the development tasks) are addressed only with respect to the iteration under discussion. In addition, the planning game enables the developers to see the way in which the system is composed of its components. Being part of the entire process, one can see the entire picture and at the same time observe the process through which the system is built up from its parts. This stands in contrast to a situation in which programmers are required to implement components that have been planed or designed by others. All of the above illustrates how the planning game is one of the XP practices that encourage developers to move between levels of abstraction - a transition which is inherent in software development processes and which is difficult to apply in the absence of specific practices that lead such a process - thus helping to bridge the abstraction chasm.

Coding Standards. Since programmers must write all code in accordance with rules that emphasize communication through the code, they must curb their tendency to write code in a way that is comprehensible to them alone. In other words, the coding standards practice leads one to overcome his or her individual needs in order to fulfill collective needs, thereby supporting the bridging of the satisfaction chasm.

Testing. In addition to the huge contribution of this practice to the correctness of software, this practice (with its strict and rigid implementation in XP) helps the individual bridge the satisfaction chasm. Testing helps the programmer avoid perceiving any code that runs as a complete code and prevents him or her from leaving any piece of code before all tests, written for it in advance, are passed successfully.

Furthermore, by the implementation of the XP practice of testing coding becomes a series of manageable steps through which small pieces of code are added to the application. Thus, testing helps one remain on a low level of abstraction when appropriate. This approach stands in contrast to situations in which the process of testing requires the mental manipulation of large amounts of code, a process that requires simultaneous consideration of the code on different levels of abstraction. This is of course very difficult and may explain the negative feelings that people associate with software testing. Not surprisingly, in XP development frameworks these negative feelings towards testing are transformed into more positive feelings.

Metaphor. In his talk *The Metaphor Metaphor*, given in OOPSLA 2002, Kent Beck said that "[o]f all the aspects of Extreme Programming, the suggestion that customers and developers share a common metaphor or metaphors for the system is the most problematic." We would like to present this practice as a means by which the bridging of the satisfaction chasm is assisted. Specifically, this practice encourages developers to look at the other person's perspective (customer, teammate) while engaged in development of the software. Instead of being "trapped" in one's own conception of the software development process, programmers must also take into consideration the perspective of the others in order to help everyone involved in the development process understand the elements of the software and the relationships between them. The chasm is especially noticeable when dealing with customers who are not always familiar with the technical jargon used by software developers.

Collective Ownership. As it turns out, since programmers know that their work will be examined by others and improved upon if required, there is a tendency to postpone immediate personal satisfaction and improve the code prior to its integration. Thus, the bridging of the satisfaction chasm is supported. In addition, when refactoring codes written by other developers, one must adopt the other's perspective in order to enhance his or her own understanding of the code.

Refactoring. In addition to the fact that refactoring improves communication and code simplicity, it also helps bridge the abstraction chasm throughout coding phases. This can be simply observed from the fact that in order to improve a piece of code one must examine it on a level of abstraction that is higher than that in which it was written.

Furthermore, refactoring also helps bridge the satisfaction chasm. According to this practice, it is not sufficient that the code pass all the tests. The code must also be restructured and improved upon in order to enjoy the benefits of long-term activities that are to be performed on the code, either by the developer who originally wrote the code or by other developers. In other words, the investment of a greater deal of effort now (that is, postponing individual's current desire to move on), will save time and effort in the future.

Simple Design. Like refactoring, this practice also aims at improving communications between the teammates working on the same software. This practice, too, promotes transition between different levels of abstraction. This is achieved by examining the code (low level of abstraction) by a higher level of abstraction (the simple design). Furthermore, the practice of simple design also helps to bridge the satisfaction chasm. It is not sufficient that the code pass all the tests, its design must also be simplified as much as possible.

4   Conclusion

This paper examines how XP practices support the bridging of two chasms that exist in software development - the abstraction chasm and the satisfaction chasm. In the case of the abstraction chasm, XP practices guide software developers to move between different levels of abstraction, or alternatively to stay at the same level of abstraction, all according to the case. In the case of the satisfaction chasm, XP practices guide software developers to postpone satisfaction of their own needs and, when appropriate, to invest more efforts in fulfilling the needs and expectations of others. We suggest that this observation can explain the rapid acceptance of XP by the industry. In our current work we expand this discussion and illustrate additional ways by which XP practices can reduce cognitive and social complexities of software development.

References

1. Beck, K.: Extreme Programming Explained: Embrace Change. Addison-Wesley 2000
2. Hazzan, O. and Dubinsky, Y.: Teaching a software development methodology: The case of Extreme Programming. In The proceedings of the 16th International Conference on Software Engineering Education and Training. Madrid, Spain 2003

A System Dynamics Simulation Model
to Find the Effects of XP on Cost of Change Curve

S. Kuppuswami[1], K.Vivekanandan[2], and Paul Rodrigues[3]

[1] Dept. of Computer Science, Pondicherry University
Pondicherry - 605014, India
skswami@yahoo.com
[2] Dept. of Computer Science & Engg. and Information Tech.
Pondicherry Engineering College
Pondicherry - 605014, India
kvivek27@yahoo.com
[3] Nature Soft, Chennai - 600004, India
paul_r@naturesoft.net

Abstract. The constant nature of cost of change curve is claimed to be one of the important benefits of eXtreme Programming (XP). In order to find the effects of XP on cost of change curve, we propose a system dynamics simulation model of XP software development process. We also describe the steps to be followed to construct cost of change curve using the simulation model.

1 Introduction

The software development life cycle consists of the following phases: analysis, design, coding, testing, release and maintenance. Normally, requirements for a project are finalized before starting the software development process. However, in practice the customers come up with requests for changing the already finalized requirements. The request for change in requirements is called change request. The change request may be any one of the following three types: (i) already implemented functionality to be dropped, (ii) already implemented functionality to be modified and (iii) new functionality to be added. The change request may occur, in any phase of the software development cycle. Boehm presented the relationship between the cost of implementing the change request and the phase in which it is introduced. It is of exponential in nature as shown in Fig. 1 and the curve is called cost of fixing error curve [1]. Later Kent Beck called this cost of fixing error curve as cost of change curve [2].

From Fig. 1 it is seen that the cost of change is very high and is of exponential in nature when software process comes closer to the end phases. This is due to the fact that, all the steps in the previous phases have to be repeated to implement a change request that would occur later.

This rework effort is quite high as the traditional methods require lot of effort in analysis and design phases. Hence, it is desirable to think of a software development

M. Marchesi and G. Succi (Eds.): XP 2003, LNCS 2675, pp. 54–62, 2003.

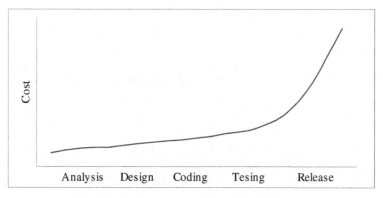

Fig. 1. Cost Change Curve of Traditional Methods

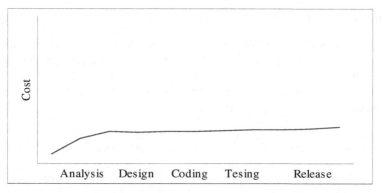

Fig. 2. Cost of Change Curve of XP

methodology which would flatten the cost of change curve. Kent Beck proposed XP methodology which could result in a constant cost of change curve as shown in Fig. 2 [2]. Here, the cost for implementing the change request is same irrespective of the phase in which the change request is introduced.

1.1   The Cost of Change Curve of XP

The reasons for the constant nature of cost of change curve in XP are given below:

- Simple design emphasizes to do things that are required today. Major parts of the design decisions are done at later stage, especially at coding stage [2].
- The small releases practice advocates incremental development of software. It is always easier to implement change requests in incremental software development model.
- Refactored code provides an opportunity for the developers to reuse the existing code for implementing new requirements [3].
- The requirements are defined in terms of stories. As far as possible the stories are framed as independent modules. So change in one story does not propagate to other stories.

- All the developers are familiar with the complete system through collective code ownership, pair programming and coding standard practices. Hence, the developers understand the change requests easily and implement them quickly.
- Continuous testing, onsite customer and continuous integration practices ensure early detection of misunderstanding of the requirements and bugs[3] [4].

Even though it is claimed that XP process and practices flatten cost of change curve, no proof is found in the available literature either in the form of case studies or survey. The correctness of constant nature of cost of change curve of XP has also been questioned by some developers [4]. Hence, the effects of XP on cost of change curve have to be investigated using an appropriate method. In this paper, we propose a system dynamics simulation model to find the effects of XP on cost of change curve.

2   Investigation Method

The survey, case studies, controlled experiments, executable process, cost estimation and simulation models are some of the important methods available for investigating software development process [5] [6] [7]. Simulation model is found to be more suitable for investigating XP software development process as the other methods have the following constraints [6] [8] [9]:

- The task of collecting data to construct cost of change cost curve requires a high level of control and monitoring of project variables. Hence, survey method can not be used.
- The controlled experiment is difficult as the experimentation is to be spread over the entire software development cycle.
- In case studies, there will be a possibility that the change requests may not have come at all during the entire period of software development project. Without sufficient number of change requests it is not possible to collect data.
- No off-the-shelf cost estimation models are available, which take into account of XP practices.

Many simulation techniques have been proposed for simulation of software development process [9]. The system dynamics modeling based simulation technique is one of them and has been used elsewhere to model software development process [7] [10] [11] [12] because it is convenient for strategic analyses and highly suitable for modeling complex, dynamic and nonlinear interactions of software development process.

The system dynamic models proposed in [7] [10] [11] and [12] can not be used for modeling XP process, as they do not take into account of procedures, practices and roles of XP.

3   System Dynamics Modeling

The system dynamics field was introduced by J. W. Forrester to apply the engineering principles of feedback and control to social systems [13]. Abdel-Hamid was the first person to use system dynamics for modeling software project management process [11]. In system dynamics a system is defined as a collection of elements that continually interact with each other and outside elements over time, to form a unified whole [14]. The two important elements of the system are structure and behavior. The structure is defined as the collection of components of a system, and their relationships. The structure of the system also includes the variables that are important in influencing the system. The behavior is defined as the way in which the elements or variables composing a system vary over time [15].

System dynamics modeling is used

- to understand how systems change over time and
- to analyze how structural changes in one part of a system might affect the behavior of the system as a whole

The software development process is highly interconnected components such as products, process and people. It also includes variables such as effort, errors, and lines of code that change over time. The system dynamics model is highly appropriate method to model software development process.

4   SD Model of XP Software Development Process

The proposed system dynamics model for XP project is illustrated in Fig. 3 and it is generic in nature. The model is created using Vensim simulation tool [16]. For easy understanding we have shown only the high level diagram.

Before explaining the model, we briefly describe the system dynamics modeling elements.

Sources and sinks: are the accumulations that are external to the system being modeled and connected to the system as input and output respectively.

Level: represents things being accumulated within system or utilized by the system.

Flows: represents the movement of accumulation. The rates are the flows, which increase or decrease the levels.

Auxiliary variables: are the fundamental variables that also describe the system.

Constants: whose values do not change.

Links: shows the connection between two model elements.

The graphical notations for the above modeling elements are shown in legend of Fig. 3.

XP Process: The input to this model is project size and output is accepted stories. The input requirements are transformed into accepted stories by adopting the following processes successively: story creation process, estimation & schedule process, design process, testing & coding process, refactoring process, integration process and acceptance test process. Story creation and estimation & schedule processes are done only once in a life cycle. The other processes are repeated for each of the small releases. The refactoring process is applied only to a part of the developed code.

Assumptions: The proposed model is developed assuming the following:

- Each story is having same complexity. The effort to implement each story is the same.
- The errors introduced in any process are found out in the same process itself.

Modeling of XP Process: In order to compute the total cost of a project, the important process elements have to be modeled. They are input to a process, output from a process, and the rate of transformation. The input and output of a process are modeled as levels. The rate of transformation is modeled as rate component of system dynamics. The number of story cards created, the number of designed stories, the number of developed and unit tested stories, the number of refactored stories, the number of integrated stories, and the numbers of acceptance tested stories are the elements that are modeled as level variables. The important rates are story card creation rate, schedule creation rate, design rate, programming rate, refactoring rate, integration rate and acceptance test rate. The rates are in turn affected by other variables and these variables are modeled as auxiliary variables. The model incorporates the influence of XP practices, by making the rate variables dependent on XP practices as shown in Fig. 3. Other variables such as onsite customer ability, XP team experience are also affecting the rate and hence modeled as auxiliary variables.

For brevity, we explain only the story card creation process of XP. The requirements and user stories are modeled as levels. The number of story cards created per day is modeled as rate variable (story creation rate). The story creation rate depends on three auxiliary variables as shown in Fig 3.

The relationship between modeling elements can be defined in the form of equations. The equations of the story creation process are given below:

story generation rate= IF THEN ELSE(Story creation   over, 0,nominal story
generation rate * onsite customer capability * XP Experience)   (1)
       Units: stories/Day

user stories= INTEG (story generation rate,0)
       Units: stories   (2)

Story creation over=IF THEN ELSE (user stories = Size of the project, 1, 0)
       Units: Dimensionless   (3)

4.1   Simulation Steps to Construct Cost of Change Curve

The simulation model generates the following variables that represent behavior of the project over time:
- Effort spent on each activity such as planning game, refactoring, programming, and integration
- Cumulative effort spent in person days

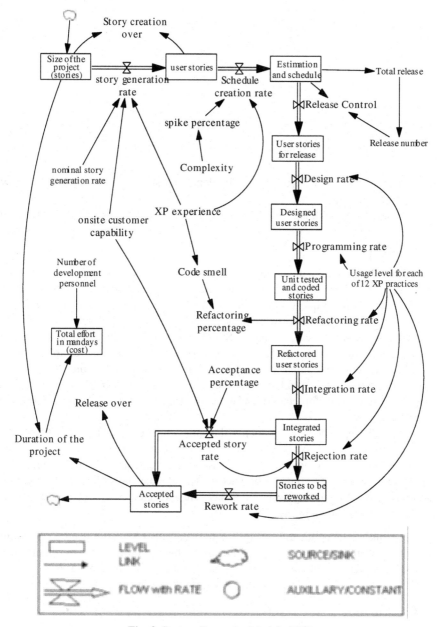

Fig. 3. System Dynamics Model of XP

- The level variables such as the number of story cards created, number of story cards designed, etc. For example, a graph showing number of user story cards created over time is given in Fig. 4.

The simulation can be stopped at any specific time to introduce change requests. The change requests may be any one of the following three types: (i) already imple-

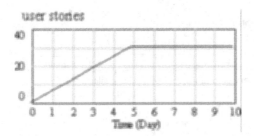

Fig. 4. Number of User Stories Created Over Time

mented story to be dropped. (ii) already implemented story to be modified. (iii) new story to be added.

It is assumed that a change request occur only once in a simulation run, but it can occur at any time of software development cycle. The simulation steps to construct cost of change curve are given below:

1. Initialize all parameters including size of the project. The project size is estimated in terms of number of story cards. Simulate the project completely without introducing any change request. Obtain the total cost and number of calendar days required for completing the software project.
2. Initialize all parameters as in step 1. Simulate the project for a calendar day and then introduce a change request, which modifies the related level variables. Now, find the total cost by continuing the simulation from second day until the completion of the project. The difference between the cost computed in the step 2 and the step 1 is the cost of implementing the change request, which is introduced at the end of first day.
3. The step 2 is repeated by introducing the same change request on 2nd, 3rd, 4th, 5th day and so on, up to the number of calendar days computed in step 1.
4. The additional cost computed in step 2 and step 3 represent the cost incurred for implementing a change request on successive calendar days of project period. A graph is drawn by plotting cost versus day. The expected cost of change curve for an XP project is shown in Fig. 5.

In the simulation model the change request can also be introduced in different phases of software development in addition to day basis. For example, the change can be introduced after the planning game or after any one of the small releases.

5   Conclusion

We have proposed a system dynamics simulation model of XP software development process to find the effects of XP on cost of change curve. We have also proposed a simulation method to construct the cost of change curve. As a case study, we are planning to make use of the proposed model to simulate a real XP project to construct cost of change curve. We are in the process of collecting project specific values of model variables, by employing metric collection program.

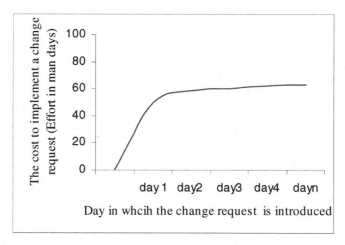

Fig. 5. Cost of Change Curve for XP

Even though, the proposed simulation model is developed to construct the cost of change curve, it also can also be also be used to find effects of individual practices on cost, development time, etc. This model is useful for project managers to perceive effects of new policies with out actually implementing them.

References

1. Boehm, B.: Software Engineering Economics. Prentice-Hall, EnglewoodCliffs, New Jersy, 1981.
2. Beck, K.: Extreme Programming Explained: Embrace Change. AddisonWesley, 2000.
3. Cauwenberghe, P.V: Refactoring or upfront Design. In: Proceedings of Xp2001 Extreme Programming, Sardina, Italy 20-23 May 2001.
4. Cockburn, A.: Reexamining the Cost of Change Curve year 2000. Online: http://www.xprogramming.com/xpmag/cost_of_change.htm
5. Kitchenham, B., Piclard, Pfleeger, S.L: Case Studies for Method and Tool Evaluation. IEEE Software , July 1995,
6. Zelkowitz, M.V., Wallace, D.: Experimental Validation in Software Engineering. Information and Software Technology 39(11), November 1997.
7. Tvedt, J.D.: An Extensile Model for Evaluating the Impact of Process Improvements on Software Development Cycle Time. Ph.D Dissertation, Arizona State University, May 1996.
8. Dewayne, E., Adam A.P, Lawrence, P, Votta, G.: Empirical Studies of Software Engineering: In: Proceedings of 22nd International Conference on Software Engineering 2000, ACM.
9. Kellner M. I., Madachy, R. J., David, R.: Software Process Simulation Modeling: Why? What? How?. Journal of Systems and Software, Vol. 46 no.2/3, April 1999.
10. Madachy, R.: A Software Project Dynamics Model for Process Cost, Schedule and Risk Assessment., Ph.D. Dissertation, Dept. of Industrial and Systems Engineering, University of Southern California, Los Angeles, California, December 1994.

11. Abdel-Hamid, Madnick, S.: Software Project Dynamics. Englewood Cliffs, NJ, Prentice Hall 1991.
12. Pfahl, D., Lebsanft, K., Using Simulation to Analyze the Impact of Software Requirement Volatility on Project Performance. Proceedings of ESCOM-SCOPE 2000, April 2000, Munich, Germany, Shaker Publ., pp. 267-275.
13. Forrester, J.W.: Industrial Dynamics. The MIT Press, Cambridge, 1961.
14. Mohapatra, P.K.J., Mandal P., Bora M.C.: Introduction to System Dynamics Modeling. University Press, 1994.
15. System Dynamics Learning Materials, Road Map 2 Online at: http://www.sysdyn.mit.edu/road-maps/home.html
16. Vensim Website at: http://www.vensim.com.

Real-Time Extreme Programming

Craig Gelowitz[1], Ian Sloman[2], Luigi Benedicenti[1], and Raman Paranjape[2]

[1] TRLabs, 108-2 Research Drive, Regina, SK, Canada
craig@reg.trlabs.ca
http://www.trlabs.ca
[2] Faculty of Engineering, University of Regina, 3737 Wascana Parkway
Regina, SK, S4S 0A2, Canada
i.j.sloman@accesscomm.ca
{Luigi.Benedicenti,Raman.Paranjape}@uregina.ca

Abstract. This paper is a research study to analyze the potential use of extreme programming paradigm for real-time programming. The analysis begins by presenting a common reference model for real-time programming and coupling with existing formalisms. The paper highlights the parts of the extreme programming approach that can contribute to the real-time development process and the aspects of extreme programming that will not work for real-time development, thus presenting a viable approach to real-time extreme programming.

1 Introduction

This paper presents an analysis of the applicability of an agile development technique, extreme programming, for real-time programming. Extreme programming (XP) is a software development methodology that focuses on several aspects such as communication, feedback, and programming in pairs [1]. It also brings software development accomplishment levels to reasonable, reachable levels that are comprehensible by all the players involved in the development process.

The use of an agile development method like XP to the development of real-time software systems is particularly attractive because it has the potential of lowering the development time while keeping a uniform and measurable quality level. Moreover, the adoption of XP in a real-time development cycle makes it possible to utilize the unique advantages proper to XP in the development of a mission critical system. These advantages include the testing mechanism, the customer focus, and pair programming.

Real-time systems require special considerations. These special considerations include not only time constraints, both on hardware components and on software components, but also the specific procedures to be followed in the development process of real-time applications.

This paper presents a modified Extreme Programming process that allows for real-time constraints. The process presented in this paper is justified only theoretically, and although an experimental development context has been set up for the validation

M. Marchesi and G. Succi (Eds.): XP 2003, LNCS 2675, pp. 63–72, 2003.
© Springer-Verlag Berlin Heidelberg 2003

of this procedure, this paper only addresses the modifications to Extreme Programming.

This paper is organized as follows: this section presents an essential literature review on real-time programming with particular focus on recent modeling attempts. Section 2 provides the requirements for a real-time development process with particular regard to XP. Section 3 contains the description of the proposed approach. Section 4 presents the conclusions and indications for future work and validation.

1.1   Building Real-Time Systems

Real-time systems are categorized specifically by time constraints placed on the execution of the system in question. A system with time constraints is considered a failure if the time constraints are not met. With respect to software, the execution of the code must progress through its functions based on a given time constraint. Conversely, most software development does not fail or depend on time constraints. In most cases software executes through the code at whatever pace the processor and operating system allows. The performance is evaluated with no regard to speed or constraints. Real-time software is restricted to perform at a given speed or to finish execution within a given time.

A hard real-time system does not accept any failure to abide to the time constraints at all times. A *soft* real-time system can accept a lower performance level for lateness, i.e., it is not catastrophic if all the deadlines are not met. It is not even essential that all events be processed to prevent malfunctioning, for example missing the occasional air ambient temperature reading would not prevent monitoring of the air temperature trend.

In terms of programming languages, both Java and C++ can not handle real-time applications without extensions. The Realtime Specification for Java – final as of 2001 Nov. 12 – extends the Java™ Platform to support real-time application programming [2]. Both hard real-time and soft real-time systems are covered by the specification. At the University of Miami a C++ preprocessor, Hard Real-Time C++, has been developed that extends C++ for specifying timing constraints for hard real-time systems [3].

1.2   Extreme Programming

Extreme Programming is a lightweight development technique that adopts specific practices to accelerate the development while maintaining a measurable assigned quality level [1]. XP has been the topic of an ongoing controversy for a few years [4]. Many of the reports on implementing XP have been the results of direct experience with it [5]. However, it is not clear whether or not XP has been more successful than traditional techniques, and the method is still too new to understand its full potential [6]. The controversy around XP is described very thoroughly in a book by McBreen [7]. Since XP is an eminently practical development technique, many efforts have been made to adapt it to specific application domains, both successfully and unsuccessfully. One of the limitations perceived in XP is the difficulty to extend the method to a large development effort – like the development of an operating system, for example.

1.3   UML and Real-Time

Modeling systems reside at a higher level of abstraction than programming languages. In recent times, the Unified Modeling Language (UML) has become well known and general enough to be applicable to a wide variety of software development efforts. In particular, UML does not require extensions or additions according to Douglass [8], although Lyons describes a set of constructs that have been combined into what he calls UML for Real-Time [9]. Douglass contends that UML already has a profile for schedulability, timeliness and performance modeling. For this paper, the material published by Douglass will be the preferred reference [8].

One more interesting aspect of UML is its expandability as a language. Although UML is generally employed as a graphical representational abstraction of a software system, there exists a complete and extensible language specification for UML. Therefore, it is possible to expand the UML notation to accommodate a semantics description of real-time constraints and activities. One such example is Executable UML.

Executable UML is a graphical specification Language combining a subset of UML (Unified Modeling Language) with executable semantics and timing rules. Executable UML can be used to create a fully executable system specification consisting of class, state and action models. An executable specification can be run, tested, debugged and measured for performance. An executable specification is built, executed and tested much like a program [10].

Each symbol of the graphical building block has a concrete definition. These building blocks operate in a framework of carefully defined timing values, allowing the timing considerations to be fully analyzed. Executable UML drives operations from action on state machines.

UML Packages, Class Diagrams, State Models, and a semantically valid action language are necessary and sufficient to create a complete, consistent, and verifiable model of an application. The Class Diagram provides the data specification, State Models provide control specifications and the action language provides the specification of the algorithm [11].

Other types of modifications to UML have been attempted [12]; of particular interest is the adoption of action semantics. Action semantics is akin to denotational semantics, but with a considerably simpler descriptive language [13]. This expands the applicability of action semantics to a large set of programming languages. Action semantics have been used to bring UML into a full temporally aware language. These UML modifications have been used successfully in several cases [14].

2   Real-Time Development Process Requirements

To make a stronger case for the application of XP to real-time development, it is necessary to analyze a real-time method and compare it to XP. The method chosen for this paper has been designed by P.A. Laplante, an engineer for avionics systems – an optimal test base for real-time constraints [15].

The phases of a typical software project usually fall within the parameters of a waterfall model. Laplante identifies those phases and are given in order of time as follows:

1. Concept phase.
2. Requirements phase.
3. Design phase.
4. Programming phase.
5. Test phase.
6. Maintenance phase.

The remainder of this section describes each phase in relation to XP.

2.1   Concept Phase

The concept phase defines the customer needs, the overall goals and the potential functionalities. In this phase Laplante asserts that most authors do not recognize this phase and confuse it with the requirements phase. No documents are created during this phase and the main goal is to define the product need and goals. Laplante also suggests the idea that the feasibility of testing the new product should be considered.

XP's approach for this phase is unclear and probably not considered because ultimately this is a customer decision. The customer must have an idea of the product before the XP process begins. This shows that XP does not conflict in any way with this phase of real-time development. Interestingly enough, the feasibility of testing that is considered in this phase parallels XP's idea that testing should be one of the first things considered.

2.2   Requirements Phase

The requirement phase is where the ideas become part of a written document or specification. The customer prepares the document. This document needs to contain all the specific information for the product. Timing and throughput, user interface, hardware/software requirements and accuracy requirements are all part of this document.

Again the integration of XP's paradigm has little or no contradictions with this. The customer's participation in the user stories of XP takes care of all of this. All the necessary requirements are part of the user stories. XP also has an advantage here because user stories can change with very little time overhead, as opposed to redoing a complicated requirements document.

Testing requirements should be part of a formal test plan at this stage. Once again XP's focus on testing first also parallels this idea, without the need for a complicated document structure.

Laplante gives rules for requirements and design documents as follows:

1. The document must be complete.
2. The document should be correct.
3. The document should be consistent.
4. Each requirement or design element should be testable.

XP shows little or no contradiction with this. The only contradiction would be that a requirements document, intended as a formal document, is not necessary. User stories should be as clear as the above specifications indicate but are not contained in a formal document.

2.3   Design Phase

The design phase consists of writing a detailed design document. The design document should include how the requirements should be met. Partitioning the functionality of the program into software modules does this. Laplante indicates that the design document should coincide with some accepted standard. He maintains that a strict design procedure is important for real-time systems. Laplante also suggests that a set of test cases should be developed in conjunction with the design document.

Conflicts, redundancies and requirements with current technology at this point may indicate problems. Changes in the requirements document at this point may have to be made.

The tasks of the design phase are thus as follows:

1. Partition software into modules.
2. Prepare detailed design document.
3. Develop test cases.

Laplante also indicates some of the considerations of partitioning software into modules by hiding the implementation of the module and only have the functionality of the module visible to the other modules. In this way, changes in the modules implementation should not affect the rest of the system.

XP's use of CRC cards are yet another parallel to this phase. The major contradiction in this case is the detailed document and adherence to an accepted standard. CRC cards are not a standard and are by no means the only way to design software in XP. The parallel to this phase despite the adherence to a standard is that the CRC cards represent loosely coupled software modules. Since XP also relies on test cases, the only missing deliverable is the detailed design document from this phase. Again, XP excels is this area with turnaround time. For example, CRC cards are easily ripped up and redone on the fly, as opposed to reformatting a formal design document.

2.4   Programming Phase

Laplante writes briefly about the programming phase. He insists that the programming phase itself should not start until the requirements and design phases are complete. He does however admit that there is some overlap in most cases. This is due to problems that are solved during programming.

Test cases are also performed during the programming phase to ensure more problems do not exist and to facilitate repeat testing of the code. The code is written in this phase and code-writing does not end until all the requirements and the integration testing are successful. Part of the programming phase also consists of management issues, like version control. This provides mechanisms for version integrity and tracking changes. Laplante does not mention the way in which programmers deal with the problems of the modules.

XP follows the same procedures mentioned above with the exception of clear delineations between phases. Test cases are used in XP extensively. Since Laplante admits that overlap exists between design and programming phases, XP can also be appropriate in this case. XP's design can change within the programming phase as problems are solved. Again, XP has the advantage here because small changes in design do not require complicated document changes. The iterative nature of XP allows for changes in design as the programming phase continues.

XP also makes reference to how programmers should attack problems. XP promotes the use of pair programming in its fundamental software development philosophy. This means that pair programming is done during the entire phase of programming. The pair programming idea is not new to programming but XP takes the idea to the extreme. Any and all programming is done in pairs, rather than traditionally only done when complicated algorithms are involved or emergency situations exist.

The advantages of this technique are immediately clear. The old saying "two heads are better than one" can be applied to this methodology. When code is created via pair programming the code is completely understood by two people rather than just one and the code is generally more understandable. Code knowledge is further shared and distributed as pairs are split and reconstituted appropriately.

2.5   Test Phase

Laplante maintains that the last phase before system delivery is the testing phase, which is an explicit phase of its own despite the fact that testing occurs throughout all the previous phases. The software is run through a formal set of tests cases developed in parallel with the software. This phase is rigid in the sense that no change to the software or documentation is allowed during this phase. The software is either successful or fails during this phase. A report is generated which summarizes the results and execution of the program. This phase consists of the following:

1. Software Validation.
2. Preparation of test reports.

In XP, this phase is not separate from the other phases since validation and testing occurs as a continual part of the methodology. Ultimately, XP requires testing as a part of its iterative process and all tests must pass in all iterations. This ensures that a final test phase is not needed. Refactoring is also part of the XP process which must also be tested continuously, to ensure operation of the product is successful.

2.6   Maintenance Phase

Maintenance consists of the following activities:

1. Product Deployment.
2. Customer Support.
3. Continuing program and error correction.

Maintenance does not end until the software system itself is no longer supported. Improvement areas are identified through out a programs life and error adjustment is taken care of through regression testing.

The maintenance phase of XP is an ongoing phase of the overall development. Refactoring is one type of maintenance that is ongoing in XP's product development. Since the customer and the programmers in XP are tightly coupled, the maintenance phase requires little adjustment for real-time XP. The only foreseeable problem with maintenance and XP is the lack of documentation. If XP is followed by the accepted definition, the code should be all the documentation one needs. XP also allows documentation for the people outside of the development team.

3   Proposed Approach

If your eXtreme Programming lifecycle does not work, modify to make it work; "making small adjustments [...] the application of XP in your environment should be the same" [5]. This credo applies to even the most formal of software development processes, such as the Capability Maturity Model; although modifying this process is part of the highest level of the process model, after all other parts of the model have been implemented. As previously stated, UML is a modeling language, not a software development process. However, UML should be able to support any reasonable process.

Each project is divided into a number of releases, each release represents an XP lifecycle, so this carries on through from the initial releases of the project, then through upgrades required to remove any software bugs found after the project goes into production, and finally on to any upgrades of functionality and QoS as may be later determined. Using this as a basis, each of the 12 practices of XP must be considered to determine how each applies directly, as well as what changes might be needed to use the particular practice in a real-time programming project.

3.1   Project Practices

On-Site Customer: A customer should be with the project from the beginning to the end, providing the programmer with the project's requirements in the form of User Stories, as well as any required further clarification during the implementation of the project.

Metaphor: Create a metaphor for the project that everybody understands; one that explains the essence of the project. Keep this metaphor in mind when naming objects/classes, functions, and variable names required to implement this project.

Pair Programming: Production code will be created by programming teams of two or three.

Coding Standards: e.g., indentation, tabs, bracket pattern, capitalization, commenting, etc.

Collective Code Ownership: All code is owned collectively; that is any programming team may correct, upgrade, or refactor any code as required.

Forty-Hour Week: "Do not work more than one consecutive week of overtime." [5]

3.2   Lifecycle Practices

Small Releases: Release early and release often. (see Planning) The release shall include whole features; this gives better business value. The release should be no longer than two months. The releases are then broken down into iterations of no more than several weeks duration. Upon receipt of the latest release, the users from the customer's company shall use the release and supply feedback to the project team.

Planning: The customer shall present the User Stories, then the project team will brainstorm the engineering tasks. Then the project team will present the customer with the stories estimates - time/cost to implement each User Story. The customer in turn shall decide the order in which the User Stories will be implemented, especially which stories will be implemented in the current release. The project team will decide which stories will be implemented in the current iteration. At this point, each programming pair will decide which stories they will take to implement.

Design: Produce only design documents that will be actually used. Do not design the whole system before you start implementing it. Use the rhythm: "design a little, test a little, and build a little." In other words, design continuously throughout the project implementation. This is applied to the implementation of the User Stories. If a problem occurs while trying to design the code for a User Story, try to 'spike' the solution; that is, try a simple program to explore potential solutions. Remember that most spikes are not good enough to be added to the production and be prepared to discard any that are not good enough. All programming pairs are to do their own design and coding.

For all important aspects of the design, the whole project team is to be involved. Do not add anything that is not necessary to complete the current iterations, i.e., do not anticipate future requirements and do not add any generalization to the code. Once you have the program functionality, and then design the timing constraints. This should be handled as a separate release or it may be handled during refactoring. Here is where the design becomes more formal. Use UML to design and document the timing constraints. Use Statecharts and Activity Diagrams to layout the timing and UML Notes to document the timing constraints. Keep the Statecharts, Activity Diagrams, UML Notes and any other UML diagrams that you use to design or document the timing constraints.

Continuous Integration: Integrate continuously, at least once or twice a day. Use CVS to track changes in integrated code. Before integration, make sure that all appropriate unit and acceptances tests have been passed.

Testing: The customer is responsible for supplying the acceptances tests. It is the programmer's job to run the tests, demonstrating to the customer that the current release works. Software development should follow the rhythm: "write a short test, run the test, write enough code to pass the test, go on to the next small portion." This handles the functionality of the code, but does not adequately address all of the issues involved with real-time applications. Extra tests will be required to demonstrate failure detection, during normal operation of the code and to verify that the code meets the timing constraints of the project.

Meeting the timing constraints should be dealt with during refactoring. Up to this point, concentrate on code functionality. The tests should be automated. Create files containing required inputs, after a manual check, include the expected outputs and compare the produced outputs against these expected results, reporting any differences.

Refactoring: Expect that early decisions will need to be changed, and do this through refactoring. Improve code structure by refactoring, remember to always rerun the unit tests to insure code functionality has not been compromised. If you are having problems writing unit tests, refactor the code to split out the behavior and rewrite the tests. In order for refactoring to be reversible, be sure to use version control (CVS, see Continuous Integration).

4   Conclusions and Future Work

It looks very much like XP can be employed to develop real-time applications. It would appear that the only changes are to the design phase, requiring a more formal design, since the User Stories tend to be to qualitative in nature. Since this has not been tried on an actual application, a starting point for further investigation would be to actually demonstrate this on a real application.

The extreme programming concept appears to be a reasonable way to develop real-time software. The concept of constant customer involvement and many iterative releases allows the customer to see any given software project evolve and take shape in the vision of the customer. Traditional methods for software development rely far more on programmers than the XP process. The problem with relying on programmers primarily for software development is the potential for time and money being spent on priorities that customers do not consider as high priorities as well as the potential for misunderstandings between programmers and customers. In a real-time programming environment, the customer's needs must be explored and reworked based on the constraints of a real-time environment. XP excels in this area, having close ties between customer and programmer as well as customer involvement and feedback.

Real-time programming using XP does not seem to conflict in many ways from a traditional waterfall method to develop real-time applications. Certain aspects of traditional real-time development are more rigid than the XP method; however, the goals remain the same. The safety aspects of a real-time application design have not been considered in this paper. This would then be a further area of investigation.

References

1. Beck, K.: Extreme Programming Explained, Embrace Change. Addison-Wesley, Pearson Education, Indianapolis (2000).
2. Locke, D., Robbins, S., Solanki, P., de Niz, D.: The Real-Time Specification for Java. Addison-Wesley, Boston (2000).
3. Pons, A.P.: Temporal Abstract Classes and Virtual Temporal Specifications for Real-Time Systems. ACM Transactions on Software Engineering and Methodology, Vol 11 No 3 (2002), 291-308.
4. Succi, G., Marchesi , M. (ed.): Extreme Programming Examined. Addison-Wesley, Pearson Education, Indianapolis (2001).
5. Jeffries, R., Anderson, A., Hendrickson, C.: Extreme Programming Installed. Addison-Wesley, Pearson Education, Indianapolis (2002).
6. Marchesi, M., Succi, G., Wells, D., Williams, L. (ed.): Extreme Programming Perspectives. Addison-Wesley, Pearson Education, Indianapolis (2003).
7. McBreen, P.: Questioning Extreme Programming. Addison-Wesley, Pearson Education, Indianapolis (2003).
8. Douglass, B.P.: "UML Lite" offers simple yet powerful tool set for even complex designs. Electronic Design, V 50 N 5, Penton Media (2002), 57-62.
9. Lyons, A.: Developing and debugging real-time software with ObjecTime developer. Real-Time Magazine, V 5, Real-Time Consult (1999), 17-24.
10. Mellor, S., and Balcer, M.: Executable UML: A Foundation for Model Driven Architecture. Addison Wesley Professional (2002).
11. Starr, L.: Executable UML How to Build Class Models. Prentice Hall PTR (2001).
12. Kleppe, A., Warmer, J.: Integration of static and dynamic core for UML: a study in dynamic aspects of the pUML OO meta modeling approach to the rearchitecting of UML. Technology of Object-Oriented Languages and Systems, 2001. TOOLS 38. Proceedings (2001) 66 -77.
13. Peter D. Mosses. Action Semantics. Number 26 in Cambridge Tracts in Theoretical Computer Science. Cambridge University Press (1992).
14. Gerson Suny•, Alain Le Guennec and Jean-Marc J•z•quel: Using UML Action Semantics for model execution and transformation. Information Systems, Volume 27, Issue 6 (September 2002) 445-457
15. Laplante, P.A.: Real-time systems design and analysis: an engineer's handbook. IEEE Press, New York (1993).
16. Wake, W.C.: Extreme Programming Explored. Addison-Wesley, Pearson Education, Indianapolis (2002).
17. Crispin, L., House, T.: Testing Extreme Programming. Addison-Wesley, Pearson Education, Indianapolis (2003).
18. Beck, K.: Test-Driven Development. Addison-Wesley, Boston (2003).

Software Development under Stringent Hardware Constraints: Do Agile Methods Have a Chance?

Jussi Ronkainen and Pekka Abrahamsson

VTT Technical Research Centre of Finland, P.O. Box 1100, FIN-90570 Oulu, Finland
{Jussi.Ronkainen,Pekka.Abrahamsson}@vtt.fi

Abstract. Agile software development methods have been suggested as useful in many situations and contexts. However, only few (if any) experiences are available regarding the use of agile methods in embedded domain where the hardware sets tight requirements for the software. This development domain is arguably far away from the agile home ground. This paper explores the possibility of using agile development techniques in this environment and defines the requirements for new agile methods targeted to facilitate the development of embedded software. The findings are based on an empirical study over a period 12 months in the development of low-level telecommunications software. We maintain that by addressing the requirements we discovered, agile methods can be successful also in the embedded software domain.

1 Introduction

Agile software development methods have captured the interest of academia and practitioners alike in the past few years. Common to the methods are the prospects of shorter lead-times, responsiveness to changes even late in the development cycle, and the promise of a continuous stream of functioning software releases from the very beginning on.

While many agile methods have been introduced (for an overview, see e.g. [1]), none of them are specifically targeted for the development embedded software. In fact, the characteristics that describe the ideal surroundings for an agile method to work best – its home ground (identifiable customer, co-located development, no more architecture design than immediately needed, object-oriented development environment, e.g. [2]) – describe the opposite of hardware-bound embedded software development. How, then, would agile development methods fit in a situation where the amount of code is not the primary scaling factor, but rather issues of performance, software reliability and constantly changing hardware requirements? This is especially the case when developing embedded systems in the telecommunications sector.

To date, there is a limited amount of literature or experiences available regarding the use of agile software development principles and methods in the domain of embedded software development. Yet, the electronics industry is the fastest growing industry sector in Europe.

M. Marchesi and G. Succi (Eds.): XP 2003, LNCS 2675, pp. 73–79, 2003.

Grenning [3] proposed using Extreme Programming [4] in the development of embedded software, but in the development he described the hardware was not a major player in the product development until late in the project. In the environment we studied, however, the hardware is available already at an early stage of a project, causing much change into the software development.

We base our work on an empirical study performed in a tightly hardware-bound environment where the aim was to improve the existing processes. The details of the study can be found in [5]. Drawing from this experience we analyze the prospects of using state-of-the-art agile methods in developing embedded software under tight hardware constraints. On this basis, we finally define the requirements for new agile methods targeted fit for this domain of software development.

The paper is composed as follows. In the next section, four essential characteristics of embedded systems development are identified and analyzed from the agile software development viewpoint. Based on this analysis, then, the requirements for increasing the level of agility in the embedded systems domain are identified.

2   Embedded Software Development: Characteristics Effecting Agility

Embedded software can be found in a wide variety of applications. The environment, requirements and constraints for different types of software in a single system vary. We focus on the problems in writing software that directly accesses hardware.

Our specific interest is in digital signal processing applications, which is a very common problem domain in the telecommunication industry sector. Data processing in such systems typically uses digital signal processors (DSPs) and application-specific integrated circuits (ASICs). They are used in performing computationally intensive signal processing tasks. DSP software allows flexibility in implementation and makes it possible to update the system through new software releases. The most intensive mathematical tasks are implemented in the ASICs.

The development of embedded systems is characterized by the need to develop software and hardware simultaneously [6]. This concurrent work is known as co-design. In our case, this means that the DSP software and ASICs are concurrently under development. The simultaneous development means that overall system functionality is constantly balanced between hardware and software implementation. This software is called "hardware-related". The concept of co-design in such a case is illustrated in Figure 1.

The dynamics of co-design – i.e. the way it effects the concurrent software development processes, has to be understood in order to enable the use of agile software development methods.

2.1   Meeting the Hard Real-Time Requirements Is the Number One Priority

The environment in which the software runs imposes several strict requirements for the software. Some of the most essential requirements concern performance. Embed-

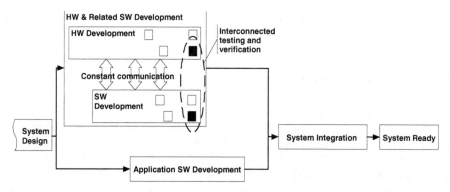

Fig. 1. Co-design timeline example [5]

ded systems often have to perform tasks within a time slot defined by e.g., a tele-communication standard. If failing to comply to the timing and performance requirements results in a risk to further system operation or in other considerable, non-correctable errors, the real-time requirements are said to be hard [7]. In hardware-related software development, the hard real-time requirements are visible most concretely in the constant need to verify the proper co-operation of DSP software and the ASIC hardware the software drives. This causes that hardware simulators are an essential tool during DSP software development.

The use of hardware simulation also makes it possible to make the final split between hardware and software functionality at a fairly late stage during development. From a software development viewpoint this means that the requirements for hardware-related software cannot be frozen before development work begins. Other notable technological constraints that cause changes during development are those of memory and power consumption. Therefore, the development method, by necessity, has to have some kind of mechanism to cope with changes in requirements during development.

A considerable deal of architecture development is practically mandatory in composing the functionality for the system. Some of the architecture emerges through experience gained during development, but preliminary architecture design cannot be avoided. Most agile methods do not encourage this. Furthermore, software design in embedded systems is largely driven by current and expected performance issues, rather than constantly added new functionality. Therefore, the concept of using "the simplest solution that could possibly work" (stated, e.g., as the "YAGNI" principle in XP [4]) must be stretched somewhat.

Another key issue is refactoring. This practice of customary rearrangement and clean-up of code in order to simplify it or to make it more understandable is an everyday practice in, for example, Extreme Programming. Refactoring high-speed hardware-related code is, however, hazardous. The interactions between the software and the hardware are very sensitive to changes in timing. Changes in code – even if the code logically remains the same – may cause slight changes in timing or other behavior, which turns into bugs that are very difficult to detect. The negative effects of refactoring can be alleviated through pervasive use of software configuration management and relentless testing, but the latter has its own problems, as will be shown later.

2.2   Experimenting Is a Part of the Development

The way the technological constraints (performance, power and memory consumption, etc.) effect code is impossible to tell exactly without hands-on experience. Therefore, the more complex the software-hardware interactions, the more the developers will experiment. This is not quite unlike the use of spike solutions in XP or prototyping in general. The difference in hardware-related software development is that the amount of code that is generated through experimenting is very significant, and much of it will evolve into actual production software.

As the development progresses, the code is required by more and more stakeholders (other software teams, hardware teams, production teams), and the effects of changes in hardware or related software ripple substantially farther than within the work of the corresponding teams. Therefore, the rigidity of software development practices has to steadily increase from what is needed in the initial, turbulent environment where changes have limited impact, to the final stages where the slightest changes have to be carefully analyzed and accepted among several stakeholders. This kind of on-the-fly adjustment of the practices is not adequately supported by current agile methods.

2.3   High Level Designs and Executable Documentation Are Not Sufficient

The information transferred between the teams implementing the system is typically very specific as regards timing, bit patterns, etc. Furthermore, embedded system development requires a wide range of expertise, which means that distributed development is a necessity. While individual teams may still reside on a shared location, the mix of different technologies involved requires communication across different teams, which means that face-to-face communication only is not enough. Also, synchronizing the teams' work requires a certain amount of up-front design documentation.

The inability to avoid up-front documentation is an obvious challenge to fully-fledged use of agile methods. The problem of keeping the documentation up to date remains, however. Therefore, the challenge for agile methods is to provide more sophisticated methods for recognizing the required amount of documentation at a given time. Due to the involvement of stakeholders of different technologies, executable documentation has its limits in the development of embedded software.

2.4   The Development Is Test Driven by Nature

The most predominant activity in developing complex embedded systems is testing. The requirements for embedded system reliability and device autonomy are generally strict [8]. In addition to the normal software tests (unit, integration, acceptance), many tests focus on the functionality of the hardware the software drives.

Some testing concepts promoted by agile approaches (the use of regression tests, for example) are already in place in hardware-related software development. Some of the core ideas (write tests first, run every unit test at least daily) are problematic, however. The test environment is usually different from the development environment, and memory or performance constraints often prevent installing and running all of the test code in the testing environment at the same time. Further still, daily testing may not be possible due to the sharing of the hardware simulation resources with hardware teams.

Despite the problems, the agile approach to testing offers promising ideas that are worth investigating in the realm of hardware-related software development. Specific solutions are required, however, for mitigating the problems of scaling the test software to different situations.

3   Requirements for Agile Methods in Embedded Systems Development

The identification of the characteristics of embedded system development shows that the problems faced in the turbulent software-hardware boundary are largely those the agile methods are intended to solve. In particular, constant change in requirements and the need to experiment already necessitate the use of an iterative and incremental development process. Testing is also vital in embedded software development, yet another highly encouraged practice in agile development methods. Finally, efficient and timely communication between hardware and software developers is paramount.

Table 1, based on the discussion above, puts forward four basic problems areas, their descriptions and the embedded domain specific requirements for the new agile software development methods.

Pervasive use of version / configuration control is one key ingredient in enabling fast-paced development work in an environment where seemingly harmless changes may cause bugs that are very difficult to locate and fix. This also has to entail relevant hardware development versions (simulation models etc.), as the functionality of software always has to be verified against the hardware, and vice versa.

Currently, existing agile methods can be most effectively utilized during the early phases of development, when even the most essential requirements may be unclear, and the availability of any working software is crucial in helping the concurrent hardware development. The key issue in adapting agile methods into usable solutions in the embedded system domain is development time scalability. What is thus required is a method with the ability to scale smoothly during development to cater for the increasing need of formal communication, change management methods, and documentation.

Table 1. Specific problems and requirements

Problem area	Problem description	Embedded domain requirements
Hard real-time requirements	The role of architecture is important, up-front design and architecture work cannot be avoided. Extensive refactoring potentially hazardous and thus not always feasible.	New agile methods should place more emphasis on the software architecture, techniques are needed for determining the extent of specification and documentation needs. Refactoring should be integrated with a workable configuration management system that includes relevant hardware versions. System-level impact analysis methods are a necessity.
Experimenting	While code experimentation (or prototyping) is generally used, the transition to well-documented production code is a challenge.	Techniques needed for progressively increasing code maturity. Various code grades for different phases of the evolution are needed..
Documentation	Existence of multiple development teams. Executable documentation alone is not sufficient. The number of stakeholders involved in the project grows gradually. Distributed development is a necessity due to presence of multiple technologies.	Techniques needed for recognizing and managing change-prone requirements. Ways to enable a gradual introduction of more rigid practices are needed. Coordination and communication methods are needed for inter-team work.
Test-driven development	Extra code for testing effects system performance and hence, test results. Capacity constraints restrict the amount of test software on the system.	Techniques for building an optimal test suite are required. Test software has to be flexible in terms of size and control – only the essential for performance, more extensive for testing program logic.

4   Conclusions

This paper has described the essential characteristics of hardware-related software development, and analyzed them from an agile development viewpoint. It was found that the development of this type of software has to face many of the same problems the agile methods were created to solve. The challenge, however, is that the current operationalization of these principles, i.e. the existing agile methods, do not suit to the development of hardware-related software as such.

The analysis was on a very limited area of embedded software development. However, since embedded system development in general is characterized by the simultaneous development of software and hardware, the problems described are not unique to the development of the most hardware-bound software. Thus, the findings are generalizable to other embedded domains as well.

Based on the analysis, we maintain that agile methods offer promising solutions for the development of embedded software. However, in order to establish a foothold in the development of embedded systems, agile methods have to focus on the specific embedded domain requirements the paper set out.

References

1. Abrahamsson, P., Salo, O., Ronkainen, J., Warsta, J.: Agile software development methods: Review and analysis. Technical Research Centre of Finland (2002)
2. Boehm, B.: Get Ready For The Agile Methods, With Care. Computer, Vol. 35(1) (2002) 64-69
3. Grenning, J.: Extreme Programming and Embedded Software Development. In: Embedded Systems Conference 2002. Chicago. (2002)
4. Beck, K.: Extreme programming explained. Addison-Wesley (1999)
5. Ronkainen, J., Savuoja, A., Taramaa, J.: Characteristics of Process Improvement of Hardware-Related SW. In: 4th International Conference on Product Focused Software Process Improvement. Rovaniemi, Finland. (2002) 247-257
6. Wolf, W. H.: Hardware-software co-design of embedded systems. Proceedings of the IEEE, Vol. 82(7) (1994) 967-989
7. Stankovic, J. A.: Real-Time and Embedded Systems. ACM Computing Surveys, Vol. 28(1) (1996) 205-208
8. Kuvaja, P., et al.: Specific Requirements for Assessing Embedded Product Development. In: International Conference on Product Focused Software Process Improvement. Oulu, Finland. Technical Research Centre of Finland (1999) 68-85

Maturing XP through the CMM

Jonas Martinsson

Lund University, Sweden and
Erisma Technologies AB, Box 8011
200 41 Malmö, Sweden
jonas.martinsson@erisma.se

Abstract. Extreme Programming (XP) and the Capability Maturity Model
(CMM) are two recently emerging models addressing the difficulty of developing and delivering high-quality software products. The CMM gives guidelines
for *what* to do at an organizational level, while XP says *how* to develop software at a project level. Together these models form a comprehensive framework for structuring the software development organization. Drawing from previous software engineering knowledge as well as personal experiences of
coaching XP teams this paper gives practical suggestions for how to combine
the two models. The paper shows that it is not only possible, but also advanta-
geous to use XP as a springboard for reaching the highest CMM maturity level
and assuring the long-term goals of the software development organization.

1   Introduction

The software industry has throughout its history been ridden with an exceptionally
high rate of failed projects. The most common symptoms of the software crisis are
overrun budgets and schedules, volatile cost and time estimates, final products crip-
pled with bugs, and increasingly complex systems. To better cope with the rapidly
changing environment of software development, different models have been tried
with varying success.

Two relatively recent developments in this field are XP (2000) and the CMM
(1991). XP is a lightweight methodology for small software development teams, introduced by Kent Beck [1]. The CMM [7] specifies 5 levels of maturity for software
organizations, ranging from the *ad hoc*-environment of level one, where most companies reside, to level 5 where products of a predictably high quality are produced. The
five CMM levels are defined by 18 Key Process Areas (KPAs), which in turn are
defined by between two to four goals each.

This paper suggests XP as a foundation for building a mature software organization
and improving upon it through modifications of the recommendations in the CMM.
For a thorough explanation of the two models, required for fully understanding this
paper, the reader is directed to the reference section at the end.

The CMM and XP are complementing each other well in the respect that the CMM
is saying *what* to do in general terms, but not *how* to make it possible, while XP is an
implementation model with explicit practical guidelines for a software organization at
the project level. This makes the CMM a prime candidate for cooperation with XP in
many organizations.

M. Marchesi and G. Succi (Eds.): XP 2003, LNCS 2675, pp. 80–87, 2003.

It is important to understand that the CMM is not mandating how to achieve the associated goals of the Key Process Areas and reach the higher levels, although it is suggesting possible routes for reaching each goal. Alternative practices may accomplish the goals of a KPA. It is important not to confuse the suggested practices with the goals, as is often the case when people are criticizing the CMM in various contexts.

2   CMM Maturity of the XP Model

Table 1 outlines how well the XP practices and roles fulfill the CMM goals. The table is based upon my own independent findings and interpretations, and it is also interesting to compare it with other analyses of XP and the CMM [2] [3] [5] [6].

Table 1. Degree of satisfaction for the 52 CMM goals by implementing an XP process.
▲: XP core practices and roles fully satisfy the KPA goal.
▶: XP core practices and roles partially or implicitly satisfy the KPA goal.
▼: XP core practices and roles do not satisfy the KPA goal.

Level	Key Process Area (KPA)	Goals 1 – 4			
2	Requirements management (RM)	▲	▲		
	Software project planning (SPP)	▲	▲	▲	
	Software project tracking and oversight (SPTO)	▲	▶	▲	
	Software subcontract management (SSM)	Omitted			
	Software quality assurance (SQA)	▲	▼	▲	▼
	Software configuration management (SCM)	▲	▶	▶	▶
3	Organization process focus (OPF)	▶	▼	▼	
	Organization process definition (OPD)	▲	▲		
	Training program (TP)	▶	▶	▶	
	Integrated software management (ISM)	▼	▼		
	Software product engineering (SPE)	▲	▲		
	Intergroup coordination (IC)	▲	▲	▲	
	Peer reviews (PR)	▲	▲		
4	Quantitative process management (QPM)	▲	▶	▼	
	Software quality management (SQM)	▼	▼	▼	
5	Defect prevention (DP)	▲	▲	▶	
	Technology change management (TCM)	▼	▼	▼	
	Process change management (PCM)	▼	▼	▼	

The actual KPA goals would be too lengthy to quote in this paper but can easily be located in the CMM specification [7]. A detailed explanation of how this table was constructed can be found in my master's thesis [4]. The "▲"-symbol indicates that core practices and roles in XP are sufficient in themselves to address and satisfy the specified KPA goal. Goals that are marked with "▶" are not fully met by the core practices and roles, but can in other ways be fulfilled by an XP implementation; either through XP's values or by using additional common practices. Guidelines for how to achieve this can be found in my thesis referred to above. "▼" indicates that XP does not satisfy the specific CMM goal.

3   Achieving CMM Maturity Using XP

As can be seen from Table 1, an XP project is not even reaching the maturity of CMM level 2 by default. However, implementing many of the suggested practices from the XP literature and other sources that are not core XP practices *per se*, will satisfy the goals that would normally only be reached partially or implicitly (marked with "▶"). Only the CMM goals that have not at all been addressed by the implementation of an XP process (marked with "▼") will be examined below. These goals, as specified by the CMM [7], are quoted verbatim in the following sections.

3.1   Reaching Level 2

Two missing goals need to be reached for an XP organization to reach CMM level 2. These are:

1. SQA Goal 2: Adherence of software products and activities to the applicable standards, procedures, and requirements is verified objectively.
2. SQA Goal 4: Noncompliance issues that cannot be resolved within the software project are addressed by senior management.

The KPA of *software quality assurance* will need to be improved upon and become more formalized in XP teams striving to reach CMM level 2. Specifically, an objective scrutiny of the software products and the activities will need to be fashioned. Examples of metrics that could be appropriate for objectively verifying the products and the process are:

- release plan adherence,
- percentage of test cases that are running successfully,
- number of acceptance tests that are running successfully,
- length of pair programming sessions,
- individual velocity,
- team velocity,
- velocity, compared with estimates.

Not all of these metrics are required to fulfill the KPA of SQA; it is more sensible to carefully examine which areas are likely to assist management in getting visibility into the state of the project at the most appropriate abstraction level. This level is not necessarily the same for different types of projects within the same organization. The responsibility for these activities could very well lie on the coach, with the assistance of the tracker. However, it is important to keep these responsibilities separated from the developers and testers. The coach or tracker that wants to take on the tasks of SQA measurements should therefore not be assigned to programming tasks within the same project.

It is also important for the fulfillment of the SQA KPA to communicate the metrics through defined channels to the affected parties and senior management. The metrics are most conveniently posted to the team using a white-board or an exposed wall in a central location. When metrics out of the ordinary occur it is important for the coach to communicate these findings, either directly to the affected party or during the daily stand-up meeting, and that these issues will be resolved. If no satisfactory solution is found the issue is brought to the customer or project manager, depending on the nature of the issue. If no solution is to be found at this level, senior management will be presented with the issue.

3.2   Reaching Level 3

Four missing goals need to be reached for an XP organization residing on CMM level 2 to reach level 3. These are:

1. OPF Goal 2: The strengths and weaknesses of the software processes used are identified relative to a process standard.
2. OPF Goal 3: Organization-level process development and improvement activities are planned.
3. ISM Goal 1: The project's defined software process is a tailored version of the organization's standard software process.
4. ISM Goal 2: The project is planned and managed according to the project's defined software process.

Common for the KPAs that are to be dealt with at level 3 for an XP team (OPF and ISM) are the needs for an *organization process definition*. This will typically be the methodology of Extreme Programming, as laid out in the books and on various Internet resources. However, companies should not feel restricted to the usage of the 12 core practices, but utilize the fact that XP lends itself very well to customizations, as long as the values and the spirit of the core practices are acknowledged. A software organization that does not exclusively use XP as the implementation model will need to address the coordination between the different models in its organization process definition at an organizational level.

A mature o*rganization process focus* will need to be developed within the company for it to be better able to customize and improve the *de facto* process. Goals number 2 and 3 of the OPF call for insight into the actual process used, and to compare it with the *organization process definition*. The CMM suggests establishing a *software engineering process group*, consisting of software engineering representatives, responsible for carrying out the tasks of managing the process used at an organizational level. It will be appropriate for this group to assess the process every few years, and from the results of this assessment come up with a comprehensive action plan for improving the organization process definition. The action plan will serve as a primary input for driving the development and improvement of the process forward according to a scheduled plan.

The 2 goals of *integrated software management* call for the *organization process definition* to be tailored and streamlined for each project's individual characteristics, into the project's defined software process, using data and lessons learned from previous projects together with changes proposed by the project as guidance. The XP process may be modified in a number of different ways, to better suit a specific project; for example:

- changing the iteration length;
- using different granularities when estimating user stories and engineering tasks;
- modifying the frequency of releases;
- using different types of metaphor(s);
- customizing the role and location of the on-site customer.

It is important to note that the process is not to be modified without restrictions. For example, it should still be possible to compare feedback data about the process between different projects within the organization. The defined process definition should also be reviewed by the software engineering process group and project manager, and approved by management, before documented and communicated to all affected parties. It is important to carefully control and manage all changes to the different process definitions. Because the defined process definition is still connatural with XP, its core practices and roles will assert the satisfaction of goal number 2 of integrated software management.

3.3   Reaching Level 4

Four missing goals need to be reached for an XP organization residing on CMM level 3 to reach level 4. These are:

1. QPM Goal 3: The process capability of the organization's standard software process is known in quantitative terms.
2. SQM Goal 1: The project's software quality management activities are planned.
3. SQM Goal 2: Measurable goals for software product quality and their priorities are defined.
4. SQM Goal 3: Actual progress toward achieving the quality goals for the software products is quantified and managed.

In order for the organization to take advantage of *quantitative process management* it must use the process performance from earlier projects and analyze these. For the XP organization it will involve extracting the estimates and actual implementation times of all user stories that may have any general significance. The velocities of the projects are also gathered in a database and analyzed. This data will serve as a model for making future estimates to similar user stories. The data should be stored in a catalogued format that enables quick retrieval and little overhead during the iteration planning meeting. The software engineering process group should be responsible for managing the data and regularly update it as new technologies and development practices emerge. By analyzing the difference between estimates and actual time spent on user stories or tasks, additional insight and knowledge into the planning game might be yielded. Other data, such as the number of failed acceptance tests, and number and severity of defects after release, should also be managed centrally within the organization.

Satisfying QPM's goal number 3 would indeed make the XP organization more mature, by making it better able to give an initial estimate for the first iteration's velocity, and thereby better fit to give a customer the cost and time frame for a given set of requirements up-front. The inability in standard XP projects to give this estimate is often quoted as a major obstacle for selling in XP to a customer or to senior management. It would still be impossible to give an exact estimate of the total cost and time of a potential project, but not more so than in any other software process model. XP would of course still enable the customer to alter the requirements very late in the project, resulting in an updated project budget.

Software quality management calls for a quantitative understanding of the software products' quality, seen from the perspective of the organization, customer and end user. The XP organization normally approaches the problem of satisfying the customer and end-user's quality goals in different ways than what the CMM suggests. XP strives to please the customer through frequent and continuous product releases, acceptance tests and communication throughout the development lifecycle, while the CMM suggests surveys, focus groups and product evaluations to find out the quality needs before the project starts. While the approaches are fundamentally different, they still try to solve the same problem. The trouble with the XP approach, seen from a CMM perspective, is that it will not lend itself very well to extracting measurable data that can be analyzed and processed during the entire development process. Fundamentally, there are two questions that will need to be answered:

1. What are the quality requirements, quantitatively?
2. How do we translate the quality requirements into process practices?

Question number one is answered by the CMM through suggested surveys, focus groups and product evaluations to find out the customer and end user's goals. XP does not even try to answer the same question, because it puts the responsibility of finding this answer on the customer while the CMM puts this responsibility on the software organization. It will be next to impossible for an XP organization to satisfy the KPA of SQM without taking responsibility for finding the answer to what the quality requirements are. Therefore, the XP organization will do best by implementing the suggested practices by the CMM mentioned above.

Question number two is answered by the CMM through suggestions like measuring how long the system is running on average between failures. XP would do best in answering this question through implementing the CMM suggestions into acceptance tests for the affected user stories. In order for the quality requirements to be translated into acceptance tests, the requirements will have to be formulated ahead of the project start (or at least ahead of formulating the corresponding user story.) It will be very important to communicate and agree on the quantitative quality requirements with the customer so that these will be successfully translated into acceptance tests. The practices above would satisfy SQM goals number one and two.

Remaining is SQM goal number three, which is somewhat tricky because XP is not taking the approach envisioned by the CMM. By continuously running the acceptance tests for the implemented user stories and track their status, a quantified measurement of the progress towards the quality goals would be obtained. It will also be necessary for this data to be continuously routed and available to the affected people in charge of the quality goals, and for them to take appropriate action to steer the measurements in line with the goals. This practice should be enough to satisfy the final remaining goal for reaching CMM level 4.

3.4   Reaching Level 5

Six missing goals need to be reached for an XP organization residing on CMM level 4 to reach level 5. These are:

1. TCM Goal 1: Incorporation of technology changes is planned.
2. TCM Goal 2: New technologies are evaluated to determine their effect on quality and productivity.
3. TCM Goal 3: Appropriate new technologies are transferred into normal practice across the organization.
4. PCM Goal 1: Continuous process improvement is planned.
5. PCM Goal 2: Participation in the organization's software process improvement activities is organization-wide.
6. PCM Goal 3: The organization's standard software process and the projects' defined software process are improved continuously.

The key process area of *technology change management* is relatively straightforward to implement in the XP organization. However, it should be noted that when a company is using TCM, it might eventually become a non-XP organization or a hybrid if an emerging new process is evaluated as superior.

TCM is best realized in the XP organization by assigning upon the software engineering process group, with the help of experienced staff with expertise in specialized areas, the responsibility to regularly probe the market for new technologies that could be suitable for the organization to adopt. Examples of areas are computer hardware, operating systems, software development platforms, development tools, programming languages, and formal methods. New and unproven technologies that are of potential value for the maturity of the organization will be tested in pilot projects, from where metrics will be collected and analyzed. The technologies that pass the test and are approved by management will be incorporated into the organization process definition or other corresponding organization-wide documents, and properly communicated and taught to the affected personnel.

Process change management is also a key process area that is relative straightforward to implement as it can be addressed in more or less the same manner regardless of implementation model. PCM is realized through the establishment of training and incentive programs.for making *everyone* within the organization aware of their responsibility and privilege to identify and communicate process improvement opportunities. The responsibility for performing and coordinating these activities once again fall upon the software engineering process group, which also develops and maintains a plan for process improvement according to a documented procedure. The suggested process improvement opportunities are examined and if found interesting tested in pilot projects, and thereafter analyzed. When actual improvements have been identified, verified and approved, these changes are made to the organization's standard software process and the defined software processes, as well as communicated through training courses within the company.

4   Conclusion

XP and the CMM are clearly complementary. Although XP does not even satisfy the requirements for reaching the second level of the CMM, it is satisfying many KPAs in different levels and using sound practices that facilitate the satisfaction of many more. By making improvements to the organization as described above, it will be feasible for an XP-practicing company to reach the highest level of software development maturity.

The most important and critical measure will be the establishment of a software engineering process group, which will be responsible for the whole organization's compliance with many of the KPAs. The most difficult (and perhaps most valuable) area to implement will be that of software quality management on level 4, but as has been shown it does not conflict with the framework of XP.

According to the Software Engineering Institute at Carnegie Mellon University, the CMM requires a long-term commitment and it may take ten years or more to reach the final level. According to this paper much of the work has already been done by practicing the XP process. Is this a paradox?

No, it is important to note that introducing XP in its strictest sense is not accomplished overnight. The process for cultivating this development process within an organization might very well take years. Implementing the remaining KPAs as described will also be a painful and time-consuming process. Still, XP should be regarded as an appealing option and a springboard for a software development company to reach higher maturity. By introducing the measures described here, most companies would be likely to improve their position on the market and reach a state where their long-term goals would be stable, and their software products would be of a predictably high quality.

References

1. Beck, Kent. *Extreme Programming Explained*. ISBN 0-201-61641-6, Addison-Wesley, 2000
2. Glazer, Hillel. *Dispelling the Process Myth*, http://www.stsc.hill.af.mil/CrossTalk/2001/nov/glazer.asp, CrossTalk, 2001
3. Jeffries, Ron. *Extreme Programming and the Capability Maturity Model*, http://www.xprogramming.com/xpmag/xp_and_cmm.htm, 2000
4. Martinsson, Jonas. *Maturing Extreme Programming Through the CMM*, http://www12.brinkster.com/jonasmartinsson/docs/MaturingExtremeProgrammingThroughTheCMM.rtf, 2002
5. Paulk, Mark C. *Agile Methodologies and Process Discipline*, http://www.stsc.hill.af.mil/CrossTalk/2002/oct/paulk.asp, CrossTalk, 2002
6. Paulk, Mark C. *Extreme Programming from a CMM Perspective*, http://www.sei.cmu.edu/cmm/papers/xp-cmm-paper.pdf, 2001
7. Paulk, Mark C. *The Capability Maturity Model*, ISBN: 0201546647, Addison-Wesley, 1995

Formal Extreme (and Extremely Formal) Programming

Ángel Herranz and Juan José Moreno-Navarro

Univ. Politécnica de Madrid
Campus de Montegancedo s/n, Boadilla del Monte 28660, Spain
{aherranz,jjmoreno}@fi.upm.es
+34 9133674{52,58}

Abstract. This paper is an exploratory work were the authors study how the technology of Formal Methods (FM) can interact with agile process in general and with Extreme Programming (XP) in particular. Our thesis is that most of XP practices (*pair programming*, *daily build*, *the simplest design* or *the metaphor*) are technology independent and therefore can be used in FM based developments. Additionally, other essential pieces like *test first*, *incremental development* and *refactoring* can be improved by using FM. In the paper we explore in a certain detail those pieces: when you write a formal specification you are saying *what* your code must do, when you write a test you are doing the same so the idea is to use formal specifications as tests. Incremental development is quite similar to the refinement process in FM: specifications evolve to code maintaining previous functionality. Finally FM can help to remove redundancy, eliminate unused functionality and transform obsolete designs into new ones, and this is refactoring.

Keywords: Extreme Programming, Formal Methods, Incremental Development, Formal Testing, Refactoring.

1 Motivation

At first sight, XP [1] and FM [11,8] are water and oil: an *impossible* mixture. Maybe the most relevant discrepancy is that while one of the strategic motivation of XP is "spending later and earning sooner" FM require "spending sooner and earning later". However, a deeper analysis reveals that FM and XP can benefit their selves.

The use of formal specifications is perceived as improving reliability at the cost of lower productivity. XP and other agile processes focus on productivity so, in principle, using FM following XP practices could improve its efficiency. In particular, *pair programming*, *daily build*, *the simplest design* or *the metaphor* are XP practices that in our view are independent of the concrete development technology used to produce software and the declarative technology and FM is just a different development technology.

On the other hand, the main criticism to XP is that it has been called *systematic hacking* and, probably, the underlying problem is the lack of a formal or even semiformal approach. But, what XP practices are liable to incorporate a formal approach? We think that *unit testing*, *incremental development* and *refactoring* are three main XP practices where FM can be successfully applied:

- When you write a formal specification you are saying *what* your code must do, when you write a test you are doing the same so one idea is to use formal specifications as tests.

M. Marchesi and G. Succi (Eds.): XP 2003, LNCS 2675, pp. 88–96, 2003.

- Incremental development is quite similar to the refinement process in FM: specifications evolve to code maintaining previous functionality.
- Finally FM can help to remove redundancy, eliminate unused functionality and transform obsolete designs into new ones, and this is refactoring.

After all, it might be possible to dilute FM in XP. We would like to point out that we are not claiming to *formalise* XP (as could be understood from the joke in the title), but just to study how the declarative technology can be integrated in XP and how XP can take advantages of this technology.

Before exploring the above XP practices from a formal approach, SLAM (our formal tool) is presented in Section 2. In Sections 3.1 and 3.3 we briefly present how formal specifications can be used in the practices of testing and refactoring. Section 3.2 focuses in the formalisation of the incremental development under the prism of FM.

2   Formal Methods and SLAM

In spite of the great expectations generated around *declarative technologies* (formal methods, and functional and logic programming) years ago, these have not penetrated the mass market of software development. One of the main causes is a deficient software tool support for integrating formal methods in the development process. Since 2001 we are involved in the development of the SLAM [9] system, a *modern* comfortable tool for *specifying*, *refinement* and *programming*.

The formal notation SLAM-SL [7] embedded in the whole system is an object-oriented specification language valid for the *design and programming stages* in the software construction process. Although the main ideas in the paper could have been presented using any other FM and its associated notation, we think that the design of SLAM-SL gives to our notation important advantages.

For this paper, other of the most relevant features of SLAM-SL is that it has been designed as a trade-off between the expressiveness of its underlying logic and the possibility of code synthesis. From a SLAM-SL specification the user can obtain code in a high level programming language (let us say Java), a code that is *readable* and, of course, correct with respect to the specification. Because the code is readable, it can be modified and, we expect, improved by human programmers.

A complete SLAM-SL description is out of the scope of this work, but let us sketch some relevant elements for the goals of the paper.

2.1   Data Modelling

SLAM-SL is a *model based formal notation* [2] where *algebraic types* (*free types* under Z terminology) are used to specify a model for representing instances. From the point of view of an object-oriented programmer, data are modelled following the design pattern *State* ([4]):

```
class Order
state pending (customer : Customer,
               product  : Product,
               quantity : Positive)
```

```
state delivered (customer : Customer,
                 product  : Product,
                 quantity : Positive,
                 payment  : Transfer)
```

Informally, an order instance can be in state *pending* so members *customer*, *product* and *quantity* are meaningful, or in state *delivered* and *customer*, *product*, *quantity* and *payment* are meaningful. Even more, *pending* and *delivered* are order constructors, and *customer*, *product*, *quantity* and *payment* are *getter* methods (the last one is partial). Automatically, the SLAM-SL compiler synthesised the following human understandable Java code:

```
class Order {
  private OrderState state;
  ...
}

class OrderState {
  private Customer customer;
  private Product product;
  private int Quantity;
  ...
}

class PendingOrderState extends OrderState {
}

class DeliveredOrderState extends OrderState {
  private Transfer payment;
}
```

Class invariants associated to every state are allowed, invariants that can be used to statically (through a theorem prover) or dynamically (through assertions) to check the specification and the implementation consistency.

2.2 Method Specification

The general scheme of a method specification is this one:

```
class A
...
method m (T₁, ..., Tₙ) : R
```
pre $P(self, x_1, \ldots, x_n)$
call $self.\mathrm{m}\ (x_1,\ \ldots,\ x_n)$
post $Q(self, x_1, \ldots, x_n, result)$
chk $T_1(self, x_1, \ldots, x_n, result)$
...
chk $T_m(self, x_1, \ldots, x_n, result)$
sol $S(self, x_1, \ldots, x_n, result)$

As we can see, a method specification involves a *guard* or a *precondition* (the formula $P(self, x_1, \ldots, x_n)$) that indicates if the rule can be triggered, an *operation call scheme* ($self.\text{m}$ ($x_1, \ldots, x_n$)); and a *postcondition* (given by the formula $Q(self, x_1, \ldots, x_n, result)$) that relates input state and output state. The formal meaning of this specification is given by the following property:

$$\forall s, x_1, \ldots, x_n. \, \text{pre} - m(s, x_1, \ldots, x_n) \, \Rightarrow \, \text{post} - m(s, x_1, \ldots, x_n, s.m(x_1, \ldots, x_n)$$

where pre and post predicates are defined in this way:

$$\text{pre} - m(s, x_1, \ldots, x_n) \equiv P(self, x_1, \ldots, x_n)$$
$$\text{post} - m(s, x_1, \ldots, x_n, r) \equiv Q(self, x_1, \ldots, x_n, r)$$

The procedure to calculate the result of the method is called a *solution* in the SLAM-SL terminology and it has been indicated by the reserved word **sol** following by the formula $S(self, x_1, \ldots, x_n, result)$. Notice that the formula is written in the same SLAM-SL notation, but must be an *executable expression* (a condition that can be syntactically checked). The SLAM-SL compiler synthesised efficient and readable imperative code from solutions. The key concept is the operational use of *quantifiers* (extending usual logic quantifiers). Quantifiers allow the expressiveness of logic while the basis for their efficient implementation as traversal operations on data.

Once it is proved that the postcondition entails the solution it is ensured the correctness of the obtained code. However, the automatically generated code could not be enough efficient and, as we mentioned previously, the programmer can modify the generated code.

Formulas prefixed with the reserved word **chk** are extra properties that will hold in the program. Each T_i must be an *executable* formula and can be considered as tests (for instance that a prime number greater than 2 must be odd). Theoretically, they are not needed because they must be entailed by the postcondition, however, important errors in specifications can be caught. They can also be completed with some values (concrete values, intervals, etc.) what can provide automatic tests to be executed during the execution. Proof obligations are generated in order to prove that every T_i holds under the given postcondition and assertions can be generated in order to check that hand-coded modifications fulfil those properties.

2.3 Support for Testing and Debugging

Executable code is obtained from solutions and using similar techniques pre and post-conditions are used to generate debugging annotations (assertions and exceptions) [6]. Notice that the postcondition can be complex enough to prevent code generation. However, test can always be checked. This feature can be used both to prevent errors in the case of programmer's modifications and to implements runtime tests. Furthermore, up to now the SLAM system is not automatically proving that the postcondition entails the solution, so test can help to find wrong solutions. Nevertheless, as soon as this feature will be incorporated to the system the automatically generated code is always correct and no test checking is needed.

3   XP Practices

As mentioned in the motivation, most XP practices are technology independent. In our opinion, the XP process could be adopted by using SLAM (or any other FM tool) instead of an ordinary programming language and tool. In other words, we propose to write formal specifications instead of programs. A number of advantages appear:

- Rephrasing a XP rule, "The specification is the documentation" because we have a high level description with a formal specification of the intended semantics of the future code. One of the bigger efforts in the SLAM development has been to ensure that the generated code is readable enough. Therefore, the "answer is still in the code" (but also in the specification).
- FM tools (theorem provers, model checkers, etc.) help to maintain the consistency of the specification and the correctness of the implementation.
- Important misunderstandings and errors can be captured in the early stages of the development but close enough to code generation.

While in Agile Methods the emphasis is on staying light, quick, and low ceremony in the process, FM could make it sometimes heavier, sometimes not. Even in the first cases we have that: i) it is still can be considered a light method in the FM area, and ii) the benefits should compensate in many cases the increase of work.

Let us focus on in three XP pieces where we consider that FM can play an interesting role.

3.1   Unit Testing

In XP the role of writing the tests in advance is similar to the role of writing a precise requirement: it is used to indicate *what* the program is expected to do. Tests in XP solves two different problems:

- The detection of misunderstandings in the *intended specifications*.
- The detection of errors in the implementation.

The perspective under both problems is completely different when using FM. The detection of inconsistencies in formal specifications are supported by formal tools, mainly by *a generator of proof obligations* and by *a theorem prover assistant*. With both tools the user get information about possible inconsistencies.

The detection of errors in the implementation is absolutely unneeded thanks to the *verified design process*: a process that ensures that the code obtained from an original specification is correct with respect to it. Notice that the use of tests do not ensure that requirements are satisfied, just "convince" the programmer that it happens. The FM approach overcome this limitation.

So we propose to replace the tests by chk formulas expressed in SLAM-SL. There are several advantages of this approach:

1. tests can be complex enough but the SLAM system takes care of the code generation is feasible,
2. tests are executed automatically every time the program is run in debugging mode,

3. testing properties can be carried out in all the incremental versions of the code, i.e. they are automatically checked in all the iterations, and
4. automated formal tools can be used to improve the behaviour, for instance proving that some test are inconsistent with the specification by using a theorem proving.

3.2 Incremental Development

In this section we present the logical properties that the iterative development of software by the incremental addition of requirements must fulfil. We have called the set of those properties the *Combination Property* and it formally establishes that the combination of the code already obtained to solve the previous requirements and the code needed to solve the new one must fulfil all the requirements. The incremental development of XP needs to ensure that: i) at every step we develop the minimal code needed to solve the corresponding requirement, and ii) this code is combined with the previous code in such a way that the old requirements still hold. To solve this goal we establish the minimal properties that must be proved to ensure a correct behaviour.

We will call $story_i$ the formula expressing requirements at step i. At every step we want to develop a *function* f_i that covers all the requirements $story_1, \ldots, story_i$. To obtain f_i we depart from:

- the function $f_{i-1}(\overline{x}, \overline{y})$ with postcondition $post_{i-1}(self, \overline{x}, \overline{y}, result)$, and
- a function $g_i(\overline{x}, \overline{z})$ that solves requirement $story_i$.

Additionally, function f_i computes "more things" than f_{i-1}, i.e. the result of f_i includes the result of f_{i-1}, and maybe more data. Formally, there exists a projection π_i that relates both results.

Let us discuss some remarks with respect to these formulas before establishing the main properties. The fact that g_i is developed for requirements $story_i$ means that its postcondition entails $story_i(self, \overline{x}, \overline{z}, result)$. We assume that some of the arguments for g_i are still present in the previous code, i.e. arguments represented by variables $\overline{x}$ are still present in f_{i-1}, while some previous arguments $\overline{y}$ are not needed for $story_i$ and some new $\overline{z}$ are required.

Now, the main property to be proved can be formulated. Let us assume that the function $f_i(\overline{x}, \overline{y}, \overline{z})$ has been specified with postcondition $post_i(self, \overline{x}, \overline{y}, \overline{z}, result_i)$. To ensure that this function is correctly defined we must prove the *Combination Property*:

$$post_i(self, \overline{x}, \overline{y}, \overline{z}, result_i) \Rightarrow$$
$$story_i(self, \overline{x}, \overline{z}, result_i) \wedge$$
$$post_{i-1}(self, \overline{x}, \overline{y}, result_{i-1}) \wedge$$
$$\pi_i(result_i) = result_{i-1}$$

Now we can formally establish that this is the only property (at every step i) needed to ensure that the final code (i.e. f_n) entails all the requirements.

Theorem 1. *For every $i \in \{1, \ldots, n-1\}$ the following formulas hold:*

$$post_n(self, \overline{x}, \overline{y}, \overline{z}, result_n) \Rightarrow story_i(self, \overline{x}, \overline{z}, result_i)$$
$$post_{i+1}(self, \overline{x}, \overline{y}, \overline{z}, result_{i+1}) \wedge post_i(self, \overline{x}, \overline{y}, \overline{z}, result_i) \Rightarrow$$
$$\pi_{i+1}(result_{i+1}) = result_i$$

The proof proceeds by induction on i.

A Simple Example

In the following example, we will show three customer stories for the development of a small telephone database ([10]). The customer wants a telephone database where information can be added and looked up maintaining two different tables: one with the persons and other one with the entries (pairs of person and phone). The specification written by development is the following one:

```
class Phone_DB
state (members : {Person},
       phones  : {(Person,Phone)})
constructor make_phone_DB
call make_phone_DB
post result.members = {}
modifier add_entry (Person, Phone)
pre  person in self.members and
     not (person, phone) in self.phones
call add_entry(person, phone)
post result.phones = self.phones + {(person,phone)}
modifier add_member (Person)
pre  not person in members
call add_member(person)
post members = self.members + {person}
observer find_phones (Person) : {Phone}
pre  person in dom(phones)
call find_phones(person) = self.phones(person)
```

In the second story, the customer asks for including a way to remove entries in the data base and this is the result of the development task:

```
modifier remove_entry (Person, Phone)
pre  (person,phone) in phones
call remove_entry(person, phone)
post phones = self.phones - {(person,phone)}
```

The combination property in this case is trivial to prove because we only have added a new operation. A consistency check is also trivial.

In the third customer story, she asks for removing the person from the database of members if its removed entry is the last one:

```
modifier remove_entry (Person, Phone)
pre  (person,phone) in phones
call remove_entry(person, phone)
post phones = self.phones - {(person,phone)} and
     if (exists phone : Phones with (person, phone)
        in phones)
     then members = self.members
     else members = self.members - {person}
     end
```

In this step, the postcondition of `remove_entry` must be proved to entail the previous postcondition. A theorem prover can automatically do the work: let A be the formula `phones = self.phones - {(person,phone)}` and B the right hand side of the conjunction, the proof obligation is

$$A \wedge B \Rightarrow A$$

what is directly the scheme of an inference rule in first order logic.

3.3 Refactoring

The declarative technology makes easier to find and remove redundancy, eliminate unused functionality and transform obsolete designs into new ones, i.e to refactor code [3]. Thanks to the reflective properties of SLAM-SL, generic patterns can be specified and it can be proved that a specification is an instantiation of such a generic pattern. The idea it is having a relevant collection of generic patterns trust the prover technology of FM were able to *match* specifications with specifications in those patterns. Some works in formalising design patterns [4] have been done using SLAM-SL [5].

However, we need to be sure that the resulting code from refactoring is still readable enough. In any case, taking into account that it is for free, the programmer can spend some time in documenting it.

4   Conclusions

We have presented how some XP practices can admit the integration of Formal Methods and declarative technology. In particular, *unit testing*, *refactoring*, and, in a more detailed way, *incremental development* have been studied from the prism of FM.

Probably there is more room for FM ideas helping agile methodologies and XP, and we will study this as a future work.

One of the goals of the SLAM system is to make FM and their advantages closer to any kind of software development. Obviously FM are specially needed for critical applications but combining it with rapid prototyping and agile methodologies could make them affordable for any software construction. Up to know we have not equipped SLAM with an automatic interface generator that precludes the use of our system for heavy graphical interface applications. The automatic generation of graphical interfaces is another matter of future work.

References

1. K. Beck. *Extreme Programming Explained: Embrace Change*. Addison-Wesley, Pearson Education, 2000. ISBN 201-61641-6.
2. H. Ehrig, F. Orejas, and J. Padberg. Relevance, intergration and classification of specification formalism and formal specification techniques. In *Proc. FORMS, Formale Techniken für die Eisenbahnsicherung*, Fortschritt-Berichte VDI, Reihe 12, Nr. 436, VDI Verlag, 2000, pages 31 – 54, 1999.

3. M. Fowler, K. Beck, J. Brant, and W. Opdyke. *Refactoring: Improving the Design of Existing Code*. Addison-Wesley, 1999.
4. E. Gamma, R. Helm, R. Johnson, and J. Vlissides. *Design Patterns - Elements of Reusable Object Oriented Software*. Addison-Wesley, 1995.
5. A. Herranz, J. Moreno, and N. Maya. Declarative reflection and its application as a pattern language. In M. Comini and M. Falaschi, editors, *11th. International Workshop on Functional and Logic Programming (WFLP'02)*, Grado, Italy, June 2002. University of Udine.
6. A. Herranz and J. J. Moreno. Generation of and debugging with logical pre and post conditions. In M. Ducasse, editor, *Workshop on Automated and Algorithmic Debugging 2000*. TU Munich, 2000.
7. A. Herranz and J. J. Moreno. On the design of an object-oriented formal notation. In *Fourth Workshop on Rigorous Object Oriented Methods, ROOM 4*. King's College, London, March 2002.
8. C. B. Jones. *Systematic Software Development Using VDM*. Prentice Hall, 1986.
9. The SLAM website. http://lml.ls.fi.upm.es/slam.
10. J. M. Spivey. *The Z Notation: A Reference Manual*. Prentice Hall International Series in Computer Science, 2nd edition, 1992.
11. J. B. Wordsworth. *Software Development with Z*. Addison-Wesley, 1992.

Agile Development Using Naked Objects

Richard Pawson[1,2] and Vincent Wade[2]

[1] Computer Sciences Corporation
rpawson@csc.com
[2] Computer Science Department - Trinity College, Dublin, IE
vwade@cs.tcd.ie

Abstract. Naked objects are core business objects that are exposed directly to the user, by means of a suitable framework. As well as offering benefits to the finished system, the use of naked objects also facilitates the use of agile development techniques. In particular, it enables the concept of an exploration phase during which users and developers prototype the user interface and the underlying business object model simultaneously. During the subsequent delivery phase, naked objects make it easier to adopt the extreme programming discipline of writing executable user acceptance tests in advance of writing the code to implement a particular story.

1 Introduction

'Naked objects' is an architectural pattern whereby core business objects (such as Customer, Product and Order) are exposed directly to the user instead of being masked behind the conventional constructs of a user interface. In a business system designed using naked objects, all user actions involve explicitly invoking methods on business entity objects.

We are aware of two frameworks that have been designed specifically to support the naked objects pattern. One is the 'Expressive Object Architecture' commissioned by the Irish government's Department of Social and Family Affairs (DSFA), and on which its new Child Benefit Administration system has been built. The second is an open-source Java-based framework known simply as *Naked Objects*[1]. Figures 1 and 2 show screenshots from applications built using these two frameworks respectively. In both cases the user interface shown is auto-generated dynamically at run-time based on the capabilities of the core business objects, which are defined in the domain model layer of the architecture. The icons on the left of each screen represent the business object classes; the icons elsewhere on screen represent individual instances, some of which have been opened to reveal their publicly accessible attributes and associations (shown as embedded icons), or right-clicked to reveal a pop-up menu of user-accessible methods. Business methods that require input parameters are invoked by means of drag an drop operations.

---

[1] Hosted on www.nakedobjects.org

M. Marchesi and G. Succi (Eds.): XP 2003, LNCS 2675, pp. 97–103, 2003.
© Springer-Verlag Berlin Heidelberg 2003

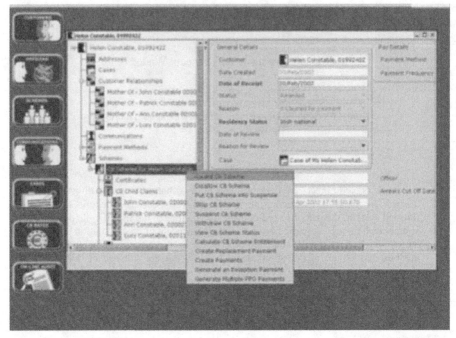

Fig. 1. User interface auto-generated by the *Expressive Object Architecture* framework

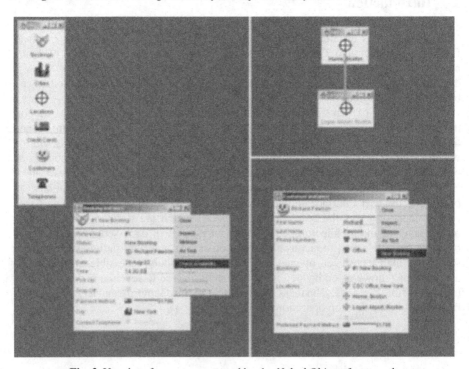

Fig. 2. User interface auto-generated by the *Naked Objects* framework

The original intent of the naked objects pattern was that it would result in business systems that were more agile, in two senses. The first, known as 'strategic agility', allows the resulting systems to be more easily accommodate future changes in business requirements. This quality derives from the fact that the naked objects pattern encourages the design of behaviourally-complete objects, which is to say that business entities are encapsulated with all of the behaviors that could be expected of them in an application. This is turn tends to localize any changes required to the code. The second, known as 'operational agility', allows the system to provide more flexibility in the day to day operations of the business that it supports. This is because the object-oriented user interface resulting from the pattern treats the user more like a problem solver and less like a process-follower. It is not claimed that this kind of interface is appropriate to all kinds of systems, nor that it is more efficient, merely that it is more expressive [5].

In use, it has become clear that the naked objects pattern can also contribute to the agility of the development process. It does this in two main ways: by facilitating communication between the developers and users, and by speeding up the development cycle. It facilitates communication between developers and users during requirements analysis, because the business objects provide a common language. We have found that end users engaging in a development process using naked objects will quickly start to express their requirements directly in object terms, requesting new methods on specific objects, new attributes or associations between objects, or new specialized sub-classes of an existing object type.

The naked objects pattern can speed up the development cycle because it eliminates the task of designing and implementing the user interface. The developer has to design and implement only the business object classes and their encapsulated business methods, and the object-oriented user interface is then auto-generated from these definitions. This can speed up the delivery of a finished system, as well as eliminating a substantial source of potential coding errors. Similar gains can, of course, be achieved by other frameworks that eliminate a specific aspect of design and/or coding, whether in the realm of the user interface or other aspects of the system.

2   A Lightweight Methodology for Using Naked Objects

Over the course of several development projects we have evolved a lightweight development methodology with the intent of leveraging these advantages. This methodology draws heavily upon the disciplines of extreme programming (XP) [2] but with considerably more emphasis placed on the idea of an up-front exploration phase.

2.1   The Exploration Phase

During this exploration phase, users and developers jointly explore the domain in question by building and using an object model to explore specific requirements as well as hypothetical scenarios. Using a framework that supports the naked objects pattern, the model is rendered into a concrete form that is immediately usable by end-users. In this sense the exploration phase feels rapid prototyping, as advocated by the Dynamic Systems Development Method [8] and other forms of rapid application development. But it is important to understand that by using the naked objects pattern during exploration, the team is not just prototyping a user presentation, but the underlying business object model at the same time – because one is a direct reflection of the other.

During such an exploration phase we have found that the users understanding of the business domain, of their highest priority requirements, and of the overall scope of the system, can change significantly. As well as permitting multiple scenarios to be explored, the executable object model itself often suggests new business possibilities that might not otherwise have been foreseen. Many users have told us that they found the process very enjoyable and instructive. The only thing that prevents it from continuing indefinitely is a firm and pre-agreed time-box (we have found 4 weeks to be adequate for most projects). Exploration itself is strongly iterative, so the team has many opportunities to decide whether to explore the domain in more depth or more breadth.

At the end of the exploration phase the team has an outline object model of the business domain, implemented in the form of an executable prototype that will have been used to test a variety of business scenarios. These scenarios include both tangible operational scenarios (akin to use-cases) and strategic possibilities ('what-if' scenarios). These will form useful inputs to the main phase of the project (which we call the 'delivery' phase), but it is important to understand that they do not constitute a comprehensive specification. Nor does this executable prototype evolve into a working system - the delivered system will be implemented from scratch, referencing the exploratory prototype for broad object responsibilities and relationships, possibly for method signatures, but not for working code.

Opinions differ as to what degree of up-front modeling is permissible within agile development. Some people seem to argue for zero up-front modeling. Others advocate developing 'spike solutions' for particularly thorny issues. Still others, exemplified by Agile Modeling [Ambler, 2002 #192] and Feature Driven Development [Palmer, 2002 #191] approaches, argue for developing a high-level domain model up front. We suggest that the naked object pattern brings benefits to these last approaches by making it easier for the users to get involved in and gain direct benefit from this up-front modeling activity.

2.2   The Delivery Phase

When the project is ready to move into the main development or 'delivery' phase we recommend that the system be coded, from scratch, based on user stories. Consistent with the XP approach, these stories are captured and prioritized during 'planning game' sessions, and then fleshed out and coded one at a time. However, adopting the naked objects pattern, and having previously conducted an exploration phase as described above, will facilitate this story-by-story approach to delivery in three ways.

First, the exploration phase will have encouraged the users to explore new possibilities for the roles of the new system, and thereby its scope. One of the criticisms leveled at XP is that encouraging the development of systems that meet only the users' articulated needs tends to discourage innovation. An up front exploration phase helps to redress this limitation.

Second, the existence of the exploration prototype can be very helpful both in identifying stories during the planning game and in subsequently fleshing them out as they are implemented. Some of these stories will have been explicitly prototyped during the exploration phase, others will not. However, even where the story has not been prototyped during exploration, the simple and consistent style of user interaction generated by the naked objects pattern makes it easy to express the new story in terms of new methods and associations on known classes, new specialized sub-classes, or, much less commonly, brand new business classes.

Third, the naked objects pattern makes it straightforward to write a test harness that will make it considerably easier to write executable user acceptance tests even in advance of implementing the functionality.

Such a test harness has now been written for the *Naked Objects* framework. Using this capability, the user and programmer sit down and verbally translate the new story into a script of user operations on the business objects. The programmer captures these, live, as a sequence of methods on specialized test classes. These test classes simulate the interaction between the *Naked Objects* viewing mechanism and the business objects. A (partial) example of such an executable acceptance test is shown below:

```
public void story2Reuse() {
    story("A booking where the previously used locations are
re-used");
    step("Retrieve the customer object.");
    View customer = getClass-
View("Customers").findInstance("Pawson");
    step("Create a booking for this customer.");
    View booking = customer.rightClick("New Booking");
    booking.checkField("Customer", customer);


    step("Retrieve the customer's home and office as
the...");
    booking.drop("Pick Up", customer.drag("Locations", "234 E
42nd Street, New York"));
    booking.drop("Drop Off", customer.drag("Locations", "JFK
Airport, BA Terminal"));
    booking.checkField("City", "New York");
    step("Use the customer's mobile phone as the con-
tact...");
    :
```

When the acceptance tests are completed for a story, the programmer(s) can then start designing and coding the necessary functionality, writing unit-tests for each of the methods created. (The *Naked Objects* framework also includes some simple extensions to *JUnit* for this purpose.) The acceptance tests also run in a manner very similar to Junit[2].

Just as with the JUnit approach to unit-testing, we have found that some programmers like to use the executable acceptance tests to guide their work: in other words

---

[2] See www.junit.org

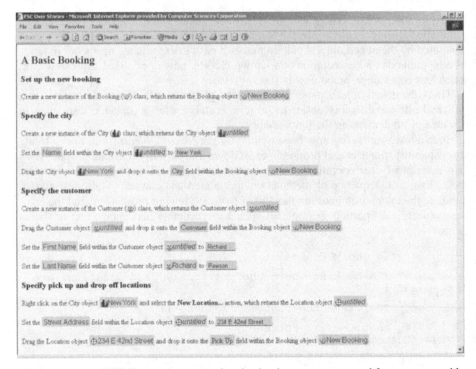

Fig. 3. Example of HTML user documentation that has been auto-generated from an executable user acceptance test

they address the errors thrown up by the tests in sequential order. When all the acceptance tests for a given story run, the story is deemed to be implemented.

The other role that the test classes and methods perform, is the ability to translate themselves into plain English. If the 'generate documentation' flag is set, then whenever a test is run successfully, it will output the English translation into an HTML file, complete with graphical icons (see Figure 3).

This capability means that is possible to auto-generate a significant proportion of the user training manual, consisting of a ready-formatted English script (other languages could easily be added) of user-operations for each test scenario - which, after all, constitute the principal business tasks. The final user manual would additionally need a small amount of up-front documentation, which can generic to all systems generated using a given framework, and an explanation of the roles of the business objects in this particular system.

Auto-generating the user manual eliminates a time-consuming task that few people enjoy doing. But the real benefit is that this user training documentation is guaranteed to be consistent with the operation of the system. An alternative way to think about this process is that when fleshing out a particular story we are asking the users to write the training manual for that story, and then we are using an executable version of the training manual as our acceptance test.

3   Conclusions

We conclude that the use of the naked objects architectural pattern, plus an up-front period of exploration using a framework that supports this pattern make a powerful addition to the practice of Extreme Programming. In particular, they may encourage more people to adopt the discipline of test-first development not only at the unit testing level but also for user acceptance testing.

References

1. Ambler, S., Agile Modelling: Effective Practices for Extreme Programming and the Unified Process. 2002: John Wiley & Sons.
2. Beck, K., EXtreme Programming EXplained. 1999: Addison-Wesley.
3. Jacobson, I., J. Rumbaugh, and G. Booch, The Unified Software Development Process. 1999.
4. Palmer, S. and M. Felsing, A Practical Guide to Feature Driven Development. 2002: Prentice Hall.
5. Pawson, R. and R. Matthews, Naked objects: a technique for designing more expressive systems. SIGPLAN Notices, 2001. 36(12).
6. Pawson, R. and R. Matthews, Naked Objects. 2002: J Wiley.
7. Raskin, J., The Humane Interface. 2000, Reading, MA: Addison-Wesley / ACM Press.
8. Stapleton, J., Dynamic Systems Development Method. 1997, Reading, MA: Addison-Wesley.

XPSwiki: An Agile Tool Supporting the Planning Game

Sandro Pinna, Simone Mauri, Paolo Lorrai, Michele Marchesi, and Nicola Serra

Dipartimento di Ingegneria Elettrica ed Elettronica, Università di Cagliari
Piazza d'Armi, 09123 Cagliari, Italy
{pinnasandro,plorrai,michele,nicola.serra}@diee.unica.it

Abstract. We present XPSwiki, a tool supporting the XP practices for requirement gathering and project management – user stories and the Planning Game.
XPSwiki has been developed in Smalltalk using Squeak Swiki technology. It is
accessed through the Internet in a user friendly agile way. XPSwiki keeps track
of multiple projects, each with its releases, iterations, user stories, acceptance
tests, and engineering tasks. It also manages teams of developers, who sign stories and tasks, and who pair-program them with another team member.
XPSwiki allows project tracking and documentation, and is at present in use
among real software firms.

1   Introduction

In Extreme Programming (XP), requirements are gathered using user stories, and the
whole development process is founded on short iterations, where incremental implementation of user stories takes place [1], [2]. XP development is driven and estimated
using the Planning Game (PG), which is in turn based on user stories. These practices
are considered among the most effective XP practices.

In their usual implementation, user stories are written by the user on index cards,
then their importance is estimated by the user, and their difficulty is estimated by
developers using story points. Eventually, the user chooses the stories to implement at
every iteration, with the constraint not to overcome the maximum number of story
points the team can implement. After each iteration, the whole PG is executed again,
accommodating changes and re-estimating team velocity and stories. The main tools
used for this activity are index cards, whiteboard,s and flipcharts visible to everyone,
acting as "information radiators" [3]. These tools are highly effective, since they are
user friendly and maximize communication.

However, the need for more structured, automated support tools for XP requirement gathering and PG is increasing, typically for two reasons:

- The software development organization has an internal or external quality certification, subject to auditing of formally defined requirements and project tracking documents.
- Software development is performed by distributed teams, and local information
  radiators are no longer sufficient to exchange information and control the process.

M. Marchesi and G. Succi (Eds.): XP 2003, LNCS 2675, pp. 104–113, 2003.
© Springer-Verlag Berlin Heidelberg 2003

Some tools have already been developed to address these needs. Among them, we may quote AutoTracker [4], Milos-ASE [5], Xplanner [6], XPCGI [7], XPWeb [8], Twiki XP Tracker [9], Iterate [10], XPPlanIt [11], and VersionOne [12].

In this paper we present XPSwiki, a new automated tool supporting the PG. This tool has been built on Wiki technology [13], using the open-source Squeak environment [14], hence its name. XPSwiki has been conceived and developed aiming to achieve the following characteristics:

- agility – the tool must be easy to use and easy to adapt and reconfigure;
- modularity and extensibility;
- Web-based – the tool must be accessed through standard Web browsers;
- interoperability – the tool should be easily interfaced to other development tools;
- open-source – the tool should be developed using an open-source environment.

In section 2 we present the requirements of XPSwiki, in the perspective of XP development practices. In section 3 we present highlights on the implementation of XPSwiki. In section 4 we present the user interface and use of XPSwiki, with the aim of giving a taste of the tool. In section 5 we conclude the paper and present our plan for future work on the tool.

2   XPSwiki Requirements

Let us briefly recall the activities and documents involved in the requirements gathering and planning phases of XP, the PG. The system requirements are gathered in the form of user stories, which are the units of implementation of the system. Each user story is written by the customer on an index card, to oblige the customer to be concise. User stories are integrated with acceptance tests, to verify whether the story has been implemented correctly or not. Each acceptance test in turn is written on an index card.

System development is performed in releases (every 2-3 months). A release is made up of a number of iterations (typically, 4-8), and each iteration implements a group of user stories. This is accomplished estimating the time to complete each story, through a score called "story points". The customer prioritizes and alters the stories, negotiating with developers, and in the end deciding which stories are allotted to each iteration. Acceptance tests are estimated and allotted as user stories.

Every user story and acceptance test is in turn subdivided in engineering tasks, which are the basic development units. Each task is subscribed by a developer, who is in charge of its correct completion.

From this short description, it is clear that the entities of the PG exhibit a well-constructed tree structure, which is shown in Fig. 1 in the form of a UML class diagram [15].

XPSwiki supports the PG model shown in Fig. 1. It allows to define one or more projects, each with a team of developers. The tool is accessed through a Web browser, and uses Wiki technology.

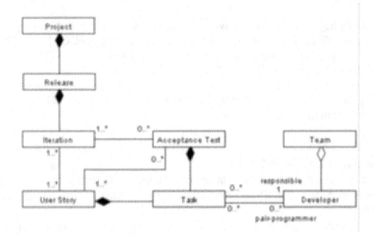

Fig. 1. UML class diagram showing the entities (persons and activities) involved in the PG. Multiplicities of aggregation and composition relationships are not explicitly shown, since they are always 1-1.*. In this model, we allow user stories and acceptance tests belonging to more than one iteration, and a user story may have no acceptance test. Usually, a user story and an acceptance test belong to only one iteration, and a user story has at least one acceptance test.

A Wiki [13] is an open Web site, where users can navigate freely through pages, add new pages, modify existing ones, and search pages by words contained. It is a tool for exchanging information on the Internet. Swiki is the Squeak implementation of a Wiki, and is used to add structure to given pages, defining input forms for each page. In this way, in a Swiki it is possible to have both pages constrained to a given structure, which is used to hold structured information, and free-format pages freely added to existing pages, which act as Post-it notes. The overall approach is very agile and user-friendly.

In the case of collocated teams, XPSwiki does not substitute the use of index cards in brainstorming sessions around a table, but can be used to keep a permanent track of the decisions taken during these meetings. It is worth noting that the Swiki logs all the changes to its pages, so it can be freely modified without the burden of explicitly tracking the changes made to the PG. If needed, these changes, or a snapshot of the project status at a given time, can be easily retrieved from the logs.

Other XPSwiki requirements are to show to developers the completion status of projects, releases, iterations, stories, and tasks, and to highlight inconsistencies, for instance iterations whose stories have more story points than allowed.

3   Implementation

We developed XPSwiki using Squeak [14], an open-source implementation of Smalltalk. We choose SWiki since it had many built-in features, which are very useful to our purposes, such as the ability to associate input forms to pages easily, a high portability on different operating systems (Windows, Linux, Mac-OS, many Unixes), a complete access to its source, the use of XML to store page information, and the power of the Smalltalk development environment.

On the other hand, SWiki has the drawbacks of being poorly documented, and consequently, we had to study and document the system ourselves.

We developed the first version of XPSwiki using the native data structure of Swiki pages. In this implementation, the information relating to the entities shown in Fig. 1 was simply held in the corresponding pages, and the relationships among them (for instance, the relationship among an iteration and the user stories implemented during it) were recorded using the hyperlinks between pages. This allowed to develop the tool rapidly, and obtain an early feedback on this version. However, the data structure was clearly inflexible and not very suitable to complex queries and further extensions.

In the second version of the development, in Squeak we implemented the object-oriented data structure of Fig. 1, giving each class the capability to store and retrieve its data into and from the corresponding Swiki pages. In this way, the computations are made directly on a modular object structure, easing their implementation and extensions, while permanent data storage maintains the advantages of existing XML implementation.

XPSwiki has been implemented with an XP approach, starting from a specification with user stories and acceptance tests. The project has been tracked since the beginning using the earliest version of the tool.

At present, the project consists of 25 system classes and 25 test classes. It cooperates with 20 Squeak Swiki classes, including the classes that hold page information in an XML repository.

The present status of the project has just completed its third release. XPSwiki is being used for internal purposes, and has been installed on the site of an industrial partner of ours. More details on XPSwiki implementation are reported in [16].

4   Use of XPSwiki

The starting page of XPSwiki shows a list of all current projects, with their completion percentage. By clicking on the project name, one can access the project home page (Fig. 2).

In its upper part, there are links to the pages showing its team members, releases, iterations, user stories, tasks, and acceptance tests. In its lower part, the completion status of the project can be seen at a glance, referring to its releases, iterations, and user stories, as well as the average team velocity, in terms of average implemented story points per release, iteration, and working day.

The icon bar on the left is a standard Swiki bar, used in all XPSwiki pages. From top to bottom, the icons allow to return to the current page, edit the current page, upload files into the current page, list all updates to the current page, go to the project home page, list the most recent changes to the project pages, perform queries on the project, and obtain help on Swiki usage. Depending on the context, one or more icons can be disabled. The small arrowhead pointing to the icon shows the present interaction status with Swiki.

Each page displaying the project process entities of Fig. 1 contains a list of the lower-level entities held, showing their status, present velocity, possible problems, and inconsistencies. For instance, a release shows its iterations, an iteration shows its stories, and so on. By clicking on the entity name, its page can be accessed.

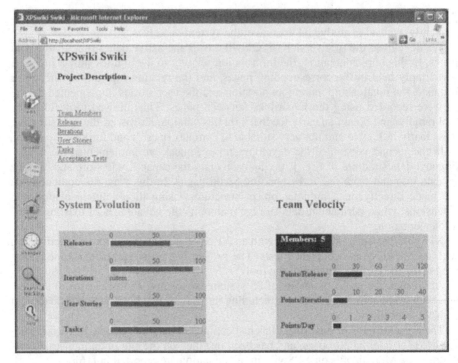

Fig. 2. The starting page of a project, allowing access to its entities, and showing the project completion status and average team velocity.

Fig. 3 shows the page of user story S10, "Iteration Editing", taken from user stories describing the XPSwiki system itself.

The upper part of the page reports synthetic information about the user story – the percentage of its implemented tasks and acceptance tests, and the story attributes. The state may be *to do, in progress,* or *done*; the priority may be *must have, should have,* or *could have*; the risk may be *high, medium,* or *low*. The story points are also reported.

Under this information, there is the story description. It is written in free format text, and could have links to other pages, include embedded images, or even hold uploaded files to download. After the description, information on story iteration, responsible developer, creation and last change dates are reported.

Then, a list of user story tasks follows, reporting task name, programmers, points, and current state. Task names are links to their pages. Acceptance tests related to the story are reported under tasks. In the example of Fig. 3, no test has yet been associated to the user story.

In the lower part of the page, the "Track Table" reports information about user story completion and possible problems. If the story had inconsistencies, for instance between the story's estimated points and the sum of the points of its tasks, this would be highlighted in red.

The pages showing information on releases, iterations, acceptance tests, and tasks are similar to the story page shown in Fig. 3. They present the description of the process entity, its status, other linked entities, and information about its completion.

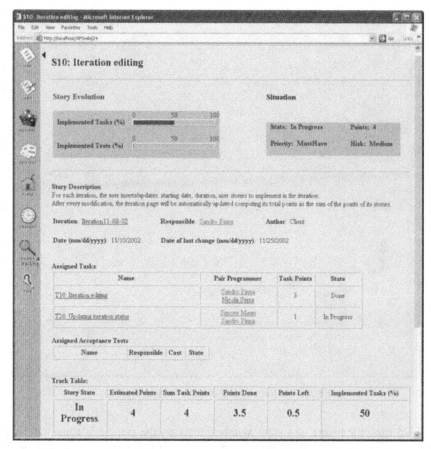

Fig. 3. A user story. The story status is shown in the upper part of the page. The story description, the persons responsible, and the attributes are shown in the middle. The task lists and track table of the story are shown at the bottom of the page.

To edit one of these pages, the user presses the "edit" icon on the left bar. Fig. 4 shows the form that appears when entering the edit mode on the user story shown in Fig. 3. The form allows editing of free-format descriptions using text editor panes. Other attributes are edited using standard input fields and combo-boxes. The changes can be saved by pressing the "save" button, while updating the user story description.

A Wiki page can also be locked using a password, and an e-mail address can be associated to it, so that an e-mail is sent whenever the page is updated.

If the user wishes to insert links to other pages, he/she can do so in the user story description, using standard Wiki syntax. If he/she wishes to upload files or images to the page, he/she must first use the corresponding icon, and then put the proper link in the description.

It should be pointed out that the editing form of a user story does not show any widget concerning its tasks. This because it is in the task page that a user story is assigned to the task, and not vice-versa. Moreover, a lot of information presented in the user story page is computed, and cannot be edited directly.

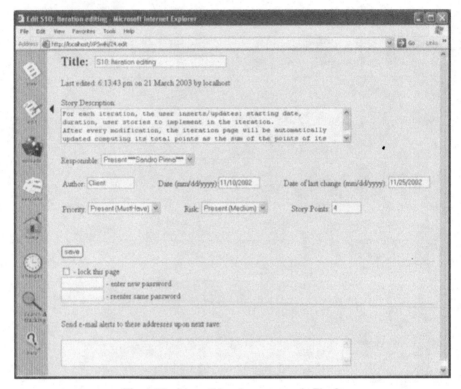

Fig. 4. The form editing the user story in Fig. 3.

Fig. 5 shows the page of a team member. It shows the member's name and basic information in the upper part. Then follows the list of all the tasks the member is involved in, both as responsible and pair programmer.

The bottom of the page holds a free-format text field called "Notes", where an image of the developer is shown, to demonstrate Swiki's ability to manage this kind of information easily.

Fig. 6 shows the form that appears when the "search and tracking" icon is clicked on. It should be noted that in the presented XPSwiki version, this feature is quite limited. The Swiki pages can be queried looking for matching words in their descriptions. This is done with the input fields and radio buttons shown in the upper part of the page.

Using the combo-box and the button in the middle of the page, a list of all the user stories in the project can be obtained ordered according to one of the following features: cost, iteration, priority, risk, or state.

It is also possible to obtain a list of all the tasks of the project, ordered according to one of the following features: start date, user story, responsible, risk, or state.

XPSwiki is a tool that is easy to use and update, that takes full advantage of Web and Wiki technology. The project is evolving rapidly considering the comments of internal and industrial users.

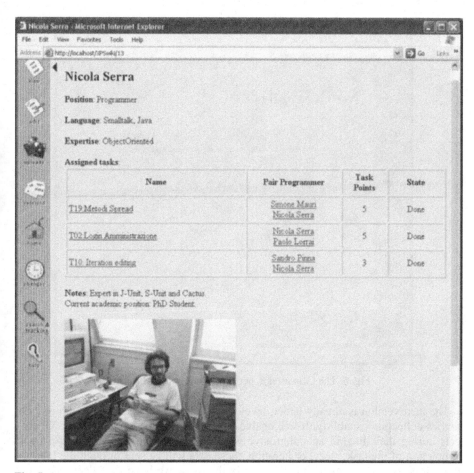

Fig. 5. A team member page, showing his skills, present involvement, and free-format description including an image.

5   Conclusions and Future Work

We have presented the design and implementation of XPSwiki, a tool supporting XP planning game. The tool is currently being used by our team, and by a number of partner software firms in Sardinia, which use it mainly to track Java development projects. We are actively gathering feedback from our partners, in order to include in XPSwiki the features needed for a fruitful and effective use in industrial environments.

The present XPSwiki version allows project tracking and estimation. As reported by our partners, it is very useful to XP developers that are starting to learn the PG, since it obliges them to use the PG. Expert XP developers are in a position of carrying out projects without these tools. But XPSwiki helps keep track of project activities, satisfying management, and contributing to the adoption of XP in firms.

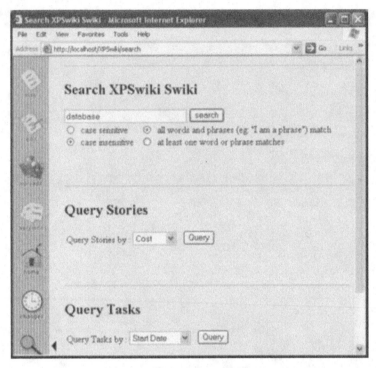

Fig. 6. The form used to perform queries on the project.

The next version is already under development, and will be provided with process metrics collection capability. It will enable us to gather data continuously on XP projects during their life, in an unintrusive way. At given time intervals and/or upon completion of the task, story, or iteration, these data will be sent through the Internet to a server devoted to metrics collection. In this way, we hope to collect many real world data on software development, with the aim of proving (or disprove) the effectiveness of XP quantitatively.

Further work on the tool will be entirely driven by our partners' needs. They include:

- Reporting modules, producing good-looking printing in PDF and/or RTF format of project tracking documents, including graphics. This feature is especially required by ISO-9000 certified organizations wishing to adopt the XP process without giving up their certification.
- Interface to the CVS configuration management system, in order to associate with each task the code actually written every day.
- Interface with popular development environments, such as Eclipse, and with project management tools like Microsoft Project.
- Development of modules to support other agile methodologies, such as Scrum [17] and Feature Driven Development [18]. This will be greatly facilitated by the flexibility of the modular structures of Swiki and XPSwiki.

References

1. Beck, K.: Extreme Programming Explained, Addison-Wesley, Reading, MA (1999).
2. Beck, K., Fowler, M.: Planning Extreme Programming, Addison-Wesley, Reading, MA (2000).
3. Cockburn, A.: Agile Software Development, Addison-Wesley, Reading, MA (2002).
4. Auer, K., AutoTracker, Position Paper for OOPSLA 2000 Workshop: "Refining the Practices of Extreme Programming", online at
   http://www.rolemodelsoftware.com/moreAboutUs/publications/autoTracker.php
5. Maurer, F.: Supporting Distributed Extreme Programming, in Extreme Programming and Agile Methods, D. Wells, L.A. Williams (Eds.), Proceedings of XP/Agile Universe 2002, Chicago, IL, USA, August 4-7, 2002. Lecture Notes in Computer Science 2418, Springer, Berlin Heidelberg New York (2002).
6. XPlanner, http://www.xplanner.org.
7. XPCGI, http://xpcgi.sourceforge.net.
8. XPWeb, http://xpweb.sourceforge.net.
9. Twiki XP Tracker, http://twiki.org/cgi-bin/view/Plugins/XpTrackerPlugin.
10. Iterate, http://www.diamond-sky.com/products/iterate.
11. König, D., Cunningham, G.: eXtreme Programming (XP) – What is it?, online at: http://www.xpplanit.com/article.pdf.
12. VersionOne, http://www.versionone.net.
13. Bo, L. Cunningham, W: The Wiki Way. Addison-Wesley, Reading, MA (2001).
14. Gudzial, M.: Squeak: Object-Oriented Design with Multimedia Applications, Prentice Hall, Upper Saddle River (2001).
15. Booch, G., Rumbaugh, J., Jacobson, I.: The Unified Modeling Language User Guide. Addison-Wesley, Reading, MA (1999).
16. Pinna, S., Lorrai, P., Marchesi, M., Serra, N.: Developing a Tool Supporting XP Process, submitted for publication.
17. Schwaber, K., Beedle, M.: Agile Software Development with SCRUM. Prentice-Hall, Upper Saddle River (2002).
18. Coad, P., de Luca, J., Lefebvre, E.: Java Modeling in Color with Uml, Prentice Hall, Upper Saddle River (1999).

CruiseControl.NET:
Continuous Integration for .NET

R. Owen Rogers

ThoughtWorks, Inc.
Peek House, 20 Eastcheap
EC UK London, United Kingdom
orogers@thoughtworks.com
http://www.thoughtworks.com

Abstract. With the release of Microsoft's .NET framework, a large number of agile tools are being ported to take advantage of the new platform. To support development on its .NET projects, ThoughtWorks has produced a functional port of CruiseControl, its popular continuous integration build server, to the .NET platform. CruiseControl.NET replicates the majority of the functionality included in the latest 2.0 release of CruiseControl and adds a number of new features to provide integration with .NET tools and technologies. CruiseControl.NET has recently been released as open source by ThoughtWorks under a BSD-style license and is freely available for download at http://ccnet.thoughtworks.com/.

1 Introduction: Automating Continuous Integration

CruiseControl.NET is a build server that enables development teams to simplify and automate the practice of continuous integration on their projects. XP and other agile methodologies advocate the benefits of a regular build, test and deployment cycle to minimise the complications associated with software integration. Integrating regularly ensures that the latest sources are always working and available to anyone who wants them; it encourages developers to communicate regularly and keep their efforts synchronised; and it helps expose integration bugs between code modules or subsystems. Typically, development teams are encouraged to perform an integration cycle once every few hours. However, relying on a manual process to ensure that regular integrations are performed requires tremendous diligence on behalf of the development team. Alternately, this process can be automated by using a continuous integration build server such as CruiseControl[1].

A continuous integration build server automates the integration cycle by monitoring the project's source control system directly. Any time modifications

---

[1] CruiseControl is the original open source continuous integration build server. Implemented by ThoughtWorks, CruiseControl continues to be the *de facto* continuous integration build server. For more information on CruiseControl, please check the CruiseControl web page at **http://cruisecontrol.sourceforge.net/** or the "Continuous Integration" white paper [1].

M. Marchesi and G. Succi (Eds.): XP 2003, LNCS 2675, pp. 114–122, 2003.
© Springer-Verlag Berlin Heidelberg 2003

are checked in, the server initiates a new integration cycle by checking out, building, testing, and deploying the software, and publishing the results of the integration to the development team. Automating the integration process produces a number of tangible benefits:

1. **Guaranteed integration cycles:** because the process is automated, integrations will not be neglected and forgotten.
2. **Integrations get fixed:** the development team is immediately notified of the status of the integration. If the integration fails, fixing the integration is the top priority; otherwise, the team will be repeatedly notified of the broken build until it is fixed.
3. **Culprit detection:** as the integration is triggered by a developer checking in code, it is easy to detect the individual responsible for breaking the build. By clearly identifying the guilty parties, developers are discouraged from adopting practices that are likely to cause the build to break.
4. **Automated test coverage:** the build is only as good as the tests that validate it. Because the build is automated, the tests must also be automated.

As the benefits of continuous integration are recognisable and attainable in almost any software development project – irrespective of whether the development team practices agile or not – a continuous integration build server, like CruiseControl.NET, has very wide appeal. Establishing a continuous integration environment is often a key stepping stone to introducing other agile practices such as automated testing (which in turn, encourages collective code ownership, which then encourages refactoring and pair programming). The development team then finds that they have adopted a number of agile practices without realising it. As a result, setting up a continuous integration build server can be an excellent way to introduce agile "under the covers", especially for clients that may have an initially adverse reaction to the idea of agile.

2   CruiseControl.NET Overview

CruiseControl.NET consists of a continuous integration build server and a number of client interface applications. The CruiseControl.NET server is available both as a Windows Service and as a command-line console application. By registering CruiseControl.NET as a Windows Service, the server can plug into the Windows Service management framework. This simplifies the management of the CruiseControl.NET server as the service can be started or stopped via the Services Controller Manager and can be configured to automatically start when the machine boots up. Alternately, the CruiseControl.NET console application provides a quick and easy mechanism for setting up and launching an instance of a CruiseControl.NET server from the command-line. This approach is ideal if multiple server instances are required to run on a single machine; however, this benefit comes at the cost of the management advantages derived from the Windows Service version. Both types of server are included in the standard distribution, and both simply represent a thin wrapper for the same underlying server implementation.

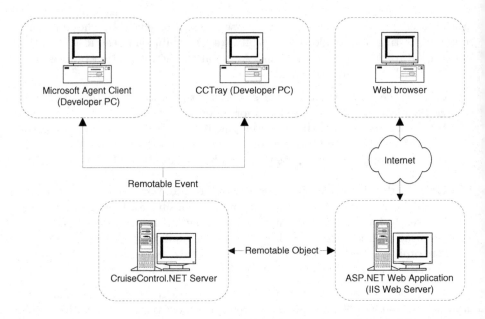

Fig. 1. Remotable client-server architecture for CruiseControl.NET.

CruiseControl.NET currently provides three client applications for interacting with the build server and for obtaining integration results. One client is an ASP.NET web application. It provides a web page for viewing the results of current and previous integrations, and for analysing statistics related to the build process. It also provides an administrative interface for remotely managing and configuring the build server. Another client, called CCTray, is a remoting client that shows an icon in the system tray indicating the status of a monitored build server. The icon will change depending on whether the build succeeded, failed or is in the process of running. There is another remote client that plugs into Microsoft Agent (the little animated helpers that are the bane of many Microsoft Office users) that pops up and provides voice notification of the results of the last integration. Somehow, the novelty of having an animated parrot pop out and squawk out "You broke the build" never seems to wear off. Under development is a plug-in for Visual Studio.NET that provides similar visual notification of the status of the current build.

All communication between clients and server is accomplished via .NET Remoting. .NET Remoting is a powerful framework for unobtrusively constructing remotable objects that can be used to proxy and transport data between remote sources and to handle remote method invocation. Using remoting to separate client and server keeps the two clearly decoupled. Figure 1 shows the connection between the CruiseControl.NET server and the described clients.

The CruiseControl.NET server provides support for two types of remoting clients. The first is a publish-and-subscribe mechanism for transmitting events to remote clients. This approach is used by the CCTray and Microsoft Agent

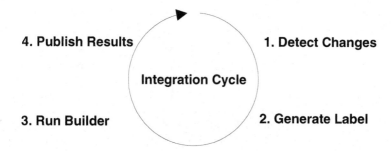

4. Publish Results   **1. Detect Changes**

Integration Cycle

3. Run Builder   **2. Generate Label**

Fig. 2. The standard CruiseControl.NET project workflow.

clients as they are subscribe-only. The ASP.NET web application uses server-activated remotable objects to interact directly with the objects running on the server. This enables the ASP.NET client to perform actions on the server such as start and stop particular builds.

3   CruiseControl.NET Architecture

3.1   Project Workflows

CruiseControl.NET automates the continuous integration process for software projects by representing their integration cycle as a configurable *workflow*. This workflow consists of a series of *tasks*, corresponding to the various steps in the build, test and deploy integration cycle. By default, CruiseControl.NET provides a standard workflow that is useful in most common integration scenarios. Currently, this workflow consists of four main types of tasks:

- **Source Controls:** detect modifications in the source control system and check out the changes.
- **Builders:** compile, test and deploy the software.
- **Labellers:** label the build output and tag the source control revision.
- **Publishers:** send out notification of the build results.

These tasks are linked together in a workflow as shown in Figure 2. First, the source control task is invoked to determine whether changes have been checked in since the last build. If changes are detected, then the latest version of the source files are checked out and the builder will then be invoked to compile and test the retrieved code. The build will then be labelled depending on its success or failure. Finally, the publishers will send out the build results to the development team. Once this is complete and after a suitable timeout, the workflow will be restarted and the integration cycle will begin again.

This default workflow is sufficient for most simple development projects; however, as projects start to scale in size and complexity, it is often necessary to customize and augment the default workflow. To accommodate this, CruiseControl.NET provides a mechanism for pluggable project workflows. Developers

Table 1. Tasks currently included in the CruiseControl.NET server distribution.

Task Name	Task Type	Task Description
NAntBuilder	Builder	Invokes NAnt[2] to compile, test and deploy a project.
DevenvBuilder	Builder	Invokes the Visual Studio.NET development environment engine to compile a solution file.
Cvs	SourceControl	Monitors a CVS repository for changes.
Vss	SourceControl	Monitors a Visual Source Safe repository for changes.
P4	SourceControl	Monitors a Perforce repository for changes.
StarTeam	SourceControl	Monitors a StarTeam repository for changes.
PVCS	SourceControl	Monitors a PVCS repository for changes.
FileSourceControl	SourceControl	Monitors a file or folder for changes.
AssemblyLabeller	Labeller	Constructs a build label from an assembly version.
EmailPublisher	Publisher	Emails integration results to a group of developers. Developers can sign up to receive emails after every build or only after builds initiated by their changes.
XmlLogPublisher	Publisher	Generates an XML log file of the build results. These log files are used as the basis for reporting build results using the ASP.NET client.
YahooPublisher	Publisher	Sends notification of build results to Yahoo! Instant Messenger clients. Supports configurable notification groups similar to the EmailPublisher.

can create their own custom workflow classes and plug them into the CruiseControl.NET server to handle their specific implementation requirements. Creating and configuring pluggable components for CruiseControl.NET will be elaborated further in Section 3.3 below.

3.2 Tasks

CruiseControl.NET comes bundled with a set of standard tasks, many of which are particularly useful for working with .NET projects. A list of these tasks is given in Table 1.

In addition to the listed tasks, active development is ongoing on a builder for NMAKE[3], support for SubVersion source control repositories, a WebDAV publisher, and an SCP publisher, amongst others.

The tasks included with CruiseControl.NET provide a solid foundation for common .NET build processes; however, the set is by no means complete. As

[2] NAnt is the .NET equivalent of Ant, the popular XML-based build tool for Java. For more details, see *http://nant.sourceforge.net/*.

[3] NMAKE is a make build tool implemented by Microsoft. See *http://msdn.microsoft.com/library/default.asp?url=/library/en-us/vcug98/html/ _asug_overview.3a_.nmake_reference.asp* for more information.

```
<cruisecontrol>
  <project name="project1">
    <schedule timeout=""60000""/>
    <sourcecontrol type="cvs">
      <executable>cvs.exe</executable>
      <workingDirectory>d:\project1</workingDirectory>
    </sourcecontrol>
    <build type="nant">
      <executable>NAnt.exe</executable>
      <baseDirectory>d:\project1</baseDirectory>
    </build>
    <publishers>
      <xmllogger>
        <logDir>d:\project1\ccnet\log</logDir>
      </xmllogger>
    </publishers>
  </project>
</cruisecontrol>
```

Fig. 3. Sample XML configuration file.

a result, CruiseControl.NET has been designed specifically to simplify and facilitate the construction and deployment of custom tasks. This simplicity is a product of CruiseControl.NET's configuration system, as described next.

3.3   Configuration

Configuration of project workflows and their tasks is handled through an XML configuration file. This configuration file defines what workflows should be managed by the build server, what tasks those workflows contain, and how those tasks are configured. A sample configuration file is shown in Figure 3. The sample configuration file specifies that the build server should generate a project workflow called **project1** that is scheduled to run every 60000 milliseconds. It will monitor a CVS repository that was been checked out to **d:\project1**. If changes are detected, the build server will use NAnt to run a build script in the specified folder. Once the build is complete, the build results will be written as XML to the **d:\project1\ccnet\log** log folder.

CruiseControl.NET uses an open source XML data binding and object serialisation tool called NetReflector[4]. NetReflector uses .NET attributes to map classes and their properties to XML nodes. When the configuration file is loaded, NetReflector will instantiate the object hierarchy defined in the XML document and will initialise their properties accordingly. Figure 4 shows a code snippet from the NAntBuilder class.

The attributes **[ReflectorType]** and **[ReflectorProperty]** are used to identify classes and their properties that are to be bound to XML elements in the configuration file. Comparing the code snippet to the configuration file above,

---

[4] See http://netreflector.sourceforge.net/ for more details.

```
using ...
using Exortech.NetReflector;

namespace tw.ccnet.core.builder {
    [ReflectorType("nant")]
    public class NAntBuilder : IBuilder
    {
        ...

        [ReflectorProperty("executable")]
        public string Executable
        {
            get { return _executable; }
            set { _executable = value; }
        }

        [ReflectorProperty("baseDirectory")]
        public string BaseDirectory
        {
            get { return _baseDirectory; }
            set { _baseDirectory = value; }
        }

        ...

    }
}
```

Fig. 4. Code snippet from the NAntBuilder class.

it is evident that the NAntBuilder class maps to the <build type="nant"> XML element, and its properties, Executable and BaseDirectory, map to the corresponding subelements.

The CruiseControl.NET builder server uses NetReflector to search through all assemblies included in the build server's \bin folder for classes that contain NetReflector attributes. Deploying a custom task is as simple as compiling an assembly containing classes marked up with NetReflector attributes and copying it into the \bin folder. Modifying the configuration file to include the XML elements for the custom task will cause the task to be automatically loaded into the workflow by the build server. As the CruiseControl.NET build server continuously monitors the configuration file for changes, the task will be activated as soon as the configuration file is changed. As a result, it is not necessary to restart the build server to deploy the custom task or to refresh the configuration data.

3.4   Multiple Workflows and Schedules

The CruiseControl.NET server is capable of running several project workflows simultaneously. Each workflow executes in a separate thread that is run according to a configurable *schedule*.

The standard schedule periodically polls the source control system for modifications. If no modifications are detected, the thread sleeps for a specified timespan before checking the source control system again. Alternately, a schedule can be configured to execute a workflow on a specific day at a specific time. For example, it is possible to get the CruiseControl.NET server to launch a build every weekday at midnight. It is also possible to instruct the CruiseControl.NET server to launch a build on-demand by specifying a project schedule that will execute once starting immediately.

Currently, support is being added to the ASP.NET web application to provide an administrative interface to remotely create and configure project schedules.

4   Rationale

It is fair to question why it was necessary to produce a .NET version of the original Java-based CruiseControl in the first place – especially as a number of projects using Microsoft development platforms already use CruiseControl to handle their continuous integration requirements. Our rationale was threefold:

- **Technical:** we needed to produce a product that would integrate with and provide built-in support for the tools and technologies that are central to .NET projects.
- **Political:** many corporate clients are wedded to a particular development platform and will not permit tools that do not run natively on that platform (i.e. they are a Microsoft shop that refuses to run Java applications or vice versa).
- **Practical:** many .NET developers have no experience with Java and would not choose to learn Java in order to set up or extend CruiseControl; our goal is to produce a version of CruiseControl that will set up and run 'out-of-the-box' on .NET platforms.

The implication of developing a separate .NET version of CruiseControl is that it risks forking the main CruiseControl development stream. As far possible, we are working to synchronise the development efforts to ensure that the two versions maintain functional equivalence. CruiseControl.NET already implements the majority of the functionality included in the latest CruiseControl release. Correspondingly, we are working on feeding some of the new functionality added by CruiseControl.NET back into the original version.

That said, CruiseControl.NET offers a large number of enhancements over the Java-version, such as:

- Pluggable, customisable workflows;
- Scheduled, concurrent project execution;
- Attribute-based configuration;
- Extensible, plug-in architecture;
- .NET-specific workflow tasks;
- Remote build server management;

- Build statistics reporting;
- Wide variety of different clients; and;
- Easy installation using Microsoft System Installer (msi).

5   Conclusion: Enterprise Continuous Integration

Long build times, large development teams, complex deployment scenarios, heterogenous platforms and programming languages, and legacy system integration are common requirements for enterprise projects. Scaling continuous integration to meet these requirements is the key challenge for automated build servers such as CruiseControl.NET.

CruiseControl.NET represents a stepping stone in the evolution towards enterprise continuous integration. By providing support for configurable workflows, a pluggable architecture and remotable interfaces, CruiseControl.NET is moving in the right direction to address these requirements. Future enterprise enhancements include support for distributed workflows spread amongst networked build servers, and remote workflow and configuration management. Check out the CruiseControl Anywhere project (`http://cca.sourceforge.net/`) for the future direction of enterprise continuous integration with CruiseControl.NET.

As it stands, CruiseControl.NET is a powerful new continuous integration server for the Microsoft .NET platform. It implements the core functionality of CruiseControl and adds a number of useful extensions and enhancements. As a fully functional, highly extensible continuous integration server, CruiseControl.NET is an essential tool for any agile .NET project.

Acknowledgements

Thanks to all of the people that have contributed and are actively contributing to the CruiseControl.NET project in various ways. Thanks also to Bill Caputo for his ideas and suggestions in defining the path towards Enterprise Continuous Integration with CCA.

References

1. Fowler, Martin, Foemmel, Matt: Continuous Integration.
   http://www.thoughtworks.com/library/Continuous Integration.pdf (2001)

Tool Support for Complex Refactoring
to Design Patterns

Carmen Zannier and Frank Maurer

University of Calgary, Department of Computer Science
Calgary, Alberta, Canada T2N 1N4
{zannierc,maurer}@cpsc.ucalgary.ca

Abstract. The abstract should summarize the contents of the paper and should Using design patterns is seen to improve the maintainability of software systems. Applying patterns often implies upfront design while agile methods rely on software architecture to emerge. We bridge this gap by applying complex refactoring towards patterns to improve software design. Complex refactorings are based on existing tool-supported refactorings, knowledge of the application to be changed, knowledge of design patterns, and the capability to generate necessary code for a given design pattern. We present complex refactorings to J2EE design patterns and describe requirements of complex refactoring and accompanying tool support.

1   Introduction

Design patterns enhance the readability, maintainability and flexibility of a software system [6]. They usually require the use of software development methodologies that implement thorough upfront design. A conflict exists when examining agile methodologies which emphasize an initial but emerging software design and architecture, and rely on tacit knowledge of said design and the YAGNI (You Ain't Gonna Need It) principle [3]. Agile methods assume that creating more flexibility than is currently needed is wasted effort while design patterns are used to increase the flexibility of software for anticipated changes.

While agile teams generate immediate feedback in the form of programmed functionality, [3], the question as to the level of comprehension each developer has of the system remains unanswered. Contrastingly, while traditional methodologies provide a basis for a developer's design knowledge in the form of design documentation, the question of the team's ability to satisfy customer requirements is prolonged until late in the life of the project. In an attempt to profit on the strengths of these conflicting approaches we ask: can we utilize agile methodologies and still create "good" design? That is, can we have sound emerging design? We propose complex refactoring to design patterns and accompanying tool support that helps developers change the design of existing software to conform to a design pattern more typically found in top-down development methodologies. We present complex refactorings, comprised

M. Marchesi and G. Succi (Eds.): XP 2003, LNCS 2675, pp. 123–130, 2003.
© Springer-Verlag Berlin Heidelberg 2003

of atomic and sequential refactorings, and which maintain design pattern knowledge, initial application design knowledge and the capability to generate code. As examples, we focus on complex refactoring to Java 2 Enterprise Edition design patterns, a popular application area. The benefits of complex refactorings and tool support therein are those typical of design pattern implementation as well as improved runtime performance. The goal of this research is to specify requirements for a tool that helps developers refactor to a given design pattern and to provide a proof of this concept. Section 2 gives some background information, Section 3 examines the definition of Refactoring, Section 4 discusses the tool's knowledge, Section 5 looks at an example, Section 6 specifies our contributions and we conclude with a look at the current state, future work and a final summary.The preparation of manuscripts which are to be reproduced by photo-offset requires special care. Papers submitted in a technically unsuitable form will be returned for retyping, or canceled if the volume cannot otherwise be finished on time.

2   Background

The Gang of Four, [6], initially defined design patterns as "descriptions of communicating objects and classes that are customized to solve a general design problem in a particular context". We focus on design patterns found in the business tier of Java2 Enterprise Edition applications. Some concerns that are addressed with these patterns in [2] are: tight coupling between the client and business tier, resulting in a proliferation of network calls; mapping the object model directly to the entity bean model; mapping each use case to a session bean and embedding service lookups in clients. The example found in Section 5 deals with the Value Object pattern and the Session Façade pattern.

3   Refactoring

The increased popularity of agile methods such as Extreme Programming, Scrum, Crystal, [1], has helped advertise a design and code improvement practice: refactoring. At the very basic level, refactoring is cleaning up code while preserving the behaviour of an application [5]. We group existing refactorings into two categories and present a third, more complex category.

3.1   Atomic Refactoring

Small changes to code such as renaming a variable, improves the readability and of software [5]. We term these 'atomic refactorings' as they are primitive refactorings comprised of only one or two operations (e.g. change name of variable, compile and test). Tool support for such operations is widely available, [4][7]. At a similar level to these atomic refactorings are refactorings such as Extract Method which moves a section of (possibly repeated) code into its own method [5]. These refactorings involve only a few more operations than the atomic refactorings previously mentioned and are thus considered atomic. Tool support for these refactorings is also easily found.

3.2 Sequential Refactoring

The complexity of refactorings quickly increases with the combination and repetition of atomic refactorings. An example of this is Extract Class which encompasses Move Field and Move Method [5]. We term such refactorings sequential as they are sequences of atomic refactorings. Tool support for these refactorings is not as easily found.

The key point to address concerning atomic and sequential refactorings is that they maintain local knowledge only, of the application on which they function. An example is Rename Variable – the rename refactoring only needs to know the name of all other variables within the scope of the variable to be renamed. At most atomic and sequential refactorings need to know names of the classes in a given package, not the structure or interaction between the classes.

3.3 Complex Refactoring

We introduce complex refactorings as an extension of atomic and sequential refactorings and distinguish them from atomic and sequential refactorings in four ways. Firstly, complex refactorings are comprised of a series of atomic and sequential refactorings. In Section 5 we describe how tool support for atomic and sequential refactoring is easily integrated into the system. From a theoretical view, these small operations are easily incorporated into a larger operation. Secondly, complex refactorings have access to knowledge of the structure of the system. Using this information as a start point, complex refactorings know what classes to change. Thirdly, complex refactorings have access to knowledge about design patterns so that they know to what structure to change. Lastly, complex refactorings have the capability to generate code for classes required in a design pattern but unimplemented in the original system. The new classes are not simply a result of moving existing code to another location in the system, but are generated from scratch.

The point to be emphasized is we view complex refactorings differently than the original definition we provided for refactoring. While complex refactorings clean up code, they also require application and domain knowledge, perform broad application transformations and generate a determinable amount of code for each design pattern. Like atomic and sequential refactorings, however, they do not modify the behaviour of the system, from an end user point of view.

4 Tool Knowledge

Tool support to achieve complex refactoring to design patterns requires three knowledge stores. First, the tool maintains an *Initial System Store* which has knowledge of the original structure of the system and the user's design decisions. The Initial System Store asks the user what files need to be analyzed, what pattern is to be implemented, any nested patterns that should be implemented, names of new classes to create and various other design attributes of the original application. Through this series of questions the system establishes knowledge of the initial structure of the application and the requirements for the target application.

Secondly, the tool maintains a *Rule Store* where it stores rules and guidelines for the domain in which we are working. The complex refactorings we discuss work with J2EE type files. The Rule Store also maintains knowledge of .jsp files such as the extension, the Java code to scan, and any flags to ignore (e.g. HTML related code) as well as information about servlet and general java files. The Rule Store maintains information about the structure of session beans and entity beans. Finally the Rule Store maintains information about design patterns and the classes that are required to be implemented for each design pattern.

The final knowledge aspect maintained by the tool is the *Target System Store*, where all the complex refactorings reside. The Target System Store accesses the Initial System Store and the Rule Store to find out what needs to be changed and how it needs to be changed. At the time of writing the steps to create a given design pattern are represented as a series of complex refactorings represented as workflow in the Target System Store.

There are numerous design decisions we made when initially working on the tool. These design decisions concern the initial and target application, not the design of the tool, and thus these decisions must be made each time a developer uses the Design Pattern Developer. Firstly, what new structure should the target application have, if any? The user needs to specify if a 3-tiered structure should be implemented or if no new structure is needed at all. Secondly, what design pattern should be implemented and what patterns (if any) should be nested? There are also various pattern-specific decisions that a developer using the tool must make before applying change. Specific examples are provided in Section 5. Figure 1 gives an overview of the change the tool performs and a specific example provided in Section 5.

5   Example

The Design Pattern Developer is implemented as a multi-page wizard, plug-in in Eclipse. The first three pages pose design questions to the user. The next four pages implement the actual changes based on information specified in the design decision pages. The Design Pattern Developer has been tested with an implementation of the J2EE business tier design patterns: Session Façade with a nested Value Object. After the desired pattern and 3-tier structure are decided, the following page specifies pattern-specific questions. For the Session Façade pattern we ask whether we need to be concerned with direct or sequential logic. We define 'direct logic' as a single line of code in the client file that needs to be moved to the Session Façade; we define sequential logic as multiple lines that must be moved to the Session Façade. We also ask for the ratio of session façades to entity beans. For purposes of application size or

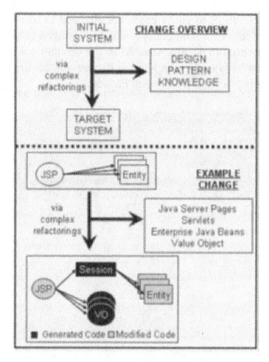

Fig. 1. Overview of the change occurring in the Design Pattern Developer; Example of Change in Session Façade with nested Value Object

business logic organization, one may wish to implement more than one Session Façade for the entity beans in an application. The last design decision that must be made is if there are any patterns that should be nested inside the previously selected pattern. In our example, we nest the Value Object pattern inside the Session Façade. Once the user has entered this information s/he can proceed to the rest of the wizard.

The fourth page of the Design Pattern Developer asks the user to select which .jsp, servlet and entity beans should be analyzed. If a new 3 tier structure was specified in the design decisions, it is implemented here. Next the name of the session bean to be created is specified (default to SessionFacade.java). If a 1:Many Session Façade to Entity Beans ratio design decision was made, the tool inserts an instantiation of the Session Façade in each of the client files and creates the actual session bean. If a Many:Many ratio was chosen the developer must then group the entity beans together and the tool creates one Session Façade for each group. An instantiation of the respective Session Façade is placed in each client file, depending on the entity bean the client file references.

The sixth page (Figure 2) defines the mapping between entity beans and value objects. At the time of writing the implementation creates one value object for every entity bean in the application. The value objects are created with all fields listed in the entity beans and accessor methods for each field. The final page lists and analyzes all client files that are changed. If direct logic was selected in the design decisions the following occurs: References to entity beans are changed to be references to respective value objects. Method calls on entity beans are changed to method calls on the session bean. If sequential logic was selected in the design decisions, the developer must select the text to be placed in the Session Façade and confirm the method name and content before it is placed in the Session Façade.

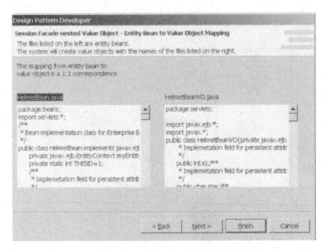

Fig. 2. Page 6 of the DPD. Entity beans to be modified listed on the left, corresponding value objects listed on the right. The code of each can be viewed.

6   Contributions

Tool support for refactoring is widely available ([4][7][10]). The concept of refactoring to patterns is not a novel one either ([6][7]). The novel contributions of this work, then is as follows:

1. We focus on integrating existing refactorings that have already been proven to be behaviour preserving.
2. We focus on J2EE applications, where we abstract the initial and target applications and place this abstraction in a separate package.
3. We access design pattern knowledge and specify the access of this information as being separate from the information that existing refactoring access.
4. We provide three definitions of refactoring based on the scope of the change that occurs and the information required to implement the change.

7   Current State and Future Work

To date we have implemented and are working on Session Façade, Value Object, Service Locator, Session Façade with nested Value Object and/or nested Service Locator [2]. The development environment, Eclipse, [4], was chosen it for its availability of code and potential for refactoring expansion. Eclipse contains refactoring wizards, refactoring classes and change classes to support atomic and sequential refactorings, all of which can be used to manipulate low-level refactorings within the complex refactorings.

We have performed preliminary testing of all these patterns on a J2EE application and also tested Value Object on a larger J2EE application, M-ASE [9]. In the former situation the Design Pattern Developer created a session bean (and/or value objects depending on the pattern applied) with references to a single entity bean. In the specified .jsp files, the tool also created an instantiation of the Session Façade and changed all returned variable references to the entity bean to value object references. Method calls on the bean (e.g. getters) were changed to calls on the Session Façade and the necessary methods were implemented in the session bean. Finally the tool created a value object corresponding to the entity bean we specified.

Immediate future work includes testing practicality and proficiency of the tool with a group of junior developers. A proposed study is to allow a student group to manually change an application to match a design pattern and to change the application using the tool. Time required, errors introduced and overall comments on the tool will be gathered. Run time of the target application will also be compared with the initial application.

8   Concluding Remarks

Traditional software development favours sound up-front design. Agile software development favours emerging design. We profit on the strengths of each approach by helping developers change the design of a existing software, regardless of whether the design was established up front or allowed to emerge throughout the development process. We propose complex refactorings that access knowledge of design patterns, design decisions, and the initial structure of the application as well as maintain the capability to generate code required to fulfill the requirements of a design pattern. The accompanying tool combines atomic and sequential refactorings to create these complex refactorings that access knowledge of an initial system, knowledge of design patterns, knowledge of how to change to a given design pattern and the capability to generate code. The domain is J2EE applications and preliminary tests have begun on two J2EE applications. The Design Pattern Developer can be extended to accommodate numerous complex design patterns, and assumes the user has knowledge of the motivation behind using each pattern. The desired goal is improvement in the following areas: readability, flexibility, understand-ability, development process and run-time.

References

1. Agile Alliance http://www.agilealliance.org/home (Last Visited: Dec 9, 2002).
2. Alur D, Crup J, Malks D; Core J2EE Patterns Best Practices and Design Strategies; Sun Microsystems Inc. Upper Saddle River, NJ; 2001; p.54-71, 104-112, 246-420.

3. Beck, K.; Extreme Programming Explained: Embrace Change; Addison Wesley Upper Saddle River NJ, 2000; p.103-115.
4. Eclipse www.eclipse.org (Last Visited: November 15, 2002).
5. Fowler, M.; Refactoring: Improving the Design of Existing Code; Addison-Wesley ; Upper Saddle River, NJ 2000; p. xv-xxi,110-116, 142-153, 227-231, 273-274.
6. Gamma E. Helm R. Johnson R. Vlissides J; Design Patterns – Elements of Reusable Object Oriented Software; Addison Wesley; Reading MA, 1995; p.1-3
7. IntelliJ IDEA www.intellij.com/idea (Last Visited: November 15, 2002).
8. Kerievsky, Joshua; Refactoring to Patterns; Industrial Logic www.industriallogic.com/papers/rtp015.pdf (Last Visited: November 15, 2002).
9. M-ASE http://sern.ucalgary.ca/~milos/ (Last Visited: November 15, 2002)
10. Roberts, D., Brant, J., Johnson, R.; A Refactoring Tool for Smalltalk; Department of Computer Science, University of Illinois at Urbana-Champaign

Experiences in Learning XP Practices:
A Qualitative Study

Bjørnar Tessem

Department of Information Science, University of Bergen
P.O.Box 7800, 5020 Bergen, Norway
Bjornar.Tessem@uib.no

Abstract. Extreme programming (XP) is one of the new agile methodologies for software engineering that has earned a lot of interest the last few years. Through a field study where a group of researchers and students aimed to learn XP through practice, we gathered qualitative data about the different practices of XP and programmers' impression of them in order to do get knowledge on how the different practices work. Findings regarding the most well-known practices are presented in this paper and to a great extent seem to verify claims from the literature. However, some difficulties in the practices are reported.

1 Introduction

Agile software development methodologies[2] have become quite fashionable in software engineering businesses the last few years. One of the most prominent of these methodologies is extreme programming (XP), as described by Beck[1].

XP consists of a set of (normally 12) practices, that together should enhance quality of work, learning, and communication in a software development organization. The practices usually mentioned are *the planning game, small releases, metaphor, simple design, testing, refactoring, pair programming, collective ownership, 40-hours week, on-site customer,* and *coding standards.*

There are some empirical studies on XP using quantitative approaches and practices, mostly to be found on the conference sites or proceedings[7] of the Agile/XP universe conference[9] and the XP conference[8].

Qualitative research approaches to software engineering are few, even though some do exist, for instance, by Seaman[6]. As for qualitative research in XP, it is worth mentioning Gittins et al.[4] who have studied the use of XP in a medium sized software business, and Karlström[5], who reports on the introduction of XP in a small software company with newly educated students. Cockburn et al.[3] also present some qualitative research work together with quantitative results on pair programming.

In this paper I will describe some findings from a qualitative analysis of data collected from a field study done with students and researchers at the University of Bergen, Norway, where the aim was to get experience with XP and the practices.

In the next section I describe the setting of the project. Then there is a description of the collected data used for analysis. The analysis section consists of five subsections describing findings on some of the more well-known practices of XP. Then there is a short discussion of validity before the paper concludes.

M. Marchesi and G. Succi (Eds.): XP 2003, LNCS 2675, pp. 131–137, 2003.

2   Setting

The goal of the reported field study of XP was first to get experience in an agile software development methodology for us as a group of researchers in software engineering and artificial intelligence. A long term goal for us is to develop intelligent software that supports software processes. Even though the use of such support systems may seem to contradict the lightweight perspective of agile methods, they may be necessary to obtain agility in projects where the programmers are geographically distributed or the development team becomes too large to be co-located. Such technology may help us to extend the boundaries of the set of projects that fit agility.

The second goal was to establish knowledge on how newcomers to XP practice the methodology and how they improve their XP practice through doing it over some time. In this context it was also our goal to understand areas where practitioners may have problems with XP and get clues on how to improve practice through intelligent support.

The project was organized in a standard XP laboratory with three development PCs, an integration computer, and one computer for personal activities. We had several whiteboards, a flip-over and a table for discussions, etc.

The six programmers had somewhat different experience ranging from very experienced programmers who have done programming in commercial projects and/or university research projects to master students whose experience mainly was coursework and teaching assistance in programming courses. I was myself a programmer in the project.

The system we were to construct was a web application for doing group work in university courses. The vision was to make a system that would make it possible for a group to make a virtual room for the group's students where they could upload their documents, pictures, models, or similar artifacts for annotation and discussion. It was developed using Java and public domain and commercial IDE-s for Java. The application was based on the use of servlets. For database we used MySQL. For version control and automatic integration we used CVS and CruiseControl.

The customers were representatives for a center for ICT in education at the University of Bergen. In that sense they were not real users, but we believe that they have sufficient knowledge of real users and their needs. A more severe problem was their willingness to be on-site continuously. We had daily meetings with them and we also had the possibility to call them over for help when we needed that. However, they were not on-site most of the time.

The project lasted only three weeks. We had two deliveries through the project. It was planned for three, one at the end of each week. However, since we did severe underestimates in the beginning and thus had not made a useful application ready by the first delivery day, we decided to deliver only twice. It is also worth mentioning that one of the programmers quit in the last week, and this lead to some problems that are commented later.

3   Data Collection

The data collected for analysis in this paper consist of two types of documents. Firstly, it is a diary that I myself wrote during the project. In this diary I tried to describe what happened and relating it to the different practices. To get some distance to the diary I waited two months from the project end before I did any analysis. It would of course have been better to have a similar diary from all or more than one of the programmers. However, this was not done, so we have to accept this single diary, and be aware of its limitations.

Secondly, it consists of questionnaires filled in by the six programmers, where they comment on the twelve practices of XP, the most common roles in such projects, and also the equipment and physical setting of the project.

The project was also studied by an ethnographer who videotaped, recorded conversations, stored screen dumps, and took notes. These data are not yet ready for analysis, and will by used to establish an ethnographic perspective on what happened in the project. However, they may also be highly relevant for a more thorough analysis of XP practices.

4   Analysis

In the analysis I have read through the documents several times, each time marking sentences relevant for one particular practice which is in focus. After extracting these sentences, each of them has been marked as referring to as an example of a practice, a wrong practice, a problem, or a solution. In addition I also counted the number of sentences with negative or positive connotations.

In this analysis only six practices are discussed, as I consider the data collected to be too small to see any interesting patterns for the rest of the practices. After the analysis of each practice my results are compared to the findings of Gittins et al.[5] and Karlström[4].

4.1   Pair Programming

Pair programming is the practice that I got most the data about. Most of the coding was done as pair programming. All programmers reported that they found pair programming a positive experience, enhancing learning and also leading to higher quality. However, this is somewhat contradicted by three of the programmers who also use negative phrases like "extremely inefficient", "very exhausting", "waste of time", and "tiresome". This indicates that it is not obvious that pair programming is more efficient than single programming, and that pair programming is so demanding that rest periods are needed to get full effect of this technique.

Towards the end of the project one of the programmers quit the project, and consequently there was more of single programming. In this same time period we got relatively more occurrences of sentences in the diary that mentions problems, wrong practices, and errors. The data seem to suggest a connection between single programming and more occurrences of problems. One situation illustrating this is that one of the less experienced programmers lost one day's work because of an error in the use of the versioning system. He was sitting alone, and a more experienced programmer sitting behind him would probably have hindered that mistake.

Other problems mentioned are communication problems within pairs and pairs that lost focus on the tasks they had committed to. Several of the programmers mention that the only way to solve the communication problems is to show more courage in criticizing your partner's work and more acceptance of criticisms. The data also suggest that frequent partner changes are necessary to get optimal learning and also to increase the feeling of collective ownership.

The investigation by Gittins et al. also mentions a couple of the problems observed here. The programmers find it taxing and some pairs do not communicate well. The programmers of Gittins et al. believe this can be solved by restricted use of pair programming. However, if we look at Karlström's report, we find that they also experienced more problems when doing single programming.

Cockburn et al.[3] show an economic cost of 15% using pair programming, and argues that this cost is more than repaid through higher quality, more learning, etc. Cockburn et al.'s work also mentions the problems observed here and in Gittins et al., but they argue that the economic gain from pair programming is so high that the practice should be enforced anyhow. Sooner or later reluctant programmers will adapt to it.

4.2   The Planning Game

This practice was not experienced equally positive as pair programming. The reasons for that may be that the planning game is a form of communication that involves more people, and hence requires more attention to how the activity is performed. Planning activities were done daily, both with and without customers. Activities involved design discussions, estimates, customers' priority meetings, etc., but most of it were task assignments for the day.

If we look more thoroughly at the data most of the reported problems were due to bad estimation. In the beginning of the project the user story time estimates were about one third of what turned out to be correct. This could be due to the rather coarse user stories, as one programmer mentioned. However, most programmers believed that the reason was the lack of experience in estimation in general and in particular within XP.

As the project ran, our estimates improved. In the beginning of the last week we re-estimated some of the user stories. After having finished these user stories, the new estimates showed to be on target.

Another issue mentioned by several was the lack of design and architecture discussion during the project. Two programmers attribute the bad estimates to too little time spent on design issues. Still, many design activities were reported in the data, so what is needed is probably some more design and architecture discussions in the first days of the project in order to get better estimates.

Gittins et al. referred to the use of 'spike solutions' as a way of handling the estimation problems. This is a technique used to build a course architecture in order to get estimable user stories, and as such could probably have been of help in this project. Karlström reported the same problems with estimation that we experienced, and also that quality in estimation improved within a few weeks.

4.3   On-site Customer

As mentioned earlier, we had not full time access to a customer. We had daily meetings with them, they were accessible on the telephone, and showed up when we called for them. They wrote most of the user stories the first day, and made their priorities in the start of each of the two iterations done.

The work the customers did was considered very valuable by all programmers. They gave good feedback on the application as it developed, and helped when we needed more precise understanding of what they wanted. So their contribution was important for the project.

The main problem mentioned was that they were not fully available all the time. They also showed up very late on the two delivery dates.

One important issue is the writing of functional tests, which was found difficult. The customers should be able to give better descriptions of the functional tests, with the aid of an experienced tester.

It was also mentioned by a few programmers that the customers were too kind. There were not much economic resources at stake, so it was questioned whether their behavior would be as friendly in a commercial setting.

Both Gittins et al. and Karlström report that they had not full time access to a customer. Gittins et al. even less than we experienced. However, they both report that the customer's participation contributed to improved quality and less failures. Karlström also reported that the customer improved when it came to writing of user stories as the project developed. Our project had too short time frame for this to be visible.

4.4   Testing

The testing approaches of XP were also considered to be a positive experience among all the programmers. The unit tests were running well, and test-first programming contributed to higher quality in code.

The problematic issue was the functional tests. We did some attempts at setting up these, but it was not done in a satisfactory way. Almost all of the negative statements in the data regarding testing were about the functional tests. It was unclear who was responsible for the functional tests, and we did not involve the customers enough in this work.

Other issues that were mentioned in the data were that there were a few occasions when people did not write test before code, and also testing of servlets.

Both Gittins et al. and Karlström reported that it was difficult to implement early unit testing in their project, which contrasts our observations. Karlström mentioned that functional testing was done by the customer running the system. No automatic functional tests were made.

4.5   Simple Design / Refactoring

I have chosen to group data on these two activities together as they are closely related.

As for the on-line customer practice and testing issues these practices were considered to be very valuable by all programmers. Several mentioned that the complexity of the system in the beginning was low, but that it grew more complex throughout the project. We did a lot of smaller refactorings to handle this. It is not clear from the data whether the programmers feel that the application design was not simple enough, or that the complexity stems from what naturally occurs because of mere complexity in functionality.

A lot of design issues were discussed over the table during the project. In contrast, only a few pure modeling activities using a whiteboard or flip-over are mentioned. Thus, it is an open question whether pure modeling activities would contribute to a simpler design.

Almost all problems referred to on these issues were related to a big redesign of the servlet hierarchies initiated by two of the programmers. This showed to be a miss, and cost us a lot of time. About five days worth of pair programming work was done on this redesign. It was started as a larger refactoring project. However, it soon became obvious that it was too complex to handle as a refactoring run as a lot of smaller refactorings and continuous integration.

The simple design and refactoring practices were not realized to a significant extent by the development group described by Gittins et al. Only a little refactoring was reported. In Karlström's report the software developers reported that they were trying to make design as simple as possible, and the programmers believe that there has been time saving because of this. Only minor refactorings were performed in that project, as in ours.

5   Validity

It is worth mentioning a couple of objections to the validity of these findings. The first is how much the findings transfer to commercial projects lasting longer than three weeks. The findings of Gittins et al.[4] and Karlström[5] seem to be confirmative of what we have seen here, except for the testing practice. Some programmers mentioned that the lack of economic incentives could weaken the motivation. However, in my experience the group seemed equally motivated to programmers I have worked with in commercial settings. I thus feel comfortable with regard to how general the results are.

Another issue is the data used in the analysis. The diary was written by myself and afterwards analyzed by myself. This is similar to how ethnographers and action researchers work in many situations. And thus, many of the problems they have with truthworthiness transfer. One has to be aware of this when assessing the findings of this study.

6   Conclusion

This paper has presented a qualitative investigation of experiences among a group of programmers learning extreme programming through a three week project.

The findings are based on analysis of data from this project held together with findings in similar studies by Gittins et al. [4] and Karlström[5]. The findings are:

- Pair programming is felt to be a positive experience, but sometimes tiresome and inefficient. Problems seem to increase when doing single programming, so pair programming is a useful practice. Quantitative studies verify the value of pair programming.
- The planning game is something that must be learned, particularly the estimation activities. Estimation is, however, learned through practice. It is useful to have some basic architecture fixed before estimation.

- Customer on-site is very valuable although often difficult to obtain. Customers also need to spend time on learning to write user stories and functional tests.
- Unit testing works well if practiced the right way. Functional tests seem to be difficult to implement.
- Simple design and refactoring are valuable practices. It is, however, difficult to evaluate the simplicity of design. Minor refactoring techniques are easy to use, whereas major refactorings are hard to do without knowing the techniques well.

It must be noted that these findings can only be verified by more thorough studies including quantitative methods. However, they seem to confirm some of the claims made about XP and agile methodologies in [1,2].

References

1. Beck, K. Extreme Programming Explained: Embracing Change. Addison-Wesley, 1999.
2. Cockburn, A. Agile Software Development. Addison-Wesley, 2002.
3. Cockburn, A. and L. Williams, The Costs and Benefits of Pair Programming. http://Collaboration.csc.ncsu.edu/laurie/Papers/XPSardinia.PDF
4. Gittins, R., S. Hope, and I. Williams. Qualitative Studies of XP in a Medium Sized Business. XP2001 Conf. Cagliari, Sardinia, Italy. http://www.xp2003.org/conference/papers/Chapter28-Gittins+alii.pdf
5. Karlström, D. Introducing Extreme Programming- An Experience Report. XP2002 Conf, Alghero, Sardinia, Italy. http://www.xp2003.org/xp2002/atti/DanielKarlstrom--IntroducingExtremeProgramming.pdf
6. Seaman, C.B., Qualitative methods in empirical studies of software engineering, IEEE Trans. on Software Engineering 25(4):557-572, 1999.
7. Wells, D. and L. Williams (eds.) Extreme Programming and Agile Methods – XP/Agile Universe 2002. Proc. Of 2nd XP Universe and 1st Agile Universe Conf., Chicago, IL, August 4-7, 2002. LNCS(2418), Springer-Verlag, Berlin 2002.
8. http://www.xp2003.org/
9. http://www.xpuniverse.com/ Object Mentor, Inc.

Swimming around the Waterfall: Introducing and Using Agile Development in a Data Centric, Traditional Software Engineering Company

Donald Howard

eFunds, 7805 Hudson Road, Woodbury, MN 55125, USA
`donald.a.howard@efunds.com`

Abstract. This paper presents ideas on how to effectively introduce and use agile development within a company that has a strong connection to waterfall-style development. It addresses the shifts in business and technical areas the company and others face today and examines the impact those shifts have on the software development process and the thinking about that process. It also characterizes the experience of an Extreme Programming project within the company and offers recommendations based on that experience.

1 Introduction

It was tough news to hear. We were nearing the end of phase one of what had become a two-phase software development project. Phase two involved development of an interactive Web site to access phase one's business-to-business service. Our business sponsor, perhaps serious, perhaps just venting, decreed that phase two *will not* take as much time nor cost as much as we estimated or he would seek outside bids ("He can't really do that, can he?" we asked ourselves).

Although initially displeased with the tone and timing of the pushback, I began to see it as an ideal opportunity to bring about what I and others had been advocating: the use of an agile development methodology like Extreme Programming (XP) instead of again using the waterfall development methodology that to my mind had contributed significantly to the predicament we were in.

2 The Company

Our company, a maker and distributor of software and software services for the financial industry, has characteristics that are likely common for software companies that survived the dot com bust of two years ago and the hard times that have followed. We have one foot firmly established in legacy software – representing the core revenue generation through the rough times – and one foot in the new world of Web development. Our mainframe group develops Cobol programs that access DB2 relational databases that are terabytes in size and that connect directly to customers' mainframes. Our Web delivery group develops Java programs that support Web-based access to

M. Marchesi and G. Succi (Eds.): XP 2003, LNCS 2675, pp. 138–145, 2003.

the mainframe applications via XML information exchange or directly via browser-based applications.

While the work of each group is essential to the long term viability of the company, not to mention most individual projects, it is difficult to imagine two software development groups more dissimilar in terms of technology and technical concerns, communication patterns and needs, even in the understanding of and approach to market opportunities. The predominant view in the company held that software development is an engineering activity best served by complete initial requirements articulation, big upfront design, and document-centered communication between specialists focusing on design, database, or construction activities.

However well this suited the company in its established technical and business areas, we felt it was not serving us in open systems web development. The view we felt was more appropriate, and one we felt web projects should be organized around, is better expressed by Cockburn. He says that to call software development an engineering activity is to "[confuse] the act of doing engineering work with the outcome of doing engineering work" and that essence of software development is not explained by the engineering metaphor but by a "cooperative game principle" that states that "software development is a cooperative game of invention and communication." [1]

3   Gaining Traction for the Idea of Agile Development

I think circumstances sell agile development more effectively than any advocate can. But it takes an advocate to make the association between the pain of circumstance and new ideas about a solution. I had conducted low key education efforts for a year for anyone interested in agile development. Some venues were the new employee training sessions, an "Extreme Hour" simulation for our Java development team, and a company-wide process definition effort culminating in a company-wide presentation. In addition to maintaining visibility for the concept I found these sessions very valuable for identifying who was for, against, or neutral to the idea.

From those who were neutral to the idea I solicited information on what reservations they may have had. Typically, the reservations were based on a misunderstanding of agile development and were resolved in personal "lobbying" sessions. To those who were for the idea I passed along books and articles with the hopes that they would add to the body of agile development knowledge at our company and take up the fight along with me.

I had no idea how to approach those dead set against the idea. An explanation put forth by Cockburn about people's reaction to risk sheds some light on that response: "...people generally are risk-averse when they have something in their hands that they might lose and risk-accepting if they are in the process of losing something and may have a chance to regain it..." [2] My group and I felt we were already losing in a way that was directly attributable to the waterfall process. To the risk-averse group the standard process represented "something in their hands that they might lose" and made them risk-averse.

I had little trouble summoning personal motivation after a year of Web development under waterfall rules. With its uncertainties and difficult problems I was left with no doubt about which was the better suited process.

4   The Project Gets the Go-Ahead to Use XP

Kent Beck says that one way to bring XP into a company is to take the hardest problem and solve it the XP way. [3] For a company like ours we needed to be more choosy. We needed a project that involved mostly Java development because the sheer amount of education to do and resistance to overcome in a project that had wider development group participation would have prevented it from ever getting off the ground. The upcoming phase two project, development of the interactive Web site to access our business-to-business service, fit the bill. That it started out with a stern warning to be in effect "faster, better, cheaper" gave it the necessary ingredient of a hard problem that Beck referred to.

My XP education work of the previous year combined with the circumstances of this particular project led to a decision point that went in favor of using XP – we received the go-ahead.

We judged that work done to date for the requirements phase of the waterfall put us somewhere near the end of the exploration phase of XP. We converted the requirements to stories, estimated the stories, and brought them back to the business sponsors for iteration and release planning. They put the stories into five two-week iterations that magically fit the team's estimated velocity. All the key players for the project were on board with the methodology and although we acknowledged the value of bringing in outside XP expertise, a budget crunch that set in right at that moment ruled out any additional outlays and we were forced to rely on books, conferences that I had attended, and our creativity and desire to make XP work.

5   Project Team Composition

Our core team consisted of a business sponsor, project manager, business analyst, user interface designer, technical writer, three testers, and six Java developers. I include myself as one of the Java developers which made me a "player/coach" since I took on the role of coach too. One challenging aspect of our team was that two of the developers and one of the testers were in Chennai, India. To have "offshore" developers who are expected to be fully integrated into the team is now commonplace and we did what we could to meet the difficulties of that arrangement head on. We had a common development area called the "pod" where all the U.S.-based Java developers worked. Other U.S.-based team members did project work out of their cubicles but visited the pod frequently.

6   Misconceptions Starting Out

This was not my first XP project. While working for a different company I had the opportunity to lead a small XP project that involved three Java developers, an Oracle database administrator, and one customer representative. The application itself consisted of a few simple web screens with an Oracle backend that we completed in three two-week iterations. While it did give me some valuable exposure to ideas, that experience plus my take on experiences reported in XP literature set up some expectations that turned out not to be valid for this project. My leading misconceptions starting out on this project were as follows:

- Good, commonly understood design will emerge while doing tasks as planned during iteration planning meetings
- Biweekly iteration planning meetings and daily conference call standup meetings will be sufficient communication for distributed developer teams
- Elaboration of detail during iterations and feature change is hardest on developers
- XP practices will come naturally and easily
- The team will settle into a sustainable development pace.

Please note that I am representing these items as my personal misconceptions not fallacies of XP. They underscore areas of challenge in our company that may or may not be present in other companies. We had mixed success in overcoming these challenges on our first project, as you will see, but what we learned makes us optimistic that we will overcome them in the next project.

7   The Journey Begins

Weeks one through four were characterized by intensive basic learning. We were learning technology basics: the code framework upon which we were basing our work was new to all of us. We were learning XP practice basics: test-first programming was new to us, refactoring was still negatively associated with failure to get it right the first time, and our integration efforts could not be described as anything near continuous. And we were learning team dynamics basics: the first iteration planning meeting barely completed task planning for a single story within the first three hours but the second one finished task planning for all stories in a little over half a day.

We delivered the features of the first iteration's stories at the end of two weeks and turned them over to the QA to test. A flood of issues reported by our testers confirmed what we suspected: that we made the features work but just barely. Too much learning, not enough time – even with the weekend work that I reluctantly requested of myself and others.

Iteration two found us starting out with fresh resolve and the confidence of a completed cycle under our belts. I tried to focus on teaching JUnit and promoting test-first programming as a fundamental practice but was stymied by the nature of our early work (servlets and JSPs) being incompatible with JUnit. I pair programmed with teammates in Chennai, according to plan, by doing several 11:00 PM to 3:00 AM sessions. For these distributed pair programming sessions we made effective use of simple technologies – a telephone and software that allowed us to connect two computers across our network. My Chennai teammates felt sorry for me after awhile having to work late into the night and volunteered to adjust their work hours to their early afternoon through evening. In doing so, they took on most of the burden of maximizing the overlap time (there is an 11 hour, 30 minute difference between Central Standard Time and India Standard Time). Sharing the burden of shifting schedules to support direct communication is an inescapable challenge of U.S./India distributed agile development.

Although our communication level seemed good, it became obvious we were pulling the design in different directions. And the code, as I now had climbed the learning curve of our chosen framework to understand its context, had key problem indicators of duplication, inexpressiveness, suspect classes, and straightline code.

We delivered the functionality, or most of it, for the stories of iteration two just about on time [1].

8   The Turning Point

Week five started a new iteration that was building on an incremental system that, well, wasn't holding up. The main problem was the newness of everything that we were working with and the lack of ready solutions to choose from. We were not having problems with team inventiveness, rather we were having problems with too many separate inventions. The only solution short of calling a month-long timeout on the project was to centralize design leadership within the most experienced OO developer-me.

I proposed object based solutions to problems we were trying to solve by big case statements in JSP code. They were completely testable using JUnit and I insisted we adhere to the test-first programming rule. We refactored fearlessly and when the going got rough we focused on making and testing one micro-change at a time. While our local team in the U.S. seemed to be making significant progress, our remote team in India seemed to be becoming less involved – the downside of centralizing design control.

Away from the development team things seemed to be making more steady progress. Our meeting routine had settled and so had the interactions between the business sponsor, analyst, UI designer, and everybody else. Some friction remained, however, in the area of formal design reviews. In the waterfall process a formal review is, among other things, a mechanism for gaining approval of a big software model document from a wide range of different groups. We attempted to meet these review expectations at the end of each iteration by producing and presenting a document called "Compilation of Essential Models Reflecting Design to Date." Unfortunately that exercise made none of the participants happy. The burden of documenting models for external communication above and beyond what existed for internal communication was high yet still fell short of expectations. The fact that the design being reviewed was already coded opened up new issues on what was fair game for review. After several difficult iteration design review sessions we asked the next level managers to help us resolve the problem and together we decided to substitute ongoing consultation and a final technical system document for formal reviews.

We delivered a much higher quality set of features for iteration three on time.

---

[1] I was well aware of the fundamental XP principal of not slipping delivery dates – that one should negotiate trimming of the feature set as soon as it became apparent that all features cannot be delivered. I consciously decided to play the weekend hedge – a Monday afternoon delivery rather than a Friday end of day delivery – and I requested that some small low priority features be factored into the next iteration. While that seemed the best decision at the time, it dodged the issue of balancing demand and supply and was our first encounter the "sustainable pace" issue that challenged us the entire project.

9   The Development Team Hits Its Stride

With the core design in place, new functionality seemed to drop into place much easier in iteration four. I took a week off for a long planned summer vacation and returned to a smoothly running iteration. We hit our target and enjoyed a lull in error reports from the testers. Too good to be true? Yes. We found that QA had fallen behind a bit in their story acceptance testing (complete testing and defect correction were on a half-iteration lag meaning that by the halfway point of any given iteration all of the previous iteration's stories were to have been tested and fixed) and the online report functionality that we'd been building since iteration three, with its maddening amount of low level detail, did in fact have a few problems. But nothing of major significance.

Our JUnit test count had been growing quite nicely but mostly from the local developers. I finally had an opportunity to mentor the remote developers in test-first programming and was pleased to find the approach, once understood, took hold quickly.

The later iterations involved integration to a separate subsystem under development by an allied "subteam." Having one subteam follow agile development and another follow waterfall development put the overall project in the "hybrid" category. Late stage integration (not that we had much choice, remember, schedule expectations were very aggressive) across subteams proved to be a problem and the effects of it carried into and disrupted the agile development rhythm that had recently begun to be so smooth. Progress slowed, stress rose. QA's testing effort took the main hit as the system went down frequently and stayed down while someone pinpointed and corrected the problem. In contrast to "synergism of positive effects" of the twelve XP practices, I noted to myself one day a "synergism of negative effects" that was happening where system instability, delays in completion, demands on attention at or exceeding capacity, and miscommunication all play on each other causing strain between individuals and groups.

10   Nearing the Release Date

In contrast to the difficulty we felt moving through subteam integration issues, we felt an ease and facility in adding new features to code that was completely under our control. With one exception: in coding a story about printing we were blazing new ground again with XSL-FO and one of its implementation frameworks and finding the going rough.

Aside from that we were pleasantly surprised to be able to meet requests for change with relative ease by "snapping" our well coded, tested, and designed objects together in different ways. While there was still a wicked problem or two to be solved the solutions generally simplified the design and left people feeling better about the code.

The Java developers receptive attitude towards change was not universally felt across the team at large. Information on change did not diffuse equally to all affected groups and those hearing it late or by secondhand means felt justifiably slighted. The pod had become the focal point for informal discussions and given that total co-location (see the section on "Project Team Composition" above and "Bright Ideas For the Next Go Around" below) was not achieved in the pod, some of the information that should have diffused to everyone never did.

We brought the final iteration to a close with a well satisfied business sponsor and we eased into a final productionizing iteration followed by some very helpful project retrospectives.

11   Conclusions

I list some of conclusions coming out of our retrospectives in bullet form with the obvious disclaimer that they may not be relevant to your situation. Hopefully I've provided you with enough background to judge the similarity of your situation to ours and hopefully some of the conclusions in context will resonate with you and prove helpful as you move into agile development methodologies.

11.1   Most Important Conclusion

There was a consensus among those who participated in the retrospectives that agile development played a large role in the success of the project and should be used again within the company.

11.2   What We Wish We'd Done Differently

- Deployed high level development tools like the WebSphere Application Developer/PVCS integration tool and the ANT automated build tool before starting in.
- Supplemented spikes of new technology done in technical literature with our own spikes that better captured the essence of the problem for us
- Directed more effort at improving everyone's object oriented testing, coding, and design skills as a solution to communication and quality problems

11.3   Interesting Discoveries

- Large-scale refactoring worked – it effectively drove out fear of change.
- Regular release of incremental functionality was a great way to boost trust both within the company from business groups and outside the company from customers.

11.4   Bright Ideas for the Next Go Around

- Achieve better more focused communication by co-locating all people committed full time to the project and by giving those committed part time or who are offsite access to an up to date summary of primary reference material and change announcements on a "virtual project wall" using an electronic site.

- Help testers and developers collaborate better instead of adhering to traditional boundaries, create a culture of quality and attention to detail in developers, pair testers with developers during unit test creation, declare a "QA day" in which a developer takes on the tester's role, declare a "bounce on it" day in which upper managers try to break the application as it exists.
- Formulate a story point multiplier based on the development team's experience in doing something similar to a given story, the number of different systems crossed, or organizational boundaries crossed for the story; apply that multiplier against the story points for a more realistic story estimate.
- Adapt XP to our company's needs where pursuit of an XP ideal did not pan out – we have come up with ideas on highly company- and group-specific adaptations that tie back to the misconceptions listed earlier and we keep in mind that each adaptation needs to be viewed critically for consistency with agile development principles.

Acknowledgements

I thank my many colleagues and friends at eFunds for actively supporting me and agile development or at least suspending disbelief long enough for us to make a go at it.

References

1. Cockburn, Alistair: Agile Software Development, Pearson Education, Inc. (2002) 29-31
2. Cockburn, Alistair: Agile Software Development, Pearson Education, Inc. (2002) 49
3. Beck, Kent: Extreme Programming Explained, Addison-Wesley (1999) 123

Cross-Continent Development Using Scrum and XP

Bent Jensen and Alex Zilmer

SAS Institute A/S, Købmagergade 7-9, DK-1150 Copenhagen K., Denmark
{Bent.Jensen,Alex.Zilmer}@sdk.sas.com

Abstract. This paper presents the experiences gained from adopting XP and later adding a Scrum wrapper in SAS Institute Inc's Danish development department. The paper will highlight our introduction of XP into the development group, modifying the process and negotiating a common set of practices between our group and other closely related groups and how we have applied a Scrum wrapper around our XP-practices 6 months ago.

1   Introduction

Software development projects that are carried out across large distances and many time zones pose certain challenges, in addition to the many challenges of software development in general. In general the emphasis on closeness and communication, which is the foundation of many Agile methodologies, including eXtreme Programming and Scrum, tends to lead one to the conclusion that these methodologies cannot be suitable for dispersed teams.

Our experience is that, at least under some circumstances, Agile methods may be a good choice for a development group operating remotely from its project counterparts. Some of the inherent problems in this kind of software development, e.g. communication barriers and a structured way of working with requirements, may even be easier to negotiate with the right mix of Agile methods.

For about the last 10 years, the authors have been engaged in software development in SAS Institute – during the whole period as a remote development unit. The relationship between ourselves and our head office in Cary, North Carolina, USA, has taken on different forms over the years: from having responsibility for an end-to-end product, and thus having substantial autonomy, to gradually becoming more deeply integrated into a larger development group. Today we are a group of 10+ developers out of a total of 80+ software developers, comprising one division (within the 9000-strong company). We operate by and large in exactly the same way as groups who are located in the US, with the main exception that we are working at somewhat different hours, and that we are using XP and Scrum as our software development method.

The rest of our division uses a slightly different set of development methodologies. These have been gradually shaped and have arrived at their current form over two decades of software development. It is our experience that it is possible to establish an interface to other groups allowing different methodologies to combine – in many large organizations this hybrid structure is the only viable way to proceed, since changing a large software development machinery to a different set of methods across the board is a risky and very difficult undertaking, and one that most organizations will be resistant to.

M. Marchesi and G. Succi (Eds.): XP 2003, LNCS 2675, pp. 146–153, 2003.

In this paper we will describe the working relationship between our group and the rest of the division, showing how technology, methodology, and awareness of the traps of virtual teamwork have helped us build up an excellent working relationship to the more centrally-placed groups of our division. The next section describes the history of XP and Scrum in our group.

We view the implementation of Agile methods as an ongoing journey where we will probably never reach the final destination. Until now the journey has yielded very promising results, but there are still a great many challenges related to coordination within the larger group as well as internally in our own group. We will in the final section describe these difficulties and the measures we have taken and outline the ongoing discussions.

2   The Virtual Team

2.1   The Project

The current project we are working on is a large, mostly Java-based project, involving in all 400+ people. The parts of the project that are carried out in Denmark entail Java component development for the mid-tier. These components utilize components built elsewhere in the division and are in turn used by applications, also built elsewhere. It should be clear that such a set-up requires firm cooperation between groups to ensure that things are built in the right order and in a way that will meet requirements and specifications.

2.2   Communication and Trust – Key Elements

The key to success in any project involving a large number of people is good communication between the involved parties. This applies even more so in a complicated software project with a loosely coupled-relationship between the groups undertaking the project. Normally, good communication is facilitated by the proximity of people. The Agile methodology emphasizes and formalizes good communication through daily meetings [1] or Scrums [2]. A special challenge for Virtual teams is the building up and maintenance of a high level of trust among the geographically distributed parties.

"It is easier to form, launch and sustain virtual teams in an environment rich in 'the features of social organization... that facilitate coordination and cooperation for mutual benefit'" [3]

Technology is one of the foundations for making this happen in our environment. In addition to a lot of email and telephone conversation, we have video conferencing equipment, that allows us to have meetings where we can see each other face to face. We also use instant messenger software quite intensively. These four pieces of technology in each their own way replace elements of normal face-to-face communication. Email is useful for neutral information, it has a low bandwidth but can cope with complex contents. The telephone has a slightly higher bandwidth – being able to hear the voice of the person talking creates a nearness that email cannot provide. Often problems and misunderstandings are easily solved over the telephone. The instant messengers create the feeling that participants are physically very close. It is possible to see when people arrive at work and start up their computers. Quick questions and small talk, similar to when people meet in the corridor in the morning, can be facilitated in this way. Finally, video conferencing has a bandwidth that is close to a real physical presence.

To achieve the benefits of the technology, people need to meet regularly in a real physical face-to-face environment. Usually a group of developers and managers come together approximately every second month. These close encounters serve as planning sessions that look ahead, but at the same time they serve as a kind of "relation recharging". It has very often been observed that the problems involving tension between individuals or difficulties in communication around certain project areas have improved greatly after the parties have been together in person. After recharge of this kind – all other communications are enriched for a long period of time.

Lately we have raised attention and awareness of what seems to be a common phenomenon: distance (in terms of communication and interactions) is inversely proportional to the level of trust between groups of people. It is much easier to blame a person far away for ruining my day because of some mistake than it is to blame my close colleague making the same mistake. Having a shared value of always assuming that all behavior has a positive intention works as a safeguard against the unproductive state of distrust.

2.3   Description of the Daily Work Cycle
between Remote Team and Headquarters

A common initial reaction we have often met when implementing collaboration with a group in our head office is the argument that the time difference will make this collaboration impossible.

Now most people have realized that we have created a set-up that minimizes the down-sides of the time difference and that the time difference to some extent does provide genuine advantages.

9 a.m. EST – the day starts with a managers' daily meeting using video conferencing equipment. This daily meeting serves the same purpose as the Scrum of Scrums [2], a daily observation of the process, with the purpose of prioritizing efforts and removing impediments between teams. In this, and the following hours, a lot of communication occurs – video conferences, phone calls and mail exchanges, where the main purpose is for the Danish team to deliver what has been finished during the day to colleagues in the head office, and to resolve uncertainties regarding what tasks we have, or are about to receive.

A positive use of the time difference comes from verifying and testing nightly builds in the Danish morning – thus allowing a precise assessment of the state of the software when the work day starts in the US.

At 11 a.m. EST the Danish working day is at its end, and after having pushed new code to the central common code repository – apart from any email communication in the evening taking place from home – our working day is over.

At the end of the US working day new code is pushed, and any outstanding issues are reported using email and our defects systems. These issues are thus ready for us to take up when we arrive at work the next day.

During the US night a full build of the software is run using the code from our common repository. When we start the next working day (it is 3 a.m. in the US), we verify the nightly build. The results of the verification are thus ready for the US teams when they arrive at work.

During the Danish working day all developers, testers and the team manager attend our daily meeting (Scrum, XP meeting), which is used for going through the status of all open tasks, prioritizing any new alert issues, and assigning developers to new tasks. All impediments are placed on the manager's shoulders to be presented and hopefully solved in the Scrum of Scrums later that day (see our description of this above).

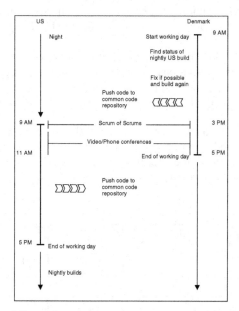

Fig. 1. The daily work cycle between remote team and headquarters

3   Adopting XP and Scrum

3.1   Background

Having developed software for several years, it seemed that gaining more experience in itself did not lead to better results. We felt that the quality of what we produced depended too much on the individual developer writing the code, and that we spent far too much time fixing defects instead of advancing the software.

At that time we were an autonomous group, and improving our practices was an internal matter for our group. Studies in literature, gave us the choice between either atomic non-related practices, or a heavy, rigid system. Neither appealed much to us – but forced with a choice, we tried to design our own process out of well-known practices. One of the techniques we looked into was formal code reviews: this was praised as the one most effective quality improvement technique. While discussing this practice, one person drew our attention to eXtreme Programming, where review is taken to the extreme by reviewing all code, all the time, using pair programming.

That was the start – after two weeks of evaluation, the team by itself decided to implement XP in full. One important thing about this was that, being at our level of maturity, moving from designing our own methodology to having a ready-made recipe eased the implementation considerably. In the beginning we simply did it by the book – one practice at the time, until we had most of XP up and running in our environment.

- Pair programming, unit tests and daily meetings comprised the first wave
- Code standard and common ownership followed shortly after
- Stories, estimates and velocity assessment were the last things to fall into place.

For a long while we did not have a direct customer – we were developing a set of Web components that was to replace a desktop solution we already had.

Aspects of XP were easy to implement, and worked immediately, other practices were more difficult, and still others continue to present challenges for us even after two years.

We had no difficulty adhering to a code standard and to the sharing of all code. Daily meetings required some adjustment before we got them working, but they have now to a great extent found their form. Registering time in order to calculate our velocity was perceived as a burden, and did not really bring us much more than confusion.

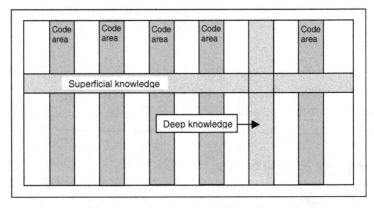

Fig. 2. Use pair programming to let developers gain a broad superficial knowledge or a narrow deep knowledge

A more difficult and deeper-rooted challenge had to do with pair programming, the transfer of knowledge and rotating both working partner and responsibility for a particular area of code. In the beginning where we deliberately moved people around both in the pairs and in the different areas of the software we kept hearing a wish expressed for having one area to specialize in. The statement often heard was that it was not rewarding to have to work on so many different things without understanding any of them fully. We have now allowed one or two developers to work for a longer time in one area of the code, thus allowing some specialization. The down-side of that

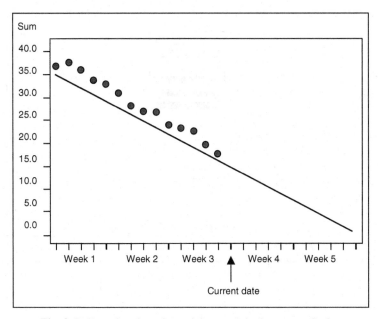

Fig. 3. Daily estimation of remaining work in the current Sprint

is that the value of the pair programming seems to be less when people have worked together for too long. It is as though the effect of being critical evaporates somewhat when people get too used to each other's way of thinking. The other down-side is that people seem to drift towards certain areas of the code, more and more often leading to them not doing pair programming.

We have not found the best balance for this yet, but clearly there is some balance to be reached between having only superficial knowledge of the system and having a deep knowledge of certain aspects.

3.2   What Didn't Work for Us?

XP didn't help us much when we had to coordinate and prioritize work between our Danish team and the 4-5 other teams at the head office.

3.3   Introducing Scrum

The text on the back cover of Ken Schwaber & Mike Beedle's book "Agile Software development with Scrum" reads: "Learn how to simplify XP Implementation through a Scrum Wrapper". This immediately sparked our interest – finding a chapter in the book that actually was about this subject was more difficult. Clearly the Scrum book was written without XP in mind, with the need for relating it to XP obviously arising at a later point. But nonetheless, in terms of simplification of process, the book as a whole describes the perfect project management framework to apply to an XP team, and to any other Agile team. Basically Scrum describes a way to maintain and bring

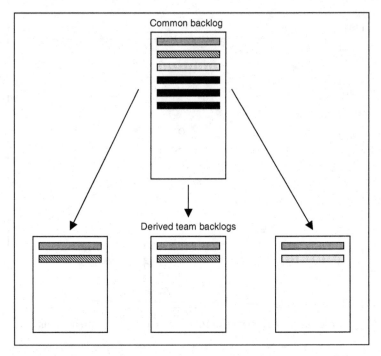

Fig. 4. Deriving team backlogs from mature items in the common backlog

forward requirements in a manner that is very different from XP's planning game. Scrum assigns a product owner, who maintains a backlog of items to be implemented in the software. The order of items in the list describes the order in which work has to be done. A set of items is then picked for an iteration and moved to the Sprint backlog, where the work is also unfolded into smaller tasks that are estimated with regard to resources. During the sprint (Scrum name for an iteration), estimates are updated daily, thus allowing assessment of whether the team is on track or not.

The nice thing about Scrum was that it made our planning, estimation and tracking much simpler while still yielding the same results.

Also the role of management (the Scrum master) was popular in the team. In Scrum the main role of management is to remove impediments for the team. In general the team takes responsibility for the Sprint and the manager has to help them.

Shortly after adding Scrum to the bag of practices, we started having daily meetings between the team managers using video conferencing. That one element greatly improved cross-team project management.

3.4   Next Steps

The natural next steps will be to have key Scrum elements applied across several teams. The main improvement potential lies in having one common backlog for all teams. Each line in that backlog should describe some functionality in the software that we are developing. Some of these requirements will map onto the work for only one team while other requirements will map onto the work for several teams.

Defining a process of maturing the backlog, by letting elements move up through it, will help teams to focus on only implementing code when a sprint has started. A "ripe" backlog item will contain a list of teams needed to fulfill it, and each team's work item(s) and estimate(s), use cases, U.I spec and other descriptions will be available. This concept will allow efficient coordination between teams AND focus on what lies just ahead of the team instead of what lies further on down the road.

References

1. K. Beck, Extreme Programming Explained: Embrace Change. Reading, Massachusetts: Addison-Wesley, 2000
2. Schwaber Ken, Mike Beedle, Ken Schwaber, Robert C. Martin, Agile Software Development with SCRUM, Prentice Hall; 1st edition (October 15, 2001)
3. Lipnack and Stamps, Virtual Teams: People Working Across Boundaries with Technology, John Wiley & Sons; 2nd edition (September 2000)

Coaching Coaches

Görel Hedin, Lars Bendix, and Boris Magnusson

Department of Computer Science, Lund Institute of Technology
Box 118, SE-221 00 Lund, Sweden
{gorel,bendix,boris}@cs.lth.se

Abstract. We have developed a tandem of undergraduate courses for teaching XP and coaching of XP teams. This paper focuses on the coaching course and the coaching practices we have developed. The tandem of courses enables us to give a challenging and interesting course for the coaches, and, at the same time, allows us to afford on-site coaches for the younger students, providing them with a high quality environment for learning XP. We also describe our experiences from the first instance of the courses and how we have tackled the bootstrapping problem.

1 Introduction

At Lund Institute of Technology, we have introduced extreme programming (XP) into the curriculum of our 4.5 year computer science and engineering program. The students are introduced to full XP in their second year, using XP as a vehicle for teaching basic principles of software engineering [5]. In the practicum part of this introductory course, the students run a scaled down extreme programming project during a 7 week study period. The project is run as 6 weekly iterations, each comprising one full day of production programming (a "long lab"), a 2-hour planning meeting, and 6 hours of individual experiments ("spike time"). The students take this course in parallel with other courses. Last year (2002), 107 students followed this course, and were divided into 12 teams of 8-10 students during the practicum part. The project scenario is that the 8-10 students are "newly hired staff" that ramp up the initial team consisting of a pair of senior developers (the coaches).

In addition to the basic 12 XP practices [1], we found two practices to be fundamental to teaching XP successfully. One is TeamInOneRoom, i.e., the whole team is present in the same room during the "long labs". The other is CoachOnSite, i.e., each team has a coach that is present during the "long labs" and actively coaches the team. See [5].

How should one go about coaching such teams, and who should be the coaches? We needed to develop coaching practices and train people to the coaching role.

One alternative could be to use faculty as coaches. They are, however, very expensive and, furthermore, their role is easily perceived as "teaching", i.e., examining the team rather than a leadership role that is part of the team. Another alternative would be to let one of the students on the team take on the role of a coach, but we never

M. Marchesi and G. Succi (Eds.): XP 2003, LNCS 2675, pp. 154–160, 2003.

considered this alternative since these students are, in general, too inexperienced. We settled for a third alternative, namely to run a second course, a coaching course, for senior undergraduate students, and let them coach teams in the introductory course. In addition to allowing us to afford on-site coaches, this provides us with an opportunity to give an advanced software engineering course where the students can make use of their team for practicing leadership, practicing software architecture issues, and learning about agile methods in more depth. To train the coaches, the coaches are themselves coached by faculty.

The rest of this paper describes the structure of the coaching course, the coaching practices we have developed, and the bootstrapping process of running the first instances of both courses. Finally, we draw some conclusions and reflect on how our practices might apply in industry.

2   The Coaching Course

The coaching course is a one-term pass/no-pass course corresponding to around 1/3 time studies (the students take other courses in parallel). It consists of three parts: a theory part followed by a practicum part in parallel with an in-depth study.

The theory part consists of seven 2-hour lectures and discussion seminars. There are also some short lab sessions for trying out techniques and tools. Topics include design and architecture covering test-driven development [2], design patterns [6], and software architecture based on FirstIteration [8], patterns generating architectures [3], and multiple views [7]. We also review the basic XP practices, and go into more depth on specific topics, in particular testing and planning. There is also some theoretical material on coaching as such, although there is not much literature available yet on this subject, and the actual coaching is taught mainly through the practicum part. The theory part ends with a one day lab session where the coaches develop the first iteration of the product in pairs. This first iteration is then used as the starting point for the teams in the introductory course.

The practicum part is the actual coaching where the coaches take care of teams of students from the introductory course. The coaches lead the planning meetings and they coach actively during the one-day long lab iterations. They also have the responsibility of tracking the evolving architecture of the product and to document it in the end. The coaches meet once a week together with a faculty supervisor in order to share experiences from their coaching, to get advice, and to reflect on their own role.

During the practicum part, the coaches also perform an in-depth study of a specific topic of their own choice. Each study is documented as a small report written in article style. Examples of selected topics include pair programming experiences, refactoring-aware versioning, and surveys of agile methods. Many of the coaches take advantage of their team in the study for conducting small experiments and surveys.

3   Coaching Practices

We have run one instance of both the introductory course and the coaching course during the study year of 2001/2002, and are currently (March 2003) in the midst of the second instance. During the first instance of the course we have developed a number of coaching practices that are discussed briefly below.

Coach

The coach should know the basic XP practices and be able to explain and motivate them to the team. Being a slightly more senior student, the coach also sometimes has technical knowledge that is of help to the team. However, the coach does not know everything, so the main role of the coach is to help the team to; learn the XP practices, develop the practices, learn to communicate, and to help them learn from each other. In essence, the goal of the coach is to help the team to help themselves. This is done by being an ActiveTrackingCoach and by TriggeringCommunication.

ActiveTrackingCoach

The coach is active in the sense that he/she actively follows the activities of the team, and in practice works as a tracker. The coach keeps track of what each programming pair does, how their work progresses, and how the code evolves. This allows the coach to act proactively, already when problems start to arise, rather than after the fact. If the coach spots a problem, it can often be solved by TriggeringCommunication between team members.

TriggerCommunication

In a team learning XP, communication within the team does often not arise spontaneously, but needs to be learnt. Initially, the team members do not know each other well and are hesitant to communicate. Also when they know each other well, they may be hesitant to ask for help because they are not yet a functioning team. A typical sign is that a pair does not ask for help when they have gotten stuck on some technical problem. Sometimes, the coach can help to solve the problem, but more often, the coach can explain that it is a practice in this case to ask other programmers on the team for help, or to switch pairs. Another common case when communication is needed is when two pairs are working on the same code without being aware of this. If a problem is of relevance to all of the team, the coach can take a TimeOut.

TimeOut

For any kind of problem that occurs in the team, if the coach cannot solve it easily and directly, a good way of tackling the problem is to take a TimeOut, i.e., to bring the team together for a brief stand-up meeting, and let the team solve the problem together. This works for technical problems, where someone on the team might have skills in a certain area, or where the team can brainstorm possible solutions or ideas for experimental spikes for solving the problem. A TimeOut is also useful for process problems where the team needs to agree on what practices to follow. Basic XP practices are given by the course material, but the team needs to reason about these practices in order to understand and accept them. There are also lots of little subpractices that need to be developed by the team itself. Often such subpractices emerge spontaneously and can be turned into a more permanent practice at a TimeOut. As an example, several teams developed the practice of switching pair programming partners after lunch. This practice had the advantage of getting the team members to know each other in a short time, and turned out to be logistically easier in the scaled down project than the normal XP practice to switch partner after the completion of a task or story.

PairCoaching

Usually, the students coach in pairs. While this might be inefficient in a commercial setting, it has many benefits in an educational environment. The coaches appreciate having someone to share the coaching with. It also allows a greater number of students to take the coaching course, a greater flexibility in the exact number of coaches needed, and finally it gives a redundancy that is good to have in case of temporary illness, since the coaches are crucial to the team.

CoachIsCoached

Each iteration, between the long lab and the next planning meeting, all coaches meet for 2 hours of reflection and advice. During this meeting, the coaches share their experiences from the previous long lab, and many good ideas emerge among the participants on how to handle various kinds of problems. These meetings are coached by faculty who also give advice on what to focus on during the next iteration. For example, the first iteration might focus on just getting started; the second one on team building, e.g., by switching pairs often; the third one on making sure that a swift release process is developed; the fourth one on checking extra carefully that testing is done in an appropriate way; etc. What to focus on need not be fixed in advance, but can be a reaction to what kind of problems that arose in the previous iteration.

CoachIsArchitect

The students taking the introductory course have previously studied programming, algorithms and data structures, and object-oriented modeling and design, but have previously only had assignments of small programs of a few hundred lines of code. They are thus quite inexperienced programmers. The product to be developed by the team is, in general, their first larger program, and there is a need for someone on the team to take a more senior role concerning the software architecture. We solve this by letting the coach take on the role as an architect as well.

During the project, the coaches have the responsibility of taking the initiative to architectural discussions during the planning meetings, they keep track of the evolving architecture, and document it at the end of the project. This allows the coach to practice software architecture in a realistic, albeit small, project.

The architect role here is very different from the traditional one of prescribing an architecture before implementation. Here, the architect role is rather to take the responsibility of keeping track of the architecture, verbalizing it and maybe visualizing it to allow it to be communicated among team members and, if needed, to take the initiative to architectural refactorings.

4   Bootstrapping the Courses

The description of the course above refers to the second instance where the coaches have already taken the introductory course and are familiar with the basics of XP. During the first instance, we did, however, not have coaches that were experienced with XP. In order to bootstrap the courses we had to train a first batch of coaches. To this end, the persons following the first coaching course instance was a combination of faculty staff, graduate students, and a few handpicked senior undergraduate students. This allowed us to train staff at the department as well as try out the course on a few student coaches.

This course instance used the same format as described above, with a theory part, a practicum part, and an in-depth study. However, the contents of the theory part were different, focusing on introducing the basic XP practices.

The first instance of the coaching course also served to bootstrap the introductory course. The theory part of the coaching course was then given prior to the theory part of the introductory course, and much of the lectures and short lab material (e.g., on version control and unit testing) could carry over from the first coaching course to the introductory course.

In the second instance of the coaching course, the situation is more like we planned. The course is a part of the regular curriculum and essentially all participants are undergraduate students, although the course is open to graduate students and interested faculty as well. The coaching students already know the basics of XP and we now take the opportunity to bring in more advanced material into the theory part. In particular, we found it beneficial to add a strong focus on architecture.

In the first instance of the coaching course the coaches developed the initial architecture in the first iteration, but many did not track the evolving architecture very closely, and later became somewhat frustrated that they did not know enough about the actual implementation. Their experience was that this made it more difficult to coach. This was one reason for developing the CoachIsArchitect practice and we expect that the active work with the architecture will allow the coach to stay in touch with the code although he/she does not do any production programming, thereby making the coaching itself more interesting and of higher quality.

The second instance of the introductory course is essentially the same as the first one. There are, however, some minor changes, such as adding a new short labsession on refactoring tools, using the Eclipse Java development tools [4]. Since this is new material to our new coaches too, we have included that in the current coaching course as well. This way, we can continually make use of the coaching course to try out new teaching material in a small group before running it in the large introductory course. We expect such smaller changes to be useful also in future instances of the courses, as the field and practice of XP evolves.

5   Conclusions

The idea to have older students studying coaching by actually coaching younger students, is in our experience a fruitful solution and, to our knowledge, has not been tried before. This tandem of courses enables us to give a challenging and interesting course for the coaches, and, at the same time, allows us to afford on-site coaches for the younger students, providing them with a high quality environment for learning XP.

In this educational setting, there is a need for a streamlined process for learning how to coach, and development of coaching practices. We have described the main practices that we have developed to this end: Coach, ActiveTrackingCoach, Trigger-Communication, TimeOut, CoachIsCoached, PairCoaching, and CoachIsArchitect.

Although we have developed these practices for student coaches, we believe that many of them are useful also in an industrial setting: Coach, ActiveTrackingCoach, TriggerCommunication, and TimeOut, are all general coaching practices that have to do with learning communication, and about learning and evolving the process. The essence of the CoachIsCoached practice is the reflection and sharing of experience concerning the actual coaching. This should be useful also in industrial settings where people are learning to coach. The PairCoaching practice is mainly motivated by the educational setting, but might be useful when introducing XP in industry as well.

The CoachIsArchitect is also mainly motivated by the educational setting where the developers are inexperienced programmers and where the combination of architecture with coaching provides more depth and challenge to the coaching course. However, we believe that also in many cases in industry, it is natural for project leaders to combine these two roles of coach and architect. In particular, the tracking architect role (rather than the traditional prescribing architect) that we envision should be of use for project leaders that wish to stay in close touch with their agile project.

The coaching role still has the association of self-learned guru in the XP world. Our experience shows that it is quite possible to teach coaching in a systematic way, even to fairly inexperienced programmers. The coaching practices we have developed to this end will certainly evolve as we get more experience, and should be thought of as protopractices that need to be further elaborated and evaluated. Nevertheless, we have tried them out with success and believe that other educators will be able to use the same techniques. The coached teams were very satisfied with their student coaches, and the coaches themselves found the course very interesting and stimulating.

Acknowledgements

We are in great depth to all the faculty, graduate students, and undergraduate students that followed the first instance of the coaching course, in particular for all ideas and feedback that surfaced at the coaching meetings.

References

1. K. Beck: *Embracing Change with eXtreme Programming*, IEEE Computer, 32(10): 70-77 (1999).
2. K. Beck: *Test-Driven Development*, Addison Wesley, 2002.

3. K. Beck and R. Johnson: *Patterns Generate Architectures*, in proceedings of ECOOP 1994: 139-149. LNCS 821. Springer Verlag.
4. *The Eclipse Java Development Tools subproject*, http://www.eclipse.org
5. G. Hedin, L. Bendix, B. Magnusson: *Introducing Software Engineering by means of Extreme Programming*, in proceedings of the International Conference on Software Engineering, Portland Oregon, May 5-8, 2003.
6. E. Gamma, R. Helm, R. Johnson and J. Vlissides: *Design Patterns: Abstraction and Reuse of Object-Oriented Design*, in proceedings of ECOOP 1993: 406-431. LNCS 707. Springer Verlag.
7. P. Kruchten: *The 4+1 View Model of Architecture*, IEEE Software 12(6): 42-50 (1995).
8. W. C. Wake: *Extreme Programming Explored*, Addison Wesley, 2001.

Where Do Unit Tests Come from?

Jing Yuan*, Mike Holcombe, and Marian Gheorghe

Department of Computer Science, University of Sheffield
211 Portobello Street, S1 4DP, UK
{j.yuan,m.holcombe,m.gheorghe}@dcs.shef.ac.uk

Abstract. In Extreme programming unit testing is organized so that the unit tests are written before coding commences. For many programmers the selection of the test cases is something of an 'ad hoc' process. Where programmers are experienced in writing test sets it is common for them to use white box or structural test techniques. However, these rely on the structure of the code being available which is not the case with XP. This article describes a principled way of creating powerful, functional unit tests from informal descriptions of the units.

1   Introduction

Developing unit tests before writing the code is an important part of Extreme Programming (not always widely accepted [5]). These tests provide immediate feedback to programmers on the quality of the component code that they then write. Such testing is complementary to the functional integration testing applied to the increments of the system at release stages. For many programmers the selection of the unit test cases is something of an 'ad hoc' process; Though there are several commercial unit testing tools for XP such as JUnit, PhpUnit etc, which are very useful in supporting testing automation through providing an environment to express, load and manage the test cases, They don't give any guidelines for how to choose the test data to produce a test case, or if current test cases are enough for a specific class. Therefore there were created methods to systematically generate complete and consistent test units [6]. In traditional development processes where programmers are involved in testing it is common for them to use white box or structural test techniques. However, these rely on the structure of the code being available which is not the case with XP.

For each class we are building thought should be given to how the class is to be tested. As we have seen the eXtreme Programming approach suggests that test sets should be created before any coding starts. This is not as simple as it seems because at the start of the coding of a unit it may not be entirely clear how it will be written and some important tests may not be easily defined. Furthermore, many of the popular types of testing such as the white box testing techniques are based on the structure of the code. But we have no code as yet so this won't work. The lack of discussion of this point is one of the weaknesses of some treatments of XP. What is important here is that a basic framework for testing the unit is defined and this will be developed into

---

* Visiting Researcher from China Xi'an Satellite Control Centre.

M. Marchesi and G. Succi (Eds.): XP 2003, LNCS 2675, pp. 161–169, 2003.
© Springer-Verlag Berlin Heidelberg 2003

a more detailed set of tests in tandem with the coding. At the end of the initial exploratory coding stage a complete set of tests should then be available so that thorough testing of the class is possible. Given the outline description or structure of a class we have to identify two important things: a) what are the ways in which the method will be accessed and what, if any, are the preconditions on the data that is supplied to it? b) What are the ranges of values that need to be provided for the methods? Once we have identified these aspect the expected outputs have to be considered and, in particular, action taken to ensure that the output information of interest can be read or displayed in an appropriate form.

We will be writing some test scripts that will be used in conjunction with the class code to establish whether it is behaving in a desired manner. These scripts, themselves forming classes or modules in the language concerned, will provide the basis for automating many of the tests but it is unlikely that all the tests can be done automatically, especially if the output is of a graphical nature.

The test scripts will have to provide the information needed to prepare the class for testing and this will involve identifying the entry points to the method and supplying suitable data to make the test work.

2   Testing Simple Cases

In any method that we want to test there will be some data input values needed from a defined data structure or type. It is important to ensure that the data selected for this purpose is sufficiently varied to expose the method to all possible types of failure as well as success. We are trying to do two things during testing - gain some confidence that the method works and at the same time trying to break it. Only then can we be sure that the class is trustworthy enough to be considered for integration into our existing working system.

Most values of data will be defined in the context of limits or boundaries which describe their validity so that, for example, we may have taken the decision earlier that a particular data value that is a string must be between 1 and 30 characters long and that falling outside that range will cause an error and some suitable recovery mechanical should be provided – perhaps inviting a user to try again if it is a data input through some user interface. Numerical values might also be restricted and it is useful to be proactive in this respect and not rely on the system to deal with out of range values.

When choosing numeric data values for using in unit testing it is useful to consider the following simple categories of data values, where we are assuming that there are upper and lower boundaries on the values:

- a value below the lower boundary;
- a value equal to or at the lower boundary;
- a mid range value;
- a value equal to or at the higher boundary;
- a value above the higher boundary;
- a value in an incorrect format;
- a null value or no input.

If we are dealing with the type of a string of literals that must be of length between 1 and 30 then we could generate distinct tests in Table 1.

Table 1. Tests for the type of a string with length between 1 and 30

\<return\>
A
Abcdef
abcdefghijklmnopqrstuvwxyz1234
abcdefghijklmnopqrstuvwxyz12346
%`¬*&
nul_input

If the algorithm used in the method needs to deal with some valid range data differently then tests with all the types of data that will exercise all the paths through the program graph of the method should be used. This issue is explored in the next section.

If the input data to the method consists of several different types of values for different parameters in the method then all combinations must be considered. It is possible that some combinations should not be valid during the operation of the method in the software overall. It is a false economy, at this stage, to ignore these aspect. Such combinations can cause problems when the code is integrated if there are undetected errors that cannot be found easily during integration. It will help debugging if care is taken at the unit testing stage to create tests that will report the results in a suitable way.

3 Testing More Complex Units

Not all the classes developed will fit into the simple pattern of a few independent methods that can be tested independently. More complex structures are likely and we need to identify how these might be dealt with. Luckily we can capitalize on our some simple modeling and test generation techniques. Even if most of the methods are very simple, it is hard to test a method without the class context, and the context is usually very complicated since there are many possible errors that could occur during its operation in a complete program. This means that even when each method in a class has been tested individually and extensively, the class may still be unreliable. In order to detect as many errors as possible from the coordination within a class, the methods' test is put into the class test. Even so, there is a possibility of high coupling between some classes (though the intent of any design should be low coupling, but sometimes we have to keep this in balance with other factors), it would be hard to test each one of them independently, in such cases, integration testing at this level needs to be done for small groups of independent classes, but such tests should not be left until integration or system testing, it should be completed during the unit testing phase.

Each class has its own life cycle, its operations have specified active sequences (during correct use) that must be obeyed by its clients. On the other hand, a class cannot control the access sequence of its clients. It is never known when an operation will be called. In such cases, to assure the correctness of the system, error handling must be used to deal with incorrect or unexpected use and complete fault coverage methods should be adopted in testing.

The W [7] and Wp method [8] are thought to be able to provide complete fault detection capability while the Wp-method produces shorter test sequences [9] if the

CFile
+GetFileName : String +GetPosition : signed short +GetStatus : bool
+CFile() +Open(in lpszName, in openFlag, out pError) +Read(in lpBuffer : void, in nCount : unsigned short(idl)) +Write(in lpBuffer : void, in nCount : unsigned short(idl)) +Close()

Fig. 1. Static structure of class CFile

specification could be expressed as an finite state machines (FSM). A Stream X-machine (SXM) [2] can be thought of as a FSM with one important difference, namely that the individual transitions are labeled by functions which take as parameters the current system input value and the current internal memory value. The internal memory is defined in any suitable form, it could be the current state of a database, attribute values of a class, or some temporary variable values etc. The transition function then returns an updated internal memory value and a system output. Such a model is sufficiently general to be applicable for the modeling of most types of software unlike finite state machines. Using such machines it is possible to create a hierarchical model of a system which allows for concise representations of the system which overcomes the problems of scalability that afflict finite state models. It is shown that if a process is modeled as a SXM, test sets can be generated by a method similar to W-method [11] and if certain conditions are meet, the complete fault coverage test set could be produced [2]. Various case studies and extended models of SXM have been investigated [2, 3, 4, 12]. Using SXM to represent the class activity can help to generate the test set more easily and completely and, potentially, automatically. Moreover in some cases we might have strong interactions between various classes that are represented as separate SXM. In such situations we need to provide these details into the model as well.

3.1   Case Example 1

This Example illustrates how to use the SXM notation to represent the active sequences of a class. The CFile is a basic file I/O class which provides non-buffered binary input/output services. The static structure of this class is shown in Fig. 1, the corresponding X-Machine model is shown in Fig. 2 (Different Open alphabets could be thought as different functions in SXM).

Based on the X-machine model, test sequences can be produced which could cover all random calls for the operation methods. Some of the test sequences are listed in Table 2 (Suppose that after calling every operation method, it could be decided if the expected result has been obtained).

3.2   Case Example 2

This is a sample application distributed with JBuilder 6 Enterprise. In this example, there are 2 classes: TCPEchoServerDemo(Server Demo) and TCPEchoDemo (Client Demo). Their static structures are shown in Fig3 and Fig 4 separately.

Table 2. Test sequences for example 1

CFile();Open(Read);Read();Read();
CFile();Open(Read);Read();Open(Read);
CFile();Open(Read);Read();Write();
CFile();Open(Read);Read();Close();
......

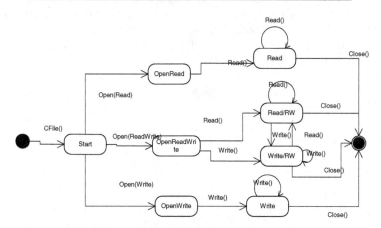

Fig. 2. An X-machine model of example 1

TCPEchoServerDemo
+startButton
+stopButton
+logTextArea
+TCPEchoServerDemo()
+main()
#startButton_actionPerformed()
#stopButton_actionPerformed()
#this_windowClosing()

Fig. 3. Static structure of TCPEchoSeverDemo

TCPEchoDemo
+connectButton
+disconnectButton
+sendButton
+textTextField
+echoMessageTextArea
+TCPEchoDemo()
+main()
#connectButton_actionPerformed()
#disconnectButton_actionPerformed()
#sendButton_actionPerformed()
#this_windowClosing()

Fig. 4. Static structure of TCPEchoDemo

These two classes communicate with each other through TCP/IP network protocol. The Server Demo receives messages from Client Demo, and then broadcasts them. At the beginning of the communication, the Client Demo must establish a connection with the Server Demo by the connectButton_actionPerformed(). But this operation can not be successful unless the Server Demon has been in the listening state as a consequence of startButton_actionPerformed(). Once the connection channel has been established, the text in the textTextField of the Client Demo could be sent to the Server Demo through sendButton_actionPerformed(). As soon as the Server Demo receives the message, it broadcasts it to the Client Demos. The Client Demos then append the message in the echoMessageTextArea to display it.

The operation sequences of class TCPEchoDemo and TCPEchoServerDemo are modeled as X-Machines in Fig. 5 and Fig. 6.

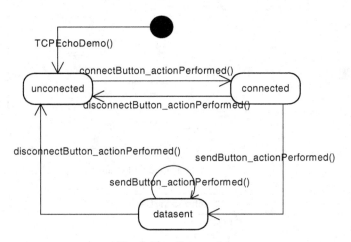

Fig. 5. The client model

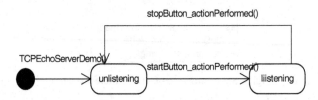

Fig. 6. The Server model

It is known from the communication process that neither could the Client Demo's tests be implemented based on the X-machine model in Fig. 5, Nor could the Server Demo be tested completely without the collaboration between them. In such cases, some ways must be found to express the interaction relationship between the two X-machine models. One of them is illustrated in Fig. 7.

In this model the dashed line indicates that there are some preconditions for the transition, that is, the methods in the square brackets should be executed before the execution of the method with the current transition; the thick line indicates that there are multiple choice operation methods leading to the next state (all methods corresponding to the same transition could be treated together as only one function in

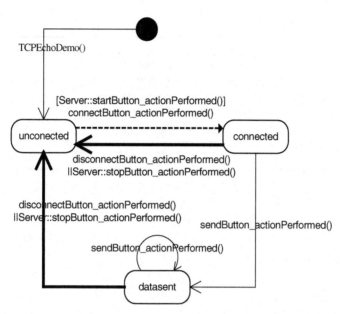

Fig. 7. Client-Server interaction model(the alphabets with *Serve* prefix are used for methods in class TCPEchoServerDemo , others without the prefix are for class TCPEchoDemo)

Table 3. Test sequences for example 2

TCPEchoDemo();Server::startButton_actionPerformed();connectButton_actionPerformed();

TCPEchoDemo();sendButton_actionPerformed();

TCPEchoDemo();disconnectButton_actionPerformed();

....

SXM). In this example, in the unconnected state connectButton_actionPerformed() must have startButton_actionPerformed() in the Server Demo as its precondition, since it cannot connect to the Server Demo unless the Server Demo starts to listen. The unconnected state can be reached either through disconnectButton_actionPerformed() or by stopping the Server from both state connected or datasent. Some of the test sequences based on this model are listed in Table 3. The JUnit program code in Java for the first 2 test cases is given after Table 3.

JUnit program code segment:

```
public void testConnectButton_actionPerformed() {

TCPEchoServerDemo tcpechoserverdemo = new  TCPEchoServer-
Demo();
```

Table 4. States-Representation Table for example 2

States	Representation
unconnected	sendButton_actionPerformed(); textsend!=textretuen
connect	sendButton_actionPerformed(); textsend==textretuen
datasent	textsend==textretuen
...	...

```
TCPEchoDemo tcpechodemo = new TCPEchoDemo();

ActionEvent ae= null ;

tcpechoserverdemo.startButton_actionPerformed(ae);

tcpechodemo.connectButton_actionPerformed(ae);

String textsend = new String("this is a test");

String textreturn = new String();

tcpechodemo.textTextField.setText(textsend);

tcpechodemo.sendButton_actionPerformed(ae);

textreturn=getReturnText();

assertEquals(textsend, textreturn); }
public void testsendButton_actionPerformed() {

TCPEchoServerDemo tcpechoserverdemo =  new TCPEchoServer-
Demo();

TCPEchoDemo tcpechodemo = new TCPEchoDemo();

ActionEvent ae=  null  ;

tcpechoserverdemo.startButton_actionPerformed(ae);

tcpechodemo.sendButton_actionPerformed(ae);

String textsend = new String("this is a test");

String textreturn = new String();

tcpechodemo.textTextField.setText(textsend);

textreturn=getReturnText();

assertTrue(textsend!=textreturn); }
```

The test sets could be automatically generated if suitable way is used to express the states into function outputs and memory values, such as Table 4 for this case example.

4   Conclusion and Further Work

The generation of unit tests in the absence of any detailed source code to guide the selection of test inputs can be achieved by using a simple and very general modeling approach based on stream X-machines. This model can be used to generate test sets with a proven excellence at defect detection. Because the model is general in its scope it is possible to test sophisticated units which involve complex communication between different classes. The method is amenable to automation and thus promises a significant advance for the creation of high quality test sets that can be applied through test application tools such as JUnit.

Future work includes carrying out more extensive evaluation of the method in an industrial setting. Early experiments have indicated that in one particular application domain the method generated tests that, in comparison with the industry standard method used were both more efficient (running time of 2 seconds as opposed to 27 hours!) and detected 30% more faults under controlled conditions [13].

References

1. M. Holcombe: X-Machines as a Basis for Dynamic System Specification. Software Engineering Journal, 1988, Vol3, 69-76.
2. M. Holcombe and F. Ipate: Correct Systems: Building a Business Process Solution, Springer Verlag, Berlin, 1988.
3. T. Balanescu, T. Cowling, H. Georgescu, M. Gheorghe, M. Holcombe and C. Vertan: Communicating Stream X-Machines Systems are no more than X-Machines, J.UCS, 1999, Vol. 9, 494-507.
4. M. Holcombe, K. Bogdanov and M. Gheorghe: Functional Test generation for Extreme Programming, Second International Conference on extreme Programming and Flexible Processes in Software Engineering XP2001, Sardinia, Italy, 2001, 109-113.
5. M. Muller and W. Tichy : Case study: Extreme programming in a university environment. 23rd International Conference on Software engineering, Toronto, Canada, 2001, 537-544.
6. D. Stotts, M. Lindsey and A. Antley: An informal formal method for systematic Junit test case generation, in D. Wells and L. Williams (Eds), XP/Agile Universe 2002, LNCS 2418, 2002, 131-143.
7. T. Sun Chow: Testing Software Design Modeled by Finite State Machines. IEEE Transactions on Software Engineering, May 1978, Vol.SE-4(3), 178-187.
8. S. Fujiwara, G. von Bochmann, F. Khendek, M. Amalou and A. Ghedamsi: Test Selection Based on Finite State Models. IEEE Transactions on Software Engineering, 1991, Vol.17 591-603
9. T. Ramalingam, A. Das and K. Thulasiraman: Fault Detection and Diagnosis Capabilities of Test Sequence Selection Methods Based on the FSM Model. Computer Communications, 1995, Vol.18, 113-122.
10. S. Eilenberg: Automata, Languages and Machines.1998, VolA, Academic Press,New York.
11. F. Ipate: Theory of X-Machines and Applications in Specification and Testing. PhD thesis, Department of Computer Science, University of Sheffield, July 1995.
12. A. Cowling, H. Georgescu, C. Vertan: A Structured Way to Use Channels for Communication in X-machine System. Formal Aspects of Computing, 2000,Vol.12,458-500
13. S. Vanak: Complete Function Testing of Hardware Description. PhD thesis, Department of Computer Science, University of Sheffield, 2002

Three Patterns in Java Unit Testing

Eric Nickell and Ian Smith

Palo Alto Research Center, 3333 Coyote Hill Road, Palo Alto, CA 94304
{nickell,iansmith}@parc.com

Abstract. This paper discusses three unit-testing techniques. These are test probe, ipecac, and test hierarchies. Each of these patterns [1] explores a different area of the interaction of white- and black-box testing. The first two techniques, test probe and ipecac, allow internal implementations to be conveniently exposed to test code without compromising production code integrity. The latter provides a pattern for testing class hierarchies in production code, and a way to move from white-box to black-box testing while refactoring.

1 Introduction

We present here three techniques that may be used by developers to create more effective unit tests in some situations:

- Test probe: a way to expose some of the internals of a class being tested in order to write white-box unit tests, without exposing those internals to production classes.
- Ipecac[1]: A way to test the intermediate state of a parsing system in progress.
- A process for refactoring test code while refactoring production code.

Throughout the paper, we use the terms "testing" and "test code" to refer to the XP practice of writing automated tests which are used to determine whether production software is performing as expected. The testing patterns described are more applicable to unit tests than functional tests.

2 A TestProbe to Expose Details to Test Code

Use a non-static inner class ('TestProbe') to provide access to private fields and methods of the outer production class via delegation.

Both black-box (closed-box) and white-box (open-box) testing are useful tools in their appropriate contexts. In general, we believe that white-box testing, being tied more tightly to a specific implementation, is easier to write, is more likely to be rigorous, is more likely to test the corner cases where a specific implementation might fail, and is not significantly more expensive to maintain than black-box testing. But white-box testing may require that test code has access to information hidden from most clients.

---

[1] A drug prepared from the ipecac plant for use in treating poisoning by inducing vomiting.

M. Marchesi and G. Succi (Eds.): XP 2003, LNCS 2675, pp. 170–179, 2003.
© Springer-Verlag Berlin Heidelberg 2003

Existing ways to access hidden fields or methods in a class being tested include:

(1) Expose the hidden information, but document it as being reserved for testing only.

(2) In the case of a hidden field, allow the calling code (via setter or constructor parameter) to provide that value. If production code does not otherwise supply this value, then the constructor or setter should be so marked. Test code can then supply a value it can probe, such as a mock object [2], i.e.

```
public class Foo {
    public Foo() {...}
    /** For TESTING only! */
    public Foo(Map TESTING_cache) {
        cache = TESTING_cache;
    }
    private Map cache;
    ...
}
```

(3) Make the test code a static inner class of the production.

(4) Provide a method to expose the member via delegation, but whose name suggests it should only be called by test code, i.e.

```
private Map cache;
Map TESTING_cache() { return cache; }
```

Methods (2) and (4) are usable when the hidden information is embodied in a few private members, but they are less usable when there is a significant amount of computation involved, such as when a private method performs a complex, intermediate calculation. And while method (3) is workable, it incurs some practical disadvantages of production code and test code being tied together in one source file, and also does not allow the developers to control the test code's access to the production code internals.

We suggest instead using a test probe to access these hidden fields and methods.

```
public class Foo {
    private Map cache;
    private int itemsInCacheMatching(String pattern) { ... }

    /** For tests only. NOT TO BE USED BY PRODUCTION CODE. */
    public class TestProbe {
      public Map cache() { return cache; }
      public int itemsInCacheMatching(String pattern) {
        return Foo.this.itemsInCacheMatching(pattern);
      }
    }
    ...
}
```

The methods in the TestProbe are often the thinnest possible veneer over the private fields and methods of the outer class, even to having the same name. In rare cases, we have provided both getters and setters to some private fields. When two or more test classes (TestCase's when using jUnit) need to share testing logic concerning the object with the probe, it makes sense for this to be factored into the TestProbe itself to avoid duplication. By using the test probe,

- we can test significant methods which are not exposed in the public interface directly
- we can make sure that the internal state is correct after a series of operations
- we can control the degree of access by the test code to the production code internals, exposing some of the implementation details without exposing all

- with an IDE such as eclipse[3], it is simple to determine that all accesses to the test probe are made from test code, at least within your own projects

In situations where there are concerns about production clients using the test probe inappropriately, we can ship production code which does not contain the TestProbe class.

3   Use Ipecac for Parser Semantics

Extend your parser to recognize a token which, when encountered, will cause the parser to throw a runtime exception (e.g., 'TESTException'). If necessary, the exception can be used to pass to the test code the objects for testing.

Parsers occur frequently in large systems, whether this is something as sophisticated as using a parser as an intregral part of a compiler, or as simple as using SAX to read data from an XML file. In most cases, we will want to test that the parser accepts the right grammar and rejects the wrong grammar, but we also want to test that the semantic actions being driven by the grammar are being followed correctly. [4] These semantic actions may be as diverse as construction of a parse tree as part of compilation, actions performed on a database while parsing a query language, or changes to a graphics state while parsing a page description language.

One technique for testing the correctness of the semantic actions is to supply the parser with valid sentences for the grammar, and to examine the state of the world after the parser returns control to the test code. All black-box tests of a parser would be constructed by submitting complete sentences in the grammar to the parser and verifying that the correct state had been reached. A white-box test could be constructed similarly, but of course would verify that internal (end) states of the parser or semantic actions were correct. Our technique provides the ability to do white-box testing on intermediate states of the parsing system.

We propose an additional mechanism, so that the test code can examine the state of the world at any point during the parsing of a valid prefix of the grammar. To do this, we want to be able to cause the parser to throw an exception on demand. During the parsing process, there are three tasks going on concurrently: (1) a lexical analyzer, or lexer, breaks up a stream of characters into a stream of logical tokens, (2) a parser proper examines the token stream enforces the production rules of the grammar, and (3) a set of semantic actions corresponding to the production rules, and which are initiated by the parser when the proper syntax is found.

In practice, the separation between the three tasks above may be quite rigid, or may be nearly non-existent. It is also common for the lexing and parsing to be done by a package which is not under the control of the developers, or to be done by code which is produced by a compiler compiler, such as ANTLR [5], JavaCC[6], or yacc[7].

There are three mechanisms that might be used deep in the parser to raise the exception:

1. In the case that we have control over the lexer, either in a hand-coded lexer or via a compiler compiler which allows the insertion of code, we can raise the exception when a sentinel token is encountered.

2. If the lexer is in a third-party package or is machine-produced, but provides a hook for examination or modification of tokens, we can check for the token and raise the exception at this point. Note that there may be a slight performance penalty in the production code for this.
3. We can create a production rule that will trigger the exception. The disadvantage of this technique is that we can only insert the ipecac token where it is part of a valid prefix of the grammar.

We can make this more concrete with an example. A word processor might provide a formula editor for placing mathematical formulas in a text document, but store the formulas as text strings. [8] The string "e^{x} = sum from{k=0} to{infinity} { x^{k} over {k!} }" could represent the formula for the Taylor expansion of e^x.

Example:

```
public class EquationParserTest extends TestCase {
    public void testBounds() {
        EquationParser parser = createTestParser();
        /* various other tests... */
        try {
            String eq="e^{x} = sum from{k=0} to{infinity} IPECAC";
            parser.parseEquation(eq);
            fail("Parse should have raised TESTException);
        }
        catch (EquationParser.TESTException e) {
            ssertEquals(5, e.stack.size());
            assertEquals("e^{x}", e.stack.get(0));
            assertEquals("=", e.stack.get(1));
            assertEquals("sum", e.stack.get(2));
            assertEquals("from{k=0}", e.stack.get(3));
            assertEquals("to{infinity}", e.stack.get(4));
        }
    }
}
```

If we are using a compiler compiler such as JavaCC to create the parser, then we can have the lexer raise the test exception when it encounters the sentinel:

```
TOKEN :
{
    < IPECAC: "IPECAC" > {throw new EquationParser.TESTException(stack); }
}
```

but only if the lexer has access to the information that should be passed via the test exception to the test code. Alternatively, we could have the parser proper throw the exception, but then the test code would have to have IPECAC inserted where it is syntactically valid.

```
/** Parse an expression (JavaCC source) */
EquationExpression equationExpression() :
{    EquationExpression a, b; }
{
    (
        "(" a=EquationExpression() ")"
        { return new ParentheticExpression(a); }
    |
        ...
    |
        /* For use by test code to examine internal state */
        "IPECAC" {throw new EquationParser.TESTException(stack);}
    )
}
```

This technique can be useful even when the parser is not something we are developing, but only using. For example, if we are using the SAX parser to process xml-structured information, we can raise the test exception in our code that SAX has called, and the exception will propagate up through the call stack to our test code. There are other approaches to solving this problem besides the one we have suggested here. For example, one could introduce a "state object" that the parser modifies as it proceeds through the parse. By using a mock object for testing, one could verify that the right calls are being made on the state object as the parse proceeds. This approach or others are certainly workable, but we feel our approach makes for the simplest testing harness.

This technique provides a mechanism for interrogating the internals of parsers. This white-box testing strategy uses a "signal token" or sentinel to alert the lexical analyzer or parser to the test-code's desire to check the system's internal state.

4   Use Test Hierarchies to Test Hierarchies

As production classes are refactored into a class hierarchy, refactor the test classes into a parallel hierarchy.

As we mentioned earlier, we find white-box testing effective. That is to say, we believe that the developer should use all that he knows about the details of the implementation to design tests which stress exactly those parts of the implementation which he feels might be at risk. This is consistent with Beck's notion of tests as bets [9, pg 117]: when there is a single implementation for the informal interface implicitly defined by the class' public methods, then the developer's time is best spent writing tests based on all he knows about what might go wrong with the implementation, rather than the more difficult task of developing test code which is implementation-independent.

That said, there are situations where black-box (closed-box) testing is preferred. When refactoring produces an interface or abstract class with concrete subclasses in the production code, the test code should be arranged as a parallel hierarchy comprising an abstract test class and concrete extensions. This is especially true if the concrete production must satisfy a testable contract guaranteed by the abstract production class or interface. The abstract and concrete test classes share responsibility: The concrete test class is responsible for creating objects to test, and the abstract test class is responsible for testing the objects so created to make sure that they pass the contracts.

The pattern here is the parallelism between the class hierarchies in the production and test code. We will not discuss here the relative merits of inheritance versus composition. Instead, we assume that inheritance is sometimes preferred, and give a testing pattern to use when this is so. In an XP project, however, subclasses in the production code should arise only for specific reasons, and at specific points in the XP cycle. For this reason, this test pattern is useful at just that point in the process, and we present the pattern in the context of the process by which it is created.

For purposes of illustration, we will create a contrived example that assumes we are developing classes equivalent to some of the standard *Collections* classes. Let us assume that our system contains the class ArrayList, and that we need to supply a linked list capability to our system, and that we need six capabilities: insert an object at the end of the list, insert an object at a given position, remove the item at a given position, determine the current size of the list, and determine whether it is empty. Obviously, we'll need a way to create a new list, so we add that to our tasks as well. We suspect that ArrayList and our LinkedList-to-be are similar, and will share many of the same methods. Thus, we are motivated to make the most of this similarity. To do this, we will try to extract a new superclass, AbstractList, from ArrayList. AbstractList will contain the intersection of the functionality between ArrayList and our LinkedList-to-be. In *Test Driven Development* [10], Beck describes an approach that would lead to a similar structure via very fine-grained refactoring. We have omitted many intermediate steps in the interest of space.

We need tests for each of the capabilities on our task list. Suspecting that our LinkedList-to-be will parallel ArrayList, we first scavenge ArrayListTest to see if there is code we can refactor or mine for ideas. There we find tests that would seem to work for all six capabilities we need for LinkedList: testSize, testIsEmpty, testGet, testAddObject, testAddIObject, and testRemove. There are also tests for features of ArrayList that are not needed for LinkedList, such as testEnsureCapacity. Let's focus on testGet and testAddObject. Before we start, ArrayListTest contains:[2]

```java
final private static Object obj0 = "First object added";
final private static Object obj1 = new Object();

protected ArrayList standardSetUp() {
    ArrayList list = new ArrayList();
    list.add(obj0);
    list.add(obj1);
    return list;
}

public void testGet() {
    ArrayList list = standardSetUp();
    assertEquals(obj0, list.get(0));
    assertEquals(obj1, list.get(1));
    ensureIndexInvalid(list, -1);
    ensureIndexInvalid(list, 2);
}

public void testAddObject() {     //test add(Object)
    ArrayList list = standardSetUp();
    list.add("obj2");    //add at end
    assertEquals(3, list.size());
    assertEquals(obj0, list.get(0));
    assertEquals(obj1, list.get(1));
    assertEquals("obj2", list.get(2));
    ensureIndexInvalid(list, -1);
    ensureIndexInvalid(list, 3);
}
```

Like the other tests, testGet and testAddObject look like we could reasonably copy these into a LinkedListTest. Instead, we will promote them into an abstract test class common to ArrayListTest and LinkedListTest. Obviously, we have to promote obj0, obj1, standardSetUp, and ensureIndexInvalid, which the tests depend on.

Let's create an AbstractListTest to contain the test machinery common to ArrayListTest and LinkedListTest, and insert it into the class hierarchy between ArrayListTest and junit.framework.TestCase. Now we promote the target test methods and the fields and methods they depend on. AbstractListTest should not be testing instances of ArrayList, but of some interface or class common to ArrayList and LinkedList, which we'll name AbstractList. So we'll change every use of ArrayList in AbstractListTest to use AbstractList. Even after we create class AbstractList, and change Ar-

---

[2]Source code for this example in its entirety can be found on http://miraloma-park.com/xp2003examples/ .

rayList to extend AbstractList, AbstractListTest will still not compile, since Abstract-List has no methods. When we add abstract method signatures to AbstractList for all six methods, all but two errors in AbstractListTest go away. Both of these come from trying to instantiate a new AbstractList, which is not possible since AbstractList is abstract. We need a way to create a concrete instance of an AbstractList – either an ArrayList or a LinkedList instance depending on what we're testing. The classic factory method design pattern can help us [11]. In both places where we have the expression, new AbstractList(), we change this to create, and add an abstract method, create, which returns an AbstractList. ArrayListTest and LinkedListTest will each be responsible to implement this method. After this change, AbstractListTest compiles. Here is part of it:

```
final protected static Object obj0 = "First object added";
final protected static Object obj1 = new Object();

protected abstract AbstractList create();

AbstractList standardSetUp() {
    AbstractList list = create();
    list.add(obj0);
    list.add(obj1);
    return list;
}

public void testGet() {
    AbstractList list = standardSetUp();
    assertEquals(obj0, list.get(0));
    assertEquals(obj1, list.get(1));
    ensureIndexInvalid(list, -1);
    ensureIndexInvalid(list, 2);
}

public void testAddObject() {     //test add(Object)
    AbstractList list = standardSetUp();
    list.add("obj2");   //add at end
    assertEquals(3, list.size());
    assertEquals(obj0, list.get(0));
    assertEquals(obj1, list.get(1));
    assertEquals("obj2", list.get(2));
    ensureIndexInvalid(list, -1);
    ensureIndexInvalid(list, 3);
}
```

But ArrayListTest still doesn't compile. First, we must implement create:

```
protected AbstractList create() { return new ArrayList(); }
```

Secondly, there are places where a method in ArrayListTest is calling a method that has been promoted to AbstractListTest, and that method returns an AbstractList rather than an ArrayList. The simplest thing to do is to cast these back into an ArrayList, knowing where they come from. For example,

```
public void testTrimToSize() {
    ArrayList list = (ArrayList)standardSetUp();
    //a white-box test
    list.trimToSize();
    assertEquals(2, list.getCurrentCapacity());
}
```

At this point, ArrayListTest should not only compile, but should pass all the tests! Thus, we are ready to begin writing tests for LinkedList.

To digress for a moment, why is it possible to reuse a test designed to test Array-List to test LinkedList as well? It's because a *testable contract* exists between callers and implementors of a class. Any subclass of AbstractList tested by a subclass of

AbstractListTest must ensure that, e.g., size() has the right meaning – and Abstract-ListTest ensures this. If we were refactoring, say, an output stream writer, how would we test that a newly-implemented writer was satisfying the contract for output writers? We couldn't, at least not by testing the abstract stream writer. There's a contract there, but it's not testable at the abstract level.

Returning to writing tests for our linked list, we create LinkedListTest by extending AbstractListTest and implementing create().

```
public class LinkedListTest extends AbstractListTest {
    public LinkedListTest(String name) { super(name); }
    protected AbstractList create() {
        return new LinkedList();
    }
}
```

To get LinkedListTest to compile, we create LinkedList:

```
public class LinkedList extends AbstractList { }
```

which doesn't compile, of course, since we have not implemented any of Abstract-List's abstract methods. One simple way to get everything to compile quickly is to add stubs for all the needed methods which raise an exception:

```
public class LinkedList extends AbstractList {
    public void add(int index, Object element) {
        throw new RuntimeException("Not yet implemented.");
    }
    ... (likewise for add, get, isEmpty, remove, size)
}
```

This compiles, and all the tests fail for LinkedListTest, which is a good thing.

So where are we exactly? We have refactored ArrayListTest into three classes, so that we can reuse many of the tests originally in ArrayListTest to test LinkedList as well. We now have a LinkedListTest with six good tests which are all failing, and a stubbed-out skeleton for LinkedList.

Once compiling, our priority is to get the tests working as quickly as possible. At present, LinkedListTest is inheriting all its tests from AbstractListTest. All the tests happen to call standardSetUp, which uses add(Object) to add two objects to the list:

```
AbstractList standardSetUp() {
    AbstractList list = create();
    list.add(obj0);
    list.add(obj1);
    return list;
}
```

So it makes sense to implement add(Object) early, since none of the tests will pass until it's working. For each stubbed-out method in LinkedList, we should look at its corresponding method in ArrayList to see if that method can be promoted. ArrayList's add(Object) looks like:

```
public void add(Object element) {
    ensureCapacity(size + 1);
    data[size++] = element;
}
```

This is specific to ArrayList, but we could refactor it to
```
public void add(Object element) { add(size(), element); }
```

defining add(Object) in terms of add(int, Object). Then we pull it up into Abstract-List, removing the stub in LinkedList. But now we must implement both size() and add(int,Object) before any of the tests will pass. Both of these require real implementation, which we will skip here, but once implemented, LinkedList.testSize will pass. LinkedList.get also needs a real implementation, after which all the tests pass except testIsEmpty and testRemove. We can promote isEmpty from ArrayList:

```
public boolean isEmpty() { return size() == 0; }
```

After implementing remove, all tests pass, and we are done. Let's review the significant points:

1. A production class was going to be refactored into a class hierarchy (or its equivalent: two classes implementing the same interface). Be careful not to create a complex class hierarchy unnecessarily: it is usually preferred to add functionality to one class rather than spawning multiple classes.
2. Upon inspection, it appeared that many of the tests for the existing class could be refactored for double-duty. This implied the presence of a testable contract. The abstract test class became the embodiment of that contract on all the subclasses of the abstract production class.
3. We can refactor the test class and get the existing tests to run. Then we can create a new test class which provides a clear road map of what needs to be implemented in the new class.
4. Once we have failing tests, we continue implementing/refactoring as usual.
   Here are some final thoughts on this topic:
   - Although it did not appear in our example, it is normal to add some tests to the concrete test classes that are specific to the production class being tested. Similarly parallel to the class hierarchy, the concrete test class should contain additional code that tests the additional contracts of the concrete production class.
   - If the natural refactoring is to have one production class extending another concrete class, the natural test hierarchy will be the same – one test class extending another concrete test class.
   - The test hierarchy may parallel the production class hierarchy even when the latter is more than one abstract class and its subclasses. (Think of the Collections framework.) Specifically, it should normally be the case that for every class in the production class hierarchy you are testing, there is a TestCase in a precisely parallel test hierarchy. Moreover, when a production class in the hierarchy is abstract, its corresponding test class should also be abstract. The abstract test class hierarchy should have tests at each level appropriate to the testable contract at that level.
   - When the production code has a testable contract (that is, testable at the abstract level), that contract should be tested with a test method in the abstract test class. Although not shown in our examples, it is best if the test method is made final. The concrete test class should have no need to override the test method as long as the concrete production class satisfies the contract, and as long as the test method in the abstract test class accurately tests the contract.
   - When the production code has a non-testable contract (that is, not testable at the abstract level), it should be possible to delegate responsibility for testing the contract to the concrete test class (template method pattern [11]), so that the same tests can be used across multiple subclasses. This can be done by creating a test method in the abstract test class which calls abstract methods which the contrete test class must supply, or more simply by creating an abstract test method in the abstract test class as a helpful reminder to the concrete test class

implementor. Notice the difference: When the contract is testable, responsibility for testing correctness can lie in the abstract test class. When the contract is not testable, only the concrete test class has sufficient information to test for correctness.

Acknowledgments

We thank our management (Richard Burton, Sharon Johnson) for their continuing support of our foray into XP.

References

1. Marick, Brian. *Software Testing Patterns* Web Site. On-line at:
   http://www.testing.com/test-patterns/
2. Mock Objects Web Site. On-line at: http://www.mockobjects.com
3. Eclipse Web Site. On-line at:
   http://www.eclipse.org
4. Aho, A. V., Ullman J.D. *The Theory Of Parsing, Translation, and Compiling*, Prentice-Hall, Englewood Hills, N.J., 1972.
5. ANTLR Web Site. On-line at:
   http://www.antlr.org
6. WebGAIN Web Site. On-line at:
   http://www.webgain.com/products/java_cc/
7. Levin, J.R, Mason, T., Brown D. *Lex & Yacc*. O'Reilly & Associates, Sebastopol, CA., 1992.
8. Open Office Web Site. On-line at:
   http://www.openoffice.org
9. Beck, K. *Extreme Programming Explained*. Addison-Wesley. Boston, MA., 2000.
10. Beck, K. *Test Driven Development: By Example*. Addison-Wesley, Boston, MA., 2002.
11. Gamma, E., Helm, R., Johnson, R., Vlissedes J., *Design Patterns*, Addison-Wesley, Boston MA., 1995.

XP with Acceptance-Test Driven Development: A Rewrite Project for a Resource Optimization System

Johan Andersson, Geoff Bache, and Peter Sutton

Carmen Systems AB, Odinsgatan 9, SE-41103 Göteborg, Sweden
geoff.bache@carmensystems.com

Abstract. In his recent book "Test-Driven Development" [1], Kent Beck describes briefly the concept of "Acceptance-Test Driven Development", and is broadly sceptical to whether it will work. After a successful project that used this technique, we wish to argue in favour of it and the TextTest [7] tool that we have built up around it. We have found that a working XP process can be built based around using only automated acceptance tests, and not doing any unit testing. In this paper we explain and analyse our XP process, its strengths and limitations, and by doing so we hope to inspire others to try and make it work for their projects too.

1 The Project

Carmen Systems has been producing planning systems for the airline and railway industries since 1994. By 2000 the C source code for one of the products was showing signs of becoming increasing difficult to maintain. After some consideration the decision was taken in 2001 to rewrite rather than to refactor the code, re-using the code base of another Carmen product written in C++. Therefore a team was created consisting of four software engineers and one product manager (acting as the customer). The team worked for over a year with the challenge of both capturing the behaviour of the legacy system and dramatically improving its run time speed. We used a process that was heavily based on eXtreme Programming.

2 The Process

2.1 Description

On most points we have followed XP fairly faithfully, but in certain aspects we have differed. These practices were followed more or less as described in Extreme Programming Explained [2]:

- 2-week iterations following the Planning Game
- Daily stand-up meetings
- Pair programming mandatory for all production code

M. Marchesi and G. Succi (Eds.): XP 2003, LNCS 2675, pp. 180–188, 2003.
© Springer-Verlag Berlin Heidelberg 2003

- Simple Design
- Refactoring
- Integration several times a day
- Coding standards
- Collective ownership of all code
- 40-hour week (in keeping with Swedish working culture!)
- Co-location (in adjacent 2-person offices)

At this point the enthusiasts count up and work out that four of the twelve practices remain. Here our process differed from Extreme Programming as you know it.

On-site customer – as a product company we have many customers, and this role hence became an internal one fulfilled by the product manager. His job as customer was to establish the requirements based on what the old system did, provide a rough priority order so that it could be implemented incrementally and also liaise with the real customers about needed improvements and features that could be dropped.

Metaphor – The legacy system served fairly well as a replacement for a metaphor

Testing – This was based entirely upon acceptance tests written by the "customer" and a story was not regarded as done until he signed off the test as working correctly. Acceptance tests had to run flawlessly before development could continue - 100% or bust, unit-test style. Unit testing itself was not used at all.

Small releases – really became continuous releases because of the way we did testing. The philosophy was that we pretended the system was in production with all features implemented so far at all times. Note that this refers to "internal releases" due to the fact that the customer was an internal role. "External release" only occurred relatively late in the project when the system was as good as the one it was trying to replace.

And then we added some entirely new practices...

Diagnostic debugging – We implemented a logging framework in the spirit of log4j [4], which allowed permanent debugging statements to describe in detail what particular modules were doing. These module diagnostics could be easily enabled independently of each other, and provided the fine-grained analysis we needed in the absence of unit tests.

Usage-First Design – We simulated Test-First Design by insisting that new code was always written "usage-first". This means that if a new class was required, we would first pretend it existed and write the code that would use it. Only when we were happy with this usage code would we attempt to implement the class.

2.2   How the Process Came about

We evaluated several development methodologies including the Rational Unified Process and XP, and the consensus proved heavily in favour of XP or something like it.

However, a certain amount of process-related activities, chiefly the testing approach and the emphasis on diagnostic debugging, came with the product whose codebase we re-used. As these approaches had been working well there, a decision was also taken to continue with them for the moment and to work on adopting other aspects of XP, with the expectation that we would change over when these aspects became our worst problem.

However, as time went on, the conviction that we had a process that worked really well grew, and these aspects have therefore stayed. We made a brief experiment at working with unit tests and CppUnit [5], but this felt to everyone involved like it was slowing us down rather than speeding us up, so it was abandoned.

By the end of 2002 the project was a success with the software in use at several major airlines with more to follow. The development team has now grown to eight software engineers and has moved on to work with other Carmen software products, using the same process.

2.3   Frequently Asked Questions

The practice of using Acceptance Tests alone was described in our XP2002 Practitioner's Report [6]. Space there did not really allow us to expand fully, and we received many questions at last year's conference on the subject. Here, then, is a description based on the most common questions.

1. *How did the customer manage to write acceptance tests?*
   The process is something like this: he finds appropriate input data for testing the feature in question and informs the developers of broadly what he expects it to do. They go off and implement it. When they have a result that satisfies them, they come back to him and show him what it does. If he isn't happy, the process iterates. If he is, that input data, along with the output and the log file produced by the program, is checked into the version-controlled test suite.

2. *How did you automate the acceptance testing?*
   The program executes in batch mode: i.e. it takes a bunch of input data (typically some flights and some crew), plans for a while, and then produces some output data (a plan). This made automating acceptance testing easy: it is fully text based. The log file and the output solution are compared using a diff tool against what it did when the customer accepted it, and any difference at all (barring process ID, timestamps etc.) is registered as failure. In addition, the performance is compared to the expected performance and failure reported if it differs by more than a preset amount (say 10%).
   Over time, our automated test suite has grown from a small, highly product-specific UNIX shell script to become a fairly sophisticated application-independent framework for this kind of testing. It is now called TextTest, is written in Python, and is (or will soon be) available for free download from Carmen's website [7]. See the Appendix (section 5) for more details.

3. *How do you get the test suite to be fast enough to run regularly?*
Insist that lots of fast tests are added to the test suite, and ask the customer not to provide large data sets (which imply long runtimes) unless they're really needed to prove that the functionality works. The tests are then run in parallel over a network using the third party load-balancing software LSF [3]. Because running all tests at every build would take too long, developers pick a time up to 15 minutes and run all tests that take less than that time, before checking in. This number depends on how radical they believe their changes are, and averages around 3-5 minutes for "normal-risk" changes. All tests that take less than 3 hours are run automatically overnight and a report generated, and any failures are the first thing to be fixed in the morning. Any tests longer than 3 hours are run only at the weekend.
In this way we maintain very short cycles in our development, and the "time-to-green-bar" is kept very low. Essentially the fastest acceptance tests are treated by the developers in a similar way to unit tests: they are run at every build and failure is treated as a sign to stop work and fix it.

4. *Doesn't it take ages to find and fix bugs without Unit Tests?*
Fortunately not, because the text-based philosophy extends to debugging, in our practice of "Diagnostic Debugging". When we need to examine some code in more detail, we write diagnostics for that code so that we can see in detail what it is doing, and these diagnostics are kept so that they can be reused in the future. Over time a large amount of these diagnostics are written, and then new diagnostics are only needed for new code.
When debugging, the first behaviour difference from the log file tells you what was going on when it went wrong, and hence which diagnostics should be enabled (note that diagnostic data, unlike logfiles and solution data, is not version-controlled, there would be way too much of it). It's then a simple matter of running the checked-in code with the diagnostics, then running the new code, and seeing in detail what has changed. Hopefully this will lead to the error. Sometimes it won't, and then we must write new diagnostics, which are checked in when the bug is fixed. To quote the log4j manual: "Debugging statements stay with the program; debugging sessions are transient." [8]

5. *Without tests being isolated from each other, surely an error can break thousands of tests at once?*
Yes it can, and frequently does. The approach then is to take the simplest, smallest test that failed and fix it. Then re-run the tests and repeat as required. So long as you don't expect that one bug will always produce exactly one test failure, it isn't a problem.

6. *Don't you miss the benefits of Test-Driven Development?*
The practice of writing unit tests before writing the code (now known as Test-Driven Development [1]) is understood to have five main benefits:

- Verification that code works
- Low-level information about test failures making debugging easier
- Design driven by tests tending to exhibit high cohesion and loose coupling ("Test-first Design")

- Predictive specification of what code will do, independent of the existence of the code itself.
- Documentation of the design

We have a testing approach that could perhaps best be described as Acceptance-Test Driven Development (ATDD)[1] in contrast to the more standard XP approach of driving development with Unit Tests. We believe that ATDD has covered and in some cases surpassed the benefits described above in our recent project. This is described in more detail below.

2.4   Comparison with Unit-Test Driven XP

Verification

Acceptance tests are written by the customer and utilise the system at a much higher level. They are thus a far stronger verification of system correctness than unit tests. Moving them into the centre of the process will therefore strengthen the verification. Of course, even when development is driven by unit tests, acceptance tests are also meant to be present as verification. However, because they are not central to the "rhythm of the process", the verification they provide is somewhat postponed at best, and in practice we believe many practitioners are relying entirely on unit tests for verification.

Refactoring

Acceptance tests are entirely independent of the design, because they do not interact with it. This means that they form a solid rock to lean on when doing refactoring. Interface-changing refactorings, as has been pointed out [9], will require the unit tests themselves to change, rendering them questionable as verification of the correctness of the refactoring, and in large numbers they will therefore exhibit a tendency to act as a brake on the mobility of the design.

Design

We have observed that the benefits described for Test-First Design - high cohesion and loose coupling - have emerged with our practice of Usage-First Design. We also feel that the pressure to isolate everything that comes with TFD is in some sense an artificial pressure, resulting in the creation of many "mock objects" [10]. Applied to extremes, it seems to lead to a system where every class which is depended on by another class will need an interface, a real version and a mock version, and we do not believe that constitutes a good design.

Isolation of classes from each other, we feel, is something that should be done when the design demands it for some reason. It is not something that should always be done up-front as an end in itself.

Help with Time-to-Error when Debugging

Debugging with easily-disabled log statements has long been advocated in various circles (e.g. [8]) and it has worked well for us. It has the advantage that effort can be spent as it is shown to be necessary rather than up-front, and also that it can be applied easily to any design, not just one of the form discussed above. This makes it much easier to apply to legacy systems, amongst other things.

Predictive Specification

A unit test makes a predictive specification about what the code will do. Applied test-first, this prediction is made before the code is written. An acceptance test may or may not: it can do anything from no prediction through vague general predictions to very precise prediction of a test.

Its verification is chiefly regressional, of course: based on the fact that program behaviour can be manually verified as correct by the Customer and then maintained unchanging indefinitely. In practice we have made use of predictive general specifications about what the system will do and not do in all tests - for example enforcing that the text "Internal Error" is never produced, that all solutions are reported as legal in the logfile, etc. We generally do not try to predict what specific tests will do before code exists: partly because our domain does not really allow solutions to the problems to be constructed by hand (which is the whole point of the software).

There is no doubt that there is a psychological aspect of being able to "test-first" (as discussed in [1]). Going in to development knowing that a test is already in place that will say immediately whether or not the behaviour is correct when the code is written gives a powerful feeling of security. We, however, understand predictive specification as a sliding scale: and verifying new features is nearly always a mixture of prediction and reaction. Up-front prediction requires effort spent on it: and we feel there comes a point when that effort is no longer justified in terms of the gain versus reacting to the behaviour when you have it. Prediction that can be applied to all conceivable tests is thus very good in terms of payback versus effort invested.

We feel that the biggest problem in software quality is usually that changes break existing behaviour. If your changes never do that, then the quality can only go up, and then you will have very good quality pretty soon.

Documentation

A unit test is a design statement. An acceptance test is a statement of the correct behaviour of the system. Therefore, it seems logical that unit tests act in some sense as design documentation, whilst acceptance tests document system behaviour.

Both of these things are of course valuable. In the absence of unit tests another way to document the design is needed: in our case we have used "Doxygen" [11], which is a Javadoc-like tool for C++.

2.5 Applicability and Limitations

The approach to testing proposed above is focussed on keeping an extremely firm control on the behaviour of the program as it is currently used in practice. For us, this has proven to be an excellent way to ensure the quality of the system stays high, while moving quickly due to not investing lots of developer effort thinking of tests up front. Of course, we cannot know how many defects exist that no customer usage has yet found: our premise is simply that it is hard to control this anyway and hence not worth investing the time trying. The evidence from the few reported defects we have from production bears this out: almost all were crashes on incorrect input to the system (and of course all resulted in a new test, so in future will result in graceful exit-with-error instead)

The fact that this approach works well for us is in some way because it is easy for us to manage and predict how the system will be used. Before it is taken into production with a major airline, a controlled implementation process will take place where we will have access to that airline's data and will know broadly what features they intend to use. This allows our "XP customer" to create tests accordingly. A company that, for example, developed "shrink-wrapped" software would be unable to do this: much more up-front effort on testing is required as many people will be using the software in unpredictable ways.

The Carmen applications and their usage are well suited to writing automated acceptance tests. There are products which are much more dependent on variations in hardware, operating system and network platform. For these, fully automated acceptance tests are not possible without replicating many of those variations, which might well be practically and economically impossible.

There are also products (such as interactive GUIs) whose natural mode of operation is not batch. The challenge of being able to re-use the technique then rests on being able to simulate the interactive part using some sort of script. Tools (such as playback tools) exist to do this, though these have a reputation of being somewhat fragile under code changes. We haven't really tried them ourselves beyond small prototypes.

As a bottom line, it can be done "by hand" by creating a scripting interface that slots in just beneath the GUI layer itself. Carmen's own user-interface team has just completed creating such an interface, though more investigation is clearly needed into the effectiveness of this.

3   Reflections

3.1   Reflections of a New Team Member (Johan Andersson)

In the autumn of 2002, Johan Andersson joined Carmen Systems and the team. Here are his reflections based on his earlier experience with XP and more traditional unit tests.

Before I joined Carmen Systems I was developing a network security product within an 8 person development team. This team had been trying to use XP as its development methodology for two years, and had been fairly successful in doing so. As this team were doing traditional unit tests, I believe I am qualified reflect on the differences in the approach of the Carmen Systems team.

Having done unit tests and Test First Design, I find the process of using acceptance tests only (with "Usage-first Design") to be an application of the

'You Ain't Gonna Need It' principle. My experience is that the vast majority of unit tests never break alone. From an error detection point of view, if a test never breaks alone it is not needed. That is, if two tests always break in unison, you need only one test. Therefore, if a broken unit test is always accompanied by a broken acceptance test, then one of them is not needed.

You could argue that having many smaller tests would help in pinpointing the cause of the error, but then you would be saying that some work now in creating these tests could possibly save some debugging work later on. I do not think that is in the spirit of XP.

In practice this speeds up the development process. The Carmen team gain this speed by sacrificing detailed failure information and checking of borderline cases in the code, as given by unit tests, while still keeping the failure indication and verification of the actually used functionality as given by the acceptance test.

3.2 Reflections from the Customer (Peter Sutton)

The customer accepts full responsibility for the behaviour of the system - even under unusual circumstances. As a result the customer gains full control over time spent developing all aspects of the system. If the customer wants the software to act in a particular way when the input data is incorrect then the customer needs to write a story specifying what that behaviour should be and provide a test case.

The advantage of this approach is that these non-functional requirements are made explicit and are prioritized along with other stories. The disadvantage is that the customer has to think of all possible things that could go wrong - an impossible job. The customer needs then to be able to accept that when something unexpected happens it is his responsibility to determine the significance of the problem and determine whether to create a new story or not. There is thus an attitude of "learn as you go" and an assumption that it will be possible to further update the software even after it has been deployed.

4 Conclusion

Given a business environment where implementation is a controlled process, and an application that runs or can be made to run in batch mode, we believe that Acceptance-Test Driven Development is an effective means of carrying out testing within an XP project. We also believe that it is within the spirit of XP, in that it is simpler and involves less effort invested up-front in the hope of a later pay-off. We hope that our success can encourage others to try out this approach.

5 Appendix – TextTest

TextTest is an application-independent configurable framework for text-based functional testing, primarily regression and performance testing, but also stress testing.

The expectation is that tests are written, run and configured using simple text files only, and that information in the file system itself is used wherever possible. It is not intended that new code should need to be written when a new test is created.

To be tested using TextTest, an application needs to be runnable from the command line using standard options and/or information in standard input. It needs to be runnable in batch mode so that fully automatic tests can be created. It also needs to produce meaningful output that is, or can be converted to, plain text. It will then use this text to monitor and control the behaviour of the application.

Structurally, it is composed of a core framework that is mainly concerned with managing and interpreting the files and directories that constitute a TextTest test suite, and a range of extendable configurations that manage how tests are run and when, which files are compared, how to create reports and so on. This allows users to write their own configurations to take advantage of local circumstances, and also provide platform specific configurations.

It is written in Python. The intention is that it will be available for free download from http://www.carmensystems.com by the time this paper is published: at least a mailing list will be set up for interested people.

References

1. Beck, K.: Test-Driven Development, page 199. Addison-Wesley, 2003.
2. Beck, K.: Extreme Programming Explained : Embrace Change. Addison-Wesley, 1999.
3. LSF is available from Platform Computing at http://www.platform.com
4. log4j can be found at http://jakarta.apache.org/log4j/. A C++ version, log4cpp, exists, but licensing difficulties meant that we were unable to use it.
5. CppUnit can be found at http://sourceforge.net/projects/cppunit/
6. Bache, G. and Bache E.: "One Suite of Automated Tests: examining the Unit/Functional divide" in Proceedings of the 3rd International Conference on Extreme Programming and Flexible Processes in Software Engineering (XP2002). Italy, 2002.
7. TextTest is free and can be found at http://www.carmensystems.com
8. http://jakarta.apache.org/log4j/docs/manual.html. The passage concerned is itself quoting Brian W. Kernigan and Rob Pike's book "The Practice of Programming"
9. van Deursen, A. and Moonen, L.: "The Video Store Revisited - Thoughts on Refactoring and Testing" in Proceedings of the 3rd International Conference on Extreme Programming and Flexible Processes in Software Engineering (XP2002). Italy, 2002.
10. Mackinnon, T., Freeman, S. and Craig, P.: Endo-Testing: Unit Testing with Mock objects, in Extreme Programming Examined. Addison-Wesley, 2001.
11. Doxygen can be found at http://www.doxygen.org

A Customer Test Generator
for Web-Based Systems

Rick Mugridge, Bruce MacDonald, and Partha Roop

University of Auckland, New Zealand
{r.mugridge,b.macdonald,p.roop}@auckland.ac.nz

Abstract. Customer (or acceptance) tests enable the customer to drive
the overall design of a required system. We introduce an approach to developing customer tests for web-based applications. The customer specifies such tests through sample web pages. A test may consist of a traversal through a sequence of HTML pages in the required system. This is
specified as a trace, defined by following prescribed links or form-submit
buttons on each of the pages of the sequence. *Isis* generates customer
tests in Java to verify that each trace occurs in a target system.

1 Introduction

Customer (or acceptance) testing is an integral part of XP, where the customer
develops a set of tests for stories before they are implemented in a system [1].

Such concrete tests serve a similar role to unit tests in driving the design,
but at the level of the overall system operating within an organisational context.
As the system evolves, the customer gains feedback on the value of the stories,
which may lead to changes in the overall design and in the details of the customer
tests.

There are several approaches to the customer testing of web-based applications. However, most suffer from the problem that the tests are not in a form
that is easy for the customer to create, understand or alter. The simplest approach is to test the application model without regard to the user interface, but
this will not pick up problems in the user interface itself, and may not be easy
for the customer to manage because it is less concrete.

Another approach is to generate XML from the application model, which is
used for testing; the XML is mapped into HTML for the user interface. However,
this approach doesn't fit well with web delivery frameworks such as Java Server
Pages [5], where the HTML pages define the structure and include references
into the underlying Java model.

Scripting customer tests of served web pages can be rather daunting, as
a single page may contain considerable detail to be checked. A trace through
many pages can require large numbers of tests, including those that check that
previously visited pages have changed only where expected. Such effort is a
disincentive to comprehensive tests being written and altered as the system
evolves.

M. Marchesi and G. Succi (Eds.): XP 2003, LNCS 2675, pp. 189–197, 2003.

Isis generates customer tests from sample web pages. Given the range of HTML editing tools available, little technical skill is required to create the customer test pages. Such pages create the very first system prototype, and allow the user to express the functionality and the layout of the pages that make up the required system.

The dynamics of the system are defined through traces, which are a traversal of a sequence of web pages. A trace is defined by following prescribed links or form-submit buttons on each of the pages of the sequence.

In the following, we use several example pages from a web-based Vacancy system for managing job vacancies. This system was developed as a year 2 Software Engineering project for Orion Systems, a local software company. A Human Resources (HR) person creates a new vacancy, specifies the extra questions that an applicant is to answer for this vacancy, and specifies ranking rules which sort applicants into various categories according to their answers. Applicants apply over the web. HR personnel can view all of the applicants for a vacancy, as well as search for candidates that match some criteria.

We begin with related work. Section 3 describes the sample web pages that *Isis* uses. Section 4 details the generation of the testing code from the sample pages. Section 5 discusses future work. Section 6 concludes.

2   Related Work

Several web testing tools provide scripting languages to specify the strings, forms, tables, and other components that are expected on a particular page, and to specify navigation from one page to the next through links and form actions.

Many of these tools will automatically provide for regression testing by gathering data on the use of an existing system and generating scripts to check that the system responds in the same manner on future occasions. But this does not help with the development of customer tests before the system is built, and such scripts can be difficult to maintain as the requirements of the system evolve.

HttpUnit [6] allows tests to be programmed in Java, emulating a web browser and providing access to pages and their components: forms, tables, sub-frames, links and text. Tables in turn have cells with embedded structure. It is simple for a programmer to write code to check that various parts of a page are present, including text, links with valid URLs, etc. It is straightforward to emulate a user entering data by setting the values of form components and then emulating the click of the submit button.

In programming tests in HttpUnit, it is necessary to write much detailed code to access and test the internal structure of web pages (tables, forms, etc). With traversal over a sequence of pages, it is especially tedious to craft the large amounts of code to do the testing. A programmer is required to specify and change the tests, which are difficult for a customer to understand.

Hieatt and Mee [7] use XML to express system operations and expected results, generating automated tests. They found XML description cumbersome, and developed a domain-specific language ESP to describe the tests. Though

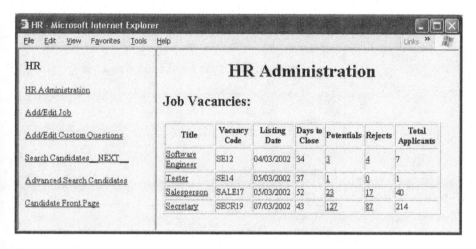

Fig. 1. First Sample Page with "__NEXT__"

complementary, we believe that this approach is less direct than ours. It will be harder for a customer to create, read and alter language-based tests as compared to managing sample web pages.

Ricca and Tonella [10][9] model the web application in UML and use white-box testing criteria to generate regression tests semi-automatically. Similarly, in Gao et al [4] an abstract behavioral model of the system is constructed, from which acceptance tests may be generated. However, these approaches are unlikely to be straightforward for a customer to use.

3 Sample Pages

Isis generates tests from sample web pages. The customer develops these web pages in HTML and chooses critical traversals through the system under development, identifying these sequences as traces.

A sample page may have multiple links and buttons for submitting forms. A link that is to be followed in a trace is simply marked with the string "__NEXT__" at the end of the link text. The corresponding link in the actual system is not marked in this way.

A submit button that is to be followed is marked with "__ENTRY__". This leads to an entry page that is the same as the first, except that the form data is updated to show what data was entered (emulating the end user's actions). The submit button on the entry page in turn is marked with the string "__NEXT__", and leads to the sample page that is expected after the submit.

For example, consider a simple traversal through three pages of the Vacancy system to search for a particular job applicant. In the required system, the end user first clicks on the *SearchCandidate* link in the left-hand frame. They fill out the form, submit it, and then see the results of the search.

Four sample pages are created by the customer, with the first as shown in Fig. 1. Here the *SearchCandidate* link is marked to signify to the customer and

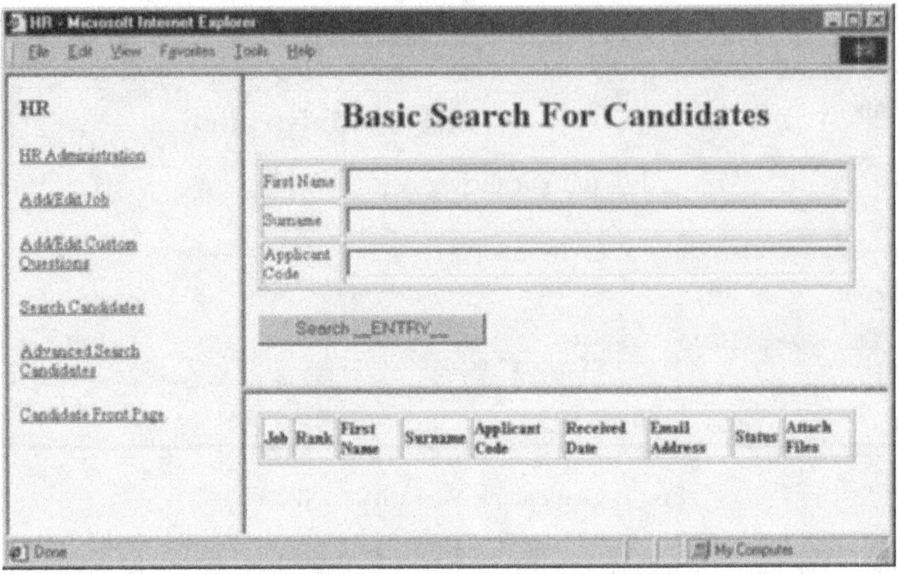

Fig. 2. Second Sample Page Prior to Data Entry

to *Isis*, for this trace, that the emulated user will first click on that link. When the customer loads the first sample page into a browser and clicks on that link, the second sample page with a form for search is loaded. Fig. 2 shows that page with the *Search* button marked.

When the customer clicks on the *Search* button, the third sample page, in Fig. 3, is shown, with the data entry in the *Surname* field already made. When the customer clicks on the *Search* button again in the third page, the fourth sample page that should result from the search is loaded, as shown in Fig. 4 (this assumes a pre-loaded database).

While there are four sample pages involved in this trace for search, the end user will see three pages in the system under test. The sample page in Fig. 3 is simply used to define the form input.

As we have shown, when a sequence of sample pages has been formed through links and submits, the customer can easily experiment with the sample system by accessing the web page files through a browser and following the various links and submits that make up the different traces. It is clear which links/buttons lead to the next step in a trace, and what data entry has been carried out with forms. Such pages act as a prototype, enabling discussion of a concrete system among customers, potential end-users and developers.

4 *Isis*

Provided with a URL for a sample page (such as for an HTML file), *Isis* generates a Java program for checking test traces against a target system.

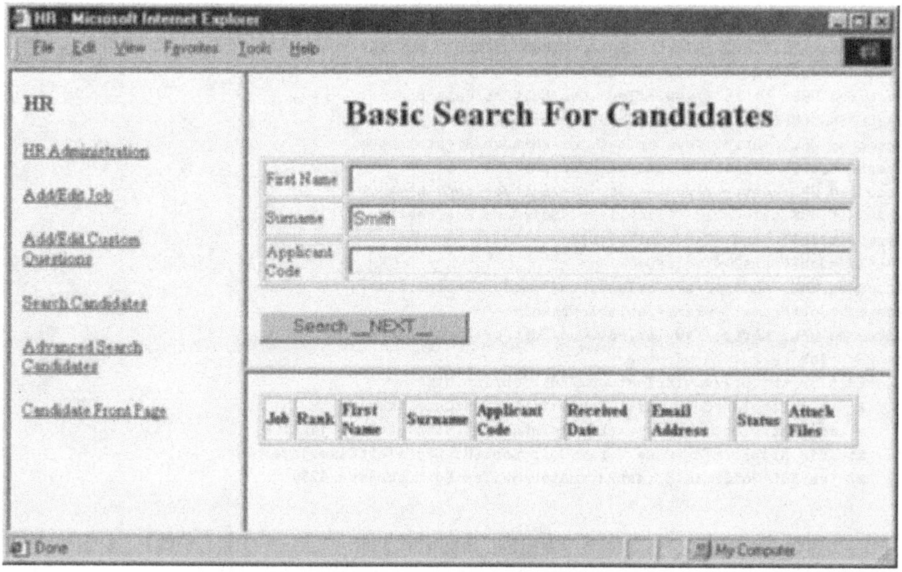

Fig. 3. Third Sample Page After Data Entry

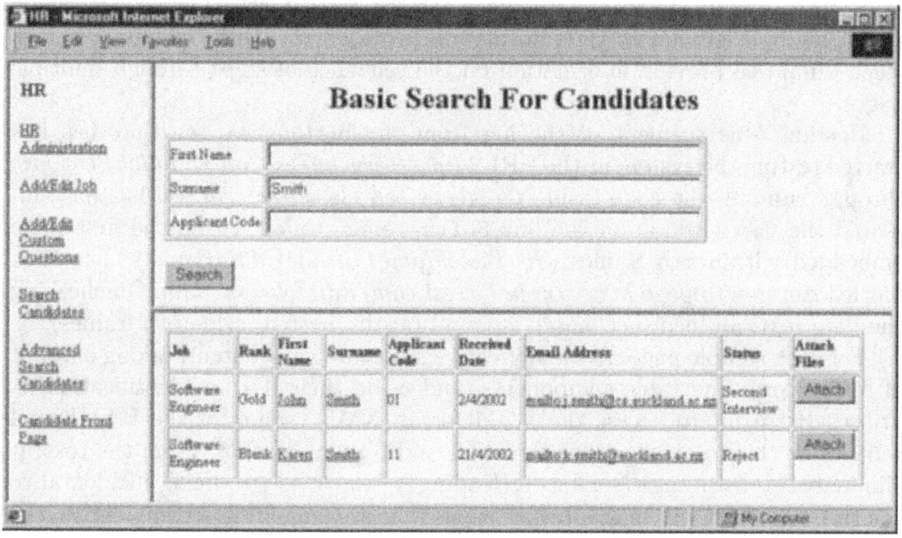

Fig. 4. Fourth Sample Page that Results from Search

When the generated program is run with a *target* URL for the system under test, it checks that the target page matches the sample and it follows each trace, checking each page along the way in the trace. Any mismatches are signalled through a log with appropriate contextual information to allow a component (eg, a table) of a web page to be identified, even though the page is one of a long sequence.

```
 . .
22) AddEditJobForm(TestEditJob$Form18)junit.framework.AssertionFailedError:
Component 'listingDateText' expected:<04/03/2002> but was:<04/03/02>
TestEditJob$Frame15 <Form:AddEditJobForm>
Accessed URL: <http://www.hrTest.com/EditJob/Data-b.htm>
TestEditJob$Frame12 <Frame<JobDataFrame-a>>
Accessed URL: <http://www.hrTest.com/EditJob/Right-a.htm>
TestEditJob$NewPage10 <Frame<MainFrame>>
Accessed URL: <http://www.hrTest.com/EditJob/top2.htm>
TestEditJob$TableCell6 <Click link:<Software Engineer>>
TestEditJob$Table4 <TableCell(1,0)>
TestEditJob$Frame2 <Table#0>
Accessed URL: <http://www.hrTest.com/EditJob/Table1.htm>
TestEditJob$Frame1 <Frame<JobTableFrame1>>
Accessed URL: <http://www.hrTest.com/EditJob/Right.htm>
TestEditJob <Frame<MainFrame>>
TestEditJob <http://www.hrTest.com/EditJob/Top.htm>
    at isis.HttpTestCase.failInContext(HttpTestCase.java:76)
    at isis.HttpTestCase.assertEqualsInContext(HttpTestCase.java:99)
    at isis.HttpFormTestCase.verifyComponent(HttpFormTestCase.java:68)
    at TestEditJob$Form18.testParameters52(TestEditJob.java:428)
    ...
```

Fig. 5. Sample Log

For example, the segment of a log in Fig. 5 shows an error that is found in some of the text on the second web page of a live system visited by Isis in a single test. The log is similar to the information provided by JUnit, including a Java stack dump, to provide information on the sequence of steps through multiple pages.

Reading this segment of the log from the bottom, we see that Isis has started testing the system at the URL *http://www.hrTest.com/EditJob/Top.htm* through running the code inside the generated class *TestEditJob*. Isis has emulated the user clicking on the link **Software Engineer** within the first table embedded within two frames (*JobTableFrame1* inside *MainFrame*). The click has led to the web page *http://www.hrTest.com/EditJob/top2.htm*. On checking the date text, an incorrect match is found (again, nested inside two frames).

For each sample page, *Isis* analyses the structure and content, taking account of frame, form and table components, and using their IDs for identification. It utilises HttpUnit to access the DOM for an XML version of the HTML and walks over this to abstract the structure and textual content. From the text, it eliminates stylistic tags (such as <Heading1> and <b>) as being incidental to the tests; hence it will match target pages that are embellished compared to the sample page.

It generates code to check that each component exists in the same structure in the target, each link exists and refers to a valid page, each form has the appropriate fields, each table has the appropriate sub-structure (such as nested tables, forms and text), and that the text exists in the sequence defined in the sample page. A complex page will result in a large number of individual tests. *Isis* utilises the link and submit button markers to generate test code that emulates the traversal and data entry of a trace and tests the pages at each step of the trace. When it finds a "__NEXT__" marker on a link in the sample page, the generated code expects to find a corresponding link in the target to follow (identified by the name of the link, without the marker).

When *Isis* finds a "__ENTRY__" marker on a submit button in a sample page, it follows the action of the corresponding form to determine the data that is to be entered when testing the target system. It generates code to set the appropriate form fields and to then "click" the submit button. *Isis* requires that the forms be named in each of the pages (and in the target pages) so that it can identify the forms appropriately.

Given that there may be multiple traces defined through a single web page, a directed acyclic graph of traces results. Each of these traces need to be tested in turn, starting from a known state of the web application.

5 Future Work

In developing the sample pages as customers, we found that it was difficult to keep them consistent. Standard HTML editors have no support for the construction of pages that have parts in common, so that the redundancy has to be handled through copy and paste or with frames. With tool support to structure pages and manage their commonality, it will be easier to create and change the sample pages.

With clearer structure, the sample pages could be used to generate and evolve parts of the required system itself, in a test-driven manner [2]. Given that the required system acts as a generalised mirror of the customer tests, any differences between a test and the system could be used to drive the alteration of either the test or the system interface, depending on which was deemed to be incorrect. This would serve an analogous role to a refactoring tool, but could only work if the incremental changes were small and thus easily identified automatically.

There is scope for improvement of *Isis* in the web page matching process. It is inconvenient to have test errors raised with every minor change to the pages of the system. But what counts as incidental for matching in one system will be significant in another. Here are some examples of structure or content that may be incidental in a page under test:

- It doesn't matter whether the text "Friday" in the head of a table is bold or not
- Extra text at the bottom of a page can be ignored
- The link text contains the string "Software" as a substring; the rest is irrelevant
- Any one of the rows in a table can match the row we're interested in; the rest are ignored
- The table structure should be ignored completely
- Expected text strings can occur in any order
- The current date on a page needs to be matched as a date, rather than as "5May2003"

We have experimented with including extra information in the sample web pages to tailor the matching, but a more general approach is needed. Rather than using HttpUnit to access some of the page components and the XML DOM for the rest, we plan to generalise the matching process for a single page and just use XML. This will allow us to avoid the need to name components, while permitting different sequencing of components between a sample and target page. It will also allow for matching of arbitrary hierarchical structures, not just web pages.

Improvements could also be made in error reporting, as textual logs are awkward to follow if there are matching errors in large traces over complex web pages. A better approach would be to add the error reports to a copy of the web pages themselves, so that they are within context. This is the approach used in FIT for table-based tests [3].

A web based system will have an infinite number of possible traces. Consider an abstraction of a web site where pages are considered to be states and links are transitions in a state transition model. An extended notion of bisimulation equivalence [8] can be employed for checking the equivalence of the sample pages and the system under test. This checking can be effectively employed to detect any missing links, invalid URLs and so on. Given such a model for a web-based system, a subset of traces for *Isis* can be generated automatically, leading to a useful combination of bisimulation checking and *Isis*.

6   Conclusions

Customer tests are a crucial element of eXtreme Programming, allowing the customer to drive the development of the overall system and providing concrete goals for the developers to meet in satisfying the stories.

Although several tools for customer testing of web pages are available, they are limited. Generally, they either require scripting expertise or an implementation of the actual system before testing can be defined. We have presented an approach to customer testing of web based systems based on sample web pages. *Isis* takes traces of sample HTML pages as input and automatically generates Java code to test whether the sequence of pages in the system under development meet the requirements implied by the sample pages.

Isis has been used by student project groups in the development of the Vacancy system. They used it to test their software against 260 sample pages that we provided as customer tests. From these pages, which largely make up short traces, *Isis* generated 13,000 individual tests for the pages served by the system under test and the traversal between them. This shows the power of this approach.

Acknowledgements

Thanks to Orion Systems for supporting the year 3 project.

References

1. K. Beck. *eXtreme Programming Explained*. Addison Wesley, 2000.
2. K. Beck. *Test Driven Development: By Example*. Addison Wesley, 2002.

3. W. Cunningham. Fit: Framework for integrated test. http://fit.c2.com/.
4. H. P. Gao, J. Samuel, J. Kung, D. Toyoshima, and Y. Chen. Behaviour-based acceptance testing of software systems. In *Annual International Computer Software and Applications Conference (COMPSAC'94)*, pages 293–298, Los Alamitos, CA, USA, 1994. IEEE Comput. Soc.
5. D. M. Geary. *Advanced JavaServer Pages*. Prentice Hall, 2001.
6. Russell Gold. HttpUnit. Opensource JAVA API for Automated Website Testing.
7. E. Hieatt and R. Mee. Going faster: Testing the web application. *IEEE Software*, March/April 2002.
8. R. Milner. *Communication and Concurrency*. Prentice Hall International, 1989.
9. F. Ricca and P. Tonella. Analysis and testing of web applications. In *23rd International Conference on Software Engineering (ICSE'01)*, pages 25–34, Los Alamitos, CA, USA, 2001. IEEE Comput. Soc.
10. F. Ricca and P. Tonella. Building a tool for analysis and testing of web applications: problems and solutions. In *Tools and Algorithms for Construction and Analysis of Systems (TACAS'01)*, volume LNCS- Vol. 2031, Berlin, Germany, 2001. Springer Verlag.

A Framework for Testing at the Edge –
An Experience Report

Alwin Ibba and Carsten Ohlemeyer

Lebensversicherung von 1871 a.G., Maximiliansplatz 5, 80333 Munich, Germany
{alwin.ibba,carsten.ohlemeyer}@lv1871.de

Abstract. We are developing an application for the insurance business in Java
and started to use JUnit for testing our application. But soon after, we discovered several areas which were hard to test. These areas were mainly on the edge
of our application like interfaces to presentation, printing and legacy systems.
In order to cover these parts with tests we developed a framework by extending
JUnit. It allows us to test servlets and JSP, struts [1], XSLFO [2] and FOP [3].
In addition we enabled the business people to write and run functional tests by
themselves. In this presentation we report from our findings developing and using this framework. We believe that most business application developers face
the same challenges and might therefore benefit from our report.

1 Introduction

We are developing an application in the insurance business using extreme programming. The application enables our insurance agents to offer individual proposals for
life insurance products for the customers.

In the course of the project we recognized the difficulties in writing unit tests for
many parts of our code. We were not able to write tests for several parts of our application, especially the XSLFO-based PDF-generator and the other XML-based technologies. Furthermore, using the available mockobjects and frameworks in order to
write tests for our servlets and struts actions we realized our test suite was getting too
slow.

Therefore, we decided to implement our own test framework that allows the developers to write well performing unit tests for all parts of our application. To write
tests for the XSLFO files it offers an XML navigator and an XML validator. The
framework consists of different components, especially factories for mockobjects and
domain objects in order to simulate the state of the application by creating all necessary session objects. To provide similar assertions as JUnit [4], our framework supplies validators for different technologies like servlets and struts.

To verify compatibility with future versions of our application the framework is
able to validate if the attributes in the persistent classes are still present.

Our framework allows to write all the tests in Java similar to regular JUnit tests.

M. Marchesi and G. Succi (Eds.): XP 2003, LNCS 2675, pp. 198–204, 2003.

In addition to the unit test framework, we implemented a framework for functional tests. We modified the FIT-framework [5] for our needs to enable the customers to specify and run their acceptance tests on their own.

2   Application

The application is entirely written in Java and was designed as a lightweight web application. It is used to govern customer- and insurance data and can be used offline on a single machine or online in a network. The common struts framework serves as the base for the presentation. We extended struts in several ways using our own `Ac-tionServlet` and some selfwritten tags. The insurance proposals as well as other data can be printed in PDF. The PDF is generated at runtime with XSLFO using FOP. Besides generating PDF at runtime we also use exisiting PDF-documents and fill in the data using FDF [6].

We store our data in an XML-based repository using the Castor [7] framework. The application runs in the Tomcat [8] server or any other J2EE compliant server.

We are using Eclipse [9] as the development environment which provides the JUnit-plugin.

3   Test Framework

Our test framework extends JUnit and provides several base classes for the different types of tests. All JUnit methods like `setUp` and `tearDown` can be used as normal. The overall base class `BaseTestCase` inherits from JUnit's `TestCase`. It contains the methods to obtain different types of factories, especially the mockobject factory and the domain object factory.

We used the mockobjects from [10] whenever possible. In many cases we had to adapt them to fit our needs. As [10] does not provide mockobjects for all technologies we use, we had to implement some on our own. The mockobjects simulate the behaviour of the servlet and struts classes. They depend on eachother, e.g. a `MockHttpSession` keeps a reference to a `MockServletContext`. The framework maintains these references. It's recommended to use the mockobjects provided by the factory in the test cases to be sure that they are up-to-date. They can be used to test struts actions as described later.

The main purpose of the domain object factory is the creation of complete domain objects and the calculation of insurance related data. Most parts of the application need the calculated data to work properly, so the domain object factory can be used to simulate a specific state of the application. The domain object factory itself uses mockobjects in order to keep all session objects up-to-date. Usually the mockobjects provided by our framework are used, but one can create own mockobjects for special purposes.

The following sample demonstrates the use of the domain object factory:

```
public void setUp()
{
    DomainObjectFactory objFactory = getDomainObjectFactory();
    objFactory.createProduct(Products.TYPE_R1);
        objFactory.calculateProductInSession();
        product = objFactory.getProductFromSession();
}
```

4   XSL Tests

The `BaseXMLTestCase` class is used for the XML tests and inherits from `BaseTestCase`.

The main purpose of the XML test class is to test the XSLFO files. An XSL transformation generates these files by applying some business logic. To test this logic, the desired state of the application is prepared by the domain object factory. Next, the XSL transformation is performed resulting in an XSLFO stream that can be used as input for our XML test framework. It is desirable to refactor the XSLFO generation by extracting the business logic from XSL and implement it using Java. To enable this refactoring, XSLFO tests are mandatory.

Our XML test framework can be used to test any XML structure, provided that the structure consists of wellformed XML and therefore is parsable by XML parsers. Some parsers allow the plugin of special filters to parse files that are not wellformed. An example is JSP, which is usually not wellformed. With the filters it is possible to parse JSP and use it as an input for our framework. This approach enables us to test JSP.

In order to use the framework, one has to deliver an XML stream. Our framework parses the stream and creates a navigator instance that can be used to step through the XML structure. Navigation can be done in an absolute manner using any matching criteria of a tag block, e.g. an ID or the like. It is also possible to navigate in a relative manner, using for example a number of steps from the beginning of any matching tag.

To verify a block, the validator can be used to check tag names, attribute names and values, tag content and any specified test criteria. If a test fails, the validator throws an exception similar to the other validators.

The following code snippet is an example how to use the framework. It does not show the `setUp` method, which contains the code for creating the domain objects and for generation of the XSLFO:

```
public void testSalutation()
{
    assuredPerson.setTitle(Titles.DR);
    assuredPerson.setLastName("Miller");
    Element element = navigator.findElementByName("salutationId");
    navigator.setCurrentElement(element);
    navigator.setNextChild();
    validator.verifyCurrentElementTextContains("Dear Dr. Miller");
}
```

XML schematron [11] is an alternative to our framework. XML schematron is a pure XML based approach, i.e. the tests itself are written in XML. Our solution makes it is easier to adapt to application specific needs by implementing search and test criterias. In order to create the XSLFO output, we need domain objects and the corresponding calculation results. This is done in Java, thus it is much easier to implement the XML tests in Java as well. Furthermore our approach is much faster than pure XML solutions, because we do not need to parse test cases written in XML and we do not need to switch between Java based business logic and XML based tests.

5   FDF Tests

FDF [6] is a technology that can be used to fill in data in PDF documents programmatically. We use the FDF-Toolkit [12] from Adobe to fill our existing proposal documents with the user data.

The fieldnames provided in Java must match the fields in the PDF document. It is desirable to test this error-prone procedure by comparing the fields in Java and PDF in order to report any discrepancies. We are currently working on a solution doing this.

It is not possible to export all specified fields in the PDF document with the FDF-toolkit or the other Adobe PDF-Tools. So we have to parse the PDF document on our own and extract all the fields. The open source PDF parser from [13] would be the right choice doing this. We haven't integrated the FDF feature in our test framework yet, but we plan to do so in a future version.

6   Struts Tests

The struts tests are performed by the `BaseStrutsTestCase` class extended from `BaseTestCase`. It can be used similar to the `StrutsTestCase` framework [14] but uses a different approach. Instead of reading the strutsconfig-file and preparing a request for the real `ActionServlet`, it creates an instance of the action class and the appropriate form bean. Our framework uses the mockobject factory and the domain object factory for preparing the state of the application and simulates the mechanism of struts by populating the request parameters directly.

This approach is much faster than the mechanism used by the `StrutsTestCase` framework. Furthermore all mockobjects and the form bean can be manipulated during the test execution. It is even possible to provide own implementations of mockobjects for some tests, which is not possible with the `StrutsTestCase` framework.

The purpose of `BaseStrutsTestCase` is to test one action or one form bean. It is not meant to test the correctness and consistency of the strutsconfig-file. There are other ways to do this, namely the XML-Framework described above.

The `BaseStrutsTestCase` can be used to obtain a struts validator that contains methods to verify the execution of the action. The result and the action errors can be accessed, manipulated and verified. In case of an error the framework throws an exception similar to `StrutsTestCase`.

Our framework can be used to test a form bean without the creation of an action simply by providing the necessary request parameters and calling the appropriate test methods.

The following code sample is an example how to use `BaseStrutsTestCase`. If you are familiar with the `StrutsTestCase` framework you can see that it is similar to use:

```
public void testPopulateAction()
{
addRequestParameter("entryDate", "ABC");
actionPerform(PopulateAction.class,MainForm.class);
    verifyActionErrorPresent("error.date.format");
verifyForward("failure");
addRequestParameter("entryDate", "12.12.1999");
actionPerform(PopulateAction.class,MainForm.class);
verifyForward("success");
}
```

7   Reference Tests

Our reference test framework is used to test the compatibility of different versions. It is actually a framework for regression tests. All the work is done by the class `BaseReferenceTest`. Each release we create reference files with all properties of the domain objects. The framework checks the compatibilty of the current version against the referential version.

A short snippet of a reference file may look like this:

```
#de.lv1871.model.KL2
#Thu Dec 12 11:27:11 GMT+01:00 2002
entryDate=de.lv1871.common.Date
name=java.lang.String
additionalData=de.lv1871.model.AdditionalData
timeLastSaved=java.lang.Long
```

However sometimes, it maybe necessary to change the referential version and develop a migration mechanism. Migration has not been considered yet in the reference test framework. So the framework has to be extended to fit these migration needs.

8   Acceptance Tests

"Our goal is to facilitate cooperation between customers, testers and developers who share the values of communication, simplicity, feedback and courage. " [5]

We implemented an acceptance test framework to ensure that the customers can write their own complex test cases which verify the implementation without the help of the developers. They fill in a spreadsheet providing all input data and expected output values.

Therefore we adapted the FIT-framework. The FIT-framework is described at [5]. It takes input values and expected results from HTML-tables. The values in the table are passed to fixture classes which perform an operation or calculation and return the result. The result is compared with the expected value from the HTML-table. The output is an HTML-page with green marks for good tests and red ones in case of failure.

Our extension takes Excel spreadsheets as input, convert them to HTML and performs the fixture test. We ensure that the values are passed to the corresponding domain objects, the calculation is started and the results are compared to the expected output values.

For better support of our customers we developed a separate web application which allows to upload and run the test spreadsheets. Results are published as an HTML page.

The following screenshot shows the mainpage of our FIT web application:

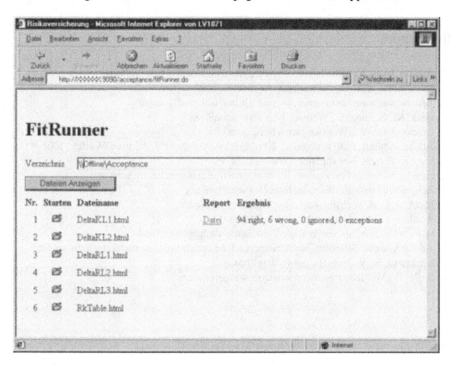

9   Conclusion

Our application consists of several parts containing business logic. In order to test this logic we had to write a framework. The main advantage of our framework is its performance. We found it valuable to have a well performing test suite. A slow running test suite is a disadvantage which should not be underestimated: developers tend to skip executing the test run, if it is too slow.

Our framework is similar to JUnit and all tests can be developed in the same way. This makes it easy to use and encourages developers to write tests.

The acceptance tests ensure the involvement of the business people, especially if they can modify and run their tests by themselves.

10   About the Authors

Alwin Ibba is a developer in the XP team with several years of experience in software development. He specialized in web based technologies and frameworks in the J2EE environment.

Dr. Carsten Ohlemeyer is a team leader in the LV1871 and has been developing insurance applications for 3 years.

References

1. Apache Software Foundation, Website, http://jakarta.apache.org/struts
2. Pawson, D., XSL-FO, O'Reilly & Associates, 2002
3. Apache Software Foundation, Website, http://xml.apache.org/fop
4. Beck, K., Gamma, E., Website, http://www.junit.org
5. Cunningham, W., Website, http://fit.c2.com
6. Adobe Systems, PDF Reference, Third Edition, Version 1.4, Addison-Wesley, 2001
7. ExoLab Group, Website, http://www.castor.org
8. Apache Software Foundation, Website, http://jakarta.apache.org/tomcat
9. Eclipse Consortium, Website, http://www.eclipse.org
10. Mock Objects, Website, http://www.mockobjects.com
11. Academia Sinica Computing Centre,Website, http://www.ascc.net/xml/resource/schematron/schematron.html
12. Adobe Systems, Website, http://partners.adobe.com/asn/developer/acrosdk/forms.html
13. Litchfield, B., Website, http://www.pdfbox.org
14. Seale, D., Website, http://strutstestcase.sourceforge.net

An Empirical Analysis on the Discontinuous Use of Pair Programming

Andrea Janes, Barbara Russo, Paolo Zuliani, and Giancarlo Succi

Center for Applied Software Engineering, Faculty of Computer Science
Free University of Bolzano-Bozen, Dominikanerplatz 3 Piazza Domenicani
I-39100 Bozen, Italy
Giancarlo.Succi@unibz.it

Abstract. Pair Programming has been shown to increase communication and teamwork skills and to provide better code. The aim of this work is to show the efficacy of Pair Programming in transferring knowledge and skills over an environment where people met only occasionally. In a quasi experiment, we find that Pair Programming is effective in sharing knowledge among 15 students who met once a week for a half day, and did their internship individually or in couple for the remaining 4 half days.

1 Introduction

Pair programming has usually considered non effective for distributed teams, not working most of the time together ([3], [4], and [8]). In this paper we discuss the effectiveness of Pair Programming at transferring knowledge and skills among students that met only occasionally and worked mostly independently.

The effect of geographical distance between pair programmers has been already addressed by Baheti *et al.* ([5]). They performed an experiment on a graduate class to assess whether it is feasible to use distributed PP to develop software. It turned out that distributed (i.e., geographically distant) pair programming teams can effectively develop software, that is, with productivity (in terms of LOC/hr) and code quality (in terms of grade awarded to the project developed) comparable to those of close-knit teams.

Kircher *et al.* ([2]) identify the aspects of XP which require co-located programming teams. The authors analyze these aspects in the distributed development of software for collaborative productivity. They found that the effectiveness warranted by physical proximity could not be completely substituted by any communication tool, though various combinations turned out to be quite effective. However, their findings are based only on the personal opinions of the participants, the authors themselves, and no empirical evidence is provided.

We report on the experience of a group of fifteen students doing a summer internship experience at the end of their first year of a first degree in Applied Computer Science at the Free University of Bolzano-Bozen (Italy). For three months students worked either in companies or research centers the whole week but Friday afternoons, when they met altogether in a university laboratory. Here, they worked on a different

M. Marchesi and G. Succi (Eds.): XP 2003, LNCS 2675, pp. 205–214, 2003.

project using PP. Our aim was to monitor the knowledge they acquired from such a structured context. Even if such an environment is not distributed in the genuine sense of the term, similar factors may affect the success of the project. Indeed problems with non-continuous use of the same software practices, difference of environments and requests and geographic distance can be equally experienced.

This paper is organized as follows. In Section 2 there is a discussion of the structure of the experiment, including a GQM schema, the questionnaire used to gather the data, the description of the sample and of the environment. In Section 3 there is a presentation of the results, with specific analysis of the effectiveness of communication tools, of pair programming as a vehicle for knowledge transfer. In Section 4 we draw some conclusions.

2   Structure of the Experiment

As mentioned, this research deals with a group of fifteen (volunteer) students doing a three-month summer internship.

Eleven students worked in local companies for all the working days but Friday afternoons, when all of them met in a university laboratory for four hours to share their experience. A group of four students worked for a research center of the Faculty - joining the others on Friday afternoons.

The environment was distributed in the sense that the students had the chance to work together only one afternoon per week, spending the rest of the week working in geographically distant places.

In the Friday afternoon meetings all the students had the possibility to share their knowledge and skills by developing software using Pair Programming. This work was completely independent from what they were doing over the rest of the week. In all the companies there were no special indications to use Extreme Programming practices except for students working for the university lab, where XP was continuously adopted.

Altogether, the use of Pair Programming was non-continuous – only on Friday afternoons – and alternated with other coding styles.

At the end of their experience students answered to a questionnaire.

2.1   GQM of the Experiment

To properly structure the experiment, we use the well known Goal-Questions-Metrics (GQM) paradigm ([6]) according to the guidelines of [7]:

Goal:
- Monitoring skills acquired in using PP in order to investigate:
- Knowledge transfer
- Effectiveness of a non continuous PP practice - alternated with a different programming methodology
- Integration of XP skills learned at University and practices acquired during an industrial internship

Questions:
- How much effective is the use of PP in transferring knowledge in a distributed environment?
- How much effective is PP in a non temporary continuous work alternated with other practices?
- How much effective is the use of PP in integrating University studies and applicative practices of a company of an industrial environment?

Metrics:
- Final questionnaire

2.2   Structure of the Questionnaire

The final questionnaire was developed according to standard questionnaire-writing styles. It consisted of three main parts: the first described the student's status – work experience and skills, the second dealt with the Internship experience and the third reported the students' opinion on the PP style. The questionnaire was structured by several multi-choice questions alternated with some rating and free-style questions. It covered topics listed in Table 1.

Table 1. Main subjects of the questionnaire

Topics		
1.	General work experience	7. Internship: Communication tools
2.	Skills in Computer Science	8. Internship: PP Best Aspect
3.	Skills in some PP features	9. Internship: Benefits
4.	Internship: Project knowledge	10. Evaluation PP: Hardest Thing
5.	Internship: Project structure	11. Evaluation PP: Non Effectiveness
6.	Internship: Project support	12. Evaluation PP: Most Important Aspect

In the first three points of Table 1, the student's work experience in computer science is evaluated. It was measured by common questions on work experience and on some aspects of team working.

Points 4 to 9 of Table 1 describe the environment of the internship. Point 4 focuses on what of the project was known before the Internship experience, such as tools (NetBeans, …), languages (Java, PHP, …) and approach to the problem - how to translate requirements into code.

To evaluate the students' degree of comprehension of the project, point 5, 6 and 7 asked students to describe the project – structure, and technical and human support – and the communication tools they used during the experience.

Points 8 and 9 measured the PP practice rooted in the students' experience, while points 10 to 12 asked students to give an opinion on the PP style independently from the project.

In Table 2 we reproduce the acronyms of the measures. Besides each acronym we put the reference number of Table 1. Points 8, 10 and 12 were in the form of free-style questions, so they are not included in Table 2.

Table 2. Acronyms of measures

1-2	WS	Working student
	WE	Work experience
	WECS	Work Experience in Computer Science
	WTE	Experience in Working in Team
	WPE	Experience in Working in Pair
	PPW	If WPE: Is Pair Programming worth?
3	PSC	Experience in working in pair sharing the same computer
	SC	Experience in working on the same code
	WD	Experience in work division
	SE	Experience in sharing experience
4	TL	Project Tools knowledge
	PA	Knowledge on how to translate requirements in code – Problem Approach
5	SP	Switched partner more than two times
6	CP	Customer's physical presence
	PS	Reference Instructor's technical support
7	T	Use of Telephone
	NM	Use of NetMeeting
	IM	Use of Instant Messenger
	EM	Use of e-mail
9	LC	Increasing Learning and Comprehension
	CT	Increasing Communication and Team working
	TM	Increasing Time Management
	OE	Increasing Opportunity of experimentations
	SR	Increasing Self-Reliance
	PSST	Increasing Problem Solving and Strategy Thinking
11	SAFYC	The use of PP is not effective Soon After a First Year Course
	STE	The use of PP is not effective for a Short Experience
	BPEC	The use of PP is not effective if Both Partners are not Equally Competent
	PU	The use of PP is not effective if the Project is Unknown

2.3   Details on the Sample

In this section we characterize our sample by studying the answers to the first part of the questionnaire and the cross-correlations among them.

Fifteen students volunteered for this project. Eleven were full-time students with some previous work experience, while four were part-time students (with part-time jobs). In Table 3 we report the frequencies for the answers of the questionnaire regarding the students' previous skills and knowledge. The frequencies are based on a sample of size fourteen, as one questionnaire was not returned. Frequencies, Pearson's cross-correlation coefficients and p-significance (as usual, we consider $\alpha < 0.05$) are calculated using SPSS, a well-known statistical tool.

We also note that the sample of the PPW variable has size five, that is, the number of students who answered "yes" to the "Experience in Working in Pair" (WPE) question.

Table 3. Frequencies of the previous skills and knowledge of the sample

(%)	General working experience (1-2)					
	WS	WE	WECS	WTE	WPE	PPW
no	71.4%	14.3%	64.3%	42.9%	64.3%	20%
yes	28.6%	85.7%	35.7%	57.1%	35.7%	80%
n/a	0%	0%	0%	0%	0%	0%
(%)	PP aspects experience (3)				Project Knowledge (4)	
	PSC	SC	WD	SE	TL	PA
no	50%	57.1%	14.3%	28.6%	28.6%	21.4%
yes	35.7%	28.6%	71.4%	57.1%	71.4%	78.6%
n/a	14.3%	14.3%	14.3%	14.3%	0%	0%

Table 4. Correlations between different aspects of students' know how

	WTE	WECS	CP	PSC	SC	WD
WS		0.85 p=0.000				
WE	0.57 p=0.032					
PSC			0.60 p=0.023		0.92 p=0.000	
WD				0.77 p=0.001	0.74 p=0.002	
SE				0.69 p=0.007	0.64 p=0.015	0.88 p=0.000
WPE				0.65 p=0.012	0.53 p=0.050	

From Table 3, we can infer that the majority of the students had a previous work experience (WE), a few of them in Computer Science (WECS). More than 70% had a good knowledge of the project they were going to start (see TL, PA in Table 3). Some students (WPE 35.7%) had already practiced PP in the past, and most of them found it worth (PPW 80%). Students with work experience (WE) have more experience in teamwork (WTE) than working in pair (WPE).

The cross-correlations resulting from the first part of the questionnaire (Table 4) confirm the students' curricula. Again, we see that students' work experience is mainly in computer science. General team working has a good correlation with work experience.

From Table 4 we may infer that students who experienced a general work in pair, know and appreciate the PP practice in some of its aspects – "Experience in working in pair sharing the same computer" (PSC) and "Experience in working on the same code" (SC).

Table 4 also shows that the four different aspects of PP are each other correlated. This might mean that students had a somehow "homogeneous" experience of PP (i.e. they did not practice just one aspect).

2.4   Details on the Environment

The companies selected for the internship were mainly local businesses. Some were software houses, others non-IT organizations with an EDP department. Students selected the companies on a First-In-First-Out basis.

To take full advantage of the internship, students were introduced to the project with several seminars related to the experience they were about to begin. Different subjects were presented: legal rights and duties, role of the unions, importance of, and techniques to communicate within corporate organizations, how to secure funds to create a start-up and so on. They were also introduced to team working by role play. They were taught time and stress management, how to support a talk and how to give priorities.

At the beginning of the internship, each company assigned a task to the student. Most of the time company assignments were part of a big project already started. Since the students had attended a course on Java during the previous semesters, all of them were not only able to use Java, but also to learn new languages and tools.

A company-internal reference person was selected to act as internal "tutor" of the student. Additionally, some selected members of the Computer Science Faculty provided technical and social support to students and monitored the overall experience.

So, almost every week a member of the University staff visited the student in the company and reported on the student's situation. Reports were published on an internal web site, so each instructor could access them. Students and companies were aware of the dates of the visits in advance, so that the internal tutor could be present to the visit.

In the Friday afternoon meetings all the students gathered in a university laboratory and worked, using Pair Programming, on a project different from what they were working on in the rest of the week. Therefore, in such meetings all the students had the chance to communicate, to compare and to analyze their weekly experience, evidencing similarities and differences. In this way they had the possibility of increasing their skills by knowledge transfer.

An instructor and a "virtual customer," i.e., a faculty member acting as the customer, were always present in the room.

The Friday afternoon project was divided into independent subprojects, each assigned to a group of four students experiencing PP. They periodically switched partners in the team.

In each of the four teams there was a member of the group of students working for the CASE, i.e., a student who was experiencing PP the whole week.

3   Results

In this section we present a summary of the results of the questionnaire. We analyze the results in two parts. First, we study how communication tools were used. Second, we report on how PP was effective in transferring knowledge and skills among participants.

As usual, we only consider Pearson's correlation coefficients whose p-significance is less than 0.05.

Table 5. Use of Communication Tools

(%)	Communication Tools (7)			
	T	NM	EM	IM
no	57.1%	85.7%	21.4%	57.1%
yes	42.9%	14.3%	78.6%	42.9%
n/a	0%	0%	0%	0%

Table 6. Cross correlations between Use of Communication Tools and Knowledge of the Project

	Cross Correlation		
	TL	PA	SR
T	-0.73 p=0.003		
NM		-0.78 p=0.001	
EM		0.58 p=0.031	
IM			-0.58 p=0.031

3.1 Use of Communication Tools

The two tables below provide some understanding on the use of communication tools. The most used communication tool has been e-mail, but telephone and instant messenger were also adopted - Table 5.

The use of telephone is negatively correlated with the tools used for coding during the Internship - Table 5. This means that students used telephone when they had troubles with the software tools. In the same way we may say that NetMeeting was used by students who initially knew little on how to approach the project. The use of Instant Messenger is negatively correlated with "Self-Reliance" (SR) - Table 6. These three facts might indicate that the more students think they have increased skills, the less they use "synchronous" communication tools.

On the other hand, "Use of E-Mail" (EM) has a good correlation with the initial ability in approaching the project (PA). From this we may instead infer that students with increased skills preferred to use "asynchronous" communication tools.

To summarize, the results of this part of the questionnaire indicate that students preferred synchronous, real-time communication tools when they knew little about coding tools or problem approach, otherwise, e-mail was the most used communication tool.

3.2 Knowledge Transfer and Effectiveness of PP

In this section we assess the effectiveness of PP in transferring knowledge and skills.

We omit frequencies On Internship benefits and non effectiveness of PP, 80% of the students answered positively on each benefit listed in Table 7.a (except for the last two items, for which slightly less than 50% gave a positive answer). This entails that students actually experienced a transfer of knowledge and skills. In Table 7.b less then 50% of the students considered Pair Programming non effective whether the kind of project is unknown and even less considered Pair Programming unfeasible for a short time experience.

Table 7. Ranking internship benefits (a) and conditions for non-effectiveness of PP (b)

a. Benefits of Internship		b. Conditions for Non-Effectiveness of PP	
High	Communication (CT)	**High**	Unknown project (PU)
↑	Problem solving (PSST)	↑	Experience soon after a first year course (SAFYC)
	Learning and comprehension (LC)		
	Time management (TM)		Member of pair not equally competent (BPEC)
	Self-reliance (SR)		
Low	Opportunity to experiment (OE)	**Low**	Short experience (STE)

Table 8. Cross-correlations with Internship Benefits

	PSST	OE	SP	CP	EM	IM	STE
LC	0.78 p=0.001		0.59 P=0.026				
CT				0.68 p=0.008			
TM							-0.74 p=0.002
SR						-0.58 p=0.031	
PSST		0.57 p=0.032	0.57 p=0.032				
OE						-0.55 p=0.042	

From Table 8, the two abilities "Increasing Learning and Comprehension" (LC) and "Increasing Problem Solving and Strategy Thinking" (PSST) are both correlated to each other and with "Switch partner more then two times" (SP). This might mean that switching partner more than two times during the Friday afternoon PP sessions had a good influence in increasing global comprehension of the project and maturity of the students.

"Communication and Team working" (CT) is positively related with the "Virtual Customer's physical Presence" (CP). From this we might infer that the on-site presence of the customer (one of the XP practices) influenced favorably the communication and teamwork skills of the students. This also suggests that PP should always be practiced with a strong presence of the customer.

The ability to manage time is highly and significantly negatively correlated with the non-effectiveness of a brief PP experience. By the frequency of the positive answers (72%) to "Increasing Time Management" (TM) we may infer that students think that PP helps to manage time better.

The last part of the questionnaire provided the students with the possibility of giving a personal opinion about PP independently from the project. In Table 9 we report the most significant cross-correlations between variables that we have extracted.

Table 9. Cross-correlation - Condition for non-effectiveness of Pair Programming

	SAFYC	STE	TM
SAFYC		0.64 p=0.014	
STE			-0.745 p=0.002
BPEC	0.54 p=0.046		

The correlation of "Considering the use of PP not effective soon after a first year course" (SAFYC) with "Considering the use of PP not effective for a short experience" STE and "Considering the use of PP not effective if both partners are not equally competent" (BPEC) confirm well known results on the XP practices.

By the students' answers to the free-style questions and by the individual meeting with a faculty member we inferred that at the end of the experience the students were conscious of the limitations and benefits of PP. In particular, conflict of personalities and difference in skills caused most of the problems in Pair Programming. The most common answer to the best aspect of PP has been – as students said – "two minds working on the same code". This might mean that although PP attracts students, they realize that this coding style is really involving.

To summarize, we saw that the vast majority (80%) of the students benefited from the experience in four ways: "Learning and Comprehension" (LC), "Communication and Teamwork" (CT), "Time Management" (TM) and "Problem Solving and Strategy Thinking" (PSST). We saw from Table 9 that these four benefits are correlated with PP aspects, namely "Switched partner more than twice" (SP), "Virtual Customer Presence" (CP) and "Use of PP is not effective for a short experience" (STE). From this we may infer that the benefits which participants received came from experiencing PP.

4   Conclusions

This paper aimed at investigating the effectiveness of Pair Programming as a tool for experience exchange. We performed a first analysis of the experience of a summer internship program run on a group of fifteen students. The goal was to assess the transfer of knowledge and skills when using Pair Programming (PP).

The peculiarity of this case study consisted in the kind of distributed environment and in a methodology approach in which PP was alternated with other programming styles. Most of the students worked in separate companies the whole week but Friday afternoons, when they met in a university laboratory to work on a different project using Pair Programming (there were no special indications to use PP when working for the companies).

Increased communication ability was the benefit that 92% of all the students felt to have gained. Also, the vast majority of students found their problem-solving, time management and learning abilities improved. These benefits are correlated with the practice of PP. Therefore, Pair Programming was effective at transferring knowledge and skills. We also found that the students' levels of self-reliance and project knowledge affect the use of communication tools: the more students become conscious of their abilities the less they use communication tools (and the more they think that meeting the partner once a week is enough).

Our results confirm previous empirical evidence about the benefits and the good resistance to distance hampering factors of Pair Programming. We gathered new empirical evidence which shows that PP keeps its effectiveness also when alternated with other coding styles. Our findings might be of help to people involved in the distributed development of software projects (*e.g.*, open source software), as well as to educators for planning and running programming projects with teams composed of distance-learning students.

Acknowledgements

The authors would like to thank the ESF office of the Province of South Tyrol (Italy) and its chairman, Dr. Barbara Repetto, for providing full support to the experience. The authors would also like to thank all the participating students and companies.

References

1. Kircher, M., Jain, P., Corsaro, A., Levine, D.: Distributed eXtreme Programming. Proceedings of XP2001 May (2001). Available at http://www.xp2001.org
2. Cockburn, A., Williams, L.: The Costs and Benefits of Pair Programming. In: Succi G., Marchesi M. (eds.): Extreme Programming Examined. Addison Wesley Professional (2001) 223-248
3. Williams, L., Kessler, R., Cunningham, W., Jeffries, R.: Strengthening the Case for Pair Programming. IEEE Software. 17 (2000) 19-25
4. Baheti, P., Williams, L., Gehringer, E., Stotts, D., Smith J.: Distributed Pair Programming Empirical Studies and Supporting Environments. Technical Report TR02-010 Dep. Computer Science Univ. of North Carolina at Chapel Hill 15 (2002)
5. Basili, V., Rombach, D.: The TAME Project: Towards Improvement-Oriented Software Environments. IEEE Trans. of Software Eng. 14 (6) (1988) 758-773
6. Wohlin, C., Runeson, P., Höst, M., Ohlsson, M. C., Regnell, B, Wesslén A.: Experimentation in Software Engineering: An Introduction. Kluwer Academic Publishers, December (2000)
7. Succi, G., Marchesi, M., Pedrycz, W., Williams, L.: Preliminary Analysis of the Effects of Pair Programming on Job Satisfaction. Proceedings of XP2002 May 2002. Available at http://www.xp2002.org

Pair-Programming Effect
on Developers Productivity

Sven Heiberg[1], Uuno Puus[2], Priit Salumaa[3], and Asko Seeba[4]

[1] Post-graduate student, University of Tartu
Research Engineer, Cybernetica
+372 5059627, Sven.Heiberg@cyber.ee
[2] Post-graduate student, University of Tartu
Head of Laboratory, Cybernetica
+372 5142594, Uuno.Puus@cyber.ee
[3] MSc student, University of Tartu
Software Engineering Specialist, University of Tartu
+372 55571484, Priit.Salumaa@ut.ee
[4] Post-graduate student, Helsinki University of Technology
Software Development Manager, Cybernetica
+372 5105744, Asko.Seeba@hut.fi

Abstract. This paper gives an overview of a pair-programming experiment designed to verify how pair-programming affects programmer's technical productivity. The experiment took place at the Institute of Computer Science, University of Tartu (UT), Estonia. The paper includes the problem statement, description of the experimental design, the experiment results, and a discussion about the validity of the results. During the experiment pair-programming worked well in getting early testable programming results, pair-programmers and non-pair-programmers performed with similar final results.

1 Introduction

Pair-programming is a programming technique according to which two programmers are working together on the same task behind one computer [12]. It is believed that pair-programming helps to avoid defects in the software; helps to improve the design of the software; makes developers feel more confident about their work; helps to build a development team; and supports knowledge transfer among the developers in the team. Most common objections to pair-programming are that two people doing the work of one waste time and double the project costs; two people together are not more effective than one; and sooner or later the work atmosphere is destroyed by chatting.

There have been studies to prove the efficiency of pair-programming [2,5,6,8,9,10,11,12]. The papers describing these experiments, the benefits and disadvantages of pair-programming have raised a lot of questions still not answered. The main considerations are related to generalizability of the results to real world settings and measuring the performance of pair-programmers and non-pair-programmers adequately comparably.

M. Marchesi and G. Succi (Eds.): XP 2003, LNCS 2675, pp. 215–224, 2003.

Authors of the paper have started another experiment with a primary goal to investigate the pair-programming, and with the secondary goal to eliminate the problem of inadequate measurement and as such provide a basis for replication experiments that eliminate generalization problems. The experiment objectives are the following:

- To experience the effect of pair-programming.
- To find out what the usefulness of pair-programming might mean, that is what aspects of the software projects could be improved in terms of technical productivity by pair-programming.
- To explore the ideas about under what circumstances pair-programming could be applicable in real projects in real world.
- To study empirical research methods in software engineering.

2   Experimental Design

The goal of the experiment is to find out what kind of influence pair-programming has on the technical productivity of the developers. In other words the goal is to find out whether two people behind one computer have different technical productivity than two people behind two computers, and if yes, then what is the difference. *Technical productivity of developers stated by the experiment team, is measured as percentage of correctly implemented test-cases during the given time.*

So, the more precise statement of the goal for experiment is to test the following **hypothesis**: *The programmers using pair-programming technique have higher technical productivity than the programmers using traditional teamwork techniques.*

In addition to the main goal the experiment has also an exploratory nature. The experiment team gathered data about satisfaction with the programming technique, and tested the personalities of test subjects. The goal is to discover the unknown relations between personalities, productivity and attitudes towards pair-programming.

2.1   Structure of the Experiment

The experiment was set up at the Institute of Computer Science, University of Tartu (UT), Estonia. The subjects of the experiment were initially c.a. 110 students of the spring term 2002 Object-Oriented Programming course at UT. They were mostly first year students, having very little experience of teamwork and even programming, but they had taken Java Programming at least for one semester.

The experiment had factorial design [7]. Students were divided to groups A and B, and into pairs inside the groups. All the pairs got the same exercise. Pairs of the group A solved the exercise using the pair-programming technique, pairs of the group B solved the exercise using the traditional teamwork techniques.

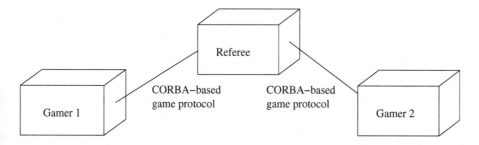

Fig. 1. A game environment

The groups A and B and the pairs were generated randomly. The first phase (*Phase 1*) lasted for two practice sessions, once a week.

At the beginning of the second phase (*Phase 2*) both groups were re-divided into pairs – each programmer got randomly a new partner from the same group. The composition of the groups A and B remained unchanged but this time the pairs in group A used traditional technique and the pairs in group B used pair-programming. All pairs received new exercise that again was the same for every pair.

To ensure that all teams have the same basic understanding about software development process a set of guidelines was produced for the pairs. This set of guidelines consisted of the description of level 0 Collaborative Software Process [11] for pair programmers and the modification of it for non-pair-programming. The modification contained the same basic steps – design, coding, testing – but excluded the pair-programming specific parts of the process.

In the last session of both phases the subjects had to fill in a questionnaire that contained quantitative and qualitative questions about their attitude towards their working style (pair vs. non-pair), partner, result and experiment.

2.2 Programming Task for Participants

All the teams had to solve the same exercise – implementing a component with pre-defined CORBA interface for a larger system – a referee for a strategy game environment. In this environment two gaming programs (*gamers*) can play a predefined strategy game with a rule-checking program (*referee*) as a mediator (see Fig. 1).

Two gamers connect the referee. A gamer sends its move to the referee according to *game protocol*, the referee checks the rules and forwards the move to the other gamer or decides that the game is over for some reason.

The students were responsible for creating the rule-checking referees in the *Phase 1* and the protocol implementations in the *Phase 2*. The experiment team prepared an interactive gamer for testing. As a proof of concept the experiment team also prepared a demo-referee with protocol implementation.

To be able to measure technical productivity a testing environment was developed by experiment team. Requirements were translated into automated test cases, which were used to evaluate the quality of the solution. Testing environment (*tester*) consists of a program simulating two gamer programs. This tester has a database of tests that consist of series of moves presented to the referee. The answers of the referee are validated automatically. The results are also stored in the database for analysis. Tests cover both valid and invalid game situations according to the game rules and communication protocol.

During the coding the experiment subjects had access to test-database through their supervisors. They could improve their implementations according to the information they received by continuously verifying their solution with the pre-implemented tests. As one may notice, it partially resembles XP test-first approach but also differs – tests were not implemented by students themselves but by experiment conductors prior to the coding. So the tests were a part of requirements specification together with documentation describing game protocol and rules.

One may ask, why the test-first approach was distorted such a way. The answer is that actually the aim of experiment was not to study the test-first approach, but certain traits of pair-programming, and the preimplemented tests were tools for measuring the experimental results on some unified basis.

It was decided to let students program the referee, not gamer, because of the following reasons:

1. The creation of automatic gamers would require a lot of creative work in designing the gamers AI. It is very likely that the creative work would resemble the pair-programming by all the teams. This would make the measuring of technical productivity difficult, because it would make it hard to differentiate between experimental group and control group.
2. The tasks of the referee are very clear and it is easy to create automatic testing system to validate whether the referee is behaving correctly or not.

3   Current State and First Conclusions

The active phase of the experiment is over and there are already some known results, but some data is not analyzed yet.

3.1   Productivity in General

Numerical Data. The numerical data about productivity collected during the experiment is represented in the Table 1.

The table represents data about answers to two questions:

Q1: *How many solutions provided by pairs in given group satisfy any test cases at all?* Answer is given as percentage from total number of pairs in this group.

Q2: *What is the average percentage of satisfied test cases per pair in given group?*

Table 1. Numerical data about productivity collected during the experiment

		Phase 1		Phase 2	
		Sess. 1	Sess. 2	Sess. 1	Sess. 2
Q1	pp	43,5%	73,9%	18,0%	62,5%
	np	26,3%	78,9%	0,0%	47,1%
Q2	pp	14,9%	66,1%	2,2%	24,7%
	np	8,0%	72,7%	0,0%	25,0%
#pairs		19np, 23pp		17np, 16pp	
#tests		78 test cases		79 test cases	

Answers for both questions are grouped by experiment phases (*Phase 1, Phase 2*), practice sessions (*Sess 1, Sess 2*) and programming technique (*np* – non-pair-programming, *pp* – pair-programming).

The last row of the table represents the number of pairs and the number of test cases in both phases (less pairs in *Phase 2* means that some students dropped out during the course).

First Conclusions. Let us assume that the experiment is internally valid. *Experiment is internally valid* when the differences in results of experimental and control group are caused by differences in controlled treatment variable, not anything else [1]. Then we can verify that *pair-programming works well in getting early testable programming results* – in first session of

- *Phase 1* 1.7 times more pair-programmers passed first test cases than non-pair-programmers.
- *Phase 1* the average number of passed tests-cases per pair was 1.9 times higher at pair-programmers.
- *Phase 2* non-pair-programmers passed no test-cases.

At first glance the table may indicate some difference in results of first sessions of both phases, but actually there are no statistically significant differences between behavior of pair-programmers and non-pair-programmers because of "bad" distribution of raw data. This statement is based on the classical statistical significance test (Mann-Whitney-Wilcoxon rank test [4]) where the probability of result being wrong is 0.05. This means that *the results of pair-programmers and non-pair-programmers are statistically equivalent (at significance level 0.05)*.

Although the excercises differed in two phases and there was one more test case in *Phase 2*, we can basically concatenate the results of two phases. In this case, if we would ease off the significance level from 0.05 to 0.1, the difference would be significant for the result of the first session of the phases – pair programmers were better after first week.

The possible explanation for better results of pair-programmers at the end of the first session, and not considerably different results at the end of the second session is that non-pair-programmers had to do more pre-programming design work and task splitting to get started, and if well done, they would catch up pair-programmers. Although the experiment does not support the stated hypothesis, the important statistically significant positive result is that *pair-programming is not less productive, than non-pair-programming.*

Experiment is externally valid if the obtained results can be extrapolated to situations outside the experiment [1]. If we could assume also some degree of external validity, the finding that pair-programming gets first results earlier might make it a good technique to use in iterative development, where early delivered testable functionality is vital. Care must be taken in such extrapolating because the catch-up by non-pair-programmers suggests also, that with longer time schedule they might pass pair-programmers.

3.2   Personality Findings

It is possible to study two perspectives about relationship of programmers personalities and pair-programming effects:

1. How the personality of a single person affects the results of using pair-programming in general?
2. How the combination of personalities in a single pair affects the results of using pair-programming?

In current paper the first perspective is addressed. Studying the second perspective is planned for future work. In dealing with the first perspective the authors of the paper have stated three practical questions:

Q1: Project manager has a project where pair-programming is used as a general practice. He/she has to compose the team and has given the pool of applicants from where to select the programmers who perform well in pair-programming setting. The question about non-pair-programming performance is not important. The concluding technical question for studying the personalities is thus *what are the personalities of the programmers who perform well in pair-programming setting.*

Q2: Project manager has a given development team. Now he/she has to decide which programmers should use pair-programming technique and which of them not, taking into account the programmer's individual predisposition on given programming technique. One concluding technical question for studying the personalities thus is, *what are the personalities of the programmers who perform well in pair-programming, but badly in non-pair-programming setting.*

Q3: The situation is the same as in Q2, but the second technical question according to the situation is, *what are the personalities of the programmers who perform well in non-pair-programming, but badly in pair-programming setting.*

Authors defined a person to perform well in pair-programming setting if the result of the student is above median of pair-programming results of all students, and badly if below the median. Analogously for non-pair-programming.

Table 2. Relationship of Personalities and Programming Techniques

Factor	Q1	Q2	Q3	QG
N	83	87	85	83
E	110	106	113	109
O	113	116	122	111
A	112	112	123	112
C	107	96	104	107
#subjects	20	8	13	82

For getting information about students personalities, authors used NEO PI personality questionaire [3]. This questionaire describes personality as consisting of five general factors: Neuroticism (N), Extraversion (E), Openness(O), Agreeableness (A), Conscientiousness (C).

Table 2 represents the average scores of personality tests for each question described above. The column QG gives the average scores of personality factors of all students who returned personality tests. The last row of the table shows the number of students corresponding to the conditions of the according question. To get the information for Q1, Q2 and Q3 we can consider only the students who took part in both phases. There were 50 students who satisfied that condition.

The differences in the table are statistically insignifficant, which means that the individual personality traits considered in isolation from partner's personality, does not have significant consequences to pair-programming performance in general. This does not mean that the personality does not affect the results in some specific manner, for example, in combination with partner's personality.

4   Validity of the Results

4.1   Strengths of the Experimental Design

One of the main strength in the design of this experiment is the way the measurement of programming results is arranged. The quality of solutions is measured by automated test cases and the same testing system is applied to both groups, thus eliminating any measurement bias that might exist if using human assessor(s), and giving clear and unambiguous definition for measurement process.

The experiment does not compare the productivities of pairs vs. individuals. It compares the productivities of pairs vs. pairs. As such it gives exactly the answer whether the pair-programming is more productive or not, without any additional noise caused by differences of team sizes.

The sample is quite large compared to other experiments known to authors [5], [6], [11], [12]. In *Phase 1* solutions were submitted from 42 pairs and in *Phase 2* from 33 pairs.

According to factorial design of the experiment, all subjects get both treatments – pair-programming and non-pair-programming. At the beginning of *Phase 2* each programmer also got randomly a new partner. Human behavior is often influenced by more than one factor. Factorial design enables to study more than one factor at the same time economically in terms of the number of participants and the total experimenter effort [7]. In current experiment the additional factors to study are how the pair-programming is affected by the personalities and the attitudes of the partners working together.

During designing the experiment the research team got consultation from experts of social sciences, who provided a lot of valuable information for increasing the validity of the experiment results by enhancing the experimental design.

4.2   Internal Validity Issues

Students got their tasks at the beginning of the first practice session in both phases. While there was one session per week, there was a whole week between the first and second practice session. Although the experiment team urged the students to deal with the task during practice sessions only, the students' time usage between the first and second practice session was not actually under experimenters' control. It is possible that some students solved the programming exercise at home. It might add some unanticipated factors that interact with treatment in favor of some group. If these unknown factors favored non-pair-programmers, it might explain away the catch-up by non-pair-programmers at the end of the second session. For example, it is possible that non-pair-programmers were frightened by the low results at the end of the first session, and that motivated them to solve the programming task meantime at home.

To get rid of this internal validity problem, one should arrange an experiment setup where it is very difficult, if not impossible, to solve the experimental task outside experimental environment.

4.3   External Validity Issues

The programmers were beginners. There is no firm evidence about how the results with the first-year students could be generalized to professionals. Authors of the article have found one experimenter replicating the experiment with professionals and obtaining positive results [6], but one experiment does not provide quite firm evidence.

It is also possible to explain away differences of treatment and control group results by enthusiasm of using new working technique. To get rid of this external invalidity problem, one should arrange an experiment with longer time schedule that would resemble real life setting more.

While actually the primary goal of any software implementation is the useful software for customer, the practical consideration of any programming method is whether it adds some value to the customer. One may ask if measuring productivity by number of satisfied test cases is an adequate measure of customer satisfaction. The software quality assurance consists of lot of tasks, including *validation* and *verification*. Validation means checking whether the requirements specified describe the software that the customer really needs. Verification means checking whether the software meets specified requirements, and is done mostly by testing. To the customer the value of validation is getting the right solution, and the value of verification is to get the stable and flawlessly working solution. The pair-programming effect on software validation process is out of scope of current study.

5 Future Work

5.1 Pending Issues of Current Experiment

The pending issues are related to the exploratory part of the experiment. The personalities of test subjects were tested. There are answered some exploratory questions about relationships between programmers personality and perfomance. These deal with how the personality of a single person affects the results of using pair-programming in general. There are not yet answered any questions about how the combination of personalities in a single pair affects the results of using pair-programming. Another goal is to find out how the personalities and the attitudes of the partners working together affect pair-programming. The data about satisfaction with the (non-)pair-programming is gathered and is being analyzed. We intentionally do not have any pre-stated hypothesis for it – the goal is to explore.

5.2 Questions for the Replication Experiments

One very pragmatic question authors of the paper have not answered is how pair-programmers react to changes in requirements to existing system, both in terms of changing existing test cases and adding test cases. There should be an experiment to measure the speed of programmer's reaction to changes. The measuring would increase the external validity of experiments because in real world the requirements change continuously. Such experimental design would pay attention on the question about internal quality of the software and its design. The current experiment does not uncover any facts about long-term software maintainability.

To increase external validity in real world situations, an experiment should involve more experienced programmers, larger teams (current experiment involved 2-member teams) and longer time-schedules.

Also, the replicating experiment should avoid weaknesses related to internal validity of current experiment.

Acknowledgements

Authors of the paper would like to thank all the people who helped to reach the point so far: Laurie Williams (North Carolina State University) for giving valuable feedback on the questions related to the earlier experiments; Ahti Peder (lecturer of OOP course at UT) and Jüri Kiho (Proffessor of Software Systems at UT) for providing access to selection of students; Aavo Luuk (Associate Professor of Department of Psychology at UT) and Aire Raidvee (undergraduate student at Psychology at UT) for helping in validity issues of the experiment; Tiia Arro and Anu Roos (master students at Institute of Mathematical Statistics at UT) for statistical analysis; Klaus-Eduard Runnel, Vahur Vaiksaar, Eva Valk, and Madis Priilinn (undergraduate students at Computer Science at UT) for implementing the automated testing environment for the experiment; Cybernetica AS, the software development company employing three authors of the paper, for urging workers to pursue also their academic undertakings; Casper Lassenius (Professor of Software Business and Engineering Institute at Helsinki Technical University) for urging to submit a paper about the experiment to XP2003, and last, but not least, the students of OOP lecture who acted as the selection.

References

1. Campell, Donald T.; Stanley, Julian C., Experimental and Quasi-Experimental Designs for Research, Houghton Mifflin College, 1966.
2. Cockburn, Alistair; Williams, Laurie; The Costs and Benefits of Pair Programming, XP2000, 2000.
3. Costa, P. T., Jr., McCrae, R. R., Normal Personality Assessment in Clinical Practice: The NEO Personality Inventory. Psychological Assessment, 4, 5-13, 1992
4. Hettmansperger, Thomas P., Statistical Inference Based on Ranks, John Wiley & Sons, 1984
5. Nawrocki J.; Wojciechowski, A., Experimental Evaluation of Pair Programming, in: K.Maxwell, S.Oligny, R. Kusters, E. van Veenendaal (eds.), Project Control: Satisfying the Customer, Shaker Publishing 2001, ESCOM 2001, 2-4 April 2001 London, 269-276.
6. Nosek, T. John; The case for collaborative programming, Communications of the ACM, vol. 41 (1998), No. 3, 105-108.
7. Ray, William J; Methods Toward a Science of Behavior and Experience, Wadsworth Thomson Learning, 2000.
8. Williams, Laurie; Kessler, R. Robert; All I Really Need to Know about Pair Programming I Learned in Kindergarten, Communications of the ACM, 2000.
9. Williams, Laurie; Kessler, Robert R.; Cunningham, Ward; Jeffries, Ron; Strengthening the Case for Pair Programming, IEEE Software, 2000.
10. Williams, Laurie; Kessler, R. Robert; Experimenting with Industry's "Pair-Programming" Model in the Computer Science Classroom, Journal on Software Engineering Education, 2000.
11. Williams, Laurie; The Collaborative Software Process, University of Utah, 2000.
12. Wilson, D. Judith; Hoskin, Nathan; Nosek, T. John; The benefits of collaboration for student programmers, Proceedings of the twenty-fourth SIGCSE technical symposium on Computer science education, 1993, Indianapolis, Indiana, United States pp. 160 164.

When Does a Pair Outperform Two Individuals?

Kim Man Lui and Keith C.C. Chan

Department of Computing
The Hong Kong Polytechnic University
Hung Hom, Hong Kong
{cskmlui,cskcchan}@comp.polyu.edu.hk

Abstract. This paper reports experimental measurements of productivity and quality in pair programming. The work complements Laurie Williams' work on collaborative programming, in which Pair Programming and Solo Programming student groups wrote the same programs and then their activities were measured to investigate productivity, quality, etc. In this paper, Pair and Solo industrial programmer groups are requested to complete algorithm-style aptitude tests so as to observe the capability of solving algorithms in singles and in pairs. So doing is independent of the familiarity of a programming language. Besides, we also take another approach to examining pair programming. A single group of industrial programmers carries alternately out Pair Programming and Solo Programming. All these demonstrate that productivity in pair programming hinges upon algorithm design at all levels from understanding problems and implementing solutions. In addition, we reach similar conclusions to Williams. Our findings indicate that simple design, refactoring, and rapid feedback provide an excellent continuous-design environment for higher productivity in pair programming.

1 Introduction

Many veteran software development managers by experience learn the following phenomenon. A newly employed developer takes days to complete a program. If he continues to work on other programs of similar types, the time for algorithm design is substantially reduced even if he writes them from scratch, i.e. without referring his previous source. Two months later the developer will be able to finish a program of that kind in a day, whereas in the past it would have taken him several days. The time reduction is obvious. As time passes, he becomes mastering the technique of coding that problem. However the amount of time that is required to write that program remains more or less constant. The time reduction is much less significant when compared with earlier.

Taking the above phenomenon to an extreme, we conduct an experiment in which a subject is asked to write the same program 8 times. Figure 1 illustrates the result. At the beginning, it takes him around 6 days to complete. Then he can complete it faster because he has been learning about the problem and becoming familiar with converting the problem into a computer algorithm. The more times he writes the same pro-

M. Marchesi and G. Succi (Eds.): XP 2003, LNCS 2675, pp. 225–233, 2003.
© Springer-Verlag Berlin Heidelberg 2003

gram, the less time he needs to think about the algorithm. Thus eventually, when he starts writing the same program again, his mind already has a full picture of what the algorithm and the structure of the program are. Then he just sits down and codes it without pausing for thought. In Figure 1, the bigger time difference between the first and the eighth times of writing a particular program means that a developer has spent much effort on designing the algorithm and planning the structure of the program. For some other programmers, they might take five days at the first time and eventually take two days at the eighth time. However, the curve remains steadfast in its shape, meaning that the relationship is always held independent of capability of people and complexity of programming.

Fig. 1. How much time can be reduced to write a program between the first time and the eighth time?

Let us consider two situations. First, a programmer collaborating with another guy works on coding a brand new problem. Second, a programmer collaborating with another guy but works on a problem that similar ones has been worked on for the eighth time. Which one is more productive? Using pair programming when developers encounter an unfamiliar problem can be much more productive than when they have handled a familiar problem. According to Figure 1, having more people does not help any time improvement when the problem was developed at the eighth time. But there is a room for accelerating the work at the first time. It can then be realized that pair programming will help to speed up programming a problem at the first time more than at the eighth time.

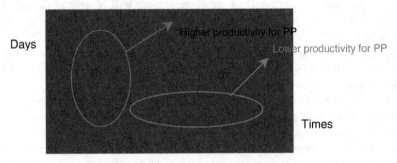

Fig. 2. Productivity for Pair Programming (PP)

Figure 2 shows when pair programming can achieve higher productivity regarding to Figure 1. Based on Figure 1, we can further interpret it as a case in which we achieve *higher* productivity and *better* quality if there is a significant time difference between two consecutive writings for the same problem being programmed.

This paper investigates quality and productivity in Pair Programming. Many experiments were conducted to establish that pair programming improves algorithm design (i.e. semantics and logic of a program) more than use of a computer language (i.e. syntax of a program).

2 Background

A pair spends an insignificant 15% more time than individuals on the same task, yet pair programming achieves a higher quality [1, 2]. These findings were based on an experimental work in which pair-programming and solo-programming student groups were formed and asked to write the same programs so their results could be directly compared.

This paper investigates if there is a repeatable, measurable test that can show substantial differences of "productivity" and "quality" between solo programming and pair programming. Such a test helps to gain insights into pair programming. Thus, we launched a research project aiming at understanding when pair programming is effective. In order to have new contributions and less arguable to our findings, two requirements must be satisfied. First, we tried to make our experiments as closed as an industrial environment. Thus, subjects who participated in this project were full-time industrial programmers. They did programming at least 40 hours a week. Second, we endeavored to make our experiments and results repeatable, so that those who are skeptical of the idea of pair programming can repeat them to judge for themselves.

3 Pair Programming

The fact that instruction in computer programming (i.e. computing algorithms) improves problem solving ability is supported by empirical data and experimental studies [6]. In addition, collaborative learning was found to enhance problem-solving skills [5]. From these, we formulate our hypothesis that people working in pairs can improve problem-solving ability; therefore, pair programming reduces bugs and increases productivity.

We need to establish that people in pairs significantly help solve an algorithm, *the basic element of a computer program*, better and faster. This should not be confused with better knowledge of a particular computer language. Of course, a pair of programmers can help each other to master the computer syntax. However, the key value of talented programmers is their skill in analyzing a problem and devising a computing algorithm for it better and faster. Therefore, we devised our experiments in which subjects in pairs and in solos are asked to solve (1) deduction problems and (2) procedural algorithms, *instead of writing a program*. This way eliminates a factor of how well those subjects are used to particular languages such as Java. In fact, should pair programming be merely beneficial for the use of language commands, two persons could work independently and sit very closely so that they can talk and share their knowledge of language syntax and command.

Deduction problems in connection with programming can be best explained by Game of Live shown in Figure 3, which was introduced by the mathematician John Conway [3]. Solving this deduction problem requires working out an algorithm that describes the problem. Game of Live can easily be programmed into a computer if its algorithm is figured out. The deduction problem can measure a developer's capability of problem reasoning, formulation and representation. Given a problem, we first solve it, then devise an algorithm (a pseudo-program) and lastly code it using a particular language.

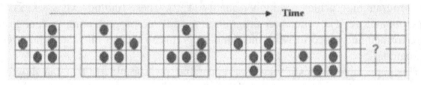

Fig. 3. Does a pair solve a deduction problem like "Game of Live" faster than an individual?

Procedural analysis is an extension of tests for aptitude in logical thinking and progress operations, which were actually designed to access aptitude in areas of competence essential to computer programming. The Procedural analysis measures a developer's capability of coping with complexity. Figure 4 shows an excerpt of a procedural algorithm selected in [4].

Fig. 4. The analysis of the flow chat demands the same type of intellectual activity in programming

We now describe our experiments. There are two approaches to conducting them. One is to divide subjects into pair and solo groups and compare their results. Another is to ask all the subjects to alternatively work in pairs and then work individually in an alternating style.

3.1   Research Methodology I

Fifteen hands-on programmers from different companies were invited for the experiment at our software laboratory. They had a diversity of backgrounds including database systems, Web applications, etc. Table 1 shows their numbers of years of experience in software development.

Table 1. Background of Subjects

Years of programming experience	1	2	3	4	
Number of Subjects	4	9	1	1	Total=15

Key process areas of CMM and practices of eXtreme Programming (XP) were introduced to the subjects for six hours and five hours, respectively. It should be noted that CMM was introduced to allow the subjects to comprehend XP from a CMM perspective. After introduction to CMM and XP, they were organized in three XP teams (of six, five and four people) and each team was asked to write an inventory system in 17 hours. A business analyst well-versed in operations of sales and distribution was invited to act as an on-site customer.

The purpose of tutorial and workshop is to provide enough hand-on practice to the subjects so that they would do our experiment in a manner of pair programming. Although our control experiment could be performed on subjects without receiving XP training, we believe that XP training is necessary because the subjects learn how to collaborate with a teammate. Measurements for two programmers, never working in pair before or , do not truly reflect the productivity of pair programming.

Now the experiment started. The subjects were grouped into ten units: five pairs and five individuals. The units were asked to complete fifteen multiple choices of procedural algorithm that we extracted from [4]. At the first completion of those questions, we told each subject unit about how many answers were correct. However, we gave no hint on which question were correctly answered. This kind of feedback is shown by " ● " in Figure 5.

Fig. 5. Visualization of the process of experiment I (Note: where ● and ▲ are two types of checkpoint.)

After the subjects received the feedback, they had to continue to spot wrong ones and figure the answers out. At the second completion, subject units submitted _only_ those answers that they previously identified as incorrect. Then we provided feedback on whether all those answers were correct or not, and whether all the problems have been solved, shown in Table 2. The feedback is indicated by " ▲ " in Figure 5. The process was repeated until the subjects could solve all the questions. The completion time for each repetition was recorded. The feedback mechanism was designed to emulate error messages given by a computer and to minimize the chance of guessing the answer from the feedback

Table 2. Feedback mechanism

Try	Submitted Answer	Feedback	Solved
1	1 A 2 A 3 C 4 D 5 C	3 correct	No
2	1 B 3 B	Incorrect	No
3	1 C 4 A	Incorrect	No

It should be noted that the whole experiment was actually organized as a competition. Subjects were told that they should use less number of submission and less time to _win_ it. For those solo units, their personal pride would drive them to challenge pair units. In this sense, solo units in fact were in competition with pair units, more than an experiment. Psychologically, solo units had a strong desire to win whereas pair units simply did not want to lose.

Result 1
Productivity in pair programming can be studied by comparing the results of pair groups and solo groups. At the first attempt, pair groups finished all the algorithms in 13.3 minutes on average, whereas solo groups required 22 minutes. A pair spends 20.9% more time than do individuals on the same task. This was close to what Williams reported of 15%.

So far we have not considered quality. Thus, it is important to compare the time required to correctly tackle all questions, which is the sum of each time of duration. The total time for the pair group was 18.2 minutes and for solo group was 38 minutes.

In consideration of the same quality (i.e. all algorithms being solved), a pair spent 4.2% less time than did individuals on the same tasks. Pair programming is strong on the design of programming algorithms. A pair outperforms two individuals for the design-driven activity.

3.2   Research Methodology II

The objective of the second experiment was to observe the behavior and performance of the same group of people working both in singles and in pairs. Thus, subjects were not divided into pair and solo groups. They work in both groups in shift (see Figure 7). This configuration minimizes the influence of differences of people intelligence and experience.

We prepared two sets of deduction problems, denoted "A" and "B", respectively. Unlike the algorithm problem (Figure 4), _none_ of the deduction problems were multiple choices (Figure 3). First, subjects were formed into pairs and attempted to complete the "A" set of problems. After completing the exercises, then the pairs were separated into individuals and each of them complete the "B" set of problems. Then individuals were formed back to pairs to correct any mistakes in their answers to the set "A" problems. The process was repeated until all problems were correctly solved. The feedback mechanism was the same as in Research Methodology I. Figure 7 depicts the process of this research methodology.

Fig. 7. Visualization of the process of experiment II (Note: where ● and ▲ are two types of checkpoint.)

Result 2

At the first attempt, on average, the groups in pair spent on 65 minutes for the set "A" whereas they in singles completed another the set "B" in 75 minutes. Thus, the pairs spent much more time to complete the deduction problems than did individuals. However, the pairs achieved 85% of correctness and the individuals only reached 51%. Thus the pairs could solve all the deduction problems at the second attempt, whereas the individuals needed more attempts and time to carry out spotting and reworking. It was doubtless that a pair has an increased mental capability since it can search through larger spaces of alternatives [1, 2].

Pairs spent 5.3% less time than individuals on solving their deduction problems. The result also shows that better quality is obtained with pair programming.

4   What Is the Worst Case in Pair Programming?

The intuition judgment of many people would be that pair programming spent about 100% more time on the program than the individuals [1,2]. According to the previous, when *ignoring* the quality, pairs did spend much more time. Therefore, we are interested in discovering what the worst situation in pair programming might be. Suppose that coding a program takes an experienced programmer 10 hours and an inexperienced programmer 20 hours. How long would it take to write the same program if both worked collaboratively?

Subjects were asked to write a Transact SQL program. The fast, the middle and the slow programmers are labeled *A*, *B*, and *C*, respectively, in Figure 8. Note that some developers were not familiar with Transact SQL, so wrote more slowly than the others. There was a three-hour gap between the fast and the slow. Then *A* and *C* formed a pair. The pair and *B* were requested to finish another program using Transact SQL.

Comparing B's performance with the pair, we conclude that the worst case in pair programming is around the same productivity as the smarter guy of the pair working alone. However, his less-experienced partner can significantly improve his skill at programming.

Fig. 8. The productivity of a pair to write a program in the worst situation is the same of the more talented or experienced person of that pair to do it. However, his partner can learn it from him and improve his skill in programming.

5   Conclusions

This paper provides several experimental results to establish a statement that a pair outperforms individuals in working on computer algorithms in terms of quality and productivity. Pair programming excels in procedural problems and deduction questions, which are key elements in programming algorithms. We can conclude that pair programming achieves higher productivity when a pair writes a more challenging program that demands more time spent on design. The finding explains that it is effective to write a program in pair for rapid changing requirements because it demands that programmers concentrate on changing (or continuous) design. In addition, this paper confirms Willam's result.

Our primary contribution, however, is to show when a pair outperforms two individuals. A problem that is new to developers can make pair programming higher productivity because pairs excel to design algorithms faster and better through learning the problem together and exploring larger space of alternatives. pair learning is prolific. In XP, small design, refactoring, rapid feedback altogether forming a continuous design environment for software development also cause pair programming higher productivity because developers are heavily involved in working on algorithms and structures of programs.

Finally, the two methods presented in Section 2 can easily be repeated by those readers who would like to explore more about pair programming in particular and eXtreme programming in general.

References

1. Williams, L. *The Collaborative Software Process*, Ph.D. dissertation, University of Utah, (2000)
2. Williams, L. Pair Programming: Why Have Two Do the Work of One? *Extreme Programming Perspective*, Edited by Marchesi, M, Succi G, Wells, D and Williams, L p.p. 23-33, Addison Wesley, (2002)
3. Kennedy J and Eberhart R, *Swarm Intelligence*, Morgan Kaufmann Publishers, p.p. 17-19, (2001)
4. Munzert, A. Part IV: Computer I.Q. – Program Procedure *Test Your IQ, third Edition,* p.p. 112-117, Random House, (1994)
5. Gokhale, A. Collaborative Learning Enhances Critical Thinking, *Journal of Technology Education* Volume 7, Number 1 Fall (1995). On-line at http://scholar.lib.vt.edu/ejournals/JTE/
6. VanLengen, C and Maddux, C. Does Instruction in Computer Programming Improve Problem Solving Ability? *Journal of IS Education* 12, (1990). On-line at http://gise.org/JISE/

Being Jane Malkovich:
A Look Into the World of an XP Customer

Angela Martin[1], James Noble[2], and Robert Biddle[1]

[1] School of Information Management, Victoria University of Wellington
Kelburn Parade, Wellington, New Zealand
angela.martin@paradise.net.nz
robert.biddle@mcs.vuw.ac.nz
[2] School of Mathematical and Computing Sciences, Victoria University of Wellington
Kelburn Parade, Wellington, New Zealand
james.noble@mcs.vuw.ac.nz

Abstract. One of the pivotal roles in XP is the customer, but little guidance is provided in the literature on the practicalities of succeeding in this role. We used an interpretative in-depth case study to explore a successful XP project. We obtained multiple perspectives on the implementation of the customer role, and this paper includes excerpts from interviews with the customer and other development team members. We found that the interviewees provided a consistent picture of the XP customer role and they agreed that the XP customer role, especially for larger organisations, is very demanding. It requires preparation, skills, attention to detail, and the ability to make critical decisions.

1   Introduction

"All the best talent and technology and process in the world will fail when the customer isn't up to scratch" [3, p. 17]

Most of us, based on our experience, agree with this statement, irrespective of whether the statement concerns an XP project or not. But how do we know when a customer is 'up to scratch' for the XP on-site customer role?

The initial XP books [2, 3] provide little guidance on the practicalities of succeeding in this role. Some experience reports [5, 8, 13] have provided valuable insights into the issues encountered during the implementation of XP, including that of the customer role. However, none of the XP literature to date has focused on the required characteristics and skills of the customer, or explored the day-to-day challenges encountered in this role.

Our research is beginning to explore the practicalities of succeeding in the implementation of the XP customer role, and this paper outlines some of our initial findings. We have used an interpretative in-depth case study to explore a successful XP project, and we have obtained multiple perspectives on the implementation of the customer role, including both the customer and programmer perspectives. We have found that the interviewees agreed that the XP customer role, especially for larger

M. Marchesi and G. Succi (Eds.): XP 2003, LNCS 2675, pp. 234–243, 2003.

organisations, is very demanding. It requires preparation, skills, attention to detail, and the ability to make critical decisions.

In the next section we outline our three research hypotheses generated based on advice in the XP literature. In the third section we describe the context of the case study, including the project background and purpose and an overview of the XP team's experience in both general software development and XP. In the fourth section we discuss the results of the case study and compare the well known advice concerning each hypothesis with what our interviews found. Finally, we present our conclusions.

2   Research Hypotheses

Our research hypotheses were established from the advice provided by the XP founders or respected practitioners, and cover the characteristics of the customer, the skills of the customer, and the location of the customer.

2.1   Characteristics of the XP Customer

Beck & Fowler provide some initial guidance on selecting a good customer in the XP planning book [3]. Their guidance consists of a list of the characteristics of a good customer:

> *"Understands the domain well by working in that domain, and also by understanding how it works (not always the same thing)*
> *Can understand, with development's help, how software can provide business value in the domain*
> *Is determined to deliver value regularly and is not afraid to deliver too little rather than nothing*
> *Can make decisions about what's needed now and what's needed later*
> *Is willing to accept ultimate responsibility for the success or failure of the project." [3p. 18]*

We used this suggested list of customer characteristics to generate our initial research question: *How did a customer on a real XP project measure up against this list of ideal characteristics?*

2.2   Skills of the XP Customer

> *"One of the things that is unsaid in the XP literature is how to be a customer (analyst)" [7]*

To describe 'how to be a customer' we need to understand the tasks the customer will need to perform. Once we understand the tasks we will be able to establish the skills that the customer will need, to either possess or be trained in, in order to perform their role effectively. The second research question we generated, based on this reasoning, was a double barrelled question: *What tasks did the customer perform on a real XP project and what skills did the customer need to perform these tasks well?*

2.3   Location of the XP Customer

The XP customer role is named the *on-site customer* role and Beck [2, p. 60 - 61] notes:

> *"A real customer must sit with the team, available to answer questions, resolve disputes, and set small scale priorities [...] The on-site customer will have the disadvantage of being physically separated from other customers, but they will likely have time to do their normal work." [2, p. 60 - 61]*

We were interested in understanding: *How did a customer on a real XP project implement the on-site requirement and what were the flow-on effects of this decision to both the project and the business?*

2.4   Research Method

Information Systems Development (ISD) methodology researchers [6, 11, 12] have expressed a growing concern that existing ISD methods do not meet the needs of today's business and software development environments. Studies [1, 10, 11] in this area have begun to explore practices in natural settings in order to begin to address these issues. Given this trend, we have used an interpretative in-depth case study to explore our research questions within the natural setting of *one* successful XP project. We used semi-structured one-on-one interviews to collect the data for this paper. The five interviewees covered the spectrum of the XP roles including the customer, programmer, coach and tester. All interviews were taped and later transcribed in detail. The interviewees were asked to validate both the transcriptions of the interview and the interpreted findings. We use a number of quotes from the interviews to illustrate our findings in this paper. Please see the technical report on this research [9] for further information on the research method.

3   Description of the Context of the Experience

The subject of this study was an intranet Content Management System (CMS). CMS was an outsourced software development project and involved the three organisations as described in table 1.

KiwiCorp's project lead on CMS describes the beginnings of the project below.

> *"Internet redevelopment in [KiwiCorp] had sort of been mooted for a couple of years and various people had sort of had a go but nothing really worked too well, and then my manager got handed the job of sorting out the intranet" – Customer, KiwiCorp*

Table 1. The Organisations involved in the CMS Project

Pseudonym	Project role	Description
KiwiCorp	Customer organisation	A large New Zealand corporation with employees dispersed throughout the country.
DevCorp	Outsourced software development company	A New Zealand based company specialising in providing Internet, extranet and intranet solutions. The company is wholly owned by an international consulting company.
BureauCorp	Outsourced infrastructure services company	An international information technology services company that supplies facilities management services. This company is responsible for the physical infrastructure CMS will be tested and deployed on.

CMS was established in the middle of 2001 with DevCorp as the outsourced software development vendor.

> *"We felt we could probably only do it if we used [DevCorp] ... because we had such a lot of confidence in them based on previous experience" – Customer, KiwiCorp*

Initially the project was a traditional waterfall project and was divided into three phases, planning (deciding what to build), development (building the application) and implementation (user acceptance testing, training and roll out). The planning phase focussed on gathering requirements using standard workshop techniques and involved a series of user workshops that were attended by the business users. At the end of the planning phase it was decided to use XP for the development phase. The requirements gathered during the planning phase were used as a basis for the user stories developed as part of the development phase. It was recognised that the formal implementation phase would need to remain as this approach was required by BureauCorp and meshed with the existing practices of KiwiCorp.

CMS was successfully deployed in September 2002. The interviews to collect the data for this paper occurred during the implementation phase, prior to deployment. The indications from KiwiCorp, based on the acceptance testing and training feedback, are that this project is considered a success:

> *"This development approach [has meant] we were able to track things as we go and actually discover that things aren't quite what people wanted and complete them ...The indication [from the testing] is really good ... And the training feedback has been really good too because we've done some one on one training with the key publishers – about 50 to 100 odd people ... [and] generally people find it easy to use and are going to be fine with it so that's really good" – Customer, KiwiCorp*

3.1   The Team

The development team consisted of KiwiCorp and DevCorp representatives. At its peak the XP team consisted of 11 full-time members, including the customer. The 10

DevCorp members ranged in experience from 3 years of small web development projects to 23 years of wide ranging software development experience. All of the programmers, except one, were experienced computer programmers. The novice programmer, however, was an experienced business analyst with a background in KiwiCorp's industry. The KiwiCorp customer had recently been involved in another Intranet development project gaining an insight into the software development process.

Prior Exposure to XP. All of the team members were new to XP. DevCorp had recently used XP successfully on a similar project. None of the team members on the earlier XP project transitioned to the CMS project. There was strong support in the team for adopting XP as evidenced below.

> *"I'd had good reports about it in [project name], I'd read the book and the book made a lot of sense, it was common sense. [and later in the interview] I was willing to give it a go myself but the other thing was the team was willing to give it a go, if the team had pushed back, I probably would have folded ... [goes on to note two particular team members] were very strong"* – Project Manager, DevCorp

The team gained an understanding of XP by reading the XP books, sharing XP experiences with other practitioners of XP and also by regularly reviewing their progress with the method throughout the project. The team's overall impression of XP at the end of the project is summed up by:

> *"Overall – I love this approach to development and I'd certainly like to use it again in any future projects I am involved in"* – Customer, KiwiCorp

4   Results of the Experience

Our research hypotheses were:

1. How did a customer on a real XP project measure up against the list of ideal characteristics?
2. What tasks did the customer perform on a real XP project and what skills did the customer need to perform these tasks well?
3. How did a customer on a real XP project implement the on-site requirement and what were the flow-on effects of this decision to both the project and the business?

For each of these hypotheses there is well known advice and in the tables below for each hypotheses we compare advice with what our interviews found.

4.1   Characteristics of the Customer

Beck & Fowler [3] have described the ideal preparation for someone playing the customer role. The customer representing KiwiCorp was close to the ideal, as we show in the table below.

Table 2. A comparison of the KiwiCorp customer to the ideal customer described in the literature

Ideal customer	Actual customer characteristics
Understands the domain well	The customer's librarian training, combined with her tenure at KiwiCorp, allowed her to understand how CMS must work to meet the diverse needs of the business users. To supplement her knowledge, she involved operational users of the existing system in the process.
Understands how the software can provide business value in the domain	The customer's existing knowledge of similar systems, combined with her perceived value of DevCorp's ideas (the possibilities of technology), allowed her to understand the value software could provide the domain.
Understands the importance of regular delivery	The customer perceived regular delivery as important as it allowed her to evolve the requirements and test the system with operational users.
Understands the importance of prioritising the functionality to be delivered	The customer perceived the importance of prioritisation and worked closely with her senior manager to ensure prioritisation decisions were made effectively. She quickly learnt that she needed to be tougher, earlier.
Accepts responsibility for the success or failure of the project	This aspect, as described here, was not covered sufficiently in any of the interviews to make an interpretation.
Is able to represent diverse users[1], termed "speaking with one voice"	The customer represented a small KiwiCorp project team including her senior manager, migration manager, testing team as well as the thousands of end users of the system. The initial requirements workshops sessions held during the planning phase assisted her to represent the users and make decisions on their behalf in her role. DevCorp team members all considered the customer as the sole source of requirements and decision making for KiwiCorp. No DevCorp interviewees indicated competing requirements or conflicting decisions occurred during the project. However, one DevCorp interviewee noted their concern that the customer had not consulted the users sufficiently during the process and may have relied overly much on the sessions from the planning phase to make decisions.

---

[1] Includes operational users, business management and IT operations

Summary. According to the existing guidance in XP literature the KiwiCorp customer had almost the ideal preparation for the customer role. However, as we outline in the section below, this preparation alone may not be sufficient to succeed in the XP customer role.

4.2   Skills of the Customer

We know from the initial XP books the customer will need to write user stories, test functionality and prioritise requirements in the planning game [3]. The customer on this project did not develop user stories, and a contract tester was hired to assist with the development of test scripts.

However, our customer noted that despite these tasks not being her responsibility, she was still overloaded:

> "I was the main [KiwiCorp] person on the project, I think we needed some extra roles basically. We probably needed about three of me. [and later describing the three roles she played as the customer] The main areas from a business point of view were looking after the product, looking after other issues, technical or otherwise [between the two outsourced vendors, KiwiCorp and BureauCorp], and then another major area was content migration – actually communicating with the existing site owners and working out a plan for them to migrate their staff and all that" – Customer, KiwiCorp.

The customer elaborated that she quickly realised that she was unable to fulfil the content migrator role as well as the other roles, and a full-time migration project manager was employed. During the interview the customer also considered the potential of applying this lesson on her next project:

> "[Regarding determining that a content migration manager was required] So we should have realised that up front and ...[Interviewer interjected - Perhaps next time you will?] Maybe, I mean it's all so ... I mean, money, you know" – Customer, KiwiCorp

The project, to implement CMS, at least from the customer's perspective, does not only include the development of the software, it also includes the vendor management and implementation activities including rollout, migration and training. It appears expecting the customer to be able to focus only on the requirements and testing may be unrealistic.

The customer also discussed the need for her to consider and understand the diverse needs of thousands of business users:

> "[KiwiCorp is a large organisation and has] such [diverse] needs, we had to ... all the way along I had to be thinking "is this flexible enough", you know, will it fit this person, will it fit this person [and later] when I felt that I didn't have enough knowledge to make a call then we would – I'd ask questions of other people in business"
> – Customer, KiwiCorp

The customer also elaborated on the importance of understanding how to "get things done" in the organisation:

> *"[My manager] was responsible for getting buy-in from the sort of senior level in business ... Well we knew that if we actually got peoples' formal sign-off – business people to sign-off for everything – we'd never actually get anything done. [and a little later about her understanding of how this approach mitigated that risk] ... Constantly using this development approach we were able to track things as we go and actually discover that things aren't quite what people wanted and complete them." – Customer, KiwiCorp*

Summary. Existing advice suggests that requirements and testing are the key tasks a customer will undertake. The KiwiCorp customer's activities, however, suggest there are a number of other tasks she must undertake to ensure a successful project. Further consideration needs to be paid to the other time consuming aspects of the customer role, often ones that require political sensitivity. These aspects include the balancing of multiple roles, understanding the needs of diverse users and obtaining senior managerial support.

4.3   Location of the Customer

On this project KiwiCorp and DevCorp were situated in different buildings within the central business district of Wellington, approximately a 10-minute walk apart. Beck notes the importance of the time with the developers but assumes other customer separation is acceptable. The customer realised she needed to spend direct "face-to-face" time with the developers as suggested by Beck. However, she also needed to spend direct "face-to-face" time with KiwiCorp stakeholders as well. Her time with KiwiCorp people allowed her to represent them with a "single voice" and also to focus on non-software development project activities such as training and migration. Her initial decision was to spend 50% of her time at each building.

During the project, however, approximately 50% of her time was spent resolving technical integration issues with BureauCorp. The result was that she was unable to spend a significant portion of her time at DevCorp moulding the software to meet the business needs:

> *"My life would have been easier if I could have been 100% devoted to requirements and testing ... because I would have been right there when the developers were saying "shall I do it this way or do it that way" right before it had even got to build." – Customer, KiwiCorp*

Cockburn concurs with and elaborates on the customer's suggested impact of not being available to the development team:

> *"Having a usage expert available at all times means that feedback time from imagined to evaluated solution is as short as possible, often just minutes to a few hours. Such rapid feedback means that the development team grows a deeper understanding of the needs and habits of users, and start making fewer mistakes ... with a good sense of collaboration, the programmers will test the usage experts idea's and offer counter proposals. This will sharpen the customer's own ideas for how the new system should look. The cost of missing this sweet spot is a lowered probability of making a really useable product and a much higher cost for running all the experiments."* [4, p. 150]

An alternative solution, locating the DevCorp developers at KiwiCorp, was briefly touched upon:

> *"I would make explicit the fact that typical outsourcing arrangements are what drive development away from the client's premises, thus breaking one of XP's implicit assumptions."* – Pre-sales consultant, DevCorp

Schalliol [13] also worked on a project where they encountered significant customer overload. This team introduced analysts to facilitate the communication activities involved with complex systems with a large diverse user base. This role complemented the existing XP customer role. The communication activities were also planned as part of an iteration. An "issue card" was introduced and placed into the prioritisation sessions in a similar manner to story cards. The roles and procedures introduced in this team were done for a large project, however these suggestions may be relevant to smaller projects, such as CMS, particularly when a large diverse user base exists.

Summary. It is clear that the practice of an on-site customer has obvious intended value. How to achieve this requirement and still obtain the required "single voice" of a customer over multiple locations, which is common in outsourcing, can be a significant problem.

5   Conclusions

We set out to investigate the practicalities of succeeding in the implementation of the XP customer role. We conducted an interpretative in-depth case study that obtained multiple perspectives, including both the customer and programmers perspectives, on the implementation of the customer role on a successful XP project. From these perspectives a consistent picture emerged concerning the customer role.

The customer on this project was clearly overloaded, despite her apparent ideal preparation for the role and enthusiasm for the process. The time required to represent thousands of diverse users and cover the larger project activities, including implementation and vendor management, was significant and diminished the time the customer could spend with the programmers. The impact of the diminished time affected the quality of the product and may have increased both the cost and duration of the project due to the resulting long feedback loops. The outsourcing nature of the contract may have affected this finding but it appears the predominant factor was the large diverse user base and other project related tasks such as vendor management and implementation.

We believe that our project shows that, even when most of the relevant XP practices have been followed, the customer role is difficult and requires serious consideration. XP has focused on building effective development team practices: we now need to turn our attention, given the pivotal nature of the customer role, to exploring the processes that will support the XP customer.

References

1. Baskerville, R.L. and Stage, J. Controlling Prototype Development Though Risk Analysis. MIS Quarterly, 20 (4). pp. 481 - 502.
2. Beck, K. eXtreme Programming Explained: Embrace Change. Addison Wesley, 2000.
3. Beck, K. and Fowler, M. Planning Extreme Programming. Addison Wesley, 2001.
4. Cockburn, A. Agile software development. Addison-Wesley, 2001.
5. Farell, C., Narang, R., Kapitan, S. and Webber, H., Towards an effective onsite customer practice. in Third International Conference on eXtreme Programming and Agile Process in Software Engineering, (Italy, 2002).
6. Fitzgerald, B. Systems development methodologies: the problem of tenses. Information technology and people, 13 (3). pp. 174 - 185.
7. Fowler, M. XP Customer Quotes, WikiWikiWeb, 2002.
8. Gittins, R., Hope, S. and Williams, I. Qualitative Studies of XP in a Medium-Sized Business. in Marchesi, M., Succi, G., Wells, D., and Williams, L. ed. EXtreme Programming Perspectives, Addison-Wesley, 2002, 421 - 435.
9. Martin, A. A case study: exploring the role of customers on eXtreme programming projects, CS-TR-03-1, School of Computing and Mathematical Sciences, Victoria University of Wellington, Wellington, 2002.
10. Myers, M. and Young, L. Hidden agendas, power and managerial assumptions in information systems development: an ethnographic case study. Information Technology and People, 10 (3). pp. 224 - 240.
11. Nandhakumar, J. and Avison, D.E. The fiction of methodological development: a field study of information systems development. Information Technology and People, 12 (2). pp. 176 - 191.
12. Russo, N.L. and Stolterman, E. Exploring the assumptions underlying information systems methodologies: their impact on past, present and future ISM research. Information Technology and People, 13 (4). pp. 313-327.
13. Schalliol, G. Challenges for Analysts on a Large XP Project. in Marchesi, M., Succi, G, Wells, D & Williams, L ed. EXtreme Programming Perspectives, Addison-Wesley, 2002, 375 - 386.

Using Actual Time: Learning How to Estimate

Piergiuliano Bossi

eXtreme Programming Centre
Quinary S.p.A.
http://www.quinary.com
p.bossi@quinary.com

Abstract. This paper discusses and examines the experience we have gained in using agile planning and tracking tools, with particular reference to a recent very successful project called M@rketInfo. The aim herein is to demonstrate the efficacy of alternative methods based on actual time as compared to the more consolidated methods of Yesterday's Weather, Velocity and Ideal Time. We shall also introduce some significant metrics to help the reader acquire a deeper understanding of the project and the techniques used.

1 Introduction

The M@rketInfo project [1] is one of the most important projects the Quinary XP Centre has carried out. Like all Quinary's Optional Scope Projects, this project was run using *Pomodoro* as a tool to measure both the estimates and the efforts related to each user story. Very briefly, a *pomodoro* is a particular kind of story point and corresponds to 30 minutes actual work usually performed by a pair ([2] and [3]).

From the very beginning of the project, the use of *pomodoro* was based on some essential elements:

- a tracking & planning sheet, similar to a double-entry book-keeping ledger; estimates, re-estimates and daily effort were tracked for each user story until the user story was completed;
- an open workspace in which workstations were physically apart from personal desks where, for example, the software engineers could read their email;
- a corporate organisation that permitted the XP Centre to manage the team's time without interference, thus being able to organise the day so that a suitable amount of time was allotted to stand-up meetings, learning activities, development and to a final recap;
- a contract with the client that clearly set out that the team's sustainable pace was closely tied to the number of *pomodori* available in the time window identified during the iteration;
- experience and discipline in using *pomodoro*, especially thanks to the skills gained in past projects [4].

All these points laid the foundations on which the process could be built and developed; we were able to work in a physical and mental *environment* that allowed us to actually achieve high project focus and productivity.

M. Marchesi and G. Succi (Eds.): XP 2003, LNCS 2675, pp. 244–253, 2003.

2   Reacting to Problems

While developing M@rketInfo the team had to face a number of difficult moments that in one way or another questioned the team's own definition of a development process. In the end, we made a few adjustments and with the aid of some new analytical tools we managed to increase the level of feedback and monitor how those adjustments affected the system over time. The two main aspects were:

1. Big Refactoring Monitor
2. Estimate Reliability

2.1   Big Refactoring Monitor

The first problem arose during the fifth iteration. A long big refactoring [5] session was required and that session radically changed the architecture of the GUI components that had emerged until then [6]. By spreading the big refactoring over four successive iterations the user stories delivery speed fell, without however leading to any abrupt stop in the project. In order to reach a better control of the user story delivery speed and an improvement in the reporting activities to the customer, a new analytical artefact called *Post Mortem* was introduced. It was an Excel worksheet fed by the a.m. tracking & planning sheet. The goal was to compare the effort put into each user story with the relevant estimate. The results from this comparison were:

1. the total estimate error of the user stories completed within the iteration, that is:

$$\text{estimate\_error} = (\text{actual\_time} - \text{estimate}) / \text{estimate} \tag{1}$$

2. an extension of (1), which also took into account unfinished user stories and estimated the relevant time to completion.

Post Mortem was one of the tools used at the start of the discussion during the retrospective and was only calculated at the end of the iteration.

While the first value was a sure measurement of the outcome of the completed iteration, the second one was only an error estimate and thus susceptible to change as the actual results relating to the unfinished user stories emerged. The unfinished user stories were only completed during subsequent iterations. Table 1 summarises the two values over the entire project and compares the number of completed user stories versus the planned ones.

For example, during iteration number 6 the error estimate for completed user stories was calculated at –20.59%, i.e. the time required to complete the user stories was overestimated by 1/5, which means 4 user stories out of the 5 planned. The last story was the one to which the big refactoring effort was assigned, thus leading to a total estimate error of 98.35%.

In other cases, such as during iteration number 20, the two error values showed opposite trends: the error for the completed user stories (only 3 in this case) was extremely high, 128.13%, whereas the error for the user stories still to be completed was much lower (17.70%). This means that the team devoted much more time to finishing the user stories the customer considered most important, but that were also unexpectedly time consuming. However, at the same time, the team estimated to spend proportionally less time to complete the remaining user stories.

Table 1. Estimate error over the entire project

Iteration	Pomodori	Planned stories	Completed stories	Extra stories	Estimate error (completed)	Estimate error (all)
1	97	5	3	0	10.00%	10.00%
2	89	7	7	1	-10.00%	-10.00%
3	90	7	6	0	0.00%	6.67%
4	156	9	8	0	7.86%	6.41%
5	200	15	7	0	49.50%	50.00%
6	91	5	4	0	-20.59%	98.35%
7	166	10	10	0	4.82%	4.82%
8	146	5	5	0	-14.05%	-14.05%
9	80	9	8	0	-3.38%	5.62%
10	167	12	10	0	5.26%	18.86%
11	211	11	8	0	6.87%	19.91%
12	87	5	2	0	8.33%	45.98%
13	110	6	6	1	-4.09%	1.15%
14	162	14	11	0	12.06%	9.26%
15	189	15	13	0	3.69%	10.32%
16	75	7	7	0	0.00%	0.00%
17	70	4	2	0	25.00%	55.71%
18	182	8	6	2	64.62%	22.25%
19	65	4	2	0	-2.50%	69.35%
20	305	5	3	1	128.13%	17.70%
21	235	8	6	1	9.70%	2.81%
22	268	6	4	0	-8.71%	9.14%
23	228	13	13	4	-5.15%	-2.36%
24	188	10	9	2	-2.53%	-6.05%
25	239	8	2	0	7.06%	75.52%
26	179	6	6	0	14.80%	14.80%

2.2   Estimate Reliability

The problem of estimate reliability is paramount when building a mutual trust relationship with the customer. As we had an agreement that specifically required the customer to set out the project scope, we felt estimate reliability was even more important than in a conventional process.

It was the customer himself who, as our second contract renewal term was approaching expiration, pointed out that any further contract renewal was tied to our ability to manage estimate errors. To meet this challenge we started to calculate three values for the different aspects of estimate reliability, starting from raw tracking & planning data which were updated daily:

- $FirstEstErr_i$ = error related to the first estimate made for the user story;
- $FirstPlanErr_i$ = error related to the estimate used to plan the user story the first time;
- $LastPlanErr_i$ = error related to the estimate used to plan the user story in the iteration in which the user story was completed.

$FirstEstErr_i$ was useful to manage the budget allocated by the customer; $FirstPlanErr_i$ showed the ability of the team to meet the commitments made during the iteration planning stage. More generally, it allowed us to manage the customer's precise expectations; $LastPlanErr_i$ showed the team's ability to tackle crisis situations and any over-running of initial estimates. It is obvious that for a given user story, planned and completed within a single iteration, FirstPlanErr$_i$ = LastPlanErr$_i$. Likewise, if a new user story was estimated for the first time and then immediately planned, then FirstEstErr$_i$ = FirstPlanErr$_i$.

The main difference between these error coefficients and those calculated in Table 1 lies in how we used them: we were not so interested in calculating the individual values of FirstEstErr$_i$, FirstPlanErr$_i$ and LastPlanErr$_i$, as we were in calculating their composite value as the project progressed, namely the value accrued up to the moment in which they were calculated. We called the three composite coefficients FirstEstErr$_{TOT}$, FirstPlanErr$_{TOT}$ and LastPlanErr$_{TOT}$. This was the picture we gave the customer at the end of the second contract renewal period:

Table 2. Accrued estimate error at the end of the second contract renewal period

FirstEstErr$_{TOT}$	FirstPlanErr$_{TOT}$	LastPlanErr$_{TOT}$
30.56%	25.41%	6.87%

Though the customer found these results encouraging, and thus signed up for a third contract renewal period, they did set the team a new ambitious goal: in order to manage their product release strategy more efficiently, the customer required FirstEstErr$_{TOT}$ to be set below 10% just for the last contract period. According to the customer, this reduction was to be achieved without affecting the throughput of the value delivered by the team, that is without artificially reducing the work pace just for the sake of meeting inflated estimates. This basically implied that the customer was giving us a specific mandate not to fall into *Parkinson's Law* [7], namely we were not to produce totally unrealistic estimates. Though we pointed out that it was objectively impossible to measure the value we had delivered until then (and thus monitor the throughput) we did take the challenge and proceeded to prepare the following artefacts:

- an Excel worksheet called *Estimates vs Efforts*, initially fed with the tracking & planning data, summarising the overall project performance with a specific focus on the FirstEstErr$_{TOT}$; the sheet was updated at the end of each iteration;
- an Excel worksheet called *Iteration Probe* which tracked the total estimate error (as mentioned above) on a daily basis, as emerging from the on-going iteration.

Thanks to the a.m. artefacts, adjustments could be made to the process and their effects monitored. One of the most significant things was to be able to rely on tools that helped the tracking process and allowed us to keep the project tracking times very low. Despite the additional work the average time devoted to tracking per day was below 15' [1].

One very simple change that had an extremely positive impact on the project was made during the estimate process. Before the third contract renewal, the team produced joint estimates, only superficially examining each team member's views. However, towards the end of the project, we decided to put on paper each team member's estimate of a given story card and then asked one of the software engineers who had made the lowest estimate to develop it. This meant we were pushing the concept of *Optimism wins* [8] to the extremes: not only was the lowest story card estimate selected among the ones produced by the software engineers, but also, the engineer who had made that estimate was then asked to implement it. This helped to shorten the feedback chain and made each software engineer aware of the reliability of his/her estimate. This in turn rapidly improved the overall estimate reliability as perceived by the customer.

Another particularly important change was made to the way the first estimate on a new story card was produced; this value played a crucial role in the FirstEstErr$_{TOT}$ calculation. Rather than directly trying to increase the estimate accuracy, the team started to work on the *grain size* of the evaluation units, going from a single *pomodoro* to multiples of 10 *pomodori* for user stories including up to 50 *pomodori* and multiples of 50 *pomodori* for user stories including more than 50 *pomodori*. Let us say that by increasing the unit of measurement the team suffered less in terms of reliability.

Although these changes seem to lead to a slower and more complex estimate process, the team was in actual fact able to keep the re-estimate times very low thanks to the simplicity of the estimate rules and a common agreement on the goal behind the rules. The team's total re-estimate effort was equal to 77 *pomodori* for the whole project, namely the equivalent of less than a week's work spread over a project that covered more than 10 months.

The trend in the three error coefficients throughout the project is shown in figure 1.

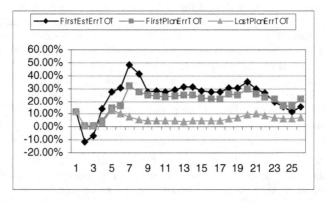

Fig. 1. The trend in the three error coefficients throughout the project

The peak between the 5th and the 8th iterations should be noted. This peak corresponds to the mentioned big refactoring. Furthermore, as of the 20th iteration (which corresponds to the third contract renewal period) a process started that affected the fairly regular trend in the three error coefficients up to that point and which, in the end, modified the three errors as follows:

Table 3. Accrued estimate error throughout the project

FirstEstErr$_{TOT}$	FirstPlanErr$_{TOT}$	LastPlanErr$_{TOT}$
15.68%	21.78%	7.24%

Lastly, it is important to underline that the FirstEstErr$_{TOT}$ – though only in the third contract renewal period – fell to 0.61%, well below the 10% target the customer had set and with the customer still feeling that the team had delivered even more value within the same time unit. This result was obviously reached through a consistent and uncompromising application of refactoring, which allowed us to keep the system fairly simple as its functionalities increased.

As far as Parkinson's Law is concerned, we feel we should mention we obtained very positive feedback from the customer. However, we should point out that when we re-estimated the stories at the end of each iteration, as an XP team usually does, the estimates the stories were planned with were frequently lower than the team's first estimates. This justifies the gap between the FirstEstErr$_{TOT}$ and the FirstPlanErr$_{TOT}$ and strikes a balance between what was possible and what was desirable. In-so-doing it is difficult to fall into Parkinson's Law. As further proof, as can be seen in Table 1, on a number of occasions the team completed the planned stories earlier than expected and thus decided to tackle extra ones - not included in the corresponding iteration plan. Lastly, even the FirstPlanErr$_{TOT}$ trend experienced in the third contract renewal period seems to confirm this conclusion; whereas it was 26.32% in the previous period (also taking into account the user stories being processed but not yet completed between one period and the next), in the third contract renewal period it fell to 16.65%, but not to zero, confirming that the team did not artificially inflate estimates in any way.

3   Actual Time vs. Ideal Time

The use of *pomodoro* may seem in contrast with one of the principles put forward by various sources (for example, [8] and [9]): an XP team should never estimate in actual time but rather refer to Ideal Time and then map out the result (namely the Velocity) by way of the Yesterday's Weather technique[1]. As a consequence, one of the possible criticisms about using *pomodoro* regards the possible loss of the beneficial effects tied to estimates carried out with Ideal Time. Moreover, if one acts in bad faith, the *pomodoro* could become nothing more than a *micromanagement* tool, thus causing the software engineer to work to a speed and under the sort of pressure that is contrary to the values inspired by XP. As such, the *pomodoro* would become a remake of Taylor's principles of productivity applied to software development.

However, our experience is quite different and confirms what is suggested in [3]. The use of *pomodoro* in an environment where interruptions due to external factors cannot occur (i.e.: meetings, email, telephone calls, etc.) will lead to total focus being placed on the project and, in turn, people will be able to map actual time against ideal time. At this point software engineers can indeed put forward their best estimates by adopting the very same approach used when estimating in ideal time. It is then essential to close the feedback loop as quickly as possible so that each engineer can correct his/her assessment of the effort required to accomplish the various tasks to complete the project. The artefacts we have mentioned in this paper, Iteration Probe and Estimates vs Efforts, go exactly in this direction, though on two different scales; the former supplies us with immediate feedback on the stories being processed in the ongoing iteration, whereas the latter provides a broader scope, as it allows us to analyse the project in its entirety. If used correctly during the iteration retrospective, together with Post Mortem, these artefacts can provide a very rich and powerful feedback.

If a team cannot create the above conditions then it is much easier to use Ideal Time. There is a risk though: the feedback on the team's estimation skills might be confused with the lack of project focus. If, on the one hand, it is clear that Yesterday's

---

[1] For a full understanding of Ideal Time, Velocity and Yesterday's Weather please refer to [8].

Weather allows us to plan effectively, it does not, in our opinion, help us learn to estimate. Rather, it might prevent us from recognising an estimate error by confusing the error with environment problems. Under such conditions, the team must be extremely careful in distinguishing the components of the estimate error, that have been caused by breaks in their work or, in any case, poor focus, from those due to:

1. incorrect evaluation of the intrinsic difficulties behind a user story;
2. poorly refactored system resistant to the introduction of new functionalities.

3.1 Comparing *Pomodori* and Yesterday's Weather

Yesterday's Weather implicitly corrects estimate errors. During past projects we tried to apply an automatic correction factor. However, the results were positive from the point of view of error correction speed, but negative as regards the ability to learn and improve our estimate skills.

In order to better explain this concept, let us try an experiment, which was also suggested by a message in the *extremeprogramming* mailing list [10]. We will try to compare the efficiency of Yesterday's Weather-based planning with that of *pomodoro*-based planning. To do this, we must convert the *pomodoro* estimates into general story points rated according to a 3-level difficulty scale (1 = simple, 2 = average difficulty, 3 = difficult). Furthermore, we will correlate the three levels so that, for example, a story with a difficulty rating of 3 would require 3 times the amount of time than a story with a difficulty rating of 1. We will then compare the story points as they would have been planned in accordance with Yesterday's Weather to the actually planned and completed story points during the iteration.

Let us take iteration 5 as our example, for which 15 user stories had been planned. As can be seen from Table 1, we were fairly accurate with our previous estimates whereas during iteration 5 we had to run a long refactoring session which necessarily slowed down the process. By mapping the estimates based on the three difficulty ratings we get a total of 20 planned story points. At the end of the iteration, we see that during the corresponding period (a little over two weeks in this case) only 10 story points were completed. During the following iteration, which was shortened to 1 week, Yesterday's Weather would have allowed to plan 4 story points only, rounding off by default. In actual fact – using *pomodori* – 10 story points were planned, 6 of which were completed at the end of the iteration. If we continue this comparison for iterations 7, 8 and 9 as well (namely those iterations when the effect of the big refactoring was most noticeable, plus the first iteration when the situation became normal), the results can be seen in Table 4.

Table 4. A comparison between *pomodoro*- and Yesterday's Weather-based planning

Iteration	*Pomodori*	Weeks	Planned story points	Completed story points	Velocity (completed story points per week)	Story point via Yesterday's Weather
5	200	2.22	20	10	4.50	
6	91	1.01	10	6	5.93	4.55
7	166	1.84	16	16	8.67	10.95
8	146	1.62	9	9	5.55	14.07
9	80	0.89	10	10	11.25	4.93

As can be seen, the use of Yesterday's Weather would, on the one hand, have led to a much faster correction of the estimate error caused by big refactoring, but also - on the other hand – to a much greater sensitivity to estimate variations. The use of *pomodoro* may therefore seem to demonstrate that there is greater inertia than with Yesterday's Weather, inertia which we feel, enhances the awareness of software engineers in the estimate process. To be quite clear on the matter, we felt that by using *pomodoro* and tying our estimates to actual time we could learn from our mistakes much more quickly and in a permanent way.

The conversion[2] of estimates made using *pomodoro* into estimates consisting of story points (using a 3-difficulty rating scale only) is arbitrary and should therefore be considered as such. Furthermore, since this conversion was performed subsequently, it has no real effect on planning, but only a theoretical one. That should be kept in mind when comparing the results. However, the team did consider the results meaningful, with a difference that could be due to two factors: lower accuracy of the scale expressed in story points (irrespective of the performed conversion) and high sensitivity to variations (volatility) shown by the Yesterday's Weather method.

3.2   Run Your Own Experiment

Should a team be practising with estimates based on actual time and wish to determine the best technique to adopt in a specific instance, they can repeat the experiment described above and adapt it to their specific requirements.

At the end of an iteration, all the team has to do is the following:

1. calculate the story points corresponding to the planned actual time (ATSP), provided it follows a linear conversion pattern, with a close level of approximation; *i.e.: in iteration no. 5, the value was ATSP = 20*
2. assess how many of the story points are originated by completed user stories (CSP); *i.e. in iteration no. 5, the value was CSP = 10*
3. calculate the Velocity (V) of the newly completed iteration, resulting from the ratio between completed story points (CSP) and number of weeks in the old iteration (WOI):

$$V = CSP / WOI \qquad (2)$$

i.e. in iteration no. 5, the value was V = 4.5
4. calculate the theoretical story points (TSP) to be planned for the subsequent iteration as: Velocity (V) times the weeks of the new iteration (WNI).

$$TSP = V * WNI \qquad (3)$$

i.e. in iteration no. 5, the value was TSP = 4.55

---

[2] Taking into account an average story size of 12.76 *pomodori* (first plan estimate) for the given period, a standard deviation of 8.29 *pomodoro* (first plan estimate), and with due regard to the fact that a pair would typically process the code of 10 *pomodori* in a full day, the team applied the following conversion rule:
- ~10 *pomodori* → rating 1
- ~20 *pomodori* → rating 2
- ~30 *pomodori* → rating 3

The effects of using Yesterday's Weather vs. actual time can be assessed by comparing ATSP to TSP. It must however be noted that Velocity has to be defined with reference to weeks, in order to allow a comparison with the actual days of the iteration (Step 3). If the team runs iterations that are always of the same size, the calculation is easier.

A decision as to which approach to adopt could even be made during the planning stage, by switching from actual time to Yesterday's Weather and vice versa, in order to meet specific needs.

4   Future Work

One very interesting future evolution of the work carried out using *pomodoro* would be the ability to assess the value delivered to the customer versus the effort required to produce that value. Had that sort of information been available to us, we would certainly have managed to better control the reduction of $FirstEstErr_{TOT}$, without having to wait for the customer's feedback. Indeed, it would have enhanced this result and offered a comparison with other metrics coming from the process. Ideally, we would like to be able to evaluate the delta of the ROI expected by the customer; however, for a number of reasons, this is only very rarely possible. The team is thus currently focusing on the possible evaluation of the amount of functionality delivered to the customer, in the hope that, over time, the customer will set priorities aimed at enhancing the project value. All of these evaluations should not in any way become an excuse for assessing the team's internal productivity and falling into the sort of regressive Tayloristic behaviour XP is designed to avoid.

5   Conclusion

A development process using XP is an on-going process where the constant improvement of obtained results is pursued. The best way to check the effects the introduced changes have on a process is to create metrics that are not misleading and that allow us to evaluate such changes. From our experience, it is possible to build simple but powerful analytical tools that allow us to control the reliability of estimates over time.

Lastly, we hope this paper has demonstrated how using actual time via *pomodoro* is definitely a way to learn to estimate. The tracking data are not used to penalise or reward the developers but to manage the customer's expectations more efficiently.

References

1. P. Bossi, eXtreme Programming applied: a case in the private banking domain, Proceedings of the 2003 OOP German conference (OOP2003), Munich, 2003
2. F. Cirillo, Exploiting Time, to be published online at http://www.xplabs.com
3. F. Cirillo, Tracking the project, to be published online at (http://www.xplabs.com)

4. P. Bossi, B. Bossola, G. Castaldi, R. Crivelli, E. Di Blasio, A. Quario, L. Ugolini, Tracking
   – A working experience, available online in the Repo Margining System - Lab at
   http://www.communications.xplabs.com/paper2001-2.html
5. M. Fowler, Refactoring: Improving the Design of Existing Code, Addison-Wesley, 1999
6. P. Bossi, G. Castaldi, A. Quario, Testing ideas and tips from the battlefield, WTiXP 2002
   Position Paper, available online at http://www.cwi.nl/events/2002/wtixp/papers/Bossi.pdf
7. C. Northcote Parkinson, Parkinson's Law: The Pursuit of Progress, John Murray, 1958
8. K. Beck, M. Fowler, Planning Extreme Programming, Addison-Wesley, 2000
9. R. Jeffries, A. Anderson, C. Hendrickson, Extreme Programming Installed, Addison-
   Wesley, 2000
10. R. Jeffries, extremeprogramming mailing list, available online at
    http://groups.yahoo.com/group/extremeprogramming/message/53239

Coaching a Customer Team

David Hussman

SGF Software Co., 3010 Hennepin Ave South
Minneapolis, Minnesota 55408-2614
david.hussman@sgfco.com

Abstract. As XP projects grow in size, the customer responsibilities need to be distributed to a group acting as a customer team. If the team is large, a customer coach can help with the coordination of information gathering, organization of cohesive collection of stories to present, monitoring story content and consistency, and synchronization with the development schedule. This paper contains topics to consider as the team prepares for the project as well as lessons learned while coaching a large customer team, both successes and failures.

1   Introduction

The contents of this paper represent the realization of ideas for coaching a team of customers for a large scale XP project. Extrapolating from experience playing the role of the customer, experience working on large XP teams, as well as general experience coaching XP teams, I started the project with a set of ideas and tactics that I thought would help jump start the customer team's efforts. Having previously worked at this particular company, I had a good understanding of the corporate culture surrounding the customer team. As there were several variations of XP being practiced company wide that would impact how this team practiced XP, I wanted to help the team by also providing a simple, unbiased experience of the planning game. Knowing that the team would need to mold XP to fit into the project's culture and the team's personality, I decided to approach the coaching effort with the following goals:

1. organize the customer team into sub-teams that would work with a sub set of developers – create initial definition of sub team roles and responsibilities
2. review, edit, and organize initial customer stories
3. help find an appropriate level of acceptance tests – provide a focus on acceptance tests as the key to clearly communicating story completion to the developers
4. help functionally decompose the project domain in a way that would help scope the project and create a bed for story creation
5. help find a level of story granularity that would work well with the developer teams
6. develop and modify iteration planning so as to find a symbiosis with developer's iteration planning
7. help recognize new stories that arise outside the customer team (from the testing or development group)
8. try to get some sort of automated acceptance testing in place from the beginning of the project

M. Marchesi and G. Succi (Eds.): XP 2003, LNCS 2675, pp. 254–260, 2003.
© Springer-Verlag Berlin Heidelberg 2003

1.1 Project Background

The project was not without pre-existing issues. Prior to creation of the first story, the project faced the age old trial of scheduling constraints created in a vacuum and imposed by upper management. All project players knew that there was a great deal of work to be done, and the proposed completion date was dangerously aggressive. The choice to use agile practices, specifically XP, came from a company wide focus to embrace XP as well as a way to manage risk and provide a view into the output of the development team.

The project leaders decided to start with one development lab. The lab members were then to be split out, sharing their knowledge and seeding new labs. Using statistics gathered from a collection of previous XP projects in the company, the project director was guessing that the customer team would eventually need to support 3 to 4 labs containing 10 developers each. Also relying on previous experience, I suggested that we shoot for a developer to customer ratio of 3:1 or less. This meant a customer team that could grow to somewhere between 10 and 20.

1.2 Known Risks

Aside from an aggressive schedule, there were several other potential issues that were addressed and worth noting. The customer team was to be internal to the company, but the sponsoring client wanted a view into the project, project requirements, and the development process in general. There was existing history with the client, and a new and higher level of trust needed to be established / rebuilt.

Most important to the project leaders (as well as the sponsoring client) was a working knowledge of the project's scope. As well as gaining a better understanding of the project, scope definition was deemed necessary to help improve the estimates for the number and size of the team(s) initially needed. As explained later, many members of the customer team would have preferred to spend more time getting a high level collection of stories / story titles prior to leaping head long into development.

2 Project Preparation

To increase the customer team readiness prior to the first release and iteration planning sessions, the team gathered several times to discuss team sub-division, the life cycle of a story, and the way in which the stories would flow in and out of the customer team, as well as to review some sample stories. We also spent a bit of time getting to know each other, sharing concerns and experiences with XP.

2.1 Practice Planning Session

Due to the diverse collection of skill sets on the team, and the number of customers new to XP, we conducted a practice iteration planning session intended to help the team form a collective vision of the planning game, learn to work together, and possibly reveal team strengths. The team presented stories and I played the role of a developer. The practice session also gave the customers a better understanding of developer interaction, possible questions asked during iteration planning, the importance of acceptance tests, the importance of story granularity and clarity, and the interactive nature of customers and developers on an XP project.

2.2   Proposed Schedule

Collectively, a proposed iteration schedule was created to clarify the lifecycle for a collection of stories to be presented during a specific iteration planning session in the future. The cycle included meetings with the sponsoring client, story selection for the iteration, creation of story skeletons, fleshing out the collective understanding of story details (and acceptance tests), presenting the stories to the developers, and story sign off. In order to be prepared for iteration planning with the developers, the customer team's planning was to be started two weeks prior to iteration planning sessions with the developers.

2.3   Story Authoring

To organize our story writing, we decided to deviate from 3x5 cards and use a simple story template which consisted of story title, story details, acceptance tests, and a small table for developer tasks and estimates. This selection allowed a large group of persons to review and modify story content with the sponsoring client (the last item turned out to be a bad idea that is reviewed in the lessons learned section of this papers). The document was also projected on a wall during iteration planning, and modifications to the document were witnessed by all.

2.4   Division of Labor

Knowing that the customer team was to serve more than one development team, we distributed and defined the tasks performed by a single customer across a customer sub-team. To do this we considered the number of sub-teams anticipated verses the customer resources available to the project, sub-team organization / roles and appropriate persons for each of the roles, and sub-team coordination and the definition of a role that might fill this void

To coordinate the customer team efforts, someone was designated to play the role I called "customer coordinator." This person was to coordinate the gathering and distribution of stories across the sub-teams and work with the project and product managers to incorporate possible project wide course corrections, gather a collection of stories for the different sub-teams, and communicate issues across to development coaches and other project leaders. We chose to create sub-teams composed of three players assuming the following roles and responsibilities:

- Story Author / Lead Customer – synchronizes with other sub-team authors and customer coordinator to gather stories for next iteration and look for story synchronization or overlap, gathers information from sponsoring client(s) or company domain expert, and crafts stories for each iteration

- Presenter / Customer – reviews authored stories prior to iteration planning, adds detail as needed, presents stories during iteration planning, and answers developer questions during iteration.
- Tester – performs all acceptance tests for iteration, meets with customer team coordinator to review defects found.

2.5   Focus on Acceptance Tests during the Life of a Story

From the beginning of the project, we discussed as a group the importance of providing complete stories to the developers. For the most part, this meant agreeing that we would not go into iteration planning without acceptance tests for the stories. We created the following list to help us find a common vision of acceptance tests during story authoring as well as usage by the developers:

1. Acceptance tests are the customer's way of concretely showing the developers a clear definition of when a story is complete. The clearer and more complete they are, the easier it will be to get stories signed off
2. When crafting stories, have an idea of one or more acceptance tests as early as possible. This will help focus on story closure from the story's inception. I suggested that the team use the following guide for authoring stories. This guide incorporates acceptance testing from the beginning and is a variation on the ideas presented in "Use Cases: Requirements In Context" [1]:
   - (Façade) - Story title; maybe a single sentence used for release planning and project scoping; create at least one acceptance test per story title
   - (Filled) - Add enough detail to the story so that the customer team can discuss the story, readying the story for presentation to the developers; for each story detail, ensure there are one or more acceptance tests (too many tests might mean the story is too large)
   - (Focused) - Review the story for clarity during iteration planning; modify the story as per the iteration planning discussion, add acceptance tests for any detail added; monitor the level of acceptances tests as a measure used to break stories into several stories; start creating any data sets needed for acceptance testing
   - (Final) - Post final version of story in the development lab; ensure readiness to acceptance test any completed stories (check in with developers as to any needs they may have to ensure stories can be acceptance tested sooner than later); create any data sets needed for acceptance testing.
3. Start acceptance testing as soon as any story is ready. Do not wait until near the end of the iteration to start acceptance testing. This will reduce the number of incomplete stories due to a misunderstanding of story content or the acceptance tests.

3   Issues Faced – Lessons Learned

As previously mentioned, I was away from the project for a period of several months. The following topics are a collection of observations regarding project change; both from my perspective and from information I gathered interviewing the customer team and other project leaders involved with the project team. Our preparations for iteration planning helped, but as expected, we encountered a collection of road blocks which called for course corrections. One of the largest issues was modifications needed to address the dynamics associated with adding more labs.

3.1   The Story Lab

Project leaders, with input from the sponsoring client, created a story lab where members of the customer team who were not yet supporting a lab would try to translate the requirements gathered to date into a collection of facade level stories. These story facades were to be used to help understand / define project scope. Upon returning to this project, after being away for several months, many of the now experienced customer team members told me that they thought this was helpful but too hurried. The customer team believed that doing this prior to starting development would have provided them a better understanding of the project, and would have better prepared them to explain functionality to the developers. When I asked about a time frame, they were happy to time-box the effort to two weeks, not too expensive for a project that will end up with thousands of stories.

3.2   Story Size and Consistency with Multiple Authors

Further complicating our ability to understand the scope of the project, the customer team struggled with multiple authors trying to create stories of similar consistency and size that would present well to the development teams. As the development teams grew, so too did the amount of work that could be included into a story. Though the customer team worked through this, and found somewhat of a steady state for authoring stories, project management was struggling with story size and the value of a story point while trying to determine how much could be accomplished by the current team.

3.3   Issues with the Sponsoring Client

During my interviews with the customer team, one of their greatest struggles involved finding when and where to let the sponsoring client into the process. Many customers thought that the story format was not a medium that worked well for both the client and the developers. A project leader suggested that next time, the client interaction with the stories should be limited to the filled level, or maybe the requirements should be presented in a different form to the client (although this made me feel a bit uneasy, translation issues and all).

Another major issue for the project was the management of scope creep. We started the project with the idea that we would track the number of stories included in the initial scope agreed upon by the company and the sponsoring client. Although this worked to some level, changing of story granularity (early in the project) and a story point, combined with the number of stories that were broken into more than one story, made managing scope difficult using stories as a metric.

3.4   Automation of Acceptance Testing - Tester and Customer Disconnect

Toward the beginning of the project, a small group met to discuss the creation of an automated acceptance test framework (ATF). Today, I would probably choose to use the FIT framework, as this is similar to what we built. As coach to the customer team, I had stressed the importance of regressively executing all acceptance tests for signed off stories. I have found this to be as important for the customer as regressively running unit tests is for the developer(s).

Upon returning to the project, I noticed that the ATF effort had been dropped. It had been determined that it would be impossible to maintain ATF due to the use of emergent design. It appears that the small group that had been assigned to implement and maintain this code simply could not keep up with the developers and the changes to the code at the point where the ATF attached.

Around the same time, with an eye on quality, someone from the group of testers started creating a collection of manual tests, their origin being functionality from the acceptance tests for the stories. Although the number of unit tests was growing, the quality of the end product began to suffer due to a lack of executing the manual tests, and possibly content previously signed off that had not made the transfer. Also, it was decided that the testers should spend time signing off on stories, or put another way, that the time to execute the manual tests conflicted with a desire to maintain or increase velocity so it was deemed less important and removed.

It is here that the project has met it worst enemy. I have found that to move forward in the name of velocity without addressing regressive acceptance testing when there is a large development team is problematic. Combine this issue with the fact that many people on or in charge of the customer team assumed that the ATF was still being used, and you have a recipe for poor quality. It is clear that, as with development, no testing reduces quality and too much testing reduces velocity. I suggest that the customer team always own the level of acceptance testing and work with the project manager(s) to determine "how much testing is enough."

The disconnection between those writing the stories and those testing the stories is now being remedied with a renewed focus on the customer coordinator role (a role that had become too focused on organizing and managing story creation).

3.5   Lack of Non-functional Stories

At the beginning of the project, I had suggested that the team try to incorporate one non-functional story (performance, security – localization). I had used this idea on smaller project and found that, as the customer, I was almost always able to pay for some non-functional development per iteration, and that the feedback it returned (i.e. performance numbers) was extremely valuable and something I could use throughout the duration of the project. I am not sure if this would have worked as well with a large team, but the project would be helped at present by some simple profiling metrics.

4   Conclusions

Embarking on this coaching effort, I planned to draw on experience and ideas garnered from previous coaching with large teams as well as acting as a customer. What I was unprepared for was the difficulties of working with a team of customers that in turn had to work with a group of representatives from a sponsoring client. Many paths chosen by the team were at odds with some of my ideas going into the project. Having left the project and returned, I was able to see those ideas that worked and, once again, learn the lesson that community based process means that the process must morph to fit into the culture of the company and the project.

As the customer team grows, it is imperative to have one or more persons helping to organize and steer. All communication issues are magnified, and meetings between the customer coach, customer coordinator, project manager, developer coaches, and other "leads" must take place to mitigate issues like lab dependencies and functional overlap to name a few. Also important is the need to sub-divide and conquer within the customer team. As described in this paper, it is crucial that this sub-division is not being done at the expense of team cohesion.

Reference

1. Daryl Kulak; Eamonn Guiney; Use Cases: Requirements in Context.

Extreme Design by Contract

Yishai A. Feldman

Efi Arazi School of Computer Science
The Interdisciplinary Center, P.O.B. 167, Herzliya 46150, Israel
yishai@idc.ac.il
http://www.idc.ac.il/yishai

Abstract. Design by contract is a practical technique for developing code together with its (light-weight and executable) specification. It is synergistic with several XP practices, particularly unit testing and refactoring. This paper investigates this relationship and points out how it can be automated (at least in part).

1 Introduction

Design by contract [1] is a practical methodology for developing object-oriented programs together with their specifications. It offers immediate benefits in terms of early error detection as well as long-term process improvement. The specifications are given as part of the code itself in the form of assertions such as class invariants and method pre- and postconditions. This allows the compiler to instrument the program to check these assertions at runtime. No less important, it allows the programmer to reason about the program with relative ease.

The first language to support design by contract was Eiffel, but the idea is gaining in popularity and several tools [2–5] have emerged recently for using this methodology when programming in Java. As implemented in these languages, the assertion language is limited in its expressive power, and does not support the full generality needed for program verification. However, it is easy to use and still offers substantial practical benefits.

Design by contract is synergistic with several XP practices, particularly unit testing and refactoring. This paper investigates this relationship, with a detailed analysis of the interactions between design by contract and refactoring. This analysis specifies the type of interaction as well as the difficulty of automating the contract modifications implied by the refactorings.

2 Design by Contract: An Example

Figure 1 shows an excerpt from a Java class RPNCalc, which emulates a simple Reverse Polish Notation (RPN) calculator (such as HP used to make)[1]. In this

---

[1] Missing in the figures shown in this paper is some of the code, as well as part of the contract. Also, some assertions have been slightly simplified. The full set of programs, with additional intermediate steps not shown here, is available at
http://www.faculty.idc.ac.il/yishai/xp-contracts.htm.

M. Marchesi and G. Succi (Eds.): XP 2003, LNCS 2675, pp. 261–270, 2003.

```
/** @inv size() >= 0
 *  @inv elements != null
 */
public class RPNCalc
{
  final protected Vector elements = new Vector();

  /** @pre size() >= 1 */
  public int display()
  {
    return ((Integer)elements.lastElement()).intValue();
  }

  /** @post size() == $prev(size()) + 1
   *  @post display() == n
   *  @post size() <= 1 || second() == $prev(display())
   */
  public void enter(int n) { elements.addElement(new Integer(n)); }

  /** @pre size() >= 2
   *  @post size() == $prev(size()) - 1
   *  @post display() == $prev(second()) + $prev(display())
   */
  public void add()
  {
    int size = elements.size();
    elements.setElementAt(new Integer(second() + display()), size-2);
    elements.setSize(size-1);
  }
}
```

Fig. 1. RPN calculator program (excerpt)

notation, the function symbol follows the arguments, and pending arguments are kept in a stack. Thus, to compute $2 + 3 * 5$ you would press the keys 2, ⟨Enter⟩, 3, ⟨Enter⟩, 5, $*$ (at which point the display shows 15), and finally $+$ to get the result, 17.

The program provides the following operations: size() returns the number of elements in the operand stack; display() and second() return the top element and the next one, respectively (these are called x and y in HP calculators); enter(int n) pushes a new number onto the operand stack; and add(), sub(), etc., perform the arithmetic operations on the top two elements in the operand stack, replacing them with the result. The implementation uses the Java Vector class for the operand stack.

The Javadoc comments of this class include the three types of assertions: class invariants, method preconditions, and method postconditions. For example, the first invariant states that the number of elements in the operand stack is never negative. Clients of RPNCalc may rely on this property. The second invariant states that the internal field elements is never null; as such, it is an *implemen-*

tation invariant, crucial to the correctness of the implementation (since there are no null tests before invoking methods on `elements`) but is irrelevant for clients.

The method `add` has a precondition that states that it may not be called unless there are at least two elements in the operand stack. It is the client's contractual obligation not to violate this precondition; any such violation is a client bug. If the client calls this method when the precondition holds, the method must end in a state where the operand stack has one less element, and the display shows the sum of the two values previously on top of the stack. (The operator `$prev` refers to the value of its argument on entry to the method.) A violation of these postconditions is a supplier bug.

The various design-by-contract tools can instrument the code to check for assertion violations. Such violations give early warnings about bugs in the program, and help identify the source of the bug, whether in the client or supplier code. The contract also has methodological implications regardless of whether it is checked at runtime or not. First, it clearly specifies the assumptions underlying re-use of existing classes. Second, it places constraints on inheritance. If B inherits from A, all instances of B are *ipso facto* elements of A as well. If B has a stronger precondition than A on some method, a client of A might inadvertently be in violation of the precondition when using an element of B polymorphically. This is clearly unacceptable, and therefore inheriting classes may only weaken preconditions. Analogously, they are only allowed to strengthen invariants and postconditions. Finally, the assertions can be used to prove the correctness of the program at various levels of rigor.

3   Contracts and XP

The implementation of a new piece of functionality is considered to be finished in XP when all the unit tests written to define it execute successfully. This practice works well when the unit tests are well-written, but no tests can completely specify the desired functionality, and it is certainly possible for a bug to slip through. Also, as code is changed (during refactoring or while adding functionality), it is possible that existing tests become invalid because they refer to an old partition of responsibilities between classes or methods, which is no longer in effect. This means that unit tests must continuously be maintained, together with the code they test [6].

Contracts are an alternative way of specifying functionality. It takes some getting used to, but experienced developers find it very natural to write a contract before the implementation of a class or method. Contracts are still not enough for testing, since additional code needs to be written to exercise the methods. However, this code is concerned with covering all interesting paths through the program rather than in checking the correctness of the results—this is the responsibility of the contracts. This has two benefits. First, less testing code needs to be written; this is like XP unit tests but without calls that check results. Second, this means that testing code can be written in larger units that exercise several methods simultaneously, instead of separate tests for each method. These two observations, taken together, mean that unit tests need to be modified less frequently when they rely on contracts for checking correctness of the results. For example, the following method is taken from a JUnit class for testing RPNCalc; it exercises all the methods of RPNCalc, and mainly relies on the instrumented contract for correctness checks. (Some global sanity checks have been added.)

```
public void test1()
{
  RPNCalc c = new RPNCalc();
  for (int i = 1; i <= n; i++) c.enter(i);
  while (c.size() > 1) c.add();
  assertEquals(n*(n+1)/2, c.display());
  for (int i = 1; i < n; i++)
  {
    c.enter(i);
    c.sub();
  }
  assertEquals(n, c.display());
  assertEquals(1, c.size());
}
```

Of course, the contract itself needs to change together with the changes in the functionality of the code. This is easier than changing the tests, since the contract gives the meaning of the class and methods, and changes we want to make in the code are naturally reflected in the contract. (Actually, this puts the cart before the horse; we should first understand what we are trying to do in terms of the contract, then translate that understanding into changes in the code.) Furthermore, contract modifications can be done in a systematic way, in the same way that refactorings are defined systematically. The rest of this paper discusses the interactions between refactoring and contracts.

4   Contracts and Refactoring

As explained above, refactorings are closely tied with contracts; whenever functionality is redistributed between methods and classes, contracts are intimately involved. One refactoring, *Introduce Assertion*[2], is all about contracts. There are a number of additional contract-related refactorings that need to be introduced; these are discussed in Section 5. However, we now focus on refactorings that involve both contracts and code, and illustrate some of the interactions between contracts and refactoring by means of an example. We start with the class RPNCalc discussed above.

In the first step, *Extract Class* is used to define a new class called Stack, which is initially empty. A new final field, stack, is added to RPNCalc. At this point, an invariant is added to RPNCalc, stating that this field can never be null. Next, *Self-Encapsulate Field* is used to encapsulate all accesses to the field, elements, that contains the vector in RPNCalc via a getter method getElements. A new invariant is added, stating that getElements never returns null. This

---

[2] Except in Section 5, refactorings mentioned in this paper refer to Fowler [7].

```
/** @inv size() >= 0
 *  @inv stack != null
 *  @inv getElements() != null
 */
public class RPNCalc
{
  final protected Stack stack = new Stack();

  /** @post $ret == stack.getElements() */
  protected Vector getElements() { return stack.getElements(); }

  /** @pre size() >= 1 */
  public int display() { return stack.top(); }

  /** @post size() == $prev(size()) + 1
   *  @post display() == n
   *  @post size() <= 1 || second() == $prev(display())
   */
  public void enter(int n) { stack.push(n); }

  /** @pre size() >= 2
   *  @post size() == $prev(size()) - 1
   *  @post display() == $prev(second()) + $prev(display())
   */
  public void add()
  {
    int size = size();
    getElements().setElementAt(new Integer(second() + display()),size-2);
    getElements().setSize(size-1);
  }
}
```

Fig. 2. Intermediate version of RPNCalc (excerpt)

directly follows from the invariant of RPNCalc that states that the elements field is never null. In addition, getElements is equipped with a postcondition that states that it returns the value of elements.

Next, *Move Field* is used to move the elements field to the Stack class (and a getter method is added for it there). In addition to the obvious changes, the postcondition on getElements now needs to say that it returns stack.getElements(). In addition, the original invariant in RPNCalc that referred to the elements field is now moved to Stack.

Now we have several methods in RPNCalc that refer to the vector through the pointer to the Stack object. We now use *Move Method* to move size, display (now renamed to top), second, and enter (renamed to push) to the Stack class. The original method bodies now delegate to the methods in Stack, and their contracts are copied to the new methods. Figures 2 and 3 show the current state of the two classes.

```
/** @inv size() >= 0
 *  @inv elements != null
 *  @inv getElements() != null
 */
public class Stack
{
  final protected Vector elements = new Vector();

  public Vector getElements() { return elements; }

  /** @pre size() >= 1 */
  public int top() {return ((Integer)elements.lastElement()).intValue();}

  /** @post size() == $prev(size()) + 1
   *  @post top() == n
   *  @post size() <= 1 || second() == $prev(top())
   */
  public void push(int n) { elements.addElement(new Integer(n)); }
}
```

Fig. 3. Intermediate version of Stack (excerpt)

The original implementation of add and similar methods made use of the methods of Vector, which give full access to all elements. These methods performed the required operation on the last two elements of the vector, and then reduced the size of the vector by one using the method setSize. As a step toward the elimination of outside access to the vector, which now resides in Stack, we use *Extract Method* to encapsulate the reduction in size by a new method, called pop. This new method needs a contract, but this contract is harder to find. We can reason as follows. First, since the body of this method sets the size of the vector to size() - 1, and the size of a vector may not be negative, we need a precondition size() >= 1. Second, a postcondition can be added stating that the value returned by size() after this operation, which is computed as the size of the vector, is one less than its previous value. Finally, the value now returned by display() is the one previously returned by second(). These reasoning steps were presented in order of increasing sophistication. It is possible that they can be discovered automatically, and we are developing a tool for this purpose [8]; however, this requires complex analysis, and needs theorem-proving capability. After extracting this method, it is moved to Stack.

We can now use *Substitute Algorithm* to complete the refactoring of add and similar methods, by rewriting their bodies to make use of push and pop. At this point, there is no further use of getElements in RPNCalc, and this method, together with the associated contract (including the invariant) can be removed.

We now have a full-functionality stack class, which we can use in other applications. Unlike traditional stack implementations, this provides access to the second element as well as the top one. We can consider generalizing this to allow

```
/** @inv size() >= 0
 *  @inv stack != null
 */
public class RPNCalc
{
  final protected Stack stack = new Stack();

  /** @pre size() >= 1 */
  public int display() { return stack.top(); }

  /** @post size() == $prev(size()) + 1
   *  @post display() == n
   *  @post size() <= 1 || second() == $prev(display())
   */
  public void enter(int n) { stack.push(n); }

  /** @pre size() >= 2
   *  @post size() == $prev(size()) - 1
   *  @post display() == $prev(second()) + $prev(display())
   */
  public void add()
  {
    int n2 = stack.top();
    stack.pop();
    int n1 = stack.top();
    stack.pop();
    stack.push(n1 + n2);
  }
}
```

Fig. 4. Final version of RPNCalc (excerpt)

read-only access to all elements of the stack (while leaving the LIFO insertion and removal policy). However, this would be adding new functionality, and is therefore outside the scope of this discussion. Excerpts from the results of the whole transformation process appear in Figures 4 and 5.

It should be noted that the testing code for RPNCalc did not need to be modified in any way during this process. Of course, the new Stack class requires tests of its own; these are easily modified from those of RPNCalc.

5   Contract-Related Refactorings

When using design by contract, there are several refactorings that maintain the contracts rather than the code. For example, when there are identical assertions on the same methods in all subclasses of some superclass, this is an indication that the assertion should apply to all possible subclasses (including future ones). In that case, *Pull Up Assertion* can be used to move the common assertion to the superclass. The opposite refactoring is *Pull Down Assertion*, which can be

```
/** @inv size() >= 0
 *  @inv elements != null
 */
public class Stack
{
  final protected Vector elements = new Vector();

  /** @pre size() >= 1 */
  public int top() {return ((Integer)elements.lastElement()).intValue();}

  /** @post size() == $prev(size()) + 1
   *  @post top() == n
   *  @post size() <= 1 || second() == $prev(top())
   */
  public void push(int n) { elements.addElement(new Integer(n)); }

  /** @pre size() >= 1
   *  @post size() == $prev(size()) - 1
   *  @post size() == 0 || top() == $prev(second())
   */
  public void pop() { elements.setSize(elements.size() - 1); }
}
```

Fig. 5. Final version of Stack (excerpt)

used when it turns out that an assertion in a superclass is too restrictive for some subclasses.

The Stack class we extracted in the example above is unbounded, since it uses a Vector for storing its elements. Other stack implementations, such as those using arrays, are bounded. It is natural to want to make BoundedStack a subclass of Stack. However, this is impossible according to the principles of design by contract, since the subclass (BoundedStack) needs to add a precondition on the push method, while the superclass has no such precondition. This is in fact a reflection of a problem in the hierarchy; the unbounded stack should be renamed UnboundedStack, and it as well as BoundedStack should both inherit from an abstract Stack class. This new superclass will have a precondition !full() on push. At this level, the predicate full is unspecified (that is, has no postcondition). In UnboundedStack, a postcondition on full specifies that it must return false, while in BoundedStack the postcondition specifies that it returns true when size() == capacity(), for example. This is called an *abstract precondition*, and is introduced by the refactoring *Create Abstract Precondition*.

6   Detailed Analysis

I have analyzed the interactions between design by contract and each of the 68 refactorings mentioned in Chapters 6–11 of Fowler's book [7]. Of course, on the simplest level, contracts are treated just like code. For example, when renaming a method, all references to it in the code must be appropriately modified; so must all references in assertions. Similarly, a method may be eliminated when it is not used anywhere, including in assertions. This is taken for granted in the analysis, and is not counted as an interaction between contracts as refactoring.

6.1 Interaction Statistics

It turns out that about 32% of the refactorings studied do not interact with contracts (except in the simple fashion mentioned above). These are mostly syntactic refactorings such as *Remove Parameter* or *Rename Method*, or those that eliminate classes or methods, such as *Inline Class* and *Inline Method*. About 55% of the refactorings require the addition of a contract for new methods or classes that they create; an additional 4% require some contract modifications or movement.

Contracts affect the applicability of some 13% of the refactorings studied. (This number includes 4% that also require contract additions and were also counted above.) For example, each new method introduced into an existing class must obey its invariant. (Of course, it is possible that the invariant itself is at fault and should be modified. This would be done in a separate step prior to the introduction of the offending method.) As a result of these constraints, it is necessary to check for possible violations before applying refactorings such as *Move Method* and *Extract Superclass*.

6.2 Automation

Some of the new contracts that need to be added when refactoring are very simple; for example, the contract of the `isNull` method created by *Introduce Null Object* specifies that it returns true for the class that represents the null object, and false otherwise. Such a contract can be created automatically by a refactoring tool. Other contracts can be derived from existing contracts; for example, the contract of a delegating method is easily adapted from that of the method it delegates to. In some cases it is more difficult to automate the creation of the new contract, as we saw in the example. In particular, *Extract Method* can take a piece of code of arbitrary complexity and make it into a new method. Even in such cases, ongoing research [8] indicates that some automation is possible, but this is much more difficult and requires careful human supervision.

As mentioned above, in some cases it is necessary to check for constraint violations. These checks can be syntactic in nature, in which case they are easy to automate. In other cases, they might require stronger theorem-proving mechanisms.

Apart from the 32% of the refactorings studied that did not interact with contracts, 39% required interactions that were judged to be easy to automate. An additional 17% were judged difficult to automate, although partial help is possible using the methods of Feldman and Gendler [8]. Another 12% would require theorem proving for constraint checking.

7   Conclusion

We have seen an example of a series of refactorings with associated contract modifications. Some of these were mechanical and easy to automate, while others required deeper understanding of the application. In any case, the understanding embodied in the contract is helpful for refactoring with confidence.

I believe that design by contract is an essential technique for producing high-quality code, and is synergistic with XP and other agile methodologies. It simplifies the creation of test cases, clarifies the design, prevents some common bugs (mostly related to the correct use of inheritance), and can even be automated to some extent. I hope this paper will encourage XP practitioners to try using design by contract in large-scale projects.

Acknowledgments

Ariel Shamir, Shmuel Tyszberowicz, and Amiram Yehudai provided useful comments on a previous draft of this paper.

References

1. B. Meyer. *Object-Oriented Software Construction*. Prentice Hall, 2nd edition, 1997.
2. R. Kramer. iContract—the Java design by contract tool. In *Proc. Technology of Object-Oriented Languages and Systems, TOOLS-USA*. IEEE Press, 1998.
3. R. Kramer. iContract home page.
   http://www.reliable-systems.com/tools/iContract/iContract.htm.
4. Parasoft Corp. Jcontract home page.
   http://www.parasoft.com/jsp/products/home.jsp?product=Jcontract.
5. Man Machine Systems. Design by contract tool for Java—JMSAssert.
   http://www.mmsindia.com/JMSAssert.html.
6. A. van Deursen and L. Moonen. The video store revisited: Thoughts on refactoring and testing. In M. Marchesi and G. Succi, editors, *Proc. 3rd Int'l Conf. Extreme Programming and Agile Processes in Software Engineering*, pages 71–76, 2002.
7. M. Fowler. *Refactoring: Improving the Design of Existing Code*. Addison-Wesley, 2000.
8. Y. A. Feldman and L. Gendler. Automatic discovery of software contracts. In progress.

Inline Method Considered Helpful:
An Approach to Interface Evolution

Tammo Freese

OFFIS, Escherweg 2, 26121 Oldenburg, Germany
tammo.freese@offis.de

Abstract. While *Extract Method* is generally considered one of the most useful refactorings, the inverse refactoring *Inline Method* is so far only documented for removing methods whose bodies are as clear as their names. This paper outlines an approach how *Inline Method* may be used in changing method signatures and behavior. Furthermore, it proposes how the approach may simplify evolving published interfaces as well as merging parallel source code changes in next generation software configuration management tools.

1 Introduction

Refactoring has grown popular not only in the Extreme Programming community. Several tools support automated refactoring, among them the integrated development environments (IDEs) Eclipse [3] and IntelliJ IDEA [7]. While both support changing the signature of a method, the tools change the return type by just replacing it with the new one. In most cases, this would lead to code that needs fixes at all the invocations of the method. This is potentially hazardous, as the fixes usually take a long time, in which the code does not even compile.

In his refactoring book [4], Martin Fowler demonstrates how refactorings may be executed in small steps. However, the book has been written four years ago when no refactoring tools for Java were available, so the steps described are focussed on standard text editors. When changing a method signature, all invocations of the old method signature have to be changed manually before the old signature can be deleted. As this may take a long time, the old signature may accidently be left behind.

This paper demonstrates an approach on how to change the return type of a method in small steps by using the automated refactoring support currently available for *Inline Method* [4]. Furthermore, it outlines how to broaden the application of the approach to other refactorings, behavioral changes, changes to published interfaces, and to development in teams.

2 Example

As an example, we will change the return type of a method in small steps. Inheritance issues will be discussed later. The example is a price calculation method `getCharge()` that currently returns a value of type **double**.

M. Marchesi and G. Succi (Eds.): XP 2003, LNCS 2675, pp. 271–278, 2003.
© Springer-Verlag Berlin Heidelberg 2003

```
public class Pricing {
    // ...
    public double getCharge(int days) {
        int additionalDays = Math.max(0, days - DAYS_DISCOUNTED);
        return BASE_PRICE + additionalDays * PRICE_PER_DAY;
    }
}
```

Let's take a look at its accompanying JUnit [8] test case:

```
public class PricingTest extends junit.framework.TestCase {
    public void testPrices() {
        Pricing pricing = new Pricing();
        assertEquals(1.50, pricing.getCharge(1), 0.001);
        assertEquals(1.50, pricing.getCharge(3), 0.001);
        assertEquals(2.50, pricing.getCharge(4), 0.001);
        assertEquals(3.50, pricing.getCharge(5), 0.001);
    }
}
```

The assertions have to use a delta for comparison, because calculations with double values may lead to small deviations. For this reason, it is strongly discouraged to use the double type to represent monetary values. Therefore, we seek a route to change getCharge() to return a Money value object instead of a double value:

```
public Money getCharge(int days) {
    // ...
}
```

This would simplify the test code, as well as other calls to the method where calculations already use Money objects. The test code would not need the delta information anymore:

```
public void testPrices() {
    Pricing pricing = new Pricing();
    assertEquals(new Money(1.50), pricing.getCharge(1));
    assertEquals(new Money(1.50), pricing.getCharge(3));
    assertEquals(new Money(2.50), pricing.getCharge(4));
    assertEquals(new Money(3.50), pricing.getCharge(5));
}
```

This is where we would like our refactoring route to end. Unfortunately, getCharge() is used throughout the system, so it is not recommended to change the signature and fix all the resulting compilation errors in one giant leap. Instead, we would like to take small steps and change the dependent code with as little effort as possible.

3   Adapt to Change

This section describes how to approach the change of a return type in tiny steps using an automated refactoring tool. While some of the steps may feel awkward at first, they will pay off in the end.

To provide an overview of the evolving code structure, we will use a simple notation where methods are represented by rectangles. An arrow between two rectangles illustrates that one method calls the other one. We start with the current signature of `getCharge()`:

```
double getCharge(int)
```

Step 1: Make Signature Available

In Java, method overloading is not possible for method signatures that only differ in their return types. The intended signature for `getCharge()` (returning a `Money`) conflicts with the existing one (returning a `double`). Therefore, our first step is to rename the existing method to make room for the new signature. As we do not want to forget to remove the old method signature, we use a name that violates our coding standard and thus catches the eye. This leads to:

```
double getCharge_OLD(int)
```

Step 2: Extract Contents

To prepare for the next step, we extract the body of `getCharge_OLD()` into a temporary method called `getCharge_TEMP()`:

```java
public double getCharge_OLD(int days) {
    return getCharge_TEMP(days);
}

public double getCharge_TEMP(int days) {
    int additionalDays = Math.max(0, days - DAYS_DISCOUNTED);
    return BASE_PRICE + additionalDays * PRICE_PER_DAY;
}
```

```
double getCharge_OLD(int)
        │
        ▼
    double getCharge_TEMP(int)
```

Step 3: Introduce Legacy Adapter

Now it is time to introduce the new getCharge() method that returns a Money value object. First we change one user of the old method to use the new signature. Motivating a new method with a test is a characteristic step in test-driven development [1] (TDD).

```
public void testPrices() {
    Pricing pricing = new Pricing();
    assertEquals(new Money(1.50), pricing.getCharge(1));
    assertEquals(1.50, pricing.getCharge_OLD(3), 0.001);
    assertEquals(2.50, pricing.getCharge_OLD(4), 0.001);
    assertEquals(3.50, pricing.getCharge_OLD(5), 0.001);
}
```

Then we implement the new method getCharge() using getCharge_TEMP(). This method is an *Adapter* [6] that converts the new signature to the old one. For this reason, we call it the *Legacy Adapter*.

```
public Money getCharge(int days) {
    return new Money(getCharge_TEMP(days));
}
```

We have changed one assertion to use the *Legacy Adapter*. Whether this preserved the intent of our test depends on the equals() implementation of our Money class. So we rerun the tests to be sure that they still pass. The current structure is:

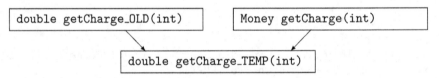

Step 4: Introduce Evolution Adapter

Now we switch over the getCharge_OLD() method to use the *Legacy Adapter*. The new implementation is an adapter that converts the other way round, from the old signature to the new one. Therefore we call it the *Evolution Adapter*.

```
public double getCharge_OLD(int days) {
    return getCharge(days).asDouble();
}
```

```
┌──────────────────────────────┐    ┌──────────────────────────────┐
│ double getCharge_OLD(int)    │───▶│ Money getCharge(int)         │
└──────────────────────────────┘    └──────────────────────────────┘
                 ┌──────────────────────────────┐
                 │ double getCharge_TEMP(int)   │
                 └──────────────────────────────┘
```

Step 5: Inline Contents

As getCharge_TEMP() is only used by getCharge(), we apply the *Inline Method* refactoring to get rid of it. This leads to:

```
public Money getCharge(int days) {
    int additionalDays = Math.max(0, days - DAYS_DISCOUNTED);
    double charge = BASE_PRICE + additionalDays * PRICE_PER_DAY;
    return new Money(charge);
}
```

```
┌──────────────────────────────┐      ┌──────────────────────────┐
│ double getCharge_OLD(int)    │ ────▶│ Money getCharge(int)     │
└──────────────────────────────┘      └──────────────────────────┘
```

Step 6: Inline Evolution Adapter

In this last step, automated *Inline Method* refactoring shows its full power: By applying it to the *Evolution Adapter*, the adapter's code is injected into all users of the old signature, changing them to use the new getCharge() method. The test case for our example is automatically changed to:

```
public void testPrices() {
    Pricing pricing = new Pricing();
    assertEquals(new Money(1.50), pricing.getCharge(1));
    assertEquals(1.50, pricing.getCharge(3).asDouble(), 0.001);
    assertEquals(2.50, pricing.getCharge(4).asDouble(), 0.001);
    assertEquals(3.50, pricing.getCharge(5).asDouble(), 0.001);
}
```

At this point, the old signature does not exist anymore. Our code is not bloated with interfaces only preserved for compatibility. We reached this point by taking small steps. After each step the code is compilable, allowing us to run our tests to gain confidence that no errors were introduced.

We still have to clean up all places where the old signature was used, as well as the new method Money getCharge(int days), because both still use the double type. These changes, too, can be applied in small steps. After cleaning up the test case, the goal of the beginning of this section is reached:

```
public void testPrices() {
    Pricing pricing = new Pricing();
    assertEquals(new Money(1.50), pricing.getCharge(1));
    assertEquals(new Money(1.50), pricing.getCharge(3));
    assertEquals(new Money(2.50), pricing.getCharge(4));
    assertEquals(new Money(3.50), pricing.getCharge(5));
}
```

```
┌──────────────────────────────┐
│ Money getCharge(int)         │
└──────────────────────────────┘
```

4   Short Cuts

Changing a return type as shown in the example above is universally applicable. In many cases, it is possible to use short cuts in the refactoring route which make the interface evolution less tedious and therefore more likely to happen. As an example, consider this implementation of `getCharge()`:

```
public double getCharge(int days) {
    int additionalDays = Math.max(0, days - DAYS_DISCOUNTED);
    Money charge = BASE_PRICE.plus(
                    PRICE_PER_DAY.times(additionalDays));
    return charge.asDouble();
}
```

As it already uses `Money` internally, four steps are sufficient to change the return type to `Money`:

1. rename `getCharge()` to `getCharge_OLD()`,
2. extract the first three lines of `getCharge_OLD()`'s body to `getCharge()`,
3. inline the local variable `charge`,
4. inline `getCharge_OLD()`.

The new method is directly extracted from the old one, thus a *Legacy Adapter* is not needed. The remainder of the old method after extraction in step 2 acts as the *Evolution Adapter* in step 4.

5   Supporting Other Refactorings and Behavior Changes

The steps used in the example are not only useful for changing a return type. They may be applied to many kinds of signature-changing refactorings, like *Add Parameter*, *Remove Parameter*, *Introduce Parameter Object*, or *Replace Error Code with Exception*. Even parts of the behavior of a method may be pushed out by inlining the *Evolution Adapter*, effectively leading to changing a method's behavior while preserving existing functionality.

The power of the approach illustrated here depends heavily on the sophistication of *Inline Method* support. If automated inlining fails for the *Evolution Adapter*, we would have to change all the invocations by hand, so that the approach would not pay off.

In our experiments with some available IDEs, we experienced problems when inlining methods that have multiple exit points. While the *Evolution Adapter* inlined in the example had only one exit point, there are of course cases where multiple exit points are required, for example *Replace Error Code with Exception*. For these, more sophisticated tool support for *Inline Method* is required.

6   Broadening the Approach

Up to this point, we only considered changing code in a private workspace. In development teams, using the illustrated approach may cause integration problems for other developers on the team. If they use the old method signature in code that they added, they will run into merge conflicts. Resolving them is a tedious task, since the old implementation of the inlined method must be retrieved from the software configuration management (SCM) tool.

The situation gets even worse if signature changes are applied to published interfaces. Every piece of code depending on the interface would not compile anymore. Therefore changing published interfaces is typically discouraged. Recommendations are to publish as little as possible as late as possible, or to make changes additions [5,2].

The author's research addresses these problems with the design and development of an SCM tool that will record the steps of TDD, especially refactorings, as operations in an IDE.

Changing Collectively Owned Code

SCM tools that only store versions of source code either cannot cope with refactoring, or have to put a huge effort in reconstructing a partial history.

The proposed SCM tool will record all refactorings that are applied to the code, so that they are known during the merging process. This will allow replaying the steps of the technique presented in section 3 on dependent code.

Changing Published Interfaces

At first glance, changing published interfaces seems to be a special case of changing collectively owned code. If we know the steps that led from the old version to the new one, a tool may use them to migrate dependent code to new versions of our published interfaces. While we assume that all members of a development team use the same IDE and SCM, we cannot expect the same for all users of a published interface. Maybe they do not use an IDE or SCM at all. So the migration tool itself should not depend on the development environment.

While we have ignored inheritance until now, at least for library development it has to be considered, since a published interface in Java often is a Java interface. To cope with inheritance, the key is to provide additional operations on source code which allow the application of the route proposed in section 3 to interfaces and all their implementations. To identify these operations, we have to look at the steps of the refactoring route.

Step 1 *Rename Method* is handled very well by current IDEs.

Step 2 extracts the method body into a new method. For inherited methods, this extraction has to be done for each implementation. After the extraction, each of them contains the same code, delegating to the extracted methods. A possible name for this refactoring would thus be *Introduce Delegate Method*.

Step 3 introduces a *Legacy Adapter* for all classes that implement the old signature. The adapter implementation is the same for all classes. Thus introducing a new method with a default implementation has to be automated.

Step 4 changes the methods introduced in step 2 to *Evolution Adapters*. The adapter implementation is the same for all classes. An automated operation is needed that replaces all implementations of a method with a new one.

Step 5 inlines the methods extracted in step 2. Each one of them is only used by the *Legacy Adapter* of its class. *Inline Method* should work for them, but it has to be extended to work automatically on an interface method.

Step 6 inlines the *Evolution Adapters*. While *Inline Method* normally leads to problems when applied to overridden methods, it should pose no problem here, because all the methods contain the same source code, just like in step 5.

So the evolution of published interfaces seems to be within reach by providing the missing operations in an IDE, and the migration tool outlined above.

7   Conclusions

This paper illustrates that the refactoring *Inline Method* deserves more attention. By using a special refactoring route, it allows changing method signatures or behavior in small steps without copying code and without keeping old signatures for the sake of compatibility.

With appropriate tool support, the technique of evolving interfaces should also be applicable in team settings as well as for published interfaces. Such tools are subject of the author's research. A prototype for the Eclipse platform is currently under development.

Acknowledgements

Thanks to Arne Harren, Frank Westphal, Jürgen Schlegelmilch and the XP2003 reviewers for their valuable comments on earlier versions of this paper. Frank pointed out the possibility to use short cuts and suggested the paper title.

References

1. Beck, K.: Test-Driven Development: By Example. Addison-Wesley (2003)
2. des Rivières, J.: Evolving Java-based APIs. http://www.eclipse.org/eclipse/development/java-api-evolution.html (2002)
3. Eclipse home page. http://www.eclipse.org
4. Fowler, M.: Refactoring: Improving the Design of Existing Code. Addison-Wesley (1999)
5. Fowler, M.: Public versus Published Interfaces. In: IEEE Software (March/April 2002)
6. Gamma, E. et.al.: Design Patterns: Elements of Reusable Object-Oriented Software. Addison-Wesley (1995)
7. IntelliJ IDEA home page. http://www.intellij.com
8. JUnit home page. http://www.junit.org

Practical Experiences of Agility in the Telecom Industry

Jari Vanhanen[1], Jouni Jartti[2], and Tuomo Kähkönen[2]

[1] Helsinki University of Technology, Software Business and Engineering Institute
P.O. Box 9600, FIN-02015 HUT, Finland
jari.vanhanen@hut.fi
[2] Nokia Research Center, P.O. Box 407, FIN-00045 NOKIA GROUP, Finland
{jouni.jartti,tuomo.kahkonen}@nokia.com

Abstract. This paper discusses the adoption level of and experiences from using agile practices in three software development projects in a large Telecom company. The use of agile practices was more emergent than planned. Project managers and developers simply used practices they considered efficient and natural. The most widely adopted agile practices were to measure progress by working code, to have developers estimate task efforts, to use coding standards, having no continuous overtime, to have the team develop its own processes, to use limited documentation, and to have the team in one physical location. The projects used conventional testing approaches. Adoption of agile testing practices, i.e., test first and automated unit tests, was low. Some agile practices can just emerge without conscious adoption, because developers find them useful. However, it seems that an emergent process aiming for agility may also neglect important agile practices.

1   Introduction

The competitiveness of IT companies is affected by how well their software development process can react to changing needs set for products [1,2]. We define agility as the ability to adapt to changing situations appropriately, quickly and effectively. In other words, agile organizations notice relevant changes early, initiate action promptly, create a feasible and effective alternative plan quickly, and reorient work and resources according to the new plan quickly and effectively.

In the Telecom industry software development has traditionally followed rather rigorous processes, typically using process frameworks such as ISO-15504 [3] or the SW-CMM [4]. As far as we know, no studies have been published discussing the use of agile methods in the Telecom industry. Thus, we believe that this paper sheds some light on the current situation.

1.1   Study Background

This study was made in a large telecom company as part of a research program, whose goal is to increase and transfer practical knowledge of achieving agility in software development. Creating a full-fledged methodology and trying to leverage it in a large organization is not feasible. However, describing a set of process patterns [5] that promote agility is more feasible. A process pattern describes a practice considering topics such as which problem it solves, when it is applicable, how to deploy

M. Marchesi and G. Succi (Eds.): XP 2003, LNCS 2675, pp. 279–287, 2003.
© Springer-Verlag Berlin Heidelberg 2003

it etc. McCormick's [6] ideas for creating a methodology for a project also support the process patterns approach: "What's needed is not a single software methodology, but a rich toolkit of process patterns and 'methodology components' (deliverables, techniques, process flows, and so forth) along with guidelines for how to plug them together to customize a methodology for any given project." Of course, the ideal content of an agile toolkit depends on the context, and the limits of agile practices are still unclear.

Before the study, we had collected a tentative list (Table 3) of agile practices that could be applicable in the company. Most of the practices are described in XP [7] and the rest in other literature [8,9]. This specific study aimed at increasing our understanding of the current level of use of these and potentially some other agile practices in the company. Based on the results of this study we will evaluate and improve the practicality and completeness of our tentative agile practice list.

The research questions for this study were:

1. Which agile practices were used in these projects?
2. What experiences were reported on those practices?

1.2   Research Method

Using the company's intranet and personal relationships, we identified several projects from the case company in Finland that were either consciously or non-consciously using agile software development practices. However, we could not identify any project that was using a complete agile methodology such as XP. From seven identified candidates we selected three projects, A, B, and C, which seemed to be most active in using agile practices. All selected projects were developing different kinds of products in different business units, and for different markets.

We interviewed the project manager and a developer from projects A and B, and only a developer from project C. The interviews covered all typical software project areas at a general level in order to identify other agile practices in addition to those we had already listed.

We quantified the level of use of the agile practices (Table 1) in order to better answer the first research question. Quantification was difficult because there are several dimensions that should be considered, e.g., number of people using the practice, duration of use, discipline of use, and aspects used. The second research question was answered by a qualitative analysis of the reported experiences.

Table 1. The quantification scale for the use of agile practices

Value	Description
3	Considerable use, e.g. it was almost a norm to use it.
2	Moderate use, e.g. several people used it for a long time.
1	Minor use, e.g. someone tried the practice for some time.
0	Practically no use of the practice.

1.3   Overview of the Projects

Project A developed a Unix based application. The mindset of the project's first two developers was towards light practices and because the project grew slowly over time, they had time to find the natural, minimal process. The success of the product and the small number of developers allowed them to keep the process as they wanted despite of the external pressure to change it to comply better with the organization's general process model. Project B developed low-level embedded software. The project manager decided the practices used in the project based on his previous experiences. Project C was a release project in which a small team worked in a larger 70-person subproject that was part of the further development of a very large legacy system. The team tried to improve the current process by deploying some aspects of certain XP practices. Table 2 summarizes the characteristics of these projects.

Table 2. Project characteristics

	Project A	**Project B**	**Project C**
Project type	Development of an evolving sw product	Integration and porting of embedded sw	Development of a part of a larger system
People	1 → 12	8	4 (of 70)
Distribution	Two teams in two countries	Co-located team	Co-located team
Duration	8 years	10 months	1.5 years
Effort	~50 man years	~6 man years	~6 man years
SW Size	590 kLOC	15 kLOC	40 kLOC

2   Results

2.1   Adoption of Agile Practices

The use of agile practices was more emergent than planned. Typically, the process or the use of individual practices was not formally defined or documented, but rather the project manager and the developers used practices that they considered efficient and natural. XP was partially experimented in project C, but others did not use any documented agile methodology as the basis for their process. The motivation for using agile practices was either experimenting with something new, e.g. some XP practices, or just working in a way that felt natural and had worked earlier in other projects. Table 3 presents the adoption level of agile practices and the following sections describe the experiences.

2.2   Use of the Practices

Incremental Delivery. Project A had a release cycle of about 6 months. Later in the cycle, pre-releases were delivered weekly to the customer. Project B planned the first release to occur 10 months after the project initiation, but the project was cancelled due to business reasons before the first release. Project C had a 6-month release cycle.

Continuous Integration. In project A, new code was checked in to the common repository as often as reasonable, typically after a few days of development. The code had to work before the check-in. In project B, developers first implemented the subsystems separately, followed by an integration phase. In project C, developers integrated their code after a few days of work.

Table 3. Adoption level of agile practices

Practice	A	B	C
Incremental delivery	2	0	1
Continuous integration	2	0	2
Measure progress by working code	3	3	2
Interactive planning	2	0	1
Developers estimate task efforts	2	2	3
Visual modeling	1	2	2
Use cases	0	0	3
Design Patterns	2	0	0
Continuously developed architecture	2	1	1
Pair programming	0	0	1
Collective code ownership	2	1	2
Coding standard	3	1	3
Refactoring	2	2	1
Write tests first	0	0	0
Automated unit testing	0	0	0
Customer writes acceptance tests	1	0	0
Limited documentation	3	2	1
Team in one location	0	3	3
Frequent team meetings	1	1	2
Customer always available	2	2	0
Team develops its processes	3	2	1
No continuous overtime	3	2	1

Legend:
3 considerable use
2 moderate use
1 minor use
0 practically no use

Measure Progress by Working Code. In project A, the current version was delivered weekly to the customer. Users tried the pre-releases and gave valuable feedback replacing the need for a detailed requirement specification. Users were committed thanks to the short feedback loop. The developers also considered it rewarding to see results soon. Project B was internally split into software milestones every 1 to 6 weeks.

Interactive Planning. In project A, the project manager continuously discussed the specifications with the customer. The presence of the relevant developers in the customer meetings was considered important for gaining a common understanding and giving a feeling of appreciation for the developers. Prioritization was made together with the customer at different levels (general direction, features) also concerning the technical feasibility of the proposals.

Developers Estimate Task Efforts. In project A, the best expert in an area performed effort estimation. In project B effort estimates originated from the functional specification phase, but the development team re-estimated them before implementation. In project C, rough effort estimates were made before the project in the feasibility study, but the developers refined them later.

Visual Modeling. In project A, the technical documentation contained only a few diagrams. One reason for avoiding diagrams was the lack of a good drawing tool. In project B, developers considered a picture of the whole system showing the parts and their connections being the most important part of architectural documentation. The developers also drew UML scenario and process diagrams of their subsystems. In project C scenario and class diagrams were used.

Use Cases. In project B, use case modeling was not used, because the project was mostly technical, low-level development. In project C, requirements were documented using use cases.

Design Patterns. Project A began to use design patterns after the first major refactoring of the product. In project B, design patterns were not considered applicable due to low-level C coding.

Continuously Developed Architecture. In project A, the architecture was developed in parallel with new features. Project B made higher-level design early based on an external specification. The design remained quite stable.

Pair Programming. In project C problems in code were often solved with a pair, but during programming tasks pairing was scarce. However, even this amount of pairing when debugging spread the knowledge of the system among developers.

Collective Code Ownership. In project A, any developer was allowed to change any part of the code if needed, but in practice they focused on their own modules. In project B, developers mostly worked with their own code. Sometimes they read others' code, but the owner made the final changes. In project C, developers were allowed to change others' code and even the platform code.

Coding Standard. In project A, a style guide was followed in naming variables, structuring the code, and organizing the code in files. In project B, instructions covered only the module interfaces. In project C, a general style guide by the company was followed.

Refactoring. In project A, architectural decay was always present as new features were added, and refactoring was exercised all the time. However, not all developers refactored consistently, causing some parts to decay quite badly. Senior people kept the code in better shape. Project B changed low-level design quite a lot during coding. Project C refactored scarcely in order not to break the existing, large code base.

Write Tests First. None of the studied projects wrote unit tests before the real code.

Automated Unit Testing. Project A tried writing unit tests without good results due to the strong GUI orientation. In project C, writing unit tests was found too difficult and time-consuming.

Customer Writes Acceptance Tests. In project A, the customer organization performed system testing. They might have had test cases defined, but the developers never saw them.

Limited Documentation. In project A, technical documentation contained a short architecture document and some technical guideline documents. These were not typically kept up-to-date. They were considered somewhat useful for new people, but apprenticeship-style hands-on training was most successful for transferring knowledge. Senior developers did not need the documents at all. Even the development at two sites did not seem to require more documents.

Project B had a short technical document of each subsystem and a general architecture description of the system. The need for design documentation was low because the size of the software was rather small and it had a modular structure. Only one person developed each subsystem and only the interfaces were of interest to others. The details and reasons behind the solutions were commented in the source code. The comments were important even for the author due to the new domain. Requirements were gathered in a short document. There was only one real user requirement and others were technical requirements.

Team in One Location. In project A a team that worked in another country was added to the project. After several months of apprenticeship in Finland, the team members started to work in their home country. The teams held frequent teleconferences, some meetings, and yearly workshops. Lead developers had own rooms and others worked in a landscaped office, which some developers did not like due to disturbing background noise. Projects B and C had adjacent two-person rooms.

Frequent Team Meetings. In project A, the team ate lunch together, and never considered it necessary to have official daily meetings. Project B had a weekly status meeting, where everyone told what he had done since the last meeting. Project C had meetings when necessary, typically 15-30 minutes once or twice a week.

Customer Always Available. In project A, there was a weekly meeting between the customer, project manager and some developers. There were also many discussions with the customer. In project B, the product manager played the customer role. His room was in another floor, but he answered questions when posed. In project C, the project manager played the role of the customer. It was difficult to identify a real customer and have proper customer involvement.

Team Develops Its Processes. In project A, the project manager created the process together with the team. The team liked the way they worked, and the lack of clear roles such as managers, designers and coders improved team spirit. In project B, the project manager created the process and discussed it with the team. The developers were most interested in developing software, so the proposed, light process did not meet with resistance. In project C, the team planned experimenting with XP practices, otherwise the process was defined outside the team.

No Continuous Overtime. In project A people worked overtime only before important releases. Project B used some overtime to speed up the first release. In project C overtime increased towards the end of the project, but was not considerable.

3   Discussion

3.1   Adoption Level

The most frequently and thoroughly adopted practices were to measure progress by working code, having developers estimate task efforts, using a coding standard, not using continuous overtime, having the team develop its own process, limited documentation, and having the team in one location.

Some practices such as interactive planning, write tests first, automated unit testing, customer writes acceptance tests, and pair programming were used almost nowhere. It may be that the familiarity with these practices was weak among the interviewees and some practices are quite exotic and difficult to adopt causing that the practices do not just emerge. It may be that the process must be created based on some documented agile methodology or a best practice list in order for these practices to be adopted. As agile testing practices are often considered as a prerequisite for many other agile practices, the low adoption of these practices suggests that more education is needed in this area.

3.2   Success Factors

We identified the following success factors in the projects. In project A, the architects stayed with the project, refactored the architecture continuously and accomplished the survival and evolution of the architecture. The first developer became the project manager, so managerial decisions were made quickly by a person who had the best technical knowledge of the software. The customer representative remained the same and a mutual trust could be built.

The personnel was one of the strengths of project B. The project manager selected developers based on their skills and traits in order to form a good team for this project. The project manager was both managerially and technically competent and designed the overall architecture.

In project C, frequent team meetings helped designing the details of the initial high-level specification. Pairing while debugging was a very useful practice and spread the knowledge of the system among the developers.

3.3   New Practices

The following additional practices were identified. *Technical authority,* e.g., a technically competent project manager improves agility because that person is able to make decisions quickly. The project manager's understanding of the technical details increases the likelihood to have the courage to decrease control elements such as managerial documents and project reviews from the process. *Team continuity,* meaning that key persons stay within the project, improves efficiency because the tacit information is preserved as happened with the architecture in project A.

3.4   Other Findings

Collective ownership improves agility by removing delays in development. If the system has a modular structure and different parts require different technical skills, the most efficient way of development may still be to let people specialize in some parts, and have one or two semi-experts as a backup for each part. Landscaped offices allow efficient and quick communication, but may disturb work requiring high concentration. Project A showed that some agile practices are viable even in a distributed project. Developers typically accepted an agile process well. This was true even in project B where they were not involved in designing the process.

3.5   Evaluation of the Research

The reported experiences of the advantages and disadvantages of specific practices were quite scarce. It may be that people have not been very conscious of using certain, admittedly vague practices that may have emerged instead of being consciously deployed. In addition, some practices, such as limited documentation and measure progress with working code actually mean not doing something, e.g., thick documents or progress reporting. Therefore evaluating the effects of these practices and discussing about the related experiences may have been hard for the interviewees.

In the interviews, the origin of the adoption of each individual practice was not explicitly asked for. Therefore, we cannot say for sure for all practices, which were consciously adopted and which just emerged.

4   Conclusions

This paper presented experiences of the use of agile practices in three projects in the Telecom industry. The use of agile practices was more emergent than planned. Typically, processes or individual practices were not formally defined. Instead, project managers and developers used practices they considered efficient and natural.

Generally speaking both the project managers and developers were satisfied with their current software development processes compared to their earlier experiences with heavier, more formal processes. They could do what they consider important (software) and see concrete results soon through frequent customer deliveries. This might explain the positive tone of the interviewees when discussing about their projects.

The adoption level of agile testing practices, i.e., write tests first and automated unit tests, whose use is typically considered a significant prerequisite for several other agile practices, was low. More information on these practices is clearly needed among the projects.

The emergence of agile practices without conscious adoption can be considered a good sign, indicating that agile practices are considered useful by the developers themselves. However, it seems that several important practices may be neglected, if a process, whose goal is to be agile is not consciously created but instead just emerges. Agile practices presented, e.g., as process patterns could help find and deploy the most suitable practices more efficiently.

References

1. McCormack, A. et al.: Developing Products on Internet Time: The Anatomy of a Flexible Development Process. Management Science 47, 1 (2001) 133-150
2. Thomke, S. and Reinertsen, D.: Agile product development: Managing development flexibility in uncertain environments. California Management Review 41, 1 (1998) 8-30

3. ISO/IEC TR 15504: Information Technology – Software Process Assessment, Parts 1-9. Type 2 Technical Report (1998).
4. Paulk, M. et al. Capability Maturity Model for Software, Version 1.1. Technical Report CMU/SEI-93-TR24. Pittsburgh, PA: Carnegie Mellon University, Software Engineering Institute (1993).
5. Ambler, S.W.: Process Patterns. Building Large-Scale Systems Using Object Technology. Cambridge University Press, (1998)
6. McCormick, M.: Programming Extremism, Communications of the ACM 44, 6 (2001) 109-111
7. Beck, K.: Extreme Programming Explained: Embrace Change. Addison Wesley, (2000)
8. Ambler, S.W.: Agile Modeling. John Wiley & Sons, Inc., New York (2002)
9. Gamma, E. et al.: Design Patterns: Elements of Reusable Object-Oriented Software. Addison-Wesley, (1995)

XP – Call in the Social Workers

Tim Mackinnon

Connextra Ltd., London, England
tim.mackinnon@pobox.com

Abstract. XP has the potential to allow a team to work on a project for a long period of time, potentially several years. At Connextra we have been carefully following the suggested XP practices for more than 3 years, and along with additional techniques such as team retrospectives and gold cards, we have proven that sustainable development is a reality. This paper outlines the history the team, the introduction and refinements of team retrospectives and an experiment in a cross discipline exchange with a qualified social worker.

1   Introduction

Connextra was founded in the summer of 1999 with 3 employees and the aim to develop a desktop product that shows contextual information relevant to what a user is viewing on their computer. After creating some initial prototypes, two of the founders began writing the application using some of the suggested Extreme Programming (XP) [1] practices. It quickly became apparent that a larger team would be required to complete the application, and full XP was chosen as a strategic methodology for accomplishing this work. The author, who had prior XP experience, was encouraged to join the project to set up the XP team and develop the product.

2   Growing the Team

With the original founders sorting out details for a growing company, it was imperative to locate some additional team members with an aptitude for XP. Contacts proved important in this search, and a previous student intern was tracked down along with another recommended student graduate. Both new team members demonstrated an ability to learn new techniques along with a well grounded programming knowledge based on object-oriented (OO) programming. With this team we were able to work with two rotating pairs and hold a planning game every 3 weeks. At this time we also invented a new testing technique called Mock Objects [6], which we used as a means of successfully applying test first programming to our problem domain.

While XP does not formally address hiring practices, we quickly noticed that collective ownership meant we were reliably able to establish whether a potential employee was a useful addition to the team. The pattern we established began with a 30-minute telephone interview and asked a few simple Java, HTML and OO questions. If successful, the next step was to invite the candidate for a face-to-face meeting at our offices where we discussed more general programming issues and talked about Ex-

M. Marchesi and G. Succi (Eds.): XP 2003, LNCS 2675, pp. 288–297, 2003.
© Springer-Verlag Berlin Heidelberg 2003

treme Programming. If the interviewee then showed a potential for problem solving and had a curiosity about XP, we then invited them to spend half a day with our development team pair programming. As this request can be quite intimidating, it was clearly explained that they would not be expected to immediately understand our code base or use our development tools to their full extent, however they would be expected to interact with their partner and use them as mentor to work on simple problems.

At our morning standup, if there was an interview, we all agreed on a good development task and roughly which team members would rotate through the course of the session. As our code base is very decoupled (due to our Mock Object discipline) it was possible to work on a small task without having to know every detail about how other parts of the system functioned. As the candidate built up tests with a partner we switched them to a new partner and looked for an ability to explain what they were trying to accomplish and what they were currently working on. At the end of the session the participating team members would have a quick discussion about the candidates' ability to write simple tests, and keep track of progress. We also looked for a capacity to learn something new during the session (typically the usage of our tools or programming techniques) as well as a sense of humor or a passion for some subject. Using this simple criterion we have successfully maintained a team of the original members. Furthermore, we have also had several candidates that have released production code in their interview, meaning that when they were hired it was actually their second day on the job.

3   Iteration History

With a running team in place, during the course of 3 and half years we have measured (and continue to measure) our velocity for each iteration (fig. 1), and used that number to drive each subsequent planning game. Initially we used an iteration length of 3 weeks, however we later adjusted this to 1-week iterations. For consistency and to compare results between iterations, fig. 1 shows a normalized velocity for a three week total based on one pair of developers. The early iterations had quite a high velocity when we didn't have any issues of support or hot staging to live servers.

Although we continued to monitor our velocity and used it as a means of planning subsequent iterations, we didn't initially use it as a way of monitoring team happiness. We viewed the numbers as a way of accommodating technical risk and reliable delivery (via yesterday's weather). Of course at each planning game we had to explain the change in numbers to our users, and as a team we would informally discuss ways of improving or maintaining our process. After working like this for over a year, we found that everyone was finding the work a little monotonous. Thus at iteration 17, we introduced the concept of Gold Cards [5] to enable developers to have planned time to research new technologies and tools. However, while the feedback we were getting was that gold cards were helping improve moral, and we were continuing to deliver new functionality, their was still a problem that seemed to be eating away at the morale fiber of the team.

Although the velocity appears to jump around, in general we have maintained a figure of 2.5 to 3 per pair (a number which includes gold card research and support tasks)

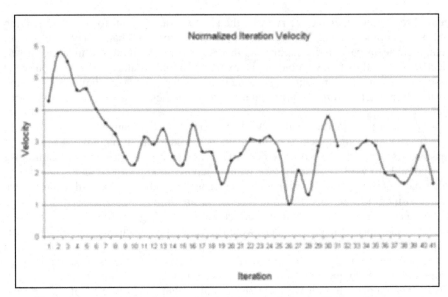

Fig. 1. Normalized Velocity (for a single pair) recorded over 41, 3-week iterations.

4   Dissatisfaction Tracking

Unable to directly identify the cause for unrest, we decided at iteration 18 to hold a new and different type of tracking activity where everyone would write cards that expressed problems, fears and issues. For 15 minutes everyone anonymously wrote out cards and put them in a pile on a table. Following this initial activity we tried to organize the cards into meaningful groups. Some groups were easy to spot and some were more difficult. Interestingly some of the cards were extremely hard-hitting and potentially hurtful. Of particular note was the card "Hypocritical management", which seemed strange given the very transparent nature of our XP process and the collective decision making process of the team. While the session was useful at resolving some of the basic problems identified by the cards, it was extremely draining for everyone involved. Along with the CTO, I vowed that we would find a way to do things differently and prevent this kind of buildup from reoccurring. In later discussing this session with a social worker colleague, I was alerted to the problem that anonymous and non-specific complaints are impossible to solve because there is nothing concrete to test against. I was encouraged to find a forum where specific incidents could be discussed and issues directly addressed.

5   Retrospectives

A solution to project dissatisfaction is recognized in some of the early XP literature [2], with references made to Norm Kerth's experiences with both large and small technical teams in his retrospective handbook [3]. I first learned about retrospectives at the XP2001 international conference, and after discussing the idea with our CTO, we decided to try one as a follow up to our dissatisfaction tracking session. We started out informally using a "Defining Success Exercise" [3] and discussed how many projects never actually deliver something (by this point we had already launched Sidewize, our first commercial product). This discussion went well, and naturally progressed into discussing the measures described in "How healthy is your organization"[3]. In reading out the characteristics of both functional and dysfunctional teams, we decided on the spur of the moment to create a chart on a whiteboard and measure ourselves on a continuum between the proposed dysfunctional and functional measurements. Our table was subsequently transcribed onto flipchart paper (and slightly abbreviate to fit) and looked like Table 1, with the middle column showing the values we recorded over 3 iterations (marked with a # character).

Table 1. Measurements of team happiness on the axis of dysfunctional to functional behavior.

Dysfunctional Indicator	Team Measure (Iterations 21-23)	Functional Indicator
Guarded Language (secrets)	-5....0..#.5 -5....0..##5 -5....0...#5	Honest Communication
Distrust of other groups	-5....##...5 -5....0##..5 -5....0.#..5	Alliance and cooperation
Well defined boundaries (loss of discussion)	-5....#....5 -5....0##..5 -5....0.##.5	Boundaries mutually discussed
Blame + Lack of respect	-5....#....5 -5....0###.5 -5....0..#.5	Appreciation + use difference between groups
Skepticism of others ideas	-5....0...#5 -5....0...#5 -5....0...#5	Group refinement of others ideas
Stick (pressure to produce)	-5....0#...5 -5....0##..5 -5....0.#..5	Carrot (encouragement to improve)
Living in the past	-5....0.#..5 -5....0.##.5 -5....0..#.5	Creating new solutions
Internal Competition (I look good)	-5....0.#..5 -5....0.#..5 -5....0.#..5	External Success (we look good)
Confrontation	-5....0.#..5 -5....0.#..5 -5....0..#.5	Constructive
No power to change	-5....0.#..5 -5....0.##.5 -5....0..##5	Empowered
Debate to win debate	-5....0.#..5 -5....0.##.5 -5....0...#5	Consensus (+support, +good enough)
Decision distrust	-5...###...5 -5....0.##.5 -5....0..##5	Decision respect (trust of skills)
Pressure to conform to standard	-5....0....5 -5....0....5 -5....0..#.5	Flexibility available for new situations

We found this exercise was challenging and very revealing, but after repeating it several times in subsequent retrospectives we found that it became less meaningful (as we achieved high functionality in most measures), and so we opted to stop using it.

Once we had completed this health chart, we then moved onto a "Time Line Mining"[3] activity and asked the questions:

- What we did well
- What we can do better
- What we have learned
- What puzzles us

These questions have formed the backbone for all of our subsequent retrospectives and have not outgrown their usefulness. Over time these titles have been truncated and slightly modified to Well, Not so Well, Puzzles, and Actions. We try to cover the positive aspects first and then move onto the items that we can do better. Often there are puzzles, and it is these, as well as actions, that drive what we will focus on in our next iteration.

Due to the short iterations involved in an XP project, we never felt the need to take the time to formally construct a time line of project events. In retrospect it may have been useful to try this the first time we attempted a retrospective, however in subsequent sessions the time gap is so short that you only need to quickly review the story cards from the earlier part of the iteration (this is a still useful activity to act as a quick refresher).

During our initial attempts at discussing the "mining" questions, we encountered the problem that everyone tried to talk at the same time. Norm described the use of a "coffee mug" as a speaker token, however all our mugs were full at the time. After a quick search I came across our shelf of holiday souvenirs and selected a small stuffed St. Bernard (slightly ironic). This dog was used for many subsequent retrospectives and had the obvious characteristic that you can safely throw it across the room to allow someone else to speak. However, an unusual side effect that we often observed was that when someone was quite emotional about a subject and began talking, they would invariably begin to unconsciously stroke the toy until they calmed down. Eventually they would realize they were doing this and then would be quite keen to give up the token to someone else.

Of course when someone has the token is discussing new issues, they don't refer back to the previous retrospectives' results until all of the mining questions have been completed for the current iteration. This prevents us from skewing our observations, and makes it interesting to compare results with the previous retrospective to see how things have changed, or how previously important actions have downgraded themselves.

Finally, while it is good to identify actions, we have also noticed that with back-to-back iterations it was often hard to get started on any of them. For this reason we successfully tried modifying our development lifecycle to 3, 1 week iterations followed by a work queue week [7]. In this 4th week we hold our retrospective on a Monday and then have time to address some of the retrospective actions as well as working on stories in a work queue fashion (one of which is gathering new stories for the next iteration).

6   The Thinking Environment

In our retrospectives, we have also tried looking for alternative approaches, one of which is using a Thinking Environment [4]. While our typical retrospectives were very similar to those described in holding a meeting using a Thinking Environment [4], there were some subtleties that we hadn't quite mastered. Obviously everyone should be given a turn to speak during a retrospective, however this can be challenging as some people are naturally more quiet and don't find an opportunity to speak up. To combat this we adopted the suggested strategy of going round a circle and asking each person to give an item that had gone well in the last iteration. We endeavored not to interrupt each other, and allowed each person to say pass if they had nothing to say. We repeated this until most of the circle had said pass, and then we moved on to things that hadn't gone so well etc.

So far we haven't explored the use of incisive questions to remove limiting assumptions, but this is definitely an area that should be explored. However, we have tried finishing off a meeting with each person offering an item of appreciation to the person on his or her left. This exercise proved to be one of the most difficult we have ever attempted in our retrospectives. It is not easy to look someone in the eye and say something meaningful to them. Equally it is also quite uncomfortable to sit and listen to someone giving you praise. As members of an XP team work particularly closely with each other, it is important to practice these skills. We certainly noticed that following this episode people were much more willing to compliment each other on a daily basis although no one has suggested that we repeat this exercise in a subsequent retrospective. I think this is a shame, but I'm sure the idea will resurface.

7   The Social Work Experiment

While we have been extremely pleased with our retrospectives, I was still noticing that there was an element of tension that never quite came out during them. Often people would mention things informally, but never together. For a long time I have thought that intense, high-energy teams should have someone around who is an expert in dealing with social situations. After researching the possibilities, and arranging a proposal, I was given the go ahead for a special retrospective to be run by a qualified social worker, which we referred to as a team development day. Both the CTO and I were both slightly nervous about the potential outcome of the day, but felt that it was time to measure our team in a different way to see if it made a difference.

7.1   The Introduction

As I wanted to be involved in the experiment I had no knowledge of how the team-building day would run, other than I already knew that our facilitator, James, was a social worker. Before the day started, James arranged the room slightly differently to our normal retrospective, moving the central table to one side and forming a circle with all of the chairs (to seat 12 people). We then began with James introducing himself as a qualified social worker who had been invited to help us run a team-building day. I was interested to note that all the team members seemed very receptive to the idea of having such a person facilitate the day and I also thought that James looked slightly relieved that everyone appeared to appreciate his presence (typically social workers are the last people anyone wants to see at a meeting).

After James' introduction, we all introduced ourselves and described our role in the company and what we hoped to get out of the day. It was interesting to hear what words people chose to describe them, as it's not something we normally do. For example, I recall one team member who has been working in the team for several years, calling himself a junior developer.

7.2   Exercise 1

Following the introductions, we divided into two random groups and began the first exercise. Each person was asked to think of 2 truths about themselves as well as one lie. One by one, each person presented their three items and the opposing team then began discussing the pros and cons of each, trying to select the lie. This exercise proved to be very popular but I wondered if the point was to give an insight into the teams' dynamics and see if there were pre-established rungs of power that would need attention. In our case this didn't appear to be the case, as everyone seemed willing to contribute and the identified lie was based on a democratic selection. I later asked James about this exercise, and he replied that actually it was chosen mainly for its merits as an ice breaking activity. However, it does give an insight into how well people know each other - as the discussions indicate levels of both professional and personal knowledge. Furthermore, it also allows the session leader to quickly learn about all the different participants. In our case, James was surprised at how well we appeared to know each other. This probably stems from continuous pair programming as well as our habit of often eating lunch together.

7.3   Exercise 2

Following the warm-up exercise we were then split into 3 groups with the task of presenting the strengths and weaknesses of the entire team. This exercise felt closest to our normal retrospectives but it worked on a higher level and got us to document skills that contribute to the "what went well", and "what didn't go well" questions. While this was a good exercise, as a team we were well practiced on this activity and so the items that we recorded were pretty much things that we had discussed over the previous year. Once again, James was surprised at how well we worked together and identified particular problems that we were able to vocalize amongst each other.

7.4   Exercise 3

After the two exercises, we had a lunch break and the mood of the group seemed very positive. When we returned, we began a third exercise to document our work process and highlight areas of communication difficulty. Again we split into three different groups and began drawing process diagrams. As you would expect from an XP team, the diagrams of the three groups looked very similar, documenting the gathering of stories, the planning game, the selection of stories and the day to day working of standup meetings, tasks and pair programming.

Different groups did have a slightly different emphasis on some items, reflecting some of the different skills in each group. For example, a support person (who pairs with a member of the team each day, to form the "exposed pair") documented some of the day-to-day support activities that take place. Another team had a graphic designer who sometimes pairs with members of the team but often works by herself. In this case she drew a separate diagram of how her processes worked, which linked back into the iteration diagram. This latter example was interesting because it was only when she stood up separately to present, that members in other teams slapped their foreheads because they had forgotten her in their diagrams. James later described to me that he had spotted that this designer was having difficulty including herself in the discussion and so had stepped in to suggest that she document her role on a separate paper. This is definitely an important lesson for dealing with mixed skill teams, as you need to encourage non programmers to include themselves in the process even if it means that they document activities that they think don't map directly to XP.

During the presentations it was also pleasing to notice that people who wouldn't normally stand up and speak directly to the group, had decided to take the floor and present. When we all had a drink later in the week, several other people in the team mentioned that they had been amazed that some of the quieter members had made a point of stepping forward to make very effective presentations. It seemed that having a social worker available as a facilitator made people more comfortable taking personal risks. Additionally, during these presentations and discussions, I noticed that James would discretely change his seat in the room. When I later asked him about this, he explained that by changing positions he was able to establish a better rapport with the group and get a different perspective on ideas being presented. He also commented that he was impressed with how closely each of our diagrams matched each other, as typically team members have radically different ideas of how their process works. Surprisingly, other team members later described how useful this particular exercise was to them, as they hadn't actually taken the time to think about our process. They knew it by rote (having joined an XP team and being immersed in that culture) but hadn't taken the time to think about the implications of each of the steps.

7.5   Triangle of Power

During the final presentation, a discussion arouse about "seeking permission" to perform certain activities. This kind of discussion had surfaced earlier in the day but the facilitator had steered the group away from it. This time however, he let the group explore this topic and it emerged that three senior team members had differing views and wanted to debate them. At this point the facilitator let the conversation continue for a few minutes and then pointed out to the rest of the group that there was an interesting triangle of power in the team that should be recognized. James further went on to comment that it was perfectly normal to have a disagreement in the team and that other members should not be afraid of this kind of situation. He then went around the group and asked everyone what there opinion on the topic was. This simple technique made a big difference to the mood of the group, and catered both to the fears of the observing team members and the frustrations of the senior members who wanted to try talking about specific trickier issues. In a later conversation with James, he explained that by identifying this triangle of opinion it made it clearer that those involved in the triangle were not necessarily arguing but debating a difficult problem. Furthermore, as a facilitator he mentioned that its important to notice when other people in the group are beginning to disengage and to bring them back into the conversation by asking everyone for their opinion. This is similar to the "Dealing With Conflict Procedure outlined by Norm Kerth [3].

7.6   Revelation

One of the most revealing items from this experiment was that James felt that as a team we were much better equipped to deal with team problems than most social work teams (who ironically have specific training for social situations). He was also impressed with the openness and enthusiasm that we have managed to maintain on the team, even after more than three years of working together.

Following this experiment, we have noticed that many more members of the team are willing to get involved in the more difficult decisions that have to be made in the evolution of the Connextra products. There is definitely a sense that some of the problems that we feared we had, have been accepted as normal and everyone is more willing to discuss the more difficult issues that remain unresolved.

8   Conclusion

While this paper outlines the history of a well-established XP team, it also describes some techniques for maintaining a stable and long lasting working relationship. From using collective ownership as a way of hiring the right staff, right through to monitoring iteration velocity for indications of unrest, you need to be ready to apply these techniques when the need arises. Just as when we resolved to never let things get so bad that anyone could even be considered a "hypocritical leader", so too must you be willing to adopt practices like retrospectives, and group appreciation. Furthermore, it should not be a scary notion to allow experts from other disciplines like Social Work, examine your process for both weaknesses and strengths. It may turn out that you will be pleasantly surprised at how well the simple XP practices can all work together to provide an enduring team. In the future, we hope to report on using the social work experiment with other teams to compare results with those described here.

Acknowledgements

The author would like to thank: the team at Connextra for being willing to try new approaches. John Nolan (Connextra CTO), who spent considerable time "after hours" in the Highgate, listening and contributing to most of the ideas presented in this paper. Alix Walton and James Blewett who were the social workers that enthusiastically agreed to try the cross discipline experiment. Marston, Thompson & Evershed who brewed the "Pedigree" that enabled many of the conversations to happen in the first place.

References

1. Kent Beck. Extreme programming explained: embrace change. Addison-Wesley, 1999.
2. C Collins, R Miller. Adaptation XP Style, Proc XP 2001
3. Norm Kerth. Project Retrospectives, a handbook for team reviews. Dorset House, 2001
4. Nancy Kline. Time To Think. Ward Lock, 1999
5. Giancarlo Succi, editor. Extreme Programming Perspectives. Addison Wesley, Aug 2002
6. Giancarlo Succi, M. Marchesi, editors. Extreme Programming Examined, Addison Wesley, 2001
7. John Vlissides, James O. Coplien, Norman L. Kerth, editors. Pattern Languages of Program Design 2. Addison Wesley. 1996

Embracing Change: An XP Experience Report

Andrew M. Fuqua[1] and John M. Hammer[2]

[1] Internet Security Systems
6303 Barfield Rd
Atlanta, GA 30328
afuqua@acm.org
http://www.iss.net
[2] Applied Systems Intelligence
11660 Alpharetta Highway, #720
Roswell, GA 30076
jhammer@acm.org
http://www.asinc.com

Abstract. The Common Policy Editor (CPE) project experienced change typical of many software development projects: the programmers, coach, managers, customers and requirements changed; the project was stopped and restarted; and the team was redirected to work on additional projects simultaneously. Extreme Programming (XP) helps teams handle change. This experience report discusses the changes this team encountered, explains how XP helped and cites several lessons learned.

1 Introduction

Kent Beck's seminal work on XP, *Extreme Programming Explained*, is subtitled *Embrace Change* [2]. Beck talks about risks that drive change, changes to the plan, changes to the requirements, the cost of change curve, and about not saving "the pictures once they have had their effect on the code."

But does XP really help teams handle the change thrown at them in a typical software development project? The Common Policy Editor Project (CPE) at Internet Security Systems (ISS) experienced plenty of change: team members were added and removed; the coach left the team; the management changed several times; the team was redirected to work on two projects simultaneously; and, of course, the requirements changed. The XP team on this project handled the change well. This experience report examines change as it happened to the team from the points of view of the engineering managers, the coach, and the programmers on the team.

2 Background

The product details do not matter for the purposes of this paper. However, a brief overview may help you understand our environment. Previously, each of ISS's security products had it's own custom policy editor. Our customers use

M. Marchesi and G. Succi (Eds.): XP 2003, LNCS 2675, pp. 298–306, 2003.

these tools to configure their security policy. Rather than continue to maintain several of these tools, we developed a "Common Policy Editor" – a single tool to replace all the others. Its internal operation is based on the principle of an XML editor: it edits XML documents that conform to an XML schema.

These editors themselves are an essential but small part of the company's offerings; so, our external customers are uninterested in answering our questions about it. Therefore, our most direct customers in the XP sense were internal. Luckily, we had 30 of them.

We built CPE in Java with two to four programmers. To date, the team has completed more than 40 two-week iterations. Our stories are small: one to five IEDs each.

3   Change the Requirements

Lesson 1 Don't try to find all stories up front, and expect to throw many away.

We discovered less than half of our stories during a four-month conception and analysis phase. (This phase was much longer than it needed to be. Our director at the time wanted to make sure we had done our homework before embarking on a multi-year investment. Still, we made good use of the time.) We discovered the next quarter of the stories during the first ten iterations and another quarter in the next ten. Of the 252 stories we have identified, we have implemented more than 180. Fifty-two are candidates for future releases and we deleted twenty. Among the reasons for the deletions were:

- We shifted responsibility for a story to another team.
- We replaced a story with a different set of stories.
- The need evaporated.
- The customer didn't need it after all.
- The output format changed so we replaced the story with a different story.
- It was something we couldn't implement.
- It didn't fit in with the rest of the application suite.
- The concept became obsolete.
- It was just a plain dumb idea.
- It was a nasty can of worms and we did not have a clear and present need.

Almost twenty percent of our stories were hard to estimate; we did not know how to implement them at discovery. There were more of these than we could spike up front, and spiking would not help much for many of them. We needed to develop more of the application before we would be able to give better estimates. To reflect this uncertainty, we gave each of those a "placeholder" estimate of 10 or 15 IEDs, a sufficiently huge number for us. By the time each of those stories became the top priority, we had learned enough to be able to split the story and estimate the pieces.

So, how did we handle these changes? We just made the appropriate adjustments to the release plan, re-prioritized and recalculated the estimated completion date. We saw the date move every two weeks, but we knew why. Knowing why the dates move, and knowing it early and often, is invaluable when managing dependencies between projects.

Lesson 2 If your customer requires projected completion dates and you have
   lots of small stories, work with blocks of stories.

Our (internal) customers needed CPE as part of their own products and depended on our timely completion of their requested features. We had long lead times in some cases because we had so many features for so many customers. Thus, our customers needed us to tell them when we would complete their features. But from all this change, how could we possibly? Projection of completion dates is discouraged in XP literature because embracing change renders the dates useless. However, we found a way to effectively use target dates in XP.

The size of our backlog divided by the velocity times the iteration size told us how long we expected it to take *if nothing changes*. Of course, something always changes. To account for that uncertainty, as well as vacation days, holidays and sick-days, we multiplied the backlog size by 1.25. This multiplier is based on Steve McConnell's [8] adaptation of Boehm's COCOMO [3]. We did this not because of poor estimates; our estimates were actually quite good [5]. And it was not because of a lack of analysis; we did lots of analysis. We did this in anticipation of changing priorities and changing requirements.

Stories fell naturally into blocks that either supported certain uber stories or satisfied needs of a particular customer. For example, "Mandatory for Mike", "Nice-to-Have for Jack", "must-have" and "cosmetic" are some of those blocks. We kept our stories in a Wiki for improved visibility for the 30 scattered customers. This allowed us to have a little javascript compute the estimated *duration* of each block.

To provide estimated *completion dates* for each block, we typed the title of each block in to Microsoft Project along with the total duration we expected to spend on that block (calculated as described earlier). MS Project would handily compute the dates for us. We never assigned stories to future iterations or put iterations or individual stories into Project. We just worked with the blocks. We never had more than 20 blocks of stories at any one time, so we could easily update the schedule. We did not use resources or any advanced features of the tool. We just used it to do the date arithmetic and to print a pretty schedule.

This worked well. The customers saw an ever growing and shuffling backlog, yet ever shrinking completion dates. Moreover, they got this update every two weeks. This gave them great confidence in our schedules and ability to deliver.

4   Change the Management

Working with blocks of stories also helps when the management changes. Our management changed three times so we got lots of practice. Our managers assumed the role of Benevolent Monarch and were called upon to prioritize. Initially, they each dove into the list of stories. They typically gave up that desire when they realized how granular the stories were. After that, they just gave us priorities at the block level.

"It was pretty easy to come up to speed on the CPE project" says Robert, one of the managers new to XP. "The project scope was laid out [in the stories] and was easy to understand. The scope of work was chunk-ified and each chunk had a description. [They were] a little cryptic but understandable. Primarily it was easy because the people in the project were competent and understood the project, scope and priorities. Therefore, I did not have to give much time to manage the project. It ran itself. It was easy to change priorities of the development by moving chunks around in time."

Lesson 3 If you have lots of stories and lots of customers, use a Wiki.

Management can't completely escape the detail: It is necessary to scrub the plan, to move stories among higher and lower priority blocks.

The CPE Project had two types of internal customers. The first was other engineers who needed CPE to configure their own product. The stories for these engineers were fine grained: support a particular type of configuration parameter or a particular user interface feature. Most of the stories had estimates of one to two IEDs. Understanding these stories was not trivial because they were numerous and they did not fit together into any larger pattern.

The second type of customer were the "Product Managers", who are the traditional source of all requirements at ISS. Although the product managers are supposed to manage the requirements, they had less interest in CPE than did the engineers. Yet, to prioritize the engineers' stories, it was necessary to interpret them in terms of business impact. Discussions with the product managers allowed prioritization of the stories. Together, we discovered that some stories had marginal value or corresponded to unlikely situations. Overall, this prioritization was a relatively minor adjustment to the project. Keeping stories on a Wiki helped facilitate this re-prioritization.

5   Stop and Restart the Project

Lesson 4 Finish the iteration.

When the economy slowed, the company adjusted with a layoff and reallocated resources to the highest priority projects. The projects put on hold were given a small amount of time to mothball their work - to make notes on the state of the code and the project so it can be picked up again later. When management told us to shut down the CPE Project, we just finished the iteration. That is a natural stopping point. We did not have to do anything extra. The state of the code was tested with no incomplete features. The Wiki and other project information showed which stories had been implemented and which had not.

Even if we had to cut the iteration short, we still could have finished whatever story we were working on – all of our stories were so short. Even if we could not have finished the story, we still would have lost no work because of the continuous integration practice. And our testing practice would have given us confidence in any code we had checked in.

Lesson 5 Clean up the design debt.

The same XP practices that helped us make a quick and orderly shutdown helped us have a successful restart. One thing we did to help get back into the swing of things was to clean up our design debt [10]. We had a handful of refactorings [4] we were saving for the next time we had to touch that code. We just went ahead and did them. This helped give us a fresh start.

6   Add a New Customer

Lesson 6 Follow the process at all times and be prepared for opportunities that may arise: Keep it working. Enforce simplicity and testing. Treat each build as if it were the last.

Another team of engineers choose CPE to meet its need for a new configuration interface. This other product, which we will call "FastAnalysis", had a rather different form and function than the others. CPE itself had to work somewhat differently in this context. Nevertheless, the FastAnalysis team integrated CPE into their product in a day or two. One of the engineers remarked to Hammer that the CPE was a dream to modify. This is a direct result of XP's simplicity and testing values.

This new customer naturally had unique requirements, which necessitated another re-prioritization of work. As mentioned earlier, changing requirements was never a problem. XP allowed us to be responsive to this new customer's needs.

CPE builds were so stable and so well tested that the FastAnalysis team was able to integrate every new version of CPE with ease. They took every iteration build that had a new feature of interest to them, and they took a few hourly builds for their most important features.

7   Add Two Programmers

Lesson 7 Handpick open-minded individuals...

We added two more programmers to the team. It is important to note that Andrew handpicked these. "As the coach, I was most interested in an open mind and the right attitude towards best practices. I did not care whether the candidate had experience with the technologies and practices we were using, other than having basic knowledge of Java, C++ or Smalltalk." That the new programmers had *volunteered* to work CPE on was key: They knew that they would be following all of the XP practices and were eager to do so. Hand picking the team members, and doing so with this selection criteria, were the most important and best decisions we made. This may be the wrong choice for "traditional" projects, but it is the correct approach for XP projects. For CPE, it was a success factor.

All we needed to do for these two was give an overview of the design and theory of operation. Our list of stories showed all of the work remaining, in detail, so we did not have to explain much about that. They learned XP on the job. They learned more about Java, XML and the code through pair programming. Pairing brought these new guys up to speed fast. They were giving good feedback on the first day.

Since the thesis of this report is that XP helps with change, let's consider how XP helped these new programmers adapt to the new team. We will start with Bob:

Bob Vincent

"I was interested in learning Java and XML, but since I had not done any independent study on either topic I felt I would be behind and hurt the team's progress. I had experience with some of the best practices described in XP Explained [2], although not many of them at once, and not all of those experiences were good ones. But the way we did XP on the CPE Project helped me deal with the changes related to joining this team.

Lesson 8 ...and pair program.

"Pair programming was a big help. It allowed me to think of the problems at hand without getting tied up in details that I did not know. At the same time I was able to learn those details much more quickly than if I was treading through on my own. Occasionally I was able to reciprocate. Overall, I could see improvements in the quality of the designs and the coding over what either person could have done on their own.

"XP pushes 40 hour work weeks. I was skeptical at first but after a year of XP development, I can't think of any time where project-panic set in. It's much easier to deal with the change of joining a new team when the team isn't in panic mode. Other practices that led to a better project experience were the continuous builds and heavy amount of testing. I'm more comfortable with making changes to a project when it has a thorough set of unit and functional tests.

"Change isn't always just something that happens to you; we drove change. Refactoring is one topic that I hear criticized quite often - why fix what's not broken? After doing plenty of refactoring, I can see how it simplified development that came later."

Chris Singer

"I certainly was concerned about joining the CPE team. What I was most worried about was not knowing the more formal practices - XP, design patterns, unit testing, etc. I knew that these disciplines were a normal part of the daily discourse on CPE. [Though I was] excited about the possibilities, I was intimidated by a feeling that I was way behind. Joining any new team is stressful and requires some ramp-up time, but I also had a new way of doing business to learn.

"Of course, it worked out well. The CPE team didn't have any unrealistic expectations and the team members were great at showing me the ropes. Naturally, pair programming is a great way to quickly bring new members up to speed. You're not just pointing them at the project in [the version control system] and saying "good luck." On most non-XP teams there seems to be a culture of independence - that a competent programmer can figure things out on his own. While that may be true, it's inefficient and often leads to missed subtleties and broken code.

Lesson 9 Manage the intensity.

"Many of the XP practices require tons of self-discipline. To test thoroughly, to estimate everything, to think through each story and break it down into tasks requires energy and commitment. Pair programming and group tasking / estimating is absolutely essential to the success of an XP project. Without the peer pressure and moral support, these annoying (albeit necessary) practices are doomed to fail. I would find XP very difficult without the all-important collaborative aspects.

"Peer pressure has its downside too. It forces everyone to operate at high intensity levels. Who wants to be the one to call for a break? Who wants to be the one to call it quits for the day? In some ways, I had a love/hate relationship with our project. On one side, the work we did was really interesting, I enjoyed working with the team and I learned a lot - but on the other side I was mentally exhausted much of the time - both from the intensity of the work itself and from worrying about how I was perceived when I'd take a break or call it quits for the day. I don't think that XP necessarily has to feel that way - I just think the intensity levels of the team members need to be well matched. Perhaps short scheduled breaks during the day would lessen the exhaustion and the feeling of being cut off from the world in the lab."

8   Add More Responsibilities

Lesson 10 Just get the job done and spare management the details.

Upper management interrupted Iteration 23. They gave our team responsibility for the Policy Management Project and wanted us to start work on it immediately. There was no reason for this to have been so disruptive. It must have seemed urgent at the time. Perhaps this was a case of them not being accustomed to iterative development or such short iterations. The team was quite unhappy about the additional responsibilities. They wanted to work on CPE - the Policy Management code was not well refactored or tested.

At first we were not exactly sure how this was going to work or how we wanted to manage it. Should we go ahead and dedicate all our efforts on the new project to get it out of the way? Should we allocate to the iteration half of the story IEDs from each project? What if the projects have different velocities and one project is short-changed? Should we adjust our split such that our actual task hours come out about even? Should we spend one week on one project and the other on the other? Or, should we put two engineers on one project and two on the other?

We were afraid upper management would want us to manage the two products a particular way of their choosing. We thought this would be an issue because in XP the work is more granular and visible than it is on traditional projects. We were afraid that if we gave them a knob, they would want to turn it. However, it turns out they were not interested in how we would go about it. They were not accustomed to the visibility. No traditional team could have given them all of these options. We eventually realized that management did not expect a choice so we did not give them one.

We began Iteration 24 with half of our IEDs from each project. After that, we noticed that our velocity on the Policy Management project was lower than our velocity on the CPE project. That is when we began to balance the amount of actual time spent on each project.

When the director asked which programmers were working on CPE and which on Policy Management, Hammer told him that they would split their effort evenly on both responsibilities. This was not the answer the director expected, but he found it represent what he wanted.

Eventually, we had completed enough of the Policy Management stories such that splitting resources evenly was no longer an issue. From then on, we just picked the highest priority stories regardless of which project they came from.

We eventually saw a good fit between what we were doing on each project and accepted, if not enjoyed, the additional assignment.

9   Loose the Coach and a Programmer

Lesson 11 Be extreme with *all* the practices. The one you neglect will be the one you need the most.

The CPE / Policy Management team lost their Coach (Andrew) and another programmer (Chris). The coach was not much of a loss, but Chris had skills the team still needed. Management granted two more iterations with Chris so we re-prioritized some stories to take advantage of this opportunity. During that time, the team paired heavily with the intent of learning everything they needed to know and of getting as many of these stories done as possible.

Unfortunately, it was a little too late. Chris knew the Policy Management code better than any one else due to some experience with it on a previous project. We had not practiced collective code ownership to the extent we should have and felt the pain after he left the team.

The fact that losing the coach was not a big deal is a measure of success. It is as Kent Beck explains [6]: "So that's my aesthetic as a coach. If I do everything perfectly, then my contribution is totally invisible to the team." If I do my job as a coach, I will have trained other team members to fill that role.

10   Conclusion

The team successfully handled every change thrown at them. The secret to the success was not just the practices and it was not just the people. The practices made the team more successful than they would have otherwise been. Yet, attempts to do these practices on other teams at ISS have not taken root. It takes a willing and able team to do XP. Thus, it is the people and the practices that make a project most successful. The critical success factors:

- An experienced coach: A "level 3" lead [1].
- The people: an open-minded commitment to best practices.
- Pair programming: "pair pressure" [9].

We firmly believe a team cannot do XP without the right attitude. There must be a strong desire to do XP and to make it work. We do not believe a below-average team can successfully implement XP because they would lack a commitment to change. Not every programmer on the team has to be a superstar, but every team member must have the XP attitude and a willingness to learn.

Finally, it would be difficult to do what we would consider XP successfully without pair programming. Pair programming is an excellent way to introduce new programmers to new software and to XP itself.

Acknowledgements

We would like to thank Matt DiIorio, Mike Nikitaides, Greg Houston, Chris Singer, Bob Vincent and Robert McEwin for their contributions to the CPE project, to this report and to XP at ISS.

References

1. Alistair Cockburn: Agile Software Development. Addison Wesley (2001)
2. Kent Beck: Extreme Programming Explained, Embrace Change. Addison Wesley (2000)
3. Barry W. Boehm, et al.: "Cost Models for Future Life Cycle Processes: COCOMO 2.0" (1995)
4. Martin Fowler, et. al.: Refactoring: Improving the Design of Existing Code. Addison Wesley (1999)
5. Andrew Fuqua: "Using Function Points in XP – Considerations". Lecture Notes in Computer Science. Springer (2003)
6. Jim Highsmith: Agile Software Development Ecosystems. Addison Wesley (2002)
7. Ron Jeffries: "Petition The King", Online at
   http://www.xprogramming.com/xpmag/PetitionTheKing.htm.
   See also the discussion online at
   http://groups.yahoo.com/group/extremeprogramming/message/56946
   particularly the two posts from Arien Malec: 57048 and 57054.
8. Steve C. McConnell: Rapid Development: Taming Wild Software Schedules. Microsoft Press (1996)
9. Laurie Williams, Robert Kessler: Pair Programming Illuminated. Addison Wesley (2002)
10. "Design Debt" online at http://c2.com/cgi/wiki?DesignDebt

Extreme Makeover: Bending the Rules to Reduce Risk Rewriting Complex Systems

Sharon Johnson[1], Jia Mao[2], Eric Nickell[1], and Ian Smith[1]

[1] Palo Alto Research Center, 3333 Coyote Hill Road
Palo Alto, CA 94304
{sjohnson,nickell,iansmith}@parc.com
[2] Computer Science and Engineering, University of California, San Diego
La Jolla, CA 92093-0114
jiamao@cs.ucsd.edu

Abstract. We describe our experience using XP to reimplement sophisticated, high-performance imaging software in a research environment. We focus especially on practices we used to derive value from the existing software, notably *reimplementation by ransacking* and *conversion as learning*. Our experience suggests that some of the classic 12 practices which define XP should be adjusted when there is a existing, well-structured system to serve as a guide.

1 Introduction

Approaching Christmas, 2001, we faced a large and daunting problem. We needed to reimplement a large, complex piece of software that has been in production use for a decade – the Cedar Imager [1 , 2]. Reengineering posed new challenges for our understanding of XP. In particular, the roles of customer and programmer needed to change to deal with the fact that the existing system specified a large percentage of the requirements and contained numerous algorithms which could (and in some cases must) be mined by the developers.

The Cedar Imager is a large system which manages the presentation of graphic images from high-level graphic shapes and fonts using abstract color models. It creates rasters of bits or bytes or similar structures for transmission to output devices. Conceived and implemented in the early 1980s at PARC's Computer Science Lab, it was first used as the imaging engine for the Cedar experimental programming environment [3,4,5]. Today, the Cedar Imager is at the core of high-performance printer controllers for monochrome and full color printers.

Developed and supported in a research setting, the Cedar Imager has been of interest to product organizations for more than a decade because of its performance and capability. However, product organizations want the ability to adapt the imaging software themselves and are reluctant to invest in developing and supporting products not written in a commercially-supported language. It was felt that PARC's imaging technology would be more valuable if it were cast in a modern, commercial language, such as Java, but only if the Imager's existing advantages could be retained.

Our project needed to determine whether it is possible to rewrite the Imager into a modern language with widespread industry support and that would retain the strengths of the existing Imager – performance, modularity, and easy-to-read source code. A

M. Marchesi and G. Succi (Eds.): XP 2003, LNCS 2675, pp. 307–314, 2003.

consistent concern was whether an imager written in Java could provide performance comparable to the Cedar Imager.

Initial work on porting the Imager to Java began in late 2001, at a time when XP was beginning to infect PARC's Computer Science Laboratory [6]. Although unit testing was incorporated from the beginning, no other XP practices were implemented during the project's first seven months. By the end of this period, some of the core functionality was in place: A Java Imager that provided basic imaging facilities that produced gray bytemaps as output, and a decomposer for Adobe's *Portable Document Format* (PDF) [7] which could parse the overall document structure for hand-constructed PDF[1].

2   Our XP Setting

In June, 2002, with the addition of a summer intern, we decided to adopt XP practices wherever possible. Our hope was to gain experience with XP during a 3 month pilot, and to see if pair programming could be used effectively with people who were only going to be involved with the project for a few months. We used one-week iterations, and six hours of pair programming each day.

The XP team consisted of four people: The full-time researcher [Nickell] and one summer intern [Mao] were the development team, while a research manager [Johnson] and an internal XP "coach" [Smith] served as customer surrogates. Our goal for the summer, as well as for the overall project, was to determine the viability of a Java Imager as a future substitute for the Cedar Imager, and to prepare an effective demonstration of this.

3   Our XP Experience

In this section we detail some of our planning game experiences, for the benefit of practitioners who may wish to compare our experience to their own.

During the first four one-week iterations, the tasks picked by our customer surrogates focused on adding basic functionality to the imager and to the PDF decomposer, and on narrowing the focus for a proposed technology demonstration near year end. Because of sharp customer focus, we spent the first few iterations adding the basic functionality needed by that demonstraction, and integrating our software into an existing printing architecture on a color printer. By the end of iteration #4, we could print a PDF document containing colored text on this system.

The planning meetings for iterations 5-7 all involved some conflict between the developers and the customers. By this time, the team had selected some target PDF documents that would be used for a demo. While everyone agreed that risk reduction and containment was a goal, the developers and customers were seeing the primary risk as coming from different directions. Each week, the customers wanted to make progress on the technical area with the largest remaining technical problems, so that the developers were working in very different domains each week, each algorithmi-

---

[1] Since we had no existing PDF decomposer in Cedar, we used standard XP practices to develop a PDF decomposer to drive our Java version of the Imager.

cally complex. The developers, however, felt that there was risk in having the developers switch between different areas of the code too rapidly. They were in favor of implementing not only basic functionality, but also addressing performance issues in that area before switching to another task. The customers won.

After iteration #7, we were printing sample PDF documents with graphic shapes, strokes, and text, but we had also collected data showing that we were running about 20 times slower than the Cedar Imager.

In the planning meeting for iteration #8, we resurrected the debate of performance vs next-piece of functionality. Keep in mind that "at comparable performance" is a critical part of the project's research question. This time around, the team agreed that low performance was now the greatest threat to the project. As such, the next three iterations, 8-10, were focused on bringing the Java Imager's performance in line with the Cedar Imager's for equivalent functionality. In iteration #8, we explored a variety of optimizations, noting any performance increases and our subjective sense how the optimization affected code smell. During iteration #9, we began selecting which optimizations to fold back into the main branch. In general, we only accepted optimizations which boosted performance by at least 20% and were localized to a couple methods in a single class or which could be isolated in a separate class.

We should note that the full-time developer went on vacation during this period, leaving the summer intern to implement the various optimizations. We still gained much of the advantages of pair programming by pairing and reviewing the selected optimizations as they were folded into the main branch. During iteration #10, we made the difficult decision to replace a compiler-compiler-based parser [8] with a hand-built parser system, to avoid a performance bottleneck inherent in the code generated by the compiler-compiler. By the end of this iteration, Java Imager performance was on par with Cedar Imager performance for our target pages.

During our final iterations, #11-12, with performance concerns addressed for the time being, the team assessed the features that would be needed to print the selected target documents for the year-end demo, and the iterations focused on implementing just those features.

4   Our Re-engineering Practice

Over time, we developed several practices to help us make the most of the existing Cedar code base while developing the Java Imager. Some of these practices were founded on assumptions we made about the Cedar Imager and its developers:

- The developers were world-class computer scientists who usually found the simplest, most elegant partitioning of the problem.
- The existing Cedar Imager core has been in constant use for nearly two decades, and the developers have good mechanisms to track and remove bugs. In our experience, it is remarkably bug-free.
- The Cedar code had been heavily optimized over a long period. Some of the optimizations were largely irrelevant for today's imaging requirements. Other optimizations were superseded at a higher architecture level and were no longer hot spots, but were left in place.
- Some code, particularly some optimizations, assumed bit-level access to the underlying memory, or relied on the ability to do pointer arithmetic. These were infrequent.

- Software that would have been implemented in Java with a small class hierarchy was implemented in Cedar with a variant record structure. This usually meant that pieces of each Cedar procedure in a module were distributed across two or more Java classes.

Practice 1: Code Size Informing Technical Estimates

During the planning game, the developers used relative sizes of Cedar modules to help us estimate time to complete tasks, as well as perceived complexity and familiarity.

Practice 2: Using an Existing System to Create Tests

When reimplementing a complex algorithm, we frequently used the existing system to compute results that we would then use to test the new system. For example, when we integrated code to rasterize embedded fonts on demand for given point sizes, device resolutions, and affine transforms, we wanted to test that the correct bits were being generated. Creating our own easy-to-test embedded font would be painful, as well as using an existing font and hand-computing the correct output pixels. Instead, we wrote code to have the Cedar Imager rasterize a sample font with different parameters, and output the results as text that we cut and pasted into an appropriate data structure in the test code.

Practice 3: Reimplementation by Ransacking

When one of an iteration's tasks was to re-implement functionality already present in the Cedar Imager, we usually neither slavishly translated each line of Cedar into the corresponding Java nor chose to ignore the Cedar code and do a clean sheet implementation. Instead, we chose something in the middle, reimplementation by ransacking.

In this approach, we would use the Cedar code as an example of how some smart people had implemented this same functionality in another setting. We would start by extending our PDF capabilities to the point that it was ready to call the Imager, using standard test-driven development. At this point we would open or create the Java class where we wanted to put this new capability, and paste in the Cedar code as comments. Next, we would identify the Cedar procedure which could provide the needed functionality, and reimplement that procedure as a Java method. At this point, assuming we understood the functionality covered by the Cedar procedure/Java method-to-be, we would translate line-by-line if that would suffice. Frequently, we would encounter a Cedar element, such as an inner procedure, that would require that we pause and consider our reimplementation options. By the time we had finished reimplementing this one procedure, we had calls from our new method to one or more other methods that also would need reimplementation, so we would repeat this process with the other procedures until the class compiled.

A frequent pattern in the Cedar was code that detected special cases which could be optimized, followed by code which implemented the general case. Here, we would only implement the general case. We also discarded other optimizations, such as object pooling.

To any method created in this way, we inserted an initial line, `assert false:` "`no test written`". This line would not be removed until we were convinced that the test code had an adequate test for that method's functionality. Also, though the Cedar language provides access modifiers for its procedures very like those for Java methods, we chose to ignore these, and instead made each reimplemented method private until we were compelled to expose it.

If a section was complex enough that we had to take a significant amount of time understanding it before we could reimplement it, then we encoded that understanding as a comment in the code. We also felt free to refactor and rename if that contributed to better understanding.

At this stage, we now have a system which compiles, but if we attempt to run the entire test suite, it fails, because the test code for the PDF/Imager bridge triggers a call to a newly-implemented method whose first line is an "assert false". At this point, we would shift from *reimplementation by ransacking* to something much more akin to *test driven development*, writing tests, removing the "assert false" and implementing missing code.

Practice 4: Conversion as Learning

Occasionally, as with iteration #6 when we were adding stroking to the Imager, we had a general understanding of the high-level task. When we examined the Cedar code, we could not immediately gain an understanding of the algorithms it was using. In these cases, we came to use *conversion as learning*. To some extent, *conversion as learning* is the converse of *reimplementation by ransacking*. In *reimplementation by ransacking*, we use our existing understanding of the task to guide our plundering of the Cedar code, working from the top down. In *conversion as learning*, we work our way through the Cedar code to build a bottom-up understanding of an algorithm to implement. Note that both approaches assume that the Cedar developers knew what they were doing.

We would choose some Cedar procedure to start converting, usually starting where we thought we understood it best. We would add assertions and comments as we translated, especially commenting the methods inputs and outputs. Assertions served as comments to us (not to mention future readers) but also helped us quickly revise our understanding if it was violated during testing. Then we would work on translating a related procedure. At some point, we would gain an insight into how the pieces fit together, either for a subsection or as a whole. That new insight would usually drive us to revisit the already-translated code and either recomment or refactor it. We would also have the option, at this point, of continuing with *conversion as learning* or switching back to our normal mode of *reimplementation by ransacking*.

5   Lessons Learned

We chose to adapt some of the XP practices in order to gain XP's over-arching goals. Some in the XP community will consider this a heresy, but if the basic problem of software development is risk [9], then we felt that we reduced the risk of increased cost or development time by modifying the practices to account for the fact that certain types of knowledge were embedded in the existing system. Thus, we needed to find ways to mine that understanding without impairing the integrity of the new system.

Lesson 1: Life without Metaphor

Instead of using a metaphor to guide all development and to guide communication between developers and customers, we used the existing system. In our case, we discussed features in terms of what could be imaged onto a page, using the existing system as a reference. To do this, the developers had to learn to articulate abstract features, such as "fill path", in terms of their visual impact on a page.

Lesson 2: Not Always the Simplest

While the developers did try to remove extra complexity as it was found, there were notable exceptions. This extra complexity arose from straightforward translation of Cedar code which did more than strictly required by the current level of functionality in the Java Imager. This extra complexity could be represented by a more general algorithm than we yet needed, or a more complex data structure. At these points, we were faced with a choice: Should we leave the excess complexity in, or strip it out? Classic XP would suggest that we remove this complexity before moving on. But if we had a task in hand for the current iteration that would require the reintroduction of the complexity, or if we were reasonably sure it would be required in the next, we chose to live with it. More precariously, there were times when our undestanding was not deep enough to know whether the code would be needed in a few weeks or not. Where practical, we would insert an assertion that would prohibit accessing the additional capabilities. This seemed like the simplest compromise between tearing out code we might eventually need, and making sure that there was no functionality without a test.

Lesson 3: Not Always Test First

As mentioned above, we often wrote our tests after writing the code.

1. Ransacking the existing system was much faster than clean-sheet design and allowed us to tackle larger chunks of functionality in a single task. But since some of our understanding was coming from the ransacking process, we were not able to write effective tests until afterward.
2. Test first in classic XP helps a pair of developers design a clean class interface. We were relying in part on the existing system to help us design this. As such, early test construction was not quite as critical.

That said, we still needed a mechanism to give us confidence that our test coverage was adequate for the current system. We could have used a task list. Instead, we chose to hobble methods developed in advance of unit tests by throw an exception as the first statement. We believe there are few, if any, untested features in the Java Imager.

Lesson 4: Using XP with an Intern

Interns usually work on a narrowly circumscribed or separable project or demo, or they work on a forked branch of a main project, or their code is carefully screened by a host before it is checked in. All of these approaches make the cost of integrating the intern's work into the larger project more expensive. One of our motivators for adopting XP was to see if we could use a summer intern effectively as a programming partner, deriving greater value long-term from their work. Our findings:

- Our permanent researcher [Nickell] perceived an immediate jump in his productivity, even during the first 2-3 weeks that our intern [Mao] was navigating and not driving. We suggest some reasons for that below.
- Even from the first day, Mao provided a second pair of eyes for typos, mistaken divergence from the Cedar source, or while debugging. By the third week, she was doing some of the driving.
- Pairing and continuous integration meant that when the intern was driving, she was able to receive prompt feedback when writing less-than-ideal code, rather than having the code buried until an end-of-summer code review.
- Pairing was a natural mechanism to transfer knowledge about the current state of the software with little cost.

We suggest that the following effects may have contributed to the perceived productivity increase even in the first two weeks:

- **Gym Effect:** Like meeting a friend at the gym, agreeing to meet at a certain time, and setting aside 6 hours each day to program with another person increased the actual hours per week writing software.
- **Email Effect:** When a solo programmer hits a difficult problem, or an intransigent bug, there is a tendency to switch tasks. There is email to be checked, or a phone call to be made. While pair programming, this would be socially awkward, so there instead the two begin discussing the problem, which often leads to a solution or an experiment.
- **Hawthorne Effect:** [10]: Workers become more productive simply by being observed. When we are pair programming, we are being observed by a partner. We suspect there is a natural tendency to want to appear astute and knowledgeable, and so we apply ourselves.
- **Meeting Effect:** In a work context where XP is rare, two people working together culturally constitute a meeting. A third party with a question for one of the pair is more likely to tread lightly, either deferring the question until later, or making a brief interruption to negotiate a later time for discussion. Our experience was that development was less interrupted.

In all, our assessment was that Mao contributed significantly to this project, more than would have been possible without using XP.

6   Conclusions

We found XP to be a powerful approach when reimplementing a complex, well-structured software system. To the degree that the expertise embedded in the existing system has value and is exploitable, it can be extracted rather than being recreated in the ongoing interactions between customers and developers. To use XP most effectively in this setting, we found it necessary to modify three core XP practices.

Acknowledgments

We would like to thank our management, Richard Bruce and Richard Burton, for allowing us to experiment with XP in this project and borrow an XP coach. We also wish to express our thanks to the Cedar, Cedar Imager, and Xerox DocuPrint developers for their excellent software and helpful discussions.

References

1. Bhushan, Abhay M. Plass. *The Interpress Page and Document Description Language.* IEEE Computer, 19(6):72-77, 1986.
2. Warnock, John and Wyatt, Douglas K., *A Device Independent Graphics Imaging Model for Use with Raster Devices*, Computer Graphics16, 3.,1982.
3. Deutsch, L. Peter, and Taft, Edward. *Requirements for an Experimental Programming Environment*, Research Report CSL-80-10. Palo Alto, California: Xerox PARC, 1980.
4. Teitelman, W. *The Cedar Programming Environment: A Midterm Report and Examination*, Research Report CSL-83-1. Palo Alto, California: Xerox PARC, 1984.
5. Lampson, B. *A Description of the Cedar Language: A Cedar Language Reference Manual.* PARC Technical Report 83-15, Xerox Corporation, Palo Alto CA., 1983.
6. Bellotti, V., Burton R., Ducheneaut N., Howard M., Neuwirth, C., Smith, I. *XP In A Research Lab: The Hunt For Strategic Value.* In Proc. Of XP 2002 (Alghero, Sardinia, Italy, May 2002), 56-61.
7. Adobe Systems Incorporated. *PDF Reference, 3rd ed., version 1.4.* Addison-Wesley, Boston, MA, 2001.
8. WebGAIN Web Site. On-line at:
   http://www.webgain.com/products/java_cc/
9. Beck, K. *Extreme Programming Explained.* Reading, Massachusetts, Addison Wesley, 2000.
10. Mayo, E. *The human problems of an industrial civilization* (New York: MacMillan) ch.3, 1933.

Component-Oriented Agile Software Development

Zoran Stojanovic, Ajantha Dahanayake, and Henk Sol

Systems Engineering Group, Faculty of Technology, Policy and Management
Delft University of Technology
Jaffalaan 5, 2628 BX Delft, The Netherlands
{Z.Stojanovic,A.Dahanayake,H.G.Sol}@tbm.tudelft.nl

Abstract. Agile Development (AD), Model-Driven Development (MDD) and
Component-Based Development (CBD) have been proposed, each on its own,
as the ways to build quality software systems fast and be able to easily adapt to
frequently changing requirements in the environment. This paper presents how
component concepts can support and strengthen AD principles and practice,
help in overcoming AD limitations, as well as bridge the gap between AD and
MDD by combining certain elements from both sides.

1 Introduction

In the past several years, Extreme Programming (XP) [1] and other Agile Methodologies (AMs) [2] have started to gain considerable interest in the IT community. The
leading agile methodologists have formed the Agile Alliance and published the Agile
Manifesto [3]. Agile Development (AD) paradigm challenges many of the common
assumptions in software development. Among the most controversial AD characteristics are its rejection of significant effort in up-front architectural design as well as
minimizing or ignoring modeling activities and documentation. AD supporters claim
that their methodologies include enough design efforts for the project to be successful, although in a different way than in traditional processes. This treatment of modeling and design is quite opposite to the current initiatives and paradigms in software
development, such as Model-Driven Development (MDD) [4]. While both AD and
MDD claim to address the challenges of high change rates, short time-to-market,
increased return-on-investment and high quality software, their proposed solutions
are actually very dissimilar. The question is whether principles and practices of both
development paradigms can be combined in order to take the benefits of both approaches.

The aim of this paper is to propose how concepts of component-based modeling,
design and development can help in bridging the gap between model-driven and agile
development. The paper shows how components can ensure and strengthen AD principles and practices, provide simple and flexible component-oriented architectural
design, as well as help in overcoming the limitations of the agile methodologies, such
as reusability, outsourcing, large teams and software, and safety critical software
development.

M. Marchesi and G. Succi (Eds.): XP 2003, LNCS 2675, pp. 315–318, 2003.

2   Components in Agile Modeling, Design and Development

Agile methodologies assume using object-oriented development paradigm. They do not define or make use of advanced software concepts such as components [5] and services [6]. In our opinion exactly components as providers of services and concepts that further raise the level of abstraction over traditional classes/objects can significantly support principles and practices of agile development.

2.1   Component Concepts

Components have been used so far mainly as implementation artifacts. However the components are equally useful and important if used as modeling and design artifacts in building the logical architecture of the system [7]. The essence of the component approach is the explicit separation between the outside and the inside of the component using an interface. A component fulfils a particular role in the context, by providing and requiring services to/from it. It participates in a composition with other components to form a higher-level behavior. At the same time every component can be represented as a composition of lower-level components. Well-defined behavioral dependencies and coordination of activities between components are of a great importance in achieving the common goal. A component must handle, use, create or simply be aware of certain information in order to provide its services properly. In order to be used in a different context or to be adaptable to the changes in its context, a component can possess so-called configuration parameters.

2.2   Components and AD Principles and Practices

Component concepts presented above represent the clear case for agile design and development. They can support the most important principles of AD, such as simplicity, good communication between stakeholders, rapid feedback, and effective adoption of changes. Service-based component concepts are equally well understood by both business and technical people, so that component-based architecture can provide a point of communication and negotiation between all involved stakeholders. Components are an excellent way to manage changes. Changes are not harmful for component-based software since they are localized inside the particular component or on the interfaces between components, so they cannot be spread across the system in an uncontrolled manner. Components can support high quality work, since if used, COTS components, or web services, are usually pre-tested and certified through a number of possible previous usage cases.

Component and service concepts can add significant value to the simple and easily scalable architectural design in agile development. Since components are defined as providers of business services at a higher level of abstraction and granularity than traditional objects, they can be used as the main building blocks of a simple architectural design understandable for all involved project stakeholders. Component concepts can support easy defining of the architecture metaphor and architecture proto-types (spikes) as the main design-level artifacts of XP. The component architecture further maps to component-based implementation providing bi-directional traceability between business needs and software artifacts. Good business-driven, component-oriented architecture design can reduce the need for further refactoring as well as for permanent customer presence in the case it is not feasible. Components can be de-scribed using different mechanisms at different levels of formality, such as natural language and sketches on the whiteboard, business vocabulary on some kind of the cards, formal specification language and contract-based theory in a CASE tool, or software code [7]. In this way the same component-approach can fit into really agile projects, as well as large, safety-critical projects and teams, depending on particular needs. Furthermore, since components are identified and defined based on use cases for which realization they are responsible, it is straightforward to define test suite for components based on use cases and conditions related to them and use these tests in building components according to AD practices. Components are well suited for incremental and iterative development. Each new iteration cycle adds more function-ality to particular components and refines the interfaces among them. Coding practice can be applied at the level of single components, their sub-components, or a set of collaborative components.

2.3   Components and AD Limitations

AD provides only a limited support for certain kinds of projects, such as projects with distributed development teams and resources, outsourcing, using legacy systems or Commercial-Off-The-Shelf (COTS) components, as well as projects involving large teams developing large or safety-critical software systems [8]. In our opinion, using the component paradigm can help in overcoming these AD limitations. Using the component way of thinking the whole problem can be divided into pieces according to cohesive sets of business functionality. These functional units called business components can be specified in informal, semi-formal or formal way, depending on a particular situation. The more formal specification of component interfaces can help in communication between team members and customers when customers are sepa-rated from developers, or a development team is distributed over several locations. Components can help in an agile project when a particular task should be outsourced to subcontractors. In that case components related to the task can be specified in more formal way than in an ordinary agile project, in order to provide precisely defined subcontracted task. Components are about reusability, so each component that nor-mally encapsulates well-defined business or technical functionality can be reused in a similar context in the future. On the other hand, well-defined component-oriented architecture provides using third-party components such as COTS components or wrapped legacy assets, as long as the interfaces toward the other components are fulfilled. By providing an effective separation of concerns the component paradigm can help in supporting the agile development that involves a larger team in building large software. Large problem can be broken down into smaller units, and then parts of the team are responsible for developing particular components in an agile manner.

System made of components can scale and be extended easily, by defining additional components or by extending the scope of existing components. Using pre-built and pre-tested COTS components can further increase the quality of the safety-critical software.

3   Conclusion

The focus of Agile Development is on effective mechanisms to adopt changes through iterative and incremental cycles, small releases, frequent testing, and the constant feedback from the customer. Although agile methodologies differ in their characteristics, mechanisms, scope and focus, they share similar concepts, principles and practices that challenge many of the common assumptions in software development and initiatives such as Model-Driven Development. While both AD and MDD claim to address the challenges of high change rates, short time-to-market, increased return-on-investment and high quality software, their proposed solutions are actually very dissimilar. This paper presents how component concepts used at the level of modeling, architectural design and implementation can effectively support the main principles and practices of agile development. Modeling and specifying components as the main building blocks of simple architecture design at a particular level of details can provide a bridge between MDD and AD. Using components can help in overcoming certain limitations of agile methodologies in relation with the type and nature of the project, such as reusability, outsourcing, large teams and building large safety-critical software systems. On the other hand, using agile values, principles and practices in current model-driven heavyweight methodologies can help in more flexible process and solutions, shorter time-to-market and products that better fulfill business needs.

References

1. Beck, K.: Extreme Programming Explained – Embrace Change. Reading, MA: Addison-Wesley Longman Inc. (2000)
2. Fowler, M.: The New Methodology. (2001). Available at
   http://www.martinfowler.com/articles/newMethodology.html
3. Agile Alliance: Manifesto for Agile Software Development. (2001). Available at
   http://www.agilealliance.org
4. OMG. Object Management Group Model Driven Architecture. http://www.omg.org/mda/
5. D'Souza, D.F., Wills, A.C.: Objects, Components, and Frameworks with UML: the Catalysis Approach. Addison-Wesley Longman Inc. (1999)
6. IBM Web Services. Web Site On-Line: http://www.ibm/com/webservices
7. Stojanovic, Z., Dahanayake, A.N.W.: A Service-Based Approach to Components for Effective Business-IT Alignment. Practicing Software Engineering in the 21st Century. Ed. Joan Peckam, IRM Press, Idea Group Publishing, PA, USA, (2003)
8. Turk, D., France, R., Rumpe, B.: Limitations of Agile Software Processes, 3th International Conference on XP and Agile Processes in Software Engineering, Italy (2002) 43-46

Unit Testing beyond a Bar in Green and Red

Rudolf Ramler[1], Gerald Czech[1], and Dietmar Schlosser[2]

[1] Software Competence Center Hagenberg GmbH
Hauptstrasse 98, A-4232 Hagenberg, Austria
{rudolf.ramler,gerald.czech}@scch.at
[2] Siemens AG Austria, Wolfgang-Pauli-Straße 2, A-4020 Linz, Austria
dietmar.schlosser@siemens.at

Abstract. The actual and appealing objective of XP's approach to unit testing is to improve quality by avoiding errors beforehand rather than to find and fix bugs afterwards. Conventional testing, on the contrary, focuses on a posteriori analysis to find errors and issues that should be corrected. Both approaches have their advantages and drawbacks, and both are valuable and necessary. This paper describes how we combined both approaches by extending our test management environment TEMPPO for unit testing with JUnit to include testers in early unit testing activities.

1 Introduction

Unit testing has become tremendously popular when it was explained as one of XP's core quality assurance measures [1, 5]. The highly iterative nature of XP projects demands such flexible and effective testing and many of XP's other recommended approaches, e.g. refactoring, rely on the existence of unit tests. Testing literature (e.g. [7, 5]) has dealt with unit testing and module testing since decades. Comparing the ideas of unit testing in XP with the principles of conventional unit testing, however, reveals significant differences. In contrast to the definition of testing as *"the process of executing a program with the intend of finding errors"* [7], XP relies on unit testing to frequently show that everything works as intended. A discussion on the unit testing practice of XP [2] concludes that XP's approach *"is not a testing technique, it's a design technique."* From the quality management point of view, this indicates that XP's unit testing is a constructive quality assurance measure, which tries to establish quality, rather than an analytical quality assurance measure like conventional testing, which primarily tries to measure the level of quality.

The contribution that XP's unit testing approach makes to the conventional testing goal of measuring the quality level is rather limited. According to the description of unit testing in XP, these tests *"always run at 100%. If one of the unit tests is broken, no one on the team has a more important job than fixing the tests."* [1]. The graphical client of the unit testing framework JUnit [4] visualizes this principle by a green or a red progress bar. A green progress bar indicates that all tests passed, a red progress bar indicates that one of the tests failed. This green and red color-coding has become a symbol for JUnit and XP's view of unit testing in general. 100% passed unit tests, however, do not mean that the tested code is 100% free of errors. Whether or not all

M. Marchesi and G. Succi (Eds.): XP 2003, LNCS 2675, pp. 319–321, 2003.
© Springer-Verlag Berlin Heidelberg 2003

the essential errors will actually be uncovered depends on the quality of the tests–whereby testing is not capable of proving 100% correctness anyway. Bad tests will miss out critical errors although passing at 100% and lull the programmer into false confidence.

Good programmers, of course, do a lot of testing when they write code. However, these tests reflect the programmers' understanding and point of view of the program. Independent testers approach testing from a different angle than programmers and so they find those bugs that the programmers have missed. Hence, programmers should cooperate with independent testers in unit testing as early as possible to bring in a different viewpoint and to apply conventional testing ideas. Thus, we integrated testers for selected parts of the program and added testers' unit tests on top of the existing programmer-written unit tests without actually shifting the responsibility for unit testing on to the tester. The following section describes our approach to integrate testers by applying test management to unit testing.

2   Test Management for Unit Testing

For the effective integration of testing know-how into unit testing activities, it is essential to gain an overview of unit testing from a testers perspective. Therefore, we extended the existing test management environment TEMPPO [3] to support unit testing with JUnit. TEMPPO is a flexible and extensible test management environment we developed for a major international industrial partner. The tool has been designed for a lightweight test process focusing mainly on system-level functional and acceptance testing [3]. The basic functionality of TEMPPO includes: Organizing test projects and test-levels, structuring tests and assigning attributes, test execution with external test tools, generation of reports and statistics, and version management for test structures, test cases, and test results. To manage unit-level testing, with TEMPPO, we had to adapt and extend the functionality of the test management environment.

Importing JUnit Tests in TEMPPO. As unit testing falls into the duty of the programmer, unit tests are usually designed and implemented in the programmer's IDE (development environment). Therefore, we developed a mechanism to import JUnit tests into the test management environment. The import wizard analyzes the hierarchical structure of the test implementation and creates a corresponding test structure in TEMPPO. In addition, the wizard allows the interactive selection of test cases as well as test packages and generates and assigns attribute values. The built-in versioning mechanism of TEMPPO is automatically applied to the imported entries.

Structuring and Attributing of JUnit Tests. Test cases and test packages are hierarchically structured according to the test code that has been imported. The structure, however, can be flexibly adopted and arranged to various semantic aspects. Furthermore, an extensible set of attributes like test objective, test type, design state, corresponding test class and test method enhances the meta-information of the tests.

Updating and Synchronizing Tests. An update mechanism keeps the test management environment synchronized to the JUnit tests. This is necessary as the application code and, thus, the test code may frequently be refactored throughout development. The changes can be tracked using TEMPPO's versioning mechanism.

Executing JUnit Tests. JUnit uses a so-called *test runner* to execute tests and to collect test results. We implemented a similar test runner that allows executing JUnit tests from within the TEMPPO test management environment. This test runner resembles the look and feel of the familiar user interface of a popular JUnit pendant.

Analyzing Tests and Test Results. The reporting capabilities of TEMPPO summarize and visualize the test results of one or more test runs. Since unit tests are expected to pass at 100%, the evaluation of test results of a single run is of limited usefulness. Therefore, custom attributes are used to augment the statistics about the test runs, to analyze trends in unit testing, and to find weak spots. Metrics are the basis for estimating the quality of the tests. Currently, we determine a static coverage measure, i.e. the number of tests for implemented classes and relevant methods, by analyzing the test structure.

3   Conclusions and Future Work

Basing conventional unit testing upon the ideas of XP's unit testing approach helps to avoid the main drawbacks we encountered in conventional unit testing. The reuse of existing, programmer written unit tests extended with further conventional unit testing allows to estimate quality with little additional effort in a simple but effective way. Therefore, we propose including testers in unit testing and extending test management to programmer written unit tests. We have adapted a test management environment for unit testing with JUnit, which our industrial partner uses in a large, security-critical XP project.

The feedback from this ongoing industrial project and our practical experience confirm the positive impact of this approach on the rate of revealed errors by more effective unit tests. Furthermore, we perceived a high correlation between the quality of unit tests and the quality of the tested code: Good unit tests led to well tested code that contains few errors and an efficient, modular design. Thus, our next step will be to improve our test management environment by incorporating additional metrics form external tools, e.g. Jester [6], to examine the quality of unit tests in more detail.

References

1. Beck, K.: eXtreme Programming explained: Embrace Change. Addison-Wesley, 2000.
2. Cunningham & Cunn., Inc.: Extreme Programming Roadmap at WikiWiki. (http://c2.com/cgi/wiki?UnitInUnitTestIsntTheUnitYouAreThinkingOf).
3. Hofman, A.: Test Management in XP Environments with TEMPPO. Technical Report, SCCH, 2001.
4. JUnit.org: The JUnit Tool. http://www.junit.org
5. Link, J., Fröhlich, P.: Unit Tests mit Java: Der Test-First-Ansatz. dpunkt, 2002.
6. Moore, I.: Jester – a JUnit test tester. in Proc. XP2001, Cagliari, Italy, May 2001.
7. Myers, G.J.: The Art of Software Testing. Wiley, 1979.

Developing Testable Web-Applications with Bugkilla

Christian Dedek[1], Dirk M. Sohn[1], Matthias Niete[1],
Sabine Winkler[1], and Andreas Spall[1]

[1] Orientation in Objects GmbH, Weinheimer Strasse 68, D 68309 Mannheim
{dedek,sohn,niete,winkler,spall}@oio.de

Abstract. Bugkilla is a tool set to create, maintain, execute and analyze functional system tests of web-applications. This research paper presents a way of using Bugkilla resulting in a IEEE 829 conformant test documentation.

1 Introduction

Developing good software, software that satisfies the needs of the users and the business, is the central goal of software-engineering. Evolving needs of the users and changing environmental circumstances lead to frequent and rapid change of system requirements.[1] Highly iterative development processes like extreme programming (XP) are a common approach to tackle this problem. [2] Functional acceptance testing is based on the functional system requirements. Therefore changes in the systems requirements implicate changes in the systems tests. Consistency between test and requirement (CTR) means:

- the existence of a test for every functional requirement
- every functional test has a corresponding functional requirement

In XP testing is of great importance not only for quality assurance but also for the measurement of progress and the tracing of requirements. Thereby regression testing is a frequent form of testing.[2]

Bugkilla is a development project for a tool set to support the efficient creation, maintenance and execution of functional system tests. Approved standards (like IEEE 829) and tools from different architectures are adopted to represent the special character of web-technology. One focus of the Bugkilla tool set is the support for CTR and tests. The other is cost reduction of functional regression testing.[3]

1.1 J2EE Specification and Testing

A variety of different problems are encountered when testing J2EE applications. Neither the descriptions of roles nor the interface specifications of the J2EE-architecture answer the questions of a standard way to define participants and system components for testing during development.[4], [5]

The J2EE architecture still leaves too many degrees of freedom in design for an easy standardization of testing[1].[5] In particular the production of code for automatic

---

[1] e.g. considering a web-centric approach there is an enormous architectural range beginning with simple servlets over modular JSPs up to MVC frameworks like Struts.

M. Marchesi and G. Succi (Eds.): XP 2003, LNCS 2675, pp. 322–324, 2003.

evaluation of test results (so-called test-oracles) is made more difficult by the great variety of possible Objects to query during the test analysis.[3] The possibilities of the J2EE architecture to distribute system components can also complicate functional testing[2].[6]

Both the problem of absence of testing standards within the J2EE architecture and the possible risks of a blindfold approach to functional testing of web applications will be tackled with a systematic and automated functional testing method[3].[7]

1.2   Bugkilla Concepts

The specification of a test case is an executable script of the interactions between the user and the system. Within the web technology the creation and maintenance of a test case can be achieved on different technological levels. The Bugkilla project is based on the idea of maintaining test cases as Hyper Text Transfer Protocol 1.1 (HTTP) communication scripts. Capture/replay tools for test cases were developed. The capture tool is called Recorder and the replay tool is called Player. The Recorder directly captures the input and output of the system at the user interface in the web container using the Servlet API 2.3. The data for test cases are stored in XML and can later on be combined with the formal specifications of state transitions in the business logic layer. The Player can execute test cases and automatically analyze the output and state transitions.

2   Functional Testing with Bugkilla

We describe a quality management (QM) process that uses Bugkilla. Within the process two roles named domain expert (DE) and Test engineer (TE) are defined. The DE is the specialist for the functional system requirements of the business side and the TE is his counterpart from the development team. The process consists of the following phases:

1. creation of test plan (TP) entries conforming IEEE 829[4]
2. development of an prototype based on the "features to be tested" defined by the TP
3. recording web-conversations of the prototype with a Recorder
4. defining comparator rules on the recorded conversation, to produce test cases
5. combining the test cases to test procedures
6. executing the test procedures
7. evaluating the test logs (production of test reports)
8. creating a "test summary report"

The following examples stem from the functional test of Java™ Pet Store Demo(Pet Store).[5] A TE and a DE start defining a TP. The feature in test could be the purchas-

---

[2]   The J2EE-architecture enforces the execution of functional tests in a fully integrated manner, which is often a not trivial challenge for testing activities
[3]   This was the motivation to start the Bugkilla project.
[4]   Institute of Electrical and Electronics Engineers (IEEE) Standard 829-1998 for Software Test Documentation

ing functionality of Pet Stores web-front-end. These tests are associated with the special Bugkilla test design specification(TDS).

This TDS, that specifies "refinements of the test approach and identifies the features to be tested", entails the fact that only items with communication between a browser and a web-server via HTTP can be tested with Bugkilla.[8] This communication can be recorded, at a prototype or a productive system, with the Recorder. Test-data-generators and comparators are connected with the captured conversation. A test-data-generator/comparator defines the input/output specification of the corresponding test case specification (TCS). A test identification part creates the associations between the TDS and the corresponding test cases.

The TCS defines a test case identified by a TDS and has a unique identifier.[8] A connection from a TCS to a Bugkilla Scenario element can be established by this identifier. Every TCS has a brief description of the corresponding items and features (e.g. a complete purchasing process over the web-GUI of the Pet Store). The input/output specifications of a TCS are made up of the captured HTTP requests/ responses and test-data-generators/ comparators created with Bugkilla.

The TE assembles TestSeries with Scenarios and specifies the order of execution. One purpose of the test procedure specification (TPS) is "to specify the steps for executing a set of test cases", therefore a TestSeries is an implementation of a TPS.[8] E.g. a TE assembles a TestSeries with the Scenarios X "complete purchasing process", Y "user registration" and Z "anonymous browses catalog".

The specified TestSeries will then be executed with the Player. The Player automatically evaluates the tests and produces test reports, that will be assembled as a part of a test summary report by the TE.

The described quality management process could easily be used in many kinds of iterative software development projects and should facilitate CTR because of its incremental character.

References

1. Booch et. al. The Unified Modeling Language User Guide RUP (1999) page 3 et sqq.
2. Kent Beck Extreme Programming (2000) p. 28,29,47,57,65,117/18
3. Dedek et. al. Dawn – Must J2EE-Webapplications be Untestable, submission to the Student Research Competition and OOPSLA Poster Session (2002)
4. Bill Shannon, Vlada Matena et.al., Java 2 Platform Enterprise Edition Specification Version 1.3 http://java.sun.com/j2ee/docs.html
5. Nicholas Kassem and the Enterprise Team, Designing Enterprise Applications with Java 2 Platform Enterprise Edition , http://java.sun.com/j2ee/blueprints
6. Helmut Balzert, Lehrbuch der Software-Technik: Software-Management (1998) p. 505-520
7. Friedewald et. al. Softwareentwicklung in Deutschland, Informatik Spektrum 24(2) p. 81-90
8. IEEE Std 829-1998 Standard for Software Test Documentation, Computer Society Press volume 4 (1999)

Extreme Programming:
A More Musical Approach to Software Development?

Andrew Johnston and Chris S. Johnson

University of Technology Sydney, Department of Information Systems
PO Box 123, Broadway, NSW 2007, Australia
{aj,chrisj}@it.uts.edu.au

Abstract. This paper considers the relationship between software development as it is typically practiced, the Extreme Programming methodology and the learning and working environment of those involved in a creative art – music. In particular we emphasise how pair programming can facilitate an increase in the overall skill level of individuals and teams, and relate this to musicians' development of models of excellence through ensemble playing. Consideration is also given to the psychology of music performance and its relevance to the pursuit of excellence in software development.

1 Pair Programming and Creative Collaboration

In this paper we contend that traditional software development working environments do not really encourage creativity. To illustrate this point we compare and contrast the typical learning and working environment of practitioners of a creative art – music – and that of software developers.

The characterization of software development as a craft rather than an engineering discipline has been proposed recently [1] and it is felt that by considering the similarities and differences between the working and learning environments of musicians and developers that some further weight can be given to calls for a more collaborative approach to software development.

First, let us consider the experiences of the typical software developer, who when at university worked alone on programming assignments. If they were relatively social, student programmers may have had discussions with other keen programmers in their course and they might have participated in online community discussions on various programming topics. However, the intensity of collaboration is likely to have remained relatively low.

When developers graduate and move into the workforce they are likely to continue to experience low levels of interaction in traditional software development environments. In such environments, developers spend the majority of their time working alone on a particular task and, if difficulties are encountered, the usual reaction is to attempt to find a solution on their own. However, as there is usually no requirement for the developer to communicate their findings to anyone else in the team, possibly useful information is often not further disseminated. Of course, the solution may be embedded in the code, but in traditional solitary development this code is 'owned' by the developer that wrote it, so the chance of this information finding its way to other members of the team is greatly reduced.

M. Marchesi and G. Succi (Eds.): XP 2003, LNCS 2675, pp. 325–327, 2003.

One of the key practices of Extreme Programming [2], pair programming, goes some way towards addressing this issue. The implications of pair programming are still being explored and several advantages have been identified. In particular, code produced by pairs is claimed to be of higher quality and have fewer defects than code produced by developers working individually. [3][4]

It would seem that if organizations are interested in improving their developers' skills and enhancing their ability to respond creatively to the challenge of developing quality software, then some consideration of the structure of their social environment is in order. While there may be a cost in terms of productivity in using two programmers on each task rather than one – and there is empirical evidence that this effect is in fact negligible and offset by improvements in quality [3][4] - there is also a cost in failing to encourage the sharing of information and skills amongst team members.

It has been observed that pair programming can help in this regard, by facilitating master-apprentice relationships between senior and junior team members and in aiding the transfer of knowledge between developers. [3]

One major benefit of pair programming is that it exposes all members of the XP team to a number of different approaches to coding and design and therefore gives them higher levels of interaction with an increased number of role models. As we contend that software development is more a craft than an engineering discipline it is felt that a high degree of interaction amongst practitioners is necessary to significantly advance development skills in an organization.

If this need is not immediately apparent, consider how a musician develops their skill. In the initial stages of learning the emphasis is usually on imitation. That is, the student imitates their teacher. After a short time, they progress to duets and finally ensemble playing, all usually well within the first year of learning.

As the student improves and gains experience in the technical aspects of playing their instrument, their ability to listen to and learn from others increases and so does the size of the pool of musical models available to them. That is, they now have far greater musical exposure and their ability to assimilate the ideas of others is increased.

At the professional level, musicians are continually exposed to new styles and approaches from the people around them. Because they work together, in the same place at the same time on the same music, they only have to open their ears to hear what's going on.

Similarly, when developers pair-program they are exposed to a range of different approaches and ideas, allowing them to extend their mental models of excellence. Research into the psychology of music learning indicates that the development of mental models is a significant factor in musical achievement [5][6] and if we accept the view of McBreen that software development is a craft [1] and not an exercise in following a predefined plan, then it makes sense to facilitate programmers' development of models of excellence in their field. Pair programming is a practical technique to help achieve this.

2   Craftsmanship, Music Learning and Pair Programming

It seems that traditionally it has been expected that programmers will simply improve with practice, and while there is significant research into music learning indicating that performance is positively correlated with practice time, practice quality is a significant factor also [7]. Another key element of successful practice is that it is goal directed, and it must be said that musicians generally have far greater exposure to models of excellence than typical software developers. As students they attend regular, one-on-one lessons with their teachers and typically participate in ensemble playing to a great extent. As professionals, the amount of ensemble playing is likely to be even higher.

Musicians typically learn their craft by working closely with teachers who serve as role models and mentors [eg. 8]. This would seem to differ from the typical learning experience of most developers, who generally participate in university courses where the relationships with teachers are less intense than those experienced by musicians in a one-on-one learning situation.

It could be observed that pair programming provides a far more interactive environment and greater scope for mentoring relationships than the more traditional solo programming.

While many organisations make efforts to train developers and encourage communication, we would argue that common practice in the real world often tends to stifle people's natural inclination to develop their skills. On the other hand, Extreme Programming and in particular the practice of pair programming, go some way towards engendering an environment where employees' skills and creativity are more likely to be enhanced.

References

1. McBreen, P.: Software Craftsmanship: The New Imperative. Addison-Wesley, Reading, MA (2001)
2. Beck, K.: Extreme Programming Explained: Embrace Change. Addison-Wesley, Reading, MA (2000)
3. Cockburn, A. and Williams, L.: The Costs and Benefits of Pair Programming. Online at http://collaboration.csc.ncsu.edu/laurie/Papers/XPSardinia.PDF
4. Nosek, J. T.: The Case for Collaborative Programming. Communications of the ACM, Vol. 41., No. 3. (1998) 105-108
5. Guettler, K. and Hallam, S.: String Instruments. In: Parncutt, R., McPherson, G. E. (eds.): The Science and Psychology of Music Performance. Oxford University Press, Oxford (2002) 303-317
6. Hallam, S.: The development of expertise in young musicians: Strategy, use knowledge acquisition and individual diversity. Music Education Research, Vol 3., No. 1. 7-23. (2001)
7. Ericsson, K. A., Krampe, R. T. and Tesch-Römer, C.: The role of deliberate practice in the acquisition of expert performance. Psychological Review. Vol. 100. 363-406. (1993)
8. Sosniak, L. A. Phases of learning. Developing Talent in Young People, ed. Bloom, B. S. 1985, New York: Ballantine.

Automated Extract Component Refactoring

Hironori Washizaki and Yoshiaki Fukazawa

Department of Computer Science, Waseda University
3-4-1, Okubo, Shinjuku-ku, Tokyo 169-8555, Japan
{washi,fukazawa}@fuka.info.waseda.ac.jp

Abstract. We propose a new refactoring "Extract Component" to support the organizational reuse of components and improve the productivity under Agile methods. Our refactoring can extract reusable components composed of classes from object-oriented programs, and modify the surrounding parts of extracted components in original programs. We have developed a tool that performs our refactoring automatically.

1 Introduction

Agile methods such as Extreme Programming (XP)[1] mainly aim to make the current project succeed, rather than improving the productivity of the entire organization. We limit this study to the use of OO language for the implementation of programs. To improve productivity, the organization has to engage in software reuse. Refactoring, which is a XP's practice, can help make software reusable. We propose a technique for transforming part of the OO classes into reusable software components automatically. In the following, we provide a strict definition of component. JavaBeans[2] is the target component system.

Definition 1.1 (Component) A component is composed of one or more Java classes that satisfy all the following requirements ($1 \sim 5$).

1. One of the classes is a Facade class, which becomes a front class for outside.
2. The Facade class implements a certain interface (the Facade interface).
3. The Facade class has one public default constructor (without any arguments).
4. All classes/interfaces necessary for instantiating an object of the Facade class are packaged into one JAR (Java ARchive) file.
5. Objects of all classes except the Facade class are not directly instantiated from outside of the classes.

The component which satisfies requirements $1 \sim 5$ has no dependency on elements outside of the component. Therefore, it is possible to reuse the classes in the form of the component. In order to obtain such components, it is necessary to transform parts of existing programs into components. We first define a class relation graph (CRG). CRG represents the relation of classes/interfaces in the target program. Next, we define a component cluster on CRG.

M. Marchesi and G. Succi (Eds.): XP 2003, LNCS 2675, pp. 328–330, 2003.

Definition 1.2 (Class Relation Graph) The multi-graph is a class relation graph, denoted $\Gamma = (V_\Gamma, \Lambda_\Gamma, E_\Gamma)$, where V_Γ is the set of class/interface nodes corresponding to classes/interfaces, Λ_Γ is the set of label names that are composed of the names of program source code and the target token locations in program source code, and E_Γ is the set of edges that are ordered trios of the source node, destination node, and label name. E_Γ is composed of the inheritance edges, refer edges, default instantiate edges, and argument instantiate edges.

The inheritance edge indicates that the class/interface inherits from another class/interface, denoted $\rightarrow$. The refer edge indicates that the class/interface refers to another class/interface, denoted $\overset{ref}{\rightarrow}$. The default instantiate edge indicates that the class/interface instantiates an object of another class by using the default constructor, denoted $\overset{def}{\Rightarrow}$. The argument instantiate edge indicates that the class/interface instantiates an object of another class by using the constructor with one or more arguments, denoted $\overset{arg}{\Rightarrow}$.

Definition 1.3 (Reachability) The node v_i satisfies the inheritance reachability with the node v_j where there is a path from v_i to v_j and all edges in the path are inheritance edges, or $v_i = v_j$, denoted $v_i \overset{*}{\rightarrow} v_j$. Similarly, $v_i \overset{*}{\twoheadrightarrow} v_j$ means that there is a path from v_i to v_j and all edges in the path are inheritance/instantiate/refer edges, or $v_i = v_j$.

Definition 1.4 (Component Cluster) The pair of the Facade node v_f and the set of nodes V_f is a cluster where CRG is $\Gamma = (V_\Gamma, \Lambda_\Gamma, E_\Gamma)$, V_f is the superset of $V' = \{v' \mid (v_s \overset{*}{\twoheadrightarrow} v') \text{ in } \Gamma\}$ for the starting node v_s, one node v_f has incoming default instantiate edges from nodes in $V_\Gamma - V_f$, and no nodes in V_f except v_f have incoming default/argument instantiate edges from nodes in $V_\Gamma - V_f$. The cluster $c = (v_f, V_f)$ is the candidate of the component that is composed of all classes/interfaces in V_f, and the Facade class of the component is v_f. The component corresponding to the cluster satisfies the above-mentioned requirements.

2 Extract Component Refactoring

When extracting components corresponding to specified clusters, the surrounding parts of clusters should use newly extracted components in order to avoid the situation where two sets of classes that provide the same function exist in the same organization/library. This modification is a kind of refactoring because this modification does not change the observable behavior of the original program. We call this refactoring, "Extract Component," and the necessary steps of this refactoring are shown below.

1) Make CRG $\Gamma = (V_\Gamma, \Lambda_\Gamma, E_\Gamma)$ of the target classes.
2) Select a class v_s that is thought to provide general/reusable functions.
3) Specify one cluster $c = (v_f, V_f)$ using v_s as the starting node.
4) Create a new Facade interface i_f. Implement i_f to the Facade class v_f.
5) Add the definitions of all public methods of the inheritance reachable classes
$V_E = \{v \mid (v_f \overset{*}{\rightarrow} v) \text{ in } \Gamma\}$ to i_f.

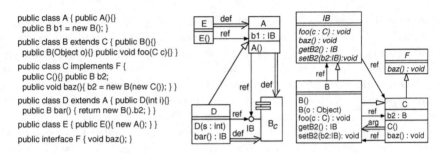

Fig. 1. (a) Code before refactoring, (b) CRG after refactoring, (c) Inside of B_c

6) Add the definitions of the setter methods and getter methods corresponding to all public attributes of V_E to i_f. Add the implementations of the setter methods and getter methods to v_f.
7) Package all classes/interfaces in V_f and i_f into one JAR file.
8) Change the types of reference to v_f in $V_\Gamma - V_f$ into i_f.
9) Change the code in $V_\Gamma - V_f$ which assign new values to attributes of V_E (or refer the values of attributes of V_E) into the code which invoke the setter methods (getter methods).
10) Insert the explicit reference conversion code, from the class/interface in V_E to i_f, into the part in $V_\Gamma - V_f$ where the implicit widening reference conversions from v_f to another class/interface in V_E exist.

For example, Figure 1(b) shows CRG after detecting the cluster $c = (B, \{B, C, F\})$ using the class C as the starting node corresponding to the program source code in Figure 1(a), and extracting a JavaBeans component B_c according to the cluster c by Extract Component refactoring. Figure 1(c) shows the inside of B_c. B_c has a new Facade interface IB and new setter/getter methods. The surrounding parts of the cluster are modified to use B_c via IB.

3   Automatic Tool and Conclusion

We have developed a tool that analyzes Java program source code, displays CRG, and performs automatically all necessary steps of the Extract Component refactoring. Using our tool, we extracted 13 components from KFC [3] (number of all classes/interfaces: 224) using all classes in KFC as starting nodes. Many of them are components with high generality, such as Button, Panel, DTD and Border. These components can be reused independently in other projects.

In conclusion, since programmers can make a component library using extracted components from a developed classes without almost any costs, our tool will support the organizational reuse of components based on Agile methods.

References

1. Beck, K.: Extreme Programming Explained, Addison-Wesley (1999)
2. Hamilton, G.: JavaBeans 1.01 Specification, Sun Microsystems (1997)
3. Yasumatsu, K.: KFC, http://openlab.jp/kyasu/

Successful Automation
of GUI Driven Acceptance Testing

Charles Lowell and Jeremy Stell-Smith

ThoughtWorks, Inc., 651 W. Washington Blvd. Suite 600
Chicago IL, 60661
{cmlowell,jeremy}@thoughtworks.com

Abstract. Acceptance Testing is a fundamental part of XP. It provides the cus-
tomer-developer "handshake" required for a project to succeed. One logical
place to do this testing is at the GUI level. However, to do so requires a GUI
testing tool. This paper will discuss the lessons we learned developing and using such a tool over the course of several projects. We believe that these lessons
are generally applicable and will lead to successful GUI-driven testing on other
projects aspiring to Agile development, whether our framework or another is in
use. We particularly wanted to share those lessons for which we paid a high
price to learn.

1   Introduction

Tools that use the graphical user interface of an application as a starting point for
testing are nothing new. In today's market there are many complex and feature-rich
packages that do this with varying levels of success. However, on two very large
XPish development efforts (30+ programmers), we found existing tools to be lacking
with respect to our requirements. In particular, we needed a tool with which it was
easy to write good acceptance tests, which was resilient to radical changes in interface
design and layout, whose test suites could be extended and refactored, and which
could also be easily automated into a continuous integration process. There are many
difficult and often non-obvious problems associated with the type of GUI testing we
were striving for [3]. As a result, we ended up distilling our own GUI testing strategies in conjunction with Marathon, an open source tool [2] specifically designed
around those strategies.

2   Tests Must Be Easy to Write

If writing tests is difficult, then people won't do it. Because of this, we made sure that
Marathon could be used to quickly and easily write GUI tests. The strategy we used
was to outfit Marathon with a recorder that automatically inserts all user actions executed on the interface, such as clicking buttons and menus into the test script. In addition to providing an ultra-simple method for the initial construction of a test script,
this strategy gives the user the most direct lesson in the scripting structure possible.

M. Marchesi and G. Succi (Eds.): XP 2003, LNCS 2675, pp. 331–333, 2003.
© Springer-Verlag Berlin Heidelberg 2003

Indeed, when it comes to learning how the scripting language works, there is no substitute for seeing a test script appear that describes the set of actions as those very same actions are being executed. However, the danger with recorders is that they often lead to write-once tests; maintainability must be a core focus.

3   Tests Must Be Easy to Maintain

Once a test is written, it must be maintained. Recording scripts with a tool makes it easy to write GUI driven tests the first time. Like other areas of the system, test scripts must be refactored to remain pertinent and to remove duplication. In the case of an agile project, maintainability of previously developed test suites is particularly important since the user interface, like every other part of the application, is volatile and subject to change. We address these issues in Marathon by paying special attention to the readability of the scripts, by making the scripts resilient to changes in layout and handling of events, and by making the language itself easily extensible.

Above all, test scripts must be easy to read, whether or not the syntax is familiar. This means they should be centered around the common GUI concepts, such as 'clicking', 'entering text', and 'producing a key stroke', etc. Marathon, for example, is really comprised of the small set of semantic functions click(), doubleclick() and select(). Unfortunately, describing playback in this simplified "user-centric" view means that the test scripts will not be 100% faithful to the actual events that occurred, because all of the events that occur in between semantic clicks will not be present during playback. This is usually not a problem since where the mouse is, or which window is active in between semantic events, is unimportant to both the user and the program. However, in those exceptional cases where it is important, Marathon can be extended to handle this correctly using its extension mechanism [5].

To be maintainable, scripts must be resilient both to changes in the way in which an interface lays out its controls, and to changes to the interface's reaction to events registered on those controls. Many GUI-driven testing tools suffer from inflexibility to changes in layout. Controls should be identified by name not coordinates. A natural side effect of naming controls is much more readable scripts. Marathon makes use of a simple (but customizable) naming scheme that makes reasonable guesses of component names when they are not explicitly set.

4   Use a Scripting Language to Write Scripts

In our experience, the most import aspect of maintaining a suite of GUI-driven tests is the ability to extend the core testing tool runtime and to refactor the tests. In Marathon we get much of this functionality for free by using jython [4], the java version of python. We originally used XML, but it proved woefully inadequate. Using XML, we had to effectively build our own scripting engine / interpreter. In contrast, jython is a fully featured interpreter that sits on top of the Marathon runtime and calls into it. In addition, jython exposes the entire java runtime, as well as application classes to test developers, enabling anything that could be done in java code to be done from a test. Finally, jython code is extremely readable. We have had remarkable success with non-programmers being able to come up to speed and begin editing our jython scripts directly, without the use of our recorder.

5   GUI Testing is NOT a Substitute for Unit Testing

Projects considering using a GUI-testing tool to drive automated acceptance tests should be warned. It has been our experience time and time again, so that we cannot say it strongly enough: Marathon test scripts are NOT, nor will they ever be, a substitute for unit testing. On every project on which we have used Marathon, there has been the tendency, especially among those team members less familiar with the concepts of unit testing and test driven design, to labor under the misconception that if a particular bit of functionality has an associated GUI test, then there is little or no need to wrap the intervening classes comprising that functionality with extensive unit tests. This is tempting, but from a merely practical standpoint, this is a dangerous attitude since testing through the GUI is several orders of magnitude slower than unit testing. For continuous integration to work well, especially, with a large team, tests must run quickly. More importantly, however, because GUI tests are end-to-end by their very nature, they are extremely coarse grained and they therefore contain a significant overlap between the code executed by different test cases.

The best strategy we have used thus far is to use GUI tests to make sure that the connections between all of the individually unit tested classes are soldered together and to test high level end to end business functionality. With our continuous build, we maintain a very small set of Marathon GUI tests, called 'smoke tests', which provide a very cursory confirmation that the components interacting to form a feature integrate correctly with each other without being too time-consuming. Next, we maintain a large set of acceptance tests that are much more thorough, extensive, cover end-to-end business scenarios, and are decoupled from the development integration cycle. Once the run is finished, the results are posted next to the build against which they were run, and if successful, development continues as normal. If this strategy is deployed correctly, the possibility of any regression errors becomes exceedingly small.

References

1. JUnit Testing Framework homepage. http://www.junit.org/
2. Marathon home page. http://marathonman.sourceforge.net/
3. Java GUI Testing Group. http://groups.yahoo.com/group/java-gui-testing/
4. Jython home page. http://www.jython.org/
5. Lowell, C., Stell-Smith, J.: Successful Automation of GUI-Driven Acceptance Testing Using Marathon, http://marathonman.sourceforge.net/papers/ Successful%20Automation%20of%20GUI%20Driven%20Acceptance% 20Testing.pdf/

Extreme Terseness:
Some Languages Are More Agile than Others

Stephen Taylor

Lambent Technology, 81 South Hill Park, London NW3 2SS
sjt@lambenttechnology.com

Abstract. While XP principles are independent of the languages in which software is developed, we can distinguish properties of programming languages that affect the agility of development. Some languages are inherently more agile than others, and the experience of developing software in these languages reflects this. A family of languages descended from the mathematics notation developed at Harvard in the 1950s by Iverson [1] shares properties of extreme terseness and abstractive power with weak data typing. The history of software development in these languages foreshadows some of the characteristics of XP projects. To these linguistic communities, XP offers the prospect of rehabilitating styles of software development that fell into disrepute with the rise of software engineering. Conversely, these languages offer XP practitioners the possibility of radical condensation of the conversation between developer and customer.

1 Introduction

Code volume affects key XP processes:

Communication. XP development places unprecedented emphasis on communication within a project and the use of code as a medium for it. The terseness of code is a reflection of a language's abstractive or expressive power. Terse code facilitates precise communication about processes and data structures in the same way that university educations and their associated vocabularies enable graduates to communicate precisely about ideas, theories and observations in their fields of study. (See Iverson on notation as a tool of thought [2].)

Refactoring. Code volume is always a significant term in the cost of refactoring, and a term independent of complexity. Terseness contributes to XP's virtuous circle of simplicity. While more work, thought and time goes into writing a line of terse code than a line in a verbose language, the code volume ratio between terse and verbose code usually has the terse code finished first. A larger benefit comes from refactoring. The lower the code volume, the less code to review, analyse and rewrite. Terseness benefits refactoring even more than initial development.

Simplicity, quality, fun. While it is still possible to write verbose code in a terse language, the abstractive and expressive power of extremely terse languages permits solutions of startling and breath-taking simplicity. (These solutions are often corre-

M. Marchesi and G. Succi (Eds.): XP 2003, LNCS 2675, pp. 334–336, 2003.

spondingly fast.) For example, a small spreadsheet, complete with GUI, can be written as 3 lines of primitive K. A single 55-character expression in J calculates and plots a Mandelbrot set. The author recently used sparse-array techniques to optimise a memory-intensive APL process; the refactoring took an hour, writing and testing just four lines of new code.

2   Communication

A recent project illustrates the effect that development in a terse language can have on communication between programmer and customer. (The project diary is available online at http://aplxp.blogspot.com.)

The project automates the preparation of letters describing the surrender value of pension policies. The processing rules are complex, to accommodate variations in legislative requirements and product specifications that have accumulated over decades. Where the sales people discard old products in favour of new ones, the maturities clerks never forget; they only accumulate more rules. New clerks take months to become proficient in interpreting the checklists that guide them through the processes.

Senior clerks train new clerks, and worked with me to identify the processing rules. Communication difficulties emerged immediately. While the trainers could *demonstrate* a process, attempts to reason about it or discuss hypothetical variations quickly exceeded their linguistic skills. I tried every kind of representation of the rules I could think of, but nothing communicated. Despite working directly with the customers, I couldn't verify any conceivable version of the rules except by coding it and asking for feedback.

So we did that, one case at a time. But using an APL interpreter enabled me to collapse an otherwise iterative process into an uninterrupted conversation.

The trainer picked a representative case; brought up the mainframe inquiry screens she used and showed me what data she was looking at. Using the APL interpreter's immediate-execution environment, it took me only minutes to replicate the data sets in ad-hoc structures in my workspace. Now she described what she did with the information, and I coded the rules. Generally, I spent less time coding a rule in APL than she spent describing it in English. I used her vocabulary to name the APL functions names. The result is that she reads the application code about as well as I read Italian: not precisely, but well enough to follow the gist.

When we completed the process I ran the code and compared the answer to hers. When we have a difference to reconcile, the APL interpreter allows us to step through the rules together, examining partial results to find where we diverge. About one time in three or four, the error is hers – the processes are *that* hard for humans to get right.

When we agree, I append the case to the acceptance test suite and we start another example, altering or expanding rules coded previously. Every time we finish a case, the test suite allows us to discover immediately if the revised rules broke earlier test cases, and to resolve any discrepancies.

The effect on our communication is radical. An entire cycle of me taking notes, writing code, her writing, loading and running acceptance tests and reporting problems, me coding corrections for her to retest – all that collapses into a single conversation, from which we emerge with both automated acceptance tests and also code that passes those tests. Moreover, my customer has unprecedented confidence in the accuracy and completeness of our code, and our ability to change the rules and the tests at need.

When we don't know something we want or need to know, we make up our own answers. Human beings do that. XP counters with high-bandwidth communication between programmers, and the importance of an On Site Customer to make frequently and quickly the decisions that only Business should make.

Shortening communication paths in a project is a valuable and virtuous circle. Here APL's terseness and abstractive power enabled a significant shift in the communication process. Some *quantitative* changes are large enough to produce a *qualitative* change. That happened here, producing levels of *involvement* with and *ownership* of the software not previously experienced or exhibited by the customer.

3   Languages Descended from Iverson's Notation

The languages listed below, descended from Iverson's original executable mathematical notation, all share the qualities illustrated above. Some of the benefits associated with agile development processes are already exhibited in the history of software development in these languages, as a reflection of the impact terseness has on the cost of change over time.

- APL
- A+
- J
- K

Links to resources for exploring these languages can be found at the web log diary for the project from which the anecdote above was taken: http://aplxp.blogspot.com.

4   Conclusion

Terseness in languages particularly suits them to agile development. Extremely terse languages participate more fully in XP's virtuous circle of simplicity. Some less well-known languages offer order-of-magnitude improvements in terseness. Agile process managers looking for more edge will consider these languages as candidates for roles in some XP projects.

References

1. Iverson, K.E.: A Programming Language, John Wiley & Sons, New York, 1962
2. Iverson, K.E.: Notation as a Tool of Thought, 1979 ACM Turing Award Lecture, Communications of the ACM, Vol. 23 (8), August 1980

EnterpriseXP:
Can the Combination of XP and DSDM Improve the Appeal of XP to the Business Community?

Mark Simmonds[1] and Barry Fazackerley (Eds)[2]

[1] Symmetrics, 127 Graham Road
Sheffield, S10 3GP
mark.simmonds@symmetrics.co.uk
[2] Xansa, Campus 300, Maylands Avenue
Hemel Hempstead, HP2 7TQ, UK

Abstract. This paper sets out a high level case for EnterpriseXP, providing a working definition, why clients, XP and DSDM can all benefit from EnterpriseXP, what differentiates it in the marketplace and the next steps to help EnterpriseXP evolve into a mature and world-class development method.

1   What Is EnterpriseXP?

"EnterpriseXP is a robust and rigorous evolution of XP to include appropriate management tools and techniques to enable it to be scalable and sustainable for projects and organisations whether small, medium and large".

The vision for EnterpriseXP is that it will bring together the energy and invention of XP with the proven maturity and commercial know-how of DSDM to produce an agile method with corporate appeal. Whilst the first iteration is captured in DSDM 4.2, future iterations could see the need for a new and distinct agile method, i.e. EnterpriseXP.

2   The Need for EnterpriseXP

The explosion of interest in the agile movement has inevitably lead to a large number of articles being written about agile methods, in particular about Extreme Programming (XP). Whilst many of these critiques are positive, some are negative and it is worth determining whether there is any credence to these arguments or whether they are simply an inevitable consequence of the rise in popularity of Agile methods.

2.1   Criticisms of XP that Enterprise XP Must Address:

The following list of criticisms of XP was found during a short search of the Web:

M. Marchesi and G. Succi (Eds.): XP 2003, LNCS 2675, pp. 337–339, 2003.
© Springer-Verlag Berlin Heidelberg 2003

- De-emphasis on up-front design work
- Reliance on refactoring and unit testing to create a design
- Lack of project governance
- Lack of scalability
- Lack of maintainability
- XP relies on above average individuals. In most companies 49.999 of people are below average...

In Autumn 2002 a group of XP and DSDM enthusiasts met together, in Birmingham UK, to talk through some of these issues and decide what, if anything, they should do. The result is a first iteration of EnterpriseXP. It is an amalgam of best practice from two existing agile methods, DSDM and XP, and we believe it starts to address many of the criticisms of earlier evolutions. When asked to comment on this initiative Kent Beck said, "The DSDM community has built a much more "corporate persona than the XP world, and it's something we need to learn. This venture is the first iteration of this learning.

Development Team:

- Keith Richards (KRIC)
- Rachel Davies (Connextra)
- Kevin Barron (Xansa)
- Barry Fazackerley (Xansa)
- Per-Magnus Skoogh (OWM)
- Mark Simmonds (Symmetrics)

- James Yoxall (Indigo Blue Consulting)
- Seán Hanly (Exsoftware)
- Rob Topley (CMG)
- Steve Ash (Select)
- Andrew Craddock (RADTAC)

3   Why EnterpriseXP?
Why Do XP and DSDM Need Each Other?

EnterpriseXP is born out of a desire to see projects succeed by delivering what the customer needs, when it is needed, at a price they can afford. Early literature for both DSDM and XP lists reasons why projects fail. Whilst both methods address these in their own right, EnterpriseXP takes this one step further.

As agile methods, both XP and DSDM have strong similarities and feature characteristic agile techniques, for example, team roles & responsibilities, timeboxing, feedback, communication, team-based planning. It was felt therefore, in developing EnterpriseXP, that it was more important to study and understand the differences between the two in order to create a new approach that was based on best practice from each.

These issues and many others were addressed by the team and are encapsulated in DSDM 4.2.

4   Key Features of EnterpriseXP

The first iteration of EnterpriseXP is available as part of DSDM 4.2 and is structured as follows:

- When to use EnterpriseXP? – A suitability filter that helps you to determine the risks of using Enterprise XP for your development.
- A Lifecycle featuring sufficient up front design activities to ensure that the business is understood and that there is a system architecture sufficient for development
- People roles and responsibilities featuring a single team involving both users and developers. YAGNI becomes WAGNI (*WE* ain't gonna need it).
- Products – A minimal set of project products to ensure management buy-in without an overwhelming array of documents
- Management Tools and Techniques – Guidance on areas such as Risk Management, Project Management, Timeboxed Planning, Prioritisation of Requirements using MoSCoW.
- Development Tools Techniques – Guidance on areas such as the use of Facilitated workshops, Pair Programming, Refactoring, Continuous Integration, Prototyping, Testing.

5   Evolution of EnterpriseXP

EnterpriseXP needs to be tried and tested in order to evolve into a mature method. The publication of our early work gives agilists the opportunity to try it out for themselves. The website www.enterprisexp.org will allow users to discuss and comment and feedback into the ongoing development of EnterpriseXP.

Using Function Points in XP – Considerations*

Andrew M. Fuqua

Internet Security Systems, 6303 Barfield Rd, Atlanta, GA 30328
afuqua@acm.org

Abstract. I set out to discover whether function points (FP) would be useful on an Extreme Programming (XP) project. I wanted to know if using function points would produce a more accurate schedule, would be a fair predictor of the iteration's ending velocity, or would be good for predicting how long it would take to implement a story. We tried function points on an XP project and found the process useful but the numbers not. After a little background on using function points I summarize statistical analysis results on the project metrics and give suggestions for practitioners as well as researchers interested this topic.

1   Function Point Analysis

Estimation using function points is more formal. Briefly, the counting process is as follows: Identify the "Logical Transactions"; identify and categorize the "Data Entity Types" referenced; identify the input and output components of each transaction; and compute the functional size [3]. The FP count for each Logical Transaction is the weighted sum of "the number of Input Data Element Types (N_i), the number of Data Entity Types Referenced (N_e), and the number of Output Data Element Types (N_o)" [3], which is computed using industry standard weights as follows: $FP = 0.58 * N_i + 1.66 * N_e + 0.26 * N_o$.

2   Summary Results

Linear regression of this project's data suggests that FPs are not as useful as IEDs to estimate how long it will take to implement a story or complete a release. Function points correlate poorly with estimated and actual task hours whereas IEDs correlate well. The analysis also shows that using function points is not as accurate as using IEDs to predict how long it will take to complete a project already underway. Finally, function points are a poor measure of velocity. A full report can be found in [2].

However, there are several issues that keep these results from being more generally applicable. First, I am a novice function point practitioner and I performed the count myself - As the author, I could have had some bias. It would have been better to have several different people perform the count, especially

---

* Thanks to Martin Fowler for expressing interest and encouragement. To John Hammer for the idea, impetus and assistance.

M. Marchesi and G. Succi (Eds.): XP 2003, LNCS 2675, pp. 340–342, 2003.

if they did not know the purpose of the experiment. Second, these FPs were counted at a much finer level of detail and with much more knowledge of the implementation than is usually available. Function points are usually counted before the application is developed. Third, our Logical Transactions may be too small. Finally, this was not a controlled experiment. Rather, the statistical model was fit to data after much of the work had already been done. More research is needed before we'll have definitive conclusions on FP's applicability to XP.

3   Suggestions

Still, I do see value in function point analysis (FPA) on XP projects. The process one goes through to identify Logical Transactions will help find important stories. FPA will help programmers produce better estimates by forcing them to consider the input, output, and entity reference components of each Logical Transaction. In addition, FPA can be useful in the hands of a skilled practitioner to *validate an initial schedule* built using estimates and velocity, even if IEDs are more effective when *revising* that schedule.

Rather than identify a separate set of Logical Transactions, I just used our stories. This approach is certainly less work, but may not produce the best FP count. Small stories are good for XP but may be too small to be good Logical Transactions. Smaller stories will have only a couple inputs and outputs and one Entity Type Reference, leading them to have similar FP counts but dissimilar XP-style estimates. If you take this approach and also split larger stories into multiple pieces for ease of development, consider recombining those for the purposes of the count – Split stories may artificially inflate the count.

Repetitive tasks may also inflate the function point count. The programmers on this project had to support editing and validation of lots of XML datatypes. They had gotten quite good at this – all of this code worked the same way. Their estimates confirmed improving skill and speed, but function points ignore efficiencies such as these [3]. The FP count for each datatype was the same, but bared no resemblance to the actual effort required.

Another factor that may have contributed to the poor results for function points is that many of our low priority stories were not suitable for function point counting. For example, basic functionality was more valuable to our customer than usability. So, we saved until the end things like consistent handling of Enter and Escape on dialogs, useful error handling, tab order, pretty icons, etc. Similarly, we treated some meetings, analysis work, defects, and refactorings like stories (we estimated them) even though they were non-functional. These are things we have to do. We know about them in advance and they affect the schedule. But they have no function points. FP counting assumes all of these things are spread out evenly over the course of the project, or are at least counted with the original story. This makes function points more useful to size a release and less useful to size iterations.

If you choose to use function points for velocity and scheduling, you will have better results if you decide up-front which of these non-functional tasks are 'in' and which are 'out' and do those all along instead of saving them until the end. If you tend to have a bunch of zero-function-point things to do at the end of your releases, you will not be able to reliably use FPs to revise your schedule.

As for what data to collect, I found it useful to analyze the following variables: story estimates, function points, task estimates, actual time taken to implement all of the story's tasks, starting velocity and ending velocity. I looked for correlations among these variables at the story and iteration level. These variables represent differing levels of detail of information, but it is interesting to see which correlate well and which do not. They also have differing error characteristics: The data is generated in various stages of the project and is collected with different processes. On my project, actual task hours had the most recording errors. Errors are likely to be those of omission - time spent but not recorded. For programming tasks, such errors should be small and evenly distributed. Most of the error in actual hours was on the non-programming, non-functional stories.

When selecting a variable to use for velocity, its predictive quality may be the most important factor. A good measure of velocity should be strongly correlated to and approximately as stable as the actual development effort.

If testing the suitability of using them together, create the FP counts and XP estimates at the same time. If contrasting the two, separate FP and XP estimation activity to keep one from influencing the other. In XP, programmers estimate more accurately as the product is developed: Re-estimating the remaining stories periodically [1] and the feedback from recording actual time improves their skill. Consider whether an experiment should treat FP counts in this same manner or have a more traditional process.

FPA is an ideal tool to measure productivity. One could compare an XP team's productivity to that of a non-XP team. FPA would be useful to compare a team's productivity before and after adopting XP. Or, compare the productivity of a small XP team with two code bases: one originally produced with XP and the other not.

The process of FPA is useful in XP even if the counts aren't. The counts and the process maybe more useful on an XP project without the issues listed above.

References

1. Kent Beck, Martin Fowler: Planning Extreme Programming. Addison Wesley (2001)
2. Andrew Fuqua: "Using Function Points in Extreme Programming". Online at http://groups.yahoo.com/group/extremeprogramming/files/XPandFPA.pdf
3. United Kingdom Software Metrics Association (UKSMA): "MKII Function Point Analysis Counting Practices Manual", Version 1.31 (Mk II FPA). Online at http://www.uksma.co.uk (1998)

Refactoring with Aspects

Granville Miller

Borland - 900 Main Campus Drive, Raleigh, NC, 27606 USA
randy.miller@borland.com

Abstract. Aspect-oriented programming is gaining in prominence in the Java community. Software engineers are realizing the value of aspects to provide reusability across the class hierarchy. As aspects become commonplace, the need to refactor existing program logic into aspect-oriented programs will become greater. Additionally, as aspects are used with processes such as extreme programming, refactoring with aspects will increasingly become necessary. This paper introduces two refactorings, extract introduction and extract advice. The first refactoring is considered to be a class level refactoring while the latter is a method level refactoring.

1   Introduction

Refactoring is a vital element of the software engineering best practices that allows us to produce better designs. While veteran developers had been refactoring their code for decades, this practice was captured and made formal by Martin Fowler's seminal work [2]. This practice is not only a formal part of extreme programming [1], but also often utilized by developers as part of other processes.

Software technology plays an important part in refactoring. While refactoring was probably every bit a part of functional programming, the introduction of object-oriented programming provided a more fertile ground for refactorings. The introduction of classes and inheritance brought modularity to new levels. New refactorings such as "Replace Inheritance with Delegation" were possible due to these modularity improvements [2].

Aspect-Oriented Programming (AOP) is another software technology that provides enhanced modularity in programming languages. Aspects are a technique for moving concerns that exist across the class structure to be centralized in a single place. Examples of areas that are well suited for aspect-oriented programming include logging, session management, performance monitoring, and built-in debugging. The decentralization of these areas that crosscut the class structure typically results in nonstandard use and redundant code.

2   Aspects and Java

Aspect-Oriented Programming is a software technology that frequently results in refactoring. Crosscutting concerns are frequently identified once the code has already been written. However, good design dictates that we group these crosscutting concerns. Additionally, most crosscutting concerns are frequently used (hence the reason that they crosscut the class structure) and will be used again. Refactoring these concerns into aspects creates better designs and makes the concern more usable.

M. Marchesi and G. Succi (Eds.): XP 2003, LNCS 2675, pp. 343–346, 2003.

AspectJ adds four new constructs for aspect-oriented programming to the Java programming language [3]. They are pointcuts, advice, introduction, and aspects. *Pointcuts* identify specific areas of the program where logic can be inserted. This logic is called *advice*. The unit of pointcut designation is the method. Therefore, we can insert advice into the beginning of a method or upon return from that method.

Introduction is a way of modifying the class structure or the inheritance hierarchy. Introduction allows you to add new members, add new methods, or alter the inheritance relationship. Introduction allows you to cleanly separate the design from the analysis logic by making it possible to inject program logic externally. For example, we often create EJBs or servlets out of our orders or shopping carts that convolute the purposes of these classes. Introduction can be used to separate the software technology logic from the business logic for a more understandable class structure.

Finally, aspects are the modular unit for consolidating crosscutting logic. Aspects define these crosscutting elements in a manner similar to the way classes provide a logical unit for the domain-related definition of program logic. Aspects are required to house advice and introduction in the same way that classes are necessary to house methods and members.

3   Refactoring with Aspects

We define two refactorings to extract aspects from Java classes. The first, *extract introduction*, defines a refactoring at the class level. Extract introduction eliminates behavior which is often captured in Java interfaces to extend class behavior. This is a common cause of code redundancy across class hierarchies.

The second refactoring, *extract advice*, eliminates redundancy in preconditions and postconditions commonly found in methods. These conditions may include timing information, traces, and assertions. Of course, there are many other types of logic that can be found at the beginning or end of a method. Extract advice works like extract method [2] but is limited to logic at the beginning or end of a method invocation only.

Extract Introduction

A reusable element exists as part of a class.

Turn the element into an aspect whose name explains the reusable element.

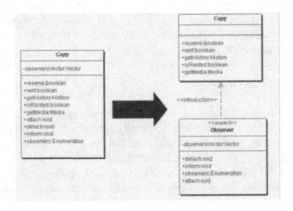

Extract Advice

You have a precondition or postcondition that can be reused.

Turn the precondition or postcondition into advice whose name reflects the value that the advice gives.

```
public void rent(Customer customer) throws IllegalArgu-
mentException {

    if (customer == null) {

        throw new IllegalArgumentException("The
argument is null");

        }

    customer.addVideo(this);

}
```

becomes

```
public void rent(Customer customer) throws IllegalArgu-
mentException {

    customer.addVideo(this);

}


public aspect NullArgumentChecker {

    pointcut check(Customer customer):

            call(void Copy.rent(Customer customer));

    before(): check(Customer customer) {

        if (customer == null)

            throw new IllegalArgumentException("The ar-
gument is null");

    }

}
```

4   Conclusion

Refactoring will continue to evolve as software technology makes more modular approaches possible. Aspect-oriented programming is a technology that increases the modularity of software. Two new refactorings, extract introduction and extract advice utilize aspect-oriented programming to provide better designs.

References

1. Beck, K.: Extreme Programming Explained. Addison-Wesley, (1999).
2. Fowler, M.: Refactoring:Improving the Design of Existing Code, Addison-Wesley, (2000).
3. Kiczales, Gr, et al.: An Overview of AspectJ, in Proceedings of the 5th European Conference on Object Oriented Programming (ECOOP), Spring, (2001).

Extreme Programming at Work

Walter Ambu and Fabrizio Gianneschi

Atlantis S.p.A
via S. Tommaso d'Aquino, 18
09134 Cagliari – Italy
{walter.ambu,fabrizio.gianneschi}@gruppoatlantis.com
http://www.gruppoatlantis.com

Abstract. This article describes our experience concerning the introduction and use of extreme programming within a research project and a commercial project with customers. After a short introduction on the two projects, the article points out how the different practices of XP have been used in both projects and which differences we have found in their implementation

1   Introduction

Atlantis is and industrial research laboratory located in Sardinia (Italy). Its aim is to become an international Innovation Excellence Centre specializing in Territorial development. Starting in Feb.2001, Atlantis increased its employees from 0 to 100 within a few months. Such a rapid growth marked out for the insertion, in the field of software development, of professional figures at their first experience, has made necessary a base formation not only on the technologies, but even on the process of development to be followed.

Comprehensive processes as RUP have appeared too heavy to be used in a context of this kind. So, we turned to agile methodologies, and specifically to Extreme Programming (XP) [1], [2]. First, we performed a pilot project to bring the development group to a suitable degree of technological and methodological skill. Then, the team applied XP to a real, industrial project.

This report presents our experience in introducing XP into our organization, comparing the issues and the findings of the pilot project to those of our first real project. We present our issues and findings for all 12 XP practices, highlighting the differences between the pilot project and the real project.

1.1   Pilot Project

The aim of the pilot project was to bring the development group, 10 programmers, to a degree of technological and methodological preparation that would allow them to bear the weight of a work order with a real customer, with real delivery terms.

The pilot project included the creation of a three tiered e-marketplace portal based on J2EE technology fully realized with open source products. Life of the project was 6 months. In an enthusiastic work atmosphere, where everybody was well disposed

M. Marchesi and G. Succi (Eds.): XP 2003, LNCS 2675, pp. 347–350, 2003.

towards XP experimentation, teaching and mentoring service made by the two senior programmers proved to be essential. Spike solution in pairs have been useful in order to acquire a better knowledge on the technologies and on the XP tools for the continuous integration and tests.

In the end, the project was successfully accomplished, and the team was ready to work on real-world industrial projects.

1.2   Real Project

The real project consisted of the development of a web portal concerning the tourist promotion of a territory with a content management system, to be completed and put into production within 5 months, with the same team and the same technology.

The team was splitted into two groups: one of them to take care about presentation (and portal), the other one about business logic and integration with database. Each group has been working in XP, but in an independent way, only sharing the help of the tracker and of the manager. The two senior programmers took up the role of the coach, while continuing the teaching activity.

The project was successfully accomplished, and the two teams delivered to the customer a working system.

2   XP Practices

In this section, we examine the 12 XP practices, presenting the experiences gathered in our pilot project, and in our first real development project.

On-site Customer. In both projects we found ourselves in a situation of shortage of on-site customers, so that we had to turn to an internal "mock" customer. We know this is not XP, but we believe that this situation is common in many real projects.

The Planning Game. No problem arose during the research project; on the contrary, in the real project the urging of delivery time and the poor agreement in targets and daily activity between mock customers and developing group, caused an ackward situation. The communication with the mock customer was inadequate and this caused misunderstandings that could be avoided.

Another requirement of the real project was the necessity to build a common infrastructure of the system without the classic customer interaction in terms of user stories definition. Prototypes were used in the first two iterations to communicate with the customer and to give feedback to the group.

Metaphor. In both projects, it was the only unused practice. For sure it represents the most difficult practice to introduce, above all in an inexperienced XP group.

Small Releases. It resulted in being the simplest practice to apply in both project types.

Simple Design. We have become aware that simplicity is a very subjective idea especially when there is a knowledge gap among developers. In the real project, the higher complexity of the problem, forced us to use simple design better than in the pilot project, so easing team work. Design patterns [3] turned out to be fundamental in the design of the system, even if someone have found their interpretation hard.

Anyway, the great importance to keep things as simple as possible clearly emerged with XP.

Coding Standard. As most of the developers were at their first experience, it was not difficult to follow the coding standards. The more experienced programmers found greater difficulties. A winning choice was the use of an automatic formatting device such as JRefactory [4].

Testing. We didn't meet big difficulties introducing and applying tests before coding concept. Nevertheless, the main problem was to produce exhaustive instead of ineffective tests. This got the most experienced programmers to a continuous monitoring. We realized that the fear of deadlines, risen only in the real project, leads the programmers to create tests only after coding.

In the real project, the good usage of testing, allowed us to find out design and architectural system defects reducing overall design complexity ("Do The Simplest Thing That Could Possibly Work").

The strength of the system proved to be the natural consequence of the good application of tests and the reduction of maintenance costs, a pleasant surprise. All these positive aspects didn't emerge in the research project.

Refactoring. The research project was useful to introduce this practice. In the real project we appreciated its effectiveness; not only did we make continuous system refactoring, but we also got to refactor the test code, improving its quality. All of that allowed us to knock down maintenance costs. Actually, every bug is now recognized and resolved in a short time.

Continuous Integration. Again, the pilot project led to the acquisition of knowledge concerning our tool of choice for continuous integration: Cruise Control [5]. The real project, unexpectedly, showed the advantages of the practice, especially in the release phase: integration between teams and inside them, let us arrive easily to the release phase of the system.

No doubt, continuous integration is a key practice of XP; we realized that it must be introduced as soon as possible on every project.

Collective Code Ownership. We found out, especially in the real project, that the attitude of the programmers to focus onto components that they made themselves, leads them to be inclined to only accept tasks and refactoring involving the same elements; it also leads the coach and the manager to feel surer if those people accept that task. This soon turns into a vicious circle which is very hard to interrupt.

Pair Programming. In the pilot project, programming in pairs turned out to be the most useful practice to teach technology to less experienced programmers and to learn XP. In the real project, we noticed that its reduced usage concentrate programmers competence on certain parts of the system, causing dangerous bottlenecks in terms of development speed. Programmers accept well a pair cooperation when they think they will acquire knowledge on new technologies; on the contrary, they are reluctant to do it when they have reached sufficient competences. Sometimes, the pressure of the deadlines causes conflicts among programmers making, as a consequence, pair programming less practicable.

Sustainable Pace. It has been the most used practice, above all on the pilot project. In the real project we worked overtime for a limited period (only the last week). The average over work was about one hour a day. The manager considered this as a success.

3   Conclusions

We especially appreciated the flexibility of the XP process, adaptable both to programmers and to the typology of the project. Nevertheless we suffered, especially in the real project, from the lack of project management tools that could help us to facilitate tracking activities and give feedback in a management comprehensible manner. Furthermore, the need of a J2EE-XP integrated development environment for testing, development and integration demonstrates to be fundamental in the present market.

XP introduction looks incompatible in a new-rising team with a real project to carry out, without previous experience on a training project. We should admit, however, that XP methodology requires a short time to be acquired and produces a lot of enthusiasm inside the team.

XP's adoption in a real project is quite different than in a research project and, with no doubt, most of its potentialities only appear in real projects.

References

1. Beck, K.: Extreme Programming Explained. Addison-Wesley Reading, MA (1999).
2. Jeffries, R., Anderson, A., Hendrickson, C.: Extreme Programming Installed, Addison-Wesley Reading, MA (2001).
3. Gamma, E., Helm, R., Johnson, R., Vlissides, J.: Design Patterns - Elements of Reusable Object Oriented Software. Addison Wesley Reading, MA (1995).
4. JRefactory, http://jrefactory.sourceforge.net/csrefactory.html
5. Cruise Control, http://cruisecontrol.sourceforge.net.

Combining Agile Practices with UML and EJB: A Case Study in Agile Development

Richard Paige[1], Priyanka Agarwal[1], and Phillip Brooke[2]

[1] Department of Computer Science, University of York, UK
paige@cs.york.ac.uk, priag16@rediffmail.com
[2] School of Computing, University of Plymouth, UK
philb@soc.plym.ac.uk

Abstract. An agile methodology, with similarities to the Rational Unified Process, and which integrates selected XP practices, UML modelling and Enterprise Java Beans is described. A case study in the domain of web-based systems is outlined, which applies and assesses the utility of the methodology.

1 Introduction

This paper reports on a case study in developing and applying an agile methodology for building web-based e-commerce systems. The methodology is novel in two respects: it integrates several of the key practices of Extreme Programming (XP) [3] with UML modelling, attempting to deal with the incompatibilities between these techniques by adopting a feature-driven development approach [6]. As well, it targets code written in the Enterprise Java Beans (EJB) [7] framework, which is particularly suited for building web-based systems. A goal of the case study is to assess the practicality and effectiveness of using both UML and EJB together in an agile manner, given a project that must be completed under strict time constraints. We claim that the technologies are compatible and can be highly effective when used together to build web-based systems under substantial time constraints.

2 Overview of the Agile Methodology

A motivation for creating the methodology was the need to construct a small web-based e-commerce system under fixed time constraints of less than a few months. The need for careful, yet lightweight modelling for *requirements understanding* was also identified, as was a desire to use EJB for implementation. Given the rapid turn-around time for delivery, and given the ultimately vague customer goals, wants, and needs, it was desired to carry out a lightweight requirements modelling and planning phase. Thus, an agile approach was adopted, integrating EJB, UML modelling, and XP practices.

EJB was selected because it is a framework for distributed systems development: developers typically need implement only business logic in order to construct a system. This is entirely compatible with agile practices, and is a key reason for selecting the technology.

M. Marchesi and G. Succi (Eds.): XP 2003, LNCS 2675, pp. 351–353, 2003.

It was desired to use UML modelling to carry out initial planning and requirements analysis, and also for explaining development iterations to the customer. A characteristic of EJBs is that the applications are often difficult to explain to customers because of the complex interactions that are usually hidden by the EJB infrastructure. Thus, UML modelling was also chosen to help with explaining the system under development to customers. At the same time, it was desired to avoid use of excessive modelling, and to carry out any modelling in a lightweight fashion.

A *feature-driven* approach [6] was adopted. Use cases were constructed based on customer interviews, and each use case (which captured a feature) was refined through to an EJB implementation. Class diagrams were produced after use case modelling, and were used for specification - rather than conceptual - modelling. Collaboration diagrams were sparingly used for trying to explain complex business logic across multiple Beans.

A hallmark of XP approaches is their emphasis on test-based based development. In the methodology, we developed acceptance tests from the use cases. This means that tests act as specifications for the methods that must be implemented in Beans. We wrote unit tests for every method. We then filled in the logic of the test case with the implementation details as we would for that method. For validation, the methodology used JUnit [5] for validating individual methods against specifications, and for further acceptance testing.

3   The Case Study

The case study that was used to experiment with and assess the methodology involved the construction of an Internet call centre. The system aimed to provide facilities for retrieving quantitative statistical data for a call management system, and to support customers' requests for information, via a web page. The system offered at least the following features: *search* for organisation details by a variety of criteria, such as name, location, etc.; view statistical data by city, category and organisation name; *authentication* via encrypted passkey facilities. Exact requirements for each service were highly changeable, making the system poorly suited for traditional development methods. Its web-based nature made EJB an appropriate implementation language.

It is not possible to include full details of the case study so herein we provide a summary. After settling on a model-view-controller architecture, work proceeded by constructing a use case diagram and carrying out release and iteration planning, prioritising the use cases based on risk, priority, and criticality. The search use case was initially chosen for development through to implementation. At the same time, acceptance tests for this interaction were constructed from the use cases. Minimal UML class diagrams were created, in part because a layered architecture based on EJB had already been selected. A collaboration diagram depicting the internal logic of the search use case was sketched, showing the normal course of events. The feature was then implemented, and testing carried out via JUnit. Testing EJBs is not straightforward since it involves traversing multiple layers in the software architecture. Thus, simulation of clients is used in, e.g., testing entity beans. See [1] for more details.

The results of this iteration were then delivered to the customer, who offered feedback and constructive criticism. The second iteration then could begin, focusing on the development of the remaining features. These proceeded along the lines described above, though typically less modelling was carried out since the architecture was by now well understood.

4   Lessons Learned and Conclusions

A number of issues are worth discussing in the context of the web-based case study and the agile methodology.

- *Was agility achieved?* Modelling was carried out before coding, since development could not start without understanding the use cases. Modelling was primarily helpful for deriving use cases that helped us understand customer requirements: these models drove development, and were particularly useful in building test cases and in test planning and resource allocation. Agility was therefore achieved at the level of use cases and feature selection: short iterations were achieved by working on a feature-by-feature basis. We also achieved agility in the use of class diagrams: simple class diagrams were constructed and mapped immediately to EJB code; the class diagrams were thereafter useful in explaining the system.
- *Lessons learned.* Modelling is essential, even in XP-based developments. It was essential in this development for identifying and understanding features, object interactions, and simple associations among classes. These models were thereafter useful in explaining the system to the customer. EJB was particularly useful in this domain for rapid application development. The framework that it provides was useful in dealing with several iterations of development, since the overall architecture of the system to be developed was not about to change. As well, the fact that EJB effectively provides a framework for development helped in producing a working system more quickly.

The case study that we carried out was successful, in the sense that the system was constructed within deadlines and satisfied its key requirements, but further case studies must be performed in order to better assess agility. Agility was achieved by using a feature-driven approach, by creating only those models that were helpful for understanding requirements and business logic, and by emphasising testing.

References

1. P. Agarwal. A case study in agile development using EJB and UML, M.Sc Thesis, University of York, UK, September 2002.
2. S. Ambler. *Agile Modelling*, Wiley, 2002.
3. K. Beck. *Extreme Programming Explained*, Addison-Wesley, 1999.
4. A. Cockburn. *Agile Software Development*, Addison-Wesley, 2002.
5. JUnit Testing Framework. On-line at http://www.junit.org. Visited October 25, 2002.
6. S. Palmer and J. Felsing. *A Practical Guide to Feature-Driven Development*, Prentice-Hall, 2002.
7. E. Roman, S. Ambler, and T. Jewell. *Mastering Enterprise Java Beans*, Wiley, 2002.

Practice Makes Perfect

Sharifah Syed-Abdullah, Mike Holcombe, and Marian Gheorghe

Dept of Computer Science, University of Sheffield
Regent court, Portobello Street, Sheffield S1 4DP, United Kindom
{s.abdullah,m.holcombe,marian}@dcs.shef.ac.uk

Abstract. This paper presents an early empirical study on Extreme Programming practices[1] employing a qualitative action research method. The study was conducted on university students doing real commercial development projects to gain an insight into the problems faced by the new developers in adopting these agile practices. The second aim of the study is to investigate the effects of the XP practices on the quality of software developed. What emerged from the preliminary analysis was the positive relationship between number of XP practices employed and the quality of software delivered as perceived by the clients.

1   Introduction

Agile software development (ASD) is synonymous with innovation and response – propagating new knowledge that delivers value to business and offering a swift response to competitive challenges[2]. Beck [1] refers to XP as a lightweight, efficient, low-risk and flexible way of developing quality software. Reports produced on XP highlighted the methodology is more people-oriented.and tools support have been developed and introduced to encourage the migration to this methodology. However, there are still resistances from several quarters especially the development teams to adopt this radical approach in software development. The main objective of this research is to identify practices that are difficult to use and to examine the reasons for these difficulties. For testing the flexibilitya and this purpose, the year undergraduate students were selected The second objective of this research is to present empirical evidence on the relationship between the number of practices and the quality of the software developed by the team. This paper discuss the research methodology employed, the lesson learned and the preliminary results obtain

2   Methodology

Baskerville and Wood[3] states that to study a newly invented technique, there must be *intervening* in some way to inject the new technique into the practitioner environment. Davison and Vogel [4] point out that the present of previous research [2, 5] provided the validated theory necessary for the application of action research approach in this study. By using this approach, the researcher is actively involved and

M. Marchesi and G. Succi (Eds.): XP 2003, LNCS 2675, pp. 354–356, 2003.

the process promotes collaboration between researcher and team members in order to support the learning cycles. A researcher starts with planning what action to take, continue to intervene with action, observes the effects of that intervention and finally, reflects the observations in order to learn how to plan better and execute the next cycle[4]. For this study, the Software Hut class was selected. The class consists of the 2nd year undergraduate students from Computer Science and Engineering degrees, and 3rd year students from Math and Computer degree. During Spring 2002, there were 10 teams using the XP methodology to develop their software for the clients. The clients selected were Small Firms Enterprise Development Initiative (SFEDI), School of Dentistry, University of Industry and the National Cancer Screening Service.

Planning between researchers (the second researcher is conducting quantitative research) was made to identify various issues, which might arise during the semester. After 2 lectures on XP methodology, a lab session on pair programming, story cards and test first coding was administered to improve the students understanding on the techniques use for the 3 practices. Initial interviews were then conducted to get a glimpse of the students' attitude and understanding on the new methodology. According to Frambach and Schillewaert [6] the insight into the adoption processes, its inhibitors and stimulators helps the supplier of innovations to market their product more effectively. During the interview sessions the researcher received mixed responses from the students but majority of them gave positive feedbacks about the XP approach. During the next 5 weeks, team-client meetings were conducted to enable the team members to interview and to identify the client's requirement. The teams were encouraged to use the story cards for this process. It was observed that the team members tend to adhere to the previous methodology in identifying the entire requirement before proceeding to coding. Second intervention was made to encourage the teams to continue immediately to test-first coding even though the requirement was not completed. It was difficult to observe test-first coding and pair programming because the teams have different schedule for their meeting. The weakness during this cycle is rectify in the second cycle by arranging a fixed lab schedule. It is hope that by enforcing pair programming practice, communication and interaction between team members will be promoted and improved at an early stage. The group members were also encouraged to rotate the team leader every week to motivate and to encourage the members to be more responsible towards the project. By having partial on-site clients, it was observed that communication and rapport between client and team members were established early. During these *interventions*, the members were encouraged to present their work to the client as frequently as possible. It was observed that only 4 groups take the initiative to seek the client's feedback other than the time allocated early in the semester. The teams were also constantly encouraged to adopt release, coding standard, and to increase visitation to the client's site.

3   Result

Due to lack of experience in action research approach, the researcher did not coach and monitor the teams properly to ensure that all of the 12 practices were strictly adhere. The lack of monitoring and coaching may have contributed to the following outcomes of the study. At the end of the semester, the follow-up interviews were conducted to gain an insight into the adoption experiences of the team members. The responses revealed a better understanding of the story cards, pair programming and test-first coding, and the project documents provided the evidence of these practices being employed especially towards the end of the development phase. The second insight revealed a low level of understanding about applying the other practices due to lack of time to research and to understand those other practices. It was insufficient to expect the team members to do an in-depth research on the practices. In the next cycle, documents and templates were prepared and hand out to be referenced during the lecturing and coaching sessions.

To investigate the relationship between the practices and the quality of software produced, the overall pattern for clients' marks was analysed through individual client's marks. These marks were chosen because individual clients set certain standards for their software product and comparison across clients did not revealed the exact comparison. The analysis revealed a positive relationship between the marks awarded by the clients and the number of practices adopted by the teams. Detail analysis on the practices adopted revealed that only 2 of the winning teams employed frequent 'presentation' during the client's meeting.

References

1. Beck, K., Extreme Programming Explained: Embrace Change. 2000: Addison-Wesley. 166.
2. Highsmith, J., Agile Software Development- Why It Is Hot!, in Extreme Programming Perspectives, M. Marchesi, et al., Editors. 2003, Addison-Wesley: Indianapolis. p. 9-16.
3. Baskerville, R.L. and A.T. Wood-Harper, A critical perspective on action research as a methods for information system research. Journal of Information Technology, 1996. 11: p. 235-246.
4. Davison, R. and D. Vogel, Group Support System in Hong Kong: an action research project. Info System Journal, 2000. 10: p. 3-20.
5. Cockburn, A. and L. Williams, The Costs and Benefits Pair Programming, in Extreme Programming Examined, G. Succi and M. Marchesi, Editors. 2000, Addison-Wesley Publishing Co. p. 223-248.
6. Frambach, R.T. and N. Schillewaert, Organizational innovation adoption: A multi-level framework of determinants and the opportunities for future research. Journal of Business Research, 2002. 55: p. 163-176.

A Designing Practice and Two Coding Practices for Extreme Programming (XP)

Mustafa Yıldız and Selahattin Kuru

Department of Computer Engineering, Işık University
Istanbul, Turkey
{mustafa,kuru}@isikun.edu.tr

Abstract. This paper introduces three new XP practices and reports the experience of applying them to web based software development. These are *issue-based programming, comment-first coding* and *just in time code ownership*. The example project is development of an on-line student information and registration software for a university.

1 Introduction

In this paper we introduce three XP practices and report our experience on them, namely, issue-based programming, comment-first coding and just in time (JIT) collective code ownership. These practices are used in a sample web based software development project, which involves the development of an on-line student information and registration software for a university [3]. Issue-based programming was used from the beginning of the project whereas comment-first coding and JIT code ownership were developed during the project. Experience on other XP practices such as pair programming, test-first coding [2] that were also used in the example application development are not reported in this paper.

2 Proposed Practices

Issue-Based Programming [3] is a designing practice where issues determine priorities. At any time instance during the software development project there are many issues to be resolve and many issues already resolved. At the early stages of development, most of the issues identified are related to requirements rather than design or implementation, whereas at later stages most issues are related to implementation. Still there are implementation-related issues at early stages and requirements-related issues at later stages. An issue table is maintained throughout the software development project and issues are identified as *closed* when they are resolved. A closed issue may become *open* later. The prioritization of issues is done regarding the requests of the customer and by negotiation between the customer and the development team.

Comment-first coding is a coding practice. It breaks the coding of a single module into two phases: coding the semantics, and coding the syntax. When coding a module,

M. Marchesi and G. Succi (Eds.): XP 2003, LNCS 2675, pp. 357–359, 2003.

first the algorithm of that code is written to the editor as comment lines in natural language. The level of detail should be such that the architecture of the algorithm should be understood at a glance and that converting each comment line to the valid syntax of the language used is easy for all the programmers in the team. After the first phase is completed, the output is a formatted text, which is easy to read and easy to convert to programming language's syntax. In the second phase, the programmer starts to code each construct following an *outside-in* approach. The reason why we call outside-in but not top-down is that the level of granularity is more or less the same at the end of the two phases.

The technique is demonstrated below step by step, on a sample module that checks if a student satisfies the prerequisite condition to take a course. The module takes two input parameters; *student* and *course* and returns a Boolean value. The past data of the student and the data about courses are kept in a database. This module also uses another public function *studentpassed(student,course)* which returns true if the given student has passed the given course successfully, and false otherwise. In the first phase, the algorithm is written in natural language, where constructs are differentiated by indents such that every construct on the same level have the same indent value. The commented algorithm for the sample module is given in Figure 1. In the second phase, the programmer starts to code each construct following an outside-in approach. In Figure 2, we see a state when the outermost loop and the first decision constructs are coded.

```
5
6    'a loop of two
7        'if it is the first pass then select the weak prerequisites and assign it to course variable
8        'if it is the second pass then select the hard prerequisites and assign it to course variable
9        'loop until course.eof
10           'set err variable to true
11           'if student passed this course set err variable to false and exit loop
12           'else select the substitutions of the course assign it to subs variable
13           'loop until subs.EOF
14               'if student passed this course set err variable to false and exit loop
15           'end of subs loop
16           'if hata is true return true -- there is a violation
17       'end of course loop
18   'end of the outer most loop
19
```

Fig. 1. Commented Algorithm of Sample Module

JIT collective code ownership can be considered as a modification of collective code ownership, which is an existing practice of XP. JIT collective code ownership is based on delaying collective code ownership until it becomes necessary. Until then code ownership is individual. The time when code ownership is switched to collective code ownership for a module depends on the difficulty of the task, effort required completing the task, and other practical factors.

3   Evaluation and Conclusion

Three new XP practices are introduced in this paper, namely issue-based programming, comment-first coding and JIT collective code ownership. These practices are used on a mid-size software development project (30 KLOC, 200 database tables, 150

```
5
6    FOR i=0 to 1 'a loop of two
7      IF i=0 THEN 'if it is the first pass then select the weak prerequisites and assign it to course
8        presql = "SELECT Prereq FROM Prerequisites WHERE Course_Code='"& cc &"' AND Min_Grade='F
9      ELSE 'if it is the second pass then select the hard prerequisites and assign it to course variab
10        presql = "SELECT Prereq FROM Prerequisites WHERE Course_Code='"& cc &"' AND Min_Grade='D
11     END IF
12     SET course = Conn.EXECUTE(presql)
13     DO UNTIL course.eof 'loop until course.eof
14       'set err variable to true
15       'if student passed this course set err variable to false and exit loop
16       'else select the substitutions of the course assign it to subs variable
17       'loop until subs.EOF
18         'if student passed this course set err variable to false and exit loop
19       'end of subs loop
20       'if hata is true return true -- there is a violation
21     course.movenext
22     LOOP 'end of course loop
23   'end of the outer most loop
24
```

Fig. 2. An intermediate state of second phase

program modules) and they were found useful and efficient. Issue-based programming is used in prioritizing tasks. Comment-first coding provides a smooth transition from algorithmic design to coding for the individual developer. It also helps him in better organizing himself, for instance, in remembering more easily where the work was left when returning to a coding task which was quitted temporarily. It also helps communication, understandability and sharing of tasks between programmer pairs. For instance, the more experienced programmer may do commenting while the less experienced does the coding. Obtaining a documented code automatically at the end of coding is another benefit of the practice. JIT collective code ownership improves efficiency of pair programming.

References

1. http://campus.isikun.edu.tr
2. Wake, W.C.: The XP series: Extreme Programming Explored, Addison-Wesley, NJ, (2002)
3. Kuru S., Yıldız, M., Erdoğan G.: "Issue based extreme programming for data intensive web applications: An example," Proceedings of the Sixteenth International Conference on Computer and Information Sciences, Antalya, (2001).

Practical Aspects of XP Practices

Teodora Bozheva

European Software Institute, Parque Tecnológico #204
48170 Zamudio (Bilbao), Spain
Teodora.Bozheva@esi.es

Abstract. This article presents the initial experience gained in 7 pilot projects experimenting with a combination of XP and PSP practices. The project is partially funded by the European Commission through the IST Programme (ref. IST-2001-34488) and by the Spanish Ministry of Science and Technology (TIC-2001-5254). It aims at collecting and disseminating best practices and lessons learned by the participating teams. Two of the organizations are ISO 9001:2000 certified. Four of the pilot projects develop e-commerce applications and two - e-business ones.

1   Introduction

XP is a challenging agile methodology applicable to small and motivated teams, with good communication between the members, thus more and more young companies are interested in adopting it. At the same time developers with little experience have difficulties to start working in a disciplined manner, to divide their tasks in subtasks, and to estimate them. Certain Personal Software Process (PSP) practices help overcoming these obstacles and as a consequence smooth and speed up the development process.

2   The Project

The *e*XPERT project[1] was established with two main objectives:

- To define a practical combination of XP and PSP, named *e*XPERT approach;
- To experiment the *e*XPERT approach in 7 pilot projects in order to validate its usability, benefits, and pitfalls.

The *e*XPERT approach includes all the XP practices, and three from PSP: time and effort recording, defect recording, task estimation by means of the Probe method, modified as to reflect customer requirement's complexity instead of LOC.

3   Current Experience

All the experimenting teams share a common satisfaction with learning about XP and PSP, and applying a combination of them in real projects. As the biggest benefit for

---

[1] http://www.esi.es/Expert

M. Marchesi and G. Succi (Eds.): XP 2003, LNCS 2675, pp. 360–362, 2003.

their organizations they point out the establishment of a disciplined manner of software development and better project control.

We see three groups of practices and our experience with them is described in the following paragraphs.

3.1   Customer Requirements Related Practices

Customer on-site seems to be a rather unrealistic principle. From 7 projects only 2 managed to get their customers on-site. However, all the teams find that the objective of this practice is to provide timely availability of the customer for discussions and question answering, as well as the customer's feedback on the latest project status. As an alternative way to achieving the goal, they (a) meet the customer as often as necessary, (b) document customer's tacit knowledge and requirements and make the documents available to all team members, and (c) use a demonstration web site showing the customer the latest status of the product developed. In 3 of the 5 pilots the whole team participates in meetings with the customer. In the others the project manager is responsible for regularly meeting with the customer and clarifying and scheduling requirements. One of the ISO certified organizations reported that the involvement of the customer during the development process shortened 30% their time to market.

3.2   Project Management Related Practices

Planning game together with *Small releases* practices are found to bring most tangible benefit to the development teams. The only slight modification made in all the pilots is that the project manager is the one who initially suggests task distribution considering the skills, and the knowledge level of the team members. The rationale behind changing the free sign-up for tasks like this is to organize the tasks to be developed so as to complete them in shortest possible time by gradually integrating new and less experienced people in the project.

Applying the adapted Probe method gradually closes the difference between the estimated and the actual implementation duration providing the team a possibility to make more realistic commitments. As a result the communication with the customer and the development process go smoother.

3.3   Software Engineering Practices

From the typical software engineering practices the ones that are the most difficult to implement are *Pair programming* and *Testing before code*.

Pair programming proves to be an excellent means to integrate new staff. It brings significant advantages, provided the pair is properly defined. The experience from the pilot projects shows that critical tasks, e.g. architecture or core programming, have to be undertaken by people with approximately equal and high professional level. Joining a highly experienced developer and a beginner for such tasks neither facilitates the work of the experienced person, nor improves much the beginner's knowledge and skills. On the other hand assigning a routine task to programmers with relatively little experience contributes to obtaining better results and faster learning.

In all the teams pair programming is applied until having a problem that is granulated down to a level where the pieces are trivial to implement. Then the pair splits and the programmers code their parts alone.

Testing before code makes a big change in the way the programmers are used to thinking and working, and thus it takes some time before implementing this practice correctly. A typical implementation deviation (perhaps reasonable) is to start writing test cases once a decision about how to implement a requirement is made, but not while trying alternatives. However, once adopted this practice becomes routine, and the developers confess they wouldn't omit it, since it considerably decreases the number of bugs produced, reduces the time for finding defects in the code and maintains it in good working condition.

The rest of the engineering practices, system metaphor, simple design, refactoring, continuous integration, and collective ownership are implemented fluently.

4   Conclusions

The XP practices have to be applied reasonably, by understanding well and trying to achieve the objectives of the practices, and relating them to the project and the organizational context.

The combination of XP with the selected set of PSP practices makes the developers more aware about their abilities to perform a particular task within a certain time frame and at a particular level of quality.

Acknowledgements

The participants are thankful to Frank Westphal and Jutta Eckstein for the great training they provided, and for transmitting the sense and the spirit of XP, not just its set of practices.

References

1. Jeffries R., Anderson, A., Hendrickson, C.: The XP Series: EXTREME PROGRAMMING Installed. Addison Wesley (2000).
2. Humphrey W.: A Discipline for Software Engineering. Addison Wesley (1994).
3. Williams L.: The Collaborative Software Process. PhD dissertation.

Scaling Extreme Programming
in a Market Driven Development Context

Daniel Karlström and Per Runeson

Dept. Communication Systems, Lund University
Box 118, SE-221 00 Lund, Sweden
{Daniel.Karlstrom,Per.Runeson}@telecom.lth.se

Abstract. This paper briefly summarizes a research project aiming at analyzing the scaling up of Extreme Programming (XP) in a market driven context for embedded software and the integration of XP towards management processes in this context. Both the scaling of XP and market driven software development issues are not addressed by the original XP methodology as it relies on developing software by simplifying the development situation as far as possible in order to do the simplest thing that could possibly work. The research project is composed of a number of steps aimed at gathering information from actual development organizations, analyzing, synthesizing, and incorporating the conclusions into the models created.

1   Introduction

The motivation for scaling an XP project is usually the need for producing a larger amount of functionality in a shorter time than a smaller team could. The size of a project can mean several different aspects of the project, for instance source code size, amount of implemented functionality, total cost, or the number of developers involved. We intend to investigate the application of the hierarchical approach [1] to scaling XP into a highly structured, very large, market driven embedded software developing organisation. The development of this type of systems requires much coordination between hardware and software organisational units, while simultaneously keeping an eye on marketing and competition. Companies in this category usually perform projects based on some form of a gate model [2] and the concept of adapting a similar model used by ABB has been briefly discussed by Wallin et al. [3].

A project using a gate based project model in the described context would typically consist of the following main phases: *Pre-study, Feasibility study, Execution* and *Completion.* In order to pass from one phase to the next the project must pass through a gate where certain prerequisites are monitored in order to certify the status of the project and a senior management decision is taken. In addition, the execution phase contains an intermediate gate as this phase is such a large part of the project. Note that the management model used in these context can appear similar to a waterfall development process, but the two are very different and should not be confused.

M. Marchesi and G. Succi (Eds.): XP 2003, LNCS 2675, pp. 363–365, 2003.
© Springer-Verlag Berlin Heidelberg 2003

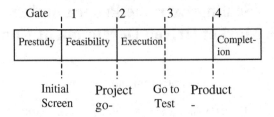

Fig. 1. Gate based project model

2   Project Steps

The project is divided into a series of steps in order to structure the work. The steps dictate a working format alternating between the academic environment and the industrial context.

Step 1 – Pre-study: This first step of the project is intended to explore the context and pre-requisites for the project. The theoretical background is explored and current practice is surveyed in the literature. Theoretical assumptions are made and issues are identified for the management of a scaled up XP project.

Step 2 – Study: During this step we intend to study in detail the decision support available at the project go ahead tollgate in an industrial application in a large software development organization at both the management and development levels in the organization. The research methods used for this will include qualitative observation and participation methods such as interviews and document analysis as well as quantitative analysis of appropriate metrics. The expected outcome of this step is a thorough case description of the situation at the specific company.

Step 3 – Analysis: The case information obtained in step 2 is analyzed and used in order to revise the management models created in step 1 so as to make these appropriate for this specific context. At this time appropriate introduction strategies, monitoring and improvement processes are also created and documented.

Step 4 – Feedback: This step involves obtaining feedback from the industrial organization on the revised model and the model is revised accordingly. Methods used for this will include structured interviews. This step is included in order to increase the validity of the conclusions and ensure that the models created are thought to work in the real world application by the actual people involved.

Step 5 – Introduction: The model or parts of it are introduced in projects within the target organization and experiences are gathered.

Further Work: Generalization of the model to other industrial settings must be done and can be performed by either introducing the model created during the course of this project or tailored versions thereof.

3   Issues Identified during the Pre-study

This section contains a brief discussion of issues identified during the pre-study step described in the previous section.

A model adjusted to accommodate agile influences would focus more on communication through working functionality instead of extensive documentation as per the XP methodology. In turn some documentation will be necessary to coordinate other teams, such as hardware and external testing teams.

In the adjusted project model the first phase, *pre-study*, would be similar to before, but as the main focus in the next phase is now to move as fast as possible towards a minimal running framework, so the prototyping work can be adjusted to focus on this.

The second phase, *feasibility*, would be quite different and would not be much different to the third, *execution*. Here the minimal framework is developed and the most basic functionality added in the first few iterations of the development. The crucial decision taken at the end of phase two is therefore taken based on an actual functioning system and planning for the remaining development can be performed using actual experience of development in the current project. Instead of a big up front design document containing the whole project we can evaluate based on the basic idea and the most important features instead.

During the third phase, *execution*, the number of developers is increased in order to limit the calendar time of the project. This implies that, in order to remain effective, the XP methodology must be adjusted or coordinated in some form. The strategy for XP team coordination has been discussed by for instance Crocker [4] by using loosely coupled teams combined with a prime team imposing a feature roll-out plan for the other teams. Rumpe and Scholz [1] discuss three forms of structuring XP for scaled up XP in software intensive companies by using terms from systems theory and applying these to an XP environment. They describe three approaches in the paper: *holistic*, *hierarchical*, and *incremental*.

During the final phase, *completion*, the product goes to acceptance testing and final productification.

The differences in testing strategy between XP, where testing is performed continuously in a structured fashion, and the actual testing common in traditional projects is an example of a further issue that has been identified during the pre-study. Another example is the fact that many industry quality certifications demand independent testing procedures not supported by the XP methodology. These issues and others will be looked at during the course of the research project in order to scale XP into a market driven product development organization governed by rigorous product management models.

References

1. Rumpe, B., Scholz, P.: "A manager's view on large scale XP projects", Third International Conference on Extreme Programming and Flexible Processes in Software Engineering, XP2002, May 26-30, Alghero, Italy, 2002.
2. Cooper, R. G.: Winning at New Products, 3rd edition, Perseus Publishing, Cambridge, MA, 2001.
3. Wallin, C., Ekdahl, F., Larsson, S.: "Integrating Business and Software Development Models", IEEE Software, November/December 2002, pp. 28-33.
4. Crocker, R.: "The 5 Reasons XP can't Scale and what to do about them", Third International Conference on Extreme Programming and Flexible Processes in Software Engineering, XP2002, May 26-30, Alghero, Italy, 2002.

Building Standard ERP Software Packages Using Self-developed Agile Methodologies

Andrea Rinaldi[1] and Luigi Benedicenti[2]

[1] Microarea S.p.a., Via Renata Bianchi 36, 16152 Genova, Italy
andrea.rinaldi@microarea.it
www.microarea.it
[2] Faculty of Engineering, University of Regina, 3737 Wascana Parkway
Regina, SK, S4S 0A2, Canada
Luigi.Benedicenti@uregina.ca
www.uregina.ca

Abstract. In this paper, we will describe the evolution of our software development techniques, and analyze actual methodologies in-depth. These are internally developed and do not refers to any standard, but they are more related to agile methodologies than standard ones. Our development techniques are strictly related to our development process. This process is slightly different from the ones of other small software houses, as we develop standard packages instead of committed projects. This raise a set of development problems, somewhat opposite to traditional committed projects ones, which can be very puzzling for small software houses.

1   Introduction

Microarea is a small independent software factory that has developed a number of standard ERP packages since 1984. One of the most important product lines for Microarea is a smart accounting package, initially produced for MS-DOS systems and later expanded both in size and in capability. This accounting package has become one of the most popular accounting packages in Italy, with over 10,000 installations in small and medium enterprises (typically with an accounting department having between 2 and 20 workstations).

The product was initially written in Pascal, an uncommon choice for an accounting package. However, at the time, it was felt that the "no-compromises" approach was needed to emphasize product functionality. This approach was upheld with the migration to the Windows environment in 1993, and the whole package was rewritten in C++. The product became a complete set of self-contained ERP systems.

Although Microarea is customer-oriented, the development of product features is not guided by customer requests. The prioritization of the features to implement must abide the market laws and happens by market consideration and competitors' analysis. Time-to-market considerations demand rapid product development and upgrading. Design errors and limitations are revealed only when the product has been al-

M. Marchesi and G. Succi (Eds.): XP 2003, LNCS 2675, pp. 366–368, 2003.

ready released and used by hundreds of customers. Moreover, since backward compatibility with existing systems and work habits must be guaranteed, the analysis process becomes very critical. Testing is also a critical point for our packages, because the cost to fix a bug in a released product entails not only a program distribution, but also the loss of trust from our customers. Time constraints and the perceived lack of productivity when writing documentation also require our programmers to maintain a thorough knowledge of our legacy packages for maintenance and upgrading.

The emphasis on analysis, thorough and early testing, and shared knowledge of legacy packages tie directly with agile methods, and especially Extreme Programming (XP). However, our development process must be kept consistent so that our productivity does not falter. It is of utter importance to maintain a successful image for our product, given that the competition in our sector is fierce. This constrains the extent to which we can effect changes to our development.

2 Injecting Agile Methods in Microarea

The development process in Microarea started in a very ad-hoc way as people discussed potential development ideas and immediately set forth to program them. With the move from MS-DOS to Windows, and then to Unix and to 32-bit computing, this simple development approach grew into a more rationalized and structured process.

The first need arising from the increasing complexity of the development task was standardized coding. This matches one of the 12 practices in XP, and also allows programmers to share their code with their peers without the need for long explanatory sessions. Code sharing begun very early in our development effort, and later evolved into version control. Today, our product is always in a "ready state" and can be built every day.

One more important feature of our process is the formalization of the conceptual phase that comes before the requirements analysis. New product ideas are collected from customers, our marketing analyses, the feedback from our retailers, and our competitors. These ideas are then connected to the requirements and summarized into a "project." Our products are feature-based, and this resembles the way in which specifications are captured in XP.

The next step in the enhancement of our development process was to formalize our design documentation. Our design documents for new programs or modules comprise four main sections: User Needs, Requirements, Coding Specifications and Testing Specifications. Complete end-user requirements often help in architectural choices, and the more the Requirements document is detailed, the less the Coding Specifications document needs to be extended. Initially, no testing documents were prepared, and as well no early testing was performed.

As a result, initially, the testing of our products was performed by experienced people (usually form Tech Support team); they would use the new release of a product testing "all" the use cases they knew and/or they could imagine, working on end user databases. Obviously this required a large amount of time and even then it was not proven to be sufficient. As the product gained more features, the risk to put regression bugs in the product grew. Complex algorithms, like MRP/II, required days of continuous tests, and the fear to lose features sometimes slowed down evolution.

For these reasons, we have recently developed a proprietary regression test methodology, together with a set of tools to perform automatic regression test. The methodology defines how to design tests for each unit (i.e., a function or a module) in three major steps. The first step is the behavioral definition of a unit. The second step defines the test cases necessary to exercise every behavioral nuance in the definition. The third step is the execution of the program according to the test case. These three steps are assisted by a few tools that automate the test execution and the comparison with the expected result specified in the test case. This kind of testing resembles the testing practices in XP.

Unfortunately, no matter how carefully the testing is done, bugs can still be found after product release. This means that a fixing strategy has to be planned. Our strategy is as follows. First, a notification must be received, accepted and classified. Second, the bug must be reproduced internally on a controlled system. The existence of workarounds, if any, should be communicated immediately back to the end user. Third, programmers find out the technical cause of the bug and fix it. Fourth, a new test is done to prove that bug disappeared. The recovery strategy is also tested. Fifth, the bug fix is included in the next fixing release. The lack of a feature, even a very important one, is not treated as a bug. This is a must in our kind of product, as thousands of customers find the need for a very large number of features, each of them very important for the single user.

As it can be glimpsed from this short account, the evolution of our development method, although not directly linked to XP, resulted in the adoption of some of XP's practices: Coding Standards, Collective Code Ownership, Small Design, Continuous Integration, and Testing. We hope that our independent experience can serve as a validation of these XP practices in terms of market value.

References

1. Beck, K.: Extreme Programming Explained, Embrace Change. Addison-Wesley, Pearson Education, Indianapolis (2000).
2. Succi, G., Marchesi , M. (ed.): Extreme Programming Examined. Addison-Wesley, Pearson Education, Indianapolis (2001).
3. Jeffries, R., Anderson, A., Hendrickson, C.: Extreme Programming Installed. Addison-Wesley, Pearson Education, Indianapolis (2002).
4. Marchesi, M., Succi, G., Wells, D., Williams, L. (ed.): Extreme Programming Perspectives. Addison-Wesley, Pearson Education, Indianapolis (2003).
5. McBreen, P.: Questioning Extreme Programming. Addison-Wesley, Pearson Education, Indianapolis (2003).
6. Wake, W.C.: Extreme Programming Explored. Addison-Wesley, Pearson Education, Indianapolis (2002).
7. Crispin, L., House, T.: Testing Extreme Programming. Addison-Wesley, Pearson Education, Indianapolis (2003).
8. Beck, K.: Test-Driven Development. Addison-Wesley, Boston (2003).

Convincing the Inconvincable

Geoff Oliphant

ThoughtWorks Inc., Peek House, 20 Eastcheap,
London, EC3M 1EB
Goliphant@thoughtworks.com

Abstract. Despite the increasing knowledge base within the IT industry world-wide about the tremendous benefits of XP and Agile processes, there is still a long way to go to convince a lot of developers. A side effect of this popularity is that XP practices may have a negative connotation for some. This may result in a reluctance to try or adopt any of these practices. This paper describes some strategies that may be employed by project team members to help those that seem "inconvincable" to recognise some of the benefits of XP. Introducing XP should be an evolution not a revolution.

1 Introduction

Moving to an XP work environment is a culture change. Those developers that have already seen the benefits that can be achieved by employing some or all of the XP tenets, as described by Beck [1], still have a difficult task convincing other developers to see the same benefits. If developers are not convinced of the long term advantages, then they will not participate. This can lead to alienation and, even the loss of a developer.

It is not always possible within a project to have the time and energy to slowly introduce XP to those that aren't interested in it. On the other hand, not doing it could have a negative effect on the whole project. By using non-threatening strategies to introduce these concepts, we will be able to generate the influence required with minimal effort to convince the development team to use these practices at every opportunity. To illustrate the use of such strategies, two practices of XP are examined, Pair Programming and Refactoring.

2 Strategies to Employ

The perception that something is difficult is often more important than the reality. If a person believes that implementing XP practices is difficult they will go out of their way to avoid it. By using some simple strategies we can introduce XP practices in a non-threatening manner and change perceptions.

2.1 Working together not Pair Programming

One of the practices is to encourage developers to help each other and to share their knowledge. This would be called *Pair Programming* [1] in the XP world, but if you call it by name then there is some inference that it has to be done in a certain way.

M. Marchesi and G. Succi (Eds.): XP 2003, LNCS 2675, pp. 369–371, 2003.

Instead it could be introduced as "knowledge sharing" rather than as writing code together. Once developers have created a bond working with each other, suggestions for improvement will be accepted.

This technique was used to great effect on a recent project where a non-XP developer was afraid of pairing with an XP developer, as she perceived that all the other developers were junior to her. Once the junior developers kept asking her to help them and she began to work with them, she found that she was learning as much about the application as they were. One day she realized that she was actually pair programming.

If a developer is uncomfortable about working with another developer, it is important that the XP developer is aware of and is sensitive to the situation. Dominating the keyboard or the chair in front of the computer (if side-by-side pairing is in use) is detrimental to influencing the other developer.

I've seen one instance where the XP developer decided that he didn't like the way that the non-XP developer had configured his IDE. By sitting down, saying, "...this is a horrible environment to develop in", changing the IDE and thereby changing the environment, the non-XP developer is offside immediately. This occasion resulted in a failure to introduce XP, simply by an incorrect implementation.

This does not mean that non-XP developers should be nurtured more than other developers nor should more time be involved in their training. Don't let a bad apple spoil the barrel [2].

2.2   Refactoring Is Improving not Fixing

Code that needs *refactoring* [1] does not necessarily mean that the original code was in error in the first place. Most developers feel that the code that they have written is designed exactly as it should be and are thus very possessive of it. If they are told that it needs refactoring then they may think that it is a comment on the work that they have done.

Working with a developer when refactoring code that they wrote is a good tactic to ensure that negative connotations are not implied. Lessons should be learnt from refactoring. Is it happening because of changed requirements? Is it happening because of a better solution? If another developer refactors their code then they could assume that the code was reviewed by others and found wanting. This is not necessarily the case, nor is the intention of the exercise.

The perception that refactoring is fixing broken code is more prevalent than the reality that refactored code is improving on the good work that has already been completed. However, sometimes it is required to remove bad code. The code may not necessarily be wrong; it may just be using bad coding practices. Refactoring should be used to improve this code and the original developer should be shown the changes to understand and learn.

I have worked with developers who make negative comments on the code that they are refactoring. This is equal to insulting the developer that wrote it. If the developer can be shown why code needs to be refactored, the application will benefit from having a better solution and the developer will learn as well.

Defining refactoring as "improving" rather than "fixing" and ensuring that the original developer is involved in the code change are two ways to make refactoring being perceived as a critique rather than a tool.

3   Conclusion

Introducing XP to developers that are not convinced of its values requires delicate handling. It is worth making the extra effort to find the novel way to implement XP so that the chances of success are maximised.

Convincing the inconvincible is not an impossible task but certainly requires more energy, thought and management.

References

1. Beck, K., Extreme Programming Explained: Embrace Change. Reading, Massachusetts: Addison-Wesley, 2000.
2. Auer, K., Miller, R., Extreme Programming Applied. Indianapolis, Indiana: Addison-Wesley, 2002.

Comparing Extreme Programming to Traditional Development for Student Projects: A Case Study

John Noll and Darren C. Atkinson

Department of Computer Engineering
Santa Clara University
Santa Clara, CA 95053-0566 USA
{jnoll,atkinson}@cse.scu.edu

Abstract. We conducted an experiment attempting to compare XP with a traditional approach to student software engineering projects. We tasked two groups of student teams with producing a simple room reservation system, one group following a traditional development process, the other using XP. We observed little actual difference between the products delivered by either process. However, in our opinion this is due to certain deficiencies in the way XP was realized in this instance, rather than fundamental flaws in the process itself.

1 Introduction

Our experience with Software Engineering project courses over the past three years showed that student project teams following traditional development processes do not consistently produce good products or documentation. Extreme Programming, with its iterative development cycle, emphasis on delivering value, and lean documentation requirements, seemed like a viable alternative. Because Extreme Programming is driven by delivering value to the customer, we hypothesized that this would help students focus on the product, rather than the individual deliverables, and therefore result in better products.

In the fall quarter of 2002, we conducted an experiment to try to confirm this hypothesis.

2 Method

The undergraduate Software Engineering course at Santa Clara University is a traditional ten week survey course, involving twice weekly lectures, a weekly lab session, and a term-long development project. We divided the class into four teams of six to eight developers; students were assigned randomly to teams. Each team was tasked with developing a web-based room reservation system that could be used to schedule classrooms in several buildings for courses and seminars. All teams were aware that they were part of an experiment to compare traditional methods with XP.

Two teams followed a "traditional" development process, based on Boehm's Anchoring Milestones [1]. These teams had three deliverables: a design document, due at

M. Marchesi and G. Succi (Eds.): XP 2003, LNCS 2675, pp. 372–374, 2003.
© Springer-Verlag Berlin Heidelberg 2003

the end of the third week; an initial operational product, due at the fifth week; and a final product, due the tenth week.

The other two teams followed Extreme Programming, with two releases comprising four one-week iterations. Production code was written using pair programming during the weekly two and one-half hour lab session; we required unit tests to be written before the lab session. The Teaching Assistant served as the "customer" for all four teams, while one of us (Noll) served as the XP coach. We conducted a brief (half hour) overview of XP for the XP teams, covering iterations and releases, test-first design, and the relationship between the customer and developers. We then proceeded directly into the first Planning Game.

3   Results

Neither of the traditional teams could install their first release on any of the target platforms; one team could not even demonstrate a working product on their development platform, and could not offer an explanation why. Both XP teams delivered first release products with minor bugs in their installation scripts; once these were corrected, both products functioned but exhibited significant failures.

All four teams managed to deliver an installable product for the second release. The XP teams delivered relatively robust products with minimal features (completing three of eight stories) during acceptance testing, although the products suffered from sloppy and difficult to use user interfaces. The traditional teams delivered more features (equivalent to all eight stories), but much less robust code.

Overall, none of the delivered products, from either XP or traditional teams, could be considered suitable for the intended application.

4   Observations

In their study of an industrial XP team, Farell, Narang, Kapitan, and Webber observed that a split between customer and developers occurred, resulting in an attitude among developers that they had to "protect their interests" from customers; they also observed that not having detailed acceptance tests early in the development process resulted in developers making assumptions about features, and a "trial and error" cycle between customer and developers trying to achieve closure on stories [2].

Both of these observations are entirely consistent with our experience. When faced with missing or ambiguous requirements, our students seemed prone to making assumptions that suit their desires, rather than seeking clarification from the customer. This was despite the fact that the customer was always available during lab sessions. According to one student, "No one wants to make changes, and we challenge you [the customer] when you request changes because we need to make sure they are worth to you the effort they will require from us."

Students also had difficulty with the concept of collective ownership: they were very reluctant to fix problems in code written by others. This seemed to be a social rather than technical problem: most were familiar enough with the entire code base to have the expertise to fix a problem, but seemed to feel that this would violate some principle of responsibility ("you broke it, you fix it").

The XP teams were reluctant to apply continuous integration. We frequently observed pairs "hoarding" finished code rather than integrating and testing it. This often resulted in a mass integration at the end of the lab period, producing confusion when inevitable problems with the build arose.

This may have been due to a lack of confidence that the features completed were actually finished; although they passed the unit tests, developers still seemed to think problems remained. They did not seem to make the connection between integration testing and discovering these problems.

5   Conclusions

Despite the inconclusive results of our experiment, we still believe that XP has potential as a pedagogical software process for software engineering project courses. We feel that the failure of our XP teams to produce significantly better products was due to two deficiencies in our application of the process: an insufficiently strong customer, and inadequate introduction to XP's values and practices. Consequently, we would adopt the following changes in future applications of XP in the classroom:

1. Provide a strong customer by having the professor play this role. This will ensure there is no misunderstanding of who is responsible for defining requirements, and that the customer has sufficient authority to insert himself into the development process when necessary.
2. Devote more class time to discussing the differences between XP and traditional software processes, in an attempt to increase student understanding of the reasons for various XP (and traditional) practices. Without adequate explanation of the reasons for XP's practices, students seemed inclined to dismiss XP as more difficult, restrictive, and therefore lacking merit. As Lappo [3] observed, it is difficult to appreciate the benefits of XP without first experiencing the pitfalls of other development processes.

References

1. Boehm, B.W.: Anchoring the software process. IEEE Software 13 (1996) 73–82
2. Farell, C., Narang, R., Kapitan, S., Webber, H.: Towards an effective onsite customer practice. [4] 52–55
3. Lappo, P.: No pain, no XP – Observations on teaching and mentoring extreme programming to university students. [4] 35–38
4. Succi, G., Marchesi, M., eds. In Succi, G., Marchesi, M., eds.: Proceedings of the Third International Conference on Extreme Programming and Agile Processes in Software Engineering, Alghero, Sardinia, Italy (2002)

XP: Good for Anything Other than Software Development?

Hans Dermot Doran

workstation ag
Europastrasse 4, 8152 Glattbrugg, Switzerland.
hans.doran@ibhdoran.com

Abstract. The author implemented XP practices in both hardware and software development projects as well as using them as guidelines for general department management. This paper describes the reasoning behind this decision and the most important results.

1 Introduction

XP is a grassroots, bottom up approach to software development. The simplicity of the practices compiled by Beck [1] into a methodology, disguise the fact that the experiences that led to this compilation are essentially universal and can be gained from development work in any engineering discipline. If these experiences are universal, then the methodology should also contain elements that are universally applicable. This train of thought led to a series of initiatives to establish XP practices, not only in software development, but also in hardware development and as guidelines for the general management of a development department. These initiatives were carried out beginning spring 2000 until the company closed in winter 2001.

In order to achieve the tasks set out in the company vision, the work in the department was divided up into three interacting categories, with decreasing resource priority. The first was release management with the product manager as the customer. The second was development, with the business development manager being the customer and the third, applied research, involving technology transfer with the local university, the customer being the CTO.

There were several benefits expected from the application of the practices on a department level. The first was to optimise the effective working time of the developers. The second was to implicitly ensure effective knowledge management across the department. The third was to explicitly ensure a high level and a high mix of knowledge, skills and expertise in, and with, the various technologies used (Java, OSGi, Bluetooth etc.). A premium was placed on buffering the developers from the insecurities associated with start-ups. In other words the practices were being applied to achieve sustainable pace, rather than sustainable pace being a practice.

M. Marchesi and G. Succi (Eds.): XP 2003, LNCS 2675, pp. 375–377, 2003.

2   Practical Experiences

2.1   Release Management

Release management was organised around the planning game. The release manager would discuss the bug list, the feature addition list and those issues which the developers wanted to refactor, with the product manager and sales team. The items on these lists were prioritised, and regular meetings were held to discuss progress. 6 weeks was set as being the ideal release cycle, it was long enough to fix bugs and improve some features but short enough that the product managers were forced to contain their creativity. Features that needed more than a release cycle to complete were considered development projects and required authorisation from higher powers. The procedure was very popular with the sales staff because it was easy to understand and allowed them higher-than-usual participation and determination rights in the technical side of product development. The system also compensated extremely well for an extraordinarily high turnover in product managers and sales staff. The team could sustain pace despite the staff turnover in an important decision making area.

2.2   Development

One major software development project was run exclusively under XP techniques, and the results reflect (good) experiences already published. Although it was difficult to generate metrics to satisfy the CTO's fellow chiefs, an important benefit was seen in watching the development team interacting with the customer. It proved to be an excellent way to deduce, from the interaction between customer and team, the teams ability to handle the task and their grasp of the subject matter.

It was expected that the acceptance, by the software developers, of the test-first practice within software projects would mean that they would consider applying it outside the pure software development realm. Unfortunately this was not the case. The rationale for testing third party libraries and interfaces (for example, OS interfaces) could not be made clear to the developers. The sense of satisfaction in having made a considerable effort to find an error and a corresponding workaround, totally overrode any sense that this could have been avoided had a test procedure been followed from the very beginning. Secondly, in the area of system design, it did not appear to occur to anybody that one could determine how a system is to be tested before it is actually built. It must be pointed out that all the development staff attended courses on XP based development.

An attempt was also made to design a hardware element using short iterations. This proved to be a costly lesson. Getting a board from finished design to actual prototype in ten days, a long period in XP terms, costs a significant amount of money and demands that all suppliers in the chain optimise their efforts. In the first instance the suppliers didn't perform as promised, which led to delays of up to over a month in getting the prototypes ready. Secondly, despite the successful completion of the initial iterations, the generation of a production-ready design, which consisted of the correction of two minor issues, suffered from severe problems. In this case the fact that the initial design hadn't been checked out of the repository properly wasn't discovered because those responsible didn't find the time to do the necessary pair-design. Whatever the specific lessons learned, the economic issues and interface with external suppliers will need to receive more consideration before XP can be successfully applied to hardware development.

2.3   General Remarks

As in [3], the desire amongst the senior developers for status symbols was a hindrance that threatened the establishment of the practices. Obviously XP requires stronger leadership than other management techniques. Difficulties were encountered in getting "old hands" to change their ways and getting "young bloods" to understand why they were supposed to work in this way. It appears that developers of a certain, median, experience level are required to apply XP successfully. On the other hand there was only one serious reaction against XP practices, out of a total exposure of about 15 development engineers.

It was expected that pair work and collective ownership would accelerate the learning curve of junior developers and lead to an higher common, knowledge and skills, denominator. On the hardware side this could not be tested due to lack of resources. In the software area, coaching was too passive, which led to the disappointing effect that, in several cases, code reviews had to be carried out. Whilst this didn't affect team performance, it significantly degraded the case for applying XP across the entire department.

The effect of high prototype and development turnover was achieved; an unusually high number of interacting features and elements could be completed in a short period of time. The effect of considering each feature a further iteration rather than a project in its own right, helped put in perspective the effort put into completing the feature which in turn helped achieve a very productive steady working state.

Applying XP department wide led to significant exposure in a political sense. The perceived lack of hard guidelines and the experimental nature of the undertaking required some hardened defense against partisan activity from some quarters. However, considering the experience two years on, the author would, if he considered the organisation could benefit from this approach, implement the techniques again.

References

1. Beck, K. Extreme Programming Explained: Embrace Change, *Addison-Wesley*, 2000.
2. Hassan, A.M., Elssamadisy, A. Extreme Programming and Database Administration: Problems, Solutions and Issues. *Proceedings XP 2002*. 2002.
3. Deias, R. Mugheddu, G. Murru, Orlando. Introducing XP in a start-up. *Proceedings XP 2002*. 2002.

Using Instructor Written Acceptance Tests
Using the Fit Framework

Daniel H. Steinberg

Dim Sum Thinking, Inc., 13938A Cedar Road #377
University Heights, OH 44118-3204
{daniel}@dimsumthinking.com

Abstract. With the recent release of the Fit framework, instructors can easily add acceptance testing into assignments in an introductory course in programming. In this paper we'll see how acceptance tests can be used by instructors to clarify the assignment and by students to check their progress. We'll also present an overview of the Fit framework and outline the differences between acceptance and unit testing in the classroom.

1   Introduction

A conversation began at XP Universe 2001 and 2002 that continued in a workshop at OOPSLA 2002 on which of the common XP practices could be easily integrated into an introductory course in programming in Java. At the top of the list were pair-programming, the planning game, and test first programming. A lot of discussion centered on how test first programming would be introduced. Some advocated using JUnit others felt that writing custom solutions that led students through the assignment would remove the burden of learning the JUnit APIs. An example of a custom solution can be found on O'Reilly's ONJava site [1].

Test first development has well documented benefits in commercial development [2], [3], and in the academic setting [4]. Benefits in the professional developer arena include more robust, flexible, and easier understood and maintained code. In the academic world, in addition to the reduced coupling and higher cohesion that is realized by all test first developers, beginning programmers don't need to impose a premature architecture by determining the entry points to their program.

Acceptance testing is a valuable tool in the commercial setting that has not been exploited in academia. The need is there but, until recently, the tools that support acceptance tests require extensive customization. Solutions often involved creating a custom language that could be easily parsed or using an existing language in which the clients could write restricted programs. Nathaniel Talbott considered these alternatives at the 2002 Ruby Conference [5].

In the past year, Ward Cunningham has released his Fit framework for acceptance testing [6] and Robert C. Martin has his Fitnesse application that incorporates Fit in a flexible, easy to use wiki environment[7]. The framework allows clients to write their

M. Marchesi and G. Succi (Eds.): XP 2003, LNCS 2675, pp. 378–385, 2003.

acceptance tests in the familiar setting of a spread sheet. Programmers can easily write the glue that allows the customer written tests to call into the application being tested. Customers can then remotely run the acceptance tests themselves and view the results.

In this paper, we'll consider how the Fit framework is successfully applied to the academic setting. The examples are taken from a tutorial in [8] that is available as a pdf file at [6]. The instructor can write the acceptance tests. Initially the instructor will write the glue layer. Later the students will take on this task. The glue layer does specify part of the, not necessarily public, interface of the application being built. Both the student developers and the instructor can regularly run the acceptance tests to gauge the progress on the assignment. Finally, it should be emphasized that acceptance tests do not replace unit testing. We'll look at the differences in expectation of these two types of testing in teaching students and address the inevitable questions of what content from the current curriculum must be dropped.

2   Accurately Specifying requirements

Typically problems that arise in describing programming assignments include the following.

- Evaluation criteria is not adequately specified in the problem description. Students are entitled to know what is important to the grading of the assignment.
- Inadvertently ill-defined problems that require clarification from the instructor after it is clear that students are misunderstanding or not understanding the problem description.
- Solution centric descriptions that lead the students step by step through the code they will need to create. Perhaps this may be appropriate in early programming assignments, students often follow the recipe provided without understanding what they have done or the reasons for these steps.

Using acceptance tests to describe a student assignment is one way to address these issues. Some proportion of evaluation can be tied to the passage of the various acceptance tests. Students can also be told that the actual values input in the final version of the acceptance tests will be changed to keep them from hard-coding solutions in. For example, an early Hello World type of program might require the user to input a name in a text field and then respond "Hello, <*input name here*>". Your acceptance test might input the name Stanley and then test that the program returns "Hello, Stanley". Students would know not to hard code Stanley into their solution because you might very well change your test data to Esmerelda. With an acceptance testing framework you can type the change in once and evaluate which student projects are resilient to this change.

Fit does not force you to specify your project more clearly or completely. It does, however encourage you to think in terms of how the software will be used and not how it is created. You will test end-to-end actions on the software. When you focus on the end user, the students are expected to problem solve to give the end user a particular experience. This tends to keep you from laying out step by step instructions of how the students will proceed. On the other hand, you will still be looking at the code the students create and can tell them that their solution must include a factory pattern, or a nested for loop, or a JTable, or whatever concept you are stressing at the time.

3   Writing the Customer Tests

Begin by downloading the fit framework from [6] or as part of the fitnesse download from [7]. On the websites you can see examples of types of tables that can be used along with fixtures that are included in the download. The framework parses the tables and maps the cell contents to method calls and variables. The first line of the table specifies the associated fixture. The fixture selection, in turn, specifies how the cells in the table are to be interpreted. Initially, there were three available fixtures. As the need arises, other fixtures such as [9] have been added. As educators begin to use Fit in our courses, we may develop our own set of supplemental fixtures that meet our particular needs.

For now, Fit ships with three basic fixtures. This first is designed to test the results of buttons being pushed and information being entered into text fields in a GUI. A second test may be used when you need to quickly set some values and check the results of performing various actions. A third type of test is used when you want to look at the characteristics of an object by querying it.

As an example, let's consider the second type of test. Here's an acceptance test for testing a cash register application.

register.CaseDiscountFixture		
unitPrice	numberPurchased	itemTotal()
800	1	800
800	5	4000
800	12	9120
800	17	13120
800	24	18240
800	29	22240
800	1200	912000
4	12	46

Fig. 1. A sample Fit acceptance test where the itemTotal() should represent the amount due for purchasing the number of items in the numberPurchased column at the individual price specified in the unitPrice column.

The first line specifies that this table will be handled by the Java class CaseDiscountFixture in the register package. The next line indicates that the first column will contain values to be input to the variable unitPrice and the second contains values to be input to the variable numberPurchased. The third column contains values that are expected to be returned by a call to the method itemTotal(). The values returned will be compared to the values in the table.

register.CaseDiscountFixture		
unitPrice	numberPurchased	itemTotal()
800	1	800
800	5	4000
800	12	9120 expected
		9600 actual
800	17	13120 expected
		13600 actual
800	24	18240 expected
		19200 actual
800	29	22240 expected
		23200 actual
800	1200	912000 expected
		960000 actual
4	12	46 expected
		48 actual

Fig. 2. The results of running a Fit acceptance tests displayed in the same table as the original specification. In a color rendering the successful tests for the first two items would result in the itemTotal() cells being colored green. For the tests that fail the cells are red and split vertically into two subcells. The top reports the expected value that was specified in the cell and the bottom reports the actual value returned by the application being tested.

If they agree then the test will indicate passage by coloring the cell green, if they don't agree then the test results will show the expected and actual results and color code that cell red. In the figure above, the top two test results have passed and the remainder have failed.

As a second example, let's look at a GUI acceptance test.

fit.ActionFixture		
start	register.MiscItemFixture	
press	miscButton	
check	display	Enter Unit Price
enter	unitPrice	800
check	display	800
press	enterButton	
check	display	Misc Grocery 800
press	timesButton	
check	display	Enter number of items
enter	numberOfItems	5
check	display	5
press	doneButton	
check	display	4000
check	totalCost	4000

Fig. 3. This Fit acceptance test exercises a GUI. The results of pressing buttons is checked and the contents of the display is verified.

Here there are four keywords, anyone of which can be used in the first column. The start keyword ties the table to the fixture that responds to the GUI commands. The top line indicates that the fit.ActionFixture class will be used to process this table. The enter and press keywords correspond to entering information in text boxes and pressing buttons. Finally, the check keyword is how we check the results of the data entry and button pressing.

4   Writing the Fixtures

Each table that you create requires a supporting fixture. It helps to think of lessons you've learned in creating GUIs. The major lesson is that the GUI should be as thin as possible. A secondary lesson is that the methods in the GUI can be public while the methods that they in turn call can be package private or private. Similarly, the fixtures should be very thin. They should call back into the application being tested.

The code corresponding to the first example, may be as simple as this.

```
package register;

import fit.ColumnFixture;

public class CaseDiscountFixture extends ColumnFixture{

    public int unitPrice;

    public int numberPurchased;
```

```
public int itemTotal(){
   Item item = new Item(unitPrice);
   item.addToOrder(numberPurchased);
   return item.totalItemCost();
   }
}
```

You can see in the code listing that very little actual work is done in the fixture. Just as with writing unit tests first, students learn that part of the interface has been specified for them. In this example, they will need to create a class Item.java that contains an addToOrder() method that takes an int and a totalItemCost() method that returns an int.

Pedagogically, this is one of the first skills I want to develop in my students. I want them to be able to see how others expect to interact with objects they are creating and what that implies about the code they are writing. Often once they leave our classrooms they will have to write pieces that interact with existing code. They will seldom be expected to write an entire application from end to end.

In this example the students will have to write the business logic that correctly calculates the cost of buying one or more of a particular item. In this case, they must also include a volume discount. The acceptance tests can help students determine that they have adequately written this logic. They should not be writing the logic in the CaseDiscountFixture class but in the client Item class and the classes that it uses.

In the second example, the fixture code does little more but act as an adapter into the production code.

```
package register;
import fit.Fixture;


public class MiscItemFixture extends Fixture{
   private ManualEntry manualEntry;
   public void miscButton(){
     manualEntry = new ManualEntry();
   }
   public void enterButton(){
     manualEntry.createItemWithPrice();
   }
   public void doneButton(){
     manualEntry.setNumberOfItems();

   }
```

```
public int totalCost(){
  return manualEntry.getTotalCost();
}
public String display(){
  return manualEntry.getDisplay();
}
public void unitPrice(int unitPrice){
  manualEntry.enterUnitPrice(unitPrice);
}
public void numberOfItems(int numberOfItems){
  manualEntry.enterNumberOfItems(numberOfItems);
}
public void timesButton(){
  manualEntry.buyMoreThanOne();
}
}
```

In introductory classes we often don't convince our students of the benefits of packaging and access modifiers. Here they can see the benefits of putting their ManualEntry class in the same package as the test fixture. They can then choose to limit the access level of their methods. As the students mature and begin to understand the structure and purpose of the various fixtures, they can begin to write their own supporting fixture code. The tables and fixture type go a long way towards specifying the interface of the corresponding fixture. They won't be ready for this responsibility at the beginning of the course but should quickly grow into this role. By the second assignment students will be writing their unit tests before they write the code that makes them pass.

5   Unit Tests vs. Acceptance Tests

Traditionally we don't introduce students to testing in a first course in programming. In this course students are introduced to testing as they are introduced to programming. This actually helps them separate the notions of unit testing and acceptance testing. For one thing, acceptance testing will be used to determine if they have minimally satisfied the requirements of the assignment. The acceptance tests are written by someone else throughout the semester while they will take over the responsibility of writing unit tests as well as the fixtures for the acceptance tests.

The relationship of the test code to their production code is very different. Many acceptance tests will be initially failing. Students will see progress as they get one after another of the acceptance tests to pass. Acceptance tests are the finish line for this week long race. Students should never ignore a failing unit test. By the time they have a suite of failing Unit tests, their code will be in need of attention that may be beyond their abilities.

In an introductory course, there may be confusion over what role the instructor is playing. The instructor acts as the customer, coach, teacher, and evaluator. The instructor may run the suite of unit tests. The students need to understand that the instructor is not doing so in their role as customer. The instructor will need to verbalize or visually denote the role being occupied so that the students aren't confused.

6   What Must Be Eliminated from the Curriculum

There is concern that if we are teaching test driven development and acceptance testing in the first course, then other material must be eliminated. In practice, we've found that working with acceptance and unit tests serve as vehicles for teaching material we have previously covered in a setting that means more to the students. As was mentioned, we have always covered packaging and access privileges, but students often didn't see the point until they had to have client code calling into their code. Once they have used and later written fixtures, they understand the advantages of placing the fixture in the same package as the class being accessed. They also understand that code in the same package may end up in different jars. This has led to students asking deployment questions that are answered, for example, by Ant. We would never have dared to introduce Ant in an introductory course before.

You will still have curricular goals. The acceptance tests provide another clear evaluation objective. In the past you, no doubt, insisted that student code compiles. Now you can also inform the students what amount of credit corresponds to having passing unit and acceptance tests. Once code compiles, runs, and passes a suite of tests, you can concentrate on the quality of the code and work with the students to refactor while paying attention to the characteristics of good coding that you are trying to impart.

References

1. Steinberg, D H, Teaching Java the Extreme Way, ONJava On-line at http://www.onjava.com/pub/a/onjava/2002/ 10/09/javaxp2.html
2. Beck, K, Test Driven Development:By Example. Addison Wesley, 2002.
3. Fowler, M et. al, Refactoring: Improving the Design of Existing Code. Addison-Wesley, 1999.
4. Steinberg, D H, The effect of Unit Tests on Entry Points, Coupling, and Cohesion in an Introductory Java Programming Course, 2001 XP Universe Papers. On-line at http://www.xpuniverse.com/2001/xpuPapers.htm
5. Talbott, N, "Are we done yet": Thoughts on acceptance testing. 2002 Ruby Conference http://www.rubyconf.org.
6. The Fit Wiki is available on-line at http://fit.c2.com.
7. The Fitnesse Wiki is available on-line at http://fitnesse.org.
8. Palmer, D W and Steinberg, D H, Hands-on Software Engineering, Prentice-Hall, 2004.
9. Martin, R C, Command Line Fixture available on-line at http://fit.c2.com/wiki.cgi?CommandLineFixture.

Teaching Team Work:
An Extreme Week for First-Year Programmers

Petra Becker-Pechau, Holger Breitling, Martin Lippert, and Axel Schmolitzky

Software Engineering Group, Faculty of Computer Science, University of Hamburg
Vogt-Kölln-Straße 30, 22527 Hamburg, Germany
{becker,breitling,lippert,schmolit}@informatik.uni-hamburg.de

Abstract. Professional software development implies team work. Therefore working in a team should be an essential part in the software engineering curriculum. We use Extreme Programming (XP) as a high-discipline software development methodology to teach software engineering within a team quite early in the curriculum. This seems not easy at first sight, as XP is aimed mainly at experienced programmers. But XP is highly motivating for students if it can be applied within the framework of a real project. After their first year of programming, students at the University of Hamburg get the chance to take part in a three week project that includes one week of intensive programming. This programming week in the middle is organized following XP principles. In this paper we describe the way we adopt XP for this week, argue about the circumstances for a compact XP-like software engineering week, and reflect on the experience we made.

1   Introduction

At which point in a software engineering curriculum should students be introduced to working in teams? Is team programming an advanced topic only for graduate students or should students start working in teams from day one? We think that programming in a team should be practiced as soon as possible, and be repeated in an iterative and incremental style during the curriculum. That is, as soon as the most basic programming skills are taught, students should be introduced to collaborative development tasks in a project-like setting.

Computer science students at the University of Hamburg in Germany start with learning logic and functional programming (Prolog and Scheme) in semester 1 and proceed with imperative and object-oriented programming (Java) in semester 2. In the summer break after semester 2, i.e., after their first year of programming, students should take part in one of several labs offered. The Software Engineering Group offers a course on object-oriented programming that is equivalent to a one-week full-time lab. The implementation part of it is organized as a project following XP principles.

M. Marchesi and G. Succi (Eds.): XP 2003, LNCS 2675, pp. 386–393, 2003.

At this stage of their curriculum, most students are not experienced programmers and have little experience with the design of object-oriented systems. Furthermore they have no experience with source code control systems, as it is typically their first time being part of a development team. Following the classification described by Cockburn [2], they are stage one programmers. Stage one programmers program by strictly *following* rules (coding standards, XP practices and the like). Following the rules takes their full attention, typically not leaving much room for reflection. After having collected substantial experience, programmers in stage two start trying alternatives. They break rules here and then, just to see if things still work, they *detach*. Finally, stage three programmers have gained enough experience to combine any given practices, as long as the combination serves its purpose - they are *fluent*.

In this paper we describe the experience we made with the stage one programmers in the course mentioned above. As with every learning person in this stage, the instructor plays an important role. Thus we also describe our view of the roles the instructors have to play under the given circumstances.

In the next section we sketch the setting of the course. In section 3 we describe the core of the project, the extreme week. In section 4 we collect the experience we made with the XP practices we integrated. Section 5 adds our thoughts on the instructor's role in a compact XP-like software engineering week, and in the conclusion we reflect on the overall experience we made using XP for this course.

2   The Setting

The lab is organized as a compact full-time project. The core of it is one week of intensive programming (the extreme week). To make this week as effective as possible, preparation and wrap-up are moved in the weeks before and after the extreme week. Therefore, the complete course is spread over three weeks. It starts with a kick-off meeting and is concluded by a wrap-up meeting.

Typically there are three parallel project groups. Each project group consists of 12 to 18 students and is coached full-time by one or two members of the Software Engineering Group (these are members of the scientific staff, most of them with professional XP experience). Each group has its own development room.

In the one-day kick-off meeting at the beginning of week one the students get only a rough idea of the project goal, a theoretical introduction to XP and an introduction to the programming environment with CVS integration, Eclipse 2.0. After this meeting the students have time to prepare for week two, the programming week. They use this time to solve some small assignments that get them in touch with the necessary libraries, technologies and the IDE. The students do this group-wise – how they organise themselves is up to them.

The programming week consists of five one-day iterations, as described in more detail in the next section, and is conducted following XP-principles. In this paper we focus on the programming week.

The wrap-up meeting at the end of week three consists of a final presentation of the running system in front of the complete group (including all coaches and students) and a reflective discussion. The time between the programming week and the final wrap-up meeting is used by the students to prepare the presentations (some still apply a final touch to their programs,).

3   The Extreme Week

One week of programming is only a limited amount of time and the students are not experienced OO developers after their first year of programming. Thus we decided to adopt only a subset of the XP practices within the programming week while keeping all the XP values and principles [1] in mind. We selected the set of practices with the teamwork goal in mind as well as pre-judging their knowledge level.

In this section we describe which XP practices we integrated into the programming week and which we left out intentionally. We use a cookbook style of description that might serve as a guideline to others.

Practices Integrated
On-Site Customer: The members of the Software Engineering Group that coach the project groups also play the customers for the projects. The customers are available all day during the whole week.

User Stories: The customers tell the stories they want the students to implement. The students write these stories down on story cards that are under control of the development team. During customer feedback meetings (see *Small Releases*) the students write additional story cards based on the feedback of the customer.

Simple Design and *YAGNI (You Ain't Gonna Need It)*: The coaches encourage the students to keep their designs simple and to not plan and implement too much ahead. The coaches follow all design discussions and comment as necessary.

Coding Standards: Coding standards are even more necessary in the given setting than they are within XP in general, as the participants are learners in stage one. The coding standards should contain lots of examples.

Pair Programming: All programming is done in pairs. Pairs have to change at least once a day. For odd numbers of students a coach can help out as a programmer.

Testing: The concepts of systematic testing, automated tests and test first have been introduced upfront (in semester 2). In the programming week the students get the chance to realise the necessity of rigid testing in a larger setting. Testing is strongly encouraged but not enforced by the coaches.

Refactoring: The students are told that refactoring can help in keeping the design simple while the system evolves. Since refactoring is hard for non-experienced programmers, the coaches offer support.

Continuous Integration: The students are encouraged to integrate as often as possible during the day - ideally about every half an hour. This trains their abilities to solve integration conflicts and eases the releases.

Collective Ownership: The coaches stress that all code in the repository belongs to all project members. Every team member should feel responsible for any code that is integrated. In this context the *truck factor* gets introduced as well, as it illustrates the difficulties that arise when a team member bails out, even for just one day.

Small Releases: The customers expect a release every evening. With each release they expect increased business value. They perform acceptance tests *live* and give immediate feedback from the customer's point of view.

Stand-Up Meeting: Every half-day a stand-up meeting is held (the instructors participate as coaches only). Each student has to give a short report (at most one minute) on what she was doing the day before and what she is planning to do next. This helps to create team awareness.

Practices Left Out

The following practices were left out mainly due to the time constraints.

Estimations: No estimations for stories are made, as the planning aspects of XP are not in the centre of interest for the course. The stories are prioritised by the customers and implemented in that order.

Metaphor: The system to be built during the programming week is too small to make metaphors really necessary. Architectural considerations are subject at a later stage in the curriculum. We decided to leave it out of an early XP project for first-year programmers. Nevertheless we definitively believe in the importance of metaphors, see [4].

4   Observations

The set of chosen practices worked considerably well in all project groups. On the one hand, the students enjoyed the programming work and they were all highly motivated during that week. On the other hand, they practised teamwork in a real-world-like project setting. They learned a lot about teamwork because the setting enforced typical problems to occur. For example: Two pairs had to implement something closely interconnected. They solved this difficult situation by talking to each other and implementing some very simple interface definitions together. After that they split up again for each group to work on its problem. The two groups kept sitting close to each other to exchange updates and changes.

Nevertheless, not all practices worked as expected. Therefore we give a short report here on selected practices and our experience with them. We also include some thoughts on what we will do differently next time.

Pair Programming

Pair programming was very well accepted by the students. However, some had problems with frequent pair changes because they could not see the advantage of it. Only at the end of the extreme week, when the application built became more complex, did they appreciate the group awareness and knowledge spread that comes with it.

We tried different ways to introduce frequent pair changes to the students. The one was to enforce changes rather strictly to cope with a certain opposition we felt every time we wanted them to change pairs: pairs had to be changed after lunch, period. The other approach was more flexible and trusting in the students' ability to organise things for themselves. The coaches just reminded them from time to time to change pairs, which they did mostly after task completions.

When changing pairs, some students complained how much it slowed them down to introduce their new pair partners to the system parts they were just working on. This occurred especially with the strict approach. All in all, we have to state that the flexible approach seems more appropriate when there is a minimum of good will among the students because it fits much better with the XP values (communication, courage).

Testing

When introduced to the students, the real benefit of unit testing was not recognised. Consequentially, they utilized it only on the most elementary level.

Later on, when larger parts of the system were restructured and changed, many programming errors could be uncovered even by those elementary unit tests. With this experience, the students made additional efforts to improve the unit test base.

As an addition, acceptance tests could be implemented by the customers. Steimann et. al. [3] describe how to structure a whole programming lab with pre-defined acceptance tests.

Refactoring

Refactoring was necessary in some groups, but only for small parts and with substantial support by the instructors. Refactoring needs a lot of experience, not owned by first year students. Consequently, one benefit of automated tests (easier refactorings) could not be experienced. Unit tests were requested by the instructors, but time was too short to let the students experience problems with missing tests. Advanced courses emphasise this practice more.

Story Cards

The usage of Story Cards led to an intensive communication between customer and developers. Many questions regarding the stories were asked and the group experienced the benefits of having a customer on-site. They experienced that it is not possible nor feasible to write everything down. That way, we managed to communicate the idea that a story card is "a promise for conversation".

The next thing we taught the students was to transform nontrivial story cards into several task cards. Those task cards were then placed on a table (in another group: on a white board) for later completion and acted as a to-do list. It seems a very good thing to establish such a special place for the task cards. It instantly meant something to the students. Once explained, the task card handling was easily adopted and successfully practised until the project's end.

On-site Customer

The most important thing for the instructors was to differentiate the customer role clearly from the role as the coach. They did so by explicitly declaring: "I now speak as your customer:...".

When the students presented releases, we assumed our customer role only. We did not give any advice on the coaching level then.

This clear separation worked very well. Even when talking to a coach, the students would start their sentences with "Our customers told us they want..." and the like.

Simple Design

The idea of simple design was supported by our strong emphasis on the customer's role. Through the customer's wishes we could stress how important it was to reach a certain functionality as fast as possible. In our role as coaches, we could use this as an argument and convince the students not to invest much time in big upfront design.

Stand-up Meeting

During the daily stand-up meetings students became aware of the whole process and of problems even if they did not experience them personally. The coaches used questions or problems raised at this meeting to introduce or discuss instructive topics such as new practices or system architecture issues.

Not only during the stand-up meeting, but the whole time, the coaches pointed out problems they observed. The students were not always able to clearly identify those problems due to their lack of experience. This way, learning was driven by experience.

5   The Roles of the Instructor

Aside of the practices used we found out that the instructor plays a major part within the project. It seems to be more important to have an experienced XP trainer than to choose the right set of practices. Therefore we also reflect on the role of the instructor within the project. This might be used as a guideline for others.

For a teaching project like ours, it is beneficial if the instructors play both the roles of the coach and the customer. It simplifies the communication for the students because they do not have to deal with different representatives. It also saves time, which is helpful within a one week programming project. For the instructors, it has the advantage that they are always fully informed about both the coaches' and the customers' communication with the students.

It is crucial that – as described before – the instructors draw a clear line of separation between their two roles.

5.1   The Coach Role in the Extreme Week

- Because the students do not have enough time to reflect on the project, the coach has to fill this gap. He has to watch the group very carefully and to intervene if necessary.

- However, the coach should not intervene all the time and not present solutions before a problem has been experienced. He introduces ideas and concepts when problems have popped up or are brought up by the students in the stand-up meetings. This makes for problem-oriented, experience-driven learning.
- From our experience, the degree of the coach's presence diminishes, even in one small extreme week.
- The students have never programmed in a team, therefore inevitably questions concerning the overall architecture and design arise. The coach's task is to guide the discussion and to help with the selection of possible solutions.
- Because the students are inexperienced programmers, the coach has to help with programming from time to time. Sometimes he should even make decisions if discussion simply takes too long.

5.2   The Customer Role in the Extreme Week

- The customer „tells" the stories and prioritises them. But there is no estimation and hence no planning game in the original sense.
- The customer represents „fate". This means that he may sometimes remove story cards or change their order which may come as a surprise to the students. These surprises make sense if the customer and coach role are assumed by the same person who knows when there are problems or violations of XP principles. The customer's action can serve to show the students their problems. Besides, a customer's change of mind is not unusual in software development reality.
- The customer provides explicit feedback when releases are presented. He has no interest in technical explanations and focuses on functionality and usability instead.

6   Conclusion

We used XP to teach first years students how software is developed within a project team. XP, with its focus on explicit communication, turned out to be a good method to introduce students to typical challenges and techniques for team programming. Especially continuous integration, collective ownership and small releases encourage the students to coordinate their tasks between programming pairs.

At the described stage of their curriculum (after their first year of programming), most students are not experienced programmers. As stage one programmers (in Cockburn's classification) they lack two important requirements for aggressive refactoring: experience and courage. We think it is hard if not impossible to improve this situation upfront. But as refactoring can easily be practiced by a single programmer on his own later on, it need not necessarily be addressed in a first year teaching project on team development.

Being stage one programmers, the students further have to rely on the guidelines and advice the instructors give them. Thus the qualification of the instructor is quite important. The instructor must be able play both the role of the customer and of the coach, but he must also be able to clearly separate the two roles.

Acknowledgements

We would like to thank the other members of the Software Engineering Group who made the Extreme Week possible. Special thanks to Martti Jeenicke for his great support and coaching. We also thank the students of the course for their motivated work during the three weeks.

References

1. Beck, K. eXtreme Programming - Embrace Change. Addison-Wesley, Boston, MA, 2000.
2. Cockburn, A. Agile Software Development. Addison-Wesley, Boston, MA, 2002.
3. Steimann, F., Gößner, J., Mück, T. Filleting XP for Educational Purposes, XP 2003.
4. Lippert, M., Schmolitzky, A., Züllighoven, H., Metaphor Design Spaces, XP 2003.

Design-led & Design-less:
One Experiment and Two Approaches

Francisco Macias, Mike Holcombe, and Marian Gheorghe

University of Sheffield, Regent Court
211 Portobello Street, Sheffield, S1 4DP, UK
{f.macias,m.holcombe,m.gheorghe}@dcs.shef.ac.uk
(+44) 114 222 1800

Abstract. This report presents an experiment comparing two lightweight methodologies. The objective of the experiment was to assess extreme programming seen as a design-less process and an agile methodology based on design. The experiment ran in a real environment. Twenty teams produced 20 systems, from scratch to the final product, in a period of one semester. They attended 4 clients. The factors of the experiment were time, quality and size. The systems written by extreme programming teams were slightly better than "agile design-based" teams. This findings show that a mature/improved version of extreme programming should be much more successful.

1 Introduction

The movement triggered by Kent Beck in 1998 has found many followers, and also has received criticises. The most evident fact so far is that this philosophy will not finish in the attic of the forgotten good ideas, but is valid to ask if this philosophy represents a panacea in the field of Software Engineering something better is still coming. At this point an empirical assessment is required.

The paper reports an experiment intended to assess the process of agile methodologies, particularly eXtreme Programming. In recent years have been done several efforts to assess some aspects of eXtreme Programming. Empirical investigation faces some important problems like the extent of the assessment (often only some aspects are assessed) or the environment of the experiment (frequently the problem to solve is too artificial). Evaluating isolated aspects of a method is difficult; evaluating a whole method is hard difficult. Dealing with a laboratory environment is also difficult. Dealing with a real business environment is even more difficult. The experiment was designed bearing in mind an assessment of the whole process embedded in a real environment.

Through this experiment we have considered two different approaches (treatments) to the software construction process, the first one is extreme Programming (XP). The second is an improved version of the traditional software construction process. It is a design based process which also emphasises first testing and the values proposed for agile methodologies. So we have a design-less (XP) process and a design-led (agile V-model) process.

M. Marchesi and G. Succi (Eds.): XP 2003, LNCS 2675, pp. 394–401, 2003.

Section 2 depicts the environment of the experiment, which includes a brief description of the projects, the skills of the students and the objective of the experiment. The next section, 3, provides the formal description of the experiment; the metrics and the collection method are also given in this section. Section 4 includes a brief description of the raw data and the results obtained from the inferential statistics. Section 5 presents the interpretation of the results.

2   Context of the Experiment

This formal experiment was carried out with the purpose to provide scientific evidence to either give support or to reject the claim that eXtreme Programming is a valid software production process, which is better than traditional approaches. Bearing in mind this purpose we identify "traditional approach" (or traditional programming) as the process that includes and emphasises the Design as a central role. The intended methodology reflects the strategy for agile processes, particularly the "first testing" practice. The students using this method should produce black box test sets then combine these sets with the requirements produced in order to obtain the specification. After this step, they should produce the "design" that leads the rest of the process, this means "implementation", "testing" and finally "delivering". On the other hand we identify eXtreme Programming as the agile process authored by Kent Beck [Beck 99-1, Beck 99-2].

The context of this experiment was a mixture of an academic and a business environment. The students at The University of Sheffield in the 4th semester have to attend a practical module called the Software Hut Project (SHP). In Spring/2002, twenty teams of students worked to produce 20 software systems for 4 real clients. The clients, referred to as A, B, C and D, were:

Client A. Small Firms Enterprise Development Initiative (SFEDI) provides advice and support to small businesses nationally. They wanted a web site for their employees that allow them to distribute general documents, policies, and procedures and make them accessible away from their main office. Some documents need only to be read while other need to be filled in. They wanted to restrict the access to certain documents according to the category of the employee accessing them. SFEDI employees have a fairly good level of computer literacy.

Client B. The School of Clinical Dentistry at the University of Sheffield conducts research using questionnaires to collect information about patients. The data generated from these questionnaires is used for a variety of purposes. The School required a system that allows them to customise the online questionnaires and subsequently produce a file containing the data submitted. Every questionnaire should have its own password. The generation of the questionnaire should be very simple and it should be usable by anyone with low computer literacy.

Client C. University for Industry (UFI) was created with its partner Learn Direct; the largest publicly founded on-line education service in the UK. In order to analyse performance and predict future trends, they need to collate and analyse information such as the number of web-site hits or help-line calls at different times of the day and the number of new registrations. The proposed problem was to construct a statistical analysis programme for UFI. The system will have two types of users: the main system user and the intranet user. Their range of ability among these users is wide.

Client D. The National Health Service Cancer Screening Program keeps an archive of journals and key articles that they provide for consulting. They required a system which was simple to use and easy to maintain that allowed them to 1) catalogue the existing collection, 2) add new articles, 3) expand the collection, 4) link associated articles and 5) find and retrieve articles quickly and effectively. A member of the staff will maintain the system. The client has no special preference for the system appearance or operation beyond the requirement that it should be easy to use, install and maintain.

The students engaged in Software Hut Project already know how to write programs, data structures, specifications, and produce web pages. They should produce a complete solution for their client during this semester. At the beginning of this semester they attend a training module either on eXtreme Programming or on a traditional (Design-led) approach.

Each team of students worked with only one client and depending on the nature of the required software they worked with Java or PHP and SQL. From the objectives stated and its connection with the background theory these hypotheses were stated:

Null hypothesis: The use of eXtreme Programming in a software construction process produces as good results (external and internal quality) as those obtained from the use of traditional processes (in the average case of a small /medium size project).

Alternative hypothesis: The use of eXtreme Programming in a software construction process produces different results than those obtained from the application of traditional processes.

These hypotheses emerge from the discussion about the validity of eXtreme Programming. These hypothesis were tuned through the pilot study that ran during Spring/2001 semester [Holcombe 01, Macias 02]. There are managers and developers [Moore 02, Putnam 02, Rumpe 02, Wright 02] who see eXtreme Programming as a suitable alternative for software production process.

3   Design of the Experiment

There were two treatments (eXtreme Programming and Traditional Approach), four blocks (clients A, B, C, and D), and 20 experimental units (the teams of students attending SHP). The students organised themselves into teams and the teams were randomly allocated among the blocks and the treatments. The experiment was organised as Randomised Complete Block Design. This means that every block (client) received the two treatments. Five teams were allocated to each client as shown in table 1.

There were three factors to measure: Time spent in the production process, Quality of the product and Size of the product. Time was measured in hours. Quality was split into two aspects: external and internal. These were quantitatively represented in a scale from 0 to 50. Size was obtained directly from the final product through counting items, it was included in the final report.

In order to gauge the Time factor we measure seven different aspects: time (in hours) spent in doing "research", "preparing requirements", "writing specification and design, "coding", "testing", "reviewing" and "other" generic activities. The values for this factor were collected every week/team automatically. Once this collection ran, we verified the data through interviews with the members of each team.

Table 1. Distribution of teams

		Treatments	
		XP	Design-led
Blocks	A	5, 7, 8	18, 20
	B	2, 6	12, 14, 17
	C	1, 9	11, 13, 19
	D	3, 4, 10	15, 16

The data of Quality factor was obtained from two different sources. The first one, External Quality, was provided by the clients. They assessed 10 aspects: "presentation", "user manual", "installation guide", "ease of use", "error handling", "understandablity", "base functionality", "innovation", "robustness", and "happiness". Client D did not assess Robustness given the nature of the required system. The second, Internal Quality, was provided by the lecturers. They assessed 7 aspects for the teams under the eXtreme Programming treatment and 6 for the teams in the traditional approach. The first 7 items were "requirements document", "test cases", "test management process", "test results", "coding standards", "user documentation" and a "general commentary". Such a commentary included log, milestones, strategies, description, and plan. The 6 items assessed for the traditional treatment were: "requirements document", "detailed design", "test results", coding standards", "user documentation" and a "general commentary". Again, the general commentary included log, milestones, strategies, description and plan.

In order to assess the size of the product we focus on the quantity of requirements and the number of test cases. The requirements split into functional and non-functional. Functional requirements were sub-classified according to the priority: high, medium, and low. Non-functional requirements included "reliability", "usability", "efficiency", "maintainability", and "portability". The test cases were not sub-classified.

The data to measure Time were collected every week. The teams were required fill in two forms (timesheets and minutes) electronically, and these forms were automatically collected. The clients and lecturers provided the data for Quality at the end of the semester. The size of the project was assessed when the projects' final version was available.

4   Results

The results of the experiment have been gathered into the three factors we have measured. The data collected from timesheets and minutes was verified through interviews with the teams. At the end of the semester those data were gathered in a single matrix. These data showed people working with eXtreme Programming spent less time - percentage- than the design based approach in the following activities: research (less than 1% vs. 3%), specification and design (7% vs. 14%), coding (36% vs. 42%), and miscellaneous activities (12% vs. 17%). On the other hand eXtreme Programming teams spent more time in these activities: testing (20% vs. 7%), review (11% vs. 1%). In requirements they spent equally (14%). The distribution of activities also showed a pattern depending on the treatment. eXtreme Programming teams started to test the code earlier during the process of construction. The analysis of variance (ANOVA) for total time vs. treatment provided the values F=6.48 and P=0.020.

The factor Quality, considered as a whole, shows better average in eXtreme Programming teams than the design based approach. The same can be observed when considering Internal and External Quality separately. eXtreme Programming present better average. But the overlapping of the Confidence Interval is higher than 50% in both cases. Running the test of Analysis of Variance (ANOVA) we obtained these results: External Quality vs. treatment F=0.65, P=0.43, Internal Quality vs. treatment F=1.87, P=0.19, and total Quality vs. treatment F=1.39, P=0.25.

The total amount of requirements was, on average, higher in teams of eXtreme Programming than Design based teams. The average of the functional requirements was higher in eXtreme Programming teams, but the average amount of Non-functional requirements was higher in Design based systems. The number of test cases was higher also for eXtreme Programming teams. The values obtained through de ANOVA test were: total amount of requirements vs. treatment F=0.02, P=0.891, and test cases vs. treatment F=1.53, P=0.232.

5   Discussion

The first challenge faced during the experiment was to ensure that teams followed the treatment. Hence the importance of the timesheets and minutes. From the results it was possible to establish that the teams generally followed their respective treatments. The teams dealing with the extreme programming treatments spent, on average, more time than the teams dealing with the traditional treatment. This fact is easy to explain as extreme programming encourages communication. A good example of this is pair programming. Pair programming requires two people working simultaneously with the same piece of code. This way of working has many advantages, e.g. the quality of the code is higher [Williams 00], the skills of the members of the teams develop more evenly, and the success of the project does not rely on a super-programmer but on teamwork.

Minimising the stage of Design in a software construction process is in itself a revolutionary step. The traditional software construction process, including a well-defined and well-distinguished Design stage, is widely accepted, and in fact, some variants of the traditional process promote the production of a very finely defined Design. Design has two mainstreams: the architecture of the system and the details for further implementation. Extreme programming substitutes architecture with an overall metaphor, and the details for implementation is with the implementation itself. The idea here is: if you have to think about and then write all these details, do it straight to code and avoid the intermediary step, this means do not write it twice [Beck 99-2, Fowler 01]. And then if the requirements change there are fewer overheads.

Extreme programming encourages simplicity, particularly in the Design. In this experiment we have seen that teams working with a Design-less production process obtain similar results (sometimes slightly better) than teams working with the traditional Design-led process. It should be expected that if you remove an important piece of construction (Design) from a process (software construction) you will not be able to obtain the same quality or complete product, but something rather strange, incomplete or a bad functioning product. This is an important result and points to the value of Simplicity and the practice of direct implementation of extreme programming.

An objective discussion should consider the uneven situation of the treatments, given the fact that one of them is more mature than the other. It is to be expected that a new procedure may lack maturity as a process. The development of the process removes unnecessary steps, emphasises relevant aspects and provides health and strength to the whole process. If it is expected that such a procedure have wide use, scope or impact the maturity process could be long and difficult. The traditional approach, design based has been generally accepted in different situations, and the general frame of Analysis-Design-Implementation-Testing-Maintenance has been accepted even further than the scope of a software construction process. Extreme programming does not have such a privilege, it is a very new idea and is only in the initial stages. From this perspective, it is surprising that extreme programming has provided as good a result as the traditional approach. We are far from being able to predict which subset of the practices could survive, maybe all of them or only few of them, maybe the practitioners will provide new practices. What we have seen is that teams working with black box testing-based analysis, testing based on requirements, simple design, planning game, pair programming, coding standards, collective ownership, continuous integration, small releases and minor scale of metaphors and refactoring have been as successful as teams working with a traditional approach which emphasised testing and standards. We are aware that no team worked either 40 hours week or with an on-site customer and so one could argue that the full extreme programming process was not used.

Internal quality factors were not related to external quality factors. External quality factors refer to those that can be detected by users and were based on the final products. Internal quality factors related to quality of process and intermediate deliverables and documents. The client assessed the external, and the lecturers assessed the internal. Two clients, the NHS Cancer Screening Program and the School of Dentistry asked for simple systems. The simpler the interface the happier the client. They required systems that were simple to learn, use, and maintain. The other two users did not look for simplicity but for more innovative systems. On the other hand, the lecturers assessed extreme programming teams and traditional teams in different aspects, according to the treatment, e.g. traditional teams were assessed on the detailed design while extreme programming teams were assessed on the specification of test cases. Neither external quality nor internal quality were always assessed exactly under the same rules for all the teams, but despite the differences the variability was low, as observed in the ANOVA results. Looking for a relationship among both quality factors, we ran a correlation coefficient test. It showed a very low (0.33) possibility of relationship among them.

There are some other factors that we can only infer, as they are not easy to measure. Among the aspects we have to consider there is the cost of the technology and the cost of the coaching required in order to maintain the practices. Technology always has a high cost, indeed, often the higher the technology the higher the cost. Extreme programming was originally thought of as a low technology requiring process [Beck 98]. Even with other added characteristics, extreme programming still remains a low technology requiring process. Such a requirement makes it less expensive than other approaches that require expensive, elaborate or more sophisticated technology. Some people [Sharifabdi 02] have found that coaching is important in extreme programming. It is important here to remember that this coaching is not a continuing cost, given the fact that extreme programming promotes the even development of skills among the members of the team, through practices like pair programming and collective ownership. Beck [Beck 99-2] suggests that the leader of the team should be rotated after certain periods of time. Based on this assumption, it is expected that after a certain period of time any member of the team should be able to coach the team.

In general terms, the validation of the equality side of the null hypothesis should not be seen as an equal situation between the treatments but as a fertile field of opportunities for this young approach.

6   Conclusion

The objective of the experiment was to assess extreme programming. With this purpose, it was compared with a design-led approach, which played the role of a control treatment. The observable practices followed by the teams in extreme programming treatment were: planning game, testing, pair programming, simple design, coding standards, collective ownership, continuous integration, small releases, and some cases of metaphors and refactoring. They did not follow "40 hours week" nor "on site customer". The teams followed an additional practice: testing based on requirements.

In this experiment, the null hypothesis was accepted, and the alternative hypothesis was rejected. This means that the results supported the fact that extreme programming teams produced as good results as the design-led approach. The implications of these results are very important. The most relevant one for the Software Engineering community is that a procedure free design provides as good results as one including design. The lack of design resulted from applying extreme programming.

Internal quality and external quality are unrelated. The behaviour of the internal quality factors was not related to the behaviour of the internal factors. This means that some systems could present good user characteristics and poor internal construction, or good internal construction and poor presentation for the user, or any other combination between external and internal characteristics. But there was not any observable pattern, according to the data from the correlation coefficient.

The rejection of the alternative hypothesis and the similar results (final product) obtained from the treatments of the experiment should not be seen as negative result. Particularly given the maturity of the processes (design-led approach is more mature than extreme programming), and the cost of the technology required (design-led approach is more expensive than extreme programming).

Acknowledgements

We would like to acknowledge our colleagues Philip McMinn and Haralambos Mouratidis for their collaboration in this project. We should also like to thank our clients who agreed work with our students on their problems. Macias thankfully acknowledges the support of CONACYT (Mexico).

References

1. [Beck 98] K. Beck; Extreme Programming: A Humanistic Discipline of Software Development; Lecture Notes in Computer Science 1382:1-16; 1998.

2. [Beck 99-1] K. Beck; Embracing change with extreme programming; Computer 32(10):70-77; Oct. 1999.
3. [Beck 99-2] K. Beck; 1999; Extreme Programming Explained: Embrace Change; Addison-Wesley; U.S.A.; p.t. 190.
4. [Fowler 01] M. Fowler; Avoiding Repetition; IEEE Software 18(1):97-99; Jan-Feb 2001.
5. [Holcombe 01] M. Holcombe, M. Gheorghe, F. Macias; Teaching XP for real: Some initial observations and plans; Proceedings of 2nd International Conference on Extreme Programming and Flexible Processes in Software Engineering (XP2001); Sardinia, Italy, May 20-23, 2001; 14-17.
6. [Macias 02] F. Macias, M.Holcombe, M. Gheorghe, "Empirical experiments with XP" in Proceedings of 3rd International Conference on Extreme Programming and Flexible Processes in Software Engineering (XP2002), Sardinia, Italy, May 26-30, 2002, 225-228.
7. [Moore 02] I. Moore, S. Palmer, "Making a Mockery" in Proceedings of 3rd International Conference on Extreme Programming and Flexible Processes in Software Engineering (XP2002), Sardinia, Italy, May 26-30, 2002, 6-10.
8. [Putnam 02] D. Putnam, "Where has all the management gone?" in Proceedings of 3rd International Conference on Extreme Programming and Flexible Processes in Software Engineering (XP2002), Sardinia, Italy, May 26-30, 2002, 39-42.
9. [Rumpe 02] B. Rumpe, P. Scholz, "A manager's view on large scale XP projects" in Proceedings of 3rd International Conference on Extreme Programming and Flexible Processes in Software Engineering (XP2002), Sardinia, Italy, May 26-30, 2002, 160-163.
10. [Sharifabdi 02] K. Sharifabdi, C. Grot; Team Development and pair programming -tasks and challenges of the XP coach; in Proceedings of 3rd International Conference on Extreme Programming and Flexible Processes in Software Engineering (XP2002), Sardinia, Italy, May 26-30, 2002, 166-169.
11. [Williams 00] L. Williams, R. K. Kesler, W. Cunningham, R. Jeffreis; Strengthening the case for pair programming; IEEE Software 17(4):19-25; Jul-Aug 2000.
12. [Wright 02] G. Wright, "eXtreme Programming in a hostile environment" in Proceedings of 3rd International Conference on Extreme Programming and Flexible Processes in Software Engineering (XP2002), Sardinia, Italy, May 26-30, 2002, 48-51.

Agile Teaching of an Agile Software Process

Vieri Del Bianco and Giordano Sassaroli

CEFRIEL, WISE Unit, Via Fucini, 2
20133 Milan, Italy
{vieri.delbianco,giordano.sassaroli}@cefriel.it

Abstract. This paper reports on the practice activity of an introductory course on Software Engineering for graduated students in Information Technology. Practices consisted of the application of the agile software development methodology for designing and implementing a simple Java application. The paper proposes an agile approach for teaching Software Engineering based on the strict collaboration of students and teachers in design activities. The paper reports results, student feedbacks, comments and observations about the teaching approach and the adopted agile software process.

1 Introduction

Software Engineering is a quite boring discipline for outsiders: usually software Engineering (SE) courses aim at teaching methodologies, tools and processes, but rarely aim at convincing students that SE is useful for practical purposes. Experience proves the effectiveness of applying these methodologies in real world, but a great step forward would be done if students could be convinced during courses.

During the Fall 2002 Semester, we taught the introductory course in SE of the fifteenth edition of the Master in Information Technology at CEFRIEL. The master is attended by graduated students with different backgrounds, most of them are unfamiliar with SE concepts and they will likely not be concerned in explicitly applying SE during their career. The course is made of ten modules of lessons and five modules of practice activity, one module corresponding to three hours.

A common mistrust on the applicability of SE to real world projects emerged from the feedbacks of students of previous editions: for this reason, we renewed the practice content introducing a real life example of software development with the adoption of an agile software process [1]. The main goal was to show students a workable use of what they learned during lessons, so that they could effectively exploit it in their future work. Anyway we had to find a compromise between fully adopting agility and including some heavy methodologies or artifacts (such as documentation) for covering all the aspects treated during the course lessons.

Starting from the solutions we adopted to face the issues that emerged from previous editions, the paper describes the agile software process that has been proposed to students, providing details on the practice activity and focusing on the management of groups, time-table and meetings. Finally, results and feedbacks are presented and analyzed, focusing on strengths and flaws of the proposed approach.

M. Marchesi and G. Succi (Eds.): XP 2003, LNCS 2675, pp. 402–405, 2003.
© Springer-Verlag Berlin Heidelberg 2003

2 Poblems and Solutions

Just One Assignment, Covering All Aspects. Past course practices were based on small problems designed for specific aspects of SE (e.g. UML exercises or testing exercises). Although this is a scalable and flexible way for managing practices, students usually perceive SE just as a set of isolated and unrelated activities that hardly fit together to effectively address bigger problems. In our vision, practices should consist of just one assignment: while designing and developing a software product, students can practice all SE activities, perceiving the purpose of each single step of the work.

Create Heterogeneous Working Groups. Students are usually left free to create their groups, resulting in homogenous groups by friendship, working area or just desk proximity. But homogeneity is unrealistic. Working groups must be created by the teachers, according to student capabilities, background experiences and interests. Competence heterogeneity among group members can accidentally lead to homogeneity among groups: each group should contain at least one experienced developer and at least one beginner.

Invest Beginners with Responsibility. Group member heterogeneity introduces the problem of cohabitation of beginners with experienced people. When a beginner finds herself involved in a working group with skilled people, she could react getting out of the way, leaving most of the work to other members and deciding that learning by observation is good enough. By this way, the practice is likely to be ineffective and to make the student skeptical about SE. Beginners are the target of teaching, so teachers should do their best to avoid that beginners are left out of the work. A good solution is investing them with the highest responsibility: being group managers, they have to be constantly updated on group activity and work progress, periodically reporting design decisions to teachers. This way, beginners are encouraged to be involved in, or at least to be conscious of, all group activities. Furthermore, during the implementation phase, group members work in pairs: given the proven effectiveness of pair programming in learning languages as well as design methodologies, we adopted it also for smoothing differences in a very heterogeneous group.

Public Monitored Project Meetings. Usually students are evaluated through the results of their work, but, given that our purpose is teaching how to properly apply methodologies and processes, we cannot state students learned anything until we see them at work. Usually the limited complexity of the problems to be solved allows the production of good results also without applying any SE methodology, and, even though they have attended lessons, students are still too much inexperienced for effectively applying concepts in a real case. Teachers must be present during group meetings, so that students are never left alone while taking design decisions: the role of teachers is to guide the meeting if the main topic is lost, to suggest best practices on high level and low level software design, to assist the members in the use of notations, etc. The teacher presence should be discreet because students are the protagonists: teachers are just assistants and observers. While a group is discussing, other groups can attend as public, observing from outside how their mates behave: from an external point of view, students can see faults and wrong behaviors they would not notice otherwise. Furthermore, the public can give suggestions on methodology and management instead of teachers, increasing the cooperation among students.

3   Practicing an Agile Software Process

The course was attended by 24 people with different backgrounds and experiences: 25% of them declared to be totally inexperienced in programming, 60% medium experienced and 15% experts. 54% declared to have no experience in software design, the remainder to be medium. Five groups were created, respecting as best we could the heterogeneity criterion; then, pairs were created autonomously by students. For each group, the least skilled student in software design was designated as group manager, while the most skilled in programming was named the internal reference on technologies and tools. In order to avoid burdening beginners with too much responsibility, we clarified since the first day that they would not have been evaluated on their practice performance, highly easing informality between students and teachers.

Our purpose was to consolidate the idea that SE is practically usable: the risk on choosing a heavy process would have been to obtain the very opposite effect. We applied the agile approach to both software process and teaching, trying to be effective and maneuverable [1]. It means that students acquire as more experience as possible from practicing, keeping the required effort of students and teachers as reasonable as possible, according to the available time table.

The software was designed and developed through an iterative process based on small steps of advancements, each iteration corresponding to one module (three hours). Iterations started with a public monitored meeting: starting from feedbacks, if any, from the previous implementation phase, students were invited, and guided, to choose and discuss a sub-problem that seemed feasible in the available time. Then, assignments to group members were decided, organizing the remaining time for implementation. The process required three iterations, preceded by an intensive problem analysis module: teachers played the role of customers and provided students with a high level natural language problem specification, in which some bugs had been artificially introduced, removing some details necessary for the problem comprehension. Exploiting the Problem Frames approach [3], students were asked to analyze the problem, finding missing elements and interviewing teachers for capturing requirements.

The assignment consisted in developing a Java application for playing the Tetris game. At the last iteration, when all other design decisions had been taken, we provided students with an implementation of the GUI: this let them focus on the application logic design, without influencing them with our view emerging from GUI and introducing worthy realistic integration issues that enriched the vision of the process.

During implementation, students were invited to practice unit testing extensively, using the JUnit framework [4]: test cases were presented as a way for increasing confidence with the code produced by other group members. Also Configuration Management was highly promoted: any electronic sub-product of student activities should be maintained on the group repository. Keeping agility as the main target, the goals of the course included also learning how to produce just the needed documentation: students were asked to document the project with the deepness they felt necessary, on the other hand complex and not agile documentation was considered a given requisite.

For what regards the adopted tools, Rational Rose [5] was chosen for producing UML documentation, Eclipse [2] as Integrated Development Environment for the implementation phase, with JUnit plug-in for software testing, and, finally, Rational ClearCase [5] was adopted as configuration management suite.

4   Comments and Results

Observing the student behavior during problem analysis convinced us of the worthiness of monitored meetings. Starting from the same problem description, three groups worked independently, while the other two made a monitored meeting, starting with a group working and a group as public and switching after half the available time. The first three groups had a lot of difficulties on autonomously applying concepts to the practical case, while the other students, with our guidance, properly applied the methodology, finding most of the artificial (and some unintentional) inconsistencies.

Public monitored meetings resulted in a very precious means for getting immediate feedbacks from students and for early correcting wrong behaviors and misunderstandings. Collaboration among the meeting group, the public and the teachers was the most valuable effect of meetings: through collaboration, beginners were not isolated and heterogeneity was effectively exploited. All students agreed on the worthiness of teacher monitoring and 80% considered being both protagonists and public very effective for learning. All agreed on the need for more time: we had to manage calendars with students attending different courses and unmodifiable time constraints, so we had to give up some aspects but we maintained a strong hold on the process.

A noteworthy feedback is that even though all students agreed on the effectiveness of applying an agile process for learning SE, 50% of them asked for more formalization on notation and documentation. Furthermore, the final score was based on a written exam with exercises and theoretical questions, so most of students asked for more exercises on specific concepts besides just applying them on the whole project.

In spite of our pressure on test driven development, there was a high resistance to write test cases, before or after coding. Most of students declared that testing is a time consuming activity and they did not test because of limited available time.

As a final remark, the experience has been fully approved by students and teachers. Although we have still to face some weaknesses, especially in time management, we are convinced of the effectiveness of this approach for enhancing the student confidence on the practicability of SE concepts in real-world projects.

Acknowledgements

We would like to thank all the students who attended the course, for all the support and valuable feedbacks they gave us. A special thank to Rational Italia [5] for providing software tools for our SE laboratory and licenses for educational purposes.

References

1. Agile Alliance Web Site. On-line at http://www.agilealliance.org
2. Eclipse Open Platform Web Site. On-line at http://www.eclipse.org
3. Jackson, M.: Problem Frames, ACM Press Books, Addison Wesley, (2001)
4. JUnit Testing Framework Web Site. On-line at http://www.junit.org
5. Rational Software Web Site. On-line at http://www.rational.com

Five Challenges in Teaching XP

Rick Mugridge, Bruce MacDonald, Partha Roop, and Ewan Tempero

University of Auckland, New Zealand
{r.mugridge,b.macdonald,p.roop,e.tempero}@auckland.ac.nz

Abstract. We have successfully run three Extreme Programming Projects with Software Engineering students over the last two years. We introduce five major challenges we encountered when running the projects with year 2 and 3 students, and discuss our (partial) solutions within the context of these projects.
We show that XP practices need some adjustment for an educational setting and that the skills required for XP need to be taught before attempting an XP project.

1 Introduction

Many institutions have an interest in teaching Extreme Programming. XP offers significant benefits as well as serious challenges in a university curriculum. We discuss five challenges we have faced over two years while running three student XP projects.

We teach in a Software Engineering (SE) programme, with two-semester project courses at years 2, 3, and 4. We have run three XP projects, one in 2001 and two in 2002. The first project built a Wiki-style web system, using Java Servlets, over the last 8 weeks in the second semester. There were 55 students in the class, and they worked in teams of 5 or 6. Two professors both acted as Customers and Coaches.

The second project was a web-based Human Resources system with the same students, now at year 3. It was over 12 weeks, with teams of 4 or 5. An HR person defines new vacancies, along with questions for candidates to answer. Ranking criteria are defined to aid in the selection from a potentially large number of applicants. Search techniques are available to select subsets of candidates. Two people from a local company acted as customers. Three professors acted as Coaches and created customer tests.

The third project, with 70 year 2 students, built a Chat system server over 6 weeks, with teams of two. One of the professors acted as the Customer, while the other acted as the Coach and assessor. We identified several challenges as we ran these projects.

2 Challenges

Challenge: Too Much to Do. As we planned the first project, it became clear we could not cover all aspects of XP, given the time available for preparation. We would need to take an iterative approach, choosing some of the practices for our first "iteration".

To begin, each student did a spike using Servlets. We ran the Planning Game with the class, over two iterations. We encouraged team members to work in pairs and use test-first programming. We assessed progress with three formal team reviews. The team

M. Marchesi and G. Succi (Eds.): XP 2003, LNCS 2675, pp. 406–409, 2003.
© Springer-Verlag Berlin Heidelberg 2003

demonstrated their system, each member answered questions, and a pair made a simple code change with help from the team. Feedback was given on test and code quality.

Some practices were not covered. We spent little time on *Metaphor*, as the domain of the project was simple enough to use directly. We did not emphasise continuous integration, as the students had not been exposed to source control tools. We ran out of time to introduce customer acceptance tests, as we had planned. We were unable to have an on-site customer, as discussed in a later challenge.

It became clear from the quality of code and tests that the students needed further background in unit testing, test-first programming, and refactoring. Their approach to integration was ad hoc and last minute, leading to problems at the end of an iteration.

The second project involved the same students in their third year. We decided that acceptance tests would provide the most value to the students (see later). Students were encouraged to use tools to help with continuous integration, but few did. We needed to make the need for using such practices more explicit in the assessment criteria.

We introduced more background material before the third project with lectures, labs and assignments on JUnit, refactoring, testing, and test-driven development. Students worked in pairs, so that more emphasis could be placed on the other practices. Acceptance tests were introduced early on and the students accepted them readily.

Taking an iterative approach to teaching XP to projects proved sensible. As expected, there was much to learn from each project, or "teaching iteration". In particular, we realized how much effort is needed for students to build up sufficient experience in the non-team XP practices prior to doing project work. The following table summarises the XP practices that we discussed and expected to be used in the three projects:

XP Practice	1	2	3	XP Practice	1	2	3
The Planning Game	Yes	Yes	Yes	Pair Programming	Yes	Yes	Yes
Short Releases	Yes	Yes	Yes	Collective Ownership	Yes	Yes	NA
Metaphor	No	No	No	Continuous Integration	No	Yes	NA
Simple Design	Yes	Yes	Yes	On-Site Customer	No	No	No
Testing (Unit/Acceptance)	Unit	Both	Both	Coding Standards	Yes	Yes	Yes
Refactoring	Yes	Yes	Yes				

Challenge: Managing Multiple Teams. We judged that resource limits would mean having the same project for each of the teams. However, this raised a challenge in keeping the teams synchronised. In the first project, teams were asked to estimate the stories. We took the smallest estimates to choose stories for the first iteration. Different teams' progress varied, making the planning game difficult for the second iteration. Some teams were unhappy about being driven by others' estimates.

Our solution, applied in the next two projects, was to stop trying to keep the teams together. We set a priority order on the stories and each team used their own estimates to determine the number of stories for the iteration. Teams in the third project reported progress half way through the iteration, and were able to re-estimate.

Challenge: Timely and Correct Acceptance Tests. In the second project, we considered having teams produce acceptance tests. It made sense to have only one test set and so we considered splitting the test creation between teams. However, to avoid serious delays in the verification of the tests, we decided it best to provide the tests ourselves.

Preliminary work with HttpUnit [3] suggested that it would be a large and tedious job to write the tests. So we developed Isis, a web-testing framework for defining acceptance tests by example. However, the framework and acceptance tests were available late in the first iteration; students had already made design decisions and were most reluctant to change their systems. In addition, many of the tests included trivial inconsistencies, which students were slow to report, and frustration developed around last minute corrections to the tests.

By the end of the first iteration, few teams had passed many of the acceptance tests. The students had instead put their effort into coding more stories. For the second iteration, we emphasised quality and passing the acceptance tests. Several teams spent all of the second iteration on these, making no further progress on the stories.

We introduced simpler acceptance tests early on in the third project. We wrote the tests in XML and developed a simple framework to run them. We built an application to ensure test correctness. Tests were accepted by most students, although a few made assumptions that were inconsistent with the tests. Although tests were supplied early, some students were still reluctant to run them. They were particularly unhappy at having to change their "working" code, even though their system failed the customer tests!

Challenge: On-site Customer and Forty Hour Week. Other coursework prevents the students working full-time on an XP project. In addition, they usually work to due dates, with long hours into the evening and on the weekend when necessary. The time spent by different students on an assignment can vary widely (reportedly by up to a factor of 10), depending on their ability and enthusiasm. For each of the three projects, students were expected to assign 6 hours per week. Some teams did not report all of their working time, as they had assumed that the number of stories completed was more important than the practices. In the third project, some teams were well ahead of the rest and were reluctant to continue working to use up their time.

Customer questions were handled in two one-hour meeting times each week, in scheduled lab times, and by email and an electronic forum. This encouraged students to make assumptions about what was required for a story, rather than asking the customer.

All of these issues raised a serious challenge to meeting the practices of On-Site Customer and 40 Hour Week. This was the greatest weakness of the three projects. Ideally, an XP project would be carried out full time by students and staff for a concentrated few weeks, with other courses running at other times.

Challenge: Ensuring Students Follow the Practices. It is difficult to ensure that students follow the XP practices. In the first project, we started with lectures and reading on XP. However, students were strongly focused on the project details. We found it difficult to align our course "acceptance tests" (assessment criteria) with XP practices.

Near the end of the first project we realised that students often had little idea about some of the XP practices. It was particularly difficult to get the students to focus on high quality, well-factored code. For the second iteration of the second project, we changed the basis of the assessment so that quantity was much less important than quality. Several teams spent all of that iteration on writing unit tests, refactoring, and meeting the acceptance tests. After the last iteration of the third project we gave the students *feedback* tests for them to run on their system for assessment and feedback.

3 Related Work

Others' experiences in teaching XP in a university setting are similar to ours. Astrachan et al. [1] made different choices of XP practices. Holcombe et al. make observations about introducing XP into their existing system, in a course that creates products for real clients [4]. After teaching XP in a Masters course Lappo feels students would better appreciate XP (and would be more likely to follow the practices) with more experience in other processes [5]. Shukla and Williams discovered a student attitude to testing similar to ours, in a senior level course, where the teaching of XP was limited to 4 weeks and they tried to cover more XP practices than us [8]. Melnik and Mauer found students were positive about XP practices [7]. Some work has focused on the effectiveness and management of pair programming (for example, [9, 2, 6, 8]).

4 Conclusion

While enjoying teaching XP in three projects over two years, we encountered several challenges. Some of these we were able to deal with successfully in later projects. Outstanding challenges are the practices of On-Site Customer and 40-Hour Weeks.

It is clear from our experience that XP cannot be taught in a single semester, nor in a single project. We recommend that prior class and laboratory time be dedicated to building experience in many of the XP practices before a full XP project is attempted. In particular, experience is needed with automated testing, test-first development, refactoring, working in pairs, and the use of source control tools.

References

1. Owen Astrachan, Robert C. Duvall, and Eugene Wallingfor. Bringing extreme programming to the classroom. In *XP Universe*, Raleigh, NC, USA, 2001.
2. Jennifer Bevan, Linda Werner, and Charlie McDowell. Guidelines for the use of pair programming in a freshman programming class. In *15th Conf on Software Engineering Education and Training (CSEET'02)*, pages 100–7. IEEE Computer Society, Feb 2002.
3. Russell Gold. HttpUnit. www.httpunit.org.
4. Mike Holcombe, Marian Gheorghe, and Francisco Macias. Teaching XP for real: some initial observations and plans. In *2nd Int'l Conf on eXtreme Programming and Flexible Processes in Software Engineering*, Sardinia, Italy, May 2001.
5. Peter Lappo. No pain, no XP - observations on teaching and mentoring XP to university students. In *Third Int'l Conf on eXtreme Programming and Agile Processes in Software Engineering*, Alghero, Sardinia, Italy, 2002.
6. Charlie McDowell, Linda Werner, Heather Bullock, and Julian Fernald. The effects of pair-programming on performance in an introductory programming course. In *Proc of the 33rd SIGCSE technical symp. on Computer science education*, pages 38–42. ACM Press, 2002.
7. Grigori Melnik and Frank Mauer. Perceptions on agile practices: A student survey. In *XP/Agile Universe*, 2002.
8. Anuja Shukla and Laurie Williams. Adapting extreme programming for a core software engineering course. In *15th Conf on Software Engineering Education and Training (CSEET'02)*, pages 184–91. IEEE Computer Society, Feb 2002.
9. Laurie Williams, Robert R. Kessler, Ward Cunningham, and Ron Jeffries. Strengthening the case for pair programming. *IEEE Software*, 17(4):19–25, 2000. Jul/Aug.

Challenges in Teaching Test Driven Development

Rick Mugridge

University of Auckland, New Zealand
r.mugridge@auckland.ac.nz

Abstract. We identify two main challenges in the teaching of Test Driven Development (TDD) over the last two years. The first challenge is to get students to rethink learning and design, and to really engage with this new approach.
The second challenge is to explicitly develop their skills in testing, design and refactoring, given that they have little experience in these areas. This requires that fast and effective feedback be provided.

1   Introduction

Test Driven Development (TDD) is a powerful technique that has evolved from test-first programming [2], one of the practices of XP [1]. Programmer tests are designed to drive the evolutionary development of a system in small steps. TDD is likely to have as much impact on programming practice in the 2000s as structured programming had in the 1970s and object-orientation had in the 1980s and 1990s.

TDD has been taught for the last two years in a second year software engineering course, SOFTENG 251, as a part of an engineering degree at the University of Auckland. SOFTENG 251 teaches advanced object-oriented programming and design and iterative development. The development of a drawing package over several steps was used as an example, with refactorings and design rationale provided.

In 2001, JUnit and unit testing were introduced, along with test-first programming [1]. The drawing package was redeveloped test-first with a larger number of steps. Assignment work involved making a series of smaller changes using a test-first approach. However, it became clear that the students needed to build their skills further.

In 2002, experience with JUnit and unit testing were provided in a prior year two course, so that the students could develop further with TDD in SOFTENG 251. A new example was used: digital circuit simulation. Refactoring of methods in a simple class was covered in labs before introducing subclassing, so that the students could better build experience with refactorings at the method level.

From this experience, two challenges in teaching TDD have been identified[1]. The first challenge is to get students to reconsider their models of learning and design, and really learn to apply TDD. With only 12 months experience in programming before this course, some students are unhappy about "starting again" with TDD when they had found learning to program the first time a demanding exercise.

The second challenge is to explicitly develop the various skills that they need to utilise TDD well, including skills in testing, design and refactoring. This requires that students are provided with fast and effective feedback on their progress.

---

[1] For an extended version of this paper, with three challenges, see [5]

M. Marchesi and G. Succi (Eds.): XP 2003, LNCS 2675, pp. 410–413, 2003.
© Springer-Verlag Berlin Heidelberg 2003

We follow with a brief introduction to TDD. Sections 3 and 4 describe the challenges and discuss what we have done to meet them. Section 5 concludes.

2   TDD

With TDD [2], frequent micro-iterations are used to develop software, in which each micro-iteration may take only a few minutes. There are generally three steps in each micro-iteration (the third is not necessary on every cycle):

- A concrete example, as an executable test, is designed, written and shown to fail
- The code is extended to pass the test while continuing to pass all other existing tests
- The code and tests are refactored [3] to eliminate redundancy

Thus abstractions are developed from concrete examples, and so the programmer doesn't have to think about all of the cases, in all their generality, all at once. A common difficulty in learning the techniques of TDD is in designing the next test, as this has a strong impact on how the program develops. Beginners especially find it difficult.

The tests act as a mirror of the developing system. Some tests are designed to expand the interface of the program and/or its components; such a test is used to design that interface. Other tests are examples that are designed to extend the capability (or boundary) of the current system, and thus lead to code expansion and generalisation.

Tests are often chosen to tackle design issues that are not too difficult and not too easy, so that something can be learned from each step. An information theoretic view of TDD would focus on the information-gathering potential of each new test [6].

This approach reflects the larger-scale cycle of XP iterations, where customer tests drive the development of the design of the whole system. This enables the customer to get feedback from the evolving system, so that the overall system design can be altered to meet the currently-understood needs of the system in an organisational context.

3   Challenge: Rethinking Learning and Design

Students inevitably bring preconceptions about learning, design and software development to a course, and these can restrict their ability to learn to apply TDD. Hence we have found it useful to explicitly address these preconceptions.

Programming is a creative act, requiring the development of a range of design and problem-solving skills. Active learning is essential, with ongoing reflection by the learner on how well they have done and how to improve.

Many students find it challenging to learn to program, but reach a level of competence that they find satisfactory. This may result in their being resistant when they have to unlearn their current approach for a new way, regardless of the perceived value of the new approach. This happened with some students in SOFTENG 251 with TDD. There is no way to avoid the pain of such change; students need to expect it as programmers and become agile learners. Maslow [4] distinguishes four stages of learning:

- Unconscious incompetence, where you are not aware that you don't know much and you don't mind

- Conscious incompetence, where you become aware of your lack of skills and don't enjoy it
- Conscious competence, where you are skillful but need to continue to put conscious effort into developing your skills
- Unconscious competence, where your skills work well without regular reflection

Design is difficult to teach and to learn, and there is considerable discomfort associated with the second and third of Maslow's stages. This is not helped by a common over-simplified model of design [6]. Often in examples of program design, a problem is clearly posed and a completed solution given. This does not take account of two issues:

- A problem may well not be clearly articulated or well understood. The design process helps to uncover a clearer view of the problem, aided by concrete examples.
- A complete solution for a realistic problem may be difficult to derive without experimentation. It may appear that an overall approach will work, but "the devil is in the detail". Appropriate abstractions and modularity may only become clear through the evolutionary development of a design.

We addressed these issues in a number of ways. Several examples of applying TDD were covered in class. The tests and code for a simple animation system (where shapes bounce around within a window) and a digital circuit simulator (with explicit gate delays) were covered in 2002, with other examples being available. Test design, refactoring and the principle of "Do the simplest thing that could possibly work" were stressed.

Assignment work involved making changes to these two systems through a sequence of explicit steps. Each of these steps required several micro-iterations and led to interesting design changes of the two systems. Students were required to hand in all of their micro-iteration steps, to show that they were applying TDD.

4   Challenge: Developing Skills

To practise TDD, a student needs to develop a range of interdependent skills:

- Write tests for an existing system, to better understand testing
- Use a testing framework such as JUnit
- Refactor application code
- Refactor tests
- Decide on areas of the application that can be extended, in order to choose a test
- Choose the next test to design, based on its intuitive merit (or economic value, in an information-theoretic sense [6])
- Design a suitable test, given the general aim of pushing the development
- Reflect on the impact of the sequence of tests that were chosen
- Make the simplest possible changes to the code (ie, don't speculate about the future)
- Understand why the code failed to pass a test (problem solving)

Many of these skills apply more generally; they are relevant to approaches other than XP. However, they tend not to be taught so thoroughly in other software development approaches.

The students had met JUnit in an earlier course in 2002, and had used it for traditional testing of several provided programs. The students had also carried out refactoring of a program where a single class was involved and all changes were to methods.

Once subtyping and subclassing were introduced, they applied refactoring in the lab to a program involving several interrelated classes. This program was a variant of the movie rental program used by Martin Fowler to explain refactorings [3]. Most of the students' practical learning of the other skills occurred when they carried out the assignment work. Simpler tasks need to be designed so that students can independently practice the various skills.

We have tried to build the needed skills incrementally, aiming to apply the ideas of TDD to the process of learning TDD. We are lacking suitable (automated and manual) tests/assessments that could be used to drive the process and to provide quick feedback to students on their progress. The correctness of the assignments was successfully assessed using the programmer tests that I had used to develop my assignment solution.

However, it's hard to assess some aspects automatically, such as the quality of the tests and the code. We have started to explore the use of simple metrics to provide automated feedback. We can compare the relative (compiled) size of the tests and code supplied by the students with the sample solution. Programs where the tests or other code are much larger than expected can be flagged, as well as those in which the size of the tests is small compared to the size of the code. We have also considered determining the code coverage of the supplied programmer tests, but this has limitations.

5   Conclusion

TDD is a powerful technique that is having a significant impact on software development [2]. It needs to be incorporated early into software curricula. TDD has been taught for the last two years in a second year software engineering course. Two challenges in teaching TDD have been identified. It is necessary to get students to reconsider their models of learning and design, and really engage with TDD. Many are reluctant to set aside the way they currently program, and "start again" with TDD when they had found it demanding to learn how to program the first time round.

The second challenge is to explicitly develop the various skills that they need in order to utilise TDD well, including skills in testing, design and refactoring. This requires that fast and effective feedback be provided to them on their progress, analogous to the role of programmer tests in TDD. A new challenge is still being planned: teaching TDD in the first introductory programming course in software engineering.

References

1. K. Beck. *eXtreme Programming Explained*. Addison Wesley, 2000.
2. K. Beck. *Test Driven Development: By Example*. Addison Wesley, 2002.
3. M. Fowler. *Refactoring*. Addison Wesley, 1999.
4. A. Maslow. *Motivation and Personality*. Harper and Row, 1970.
5. R. Mugridge. Agile learning of test driven development. Technical Report 2, Software Engineering, University of Auckland, www.se.auckland.ac.nz/tr/UA-SE-2003-2.pdf, 2003.
6. D.G. Reinertsen. *Managing the Design Factory*. The Free Press, 1997.

Filleting XP for Educational Purposes

Friedrich Steimann[1], Jens Gößner[2], and Thomas Mück[2]

[1] Universität Hannover, Institut für Informationssysteme
Appelstraße 4, D-30167 Hannover
steimann@acm.org

[2] Universität Hannover, Learning Lab Lower Saxony
Expo Plaza 1, D-30539 Hannover
{goessner,mueck}@learninglab.de

Abstract. Rather than teaching XP as a software development method, we have found that some of XP's core practices are actually viable learning scenarios. By combining these practices into a set of regulations, we have organized a well-received 200 h software practical regularly conducted during the 4th semester of an applied informatics curriculum.

1 Introduction

While learning how to program can be fun, teaching how to program is notoriously difficult. This is particularly so because programming is best learnt by doing, not by listening (or watching), thereby reducing the role of the docent to the one who assigns the right exercises (with the tutorial assistance being provided by others). Learning by doing, however, is not learning on one's own: it requires rapid feedback and gentle guidance.

Whereas the syntax of a programming language can always be internalized through trial and error (with the immediate feedback being given by the syntax editor or compiler), checking the semantic correctness of a program requires a much deeper understanding. This deeper understanding will usually be that of a peer; however, if the peer has sufficiently clear expectations of how the solution should perform, these expectations can also be cast into a test suite, making their accessibility independent of that of the peer.

Learning in small groups can be highly effective. Students can learn from each other by positive and negative example, they can join efforts to attack difficult problems, and they can learn by teaching what they have not fully understood for themselves. In addition, students are likely to have more time, to be more patient, and to have a better understanding of each other's problems than their teachers. All this makes programming in pairs seem a favourable setting for learning how to program.

It appears that test driven software development and pair programming can actually help with learning how to program. Because they are key practices of XP, what was more obvious than testing other XP practices for their pedagogical usefulness? In the following, we take a first look at the suitability of XP practices for teaching, and discuss some problems together with how they can be solved. A systematic investigation of the general aptness for XP in education however is yet to be undertaken.

M. Marchesi and G. Succi (Eds.): XP 2003, LNCS 2675, pp. 414–417, 2003.

2   A Practical Scenario for Learning How to Write Software

In order to teach programming at a university in an industry-like setting, we make our students form small "companies" (teams of six) and have each company develop a 150 person day software project. Progress and equal distribution of work are controlled by dividing the project into blocks and each block into a number of individual tasks assigned to the individual team members. At the end of each block, the solutions to the individual tasks must be integrated and turned in as one functioning program. Teams have to meet once a week for two hours, to assign tasks and perform walkthroughs (code reviews). Because programming abilities vary widely, we encourage participants to code in pairs (solving the double number of tasks per pair).

Pair Programming Fosters Collaboration and Mutual Assistance. Successful collaboration depends on many factors, personal sympathy (or antipathy) being one of them. While students find it natural to collaborate with their mates, most feel uncomfortable with co-operating with strangers, most likely because they fear exposure of their deficits. In practice, however, good (i.e., productive) collaboration even with colleagues one dislikes is indispensable. Therefore, one of the key abilities to be learnt by a programmer is a social one: being able to co-operate. We teach this ability by requiring the pairs of a company to rotate after each block.

User Stories Present Adequately Sized Tasks. In order to be able to guide students and track their progress, tasks should be cut down into chunks of small, manageable size with clearly defined outcome. On the other hand, individual tasks must be big enough so that some progress can be experienced. As it turned out, we had designed our tasks so that it took each pair an average of 25 h (or approximately three working days) per task. Thus it appears that a typical user story has about the right size for a single task. From hindsight, it would have been a good idea to present tasks as user stories, giving them a more realistic flavour. Hints on the solution of each task could then be offered as separate help (displayed from within a specially adapted development environment; see below).

Test First Enables a Constructivist Approach. XP promotes the test-first approach as one of its core practices, requiring that tests are implemented before production code is entered. Having the tests in advance allows one to experiment with possible solutions, find out how they failed, and try alternatives. If students are freed from writing the tests themselves, the so-modified test-first approach presents a constructivist learning environment, the obvious downside being that the tests must be written by someone else, namely the instructors. While following this approach students do not learn how to write tests, they learn to appreciate the existence of tests. A setting for learning how to write tests is presented in the next section.

Continuous Integration Facilitates Frequent Submission of Solutions. One problem with long-term exercises is that students tend to get lost. If the deadline is far ahead, there is only little pressure to proceed with one's work. Heterogeneous groups embracing members with different work attitudes are likely to fall apart: if some members are more determined than others, they will rather take over the work of their colleagues than wait while the deadline slowly approaches. We counteract this cause of disintegration by introducing blocks, entailing short delivery cycles.

At the end of each block, students have to turn in their solutions as a whole, i.e., they must submit the current state of the project as developed by their group by uploading their project files to the server on which they must compile and pass all tests. Although a daily build is not mandatory, the continuous integration promoted by XP is likely to prove a practice helping to meet delivery deadlines without worry.

3   Practical Problems and Their Solutions

Problems with Pairing. We found that although students were enthusiastic about it initially, actual pair programming times were much shorter than anticipated: only one third of all tasks were actually solved in pairs. Even though students appear to be open to pair programming, its actual acceptance is disappointingly low; as one student put it, "pair programming only makes sense [...] with better opportunities to meet and work together at the face". It seems that meeting is a severe obstacle to (co-located) pair programming.

To facilitate pair programming a number of students (not all, since we conduct a controlled experiment [5]) will be equipped with notebook computers with Internet access enabled via WLAN (802.11b), Ethernet cable and modem. MS NetMeeting is used as the basis for application sharing and voice communication. WLAN access points are distributed over parts of the campus and computer science buildings. Co-operation in peer-to-peer mode is also possible and the connection of choice if participants reside in close proximity, even side-by-side. It remains to be seen, however, if the ubiquitous possibility for pair programming will actually improve the acceptance of this mode of teamwork.

How to Test the Tests. Naturally, with the tests being provided students learn to appreciate the existence of tests, but they do not learn how to write them. Therefore, our curriculum of exercises must contain tasks dedicated to the writing of tests.

Following the test-driven approach to practicing software development, the tests (as a product) must be tested. Naturally, tests are tested by the application they test: if the application contains errors, the tests must find them, and if the application is error free, the tests must approve this fact. Thus, the first and most obvious approach to testing the tests is to also write the application they are testing, to introduce errors (intentionally or accidentally), and to correct both tests and application until they conform to the specification.

If writing the test is the task, however, then testing it afterwards (even if by writing the application) suffers from the same (psychological) problems as known from conventional testing: the tester is blind towards his/her own errors. Therefore, we provide with each test-writing task a set of solutions, one with no defects, the others with errors injected. A test suite is considered correct only if it finds all errors and lets the correct solution pass.

4   Discussion

Distributed Pair Programming. Distributed or dispersed XP (DXP) is a relatively new facet of computer-supported collaborative work (CSCW) that is increasingly being used across XP-style software developing companies. In DXP, programmers collaborate using voice communication and application sharing software, typically MS NetMeeting. First experiences with this setting in an educational context have been reported in [1]; our own trials are promising enough to let distributed pair programming appear a viable alternative to co-location.

Automatic Verification of Exercises. The idea of automatic verification of programming exercises has previously been put forward by Praktomat [3] and WebAssign [4], two publicly available frameworks for the conduction and evaluation of exercises. However, these systems are not integrated in a practical of our size.

5   Conclusion

Perhaps, with most of the alleged advantages of XP yet unproven, it is still too early to teach XP as a state-of-the-art programming method [2]. But if didactically valuable learning scenarios happen to coincide (or at least blend smoothly) with XP practices, then this should be sufficient justification to practise these practices in teaching. As with XP as a whole, their proliferation will depend of the personal experiences the students make, and on how successful they are.

Acknowledgements

This work has been supported in part by the BMBF Förderprogramm Neue Medien in der Bildung, Ausschreibung "Notebook-University", Förderkennzeichen 08NM222A, and by the e-Learning Academic Network Niedersachsen (ELAN).

References

1. P Baheti, L Williams, E Gehringer, D Stotts, J McC. Smith *Distributed Pair Programming: Empirical Studies and Supporting Environments* Technical Report TR02-010, Department of Computer Science, University of North Carolina at Chapel Hill (USA 2002).
2. P Becker-Pechau, H Breitling, M Lippert, A Schmolitzky "An Extreme Week for First-Year Programmers" in: *XP 2003—Proc. of the 4th International Conference* (Springer 2003).
3. www.infosun.fmi.uni-passau.de/st/praktomat/
4. http://niobe.fernuni-hagen.de/WebAssign/
5. F Steimann, J Gößner, U Thaden "Proposing Mobile Pair Programming" *OOPSLA 2002 Workshop on Pair Programming Explored / Distributed Extreme Programming* (Seattle, USA 2002).

Using XP with Children for Learning Mathematics

Maria A. Droujkova[1] and Dmitri A. Droujkov[2]

[1] North Carolina State University, 315 Poe Hall, Raleigh, NC 27695-7801 USA
maria@naturalmath.com
[2] Borland Software Corporation, 900 Main Campus Drive, Suite 500,
Raleigh, NC 27606 USA
dmitri.droujkov@borland.com

Abstract. This paper presents an interdisciplinary case study of using extreme programming (XP) in a mathematics education research project. The educational focus of the study was the use of images and metaphors by children. The practices of XP allowed researchers to access students' mathematical images and metaphors in a naturalistic setting centered on a real task, rather than in a purely education research-laboratory context.

1   Framework and Methodology

Extreme programming (XP) [1, 2] as a methodology closely parallels constructivist theories of mathematics education [4]. During our research project, students and researchers were working on designing computer games on proportionality. In effect, computer games were complex and observable metaphors that served as tools for communication, formalization and development of student's mathematical ideas. Studying metaphors presents big challenges since they are often private and unformulated [5] and thus not accessible by direct interviewing. The structure of XP processes allowed researchers working with students access students' work and their images in an intrinsic, i.e., project-related manner.

The framework for the study was based on qualitative research traditions of mathematics education studies [3]. We view metaphors, the topic of the study, as highly context-dependent phenomena. Thus our study has features of an educational ethnography: we investigated a coherent, authentic process of software development. There are also elements of the teaching experiment tradition, and the semi-formal clinical interview. Educational models presenting learning as a recursive process [4] parallel agile processes in their structure [1, 2].

2   Roles, Metaphors and Practices

Consideration of roles is a method of work used both in XP processes [1] and in some educational theories, for example, in the theory of situated cognition [6]. From the

M. Marchesi and G. Succi (Eds.): XP 2003, LNCS 2675, pp. 418–419, 2003.
© Springer-Verlag Berlin Heidelberg 2003

point of view of education, significant, intrinsic roles of learners in projects lead to meaningful learning. During the study, children took on the roles of customers, and interviewing researchers the roles of developers. Taking on roles did not present any difficulties to children, who used them quite naturally and intuitively.

We used the system metaphor in the XP sense as well as students' metaphors related to learning. In educational research, a metaphor can be broadly defined as the recursive movement between a source and a target that are structurally similar, both changing in the dynamic process of learning [5]. Establishing initial plans for their games, children followed traditional game genres, such as a quest or an arcade game. The genres were an initial metaphor that served "to jumpstart an initial understanding of the system" [1, p.35]. Parallels between mathematical operations, and actions and objects within the game, could also be considered as metaphoric tools. For example, proportional change in size of two objects was expressed in a "stretch machine" with a slider determining the amount of stretching. Conventional software features worked as basic, common metaphors for mathematical actions, for example, "slider" for "changing size." We observed iterative movement, characteristic of metaphoric thinking and supported by the XP process, between the development of student reasoning about proportionality, and the development of game features. Game metaphors allowed students to hold onto many details, formalizing their understanding of proportionality in a particular context.

All children found the practice of starting from testing quite natural. For user story cards, they made detailed screen-by-screen drawings and descriptions. For testing, they "ran through" the program by screen diagrams, modifying it as needed based on the results. This activity was highly enjoyable to students, who role-played the use of their software with artistic gusto.

3   Summary and Conclusions

The iterative, emergent structure of XP processes paralleled the way children learn mathematics, and proved supportive for their learning. XP processes may significantly contribute to the development of education research methodologies, and can be a basis for mathematics and science curricula.

References

1. Astels, D., Miller, G., Novak, M. A practical guide to eXtreme Programming. Prentice Hall, 2002
2. Beck, K. Extreme Programming explained: Embrace change. Addison Wesley, 1999
3. Creswell, J.W. Qualitative inquiry and research design: choosing among five traditions. Sage Publications, 1998
4. Davis, B., Sumara, D., Luce-Kapler, R. Engaging minds: Learning and teaching in a complex world. Lawrence Erlbaum, 2000
5. Lakoff, G., Johnson, M. Metaphors we live by. University of Chicago Press, 1980
6. Lave, J., Wenger, E. Situated learning : legitimate peripheral participation. Cambridge University Press, 1991

Using Metaphors
in eXtreme Programming Projects

Yael Dubinsky[1] and Orit Hazzan[2]

[1] Department of Computer Science, Technion, Israel
[2] Department of Education in Technology & Science, Technion, Israel

Abstract. Metaphor is one of the twelve practices of Extreme Programming (XP), and definitely among the more difficult ones to teach and use. We present our experience with the use of metaphors and conclude with suggested guidelines for teachers.

1   Introduction

Metaphors are used in order to understand and experience one specific thing using the terms of another thing ([3]). Communication which uses the metaphor's world of concepts to improve our understanding of the world of concepts of the specific thing we are trying to understand, refers not only to instances in which both worlds of concepts correspond to one another, but also in cases in which they do not. If both worlds of concepts are identical, the metaphor is not a metaphor of that thing, but rather the thing itself. According to [1], a good metaphor for XP is the process involved in learning to drive. In software development, the process is controlled by the execution of many small adjustments, similar to driving a car, but there is no teamwork involved in driving. Still, the understanding of this metaphor is worthwhile. Our own experience has led us to map the metaphor as a practice that requires a high level of cognitive awareness when implemented ([2]). When we talked about metaphors with students who are working together on software projects, it sometimes seemed that the practice is forced and unnatural. The way in which metaphor improves communications was not immediately apparent. This encouraged us to further investigate the use of metaphors in various academic courses.

2   Using Metaphors in XP Projects

We studied how metaphors were used in XP projects executed by students in three different courses. Data were gathered from the lecturer's notes, observations, videotapes, interviews, and electronic forums. Due to space limitations[1], we focus here on a specific CS-major course, named 'Projects in Operating Systems', in which XP teams of 12 students worked on a project. During the first planning sessions of one of the teams, after listening to the customer stories,

---

[1] Full version at http://www.cs.technion.ac.il/OSL/XP/Papers/Metaphor-XP2003.

M. Marchesi and G. Succi (Eds.): XP 2003, LNCS 2675, pp. 420–421, 2003.

most students were uncertain about how to think about the file navigator, the project's topic. The customer emphasized that he was not comfortable with the current tree hierarchy of files, and specifically with the lack of automatic synchronization between related files. One of the students suggested the navigator be treated as if it were an association graph. An association graph is made up of nodes that represent specific subjects, and connecting arcs, which denote equivalent relationships between the nodes. The idea was to regard each such node as representing a file, and each arc between two files as denoting a first-degree relation with respect to the file contents. The student explained that this is the way in which our mind works. During a discussion with the supervisor, in which the students used the above metaphor to explain how our mind relates to data, they began to realize how the project could be planned. Eventually, the metaphor 'File organization is Mental association' accompanied the group's discussions throughout the semester. Following are students' expressions that are instances of this metaphor: "The distance between one file and another can be infinite"; "We can ask which files have a level-2 relation to a specific file".

3   Conclusion

Following are several lessons that we find appropriate to share with other teachers. The first guideline is to be aware of metaphors. Students, like other people, use metaphors naturally, and we can learn from those metaphors about students' understanding and use it in our teaching. When we explain about metaphors, and students begin to become exposed to the understanding and new horizons that metaphors opens to them, they respond positively and want to extend their use. This leads to the need to extend the use of metaphors, talk about them and encourage their use. The second guideline is represented by the metaphor More is Better. In this case, the more metaphors we use, the more we improve the understanding of the project and get students to talk in general, and about the various aspects of the project in particular. The more metaphors we use, the more we improve our understanding of the project and of the difficulties our students might encounter during the course of the project. No special difficulties arise when using several metaphors for different parts of the project, using each one according to need. Students are willing to use different metaphors for the same topic and it does not interfere with their progress. On the contrary, multiple metaphors provide elaboration and lead to a more confident understanding. Encouraging students to provide multiple metaphors is a worthwhile practice.

References

1. Beck, K.: Extreme Programming Explained: Embrace Change. Addison-Wesley 2000
2. Hazzan, O. and Dubinsky, Y.: Teaching a software development methodology: The case of Extreme Programming. In The proceedings of the 16th International Conference on Software Engineering Education and Training. Madrid, Spain 2003
3. Lakoff, G. and Johnson, M.: Metaphors We Live By. The University of Chicago Press 1980

Doctoral Symposium at XP 2003

Paul Grünbacher

Johannes Kepler University
Altenbergerstr. 69, 4040 Linz, Austria
gruenbacher@acm.org

The goal of organizing a doctoral symposium at this year's XP conference was to provide a forum for doctoral students doing research in the area of XP, agile methodologies, and related areas. A primary goal of the event was to provide mutual feedback and guidance in completing the dissertation and to discuss future research directions. The doctoral symposium had the same scope as the main XP 2003 conference.

We are very happy that we can welcome 14 students from 9 different countries (Austria, Denmark, Germany, Israel, Italy, New Zealand, Norway, Poland, Sweden) to the symposium.

Many thanks to Giancarlo Succi for reserving some space in the conference proceedings. This gives the participating students the opportunity to publish their ongoing research results. I encourage you to read the papers to learn more about the research issues the students are interested in, their research objectives, and results achieved so far.

M. Marchesi and G. Succi (Eds.): XP 2003, LNCS 2675, p. 422, 2003.

Collaboration on Software Tasks

Hans Gallis

Simula Research Laboratory, Software Engineering Department
P.O. Box 134, 1325 Lysaker, Norway
hansga@simula.no

In pair programming (PP), two developers work together on the same task using one computer and keyboard. PP involves not just coding, but many phases of the software development process such as design and testing. PP has been proposed by several authors since the 70's, but it is primarily during the last three to four years that some of the claimed benefits have been tested empirically.

Initial results indicate many benefits in favour of PP [1, 2]. However, there are some studies that conflict with these benefits [3, 4]. One explanation of the apparently contradicting results may be differences in the context in which the studies were conducted. Existing studies on PP have so far compared PP with individual programming. However, PP is just one way in which programmers can collaborate on software development tasks. Partner programming [5] and team collocation [6] are examples of other levels of programmer collaboration. Furthermore, most studies have so far used students as subjects. There is a need for more realistic studies using professionals as subjects to ensure external validity.

Jim Haungs, a developer at the C3 project at Daimler Chrysler, attested to the success of pair programming, but at the same time he could point to instances where PP did not work or was not emphasized in this early XP project [7]. This pragmatism, using a technique where it works and ignore it where it does not work, is stated to be one of the strengths of XP. This further illustrates that PP does have its limitations, but existing studies have mostly focused on its benefits.

This motivates our main research question:

> When and how are different levels of programmer collaboration beneficial (and not beneficial)?

To answer the research question, several more and complimentary studies have to be conducted. This includes case studies in industry, surveys regarding how many and how the techniques are applied and used in practice, action research studies to directly improve the practice and the problem-solving process, and controlled experiments to study cause-effect relationships. To aid in the design of empirical studies on PP an initial theoretical framework is being developed. The initial framework is grounded on Pfleeger's [8] first out of three key steps in the sequential studies model which is to reach an "... *initial understanding, including identifying likely variables, capturing the magnitude of problems and variables, documenting behaviours, and generating theories to explain perceived behaviour...*".

M. Marchesi and G. Succi (Eds.): XP 2003, LNCS 2675, pp. 423–424, 2003.

The framework attempts to identify the most important relationships between:

- independent variable (i.e., level of programmer collaboration),
- dependent variables (time to market, cost, quality, information and knowledge transfer, and trust and morale) and
- context variables (e.g., subject, task and environment)

Voas pointed to the difficulties of having *faster* (time to market), *better* (quality), and *cheaper* (cost) as desired goals of a software development project at the same time [9]. There is a trade-off between these goals and the only combination he found achievable today was *faster* and *cheaper*. There is also a reason to believe that such and similar trade-offs are present in PP. For example, an extrovert expert driver who is paired with an introvert novice navigator will probably not lead to more effective and faster development. The introvert novice programmer would probably be made passive and thus prevented from contributing. If the goal was to train a new employee, the whole situation would look pretty different. Then the extrovert expert programmer could talk loudly and explain while he programs, and, thus, transfer information and knowledge to his partner.

Our framework tries to reveal these trade-offs by focusing on the desired outcome (dependent variable) of the PP activity and how different factors (independent and context variables) influence the outcome.

Our own research results are based on an explorative industrial case study, an industrial action research study, and a controlled experiment with professionals. Our preliminary results suggest that PP may be beneficial in terms of trust and morale and information and knowledge sharing. However, we have found no clear benefits regarding time-to-market, cost, and quality.

References

1. McDowell, C., et al. The Effects of Pair-Programming on Performance in an Introductory Programming Course. in Proceedings of the 33rd SIGCSE technical symposium on Computer science education. 2002. Cincinatti, Kentucky, USA: ACM Press.
2. Williams, L., et al., Strenghtening the Case for Pair Programming. IEEE Software, 2000. 17(4): p. 19-25.
3. Müller, M.M. and W.F. Tichy. Case Study: Extreme Programming in a University Environment. in International Conference on Software Engineering (ICSE). 2001. Toronto, Canada.
4. Nawrocki, J. and A. Wojciechowski. Experimental Evaluation of Pair Programming. in European Software Control and Metrics (Escom). 2001. London, England.
5. Cockburn, A. and L. Williams, The Costs and Benefits of Pair Programming, in Extreme Programming Examined, G. Succi and M. Marchesi, Editors. 2001, Addison Wesley.
6. Teasley, S.D., et al., Rapid Software Development through Team Collocation. IEEE Transactions on Software Engineering, 2002. 28(7): p. 671-683.
7. Haungs, J., Pair Programming on the C3 Project. IEEE Computer, 2001. 34(2): p. 118-119.
8. Pfleeger, S.L., Albert Einstein and Empirical Software Engineering. IEEE Computer, 1999. 32(10): p. 32-38.
9. Voas, J., Faster, Better, and Cheaper. IEEE Software, 2001. 18(3): p. 96-97.

Unit Testing Using Design by Contract and Equivalence Partitions

Per Madsen

Aalborg University, Department of Computer Science
Fredrik Bajers Vej 7E, 9220 Aalborg, Denmark
madsen@cs.auc.dk

Extreme Programming [1] and in particular the idea of Unit Testing can improve the quality of the testing process. But still programmers need to do a lot of tiresome manual work writing test cases. If the programmers could get some automatic tool support enforcing the quality of test cases then the overall quality of the software would improve significantly.

This approach should not be seen as an opposition to the test-driven development idea of Extreme Programming. On the contrary the test cases automatically generated should be seen as a supplement to the manually made test cases.

One step in the direction of an automated testing approach is to use the concept of Design By Contract [3]. In Design by Contract the code is decorated with assertions in form of pre- and post-conditions and class invariants. If one of these assertions is violated during the execution of a test case a potential error has been detected. In this work this approach has been named *Testing by Contract*.

The next step would be to find a way to automatically generate appropriate test cases. A promising approach would be to take the idea of Equivalence Partitions (Equivalence Classes) [2] as a starting point. If the assertions forming the contracts are enhanced with formalized knowledge about Equivalence Partitions, this knowledge can be a valuable help in the process of generating test cases. The main focus in this Ph.D. work is to identify how and to which degree this knowledge of Equivalence Partitions can be used to generate test cases.

If the Equivalence Partitions are expressed as assertions that can be evaluated during execution of a test case, it is possible to derive partition coverage statistics. This can be used to ensure that the test cases cover all partitions. Take a class implementing a linked-list as an example. A straightforward partitioning would be to split it into four partitions: empty (no elements), one (one element), small (a few elements) and large (a large number of elements). The actual number of items separating a small list from a large list will depend on the context. When executing test cases it is possible to evaluate how many test cases did actually create and use objects belonging to each partition. Notice that partition coverage statistics can be derived for both automatically generated and manually written test cases.

These partition assertions can be though of as *partition invariants*. They are like class invariants but they are only required to hold for objects belonging

M. Marchesi and G. Succi (Eds.): XP 2003, LNCS 2675, pp. 425–426, 2003.
© Springer-Verlag Berlin Heidelberg 2003

to a particular partition. This concept brings along some benefits when writing assertions. In regular Design by Contract an assertion is often repeated in similar methods. If the assertion can be written as a partition invariant instead, the assertion can be simplified by just stating that at this point the object should belong to a particular partition.

The ability to express knowledge about partitions in pre- and post-conditions and class-invariants actually provides some valuable guidelines for generating test cases. If a certain method has a pre-condition stating that it only makes sense to call the method when the object belongs to a certain partition, then it only makes sense to generate test cases that satisfies this relation. This limits the number of potential test cases. The same applies if a post-condition states that after a certain method the object will always belong to a particular partition.

An algorithm for building a connected graph where partitions are nodes and methods are edges has been developed. The graph would reflect which methods could cause an object to go from one partition to another. The graph can be used as a recipe for making objects belonging to each partition. In the linked-list example this graph would show that in order to end up in the "small" or "large" partition a method like "add" would have to be called. This graph and the ability to actually tell whether a particular partition has been reached can together form a strong tool for building test cases.

One of the main challenges is to investigate whether such a tool can automatically provide sample objects belonging to all partitions or whether this has to be left to the programmer.

A prototype Java-like language with support for Design by Contract enhanced with Equivalence Partitions has been developed. A compiler to regular Java-code as well as a tool for automatic generation of test cases is currently being build. This prototype language/tool will be used to further examine the ideas described above.

References

1. K. Beck. Extreme programming explained. Addison Wesley, 2000.
2. B. Beizer. Software testing techniques. Van Nostrand Reinhold, 1990. Second Edition.
3. B. Meyer. Object-oriented software construction. Prentice Hall, 1997. Second Edition.

Exploring the XP Customer Role

Angela Martin

School of Information Management, Victoria University of Wellington
Kelburn Parade, Wellington, New Zealand
angela.martin@paradise.net.nz

1   Research Question

eXtreme programming (XP) is one of a new breed of methods, collectively known as the agile or light methods, that are challenging conventional wisdom regarding systems development processes and practices. One of the core roles within the XP team is the Customer role. Beck and Fowler [1] describe a good customer as someone who understands the domain well and know how to use software in that domain to achieve business value using the technique of regular delivery.

The central question of this research is "How is the customer role addressed on XP software development projects?"

2   Current Solutions

Information Systems Development (ISD) methodology researchers have expressed a growing concern that existing ISD methodologies and ISD methodology do not meet the needs of today's business and software development environments [2, 4]. Studies in this area have begun to explore practices in natural settings in order to begin to address these issues [3], but practitioners have not waited for this research and have instead established agile methods.

No research, of academic rigour, has been undertaken that specifically addresses the use of the customer role in agile methods on software development projects. The proposed study will fill this gap and will do so by applying some of the suggestions coming from methodology researchers, including the use of rich descriptive studies that explore actual practice. The proposed study will also specifically address practitioner concerns regarding the practicality of implementing the customer role.

3   Results Achieved so Far

My initial research used an interpretative case study to explore a successful XP project. We obtained multiple perspectives on the implementation of the customer role within the planning process and found the following:

M. Marchesi and G. Succi (Eds.): XP 2003, LNCS 2675, pp. 427–428, 2003.

- The XP customer role, especially within larger organisations, is a demanding role. It requires preparation, skills, attention to detail, and the ability to make critical decisions.
- Obtaining regular feedback during the project allows the customer to make effective business decisions concerning the system.
- The development team must carry out key XP practices in order to provide the feedback necessary to enable the customer to make effective decisions. The customer role is a core role within XP.

4   Proposed Future Research

The initial study was exploratory in nature and it provides an initial foundation from which future research can be conducted. Suggested research would include:

- Increasing the depth of this study with a follow-up longitudinal study on the project from the initial study in six months time. We will want to find what further experiences have been undertaken by the team to facilitate the effectiveness of the customer role.
- Increasing the depth of this study by widening the perspectives. A full 360 degree review of the system and process which would include the perspectives of the project sponsor, the users of the system, the acceptance testers and the outsourced facilities management personnel.
- Increasing the breadth of this study by exploring multiple cases using a maximum variation sampling technique to increase the validity of the findings of this research.
- Increasing the breadth of this study by undertaking a quantitative investigation using the findings of this study.

References

1. Beck, K. and Fowler, M. *Planning Extreme Programming*. Addison Wesley, 2001.
2. Fitzgerald, B. Systems development methodologies: the problem of tenses. *Information technology and people*, *13* (3). pp. 174 - 185.
3. Nandhakumar, J. and Avison, D.E. The fiction of methodological development: a field study of information systems development. *Information Technology and People*, *12* (2). pp. 176 - 191.
4. Russo, N.L. and Stolterman, E. Exploring the assumptions underlying information systems methodologies: their impact on past, present and future ISM research. *Information Technology and People*, *13* (4). pp. 313-327.

Extending Testability for Automated Refactoring

Bartosz Walter

Poznan University of Technology
Piotrowo 3A, 60-965 Poznan, Poland
{Bartosz.Walter@cs.put.poznan.pl}

1   Introduction

Refactoring, one of XP core practices, aims at keeping the software design simple and flexible. It assumes changing internal structure of the code without influencing its functionality [1]. However, since refactoring is a costly and complex process, researchers and practitioners try to automate or semi-automate it (e.g. [2]), having in mind both decreasing the cost and preventing it from introducing new errors to the code. The automation is usually based on syntactic verification of well-known conditions that must be met to successfully apply a given transformation. Unfortunately, only a few among refactorings catalogued by Martin [4] are subject to full automation.

The remaining majority of refactorings require execution of the code, i.e. preparation and running unit tests [3]. The tests make a kind of formal specification that the refactored piece of code should follow, regardless of its actual implementation. They are commonly used for refactoring complex systems, but have two main disadvantages: a programmer should create them (software semantics cannot be deduced from the code itself) and they cannot prove the refactoring is correct (they discover the errors only). Therefore they make refactoring a difficult and time-consuming process, which is hardly automatable.

2   Problem Formulation

The two exclusive areas are particularly evident when considering existing programming tools and their support for refactoring: only some of syntactic ones are fully implemented and automated, and some more – partially. Most of semantics-dependent problems still require manual re-writing the code. The low level of automation is a serious drawback from refactoring.

Therefore, since many refactorings require testing, the actual question is if some of them could be tested automatically. Unit-tests are designed to run automatically, but they have to be written manually. However, in refactoring the actual problem is in tests creation, not execution, so the tests should be based on the given refactoring and derived from it, taking also into account the specific logic being transformed. The existence of such patterns for testing refactorings can improve the process and decrease its cost.

M. Marchesi and G. Succi (Eds.): XP 2003, LNCS 2675, pp. 429–430, 2003.
© Springer-Verlag Berlin Heidelberg 2003

3   Proposed Solution

Fowler in his catalogue [4] introduced systematics for refactorings, based on their functionality or complexity. In parallel to that, another taxonomy, based on the testability of refactorings, can exist. According to it, there are 3 categories of refactorings:

- **Syntactic** – based on verification of some conditions derived from the code syntax (e.g. whether a method signature is already in use or a class is finalized). In strongly typed languages even a compiler can verify their correctness, although in many cases they are automated and supported by tools available on the market.
- **Testable** – which still require testing, but the suites of required tests are repeatable and well-known, so that the tests can be generated automatically, based on the properties of the given refactoring. Introduction of this category allows extending the scope of automation and decreasing the cost of refactoring.
- **Non-automatable** – which require the tests to be designed by a programmer and are not subject to automation of any kind considered here.

In several cases the suite of required tests is purely generic, but there are many which require a meta-description of the refactored code (e.g. the border conditions). Such annotation, proposed in [5], can be embedded in the code documentation like javadoc for Java™, and help the refactoring tool to generate appropriate tests.

4   Further Research

The idea of testability-dependent systematics requires verification in practice. In the next stage of research the refactorings defined by Fowler should be categorized. The number of syntactic and testable refactorings will show if the proposed categories appear useful and actually extend the automation of refactoring. The other direction of the research is *incomplete refactoring*, which do not preserve the entire functionality of the code. They come from observation that properly set conditions the code should meet can prevent the programmer from testing cases that will never happen in practice. It can lead to further savings on testing the refactorings.

References

1. Opdyke W. F.: Refactoring object-oriented frameworks. Ph.D. thesis. University of Illinois, Urbana-Champaign, 1992.
2. Roberts D., Brant J., Johnson R.: A refactoring tool for Smalltalk. Theory and Practice of Object Systems, 3(4), 1997.
3. Gamma E., Beck K.: jUnit. http://www.junit.org/ (March 2003)
4. Fowler M.: Refactoring: improving the design of code. Addison-Wesley, New York, 1999.
5. Roock S., Havenstein A.: Refactoring Tags for automatic refactoring of framework dependent applications. Proceedings of Extreme Programming Conference 2002, Villasimius, Cagliari, Italy, 2002.

Software Configuration Management for Test-Driven Development

Tammo Freese

OFFIS, Escherweg 2, 26121 Oldenburg, Germany
tammo.freese@offis.de

Abstract. Although test-driven development is a well established part of Extreme Programming, there are still unsolved issues if using it for library development or in team environments. This paper describes how these issues may be addressed by a software configuration management tool.

1   Problem Description

Refactoring is an integral part of test-driven development (TDD) [1]. While there is extensive tool support for refactoring in integrated development environments (IDEs), refactorings applied to published interfaces in library or framework development lead to problems. Every piece of code which uses the published interfaces does not compile anymore, so it has to be adapted to the changes. Therefore changing published interfaces is typically discouraged. Recommendations are to publish as little as possible as late as possible [4], or to handle changes as additions. Although these strategies are useful with currently used development tools, they delay releases and evolution of libraries.

Additional problems arise when using TDD in a development team. Refactorings like renaming or inlining methods change existing signatures. Textual merging will fail in all cases where another developer in the team uses the old signature in new code. One possible solution is to apply global refactorings outside business hours only, but this delays necessary changes.

2   Goal

The goal of the author's PhD thesis is to provide a concept for TDD to cope with a number of changes to published interfaces as well as parallel changes in team development. To evaluate the concept, a prototype will be developed.

3   Proposed Solution

Using TDD leads to many small development steps. Each of them is either a refactoring or another change to the code. The basic assumption of the authors's

M. Marchesi and G. Succi (Eds.): XP 2003, LNCS 2675, pp. 431–432, 2003.

research is that using these steps as a foundation for a software configuration management (SCM) tool is the key to achieve the goal stated above.

To record the steps, a local SCM tool is integrated in an IDE to gather information on code change and compilation as well as test execution.

If a library is developed, dependent code may be migrated to new versions by replaying the steps recorded in library development. Most of the changes are expected to work automatically, reducing migration costs drastically.

For merging, two sequences of steps have to be mixed. Conflict identification and resolution may be done in small steps. Since the merge result should also be usable for library migration, it has to be a sequence of steps as well. So instead of changing both sequences of steps, the author's approach is to change the newer sequence to be applicable after the old one.

4   Related Work

The core of the SCM proposed here is the application of operation-based merging [5] on the steps of TDD. While there are development environments that support automated refactorings, no SCM is known to the author that stores refactorings as operations.

An approach to allow some refactorings for library migration is described in [6]. The developers add special tags to the code which describe refactorings. A migration tool then utilizes these tags for migrating dependent code. While this approach does not depend on an IDE, the refactoring information still has to be added manually, which is a potential error source.

5   Current Status

A prototype is currently under development for the Java Development Tooling in the Eclipse IDE [2]. At the time of writing (March 2003), gathering the change information works. The next step will be the transformation of the change information into a development step sequence.

References

1. Beck, K.: Test-Driven Development: By Example. Addison-Wesley (2003)
2. Eclipse home page. http://www.eclipse.org
3. Fowler, M.: Refactoring: Improving the Design of Existing Code. Addison-Wesley (1999)
4. Fowler, M.: Public versus Published Interfaces. In: *IEEE Software* (March/April 2002)
5. Lippe, E., van Oosterom, N.: Operation-based Merging. In: *Proceedings of ACM SIGSOFT'92: Fifth Symposium on Software Development Environments (SDE5)* (1992)
6. Roock, S., Havenstein, A.: Refactoring Tags for automated refactoring of framework dependent applications. XP2002 Conference (2002)

A Study on Introducing XP
to a Software Development Company

Harald Svensson

Royal Institute of Technology
Department of Computer and Systems Sciences
Forum 100, SE-164 40 Kista, Sweden
haralds@dsv.su.se

Abstract. This study investigates the effects on a company's software development process before, during and after introducing eXtreme Programming (XP). In addition of gaining empirical data, the study addresses two other issues: First, the adaptation of XP to fit the company's complex software development environment. Second, to find out if some practices in XP seem to contribute more to the software development process than others.

1 Problem Description

XP is not based on empirical research as stated in [1] and is in need of more empirical studies. Hence, this study contributes with empirical data of applying XP in the industry. Further, it is vital for a software development process to be continuously applied and integrated in the organization. Thus, it is important to gain opinions from software engineers using XP. The study addresses this issue.

It is likely in many cases that XP will not be applied under its ideal circumstances, e.g. one room, customer always at hand and so forth. The company where the study will take place is a large IT development company where the ideal requirements for applying XP most likely will not be fulfilled. This study will provide results regarding this issue.

In many cases, companies may only want to apply parts of XP. Thus, the study investigates if some practices in XP seem to contribute more to the software development process than others.

2 Goal

The goal of the research is to study the results on the software development process before, during and after introducing XP to a software development company, investigating both hard and soft issues.

3 Proposed Solution

We will introduce one practice at a time to the study group. Thus, the group will start with applying one practice and finish applying all of XP's practices. This

M. Marchesi and G. Succi (Eds.): XP 2003, LNCS 2675, pp. 433–434, 2003.

way of introducing XP appeals to the company and fulfills our research idea of studying the results on the software development process during introduction of XP. The order of introduction is decided in conjunction with the company.

At every iteration we will measure the impact on the software development process, when applying a set of introduced XP practices. The metrics will be chosen in conjunction with the company. Here, the company wants to apply metrics that concern different aspects of the software development process. For instance, when addressing quality of the product metrics like number of inserted and corrected defects could be used. Productivity or efficiency can be addressed by using metrics such as function points or XP's own metric project velocity.

Regarding the case of studying the software engineers attitude towards XP, we will conduct interviews at regular intervals. Further, at the end of each iteration we will register information that could affect the results on the software development process. Thus, we will be better prepared to analyze the results and understand why some data points may be so called "out-liers".

4   Expected Results

Regarding the case of adapting XP to the needs of the company, it is likely that some practices may be harder to realize than others. In [2], a survey was conducted on 45 companies or studies that had applied XP. Two practices were seen as especially difficult to realize in an XP project. The practices were *Metaphor* and *On-Site Customer*. We suspect that these two practices will also be hard to realize in this study since the company has a lot of different subsystems who are closely coupled. As a consequence, it will be hard to develop an appropriate metaphor, which make it hard to realize the practice *Metaphor*. The practice *On-Site Customer* will be difficult to realize since by tradition the customers do not have people at the company to help the development organization.

Regarding the impact on the software development process before, during and after the introduction of XP we really do not know what to expect, excepts some kind of improvements. The number of published empirical studies on introducing and applying XP are few so more research is motivated in this area.

References

1. Lundh, E. Compelcon, VI newsletter nr 3, 2000:XP.
2. Rumpe, B., Schröder, A. "Quantitative Survey on Extreme Programming Projects". Munich University of Technology, Arcisstr. 21, Germany.

Teaching eXtreme Programming
in a Project-Based Capstone Course

Yael Dubinsky

Department of Computer Science, Technion - Israel Institute of Technology
Haifa 32000, Israel
yael@cs.technion.ac.il

Abstract. The subject of the PhD research that the author conducts
is 'Teaching software development methodologies in a project-based capstone course'. The methodology according to which the students work in
the course is eXtreme Programming. The research is conducted at the
Technion - Israel Institute of Technology under the supervision of Dr.
Orit Hazzan.

1   The Research Targets

Following are the research targets: 1. Mapping the eXtreme programming (XP)
[1] practices according to their complexity levels with respect to learning and
teaching. 2. Building a framework, consists of social and technical practices, that
fit to be integrated into a CS-major capstone course. 3. Formulation teaching
guidelines which address the instruction of software development methodologies.

2   The Research Field

The research field is the 'Operating Systems Projects' course. This course, which
the author instructs for the last six years, is one of the advanced courses that
the Computer Science Department offers. This is a project-based capstone course
which is learned after two theoretical courses 'Introduction to Operating Systems' and 'Operating Systems Structure'. Starting in the 2002 Summer semester,
XP has been introduced into the course together with some studio elements ([3],
[6]). Since then, in the Summer 2002 and the Winter 2003 semesters XP has been
implemented in 6 studios of 12 students in each. Throughout the semesters XP
practices were taught and employed. Attendance to all sessions every week was
compulsory. Thus, the students experienced a real world situation of software
development by XP, and developed a product within a short period of time.

3   The Research Tools

The research tools used throughout the semesters for data collection are: questionnaires, video tape of studio sessions, frequent conversations with students
and supervisors, students weekly reflections, and team diaries.

M. Marchesi and G. Succi (Eds.): XP 2003, LNCS 2675, pp. 435–436, 2003.

4 Preliminary Results

Based on the data analyzing, several results have been published so far. In [2], the quality issue is addressed, and students conceptions of quality issues are highlighted. In [4], ten principles of teaching a software development methodology are suggested, while examining each from both a pedagogical and an organizational viewpoint. In [5], we present two chasms inherent in software development processes a cognitive chasm and a social chasm and describe, based on our experience, how the twelve XP practices can help bridge these chasms.

References

1. Beck, K.: Extreme Programming Explained: Embrace Change. Addison-Wesley 2000
2. Dubinsky, Y. and Hazzan, O.: Improvement of Software Quality: Introducing eXtreme Programming into a Project-based Course. The proceedings of the 14th international Conference of the Israel Society for Quality. Jerusalem, Israel 2002
3. Hazzan, O.: The reflective practitioner perspective in software engineering education. The Journal of Systems and Software 2002
4. Hazzan, O. and Dubinsky, Y.: Teaching a software development methodology: The case of Extreme Programming. In The proceedings of the 16th International Conference on Software Engineering Education and Training. Madrid, Spain in press March, 2003
5. Hazzan, O. and Dubinsky Y.: Crossing Cognitive and Social Chasms in Software Development by Extreme Programming. In The Fourth International Conference on eXtreme Programming and Agile Processes in Software Engineering. Genova, Italy in press, May, 2003
6. Tomayko, J. E.: Carnegie-Mellon's Software development Studio: A five-year retrospective. SEI Conference on Software Engineering Education 1996

Mitigating Risks in Mobile System Development

Norbert Seyff

Systems Engineering and Automation
Johannes Kepler University
Altenbergerstr. 69, 4040 Linz, Austria
ns@sea.uni-linz.ac.at

Abstract. The limitations and constraints of mobile systems need to be adequately addressed in software development. We have been developing a taxonomy of risks based on SEI's risk questionnaire and applied it during the development of a negotiation support system for a Personal Digital Assistant (PDA). In our planned research, we will explore how we can better integrate existing risk management strategies and Agile Methods (AM).

1   Introduction

Developing software for mobile systems is largely influenced by the limitations of these systems. Understanding and handling these constraints as development risks is critical for project success. Examples include usability risks caused by small displays and different human computer interaction, limited operating time, or reduced processing power, storage capabilities, and network bandwidth. In addition to these technical risks, developers are often not experts in technologies and environments for mobile system development.

2   Mobile System Development Risks

In our previous research we used SEI's Taxonomy-Based Questionnaire (TBQ) [1] to identify risks potentially affecting mobile system development. For example, the Product Engineering Class of the TBQ covers risks affecting mobile system development:

- Requirements (Stability, Validity, Feasibility)
- Design (Functionality, Difficulty, Performance, Testability, Hardware Constraints)
- Code and Unit Test (Coding/Implementation)
- Engineering Specialties (Maintainability, Security, Human Factors)

With these risks in mind we have been developing a novel PDA-based client for the EasyWinWin requirements negotiation approach [2]. Because of its flexibility we followed the spiral model for software development, a risk-driven process model generator [3], in which different risk patterns lead to the selection of the appropriate process.

M. Marchesi and G. Succi (Eds.): XP 2003, LNCS 2675, pp. 437–438, 2003.

Although XP was not the primary focus in this project, we also applied several XP practices [4], in particular the Planning Game, Small Releases, Simple Design, Refactoring, On-site Customer, and Coding Standards. Using these practices was successful, so we decided to further examine how useful XP is for mobile system development.

3   Planned Research

The planned PhD research will investigate if and how agile methods can help in dealing with mobile system development risks. In particular, we will examine XP practices and (if necessary) propose risk management extensions. Furthermore we will investigate whether existing risk management methods can be used in an XP context. For example, we will have to take a new perspective on stability risks as changing requirements play a different role in XP. The Planning Game estimates can help to identify infeasible requirements. The Small Release and the On-site Customer practices provide the customer with an additional mechanism for reducing validity risks.

References

1. Carr, M. J., et al., Taxonomy-Based Risk Identification. June 1993,
   http://www.sei.cmu.edu/legacy/risk/kit/tr06.93.pdf, (current March 2003).
2. Boehm, B., Gruenbacher, P., and Briggs, R. O., Developing Groupware for Requirements Negotiation: Lessons Learned. IEEE Software, Vol. 18, No. 3, May/June 2001, pp 46-55.
3. Boehm, B., A Spiral Model of Software Development and Enhancement. IEEE Computer, Vol. 21, No. 5, May 1988, pp 61-72.
4. Beck, K., Extreme Programming Explained: Embrace Change. Addison-Wesley, 1999.

Extreme Advertised Bidding

Peter Regner and Thomas Wiesinger

Institute For Applied Knowledge Processing (FAW)
University of Linz, Austria
{pregner,twiesinger}@faw.uni-linz.ac.at

Abstract. The award procedure in the field of advertised bidding has a great deal of influence on the software process. Therefore the choice of a qualified type of award procedure is of particular importance for the success of a software development project in the public sector. The open procedure and the restricted procedure, two types of award procedures, require a complete and detailed requirements specification, to enable the comparison of the tenders. From a software development point of view, the application of one of these types means using the waterfall model with its well known problems. One type of award procedure, the negotiated procedure, permits the application of an agile approach and is therefore the basis for all kinds of risk mitigating software processes.

1 Motivation

The choice of a qualified type of award procedure has a great deal of influence on the software process and therefore on the quality of the result. Not enough that the software process itself is risky, the award procedure is a supplementary source of complexity and risk. The award of public sector contracts is regulated by the European treaties and by European directives and national rules. Negotiated procedures, a special form of the restricted procedures, are those award procedures whereby public authorities consult service providers of their choice and negotiate the terms of the contract with one or more of them.

2 Research Goals

The goal of our work is to achieve the basic principles of agile software development in consideration of the requirements of an award procedure as best as possible. This means primarily:

- Produce only those documents which are absolutely necessary. If documents are necessary, use the information that could be reused in the agile process, for example: User Stories.
- Make the time during which people can not work together and communicate face to face as short as possible.

Our approach is to integrate the two processes, the software process and the award procedure in consideration of efficiency and effectiveness to enable a continuous process.

M. Marchesi and G. Succi (Eds.): XP 2003, LNCS 2675, pp. 439–440, 2003.
© Springer-Verlag Berlin Heidelberg 2003

3   A Short Process Example Based on XP

The negotiated procedure consists of the prior publication and the core negotiations. Its intention is to inform interested service provider about the planned software development project so that they can decide if they are qualified and capable. The prior publication should contain the project's scope and boundary conditions to give an idea of the project, acceptance criterions and User Story Cards to describe what is intended to be in the product.

Based on the prior publication, interested service provider send in a request for participation which is used to shortlist the most eligible candidates based on quantitative criterions. Now, the Story Cards of the prior publication are used to start the Planning Game with the service providers leftover. For tough problems or risky parts Spike Solutions could be used to test the problem solving competence of the candidates. After this phase, based on qualitative criterions candidates are eliminated. With about two candidates left over the first iteration is started. The iteration work will show, which service provider could do the work best.

After the award of the project partner, a contract to support XP with its Releases, like a framework contract has to be found.

4   Conclusion

In the public sector it is anymore harder to explain that a complete, explicit and neutral specification, comprising thousand of printed pages, is in worst case a matter for collapsed projects and anyway responsible for squandered money. Our work in this field should help to use an agile process like extreme programming to guide software projects efficiently and effectively in the public sector.

References

1. Beck, K., Extreme Programming Explained Embrace Change, Addison Wesley Longman, Inc., 2000.
2. Council Directive 92/50/EEC of 18 June 1992 relating to the coordination of procedures for the award of public service contracts, Official Journal L 209, 24/07/1992 P. 0001 – 0024.
3. Highsmith, J., Cockburn, A.: Agile Software Development: The Business of Innovation, IEEE Software, December 2002, p 120 – 122.

Software Effort Estimation:
Planning XP Guidelines Compared to Research
on Traditional Software Development

Kjetil Moløkken

Simula Research Laboratory, Martin Linges v 17, Fornebu, Norway
kjetilmo@simula.no

Abstract. In the "Planning Extreme Programming" framework by Beck and Fowler, they propose several guidelines for project estimation. This paper focuses on the guideline to use estimation teams. There exist several methods from software engineering research on how to do this, with varying degree of formalism involved. We present an account of earlier research on how to combine expert estimates, and compare it with the XP guidelines. It seems that the proposed framework, with some modifications, is a reasonable way to improve accuracy.

Discussion

Effort estimation is one of the main challenges when planning software development. Surveys of actual projects [1] and controlled experiments [2] continuously report on the industry's inability to provide precise effort estimates. Beck and Fowler [3] present guidelines on how to estimate XP projects. These guidelines include key elements such as conducting breakdown of projects, treating estimation as a team exercise, and systematic learning from experience.

Our research seeks to address if the guideline recommending estimation as a team activity has support in empirical research on effort estimation.

In general, earlier research on effort estimation in teams has focused on using structured team interaction, like the Delphi, the Wideband Delphi or the Estimeeting techniques [4]. These techniques follow strict procedures, and allow little or no face-to-face interaction.

The planning XP handbook [3] on the other hand, recommends using informal interactions when estimating project effort. To our knowledge, there have not been any studies that compare different methods for team collaboration, and only one controlled experiment on the performance on unstructured teams versus individual experts [4] in software effort estimation. In this study, team estimates were significantly more accurate than the average of individual estimates. The main reason for increased accuracy was the identification of more activities and project overhead.

The experiment was conducted with a traditional development project. Nonetheless, the size of the team (four experts) and the process involved (face-to-face interac-

M. Marchesi and G. Succi (Eds.): XP 2003, LNCS 2675, pp. 441–442, 2003.

tion), was similar to the handbook guidelines [3]. It seems that unstructured team estimation is a reasonable method to enhance the estimation process.

There are, however, two main problems associated with the proposed framework [3]. The first is that the procedure described refers to the estimation of individual user stories. Earlier research on estimation has shown that experts can make accurate estimates of parts of a project, when the project is broken down into tasks or activities [5]. The challenge is to estimate the complete project scope. Beck and Fowler does not address this problem properly in their guidelines. It is therefore necessary to conduct surveys to se how actual XP projects are estimated in the industry.

The second problem is the suggestion that one should use the most optimistic estimate if the team is unable to agree on a story estimate. The rationale for this guideline is to put pressure on the developers to increase productivity, and that there is always a possibility to learn from estimation errors. Since software effort estimates are more likely to be too optimistic than the opposite [1], disagreements should be resolved by using the arithmetic mean of several sources or the least optimistic estimate to reduce estimation bias.

To our knowledge, there have not been conducted any surveys that reveal to what extent projects are estimated according to the XP guidelines. Nor have there been any controlled experiments or surveys that address the precision of the estimates made with the planning XP framework, compared to other estimation methods.

We are currently conducting an in-depth survey of several major companies who differ on characteristics like customer type, company size and product platform. Several questions are addressed, e.g., to what extent XP is used in comparison with other software development methods, and the proportion and size of overruns in XP projects compared to other projects. Preliminary findings include feedback from managers that the XP framework is best suited for in-house development, where quality is a more important variable than cost or delivery date. This survey will act as a foundation for controlled experiments on team effort estimation.

References

1. Wydenbach, G. and J. Paynter, *Software Project Estimation: a Survey of Practices in New Zealand.* New Zealand Journal of Computing, 1995. 6(1B): p. 317-327.
2. Jørgensen, M. and D.I.K. Sjøberg, *Impact of effort estimates on software project work.* Information and Software Technology, 2001. 43(15): p. 939-948.
3. Beck, K. and M. Fowler, *Planning Extreme Programming.* 2001: Addison-Wesley.
4. Moløkken, K. and M. Jørgensen. *Software Effort Estimation: Unstructured Group Discussion as a Method to Reduce Individual Biases. Accepted for PPIG.* 2003. Keele, UK.
5. Hill, J., L.C. Thomas, and D.E. Allen, *Experts' estimates of task durations in software development projects.* International journal of project management, 2000. 18: p. 13-21.

Collecting Data in Web Service Development

Alberto Sillitti

DIST – Università di Genova, Via Opera Pia 13
I-16145 Genova, Italy
alberto@dist.unige.it

Abstract. This paper describes the early stages of a research dealing with measures of web services in a XP environment. The paper presents an overview of the research through the identification of the research question, the objectives, the approach, and the expected results.

1 Background

Collecting data is an important task in all engineering disciplines due to their importance in the understanding of how things work and how engineers can make changes to produce desired results, to optimize the production process, etc. Measures are extremely important in software engineering as they reduce the intrinsic uncertainty of software projects, usually much higher than in other engineering disciplines.

Till now measures of web services focus mainly on quality of service including servers internal architecture, architecture and communications among different servers (web servers, application servers, load balancers, etc.) and network performances. These measures are extensions of traditional performance analysis of web sites and TCP/IP networks. Web services are complex entities, based on web data provides and data flows, that can me compared to traditional software. The development of standard such as BPEL4WS (Business Process Execution Language for Web Service) provides a flexible way to integrate web data sources.

Web services include problems experienced in both software development and web development. There are many techniques to measure software and networks separately, but there is a lack of methodologies and tools to measure them together, as web services actually need.

Agile Methodologies require reliable measures to estimate the quantity of work completed and the quality of code produced. At present, in web service development the metrics collection task is *not agile* because developers have to use metrics designed for different purposes and results are hard to interpret.

2 Objectives and Approach

The aim of this research is the development of methodologies and tools to help developers to track the development of web services with a specific methodology and tools. The main objectives are:

M. Marchesi and G. Succi (Eds.): XP 2003, LNCS 2675, pp. 443–444, 2003.

1. Identification of suitable metrics for web services
2. Development of a framework for the collection and analysis of such metrics in a
   XP environment
3. Analysis of such metrics compared to quality of service metrics

These metrics and tools should provide to developers a way to identify problems in
the development of web services without complex post-collection elaborations.

The aim of the research is providing concrete help to developers, for this reason
data collection and analysis tools should be highly integrated in popular software
development.

To validate the identified metrics and the developed tools, the collaboration of
software firms is required. This collaboration will be useful to improve and refine the
work addressing real world needs.

3   Expected Results

Expected results of the research include:

1. A set of metrics tuned to measure web services both in quality of service and development quality
2. A set of tools to perform metrics data acquisition
3. A set of experimental data from *real* web services to validate the approach

The analysis of acquired data should provide a set of best practices in the development of complex web services. These data could help developers to build better web
services both in quality and performances without any additional effort to collect and
analyze such information.

References

1. Fenton, N.E., Pfleeger: Software Metrics: a Rigorous and Practical Approach. Thomson
   Computer Press, London (1997)
2. Humprey, W., Introduction to the Personal Software Process. Addison-Wesley (1997)
3. Menasce, D.A., Almeida, V.: Capacity Planning for Web Services: metrics, models, and
   methods. Pearson Education (2001)

Measuring the Effectiveness of Agile Methodologies Using Data Mining, Knowledge Discovery and Information Visualization

Andrea Janes

Center for Applied Software Engineering, Free University of Bolzano-Bozen, Italy
andrea.janes@unibz.it

Abstract. This paper gives a description of a research effort into the analysis of the effectiveness of Agile Methodologies using Data Mining and Knowledge Discovery methods. The motivations for this research, the used approach, applied methods, as well as expected results are presented.

1 Background

Agile methodologies try to give an answer to today's increasing demands in short time-to-market speed and development flexibility. It is stated that an improvement in development productivity, software quality, and job satisfaction can be achieved.

As an example, Extreme Programming is presented as a "lightweight methodology for small- to medium-sized teams developing software in the face of vague or rapidly changing requirements. [1]"

The effectiveness of the application of agile methodologies, possible critical success factors, dependencies between main actors, and promising usage patterns are still to be examined thoroughly.

2 Approach and Used Methods

The research includes the development of supporting tools to audit user behavior and working patterns. Plugins are developed to log user behavior in form of interaction with certain applications. The produced output is categorized using relevant metrics.

These tools are used to acquire data of developers before and after a methodological change or to compare developers acting in different professional fields.

The obtained data is analyzed to assess the variation of working patterns, the discovery of new ones, the classification of benefits and problems, the finding of dependencies between different variables.

For this reason the use of knowledge discovery methods to find "valid, novel, potentially useful, and ultimately understandable patterns/models in data" is considered fruitful. Particularly data mining is used to fit data into models or determine patterns from observed data.

To handle the potential amount of data the use of information visualization methods in combination the above methods is considered.

M. Marchesi and G. Succi (Eds.): XP 2003, LNCS 2675, pp. 445–446, 2003.

3   Expected Results

This research aims to deepen the understanding of agile methodologies, provide best practice examples, and in this way help software engineers to properly decide about the suitability of an agile method for their project.

"The primary goals of data mining are to describe the existing data and to predict the behavior or characteristics of future data of the same type. [2]", in a sense this is the aim of this work, to understand the system of interdependent variables that are to be considered when choosing a methodology for software development.

The obtained results of the overall research will include the developed tools, the collected data describing the behavior of developers and the findings of the analysis of this collected data.

References

1. Kent Beck. Extreme Programming Explained: embrace change. Addison-Wesley, 2000.
2. Usama Fayyad, Georges G. Grinstein, Andreas Wierse, editors. Information Visualization in Data Mining and Knowledge Discovery. Academic Press, 2002.

Evaluation of New Software
Engineering Methodologies

Marco Scotto

DIST, Università di Genova
Via Opera Pia, 13
16145 Genova, Italy
scotto@dist.unige.it

Abstract. This paper describes the early stages of a research dealing with measures of the software development process. The paper presents an overview of the research through the identification of the research question, the objectives, the approach, and the expected results.

1   Introduction

For several years, we had been in the "software crisis" due to two main problems:

1. Software production do not satisfy customers neither in quality nor in delivery times;
2. Software development methodologies cannot address the problem of quickly delivering quality software because they are too much heavy and rigid.

To solve these problems there are new software development methodologies called "lightweight", such as: Agile Methodologies (AMs) and Extreme Programming (XP) [1]. In order to try the effectiveness of lightweight methodologies we have to measure the software development process [2]. Software metrics [3] is an attempt to bring more scientific basis to software development. In general, there are two types of metrics – process metrics and product metrics. We are mainly interested in process metrics. Process metrics measure the software development process itself. Measures can include design time, coding time, code review, etc. These are related to the kind of measures used for project management.

In software engineering, measures are difficult to collect due to two main problems [4, 5]:

1. Collecting metrics is a time expensive task. This is a problem because software projects are often late and there is no time to spend in activities that do not produce immediate benefits;
2. Manual data collection is an unreliable activity. Too many errors or missing data badly affect the analysis process. These errors appear mostly in critical periods, when the data correctness should help to understand better the situation such as during high stress working periods.

M. Marchesi and G. Succi (Eds.): XP 2003, LNCS 2675, pp. 447–448, 2003.
© Springer-Verlag Berlin Heidelberg 2003

2   Objectives and Approach

The aim of this research is the development of an experimental tool for the evaluation of AMs and XP. That tool can help project managers and developers to track the software development process with a specific methodology. The main objectives are:

1. Identification of suitable metrics for the evaluation;
2. Development of a framework for the collection and analysis of such metrics;
3. Extraction of project specific models regarding the effects of AMs and XP.

These metrics and the tool should provide to developers a way to identify problems in the software development without complex post-collection elaborations. The aim of the research is providing concrete help to developers, for this reason data collection and analysis tools should be highly integrated in popular software development. To validate the identified metrics and the developed tools, the collaboration of software firms is required. This collaboration will be useful to improve and refine the work addressing real world needs.

3   Expected Results

You Expected results of the research include:

1. A set of metrics tuned to measure lightweight methodologies;
2. A tool to perform metrics data acquisition;
3. A set of experimental data from *real* software to validate the approach.

The analysis of acquired data should determine when AMs and XP can be successfully applied to a specific environment to achieve the best result, i.e. increased quality, reduced time to market, higher customer satisfaction, etc.

References

1. Kent Beck, Extreme Programming Explained: Embrace Change, Addison Wesley, 1999
2. N.E. Fenton, S.H. Pfleeger, Software Metrics: a Rigorous and Practical Approach, Thomson Computer Press, 1994
3. W. Humprey, Introduction to the Personal Software Process, Addison-Wesley, 1997
4. A. M. Disney, P. M. Johnson, "Investigating Data Quality Problems in the PSP", Sixth International Symposium on the Foundations of Software Engineering (SIGSOFT'98), Orlando, FL, USA, November 1998.
5. P. M. Johnson, A. M. Disney, "A critical analysis of PSP data quality: Results from a case study", *Journal of Empirical Software Engineering*, December 1999.

Evaluation of Product Metrics
Applied to Agile Methodologies

Matteo Canessa

D.I.S.T. – Università di Genova, Via Opera Pia 13, 16145 Genova, Italy
canessa@dist.unige.it

Abstract. This paper describes the early stages of a research dealing with the evaluation of new Software Engineering design and development methodologies from the product metrics point of view. The paper presents an overview of the research through identification of research questions, objectives, the approach and expected results. Keyword: code metrics, product metrics, Extreme Programming.

1 Background

Currently we talk about Software Crisis more and more insistently: software production neither satisfy quality demand nor time to market. Moreover unforeseeable costs cause economical damages to software houses.

Agile Methodologies (AM) in general and Extreme Programming (XP) in particular seem to be the best candidate to solve problems related to software development. however It is necessary, , to evaluate weather AMs and XP actually produce results. Through product metrics we have a set of tools to evaluate weather the proposed solution is really valid. Collecting metrics is a very expansive task that distract programmers from their real activity, i.e. software development, and this could be a critical aspect especially when projects are late and there is no time to spend in activities that do not produce immediate benefits; moreover manually collected data are often incomplete and errors affected and this lead to incomplete and erroneous analysis.

2 Objectives and Approach

The aim of this research is to evaluate how product metrics can improve productivity and software quality and to develop tools to help developers to collect software metrics as transparently as possible during their work.

The main objectives of this research are:

1. the development of a tool to avoid developers collecting software metrics manually;
2. testing the tool in software houses to evaluate its behavior and its functionality;
3. the analysis of collected data to evaluate developed software characteristics of quality.

M. Marchesi and G. Succi (Eds.): XP 2003, LNCS 2675, pp. 449–450, 2003.

The first objective is important due to several reasons. First of all an automated tool to collect data should solve problems exposed in paragraph 1. : it should free programmers from collecting data allowing them working only on software development and it should collect large size of correct data improving the analysis correctness.

The second objective is also important. Testing effective behavior allow collecting a lot of data and evaluating tools impact on every-day programmer's life: tools collecting data activity must be as transparent as possible to programmers and they must go on working like as they does not have the tool installed on their computer.

The third objective allows evaluating software developed quality and establishing parameters on which judging software characteristics as size, coupling, reusability and so on.

3   Expected Results

Expected results of the research include:

1. a set of new kind of metrics to measure software characteristics;
2. a tool to perform metrics data acquisition;
3. a set of real data to evaluate the approach correctness.

The analysis of acquired data should provide a set of best practices in software development to achieve particular characteristics such as reusability, robustness, coupling etc. These data could build a kind of knowledge base to help developers to produce software of better quality.

References

1. Kent Beck, Extreme Programming Explained: Embrace Change, Addison Wesley, 1999.
2. N.E. Fenton, S.H. Pfleeger, Software Metrics: a Rigorous and Practical Approach, Thomson Computer Press, 1994.
3. Hitz, M. and B. Montazeri (1995). "Measuring Coupling and Cohesion in Object-Oriented Systems," Proceedings of the International Symposium on Applied Corporate Computing (ISACC '95), Monterrey, Mexico.
4. Hitz, M. and B. Montazeri (1996) "Chidamber & Kemerer's Metrics Suite: A Measurement Theory Perspective," IEEE Transactions on Software Engineering, Vol. 22.

Coaching for Agile and Xtreme Practices
A Fishbowl with Piranhas

Steven Fraser, Rachel Reinitz, Jutta Eckstein, Joshua Kerievsky,
Erik Lundh, Rob Mee, and Mary Poppendieck

Abstract. This panel-fishbowl hybrid will discuss all aspects of coaching – becoming a coach – choosing one and describing what it means to be an (in)effective coach. A coach watches, provides feedback, and suggests subtle direction – some will argue that the coach is more – for example, an architect or team lead – but that is a matter for debate. This session will be run as a panel with two fishbowl seats – only one of which may be occupied by audience members at any one time. The piranhas (panelists) will state their positions and offer their feedback. The panel-fishbowl hybrid was conceived by Steven Fraser and facilitated by Rachel Reinitz.

Jutta Eckstein (jutta@jeckstein.com) – *The Undogmatic Coach*

Jutta uses the team's best practices as a starting line. Interviews are an excellent technique for mining the team's best practices. Alternatively one can use a specific agile process, such as XP as a starting line allowing for deviations where necessary. Although as a coach you might have experienced XP as the ideal process for a specific team, it might not work for a different team. Be flexible in the process as long as it supports the overall goal since working software providing the highest business value to the customer.

Use regular retrospectives to learn about necessary process corrections. Additionally (and more importantly) use *informal check-backs*, e.g. over coffee. Look for individual dialogs with the team members and talk with them about how they are, what they are struggling with etc. Take all information seriously as possible input for process corrections. For getting as much and quick feedback as possible, establish really short iterations. This leaves the freedom for timely corrections. A really short iteration covers one week. Don't coach the team longer than necessary - it's better to leave earlier and establish regular *check-backs* since only an early departure will empower a self-organizing team. The longer you work with a team - the more the team relies on you (and the more it costs them). Lastly, don't forget to coach the customer!

Jutta Eckstein (www.jeckstein.com,) is an independent consultant, XP coach and trainer from Munich, Germany. Jutta's experience with agile processes developed over ten years developing object-oriented applications. Jutta has worked with teams of different sizes mainly in the finance industry to help them use agile processes. Besides engineering software she has designed and taught OT industry courses. Jutta trained as a teacher and experienced leading many *train-the-trainer* programs in in-

M. Marchesi and G. Succi (Eds.): XP 2003, LNCS 2675, pp. 451–454, 2003.

dustry. She focuses on techniques which help teach OT and is a main lead in the pedagogical patterns project. She is currently writing a book on Scaling Agile Processes, which will be published in 2003. She is a member of the Agile Alliance (http://www.aanpo.org) and a supporter of the Manifesto of Agile Software Development (http://www.agilealliance.org).

Joshua Kerievsky (joshua@industriallogic.com) – *Fearless Coaching*

To be a great XP coach, you must be fearless. Fearlessness comes from knowing your stuff, walking the walk, telling it like it is, taking risks, embracing change, learning from failure and loving what you do. Fearless XP coaches don't ignore critical problems, such as personality conflicts, poor design decisions, insufficient customer support or uncomfortable work environments: they courageously help programmers, customers and managers apply XP's values and practices to solve problems and iterate to success.

Joshua Kerievsky has been programming professionally since 1987 and is the founder of Industrial Logic (http://industriallogic.com), a company specializing in Extreme Programming (XP). Since 1999, Joshua has been coaching and programming on small, large and distributed XP projects and teaching XP to people throughout the world. He is the author of numerous XP and patterns-based articles, simulations and games, including the forthcoming book (http://industriallogic.com/xp/refactoring/), *Refactoring to* Patterns.

Erik Lundh (erik.lundh@compelcon.se) – *Coaching is Not Team Leadership*

Coaching in the XP sense is a matter of helping teams to bootstrap or improve an agile development process, not team leadership in the general sense. Applying leadership outside that scope is playing with loaded dice, something a coach might do only to help the team be successful in a XP bootstrap. The coach should lead the team to a better form of work, not manage a particular project. I often find myself having to shut-up while the team figures out priorities and technology, since I have more than twenty years of experience with a variety of technologies and processes. But if I give a team too many suggestions, they will be too busy catching up with technology issues. Since I might be a particularly stupid consultant money-wise, I have optimized my coaching process so that I only do two to four half-day seminars with digestion time between, followed by one half-day project start-up where we do a 5 minute standup and then start coding. Then I coach half to one day sessions once or twice a week. I prefer half days if I can combine sessions geographically. This limited-time approach has been crucial to get approval for initial XP pilot projects in the industries where I typically coach.

Erik Lundh has developed software for products the last 20 years. These days, his work takes him inside both boardrooms and R&D labs. He equally enjoys being coach and director. Erik got involved in XP while looking for a sustainable form for cross-industrial teams, from established industries with differing engineering traditions, to work together in a rich environment. He coaches one team, including the customer. That means coaching the customer on team from a business perspective and developers from both business and technical perspective. Erik is proud that his XP-teams ship products in volumes today. Erik promotes and supports software industry/academic networks/SPINs, with international exchanges, on a national level SPIN-SWEDEN, and in his own regional SPIN-SYD, a peer network of people from 35 software companies in the south of Sweden. Erik is also instrumental in the startup of new SPINs in Sweden. (http://www.compelcon.se/index.html).

Rob Mee (robmee@ieee.org) – *Coaching on the Run*

XP coaching feels to me like sprinting in two directions at once. Going forward, I jump into the heart of the team as fast as I can: pair programming with each developer; getting to know the customers and their domain through planning; soaking up all the innumerable tidbits of coaching knowledge that every new XP team invariably teaches me. At the same time, I'm heading for the exit at top speed: identifying internal replacement coaches; taking less of a leadership and decision-making role daily; establishing each practice such that it takes on a life of its own inside the team. Needless to say, this sort of situation can lead to some disorientation for a consulting coach. It also isn't a great business model in tough economic times: the better we get, the faster we work ourselves out of jobs. Still, I feel sure that this is the way it has to be. XP really does enable self-organizing teams, once the process has taken root. Holding firm to this ethos also enables us to stand apart from so many large consulting companies whose practices and revenue models seem counter to the interests of their clients.

Rob Mee is a consultant, XP coach, and programmer from San Francisco. He recently coached with Jutta Eckstein and Kent Beck a very successful XP project in Munich, Germany. In December 2002 he was an invited speaker at the first XP Brazil conference, where he talked about patterns of XP coaching and fought Kent Beck to a draw in a hotly contested battle of the coaches.

Mary Poppendieck (mary@poppendieck.com) – *Coaching*

The first responsibility of a coach is to field a team that has a chance to win. This means that the team has within it, or has access to, the specialty areas necessary to be successful – whether it be expertise in database, usability, embedded software, or whatever. It also means that the wrong people (the naysayers and grumblers and prima donnas) are not on the team and that the inexperienced are balanced with the experienced. It means that team members are dedicated to the project if at all possible, and that they have the necessary tools to do a good job. Someone has to see to these things, and in all sports, this is the role of the coach. The second responsibility of a coach is to assure that the team has a purpose. In sports, the purpose of the game is crystal clear. In software development, a clear mission that is well understood by the team is the enabling factor that allows the team to make decisions locally. The mission must be achievable and the team must 'buy into' it. The coach's job is to be sure that the planning meetings and release planning provide the team with a clear direction. With the right people committed to clear goals, the rest will take care of itself.

The third responsibility of the coach is to make work self-directing. Coaches never take the field in a sport – the coach organizes the team so that players can handle any situation as it occurs without direction. When developers show up for work in the morning, they need to be able to decide for themselves how to spend their time. The coach's job is to organize the daily meetings, information radiators, customer access, room arrangement, pairing rules, etc. so that team members can look around and decide for themselves what needs to be done. The forth responsibility of a coach is to see that each individual finds motivation in their work. Everyone is motivated by different things – some look for accomplishment, some for recognition, some for a regular income. The coach has to understand what is important to each team member and provide it. This means making sure everyone has an opportunity to be successful. It means giving team members opportunities to brag to their management and peers about what a great job they are doing. It means creating a sustainable pace and a fun place to work. It helps if the coach considers everyone as if they were a volunteer and considers how to keep them fully engaged.

Mary Poppendieck has over thirty years of experience as an engineer, IT manager, program manager and product development manager. A twenty year veteran of 3M, she is an expert in process control, lean manufacturing systems, and commercialization of hardware and software products. She is the president of Poppendieck. LLC (www.poppendieck.com) as well as Treasurer and Managing Director of AgileAlliance (www.agilealliance.org). She is the author of numerous articles, including "Lean Programming" and "Wicked Problems" in Software Development Magazine. Her book *Lean Development; A Toolkit* will be published by Addison Wesley in April, 2003 (www.poppendieck.com).

Rachel Reinitz (rreinitz@us.ibm.com) – Panel-Fishbowl Facilitator

Rachel Reinitz is a Senior Consultant with IBM Web Sphere Services focusing on Web Services. She is also an experienced eXtreme Programming coach who has used XP practices for four years. Rachel advises customers on incorporating web services into their applications and on incorporating Agile/XP practices and tools into their development processes. Rachel spent a year as technical lead for supplier integration at the B2B marketplace builder, Ventro (Chemdex) and two years as an XP independent consultant.

Steve Fraser (sdfraser@acm.org) – Panel-Fishbowl Impresario

Steve Fraser is an independent consultant in Santa Clara California and currently serves as the Panels Chair for OOPSLA'03 and XP2003. Until 2002 Steve served fifteen years in a variety of diverse software technology program management roles at Nortel Networks including: Process Architect, Senior Manager (Disruptive Technology), Process Engineering Advisor, and Software Reuse Evangelist. In 1994 he served a year as a Visiting Scientist at the Software Engineering Institute (SEI) collaborating with the Application of Software Models project on the development of team-based domain analysis techniques. Steve is an avid operatunist and videographer.

XP Practices versus Values?

Alan C. Francis, Steven Fraser, Bill Caputo, Michael Cusumano,
Mike Hill, and Andrew Swan

Abstract. This panel will discuss the consequences of alternative characteriza-
tions of Xtreme Programming (XP): Some practitioners feel that the four values
make XP what it is, while others emphasize the explicit list of XP practices as
definitive. People who define XP in terms of its values, tend to emphasize the
humane aspects of XP - that XP is about interactions among people and so if a
team focuses on embracing the XP values the team will be successful in adopting XP, regardless of their list of best practices. In contrast, people who define
XP in terms of its practices tend to emphasize the mechanical aspects of XP -
that XP is about writing better code and so if a team focuses on correctly applying the XP practices, the team will be successful in adopting XP, even if they
have a different value system.

Bill Caputo (wecaputo@thoughtworks.com)

It might not be an understatement to say that I am a fence sitter as regards the values
versus practices debate, but it would certainly be misleading. In a sense, it seems
obvious that both the values and the practices are important: They were each included
in the definition of XP and (we may both presume and ask) that there was a reason
that those who defined it, had a reason for including them both. But at the same time,
I do think there is more to the adoption and practice of Extreme Programming than
simply saying Yup, do both. In short, my preference is toward the values as fundamental, but the practices are by no means arbitrary. As I said, my position is that the
values are fundamental. They provide a necessary perspective for successfully adopting the XP practices. This does not mean that if a team simply communicates a lot,
creates extensive feedback, considers simple solutions first and does all of this with
courage, that good software will necessarily result, but rather that the practices of XP
are going to be less comprehensible with a different value system, and a team is much
less likely to find individual alternate practices that provide similar benefits without
these goals in mind. Furthermore, I believe that the values of XP create and maintain
trust, which to me is an essential part of any collaboration (i.e. the vast majority of
professional software development projects). Thus alternate value systems for effective software development are not infinite (yet quite likely to be more than just this
one), but constrained to those that also create and encourage trust. I hasten to add
however that I also feel that the XP practices taken holistically do provide a tangible
benefit. Thus my implication that the values are a good path to practice adoption.
These are not simply individual practices, but a well reasoned collection that creates
an interdependent whole. Furthermore, an argument can be made that the values of
XP are taught more easily via the practices. I do find myself advocating that practic-

M. Marchesi and G. Succi (Eds.): XP 2003, LNCS 2675, pp. 455–458, 2003.

ing XP is the best way to learn XP. And while it is true that some of the XP practices seem to be beneficial regardless of one's value set, others (either in isolation or with a different mind set) seem capable of producing very undesirable results. Thus, I see the practices as not necessarily exhaustive or exclusive, but nonetheless important and forming an effective system stitched together by the XP values.

William E. Caputo is a Senior Programmer and IT process consultant with ThoughtWorks Inc. For the past four years he has been working extensively with Extreme Programming and Agile methods, first as a programmer, and later as both a coach and a mentor. Bill has practiced XP in several industries, including Accounting, Leasing, Securities Trading, and Insurance. He is an active participant in the Extreme Programming community and the Chicago Agile Developers group. Bill has also contributed to several Open Source Software projects, including CruiseControl (both Java and .NET), Nant, a .NET port of the popular Java Ant tool, and QuickFIX, a cross-platform C++ FIX protocol implementation.

Michael Cusumano (cusumano@mit.edu)

My view is that values without practices behind them have little meaning or utility to a software project. You are what you do. It doesn't matter to me what values a person or an organization claims to espouse. If they don't practice these values in some concrete way, they are doing no more than hand-waving. In many cases, I also think it is more useful to deduce what the core values or strategies are of a software development organization by looking at their practices first. There are many companies that tell you they are something, but when you look at what they do, there is a big gap. On the other hand, the way to influence how an organization evolves and learns is to talk about best or better practices as well as the philosophy behind those practices. People need to understand the logic behind what they are being asked to do.

Michael Cusumano is a chaired professor at the MIT Sloan School of Management, where he teaches courses on The Software Business, Strategic Management, and Innovation and Entpreneurship. He also has consulted extensively on software development methods and strategies for software companies. He is the author or co-author of 8 books, including Microsoft Secrets (1995), Competing on Internet Time: Lessons from Netscape and its Battle with Microsoft (1998), Japan's Software Factories (1991), and The Software Business (forthcoming, 2003).

Alan Francis (francis@thoughtworks.com)

The core that lies at the centre of XP is its value system. The values are the thing which differentiates XP from other methods. In fact, while there is often some confusion about exactly how many practices XP is comprised of, and what they are (pop quiz: is Open Workspace an 'official' practice?) the values remain constant. I'd even go so far as to say that you could change all the practices of XP and still be extreme (as long as you were coding, testing, designing and listening). The values are what unite programmers and bring them together. The practices bring software together, the values bring people together.

Alan Francis, despite appearances, isn't Mike Hill's little brother. In ten years, he's built software that delivers junk mail, controls dams, authors DVDs and lets you buy beer in Wetherspoons pubs. He has mentored for ObjectMentor and now thinks for ThoughtWorks.

Mike Hill (hill@objectmentor.com)

The power and elegance of XP is achieved through its particular combination of figure and ground. The figure is the practices: they provide an algorithm for those parts of software development that can be more-or-less rigidly characterized and then formulaically handled. The values are the ground of the picture: they serve as guideposts in those frequent situations that can not be addressed via formula. Programming is fundamentally a human enterprise, which means that whole great swathes of it can not be rigidly characterized and handled using formulas. The situation-on-the-ground can rarely be made to precisely match the practices, but it can always be made to match the values. No mistake here: the picture includes both figure and ground, and you can't have one without the other. But if I can only keep one, I'll keep the values and abandon the practices, especially system metaphor.

Mike Hill's chief claim to fame is that he is the older brother of Alan Francis. He has been a programmer, a teacher of programmers, and a coach of programmers for twenty-plus years. He is a mentor for Object Mentor, Inc., where he has witnessed around 50 transitions to XP, and led a dozen or so.

Andrew Swan (Andrews@owl.co.uk)

The practices give us the techniques that have proved through experience to be useful without having to discover them ourselves. The practices separate XP from most other methods. They focus on the task of producing correct, running software, rather than an abstract design. The more concrete and well defined the practice the easier it is to teach and apply (compare refactoring with metaphor). The values require someone to attain the mindset of the methodologist and hope they will develop software the same way he does. The values provide a meta-description of the practices. They provide a framework that can be used to create new practices and fit them into the overall method. There is no magic recipe for producing quality software, good software is written by good people. However practices are the best way to improve the skills you have. If someone shows me an example of duplication and a refactoring to remove it, I have learned a useful technique that can be applied whenever I see that pattern of duplication. Just seeing a different version which may be "simpler" and "communicate" more doesn't have the same effect, I just see a better solution to the problem at hand. The practices help people produce software; the values help people produce methods.

Andrew graduated in 1992 from Napier University in Edinburgh and has developed software for the last 11 years. The majority of that time was spent developing client side GUI application in C, C++ and Java. Andrew's primary interest is in improving the quality and productivity of software development.

Steve Fraser (sdfraser@acm.org) – **Panel Impresario**
Steve Fraser is an independent consultant in Santa Clara California and currently serves as the Panels Chair for OOPSLA'03 and XP2003. Until 2002, Steve served fifteen years in a variety of diverse software technology program management roles at Nortel Networks including: Process Architect, Senior Manager (Disruptive Technology), Process Engineering Advisor, and Software Reuse Evangelist. Steve served as the initiator, Chair, and Event Director of the Nortel Networks Design Forum, a proprietary global technology transfer event run by video, audio and web conferencing. In 1994 he served a year as a Visiting Scientist at the Software Engineering Institute (SEI) collaborating with the Application of Software Models project on the development of team-based domain analysis techniques. Steve is an avid operatunist and videographer.

Test Driven Development (TDD)

Steven Fraser, Kent Beck, Bill Caputo, Tim Mackinnon,
James Newkirk, and Charlie Poole

Abstract. This panel brings together practitioners with extensive experience in agile/XP methodologies to discuss the approaches and benefits of applying TDD. The goal of test driven development (TDD) is clean code that works. The mantra of TDD is: write a test; make it run; and make it right. Open questions exist, for example – how can TDD approaches be applied to databases, GUIs, and distributed systems? What are the quantitative benchmarks that can demonstrate the value of TDD, and what are the best approaches to solve the ubiquitous issues of scalability?

Kent Beck (kent@threeriversinstitute.org)

Lean Production identifies two kinds of waste. The first kind of waste (creatively titled "Type I") is pure waste--you screwed up and you knew better, or you are sitting around waiting because of poor resource allocation. The second kind of waste (wait for it, yes! "Type II") is waste that is necessary at the moment, but doesn't really add value. Inspections are a perfect example--your process creates too many defects to just ship units to customers, but you'd really rather eliminate the defects at the source, at which point you can eliminate the inspections without removing value. Customers pay for running functionality. The tests we write in TDD, then, are Type II waste--necessary at the moment but a direct addition of value. But TDD is such a big step forward from test-after, test-manually or test-never. How can we resolve this contradiction? How might it be possible to move from Test-Driven Development to Driven Development?

Kent Beck is best defined in terms of relationships. Following work by Jim Coplien and Ward Cunningham on software development process, with Ron Jeffries and the C3 team at Chrysler he invented and named Extreme Programming, resulting in the Jolt Productivity Award-winning *Extreme Programming Explained: Embrace Change*. He is the co-author of *Planning Extreme Programming* with Martin Fowler, with whom he also collaborated on *Refactoring: Improving the Design of Existing Systems*. With Ward Cunningham he wrote HotDraw, a widely copied drawing editor framework, pioneered patterns for software development, and popularized CRC cards. He channeled the Ancient Smalltalk Masters to produce *The Smalltalk Best Practice Patterns*, and is currently reviving a decades-old technique in *Test-Driven Development By Example* (Addison Wesley). He lives on a southern Oregon farm with a dwindling but still-impressive gaggle of children, his lovely wife Cindee, four dogs, and a bunch of chickens.

M. Marchesi and G. Succi (Eds.): XP 2003, LNCS 2675, pp. 459–462, 2003.

Bill Caputo (ecaputo@thoughtworks.com)

As this is a benefit and approaches panel, I have opted to take a more systemic position on the practice of TDD. As do many others, I see TDD primarily as a design technique, providing a concrete and objective bottom-up approach that compliments top-down design techniques found in the XP planning sessions and elsewhere. TDD's tight iterations, and rapid feedback are the smallest ratcheting gear of the XP process. However, I often find difficulty not in teaching the mechanics of TDD, but in explaining its role in the larger system of activities of software development. The fact that the practice centers on tests invites confusion with QA activities which also almost invariably include testing. Even within XP, Continuous Integration uses testing to increase our confidence in our progress, leading some to feel that this execution is the reason we write these tests. My position is that by presenting software development as a system of activities and showing how TDD fits in with these other uses of testing to achieve the overall aim of the system (to deliver high quality code on time under budget to customer specification) it is easier to focus people's attention on TDD as design, and helps ease their acceptance of the notion that "Yes its OK for programmers to be writing tests."

William E. Caputo is a Senior Programmer and IT process consultant with ThoughtWorks Inc. For the past four years he has been working extensively with Extreme Programming and Agile methods, first as a programmer, and later as both a coach and a mentor. Bill has practiced XP in several industries, including Accounting, Leasing, Securities Trading, and Insurance. He is an active participant in the Extreme Programming community and the Chicago Agile Developers group. Bill has also contributed to several Open Source Software projects, including CruiseControl (for both Java and .NET), Nant, a .NET port of the popular Java Ant tool, and Quick-FIX, a cross-platform C++ FIX protocol implementation.

Tim Mackinnon (tim.mackinnon@pobox.com)

Test driven development is much more than a technique for writing tested code, it is also more than a design technique - its most powerful characteristic is that it enables programmers to successfully pair together. Without TDD, pair programming is like watching paint dry.

Tim Mackinnon pioneered the use of eXtreme Programming (XP) at Dashboards Software in early 1999, and again at Connextra a year later. As a senior developer at Connextra, he led the teams that created the Sidewize, ActiveAd and Ultra-Ad products. Tim is an inventor of the Mock Objects testing technique, Gold Cards, and a founder of XPDeveloper.com - a group that encourages developers to document their experiences with XP, and runs the successful XPDay conferences.

James Newkirk (jim@nascent-software.com)

I believe that Test Driven Development works in practice because it helps guide the design process from requirements into actual running code. The act of writing a test starts the transformation. The test represents an unambiguous requirement that the program must satisfy. Since the rules state that you must satisfy this test in order to proceed you have to focus on this single requirement. This enables you as the programmer to shut off all the other requirements and focus solely on satisfying this one. Once the test runs successfully you can then take a step back, survey the landscape that was created, and touch up a few things (refactor), and then move on to the next requirement. Often in other design approaches I have used the programmers gets paralyzed because the problem that is being solved is so huge that it is difficult to know where to begin. Test-Driven Development recognizes the reality that you don't solve big problems with huge sweeping changes with little or no feedback. You solve a problem by making small incremental steps which provide crucial real feedback. These small incremental steps eventually lead to solving the large problem with a better and more verifiable solution.

James Newkirk has been a software practitioner for over 19 years. He has designed and implemented software in many different environments, from real-time micro-controllers to large-scale multi-tiered business systems. In addition he has managed groups varying in size up to 40 software developers. He has been intimately involved with the Agile Processes Community almost since its inception. In 2001 he co-wrote *Extreme Programming in Practice* with Robert C. Martin, published by Addison-Wesley. The book is a pragmatic look at what it's like to do an XP project. He has also written many articles related to Extreme Programming (XP) and Object-Oriented Design and spoken at conferences such as XP/Agile Universe and OOPSLA. He is a major contributor to the book *Agile Software Development* by Robert C. Martin, which was published by Prentice-Hall in the fall of 2002. He is currently writing *Test-Driven Development with .NET* with Alexei Vorontsov, which will be published by Microsoft Press in the fall of 2003. For the past 2 1/2 years he has been a frequent contributor to the development of NUnit, a unit testing tool for the .NET environment. In early 2002 he became the administrator of this open source project and led a small team that completely redesigned and implemented V2.0 of NUnit. The initial version of NUnit was simply a transliteration of the Java unit testing tool JUnit. V2.0 leverages more of the .NET platforms capabilities.

Charlie Poole (cpoole@pooleconsulting.com)
TDD is one of the harder things for certain folks to grasp when it comes to understanding XP practices. On the one hand, we would like to get people to use TDD from the beginning. On the other hand, insisting on it too firmly may prevent any movement toward XP in certain environments. My current solution is to try to understand clearly what the client is asking for: if it's *tell me how to do XP* then TDD is central, but if it's *how can I improve my process* then TDD may come a bit later. Others approach this differently and, of course, we all get to choose what kind of work we want to do. Aside from the tactics around adoption, the most interesting part of TDD for me is its interaction with the overall vision of the application held by the team at any given time. That overall view is the cumulative result of many decisions, some made *up front* but most emerging through TDD as the project progresses. At any given point, there is a tension between the overall design/metaphor of the project and the decisions one feels the need to make right now. It's a fact that this tension gets resolved, but the process by which it happens isn't too well understood and needs

some clarification. The practice of routinely exposing the cumulative result of all previously decisions to the team is what I call the "Big Story" practice: a translation of metaphor into something we can actually do, rather than something we simply have. By regularly telling the story of the application - the result of many prior decisions - team members are helped to maintain a common view - a theory, in Naur's usage - of what the application is about. The relation of this to TDD is that each small decision is made against a common background which is shared by the entire team. And when those emerging decisions turn out to be not quite so small, the impact they will have on the overall "Big Story" is known at the point of making the choice and can be quickly shared with the team in a form that's easy to digest. The updated design/metaphor/story of the application forms the background for the next decisions that must be made.

Charlie Poole has worked in the software development field for over 25 years, first in the IT department of a government agency and subsequently as an independent developer, coach and consultant. Charlie is a veteran C++ developer with a background in the Windows SDK and COM. He has been working with the .Net framework and C# language since the early beta releases and is one of the developers of the NUnit open-source testing framework for .Net. He is the president of the Seattle XP Users Group and is active in promoting XP in the Northwest.

Steve Fraser (sdfraser@acm.org) – Panel Impresario

Steve Fraser is an independent consultant in Santa Clara California and currently serves as the Panels Chair for OOPSLA'03 and XP2003. Until 2002, Steve served fifteen years in a variety of diverse software technology program management roles at Nortel Networks including: Process Architect, Senior Manager (Disruptive Technology), Process Engineering Advisor, and Software Reuse Evangelist. Steve served as the initiator, Chair, and Event Director of the Nortel Networks Design Forum, a proprietary global technology transfer event run by video, audio and web conferencing. In 1994 he served a year as a Visiting Scientist at the Software Engineering Institute (SEI) collaborating with the Application of Software Models project on the development of team-based domain analysis techniques. Steve is an avid operatunist and videographer.

Author Index